Lecture Notes in Artificial Intelligence 13616

Subseries of Lecture Notes in Computer Science

Series Editors

Randy Goebel
University of Alberta, Edmonton, Canada

Wolfgang Wahlster
DFKI, Berlin, Germany

Zhi-Hua Zhou
Nanjing University, Nanjing, China

Founding Editor

Jörg Siekmann
DFKI and Saarland University, Saarbrücken, Germany

More information about this subseries at https://link.springer.com/bookseries/1244

Frank Dignum · Philippe Mathieu ·
Juan Manuel Corchado ·
Fernando De La Prieta (Eds.)

Advances in Practical Applications of Agents, Multi-Agent Systems, and Complex Systems Simulation

The PAAMS Collection

20th International Conference, PAAMS 2022
L'Aquila, Italy, July 13–15, 2022
Proceedings

Editors
Frank Dignum
Umeå University
Umeå, Sweden

Juan Manuel Corchado
University of Salamanca
Salamanca, Spain

AIR Institute
Salamanca, Spain

Philippe Mathieu
University of Lille
Lille, France

Fernando De La Prieta
University of Salamanca
Salamanca, Spain

ISSN 0302-9743 ISSN 1611-3349 (electronic)
Lecture Notes in Artificial Intelligence
ISBN 978-3-031-18191-7 ISBN 978-3-031-18192-4 (eBook)
https://doi.org/10.1007/978-3-031-18192-4

LNCS Sublibrary: SL7 – Artificial Intelligence

© The Editor(s) (if applicable) and The Author(s), under exclusive license
to Springer Nature Switzerland AG 2022
This work is subject to copyright. All rights are reserved by the Publisher, whether the whole or part of the material is concerned, specifically the rights of translation, reprinting, reuse of illustrations, recitation, broadcasting, reproduction on microfilms or in any other physical way, and transmission or information storage and retrieval, electronic adaptation, computer software, or by similar or dissimilar methodology now known or hereafter developed.
The use of general descriptive names, registered names, trademarks, service marks, etc. in this publication does not imply, even in the absence of a specific statement, that such names are exempt from the relevant protective laws and regulations and therefore free for general use.
The publisher, the authors, and the editors are safe to assume that the advice and information in this book are believed to be true and accurate at the date of publication. Neither the publisher nor the authors or the editors give a warranty, expressed or implied, with respect to the material contained herein or for any errors or omissions that may have been made. The publisher remains neutral with regard to jurisdictional claims in published maps and institutional affiliations.

This Springer imprint is published by the registered company Springer Nature Switzerland AG
The registered company address is: Gewerbestrasse 11, 6330 Cham, Switzerland

Preface

Research on agents and multi-agent systems has matured during the last thirty years and many effective applications of this technology are now deployed. An international forum to present and discuss the latest scientific developments and their effective applications, to assess the impact of the approach, and to facilitate technology transfer became a necessity and was created almost two decades ago.

PAAMS, the International Conference on Practical Applications of Agents and Multi-Agent Systems, is the international yearly conference to present, discuss, and disseminate the latest developments and the most important outcomes related to real-world applications. It provides a unique opportunity to bring multi-disciplinary experts, academics, and practitioners together to exchange their experience in the development and deployment of agents and multi-agent systems.

This volume presents the papers that were accepted for the 2022 edition of PAAMS. These articles report on the application and validation of agent-based models, methods, and technologies in a number of key application areas, including simulating complex systems, agents for social good, advanced models for learning, agent-based programming, distributed data analysis, automatic planning, decision-making, social interactions, formal and theoretic models, self-adaptation, mobile edge computing, swarms, and task allocation. Each paper submitted to PAAMS went through a stringent peer-review process and was evaluated by at least three members of the Program Committee (composed of 134 internationally renowned researchers from 29 countries). From the 67 submissions received, 20 were selected for full presentation at the conference; another 15 papers were accepted as short presentations. In addition, a demonstration track featuring innovative and emergent applications of agent and multi-agent systems and technologies in real-world domains was organized. In all, 10 demonstrations were shown, and this volume contains a description of each of them.

We would like to thank all the contributing authors, the members of the Program Committee, the sponsors (IBM, Indra, Dipartimento di Ingegneria e Scienze dell'Informazione e Matematica dell'Università degli Studi dell'Aquila, Armundia Group, Whitehall Reply, T.C. Technologies and Communication S.R.L., LCL Industria Grafica, AIR Institute, AEPIA, and APPIA), and the Organizing Committee for their hard and highly valuable work. We thank the funding with the project "Intelligent and sustainable mobility supported by multi-agent systems and edge computing", Id. RTI2018-095390-B-C32). Their work contributed to the success of the PAAMS 2022 event.

Thanks for your help – PAAMS 2022 would not exist without your contribution.

July 2022

Frank Dignum
Philippe Mathieu
Juan Manuel Corchado
Fernando De La Prieta

Organization

General Co-chairs

Frank Dignum	Umeå University, Sweden
Philippe Mathieu	University of Lille, France
Juan Manuel Corchado	University of Salamanca and AIR Institute, Spain
Fernando De la Prieta	University of Salamanca, Spain

Workshop Chair

Alfonso González Briones	University of Salamanca, Spain

Advisory Board

Bo An	Nanyang Technological University, Singapore
Paul Davidsson	Malmö University, Sweden
Keith Decker	University of Delaware, USA
Yves Demazeau	CNRS, LIG, France
Tom Holvoet	KU Leuven, Belgium
Toru Ishida	Kyoto University, Japan
Takayuki Ito	Nagoya Institute of Technology, Japan
Eric Matson	Purdue University, USA
Jörg P. Müller	Clausthal Technical University, Germany
Michal Pěchouček	Technical University in Prague, Czech Republic
Franco Zambonelli	University of Modena and Reggio Emilia, Italy

Organizing Committee

Juan M. Corchado Rodríguez	University of Salamanca and AIR Institute, Spain
Fernando De la Prieta	University of Salamanca, Spain
Sara Rodríguez González	University of Salamanca, Spain
Javier Prieto Tejedor	University of Salamanca and AIR Institute, Spain
Pablo Chamoso Santos	University of Salamanca, Spain
Liliana Durón	University of Salamanca, Spain
Belén Pérez Lancho	University of Salamanca, Spain
Ana Belén Gil González	University of Salamanca, Spain
Ana De Luis Reboredo	University of Salamanca, Spain
Angélica González Arrieta	University of Salamanca, Spain

Emilio S. Corchado Rodríguez	University of Salamanca, Spain
Alfonso González Briones	University of Salamanca, Spain
Yeray Mezquita Martín	University of Salamanca, Spain
Beatriz Bellido	University of Salamanca, Spain
María Alonso	University of Salamanca, Spain
Sergio Márquez	University of Salamanca, Spain
Marta Plaza Hernández	University of Salamanca, Spain
Guillermo Hernández González	University of Salamanca, Spain
Ricardo S. Alonso Rincón	AIR Institute, Spain
Raúl López	University of Salamanca, Spain
Sergio Alonso	University of Salamanca, Spain
Andrea Gil	University of Salamanca, Spain
Javier Parra	University of Salamanca, Spain

Local Organizing Committee

Pierpaolo Vittorini (Co-chair)	University of L'Aquila, Italy
Tania Di Mascio (Co-chair)	University of L'Aquila, Italy
Federica Caruso	University of L'Aquila, Italy
Anna Maria Angelone	University of L'Aquila, Italy

Program Committee

Emmanuel Adam	LAMIH, Université Polytechnique Hauts-de-France , France
Analia Amandi	CONICET, Argentina
Fred Amblard	IRIT, Université Toulouse 1 Capitole, France
Bo An	Nanyang Technological University, Singapore
Ronald Arkin	Georgia Institute of Technology, USA
Piotr Artiemjew	University of Warmia and Mazury in Olsztyn, Poland
Matteo Baldoni	Università di Torino, Italy
João Balsa	Universidade de Lisboa, Portugal
Cristina Baroglio	Università di Torino, Italy
Nick Bassiliades	Aristotle University of Thessaloniki, Greece
Byambasuren Bat-Erdene	Mongolian University of Science and Technology, Mongolia
Michael Berger	Docuware AG, Germany
Moulin Bernard	Laval University, Canada
Vicent Botti	Universitat Politècnica de València, Spain
Lars Braubach	City University of Bremen, Germany
Sven Brueckner	ConvergentAI, Inc., USA
Javier Carbo	Universidad Carlos III de Madrid, Spain

Luis Fernando Castillo	Universidad de Caldas, Colombia
Anders Christensen	University of Southern Denmark, Denmark
Rafael Corchuelo	University of Seville, Spain
Daniela D'Auria	University of Naples, Italy
Paul Davidsson	Malmö University, Sweden
Giulia De Masi	Technology Innovation Institute, United Arab Emirates
Keith Decker	University of Delaware, USA
Yves Demazeau	CNRS, LIG, France
Louise Dennis	University of Manchester, UK
J. Andres Diaz-Pace	Universidad Nacional del Centro de la Provincia de Buenos Aires, Argentina
Frank Dignum (Co-chair)	Umeå University, Sweden
Aldo Franco Dragoni	Università Politecnica delle Marche, Italy
Alexis Drogoul	IRD, Vietnam
Ed Durfee	University of Michigan, USA
Ahmad Esmaeili	Purdue University, USA
Rino Falcone	Institute of Cognitive Sciences and Technologies, CNR, Italy
Lino Figueiredo	ISEP, Portugal
Timothy Finin	University of Maryland, USA
Kary Främling	Aalto University, Finland
Ruben Fuentes-Fernandez	Universidad Complutense de Madrid, Spain
Katsuhide Fujita	Tokyo University of Agriculture and Technology, Japan
Naoki Fukuta	Shizuoka University, Japan
Stéphane Galland	Université de Technologie de Belfort-Montbéliard, France
Qian Gao	Qilu University of Technology, China
Amineh Ghorbani	Delft University of Technology, The Netherlands
Sylvain Giroux	Université de Sherbrooke, Canada
Daniela Godoy	ISISTAN Research Institute, Argentina
Jorge Gomez-Sanz	Universidad Complutense de Madrid, Spain
Vladimir Gorodetsky	St. Petersburg Institute for Informatics and Automation, Russian Academy of Sciences, Russia
James Harland	RMIT University, Australia
Salima Hassas	Université Claude Bernard Lyon 1, France
Hisashi Hayashi	Advanced Institute of Industrial Technology, Japan
Vincent Hilaire	IRTES-SET, Université de Technologie de Belfort-Montbéliard, France
Koen Hindriks	Vrije Universiteit Amsterdam, The Netherlands

Martin Hofmann	Lockheed Martin ATL, USA
Tom Holvoet	Katholieke Universiteit Leuven, Belgium
Jomi Fred Hubner	Federal University of Santa Catarina, Brazil
Takayuki Ito	Kyoto University, Japan
Vicente Julian	Universitat Politècnica de València, Spain
Ryo Kanamori	Nagoya University, Japan
Franziska Klügl	Örebro University, Sweden
Matthias Klusch	DFKI, Germany
Nadin Kokciyan	University of Edinburgh, UK
Panagiotis Kouvaros	Imperial College London, UK
Ryszard Kowalczyk	Swinburne University of Technology, Australia
Paulo Leitao	Polythecnic Institute of Braganca, Portugal
Alessio Lomuscio	Imperial College London, UK
Henrique Lopes Cardoso	University of Porto, Portugal
Miguel A. Lopez-Carmona	University of Alcala, Spain
Rene Mandiau	LAMIH, Université Polytechnique Hauts-de-France, France
Wenji Mao	Institute of Automation, Chinese Academy of Sciences, China
Stephen Marsh	University of Ontario Institute of Technology, Canada
Philippe Mathieu (Co-chair)	University of Lille, France
Viviana Mascardi	DIBRIS, University of Genoa, Italy
Eric Matson	Purdue University, USA
Shigeo Matsubara	Osaka University, Japan
Toshihiro Matsui	Nagoya Institute of Technology, Japan
Frederic Migeon	IRIT, France
Tim Miller	University of Melbourne, Australia
Tsunenori Mine	Kyushu University, Japan
Jose M. Molina	Universidad Carlos III de Madrid, Spain
Koichi Moriyama	Nagoya Institute of Technology, Japan
Joerg Mueller	TU Clausthal, Germany
Jean-Pierre Muller	CIRAD, France
Aniello Murano	University of Naples Federico II, Italy
Juan Carlos Nieves	Umeå University, Sweden
Nariaki Nishino	University of Tokyo, Japan
Pablo Noriega	Artificial Intelligence Research Institute, Spain
Paulo Novais	University of Minho, Portugal
Ann Nowé	Vrije Universiteit Brussel, Belgium
Akihiko Ohsuga	University of Electro-Communications, Japan
Eugenio Oliveira	Universidade do Porto, Portugal

Andrea Omicini	Alma Mater Studiorum–Università di Bologna, Italy
Ei-Ichi Osawa	Future University Hakodate, Japan
Sascha Ossowski	Universidad Rey Juan Carlos, Spain
Julian Padget	University of Bath, UK
Van Parunak	Soar Technology, USA
Juan Pavón	Universidad Complutense de Madrid, Spain
Terry Payne	University of Liverpool, UK
Skobelev Petr	Smart Solutions, Ltd., Russia
Gauthier Picard	ONERA/DTIS, Université de Toulouse, France
Sebastien Picault	INRAE, France
Marco Picone	University of Modena and Reggio Emilia, Italy
Faruk Polat	Middle East Technical University, Turkey
David Pynadath	University of Southern California, USA
Sarvapali Ramchurn	University of Southampton, UK
Alessandro Ricci	University of Bologna, Italy
David Robertson	University of Edinburgh, UK
Ana Paula Rocha	University of Porto, Portugal
Sebastian Rodriguez	Universidad Tecnológica Nacional, Argentina
Antonino Rotolo	University of Bologna, Italy
Kristin Yvonne Rozier	Iowa State University, USA
Yuko Sakurai	National Institute of Advanced Industrial Science and Technology, Japan
Ken Satoh	National Institute of Informatics and Sokendai, Japan
Silvia Schiaffino	CONICET, Argentina
Holger Schlingloff	Fraunhofer FOKUS and Humboldt University, Germany
Michael Ignaz Schumacher	University of Applied Sciences and Arts of Western Switzerland, Switzerland
Franciszek Seredynski	Cardinal Stefan Wyszynski University in Warsaw, Poland
Emilio Serrano	Universidad Politécnica de Madrid, Spain
Jaime Sichman	University of São Paulo, Brazil
Toshiharu Sugawara	Waseda University, Japan
Andreas Theodorou	Umeå universitet, Sweden
Ingo Timm	University of Trier, Germany
Viviane Torres da Silva	IBM, Brazil
Ali Emre Turgut	Université Libre de Bruxelles, Belgium
Suguru Ueda	Saga University, Japan
Rainer Unland	University of Duisburg-Essen, Germany
Domenico Ursino	Università Politecnica delle Marche, Italy

Lois Vanhee	Umeå universitet, Sweden
László Zsolt Varga	Eötvös Loránd University, Hungary
Laurent Vercouter	LITIS, INSA de Rouen, France
Harko Verhagen	Stockholm University, Sweden
José Ramón Villar	University of Oviedo, Spain
Gerhard Weiss	Maastricht University, The Netherlands
Wayne Wobcke	University of New South Wales, Australia
Gaku Yamamoto	IBM Software Group and Tokyo Institute of Technology, Japan
Neil Yorke-Smith	Delft University of Technology, The Netherlands
Laura Zavala	City University of New York, USA
Jinyu Zhang	Nanjing University, China
Dengji Zhao	ShanghaiTech University, China

PAAMS 2022 Sponsors

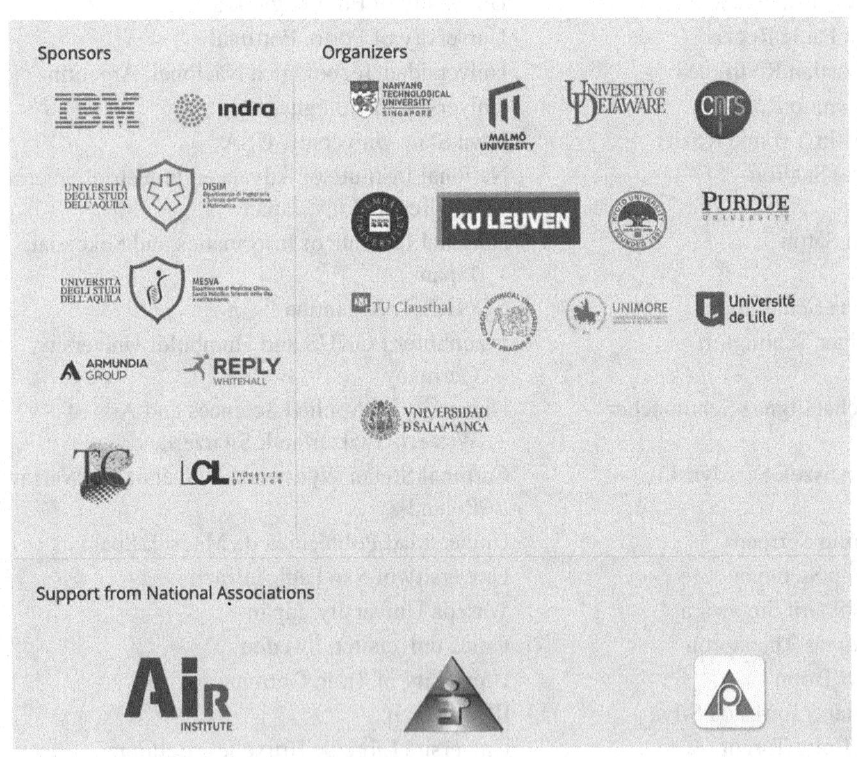

Contents

Main Track

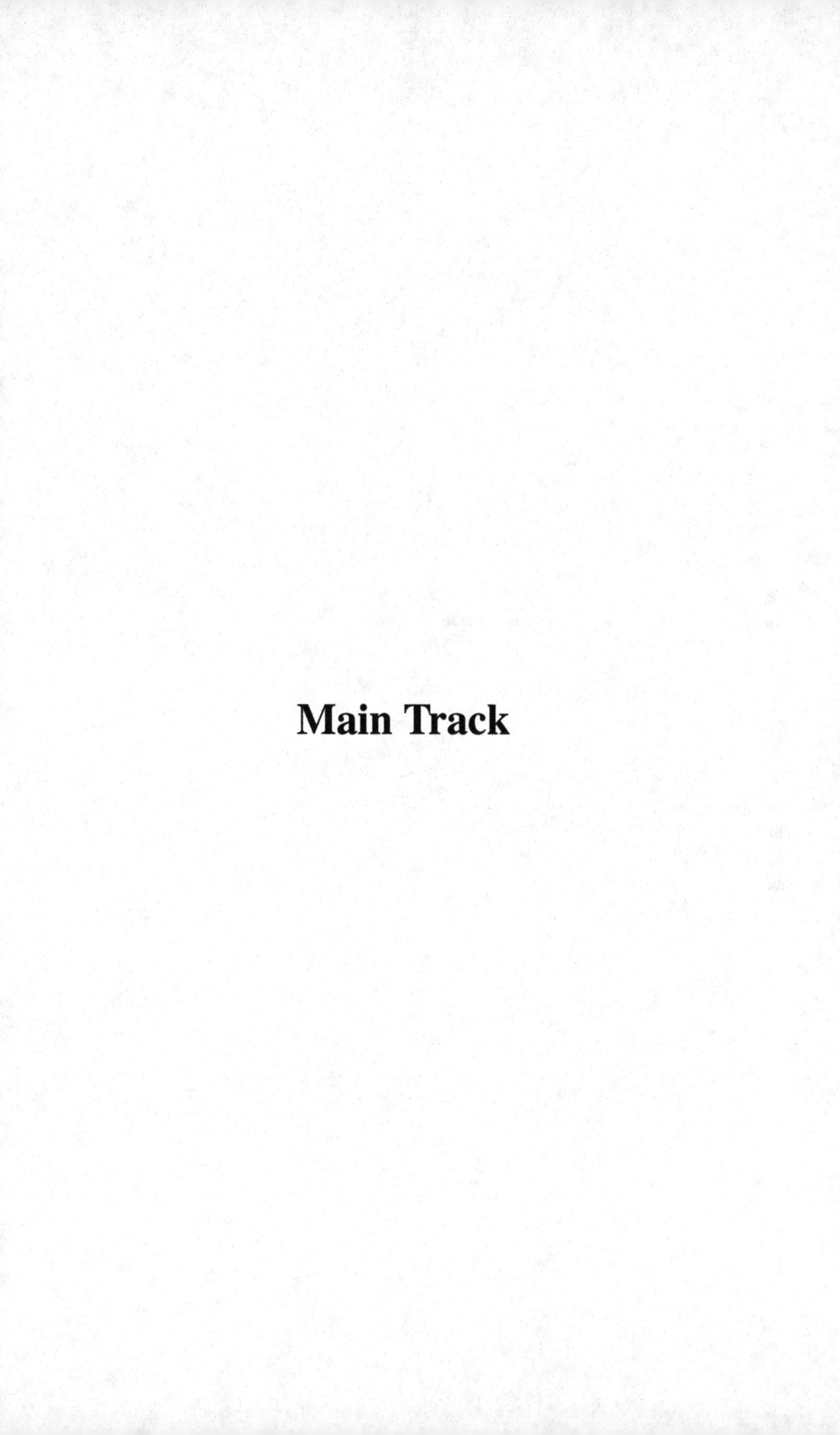

Main Track

An Open MAS/IoT-Based Architecture for Large-Scale V2G/G2V

Charilaos Akasiadis[1], Georgios Iatrakis[2], Nikolaos Spanoudakis[3(✉)], and Georgios Chalkiadakis[2]

[1] Institute of Informatics and Telecommunications, NCSR 'Demokritos', Athens, Greece
cakasiadis@iit.demokritos.gr

[2] School of Electrical and Computer Engineering, Technical University of Crete, Kounoupidiana, Greece
{giatrakis,gchalkiadakis}@isc.tuc.gr

[3] School of Production Engineering and Management, Technical University of Crete, Kounoupidiana, Greece
nispanoudakis@isc.tuc.gr

Abstract. In this paper we put forward an open multi-agent systems (MAS) architecture for the important and challenging to engineer vehicle-to-grid (V2G) and grid-to-vehicle (G2V) energy transfer problem domains. To promote scalability, our solution is provided in the form of modular microservices that are interconnected using a multi-protocol Internet of Things (IoT) platform. On the one hand, the low-level modularity of Smart Grid services allows the seamless integration of different agent strategies, pricing mechanisms and algorithms; and on the other, the IoT-based implementation offers both direct applicability in real-world settings, as well as advanced analytics capabilities by enabling digital twins models for Smart Grid ecosystems. We describe our MAS/IoT-based architecture and present results from simulations that incorporate large numbers of heterogeneous Smart Grid agents, which might follow different strategies for their decision making tasks. Our framework enables the testing of various schemes in simulation mode, and can also be used as the basis for the implementation of real-world prototypes for the delivery of large-scale V2G/G2V services.

Keywords: Internet of things · Open multi-agent systems · Smart grid

1 Introduction

In the emerging Smart Grid [2], energy and information flow towards all possible directions over distribution and transmission networks. As such, buildings but also vehicles become active consumers and producers of energy, and need to be integrated into the Grid. Not only is the Smart Grid an electricity network with diverse consumers and producers, it is also a dynamic marketplace where heterogeneous devices appear and need to connect [9]. To date, several Smart

© The Author(s), under exclusive license to Springer Nature Switzerland AG 2022
F. Dignum et al. (Eds.): PAAMS 2022, LNAI 13616, pp. 3–14, 2022.
https://doi.org/10.1007/978-3-031-18192-4_1

Grid-related business models and information systems' architectures have been proposed, but they do not always adhere to particular standards [4]. This is normal, as the energy markets involved can be global, regional, or isolated; can be based mostly on renewable energy or not; and can be regulated by a public authority or allow dynamic pricing based on demand and offer.

Such energy markets naturally reflect systems where not one player can force others to use her products; players or stakeholders can come along their own business models; and stakeholders can have diverse goals in negotiating their consumption and offer. Moreover, these systems allow for pro-activeness of the players who pursue their goals and sociability—as they can form dynamic partnerships or coalitions, but also react and/or adapt to a changing dynamic environment [13]. In addition, it is natural for participants to be generally able to freely join and leave the system at any time. All these characteristics point to agent technology and open *multiagent systems (MAS)* in particular [20].

At the same time, the advances in the domain of the Internet of Things (IoT) allow the deployment of such approaches in the real world, as IoT offers a networking layer that interconnects distributed resources, e.g. power meters and other sensors, charging controllers and similar actuators, decision support agents and various processing services [5]. A key IoT concept is that these resources, although heterogeneous, are interoperable in the sense that they exchange information and reconfigure particular parameters, crucial for their operation.

To the best of our knowledge, however, existing approaches for the Vehicle-to-Grid (V2G)/ Grid-to-Vehicle (G2V) problem do not provide functional open prototypes offering such features, or adequately exploit existing engineering MAS research paradigms. In an open system, diverse agents representing stakeholders need to use predefined protocols to interact; but also need to work the protocols with their own algorithms and/or goals. Given this, the main contribution of this paper is a novel MAS/IoT architecture we put forward for the V2G/G2V domain. Our architecture allows the different stakeholders to reuse existing agents in new deployments, or to develop new ones, according to respective goals. We propose the instantiation of such a system using SYNAISTHISI, a research-oriented IoT platform deployed in docker containers, which allows agents to connect and communicate using the Message Queuing Telemetry Transport (MQTT) publish/subscribe protocol [1]. The validity of the approach is illustrated via simulation experiments with two different dynamic pricing mechanisms and three charging scheduling algorithms inspired by the existing literature.

In the rest of this paper, we first present the necessary background and discuss related work (Sect. 2). Then, Sect. 3 presents our V2G/G2V-specific MAS-based architecture and the roles that the different agents have. Section 4 details the system development process, along with the IoT communications infrastructure and agent interaction protocols. Following that, in Sect. 5, we evaluate the applicability of our approach with realistic use case scenarios of interest. Finally, Sect. 6 concludes this paper.

2 Background and Related Work

Recent trends indicate that, in the near future, large numbers of EVs will penetrate into the electricity markets resulting to different demand patterns, altered enough to disrupt the stability and reliability of existing power networks [6]. To overcome this, researchers have introduced "smart charging", or Grid-to-Vehicle (G2V) approaches, where charging might not be initiated instantly upon EV connection, but get delayed due to various factors [3], e.g., renewable production levels, demand from other EVs, pricing, etc. Complementary to G2V, the Vehicle-to-Grid (V2G) approach takes advantage of the electricity storage capabilities of EV batteries, and allows their controlled discharging for supporting the Grid during times of energy supply shortage [15].

Research has focused on combining simulators with (possibly smaller-scale) real-world trials for the delivery of V2G and G2V services. For example, XBOS-V [12] is a system for controlling plug-in EV charging in residential and small commercial sites. RISE-V2G is an implementation of the V2G communication interface ISO 15118, i.e. a standardized communication method, which provides lower level connection infrastructure between electric vehicles and charging stations. Similar examples are the Open Charge Point Protocol (OCPP), the Open Charge Point Interface (OCPI), and the Open Smart Charging Protocol (OSCP). OpenV2G [7] implements the necessary components of the V2G public key infrastructure. The focus of the approach is to securely connect electric vehicles and charging stations and provide simulation capabilities. GEM [17], another approach, simulates the operation on both the mobility and the electricity domains. However, the simulation approach followed represents a higher level and does not include particular stakeholder types, such as a station recommender. ACN-Sim [10] is a tool for managing battery charging and performs a user- rather than a grid-level analysis.

SYNAISTHISI IoT is a research-oriented platform that brings together open-source frameworks into a unified solution with many desirable properties [1]. In particular, services and sub-modules come in docker containers, allowing scalable and operating system independent deployments. For user developed services, the platform can act as a message-oriented middleware enabling their communication and orchestration. To that end, multiple protocols are supported and can be translated to one another instantly, so that agent and service heterogeneity with respect to their implementation details is sufficiently captured. Moreover, authentication and authorization is supported for restricting access to topics holding private information, and semantic descriptions of services and exchanged information allow more sophisticated processing and knowledge extraction. These features fulfill the requirements of our proposed open system, and also enable the reusability of services for fast system redeployment at different locations.

3 System Architecture

In this section we provide an overview of our architecture. We assume that agents coexist in a microgrid infrastructure that can be interconnected with

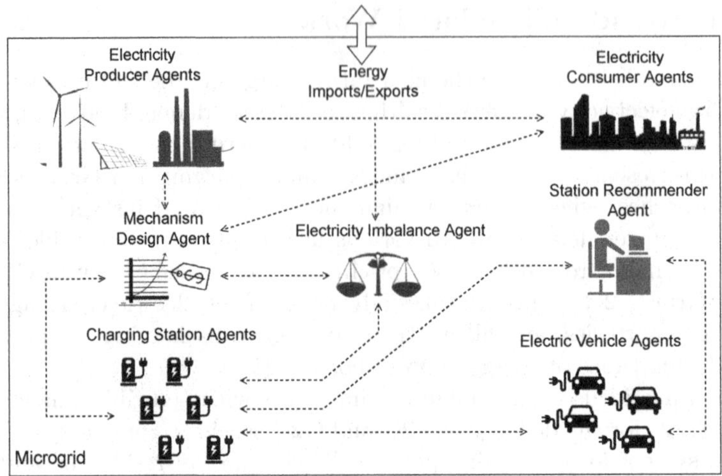

Fig. 1. Overview of the proposed MAS architecture for the V2G/G2V problem.

other parts of the Smart Grid through distribution and transmission networks. When a microgrid requires power that can not be generated locally, it can import it, while, when it has a local energy surplus, it can export it to the Grid and create additional profits for its producers, according to energy market regulations [9]. Figure 1 provides an overview of the agents and their interactions.

In particular, the agent types in our system are: the *(a)* Electric Vehicle agents (EV), the *(b)* Charging Station agents (CS), the *(c)* Electricity Producer agents (EP), and the *(d)* Electricity Consumer agents (EC). We also assume the existence of a regulatory service (possibly a for-profit private service), that consists of the following agents: *(i)* a Station Recommender (SR), *(ii)* an Electricity Imbalance (EI), and *(iii)* a Mechanism Design (MD). In what follows, we refer to this service by its three distinct agents separately. Note that each agent type may consist of certain "private" sub-modules, whose specific functionality can further differentiate agent behaviors.

EV agents aim to optimize a utility function set by the EV owner— e.g., always have enough energy to realize the next trip, achieve so by the minimum cost, etc. The *EV agent* monitors the driver's activities, models and predicts her future behavior and needs, and can contact a charging station to schedule battery charging, seek profit from participation in V2G activities, and engage in negotiations with the charging stations. Building blocks can be preference elicitation modules, responsible for monitoring the habits and behavior of the driver, and perhaps even forecast future preferences; user interfaces accessible by humans either via mobile devices or the vehicle's dashboard, to operate respective procedures and monitor their conduct, for example payments, negotiations, or browse and select recommendations. Such agents can implement alternative strategies for automatically selecting a charging schedule according to predefined needs of each driver, e.g. less cost, quicker availability, charging network preferences, location-based selection etc. An *EV agent* communicates with the *SR agent* to receive recommendations and the *CS agents* to reserve station slots.

Next, *CS agents* manage the physical gateways (i.e. connectors, parking slots) by which EVs connect to the grid and create profit by charging their batteries. They can also negotiate with *EV agents* regarding an existing charging agreement, to change some of the parameters so as be able to schedule the charging of additional vehicles. This leads to better utilization of the station infrastructure, and maximizes its profit. A *CS agent* may contain a charging scheduling module, the algorithmic component responsible for schedule charging/discharging activities over a predefined planning horizon; a negotiation decision making module for conducting negotiations; a pricing module that calculates costs and payments; and a preference elicitation module that monitors charging slots usage and updates the prices for each of them according to the needs of the station owner; A *CS Agent* communicates with the *SR*, the *MD*, the *EI*, and *EV* agents.

The *SR agent* recommends to EVs a subset of the available CS and charging slots that match most with their preferences (e.g. duration, distance). This agent can be also augmented to take into account various grid constraints in order to, e.g., help avoid herding effects. It consists of a recommendations engine module, an EV repository module that stores information about the past EV behavior in order to utilize it for future recommendations, and a charging station repository of registered CSs. It communicates with the *CS* and *EV* agents.

The *EI agent* aggregates data from the *EP*, *CS*, and *EC* agents regarding their expected energy profiles, and calculates the periods of electricity shortage and surplus. Then, it provides the imbalance levels to all interested parties, for them to plan their consumption and production activities. It employs a constraints extraction module that incorporates various measures and methods that could be relevant in such a scenario, and calculates electricity imbalance over a predefined planning horizon; stations, producers, and consumers repositories.

The *MD agent* represents an intermediate trusted third party entity, responsible for calculating dynamic prices and managing the payments of the various contributor types. Its goal is to assign appropriate, and possibly personalized rates for energy consumption and production by *CS*, *EC*, and *EP* agents. It can be equipped with pricing mechanisms that incentivize agents to be truthful regarding their statements for expected values, as well as their actual behavior.

Finally, the various *EP* and *EC* agents predict and periodically report expected production and consumption levels respectively, and their confidence on such predictions. These types of agents typically communicate with *EI* and *MD* agents. Every agent type may also have user interfaces, either for mere monitoring in case of fully autonomous operation, or for additional human interaction in semi-automatic or manual modes.

4 Agent Interactions

We followed a methodological approach to system analysis and design, based on the Agent Systems Engineering Methodology (ASEME), which has been employed in the past for modeling Ambient Intelligence applications [18] and

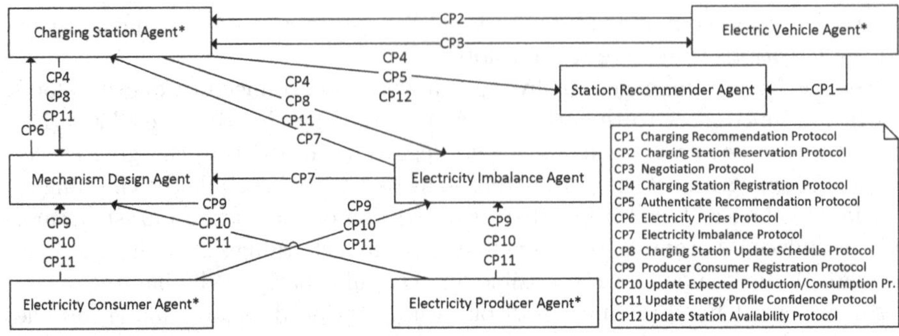

Fig. 2. The proposed architecture. (*) denotes agent types with multiple instances. Arrows start from the agent that initiates the protocol and point to the receiver agents.

referred to by the literature on modeling IoT-based MAS [16,21]. ASEME builds on existing languages, such as Unified Modeling Language (UML) and state charts, in order to represent system analysis and design models. It is agent architecture- and agent mental model- independent, allowing the designer to select the architecture type and the mental attributes of the agent, thus supporting heterogeneous agent architectures. Moreover, ASEME puts forward a modular agent design approach and uses the so-called intra-agent and inter-agent control concepts. The first defines the agent's behavior by coordinating the different modules that implement its capabilities, while the latter defines the protocols that govern the coordination of the society of the agents.[1]

In this sense the cooperation protocols were modeled as state charts. Figure 2 shows the agent types along with the protocols used for their cooperation.

CP1 Charging Recommendation: Initiated whenever an EV needs to schedule a charging session. The EV submits its preference and location to the SR and receives a list of recommended CSs and slots.

CP2 Charging Station Reservation: Follows right after CP1, for the EV to reserve the selected charging slot.

CP3 Negotiation: Optional, initiated after CP2, whenever the CS or the EV need to reschedule a charging slot.

CP4 Charging Station Registration: Registration of a new CS into the system and informs the MD, the EI and the SR about its specifications.

CP5 Authenticate Recommendation: Follows right after CP2. The EV sends the recommendation it selected to the CS, and CS requests from to the SR its validation.

CP6 Electricity Prices: Follows after CP7. Used by the MD to update prices and broadcast these to every CS.

CP7 Electricity Imbalance: Follows right after CP10 or CP8, if the expected production or consumption changes, the EI broadcasts the updated values to the MD and every CS.

[1] More detailed descriptions of the inter- and intra-agent control and a detailed description of the protocols, including the message syntax and semantics, can be found in our online repository: https://github.com/iatrakis/IoT-V2G-G2V.

CP8 Charging Station Update Schedule: Follows after CP5. The CS creates an updated *energy schedule* after an EV recommendation is authenticated, and communicates it to the EI and the MD.

CP9 Producer Consumer Registration: Registers new producers and consumers. The new stakeholder informs EI and MD about its type.

CP10 Update Expected Production/Consumption: Triggers at the beginning of each day. All producers and consumers inform the EI and MD agents about the next day's expected production and consumption.

CP11 Update Energy Profile Confidence: Triggers at the start of each day. All producers and consumers inform the EI and MD agents about their confidence regarding their forecasts (CP10).

CP12 Update Station Availability: Follows right after CP2. The CS updates its charging slot availability after each new reservation, and informs the SR.

Now, each agent is implemented in a different program that is deployed in an independent docker container, either hosted in cloud infrastructure, or locally in each stakeholder's premises. Moreover, to support research, we can set up simulations to test and evaluate different agent strategies and algorithms. This can be achieved by implementing additional orchestrator scripts that take advantage of the IoT platform's API for registering, deploying, and configuring services in batches, as well as for logging the actions and outcomes of each agent. We also need to define the duration of a simulation hour in actual time—e.g., two seconds correspond to one simulated hour, to configure the agent implementations accordingly. Similarly, each agent provides data regarding demand/charging preferences. In an actual system deployment though, the required data would be obtained in real-time, via sensor measurements, or user input forms.

Our implementation is based on the SYNAISTHISI platform, however any other IoT platform solution offering similar features could be used as well. We chose this particular one for a number of reasons. From a user perspective, it has a non-commercial license and can be used for research purposes, and allows developers to create new services of their own and integrate them into more complex applications; and from a technical perspective, it supports many application layer protocols (MQTT,[2] HTTP/REST,[3] etc.), it can be easily deployed as docker containers offering this way interoperability with other software and scalability for large-scale deployments. Also, it employs user authentication and authorization processes to restrict open access for private information.

The service interconnection is realized with the exchange of messages, in our case using the MQTT publish/subscribe protocol. Each service can subscribe to topics in order to receive messages, or publish to other topics where other services have subscribed to, for sending information and commands. To receive or send data, from and to particular topics, the service owner must possess appropriate access rights, which can be managed via the platform's GUI. The same holds for the deployment and the execution monitoring of the deployed

[2] MQTT is an OASIS standard messaging protocol for the Internet of Things, mqtt.org.

[3] REpresentational State Transfer (REST) over Hypertext Transfer Protocol (HTTP).

services. In case of mobile assets such as EVs, a wireless internet connection is required in order for the messages to be exchanged. For charging stations and the various Supervisory Control and Data Acquisition (SCADA) systems, appropriate connectors can offer an interface for the platform interconnection, provided that these too are connected via the internet.

4.1 Implemented Agent Strategies

For the purposes of evaluation via simulation, we need to test different methods and compare their effects on the system in simulation mode. To this end, we implemented two pricing algorithms used by the MD agent to observe how they contribute to grid stability, i.e. to reducing the energy surplus and deficit peaks. We also implemented three scheduling approaches that determine when and how much energy is exchanged between CS and EV agents.

Price Calculation Algorithms for the Mechanism Design Agent:

A) *NRG-Coin pricing algorithm:* This mechanism is inspired by the one in [14], and aims at incentivizing stakeholders to balance supply and demand.
B) *Adaptive pricing algorithm:* According to this mechanism proposed in [19], we estimate the evaluation of energy with respect to the cost induced by the EV agents. The mechanism can adjust prices to motivate agents to charge their EVs when there is an energy surplus on the grid.

Charging Scheduling Algorithms:

A) *First slot:* In this case, EVs charge their battery in the first available time interval, without taking into account if prices are better or worse.
B) *Lowest Prices:* In this approach, EVs are trying to reduce charging costs by choosing time periods that the energy prices are the lowest possible.
C) *V2G:* In this case EVs are able to discharge their batteries when the prices are high to provide load to the rest of the grid, and then charge it back when prices are lower, nevertheless within the periods that EVs are connected to a charger. For this purpose and inspired by [8] and [11], we used linear programming to minimize an objective function representing charging costs in the presence of constraints regarding the EV preferences and charging specifications.

5 Experimental Evaluation

In this section we show four use cases that illustrate the applicability of our proposed architecture. The use cases provide comparative evaluations of the implemented strategies discussed in the previous section. All agent implementations are in Python, while the datasets that we used are based on a collection of real data from a number of publicly available online resources;[4] and the duration of each simulation is 10 days. The simulations were performed on a PC with an AMD Ryzen 5 1500X @ 3.5 GHz processor and 8 GB of RAM.

[4] Specifically, consumption and production data originate from the ENTSOE platform, and EV data from the MyElectricAvenue project.

5.1 Simulating Algorithms and Mechanisms

The first use case is employed to compare the different EV charging scheduling methods, using the *NRG-Coin* pricing mechanism. We remind the reader that these methods are charging *(i)* during the first slots that the EV gets connected to a charger, *(ii)* during intervals with the lowest price for consumption, and *(iii)* with V2G capability, where the EV can also sell back to the grid some of the stored energy and recharge later, provided that the price difference between the discharge and recharge intervals generates profit. Figure 3a shows the average cumulative EV costs for the entire planning horizon. As we can see, the highest cost for the EV is given by the *first slot* method, which is expected as in this case the EV agent chooses to charge immediately without considering the energy price. By adopting the *Lowest Prices* method, the total cost for EV charging drops about 33% by the end of the time horizon. Finally, by allowing *V2G* operations, the charging costs drop even more, 15% lower than those of *Lowest Prices*, and by 43% compared to the *first slot* method.

Next, we account for the impact of the different charging scheduling methods on the aggregate energy imbalance. As a baseline, we consider grid imbalance without the EV demand. We calculate the sum of the absolute imbalance values among the intervals, the sum of only the positive imbalance intervals (i.e., the total exported or "wasted" energy), and the sum of only the negative intervals (i.e., the total energy imports). Table 1 shows the significant impact of EVs strategy on the energy imbalance. When using the *first slot* method, EVs affect the system negatively, by increasing the total imbalance and adding more than double to the energy that has to be produced to meet demand in the grid. In parallel, the amount of energy wasted drops, since EVs consume energy that otherwise would not be consumed. In the case of *Lowest Prices* method, the imbalance tangibly drops, and the available energy that is utilized and does not get wasted, increases by half (specifically, by 45.6%). The imports are also increased, due to the additional demand of the 100 EVs and their occasional need to charge their batteries to continue their trip without caring about high energy

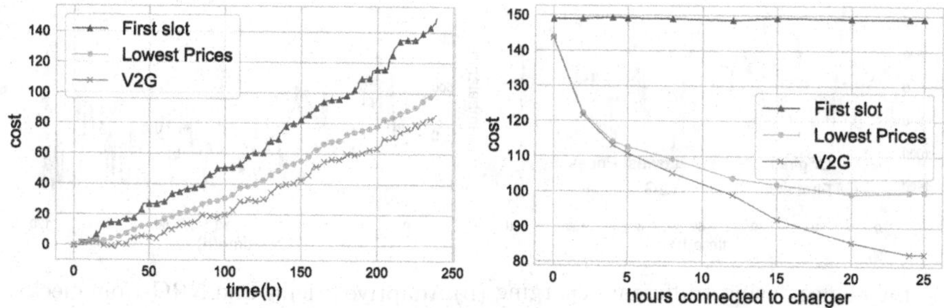

(a) Average Cumulative Cost per EV for different charging scheduling methods.

(b) Cost comparison of varying time periods that EVs are connected to chargers.

Fig. 3. Charging cost variation in different scenarios.

Table 1. Energy differences on charging scheduling methods compared to the "no EVs" baseline. The MAPE of the original imbalance curve is 63.9%.

Method	Imbalance	Wasted	Imported	MAPE
First slot	+7.0%	−21.8%	+104.2%	−12.4%
Lowest prices	−31.4%	−45.6%	+16.4%	−44.5%
V2G	−37.3%	−49.1%	+2.5%	−55.7%

prices and energy shortage of the grid. An even better picture is obtained when *V2G* comes into play, with even lower imbalance (higher imbalance reduction, reaching 37.3%); less energy wasted (waste reduced by 49.1%; while imports are increased by only a very small rate (specifically, by 2.5%). Moreover, it achieves a larger reduction in the *Mean Absolute Percentage Error (MAPE)*, than the other two methods. MAPE measures the difference of the induced imbalance from a totally flat curve with a value of zero, which resembles perfect matching between supply and demand. This is clearly visible when plotting the imbalance across the time horizon for each method, as we do in Fig. 4a. Indeed, it is noteworthy that *V2G* induces smaller peaks in the imbalance between demand and supply than the rest of the methods.

In the second use case, we measure the total cumulative cost of EVs, when increasing the duration of connection to chargers by 24 h compared to the original data, by following the three different charging scheduling methods of the first use case. The results of Fig. 3b show that by increasing the duration of connection, the *Lowest Price* and *V2G* methods manage to gradually reduce the battery charging costs. This happens since the longer an EV is connected to a charger, the higher probability it has to find the most advantageous intervals to buy energy at from the grid— and also to sell it back to the grid in the case of V2G. As anticipated, again, the *V2G* method leads to lower charging costs than the

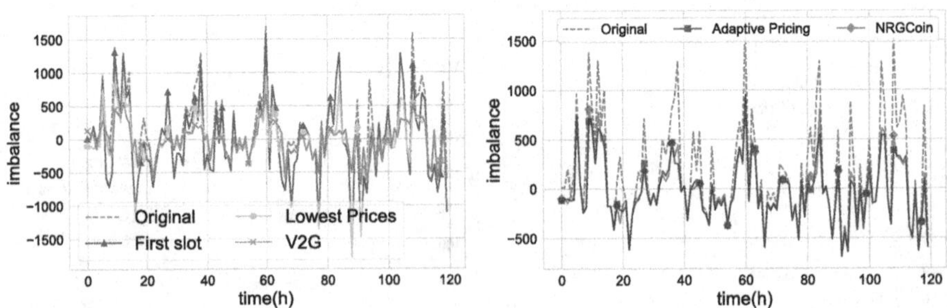

(a) Imbalance using different charging scheduling methods.

(b) Adaptive pricing and NRG-Coin mechanisms.

Fig. 4. Difference in imbalance curves in two different scenarios

Table 2. Pricing Algorithms: Energy differences compared to "no EVs" baseline.

Method	Imbalance	Wasted	Imported	MAPE
NRG-Coin	−31.4%	−45.6%	+16.4%	−44.5%
Adaptive pricing	−31.3%	−45.6%	+17.1%	−42.7%

other two, and the difference (mirroring this *V2G*'s advantage) increases as the duration of connection to a charger gets longer.

The third use case compares different pricing algorithms for the MD agent, in particular the *NRG-Coin* pricing and the *adaptive pricing*. Both methods aim to balance demand and supply, by setting higher prices for consumption during problematic intervals of negative imbalance, and lower for those with positive. The charging of EVs for this use case is performed according to the *Lowest Prices* scheduling approach. Considering that EV agents are rational and aim to reduce their expenses, the application of the two pricing algorithms results to demand being shifted to utilize the generated energy more effectively, thus leading to smaller peaks in the imbalance curve. Figure 4b shows that the algorithms have a similar effect on the stability of the grid. In Table 2, we can observe a similar behavior of reducing the wasted energy and a slightly outperform of *NRG-Coin* on imported energy and MAPE reduction.

In the fourth use case, we count the total number of exchanged messages required for the scheduling of charging using our proposed cooperation protocols as the EV population increases. We report that we observed a *linear* increase in the number of messages exchanged over a 10 days period (we do not present the results in detail due to space restrictions).

6 Conclusions and Future Work

In this paper we presented a open architecture for the V2G/G2V energy transfer problem domain, and provided implementations of agents as flexible microservices that are interconnected by an IoT platform. Our approach can be used for the exploration of various agent strategies in simulation mode, but is also readily deployable and can support real world trials. We also address the needs for openness, and the coverage of diverse business models via the definition of a number of key agent types and the development of open protocols. These can be made available to any interested party, which can subsequently build their own agents given their expertise and business cases. This is demonstrated via presenting realistic use case scenarios.

Having validated our architecture, we can now look to the future. There is much to be done in terms of populating the agents' components with actual machine learning, decision-making, and recommendation algorithms. Finally, we intend to use our system in the real-world, first as part of a pilot study. This will allow us to test the perceived openness and the usability of the system, and to identify potential extensions, as well as important business models.

References

1. Akasiadis, C., Pitsilis, V., Spyropoulos, C.D.: A multi-protocol IoT platform based on open-source frameworks. Sensors **19**(19), 4217 (2019)
2. Burke, M.J., Stephens, J.C.: Energy democracy: goals and policy instruments for sociotechnical transitions. Energy Res. Soc. Sci. **33**, 35–48 (2017)
3. Danner, D., Duschl, W., de Meer, H.: Fair charging service allocation for electric vehicles in the power distribution grid. In: e-Energy 2019, pp. 406–408 (2019)
4. Espe, E., Potdar, V., Chang, E.: Prosumer communities and relationships in smart grids: a literature review, evolution and future directions. Energies **11**(10), 2528 (2018)
5. Hossein Motlagh, N., Mohammadrezaei, M., Hunt, J., Zakeri, B.: Internet of things (IoT) and the energy sector. Energies **13**(2), 494 (2020)
6. International Energy Agency: Global EV outlook: Towards cross-modal electrification (2018)
7. Käbisch, S., Peintner, D., Heuer, J., et al.: The OpenV2G project. http://openv2g.sourceforge.net/. Accessed 22 Apr 2022
8. Karfopoulos, E.L., Hatziargyriou, N.D.: A multi-agent system for controlled charging of a large population of electric vehicles. IEEE Trans. Power Syst. **28**(2), 1196–1204 (2013)
9. Ketter, W., Collins, J., Reddy, P.: Power TAC: a competitive economic simulation of the smart grid. Energy Econ. **39**, 262–270 (2013)
10. Lee, Z., Johansson, D., Low, S.H.: ACN-sim: an open-source simulator for data-driven electric vehicle charging research. In: e-Energy 2019, pp. 411–412. ACM (2019)
11. Liao, J.T., Huang, H.W., Yang, H.T., Li, D.: Decentralized V2G/G2V scheduling of EV charging stations by considering the conversion efficiency of bidirectional chargers. Energies **14**(4), 962 (2021)
12. Lipman, T., Callaway, D., Peffer, T., von Meier, A.: Open-source, open-architecture software platform for plug-in electric vehicle smart charging in California. California Energy Commission (2020)
13. Mahela, O.P., et al.: Comprehensive overview of multi-agent systems for controlling smart grids. CSEE J. Power Energy Syst. (2020)
14. Mihaylov, M., Jurado, S., Avellana, N., et al.: NRGcoin: virtual currency for trading of renewable energy in smart grids. In: 11th International Conference on the EU Energy Market (EEM 2014), pp. 1–6. IEEE (2014)
15. Sarkar, R., Saha, P.K., Mondal, S., Mondal, A.: Intelligent scheduling of V2G, V2V, G2V operations in a smart microgrid. In: e-Energy 2020, pp. 417–418 (2020)
16. Savaglio, C., Ganzha, M., Paprzycki, M., et al.: Agent-based internet of things: state-of-the-art and research challenges. Futur. Gener. Comput. Syst. **102**, 1038–1053 (2020)
17. Sheppard, C., Jenn, A.: Grid-integrated electric mobility model (GEM) v1.0. US Department of Energy (2021). https://www.osti.gov//servlets/purl/1765949
18. Spanoudakis, N., Moraitis, P.: Engineering ambient intelligence systems using agent technology. IEEE Intell. Syst. **30**(3), 60–67 (2015)
19. Valogianni, K., Ketter, W., Collins, J., Zhdanov, D.: Sustainable electric vehicle charging using adaptive pricing. Prod. Oper. Manag. **29**(6), 1550–1572 (2020)
20. Wooldridge, M., Jennings, N.R.: Intelligent agents: theory and practice. Knowl. Eng. Rev. **10**, 115–152 (1995)
21. Zambonelli, F.: Key abstractions for IoT-oriented software engineering. IEEE Softw. **34**(1), 38–45 (2017)

Investigating Effects of Centralized Learning Decentralized Execution on Team Coordination in the Level Based Foraging Environment as a Sequential Social Dilemma

Peter Atrazhev and Petr Musilek(✉)

Department of Electrical and Computer Engineering, University of Alberta, Edmonton, Canada
{atrazhev,pmusilek}@ualberta.ca

Abstract. In this work, we investigate the effects of centralized learning decentralized execution algorithms on agent coordination in a modified version of the Level Based Foraging environment that behaves as a sequential social dilemma. We show that with individual agent rewards, Level Based Foraging becomes a sequential social dilemma. When compared with previously reported results on the Level based Foraging environment using joint rewards [13], we observe significant convergence rate improvements for algorithms that perform state action value estimation: IQL, VDN and QMIX.

Keywords: Social dilemmas · Multi Agent Reinforcement Learning · Centralized Learning Decentralized Execution

1 Introduction

Multi Agent Reinforcement Learning (MARL) has emerged as an efficient, performant tool to solve complex tasks. Most high-profile investigations focus on scenarios with joint team rewards [12,19], as the success of MARL systems relies on a clear, task-relevant reward signal.

Unfortunately, there are many potential application scenarios that do not favour or allow a joint reward function for security, privacy, implementation, or task reasons. In these situations, individual agents receive rewards that are based on their own state action trajectories, rather than being a signal that represents the performance of the team based on all members state action trajectories. This increases task difficulty due to decrease in information about team performance in the reward signal resulting in misalignment between agents and team goals. Seeing as MARL algorithms maximize reward for each agent, it is possible for the task to exhibit elements of a Sequential Social Dilemma (SSD) that could be detrimental to the completion of the task.

In a SSD, agents have to choose between two broad policy categories: collaboration with other agents or defection prioritizing themselves. When agents

© The Author(s), under exclusive license to Springer Nature Switzerland AG 2022
F. Dignum et al. (Eds.): PAAMS 2022, LNAI 13616, pp. 15–23, 2022.
https://doi.org/10.1007/978-3-031-18192-4_2

collaborate, they usually suffer a short-term penalty in exchange for higher returns. Agent defection involves prioritizing the individual agent's rewards over the long term rewards of the group. The key to solving SSDs is for the agents to learn to coordinate their policies to maximize return.

Recently, a class of MARL algorithms called Centralized Learning Decentralized Execution (CLDE) have demonstrated increases in performance on difficult coordination tasks. [15] CLDE algorithms employ a centralized learning method during training, conditioning agents on more information than the agents local observations. Therefore, CLDE algorithms result in policies are able to coordinate better with teammates, do not require shared rewards during training and exhibit higher sample efficiency.

We are unaware of literature evaluating CLDE algorithms on SSDs to determine if they are able to increase the performance of agents with conflicting goals, when compared to their non CLDE counterparts. We suspect that this is partially due to the lack of accessible SSD MARL environments with reported benchmarks [1,13]. We investigate the effects of using CLDE methods in SSD's and the effect of agents receiving individual reward in CLDE methods with the hopes of establishing a reference for the use of CLDE in SSD.

The recently released EPYMARL package contains several CLDE algorithms as well as several fully cooperative MARL environments [13], including the Level Based Foraging environment (LBF) [2,13]. This gridworld environment has agents working together as a team to collect various food items within a certain time frame. Agents and food have respective levels with food only being collected when the aggregate level of all surrounding agents is greater than its own. Agents are individually rewarded for their contribution in loading food. [13] studies LBF with joint reward.

As part of this article's contributions, we show that when agents receive individual rewards, the LBF environment is a SSD that focuses on temporal coordination of a partnership of asymmetrical agents. We record the performance of the following algorithms on four LBF tasks in which agents receive individual rewards: IQL, IPPO, IA2C, VDN, QMIX, MAA2C and MAPPO. We then compare those results to previously reported results which use a joint reward in the same scenarios. Our results show that state action value estimating algorithms achieve significantly faster convergence in the independent reward setting when compared to the joint reward setting.

2 Background

2.1 Multi Agent Reinforcement Learning (MARL)

Cooperative Tasks: We define a cooperative task as a *Markov Multiagent Environment* which consists of the tuple $M = <D, S, A, T, O, o, R, h, b_0>$ [11]. Where D is the set of agents, S is the set that describes the true state of the environment, A is the joint action set over all agents, T is the transition probability function, mapping joint actions to state. O is the joint observation set, o represents the observation probability function, R is the reward function which describes the set of all individual rewards for each agent (joint reward) $\mathbf{R} = R_t^i$. The horizon of the problem, h, is equivalent to the discount factor γ in RL literature. The initial state distribution is given by b_0. M describes a partially observable scenario in which agents interact with the environment through observations, without ever knowing the true state of the environment. When agents have full access to state information, the tuple becomes $<D, S, A, T, R, h, b_0>$ and is defined as a *Multiagent Markov Decision Process (MMDP)* [11]. When the whole team receives a joint reward value taken as the sum of all individual agent rewards $R = R^i = ... = R^N = \sum_{i=1}^{N} R_t^i$ the setting returns to the de-facto MARL setting known as the *Dec-POMDP* [11], and is known as a fully cooperative tasks.

The most prevalent difference between these two task types is that in the cooperative task each agent will experience a reduction in frequency of rewards that it experiences since it wont receive any reward from the actions of other agents on the team. Cooperative task rewards therefore are more stochastic in nature as agents that do not participate in reward events do not receive rewards, which can lead to slower convergence rates or in extreme cases, failure to converge. However, the reward that each agent experiences is now due entirely to that individual agent's policy. This can offer a truer signal for policies to be based on, leading to faster convergence rates and possibly higher rewards. The linking of reward to individual agent policy may cause agents to act greedy to their own policy rather than trying to optimize a joint team policy, which can turn a team objective into a sequential social dilemma. It is unclear if individual rewards in team MARL settings will increase team coordination or be a detriment.

2.2 Sequential Social Dilemmas

Sequential social dilemmas (SSD) are described as problems in which individual rationality leads to collective irrationality. In the multi agent setting, sequential social dilemmas are categorized into two broad categories: the provision of public goods and the tragedy of the commons, of which we focus on the latter. The commons problem involves individuals being tempted by an immediate benefit that produces a cost shared by all if all players succumb to temptation [4]. The key to solving the commons problem is for all agents to coordinate their actions to avoid premature exhaustion of a shared resource.

MARL has emerged as a empirical method for studying temporally complex SSD's that feature more than two agents [3,5–7]. These studies have produced a robust definition of the SSD and its mechanics [3,6,7]. To analyze a SSD, the joint action set A is split into the set $[C, D]$ where C is the set of collaborative actions and D is the set of defective actions. This categorization allows for the classification of policies to be collaborative or defective. If the SSD is simple or can be decomposed into a simple matrix game then there are analytical methods for proving that the situation is an SSD [7].

2.3 Centralized Learning Decentralized Execution (CLDE)

CLDE is the current state of the art method for using MADRL on fully cooperative problems. This method attempts to coordinate agents by training agent's individual policies using a centralized system that conditions over all agents observations [8,14,20]. During execution, agents only condition on their local observations and rewards. This allows for the creation of collaboration without requiring that agents share any information with each other at run time. CLDE methods fall into two categories: the centralized policy gradient methods [8,9,20] and the value function decomposition methods [14,18].

3 Related Work

3.1 MARL Coordination in SSDs

MARL Coordination in SSDs has been studied through different mechanisms by which agents can be incentivised to collaborate together without necessarily sharing information inspired by psychology and sociology. These mechanisms range from imbuing the reward function with terms that create social pressures on the agents [3], to outright enabling actions that punish other agents, allowing the creation and enforcement of taboo behaviour in agent systems [5].

Most of these methods study algorithmic effects on behavior, and focus on investigating changes in agent policy as a result of the imbued mechanism. Some of these mechanisms observe the actions and rewards of other agents which may not always be available or favourable for computation in large systems during run time.

Additionally, an active field of research is the study of environmental properties of SSDs. Leibo et al. [6] recently packaged and released a comprehensive compendium of SSDs with varying properties and made them available in lab2D [1]. Leibo et al. [6] provide a ontology of different SSDs, and although the authors caution that their classification methods are not rooted in any concrete analysis, we find it useful for the proposal and presentation of environments that have novel combinations of characteristics.

We note a lack of investigations that include CLDE algorithms in both mentioned areas of research. This is surprising since CLDE algorithms have been known to increase performance even in very challenging, fully cooperative environment such as the Starcraft Multiagent environment [15].

3.2 Learning Algorithms

This work extends EPYMARL to conduct experiments, modifying the learning algorithms where necessary to learn within the cooperative scenarios we investigate.

Independent Learning Algorithms (IL): Algorithmically identical to their single-agent counterparts, IL algorithms condition independently on an agent's local information in a decentralized manner, without access to joint information from other agents. In this work we employ three different IL algorithms. Independent Q Learning (IQL) that is based on the popular DQN algorithm [10]. Independent Proximal Policy Optimization (IPPO) based on the successful PPO algorithm [16]. Independent Synchronous Advantage Actor-Critic (IA2C) is a synchronous variant of the A3C algorithm [9].

Centralized Learning Decentralized Execution (CLDE): The CLDE algorithms used in this work include both centralized policy gradient and value function decomposition methods. Chosen centralized policy gradient algorithms are multi agent independent synchronous advantage actor-critic (MAA2C) and multi agent proximal policy optimization (MAPPO) [20]. MAA2C and MAPPO are both multi agent versions of their independent counterparts with a joint critic conditioning on all agent observations. Value decomposition methods used were Value Decomposition Networks (VDN) [18] and its more contemporary counterpart QMIX [14].Value decomposition methods train a factored joint state action value function using the standard DQN algorithm. VDN decomposes the value function as the sum of individual value functions while QMIX employs a hypernetwork conditioned on state information to factor the state-value function.

4 LBF as a SSD

We show that the cooperative version of the LBF (CLBF) task becomes a commons type SSD similar to the stag hunt problem [3]. The payoff structure is shown in Table 1. As in the stag hunt problem, agents in the CLBF environment coordinate to collect the food resources spread out on the gridworld. Agents are motivated by fear of being taken advantage of $R_d(0.7) > R_c(0.3)$. This causes two Nash Equilibria to emerge: C, C and D, D

Table 1. Individual payoff matrix for CLBF environment.

Player 1/2	C	D
C	0.5, 0.5	0.3, 0.7
D	0.7, 0.3	0.4,0.4

5 Experimental Design

In order to evaluate the effects of changing the task from a fully cooperative task to a cooperative task we chose to repeat a recent benchmark in the LBF environment [13]. By selecting a series of scenarios to study, we can directly compare the results, and can attribute most differences to the increase in task complexity due to the cooperative reward.

Tasks selected for this study are: *8x8-2p-2f-coop*, *2s-8x8-2p-2f-coop*, *10x10-3p-3f* and *2s-10x10-3p-3f*. *2s* indicates a observation radius of 2 squares, allowing the study of partial observability. *-p* and *-f* indicate the number of players and food in the gridworld. The *-coop* flag causes the game to enforce all agents be present to collect food, thereby forcing the cooperative policy to be the only policy that can be learned.

These tasks were selected because most algorithms were able to achieve maximum episode return in the joint reward context, and it is reasonable to assume that the same algorithms would also be able maximize the episode return in the individual reward setting. To evaluate algorithm performance, we calculate the average returns achieved throughout all evaluation windows during training, and 95% confidence interval across five seeds. Hyperparameter tuning was not performed for this experiment to stay consistent with the hyperparameters used for the LBF benchmark [13].

6 Results

The results of the selected algorithms are reported in Fig. 1, showing the normalized evaluation returns. Figure 2 shows results from [13] with only the relevant information from the experiments that we performed, allowing an assessment of the effects of the change from fully cooperative to cooperative tasks.

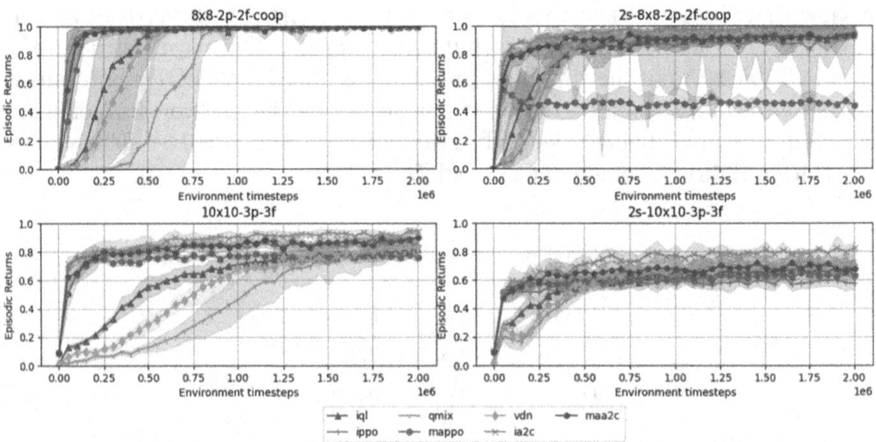

Fig. 1. Episodic returns of all algorithms on CLBF showing the mean and 95% confidence interval over three different seeds

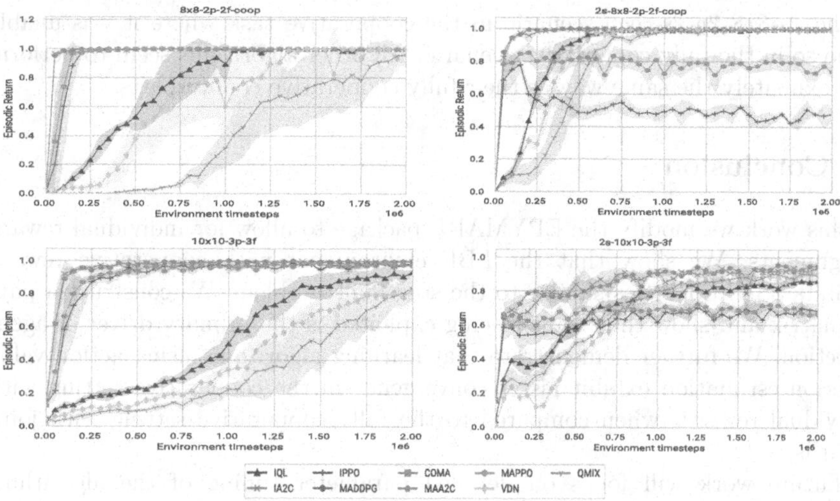

Fig. 2. Image taken from Papoudakis et al. [13] COMA and MADDPG traces have been removed and only the relevant scenarios have been kept. These results show the performance of algorithms on the fully cooperative

As a general observation, the change to a cooperative environment decreases the performance of all tested algorithms. Since hyperparameter optimization was not performed for this experiment, it may be possible that tuned agents could reclaim losses in performance. The lack of hyperparameter optimizations also makes it unclear if the slight reduction in final mean return is due to the change in the reward function or unoptimized hyperparameters. These will be studied in the future.

Fully Observable Scenarios

Methods that rely on any form of estimating the action value function seem to improve in the cooperative setting. The algorithms IQL, VDN and QMIX all show increase in speed of learning when reward is individual. While it can be argued that the improvement in IQL convergence rate is intangible, the improvements in VDN and QMIX are notable. When Figs. 1 and 2 are compared, both VDN and QMIX show signs that the training speed is reduced by at least 1/4 with some earlier training instances being reduced by 1/2. This convergence speed up is best seen in the QMIX algorithm in the *8x8-2p-2f-coop* scenario where convergence is shortened from 2 million timesteps in the fully cooperative setting to just under 1 million timesteps.

Partially Observable Scenarios

These scenarios are the ones that include 2s in the title. Most algorithms show no discernible improvements at all in these scenarios. IPPO is able to converge in the *2s-8x8-2p-2s-coop* scenario in the cooperative task where it was unable to do so in the fully cooperative scenario. All other algorithms seem to perform approximately the same way as their fully cooperative counterparts.

7 Conclusion

In this work we modify the EPYMARL package to allow for individual reward assignments. We show that the LBF environment with cooperative reward exhibits SSD properties similar to the stag hunt problem. We construct a payoff matrix and show that fear of being exploited is the primary driver of agent defection. We further demonstrate that learning algorithms using action value function estimation exhibit faster convergence in the cooperative setting with individual rewards when compared to the fully cooperative setting with joint rewards.

Future work will focus on detailed parameter tuning of the algorithms employed in this work to deeper investigate detected trends in convergence behavior. Further continuing this line of inquiry could involve adding more value decomposition algorithms that can factor more general functions, such as QTRAN [17]. Additionally, incorporating a linking layer between CEPYMARL and the MeltingPot protocol [1,6] would offer the chance to see how CLDE algorithms perform on a variety of SSDs with additional benchmarks to compare to.

References

1. Beattie, C., Köppe, T., Duéñez-Guzmán, E.A., Leibo, J.Z.: DeepMind Lab2D. CoRR abs/2011.07027 (2020). https://arxiv.org/abs/2011.07027
2. Christianos, F., Schäfer, L., Albrecht, S.V.: Shared experience actor-critic for multi-agent reinforcement learning. In: Advances in Neural Information Processing Systems (NeurIPS) (2020)
3. Hughes, E., et al.: Inequity aversion resolves intertemporal social dilemmas. CoRR abs/1803.08884 (2018). http://arxiv.org/abs/1803.08884
4. Kollock, P.: Social dilemmas: the anatomy of cooperation. Ann. Rev. Sociol. **24**(1), 183–214 (1998)
5. Köster, R., et al.: Model-free conventions in multi-agent reinforcement learning with heterogeneous preferences. arXiv preprint arXiv:2010.09054 (2020)
6. Leibo, J.Z., et al.: Scalable evaluation of multi-agent reinforcement learning with melting pot. In: International Conference on Machine Learning, pp. 6187–6199. PMLR (2021)
7. Leibo, J.Z., Zambaldi, V.F., Lanctot, M., Marecki, J., Graepel, T.: Multi-agent reinforcement learning in sequential social dilemmas. CoRR abs/1702.03037 (2017). http://arxiv.org/abs/1702.03037
8. Lowe, R., Wu, Y.I., Tamar, A., Harb, J., Pieter Abbeel, O., Mordatch, I.: Multi-agent actor-critic for mixed cooperative-competitive environments. In: Advances in Neural Information Processing Systems 30 (2017)
9. Mnih, V., et al.: Asynchronous methods for deep reinforcement learning. In: International Conference on Machine Learning, pp. 1928–1937. PMLR (2016)

10. Mnih, V., et al.: Human-level control through deep reinforcement learning. Nature **518**(7540), 529–533 (2015)
11. Oliehoek, F.A., Amato, C.: The Decentralized POMDP Framework, pp. 11–32. Springer, Cham (2016). https://doi.org/10.1007/978-3-319-28929-8_2
12. OpenAI: OpenAI five (2018). https://blog.openai.com/openai-five/
13. Papoudakis, G., Christianos, F., Schäfer, L., Albrecht, S.V.: Benchmarking multi-agent deep reinforcement learning algorithms in cooperative tasks. CoRR abs/2006.07869 (2020). https://arxiv.org/abs/2006.07869
14. Rashid, T., Samvelyan, M., de Witt, C.S., Farquhar, G., Foerster, J.N., Whiteson, S.: QMIX: monotonic value function factorisation for deep multi-agent reinforcement learning. CoRR abs/1803.11485 (2018). http://arxiv.org/abs/1803.11485
15. Samvelyan, M., et al.: The StarCraft Multi-Agent Challenge. CoRR abs/1902.04043 (2019)
16. Schulman, J., Wolski, F., Dhariwal, P., Radford, A., Klimov, O.: Proximal policy optimization algorithms. CoRR abs/1707.06347 (2017). http://arxiv.org/abs/1707.06347
17. Son, K., Kim, D., Kang, W.J., Hostallero, D., Yi, Y.: QTRAN: learning to factorize with transformation for cooperative multi-agent reinforcement learning. CoRR abs/1905.05408 (2019). http://arxiv.org/abs/1905.05408
18. Sunehag, P., et al.: Value-decomposition networks for cooperative multi-agent learning. arXiv preprint arXiv:1706.05296 (2017)
19. Vinyals, O., et al.: Grandmaster level in StarCraft II using multi-agent reinforcement learning. Nature **575**(7782), 350–354 (2019). https://doi.org/10.1038/s41586-019-1724-z
20. Yu, C., Velu, A., Vinitsky, E., Wang, Y., Bayen, A.M., Wu, Y.: The surprising effectiveness of MAPPO in cooperative, multi-agent games. CoRR abs/2103.01955 (2021). https://arxiv.org/abs/2103.01955

Agent Based Digital Twin of Sorting Terminal to Improve Efficiency and Resiliency in Parcel Delivery

Souvik Barat[1(✉)], Vinay Kulkarni[1], Aditya Paranjape[2], Subramaniam Dhandapani[3], Solomon Manuelraj[3], and Sai Prasad Parameswaran[3]

[1] Tata Consultancy Service Research, Pune 411013, India
{souvik.barat,vinay.vkulkarni}@tcs.com

[2] Imperial College London, London 69121 SW7 2BX, UK
a.paranjape@imperial.ac.uk

[3] Tata Consultancy Service, Bangalore, India
{s.dhandapani,solomon.m,p.sai}@tcs.com

Abstract. Open economy, globalization and effect of Covid19 pandemic are transforming the consumer behavior rapidly. The business is nudging consumers towards hyper consumption through online shopping, e-commerce and other conveniences with affordable cost. The companies from courier, express and parcel (CEP) industry are trying to capitalize on this opportunity by tying up with business to consumers (B2C) companies with a promise of delivering parcels to the doorstep in an ever-shrinking time window. In this endeavor, the conventional optimization-based planning approach to manage the fixed parcel payload is turning out to be inadequate. The CEP companies need to quickly adapt to the situation more frequently so as to be efficient and resilient in this growing demand situation. We propose an agent-based digital twin of the sorting terminal, a key processing element of parcel delivery operation, as an experimentation aid to: (i) explore and arrive at the right configuration of the existing sorting terminal infrastructure, (ii) be prepared for possible outlier conditions, and (iii) identify plausible solutions for mitigating the outlier conditions in an evidence-backed manner. This paper presents digital twin of the sorting terminal and demonstrates its use as "in silico" experimentation aid for domain experts to support evidence-backed decision-making.

Keywords: Digital twin · Sorting terminal · Decision making · Agent model

1 Introduction

The pervasiveness of internet, widespread acceptance of mobile technology, and Covid19 pandemic related restrictions are revolutionizing the consumer behavior significantly. Online shopping and e-commerce are becoming a new normal for most of the business sectors. Product vendors are keen to make available products worldwide at an affordable cost; suppliers are committing to just-in-time raw material supply to help manufacturers

© The Author(s), under exclusive license to Springer Nature Switzerland AG 2022
F. Dignum et al. (Eds.): PAAMS 2022, LNAI 13616, pp. 24–35, 2022.
https://doi.org/10.1007/978-3-031-18192-4_3

reduce inventory cost; and Retailers are setting up virtual product stores to deliver products in ever-shrinking time window. All these are driving the need for flawless, speedy and economic shipping. As an early indicator, the global e-commerce market is expected to reach US$ 55.6 Trillion by 2027 from US$ 13 trillion in 2021[1].

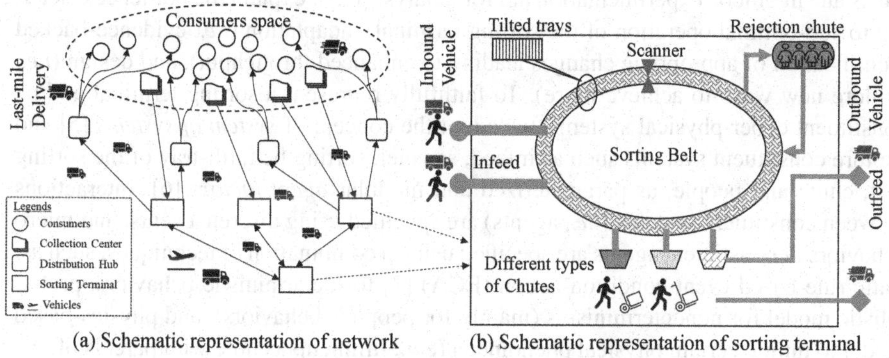

(a) Schematic representation of network (b) Schematic representation of sorting terminal

Fig. 1. An overview of parcel delivery network

However, optimally delivering large numbers of parcels of different size and characteristics across the globe with certainty in a dynamic and uncertain world is a significant challenge for Courier, Express and Parcel (CEP) companies. Until now, these CEP companies managed to fulfill shipment demands with a relatively static network of collection centers, sorting terminals, transportation, and last-mile connectivity as illustrated in Fig. 1(a). To get and manage assignments, logistic companies have strategically placed collection centers to collect parcels; transportation machinery takes these parcels to sorting terminals; sorting terminals sort the parcels identifying their destinations; transportation machinery takes these parcels to the right delivery centers; and the last-mile delivery machinery delivers the parcels to customer doorstep. To capitalize on the increasing parcel delivery demand in ever-shrinking time window, CEP companies are trying to improve their parcel delivery capabilities along three dimensions: optimum vehicle management [1, 2], efficient last-mile delivery [3], and sorting terminal throughput. While the first two dimensions can be satisfactorily addressed using sophisticated algorithms and (on-demand) vehicles/carriers as reported in [4], improving throughput of the sorting terminal is a much complex task. It calls for accurate parcel arrival forecast, automation aids, and strategies for efficient operation. CEP companies have several automation aids spread across a wide spectrum of sophistication to choose from e.g., automated in-feeds to onboard parcel to be sorted, scanners to scan the parcels, tilt-tray sorting belt, different kinds of chutes to collect the sorted parcels, and outfeeds to load parcels for transporting. Even as technologies continually improve over time, several concerns are becoming critical. For instance, identifying the best configuration of the sorting terminal for the expected payload in terms of the choices for each automation aid, deciding the number of human operators to be allocated and assigned to individual

[1] https://www.imarcgroup.com/e-commerce-market.

automation aids to maximally leverage the chosen configuration, and determining where to invest more (i.e., replace/redefine) and when in order to maximally garner the shipment demand. Precise and continuous evaluation of these concerns will help CEP companies to be more efficient and resilient in dynamic and uncertain operating environments.

Toward this end, we propose an agent-based simulatable digital twin of sorting terminal as an "in-silico" experimentation aid for: analysis (*e.g.*, explain the bottlenecks leading to sub-optimal operation of the sorting terminal), adaptation (*i.e.*, evidence-backed identification of appropriate changes leading to enhanced throughput), and design (*i.e.*, explore new ways to achieve more). To faithfully represent a sorting terminal and its constituent cyber-physical systems, we adopt the concept of *system of systems* [5] and capture constituent systems such as infeed, scanner, sorting belt, tilt-tray of the sorting belt, chute and people, as parameterized and modular *agents/actors* [6]. Interactions between constituent systems (*i.e.*, agents) are specified using discrete events, and micro behaviors of constituent agents are specified using a combination of techniques, such as: static rule-based event-condition-action (ECA) [7] for deterministic behaviors, probabilistic model for nondeterminisms (mainly for people's behaviors), and physics-based model to mimic certain physical phenomena (e.g., filling up a chute with parcels of different size). We use agent-based bottom-up discrete event simulation to understand the overall behavior of a sorting terminal that emerges from nondeterministic micro behaviors of the constituent agents and their interactions. Simulation with different parameter values of constituent agents and replacement of agents with alternate sets of agents (with hypothetical behaviors) helps experiment with candidate adaptation and design alternatives.

The rest of the paper is organized as follows. Section 2 presents complexities of a sorting terminal and evaluates the state-of-the-art optimization techniques. Section 3 introduces our sorting terminal digital twin. The efficacy of the proposed digital twin is discussed in Sect. 4. Conclusions and future work constitute Sect. 5.

2 Problem Statement

Sorting terminal will deliver optimal throughput when: the parcels spend as less time on the sorting belt as possible, the chutes get emptied as fast as possible, and as few packets remain on the belt unsorted as possible, thus necessitating human intervention (*refer* Fig. 1(b)). The key operational challenges with sorting terminal are: defining suitable equipment configuration (how many chutes of different kinds, and which infeeds need to be operational *etc.*), defining the sorting logic (*i.e.*, which parcels should get collected at which chute), and assigning workforce for chutes, infeeds and outfeeds. Current practice addresses these challenges in a manner that is largely manual and experience driven. Experts design appropriate sets of experiments that are conducted on the sorting terminal in a sand-boxed environment which is intensive in terms of time, effort, cost as well as operator intellect and experience. Moreover, it is risky as the ripple effects of outlier situations may put the entire network to risk.

2.1 State of the Art Analysis Techniques

Conceptually, defining a suitable strategy for optimal throughput of a sorting terminal for a given payload is a complex multivariate optimization problem. However, it is rarely formulated as a monolithic optimization problem due to its inherent complexities. For example, parcel payload of a shift/day is typically estimated based on historical parcel payloads, while the actual flow of parcels may differ from forecasting not only in terms of the quantum (i.e., number of parcels) but also in terms of their sizes, destinations, characteristics (i.e., hard/soft/bendable/perishable) and the order in which the parcels arrive in a sorting terminal. As a result, chutes may encounter blockages requiring a variety of interventions even with a most optimum parcel-to-chute allocation strategy. Inability to address these in a time bound manner may cause undesired micro-level disruptions. The emergence of multiple micro disruptions (e.g., chute blockages) augmented with contextual uncertainties, such as temporary resource unavailability, machine-induced fault and human fatigue-induced errors, may lead to a major disruption causing sub-optimality in the overall network.

Therefore, the state-of-the-art analysis techniques focus on well-defined and relatively bounded parts (*e.g.*, parcel to chute allocation [8]) and solve them independently using linear programming and its variants. Though these localized optimum solutions ensure high accuracy for the ideal situation, they rarely ensure the robustness of the whole sorting terminal. Moreover, they are vulnerable to several real-world events (*e.g.*, wide heterogeneity in parcel characteristics, arrival rate and the arrival sequence) and inherent contextual uncertainties (e.g., varying human productivity, unavailability). These complexities are expected to grow with the growing demand for delivering a wide range of parcels to the consumers doorstep within small time window with dynamic socio-geo-political situation. Formulation of emerging parcel delivery problem as optimization problem will be much more intellect-heavy and possibly computationally infeasible over the time. The real time experimentations to understand the efficacy of adaptation/design alternative will have greater business risk with potential revenue loss.

3 Approach

We rely on a simulatable digital twin [9] as a risk-free experimentation aid to explore and quantitatively evaluate the efficacy of various operational strategies, interventions, adaptation choices and design alternatives for maximizing throughput. To enable fine-grained analysis, we visualize the sorting terminal as well orchestrated parts, i.e., *system of systems*, and represent these constituent parts/elements as configurable and adaptable *agents*. It is important to note here that we consider agents as *adaptive* element to virtually introduce adaptation and design alternatives for what-if experimentations.

3.1 Agent Based Realization

A sorting terminal is a composite unit where parcels arrive in batches at discrete time intervals (i.e., based on vehicle arrivals) and the sorted parcels are sent to next destination point as shown in Fig. 1(b). The primary equipment of a sorting terminal is a sorting

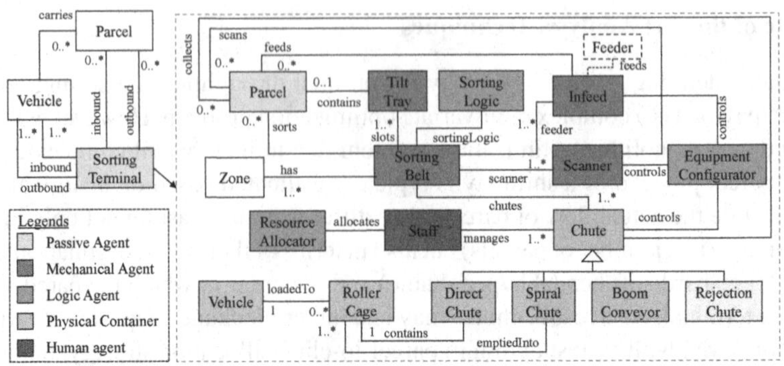

Fig. 2. A schematic view of agent topology for sorting terminal digital twin

belt, which may spread across hundreds of meters and comprises multiple tilt trays that hold parcels. The parcels unloaded from the inbound vehicles are put onto the sorting belts using a set of infeeds - a physical connector with rolling belt. The sorting belt is equipped with multiple scanners that identify the destination for parcels. The parcels are collected in the designated chute for further distribution. For operational convenience, a sorting terminal is typically visualized as a set of zones – a logical decomposition of the area for managing people (i.e., staff) and equipment. An agent topology and various types of agents describing the constituent elements of a sorting terminal are highlighted using different colors in Fig. 2.

Parcels: A parcel is a passive element with no specific behavior[2]. However, their unique characteristics (*i.e.*, weight, height and destination) contributes to the sorting logic. We capture their individualistic characteristics as a passive agent.

Mechanical Units: The equipment or mechanical units (*e.g.*, sorting belt, infeed and scanner) and their parts are governed by a set of well-defined behavioral rules with a certain failure possibility. For example, a sorting belt contains multiple tilt trays (*i.e.*, slots) and helps them to move with a pre-configured speed. A tilt tray with specific length and width carries a parcel and drops it at a designated chute (decided by the sorting logic) if the chute is not blocked when tilt tray is aligned with the destination chute. A tilt tray maintains the circulation count of a parcel and triggers a drop instruction to the rejection chute after the maximum number of allowed attempts, which is known as the *circulation count* – a configurable parameter as shown in Fig. 3(c).

An infeed has a belt that moves at a pre-configured speed to transfer parcels from the inbound area to the sorting belt and places them into a tilt tray (one parcel on one tilt tray). A scanner reads the barcode of the parcel to get the information necessary for sorting. All these machines work with a certain degree of accuracy with respect to their pre-defined rules and may encounter certain failures (i.e., *known unknown*). We capture their characteristics as configurable agent parameters, behavior as set of rules (i.e., ECA specification) and failure uncertainties as a probability function embedded

[2] Parcel behavior becomes important when it carries perishable items or one would like to explore damage propensity from sorting operation, which is out of scope for this paper.

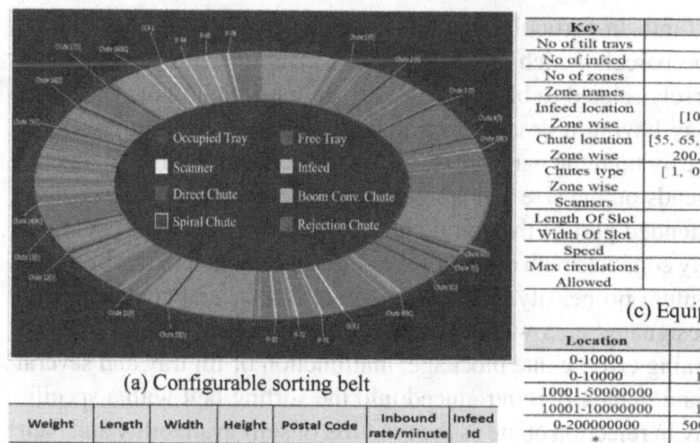

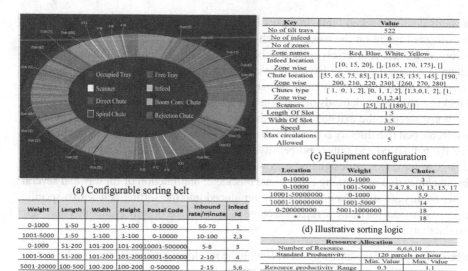

(a) Configurable sorting belt

Weight	Length	Width	Height	Postal Code	Inbound rate/minute	Infeed Id
0-1000	1-50	1-100	1-100	0-10000	50-70	1
1001-5000	1-50	1-100	1-100	0-10000	10-100	2,3
0-1000	51-200	101-200	101-200	10001-500000	5-8	3
1001-5000	51-200	101-200	101-200	10001-500000	2-10	4
5001-20000	100-500	100-200	100-200	0-500000	2-15	5,6

(b) Illustrative parcel feed specification

Key	Value
No of tilt trays	522
No of infeed	6
No of zones	4
Zone names	Red, Blue, White, Yellow
Infeed location Zone wise	[10, 15, 20], [], [165, 170, 175], []
Chute location Zone wise	[55, 65, 75, 85], [115, 125, 135, 145], [190, 200, 210, 220, 230], [260, 270, 280]
Chutes type Zone wise	[1, 0, 1, 2], [0, 1, 1, 2], [1,3,0,1, 2], [1, 0,1,2,4]
Scanners	[25], [], [180], []
Length Of Slot	1.5
Width Of Slot	3.5
Speed	120
Max circulations Allowed	5

(c) Equipment configuration

Location	Weight	Chutes
0-10000	0-1000	3
0-10000	1001-5000	2,4,7,8, 10, 13, 15, 17
10001-50000000	0-1000	5,9
10001-10000000	1001-5000	14
0-200000000	5001-1000000	18
*	*	18

(d) Illustrative sorting logic

Resource Allocation		
Number of Resource	6,6,6,10	
Standard Productivity	120 parcels per hour	
	Min. Value	Max. Value
Resource productivity Range	0.3	1.1

(e) Illustrative resource description & allocation

Fig. 3. Illustration of digital twin configuration

into behavioral specification where the probability ranges are typically derived through heuristic and/or analyzing historical occurrences. The external and internal interactions and instructions are realized as events or messages passed between agents. An illustration of the configurable elements of a sorting terminal are shown in Fig. 3(a) and their parameters are highlighted in Fig. 3(c).

Containers: The containers, such as different types of chutes and roller cages, are primarily passive elements, *i.e.*, they have capacity and no explicit behavior as such. However, they contribute to an interesting emergent behavior that may cause blockage when heterogeneous parcels start falling into them in a random order. In reality, a container is considered as blocked, typically detected through camera sensor, when no more elements can be accommodated without removing them or compressing them using some technique.

We replicate the container blockage phenomena in the virtual world by carefully reflecting on well-studied container packing problem [10]. Empirical results in the literature show that the density of a packed container may differ from 52% (loosely packed) to 74% (densely packed) based on the element size, shape and the characteristics of the container. We consider the concept of Random Close Packing (RCP) [11] and Random Loose Packing (RLP) [12] along with the established empirical findings about the possible density of the container to determine container blockage behavior. Typical sorting terminals contains four types of chutes: direct, spiral, boom conveyor, and rejection chutes. The direct chute uses a roller cage, *i.e.*, an up-side open cuboid, as a container where parcels are dropped from the top (i.e., parcel uses gravitational force to accommodate a position inside the container). Therefore, their behaviors closely match with RCP and the density at which the blockage can be observed, we term it as blockage density, typically varies from loosely packed to densely packed situations with a bias towards densely packed limit. In particular, the blockage density (between two limits) is computed based on the parcels which are dropped at a given instance, *i.e.*, number of bigger parcels is inversely related to blockage density in our digital twin. The spiral chute is a curved pathway having a descent to a lower level along with an extended open platform to temporarily hold the parcels. The behavior matches with RLP, and the blockage propensity depends on the size and weight of the parcels (as it moves against frictional force at the extended part of the spiral chute. The boom conveyor chute is a moveable belt that directly connects with outfeed – we define its characteristics by defining the belt speed and failure propensity. A rejection chute is a special container with a large volume (*i.e.*, a designated area within sorting terminal) where parcels rejected by all chutes due to scanning error, chute blockage, malfunction of tilt tray and several other factors are stored and manually reintroduced into the sorting belt with a specific delay. We model the delay in rejection chute as the function of staff availability and their productivity.

Staff: The people or staff, who interact with the machines and containers, perform well defined tasks that include a) picking up parcels from spiral chute and place them into the roller cage, b) take filled roller cages to the outfeed, c) replace roller cage of direct chute when it is full and take them in outfeed, d) inspect and rectify the issues with the parcels in the rejection chute, and e) address other mechanical blockages and faults. They perform specific/instructed activities with uncertainties. As an example, a person can lift and place 120 parcels from a spiral chute into roller cage in an hour as a standard for a sorting terminal. However, the individual productivity can vary from 30% to 110%. Moreover, the individual productivity can differ with time (due to sluggishness) and individuals can be unavailable for certain time periods. We model people as stochastic agents, where individual behavior and the associated uncertainties are specified as rules (ECA) with temporal nondeterminism and the limits of the nondeterministic behaviors are defined as configurable parameters (see Fig. 3(e)).

Logic Units: Sorting terminal has several logic units that are either closely embedded with the physical systems, such as sorting belt and tilt tray, or produce instruction for the staffs about specific task (*e.g.*, scanning a parcel on a spiral chute indicates appropriate destination roller cage for the staff). Therefore, these units are typically static or dynamic rules about performing tasks.

A sorting logic is set of rules about parcel-to-chute allocation as shown in Fig. 3(d). Equipment configuration is about deciding which machine to operate when and using what parameters (or configuration), such as maximum circulation count of parcels as highlighted in Fig. 3(c). The resource allocator is a resource planner that decides who will work where and for how long. These strategic logic units may define rules over different time scales. For instance, sorting logic is defined for a shift/day; resource allocation changes in every shift, and equipment logic is typically set for a month or more. We capture these units as parameterized rule-based temporal agents that can send events to other units based on the situation. Parameterized realization of these units helps to explore hypothetical scenarios for quantitative evaluation.

Environment Elements: We approximate the rest of the network using two agents namely: Feeder and Vehicles. The feeder agent can introduce any number of parcels with

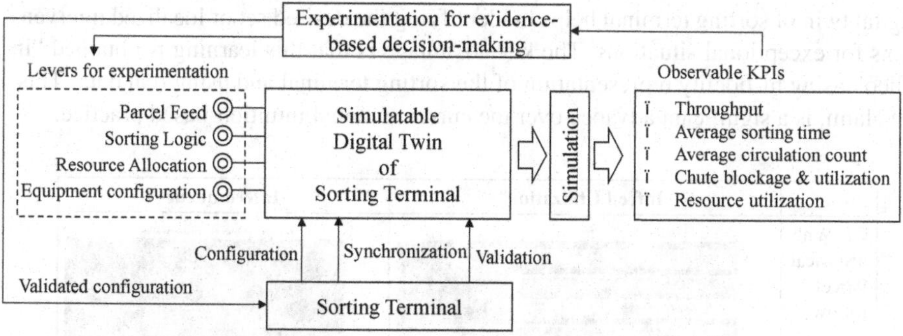

Fig. 4. Digital twin for evidence-based decision making

different characteristics at different time intervals to mimic varying inbound parcel flow, whereas vehicle agents represent the outbound flow by removing parcels from sorting terminal based on staff availability and vehicle schedule. As illustrative configuration of feeder agent is shown in Fig. 3(b).

3.2 Simulation-Led Experimentation Aid

To enable simulation-led experimentation of different strategies and configurations of sorting terminal, we capture agent topology using simulatable event-driven Enterprise Simulation Language (ESL[3]) [13]. Our experimentation method is shown in Fig. 4. As initial experimentation setup, we configure, synchronize and validate the sorting terminal digital twin. Essentially, the constructed sorting terminal digital twin is first configured to mimic the physical setup of a real sorting terminal by specifying equipment configuration that includes the number of tilt trays, infeeds, scanners and different types of chutes along with their locations and other characteristics as illustrated in Fig. 3(b). Further, it can be synchronized with the real sorting terminal to represent the number of parcels on the infeed, sorting belt, chutes, and so on as the initial state of the simulation. We adopt *operational validity* [14] to ensure the faithfulness of a sufficiently configured and synchronized sorting terminal digital twin, where we simulate multiple known scenarios (*i.e.*, historical parcel payload, resource allocations, and sorting logic) and compare simulated key performance indices (KPIs) with respect to historically observed KPIs.

The simulation of a faithfully configured, fully synchronized and validated digital twin of a sorting terminal, therefore, can explain why things are the way they are. The bottlenecks and causes for sub-optimal outcomes can be explored and evaluated by feeding different parcel payloads with varying characteristics and with suitably configured feeder agent, as shown in Fig. 3(b). Different aspects of interest can be simulated "in silico" by adapting different agents of the digital twin using the parameters related to sorting logic, equipment configuration and resource allocation agents. An iterative exploration with different parameters along multiple aspects of interest and observing simulation trends of KPIs can generate sufficient evidence for informed decision-making. Thus, the

[3] http://www.esl-lang.org.

digital twin of sorting terminal helps in identifying the desired set of localized interventions for exceptional situations. The key advantage is that this learning is obtained "in silico" using hi-fidelity representation of the sorting terminal and using real data. This, we claim, is a significant advance over the current manual intuition-based practice.

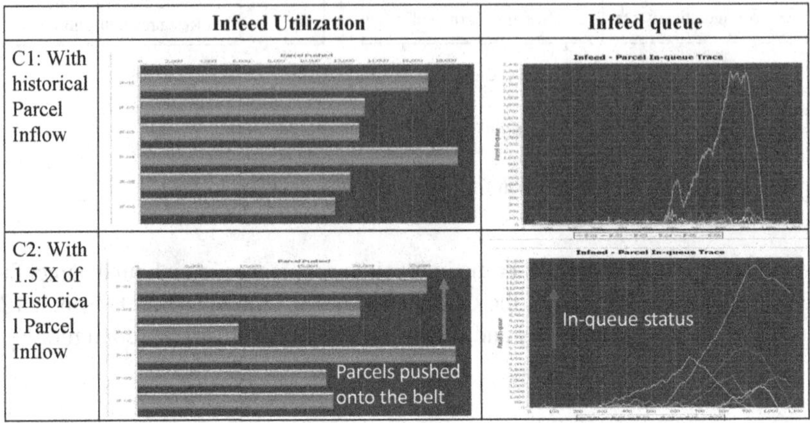

Fig. 5. Experimentation with more inbound parcels

4 Illustrative Case Study

We used our sorting terminal digital twin to understand the bottlenecks and explore effective interventions for improving the operational efficiency of two sorting terminals of a Nordic postal company. Here we present a few illustrative near-real scenarios from our real case study to demonstrate the art of the possible and the efficacy of our approach[4]. For experimentation, we considered a sorting terminal having four zones, a sorting belt with 522 tilt trays, 6 infeeds, 2 scanners, 18 chutes (4 direct chutes, 8 spiral chutes, 5 boom conveyor chutes and 1 rejection chute) with representative physical capacities, and 30 employees as shown in Fig. 3. The illustrative scenario playing demonstrating the art of possibilities are described below.

Analysis: The objective of this scenario is to assess the operational efficiency of the sorting terminal. Here, we simulated the configured digital twin with historical parcel payloads and measured different KPIs for validation. After ensuring the validity of the digital twin, we further explored using different inbound parcel volumes, sizes, characteristics and the order in which they arrive into the sorting terminal by configuring the *Feeder* agent appropriately. We observed that the sorting belt is not capable of sorting high-volume parcels – it restricts parcels to enter the sorting belt and therefore causes queues at the infeed area. As an illustration, the observation about infeed utilization and the queue formation at different infeeds for 1.5 X of as-usual inbound parcels are shown in Fig. 5.

[4] The actual case study is not presented due to the confidentiality of our engagement.

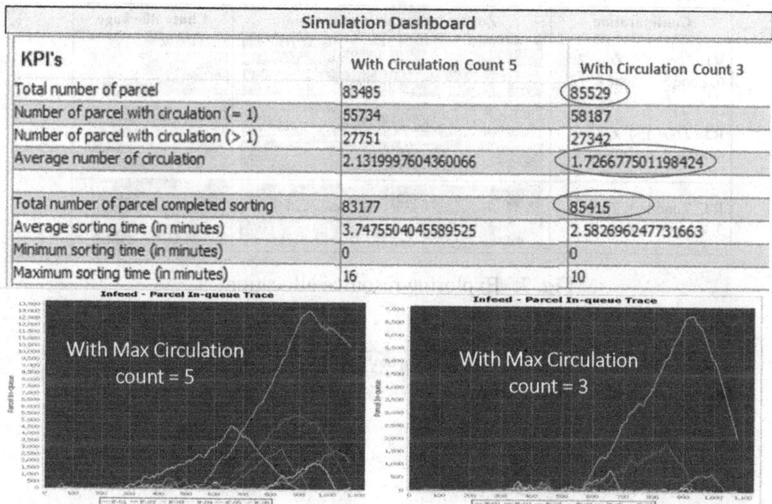

Simulation Dashboard		
KPI's	With Circulation Count 5	With Circulation Count 3
Total number of parcel	83485	85529
Number of parcel with circulation (= 1)	55734	58187
Number of parcel with circulation (> 1)	27751	27342
Average number of circulation	2.1319997604360066	1.726677501198424
Total number of parcel completed sorting	83177	85415
Average sorting time (in minutes)	3.7475504045589525	2.582696247731663
Minimum sorting time (in minutes)	0	0
Maximum sorting time (in minutes)	16	10

Fig. 6. Exploring sorting terminal configurations

Exploring Adaptation: There could be several ways to bring the system back to the desired state for 1.5times inbound payload. Configuring the appropriate maximum circulation count allowed for parcels is one such intervention as it allows parcel to spend an increased or reduced time (as necessary) on the sorting belt. A change of maximum circulation count from 5 to 3 leads to a significant reduction in infeed queue formation as shown in Fig. 6. It also helps to improve the number of parcels processed, the average number of circulations, and the average sorting time as highlighted in Fig. 6. Simulation results also indicates that the sorting logic may result into a skewed chute utilization for new payload as indicated as "with based sorting logic" in Fig. 7. We explored multiple sorting logics and evaluated their impact using our digital twin. One of the sorting logics that resulted in a better chute utilization and improved average sorting time is shown as comparative analysis in Fig. 7.

As further exploration, we evaluated resource utilization where we found the existing 30 employees are under-utilized for the current and our new payload. We explored resource requirements by reducing staff from 30 (with allocation <Zone 1: 6, Zone 2: 6, Zone 3: 6, Zone 4: 12>) to 20 (with allocation <Zone 1: 4, Zone 2: 4, Zone 3: 4, Zone 4: 8>). Simulation shows that the reduction from 30 to 20 improves resource utilization without an observable impact on chute blockage as shown in Fig. 8. However, further reduction of employees from 20 to 15 (with allocation <Zone 1: 3, Zone 2: 3, Zone 3: 3, Zone 4: 6>) causes more chute blockage.

Design: As part of the design space exploration, we explored different equipment layouts by changing the equipment agent. For example, possible effect of adding new chutes, replacing one type of chutes with another type, and moving scanners to different locations for parcel to travel a smaller distance, are explored using a new configuration of sorting terminal digital twin.

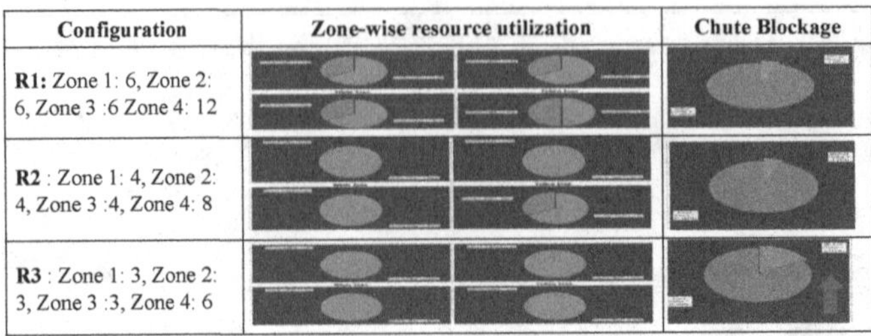

Configuration	Zone-wise resource utilization	Chute Blockage
R1: Zone 1: 6, Zone 2: 6, Zone 3 :6 Zone 4: 12		
R2 : Zone 1: 4, Zone 2: 4, Zone 3 :4, Zone 4: 8		
R3 : Zone 1: 3, Zone 2: 3, Zone 3 :3, Zone 4: 6		

Fig. 7. Exploring resource allocation

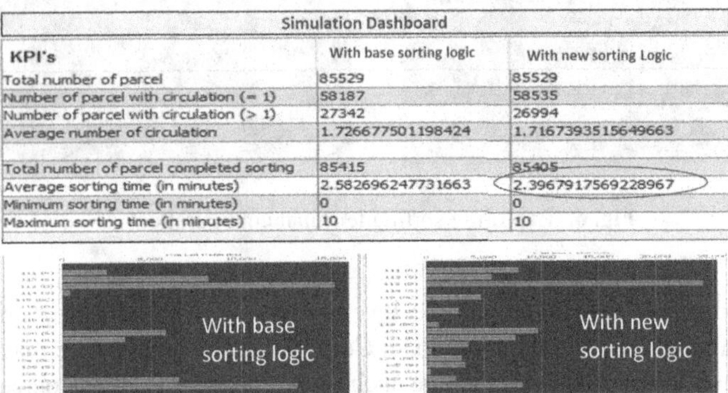

Simulation Dashboard		
KPI's	With base sorting logic	With new sorting Logic
Total number of parcel	85529	85529
Number of parcel with circulation (= 1)	58187	58535
Number of parcel with circulation (> 1)	27342	26994
Average number of circulation	1.726677501198424	1.716739351564966З
Total number of parcel completed sorting	85415	85405
Average sorting time (in minutes)	2.582696247731663	2.396791756922896 7
Minimum sorting time (in minutes)	0	0
Maximum sorting time (in minutes)	10	10

Fig. 8. Understanding efficacy of different sorting logic

5 Conclusion

Current intuition-driven practice for deciding appropriate strategies to maximize operational efficiency of sorting terminal is turning out to be ineffective to meet the growing demand. An approach based on real-time experimentation in a sandboxed environment is found wanting on the counts of agility, robustness and resilience, and carries high risk as well. To overcome these lacunae, we presented a fine-grained agent-based digital twin of a sorting terminal. We demonstrated its efficacy as an "in silico" experimentation aid through a wide range of what-if simulations to arrive at: (i) the right configuration of the digital twin, (ii) the right strategies for operational excellence, and (iii) a sort of early warning system to be prepared for possible outlier conditions for better resilience. We also discussed how the sorting terminal digital twin can be leveraged for exploring design considerations for doing more than what is possible with existing setup. The experience of using digital twin as an "in silico" experimentation aid has underlined a limitation – human expert needs to carry a heavy intellectual burden of identifying the set of what-if scenarios, interpreting the simulation results, identifying a candidate set of corrective interventions etc. Going forward, it is possible to reduce this intellectual burden. For instance, we can employ the digital twin as an 'experience generator' to train a reinforcement learning (RL) agent that can serve either as a recommender system or as a controller to maximize throughput of the sorting terminal. As a further refinement, we can make the agents 'smart' by augmenting each with a purposive RL agent. Armed with this capability, we expect to be in a better position to support self-adaptive sorting terminals.

References

1. Nagy, G., Salhi, S.: Location-routing: issues, models and methods. Eur. J. Oper. Res. **177**(2), 649–672 (2007)
2. Jairo, R.M.-T., et al.: A literature review on the vehicle routing problem with multiple depots. Comput. Indust. Eng. **79**, 115–129 (2015)
3. Joerss, M., Neuhaus, F., Schröder, J.: How customer demands are reshaping last-mile delivery. McKinsey Q. **17**, 1–5 (2016)
4. Boysen, N., Fedtke, S., Schwerdfeger, S.: Last-mile delivery concepts: a survey from an operational research perspective. OR Spectrum **43**(1), 1–58 (2020). https://doi.org/10.1007/s00291-020-00607-8
5. John, B., Sauser, B.: System of Systems-the meaning of. In: 2006 IEEE/SMC International Conference on System of Systems Engineering. IEEE (2006)
6. Carl, H.: What is computation? Actor model versus Turing's model. A computable universe: understanding and exploring nature as computation, pp. 159–185 (2013)
7. Alferes, J.J., Banti, F., Brogi, A.: An event-condition-action logic programming language. In: Fisher, M., van der Hoek, W., Konev, B., Lisitsa, A. (eds.) JELIA 2006. LNCS (LNAI), vol. 4160, pp. 29–42. Springer, Heidelberg (2006). https://doi.org/10.1007/11853886_5
8. Supratim, G., et al.: A simulation driven optimization algorithm for scheduling sorting center operations. arXiv preprint arXiv:2112.04567 (2021)
9. Grieves, M., Vickers, J.: Digital twin: mitigating unpredictable, undesirable emergent behavior in complex systems. In: Kahlen, J., Flumerfelt, S., Alves, A. (eds.) Transdisciplinary Perspectives on Complex Systems. Springer, Cham (2017). https://doi.org/10.1007/978-3-319-38756-7_4
10. Nolan, G.T., Kavanagh, P.E.: Computer simulation of random packing of hard spheres. Powder Technol. **72**(2), 149–155 (1992)
11. Desmond, K.W., Weeks, E.R.: Random close packing of disks and spheres in confined geometries. Phys. Rev. E **80**(5), 051305 (2009)
12. Delaney, G.W., Hilton, J.E., Cleary, P.W.: Defining random loose packing for nonspherical grains. Phys. Rev. E **83**(5), 051305 (2011)
13. Clark, T., Kulkarni, V., Barat, S., Barn, B.: ESL: an actor-based platform for developing emergent behaviour organisation simulations. In: Demazeau, Y., Davidsson, P., Bajo, J., Vale, Z. (eds.) PAAMS 2017. LNCS (LNAI), vol. 10349, pp. 311–315. Springer, Cham (2017). https://doi.org/10.1007/978-3-319-59930-4_27
14. Robert, G.S.: Verification and validation of simulation models. In: Proceedings of the 2010 Winter Simulation Conference. IEEE (2010)

Fully Distributed Cartesian Genetic Programming

Jörg Bremer(✉) and Sebastian Lehnhoff

University of Oldenburg, 26129 Oldenburg, Germany
{joerg.bremer,sebastian.lehnhoff}@uni-oldenburg.de

Abstract. Cartesian genetic programming is a popular version of genetic programming and has meanwhile proven its performance in many use cases. This paper introduces an algorithmic level decomposition of program evolution that can be solved by a multi-agent system in a fully distributed manner. A heuristic for distributed combinatorial problem solving is adapted to evolve programs. The applicability of the approach and the effectiveness of the multi-agent approach as well as of the evolved genetic programs are demonstrated using symbolic regression, n-parity, and classification problems.

Keywords: Cartesian genetic programming · Multi-agent system · COHDA · Distributed optimization

1 Introduction

Cartesian genetic programming (CGP) has been introduced as an efficient form of Genetic Programming (GP) [1]. Since then it has become very popular and been broadly adopted [2]. Many different use cases and applications speak for a broad applicability [3–6]. CGP uses an integer-based representation of a directed graph to encode the program. Integers encode addresses in data or functions by addresses in a look-up table. Later versions also experimented with float-based representations [7].

Cartesian genetic programs are mostly evolved using a $(1+\lambda)$-ES with mutation (on all or just on active genes) and selection only [8,9]. Although initially though of to be useless [1], crossover can help a lot if multiple chromosomes have independent fitness assessments [10]. Recently, distributed use cases have been contemplated that showed that CGP evolution can be very time consuming when solved in a centralized manner [11]. For standard GP, distributed versions exist [12]. Although, distributed GP is closely related to CGP due to representation, distributed CGP is so far missing.

We propose an algorithmic level decomposition [13] of CGP evolution and the use of an agent-based, distributed approach for solving [14]. In [15] the fully decentralized, agent-based approach Combinatorial Optimization Heuristics for Distributed Agents (COHDA) has been proposed as solution to problems that

© The Author(s), under exclusive license to Springer Nature Switzerland AG 2022
F. Dignum et al. (Eds.): PAAMS 2022, LNAI 13616, pp. 36–49, 2022.
https://doi.org/10.1007/978-3-031-18192-4_4

can be decomposed on an algorithmic level. The general concept is closely related to Cooperative Coevolution [16]. The key concept of COHDA is an asynchronous iterative approximate best-response behavior. Each agent is responsible for one dimension of the algorithmic problem decomposition. The intermediate solutions of other agents (represented by published decisions) are regarded as temporarily fixed. Thus, each agent only searches along a low-dimensional cross-section of the search space and thus has to solve merely a simplified sub-problem. Nevertheless, for evaluation of the solution, the full objective function is used after aggregation of all agent's contributions. In this way, the approach achieves an asynchronous coordinate descent with the additional ability to escape local minima by parallel searching different regions of the search space; and because former decisions can be revised if newer information becomes available. This approach is especially suitable for large-scale problems [17].

To adapt COHDA to CGP, we split the chromosome that encodes the graph representation into sub-chromosomes for each node. Assigning the best alleles to a node chromosome is the low-dimensional optimization problem of a single agent. Thus, to each node, exactly one agent is assigned. The multi-agent system jointly evolves the program with agents that can be executed independently and fully distributed.

The rest of the paper is organized as follows. We start with a recap of both technologies that are combined to distributed CGP. We describe the adaption of COHDA to CGP. The applicability and the effectiveness of the approach are demonstrated using problems from symbolic regression, n-parity problems and classification problems. We conclude with a prospective view on further use cases and possible extensions.

2 Distributed Cartesian Genetic Programming

CGP encodes computer programs as graph representation [18] and is an enhancement of a method originally developed for evolving digital circuits [19,20]. CGP already demonstrated its capabilities in synthesizing complex functions in several different use cases for example for image processing [3], or neural network training [21]. Some additions to CGP have been developed, e.g. recurrent CGP [8] or self-modifying CGP [22]. In this paper, we will focus on standard CGP as the evolution of the programs is often identical.

A chromosome in CGP comprises function as well as connection and output genes. Together they encode a computational graph that represents the executable program. Figure 1 shows an example with six computational nodes, two inputs and two outputs. The gene of a function represents the index in an associated lookup-table ($\underline{0}$ to $\underline{3}$ in the example). Each computation node is encoded by a gene sequence consisting of the function look-up index and the connected input (or output of another computation node) that is fed into the function. Thus, the length of each function node gene sequence is $n + 1$ with n being the arity of the function. The graph in traditional CGP is acyclic. Parameters that are fed into a computation node may only be collected from previous nodes or from the inputs

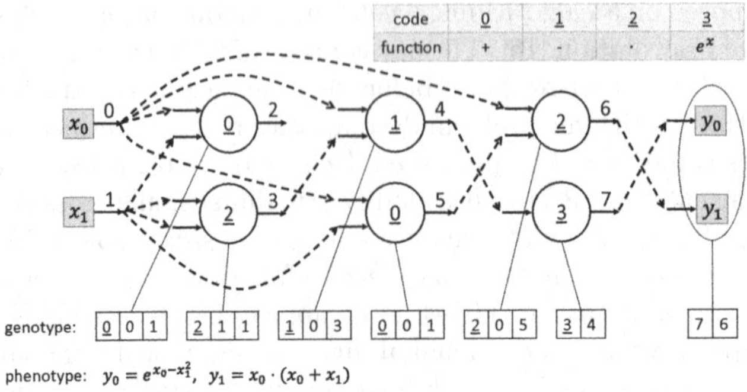

Fig. 1. Computational graph and its genotype and phenotype representation in cartesian genetic programming; modified after [11].

into the system. Thus, there exists a predefined execution order. Outputs can be connected to any computation node, or directly to any input. Not all outputs of computational nodes are used as input for other functions. In fact, usually many of such unused computational nodes occur in evolved CGP [19]. These nodes are inactive, do not contribute to the encoded program's output, and are not executed during interpretation of the program. In this way, phenotypes are of variable length whereas the size of the chromosome is static. As functions may have different arity, some genes encoding input connections may be unused. In this way, what makes CGP special is that it just rewires nodes during evolution, but using an intermediate output of an inner node is not mandatory.

COHDA has initially been introduced as solution to distributed energy management [23]. We will use COHDA for distributing the evolution of cartesian genetic programs. In COHDA, each participating agent – originally representing a decentralized energy unit in distributed energy management – reacts to updated information from other agents by adapting its own decision on some local sub-problem. Originally, agents had to select an energy production scheme that enables a group of energy generators to jointly fulfil an energy product from market as good as possible. So, agents had to decide on the local energy generation profile only for a single generator. All decisions were always based on (intermediate) selected production schemes of other agents. The general approach has meanwhile been adapted to many different problems: e.g. coalition structure formation [24], global optimization [17], trajectory optimization for unmanned air vehicles [25], or surplus distribution based on game theory [26].

Before we describe how COHDA has been adapted to train Cartesian genetic programs, we explain the underlying agent protocol. In [15] COHDA has been introduced, originally to solve the problem of predictive scheduling [27] within the Smart Grid. COHDA works with an asynchronous iterative approximate best-response behavior. All agents coordinate themselves by updating and exchanging information about each other and by making local decisions based on this information. The overall protocol is as follows. In a first step, the agents are drawn together by an artificial communication topology. For this, a small-world topology [28] has proven useful. Starting with an arbitrarily chosen agent by passing it a message containing just the global objective, each agent repeatedly goes through three stages: *perceive*, *decide*, and *act* (cf. [29]).

`perceive phase`: Each time a message is received from a neighboring agent (preceding in the communication topology), the data contained in the message is imported into the own memory. The communicated data consists of the (updated) local decision of the agent that sent the message, and the transient information on decisions of other agents that led to the previous agent's decision. After updating the local knowledge with the received information, usually a local decision is made based on this information. In order to better escape local minima, agents may postpone a decision until more information has been collected [30].

`decide phase`: Here, the agent has to conduct a local optimization. Each agent is responsible for a low-dimensional problem part. Dimension can also refer to a sub-manifold containing a low-dimensional local solutions as fraction of a way higher dimensional global solution. In the smart grid use case for example, a local contribution to the global solution (energy generation profile for a large group of independently working energy resources) consists of many-dimensional real-valued vector describing the amount of generated energy per time interval for one single device. In the CGP case, a local solution would consist of a local chromosome encoding the functions and inputs of a single node. Other agents have made local decisions before and based on gathered information about (intermediate) local decisions of these agents a solution candidate for the local (constrained) search space is sought that puts forward the group of all agents as much as possible.

`act phase`: In the last stage, the agent compares the fitness of the best found solution with the previous solution. For comparison, the global objective function is used. If the new solution has a better fitness, the agent finally broadcasts a message containing its new local solution contribution together with everything it has learned from other agents and their current local solution contributions (the decision base) to its immediate neighbors in the communication topology. Receiving agents then execute these three phases from scratch leading probably to revised local solution contributions and thus to further improved overall solutions.

If an agent is not able to find a local solution contribution that improves the overall solution, no message is sent. If no agent can find an improvement, the process has reached an at least local optimum and eventually ceases. After producing some intermediate solutions, the heuristic eventually terminates in a state where all agents know an identical solution that is taken as the final solution of the heuristic. Properties like guaranteed convergence and local optimality have been formally proven [23].

We adapted the agent approach to CGP as follows. Each agent is responsible for a single node in the program graph. In general, there are two types of agent, function node agents a_{f_i} responsible for function node f_i and output agents a_{y_j} responsible for output y_j. The task of both agent types is rather similar, but can be distinguished by the local search space. Each function node agent is responsible for exactly one node and thus internally just manages the number (look-up table address) of the function and the respective input addresses as variable number of integers depending on the arity of the function. This list of integers is just one sub-chromosome of a complete solution. At the same time, every agent has some knowledge about the intermediate assignment of alleles to chromosomes of other agents (immutable for this agent). Together (own gene set and knowledge about other's gene sets) the genotype of a complete solution and subsequently a phenotype solution can be constructed by an agent.

If a function node agent receives a message, it updates its own knowledge about the other agents. Each agent knows the most recent chromosomes from other agents. If newer information is received with the message, outdated gene information is updated; if so far unknown information arrives, additional genes are integrated into the own belief. After data update, the agent has to make a decision on the own chromosome. This decision is a local optimization process.

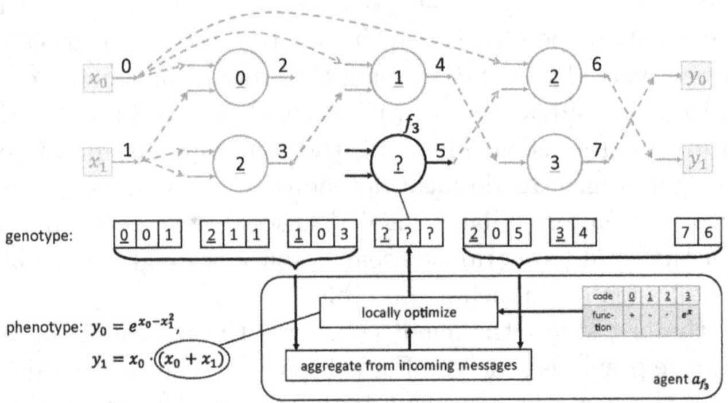

Fig. 2. Single, local optimization step (intra-agent decision) during CGP program evolution.

The known genes of the other agents are temporarily treated as fixed for the duration of the agent's current decision-making. Each agent may modify only to the own chromosome. Nevertheless, the genes of the other agents may afterwards again be altered by the respective agents as reaction to alterations. If an agent makes a local decision, it solves for the global problem of finding a good genotype but may only mutate its own local chromosome. Figure 2 shows this situation for agent a_{f_3}. This optimization could in general be done by any algorithm; e.g. by an evolution strategy. For the use cases in this paper, even a full enumeration of all solution candidates was sufficiently fast enough, because each agent has just a rather limited set of choices. Nevertheless, for larger scenarios we recommend using problem-specific heuristics. Constraints can easily be checked as the number of functions and the arity of each function is known to the agent. Currently, we set the number of rows in the graph to 1 as this convenient single row representation has been shown to be no less effective [31] and was already frequently used, e.g. in [32]. The levels-back parameter is set to the number of agents to allow input from all preceding nodes. Each agent knows its own index and may thus decide which other nodes (or program input) to chose as input for the own node.

As soon as the best local allele assignment has been found, the agent compares the solution quality with the quality of the previously found solution. If the new solution is better, messages are sent to neighboring agents. During our experiments, we found that it is advantageous to always send messages to the output agents, to enable a more frequent update of the best output. The basic difference between function and output node agents is the local gene. Output agents just manage a single gene consisting of a single integer allele that encodes the node that is connected with the respective output.

If no agent is able to make any further progress, no messages are sent and the whole negotiation process ceases. Initially, COHDA was supposed to approach an often unknown optimum as close as possible. For the CGP use case on the other hand, it is also fine to drop out of the process, if one agent for the first time finds a solution that fully satisfies a quality condition (program does what it is supposed to do). Thus, we added an additional termination criterion. If an agent discovers a solution that constitutes a success, it send a termination signal instead of a decision message and reports the found solution.

3 Results

For evaluation, we investigated three use cases: regression problems, the n-parity problem, and classification problems.

3.1 Regression

For comparison with results achieved by the original CGP from [33], we used symbolic regression of the following 6th order polynomial: $x^6 - 2x^4 + x^2$. The objective here is to evolve a program that produces the same output for arbitrary input x. The used function set was $\{+, -, \cdot, /\}$. The fitness was evaluated with 50 randomly chosen input values of x from the interval $[-1, 1]$. The program input was just x as opposed to [33], who additionally gave a 1.0 as input. Previously, also ephemeral constants had been used to support solving the problem with GP [34].

For comparison, we used statistical measures as introduced by Koza [35]. The cumulative probability of success for a budget of i objective evaluations is given by

$$P(M, i) = \frac{n_{\text{success}}(i)}{n_{\text{total}}}, \tag{1}$$

with n_{success} denoting the number of successful runs at i objective function calls and n_{total} denoting the total number of runs. M denotes the number of individuals. In our use case, M – although maybe interpretable as number of agents –

is of no use as the agent system works asynchronously and not in terms of generations with a constant number of evaluations per iteration. Instead, we simply use the budget i of the maximum number of objective functions calls allowed by all agents together and set $M := 1$. This approach is consistent with the generalization in [36].

From the success rate one can derive the mean number of independent runs that are required to achieve a minimum rate of success when the budget is fixed to a maximum of i evaluations per run. Let z denote the wanted success rate, then

$$R(z) = \left\lceil \frac{\log(1-z)}{\log(1-P(M,i))} \right\rceil \tag{2}$$

gives the number of necessary runs. The computational effort $I(M, i, z) = M \cdot i \cdot R(z)$ gives the number of individual function evaluations that must be performed to solve a problem to a proportion of z [36]. As i is a matter of parametrization, Koza defines the minimum computational effort as

$$I_{\min}(M, z) = \min_i \; M \cdot R(z). \tag{3}$$

Table 1 shows the comparison of our results with [33]. The distributed approach shows competitiveness compared with the original results achieved with a genetic algorithm with a population size of 10, uniform crossover (100% rate), and 2% mutation. In [33] the number of maximum generations was set to 8000. As this is not applicable in asynchronous agent systems, we restricted the total number of evaluations to 80000 instead. The confidence level was $z = 0.99$.

Table 1. Comparison of the computational effort for symbolic regression between distributed and standard CGP.

	COHDA	GA [33]
Success rate (80000)	0.97	0.61
Minimum computational effort	75000	90060
Independent runs (budget)	3 (25000)	6 (15000)

Table 2. Results (yielding the minimal computational effort) for several symbolic regression problems with 1-dimensional and 2-dimensional input.

$f(x)$	No. of agents	Budget	$P(i)$	$R(z)$	Min. computational effort	Mean effort
$x^2 + 2x + 1$	8	20000	0.93	2	40000	7768.4 ± 9944.6
$x^8 + x^5$	20	200000	0.83	3	600000	136833.2 ± 129852.2
$\frac{x^2}{2x-1}$	30	220000	0.67	5	1100000	786270.1 ± 791943.8
$0.2x^2 + 0.5$	20	500000	0.50	7	3500000	$538625,2 \pm 436231.5$
$2x_1^2 + x_1x_2$	15	180000	0.81	3	540000	110931.5 ± 127073.4

Table 2 shows some results for several other symbolic regression problems. Figure 3 explores the relation of the number of agents (and thus mainly functional nodes) to the mean number of evaluations and to the length of the encoded phenotype solution (number of active nodes). The experiment was conducted for the simple regression problem $-x^6$ with 100 runs for each different number of agents. Although the mean number of active nodes (calculated only for successful runs) stays rather constant Fig. 3(b), an unnecessarily high number of agents leads obviously to some outliers with bloated phenotype. The mean number of evaluations also grows. Future improvements should address these issues; maybe by starting with a rather low number of agents and by adding more agents only in case no further improvement of a solution is detected.

3.2 N-Parity

Evolving Boolean functions is a standard use case in evaluating Genetic Programming [37–39]. A special case is the even-n-parity problem [35]. The goal is to find a function, that counts the number of ones of given n bits by only using Boolean expressions, returning TRUE iff the number is even. In this way, a correct classification of arbitrary bit strings of length n having an even number of ones is sought [40]. Input to the CGP-program are the bits $b_0, \dots, b_n$. The used function set for program evolution consists of the four Boolean functions $\{AND, OR, NAND, NOR\}$. The Boolean even-n-parity function is seen as the most difficult Boolean function to evolve [35,41]. With standard GP, results for problem sizes up to $n = 5$ can be obtained [41]. For solving larger instances, techniques like automatically defined functions [42], or extended function sets are needed [38]. Some results for the COHDA-CGP-evolved programs are listed in Table 3. The number of agents and the total budget (for all agents together) are a result of sampling for the minimal computational effort (Eq. 3). Sampling has been done by grid search. So far, we were able to train CGP for up to $n = 5$. For smaller instances of the problem, also different numbers of agents (computation nodes respectively) were tested. Obviously, having larger chromosomes (number of agents in our case) as stated in [43], is not always advantageous in the distributed case.

3.3 Classification

Finally, we tested the distributed approach on classification problems. We used a problem from the energy domain known as flexibility modeling [44]. The goal is to correctly classify energy generation profiles $\boldsymbol{x} \in \mathbb{R}^d$ with x_i denoting the generated amount of energy during the ith time interval for a given, specific energy resource. A generation profile $\boldsymbol{x}$ can either be feasible (can be operated by the energy resource without violating any technical constraint) or not. This problem is often modeled as a 1-class classification problem [45].

Solutions using support vector machines (SVM) or support vector data description (SVDD) as classifier can for example be found in [46,47]. We used SVDD for comparing our approach [48]. The classifiers are trained using a set

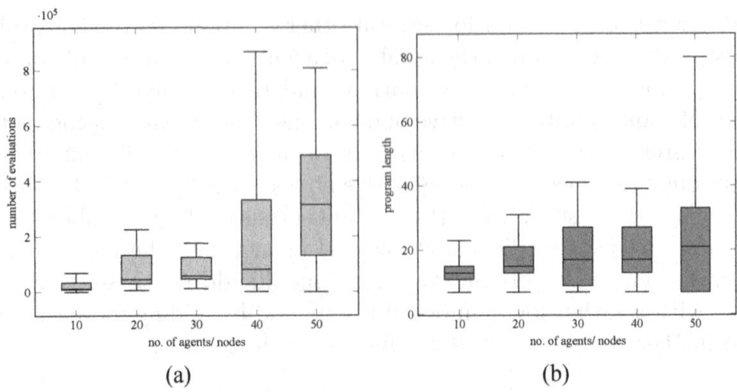

Fig. 3. Relation of number of agents and mean number of evaluations (a) and length of resulting phenotypes (measured by number of active nodes).

Table 3. Results for several instances of the n-parity problem (correctly classifying an even number of 1 in a bit string of length n) for different numbers of agents.

Size	# of nodes	No. of evaluations
even-2	10	522.77 ± 575.61
even-2	20	1640.52 ± 1900.74
even-2	30	3111.77 ± 3366.56
even-3	10	2309.05 ± 1819.84
even-3	20	7834.47 ± 8174.38
even-4	30	64772.04 ± 54501.49
even-5	40	242264.33 ± 192328.68

of feasible generation profiles that is generated using an appropriate simulation model of the energy resource. We used the model of a co-generation plant (CHP). This model comprises a micro CHP with 4.7 kW of rated electrical power (12.6 kW thermal power) bundled with a thermal buffer store. Constraints restrict power band, buffer charging, gradients, min. on and off times, and satisfaction of thermal demand. Thermal demand is subject to simulated losses of a detached house according to given weather profiles. For each agent the CHP model is individually (randomly) configured with state of charge, weather condition, temperature range, allowed operation gradients, and similar [26].

Our goal was to evolve a program that gets d values representing the amount of energy $\boldsymbol{x} = (x_1, \ldots, x_d)$ as input and outputs $y < 0$ if the profile is infeasible to operate for the energy resource and $y \geq 0$ in case the profile is feasible and can thus be operated by the CHP. For evaluation, we used a training set of 1000 generation profiles (50% feasible) generated by the simulation model. As function set, we used $\{+, -, \cdot, /, \text{AND}, \text{OR}, \text{NOT}, \text{XOR}, =, <, >, \text{IF THEN ELSE}, 0, 1, 2\}$, with 0, 1, 2 denoting constants (nullary functions).

Table 4. Comparison of results for the flexibility modeling classification problem (using a model for co-generation plants). We compare distributively evolved CGP-program and SVDD classifier.

Dimension	No. of agents	No. of evaluations	Training accuracy	Accuracy CGP	Accuracy SVDD
8	30	8351149	0.89	0.8616 ± 0.0110	0.8770 ± 0.0091
32	50	205262361	0.952	0.9569 ± 0.0085	0.9732 ± 0.0048
96	50	68825837	0.896	0.9461 ± 0.0109	0.9603 ± 0.0059

For evaluation and for comparing the classifiers, we used the classification accuracy. Evaluation during CGP evolution was done using the 1000 training instances to calculate the confusion matrix and finally the achieved accuracy. The SVDD classifier was trained with 1000 feasible instances. After a classifier program has been evolved, we compared the CGP classifier with the SVDD classifier using 100 times a test set of 1000 newly generated, so far unseen generation profile instances from identically parameterized simulation models (the same sets for both classifiers respectively). Table 4 shows the results for different dimensions d of the generation profile.

Although all CGP results are slightly worse than that of SVDD, the achieved accuracy is still estimable. The training accuracy denotes the best fitness that has been achieved during several test runs of program evolution. The best found programs had then been applied to the different unseen test set generated for newly instantiated CHP models. This generalization ability is compared between CGP and SVDD by the respective mean accuracies. Another interesting observation can be seen by the following example phenotype for 8-dimensional generation profiles as input:

$$y = +(*(x_1, x_3), \mathrm{IF}(x_7, -(/(2.0, -(\mathrm{AND}(x_0, -(/(x_0, x_7), x_7)), *(x_1, x_3))), \\ +(/(x_6, x_7), /(x_7, x_6))), x_0)).$$

Obviously, not all inputs are of interest for classification as some are always omitted. These were always the same ones in different evolved programs. This fact is also reflected by the just marginal growing number of agents compared to the faster growing dimensionality of the problem. Such identification of the smaller intrinsic dimension is an extra for the CGP program not provided by classifiers like SVDD.

4 Conclusion

We presented the adaption of a distributed optimization heuristics protocol to cartesian genetic programming. By decomposing the evolution on an algorithmic level, it becomes possible to distribute nodes and regard the evolution process as parallel, asynchronous execution of individual coordinate descent.

The results show that the distributed approach is not superior (with regard to the evolved programs) but competitive regarding solution quality and computational effort. The actual advantage is the ability to distribute computational burden. Moreover, distributed evolution of programs enables a seamless integration into distributed applications, also but not only using the example of the smart grid. Agent-based CGP constitutes a universal means to cooperative planning. Future work will now lean towards distributed use cases. Another advantage is that different nodes may have different function sets in case they represent real world nodes with different capabilities.

So far, we considered merely standard CGP. Extensions like recurrent CGP that effect rather interpretation or execution of the phenotype may already now be evolved by the distributed approach with just an adaption of the possible choices of other agents' output as input for the own node. In the same way, different levels-back parametrizations could be handled.

References

1. Miller, J.F., et al.: An empirical study of the efficiency of learning boolean functions using a cartesian genetic programming approach. In: Proceedings of the Genetic and Evolutionary Computation Conference, vol. 2, pp. 1135–1142 (1999)
2. Miller, J.F.: Cartesian genetic programming: its status and future. Genet. Program Evolvable Mach. **21**(1), 129–168 (2020)
3. Harding, S., Leitner, J., Schmidhuber, J.: Cartesian genetic programming for image processing. In: Riolo, R., Vladislavleva, E., Ritchie, M., Moore, J. (eds.) Genetic Programming Theory and Practice X. Genetic and Evolutionary Computation, pp. 31–44. Springer, New York (2013). https://doi.org/10.1007/978-1-4614-6846-2_3
4. Suganuma, M., Kobayashi, M., Shirakawa, S., Nagao, T.: Evolution of deep convolutional neural networks using CGP. Evol. Comput. **28**(1), 141–163 (2020)
5. Parziale, A., Senatore, R., Della Cioppa, A., Marcelli, A.: Cartesian genetic programming for diagnosis of Parkinson disease through handwriting analysis: performance vs. interpretability issues. Artif. Intell. Med. **111**, 101984 (2021)
6. Ahmad, A.M., Muhammad Khan, G., Mahmud, S.A.: Classification of arrhythmia types using cartesian genetic programming evolved artificial neural networks. In: Iliadis, L., Papadopoulos, H., Jayne, C. (eds.) EANN 2013. CCIS, vol. 383, pp. 282–291. Springer, Heidelberg (2013). https://doi.org/10.1007/978-3-642-41013-0_29
7. Clegg, J., Walker, J.A., Miller, J.F.: A new crossover technique for cartesian genetic programming. In: Proceedings of the 9th Annual Conference on Genetic and Evolutionary Computation, pp. 1580–1587 (2007)
8. Turner, A.J., Miller, J.F.: Recurrent cartesian genetic programming. In: Bartz-Beielstein, T., Branke, J., Filipič, B., Smith, J. (eds.) PPSN 2014. LNCS, vol. 8672, pp. 476–486. Springer, Cham (2014). https://doi.org/10.1007/978-3-319-10762-2_47
9. Goldman, B.W., Punch, W.F.: Reducing wasted evaluations in cartesian genetic programming. In: Krawiec, K., Moraglio, A., Hu, T., Etaner-Uyar, A.Ş, Hu, B. (eds.) EuroGP 2013. LNCS, vol. 7831, pp. 61–72. Springer, Heidelberg (2013). https://doi.org/10.1007/978-3-642-37207-0_6

10. Walker, J.A., Völk, K., Smith, S.L., Miller, J.F.: Parallel evolution using multi-chromosome cartesian genetic programming. Genet. Program Evolvable Mach. **10**(4), 417 (2009). https://doi.org/10.1007/s10710-009-9093-2
11. Bremer, J., Lehnhoff, S.: Towards evolutionary emergence. Ann. Comput. Sci. Inf. Syst. **26**, 55–60 (2021)
12. Poli, R.: Parallel distributed genetic programming. University of Birmingham, Cognitive Science Research Centre (1996)
13. Talbi, E.G.: Metaheuristics: From Design to Implementation, vol. 74. Wiley, New York (2009)
14. Hinrichs, C., Vogel, U., Sonnenschein, M.: Approaching decentralized demand side management via self-organizing agents. In: ATES Workshop (2011)
15. Hinrichs, C., Sonnenschein, M., Lehnhoff, S.: Evaluation of a self-organizing heuristic for interdependent distributed search spaces. In: Filipe, J., Fred, A.L.N. (eds.) International Conference on Agents and Artificial Intelligence (ICAART 2013) - Agents, vol. 1, pp. 25–34. SciTePress (2013)
16. Potter, M.A., Jong, K.A.D.: Cooperative coevolution: an architecture for evolving coadapted subcomponents. Evol. Comput. **8**(1), 1–29 (2000)
17. Bremer, J., Lehnhoff, S.: The effect of laziness on agents for large scale global optimization. In: van den Herik, J., Rocha, A.P., Steels, L. (eds.) ICAART 2019. LNCS (LNAI), vol. 11978, pp. 317–337. Springer, Cham (2019). https://doi.org/10.1007/978-3-030-37494-5_16
18. Sotto, L.F.D.P., Kaufmann, P., Atkinson, T., Kalkreuth, R., Basgalupp, M.P.: A study on graph representations for genetic programming. In: Proceedings of the 2020 Genetic and Evolutionary Computation Conference, GECCO 2020, New York, NY, USA, pp. 931–939. Association for Computing Machinery (2020)
19. Miller, J.: Cartesian Genetic Programming, vol. 43. Springer, Heidelberg (2003)
20. Miller, J.F., Thomson, P., Fogarty, T.: Designing electronic circuits using evolutionary algorithms. Arithmetic circuits: a case study. Genet. Algorithms Evol. Strateg. Eng. Comput. Sci. 105–131 (1997)
21. Khan, M.M., Ahmad, A.M., Khan, G.M., Miller, J.F.: Fast learning neural networks using cartesian genetic programming. Neurocomputing **121**, 274–289 (2013)
22. Harding, S., Banzhaf, W., Miller, J.F.: A survey of self modifying cartesian genetic programming. In: Riolo, R., McConaghy, T., Vladislavleva, E. (eds.) Genetic Programming Theory and Practice VIII. Genetic and Evolutionary Computation, vol. 8, pp. 91–107. Springer, New York (2011). https://doi.org/10.1007/978-1-4419-7747-2_6
23. Hinrichs, C., Sonnenschein, M.: A distributed combinatorial optimisation heuristic for the scheduling of energy resources represented by self-interested agents. Int. J. Bio-Inspired Comput. **10**(2), 69–78 (2017)
24. Bremer, J., Lehnhoff, S.: Decentralized coalition formation with agent-based combinatorial heuristics. Adv. Distrib. Comput. Artif. Intell. **6**(3), 29–44 (2017)
25. Tong, B., Liu, Q., Dai, C., Jia, Z.: A decentralized multiple MAV collision avoidance trajectory planning method. In: 2020 Chinese Automation Congress (CAC), pp. 1545–1552 (2020)
26. Bremer, J., Lehnhoff, S.: Decentralized surplus distribution estimation with weighted k-majority voting games. In: Bajo, J., et al. (eds.) PAAMS 2017. CCIS, vol. 722, pp. 327–339. Springer, Cham (2017). https://doi.org/10.1007/978-3-319-60285-1_28
27. Sonnenschein, M., Lünsdorf, O., Bremer, J., Tröschel, M.: Decentralized control of units in smart grids for the support of renewable energy supply. Environ. Impact Assess. Rev. **52**, 40–52 (2014)

28. Watts, D., Strogatz, S.: Collective dynamics of 'small-world' networks. Nature **393**, 440–442 (1998)
29. Nieße, A., Beer, S., Bremer, J., Hinrichs, C., Lünsdorf, O., Sonnenschein, M.: Conjoint dynamic aggregation and scheduling methods for dynamic virtual power plants. In: Ganzha, M., Maciaszek, L.A., Paprzycki, M. (eds.) Proceedings of the 2014 Federated Conference on Computer Science and Information Systems. Annals of Computer Science and Information Systems, vol. 2, pp. 1505–1514 (2014)
30. Bremer, J., Lehnhoff, S.: Lazy agents for large scale global optimization. In: ICAART (1), pp. 72–79 (2019)
31. Oranchak, D.: Cartesian genetic programming for the Java EC toolkit (2010)
32. Inácio, T., Miragaia, R., Reis, G., Grilo, C., Fernandéz, F.: Cartesian genetic programming applied to pitch estimation of piano notes. In: 2016 IEEE Symposium Series on Computational Intelligence (SSCI), pp. 1–7. IEEE (2016)
33. Miller, J.F., Thomson, P.: Cartesian genetic programming. In: Poli, R., Banzhaf, W., Langdon, W.B., Miller, J., Nordin, P., Fogarty, T.C. (eds.) EuroGP 2000. LNCS, vol. 1802, pp. 121–132. Springer, Heidelberg (2000). https://doi.org/10.1007/978-3-540-46239-2_9
34. Koza, J.R.: Genetic Programming II: Automatic Discovery of Reusable Programs. MIT, Cambridge (1994)
35. Koza, J.R., Koza, J.R.: Genetic Programming: On the Programming of Computers by Means of Natural Selection, vol. 1. MIT Press, Cambridge (1992)
36. Christensen, S., Oppacher, F.: An analysis of Koza's computational effort statistic for genetic programming. In: Foster, J.A., Lutton, E., Miller, J., Ryan, C., Tettamanzi, A. (eds.) EuroGP 2002. LNCS, vol. 2278, pp. 182–191. Springer, Heidelberg (2002). https://doi.org/10.1007/3-540-45984-7_18
37. Gathercole, C., Ross, P.: Tackling the boolean even n parity problem with genetic programming and limited-error fitness. Genet. Program. **97**, 119–127 (1997)
38. Poli, R., Page, J.: Solving high-order boolean parity problems with smooth uniform crossover, sub-machine code GP and demes. Genet. Program Evolvable Mach. **1**(1), 37–56 (2000)
39. Mambrini, A., Oliveto, P.S.: On the analysis of simple genetic programming for evolving boolean functions. In: Heywood, M.I., McDermott, J., Castelli, M., Costa, E., Sim, K. (eds.) EuroGP 2016. LNCS, vol. 9594, pp. 99–114. Springer, Cham (2016). https://doi.org/10.1007/978-3-319-30668-1_7
40. Parent, J., Nowé, A., Defaweux, A.: Addressing the even-n-parity problem using compressed linear genetic programming. In: Late Breaking Paper at Genetic and Evolutionary Computation Conference (GECCO 2005), Washington, DC, USA, pp. 25–29 (2005)
41. Muntean, O., Diosan, L., Oltean, M.: Solving the even-n-parity problems using best subtree genetic programming. In: Second NASA/ESA Conference on Adaptive Hardware and Systems (AHS 2007), pp. 511–518. IEEE (2007)
42. Koza, J.R., Andre, D., Bennett, F.H., III, Keane, M.A.: Use of automatically defined functions and architecture-altering operations in automated circuit synthesis with genetic programming. In: Proceedings of the First Annual Conference on Genetic Programming, pp. 132–140. Stanford University, MIT Press, Cambridge (1996)
43. Miller, J.F., Smith, S.L.: Redundancy and computational efficiency in cartesian genetic programming. IEEE Trans. Evol. Comput. **10**(2), 167–174 (2006)
44. Chakraborty, I., Nandanoori, S.P., Kundu, S., Kalsi, K.: Data-driven predictive flexibility modeling of distributed energy resources. In: Sayed-Mouchaweh, M. (ed.)

Artificial Intelligence Techniques for a Scalable Energy Transition, pp. 311–343. Springer, Cham (2020). https://doi.org/10.1007/978-3-030-42726-9_12

45. Bremer, J., Sonnenschein, M.: Model-based integration of constrained search spaces into distributed planning of active power provision. Comput. Sci. Inf. Syst. **10**(4), 1823–1854 (2013)
46. Pinto, R., Matos, M.A., Bessa, R.J., Gouveia, J., Gouveia, C.: Multi-period modeling of behind-the-meter flexibility. In: 2017 IEEE Manchester PowerTech, pp. 1–6 (2017)
47. Bremer, J., Rapp, B., Sonnenschein, M.: Encoding distributed search spaces for virtual power plants. In: Computational Intelligence Applications In Smart Grid (CIASG), 2011 IEEE Symposium Series on Computational Intelligence (SSCI), Paris, France, April 2011
48. Tax, D.M.J., Duin, R.P.W.: Support vector data description. Mach. Learn. **54**(1), 45–66 (2004)

Data Synchronization in Distributed Simulation of Multi-Agent Systems

Paul Breugnot(✉), Bénédicte Herrmann, Christophe Lang, and Laurent Philippe

FEMTO-ST institute, Univ. Bourgogne Franche-Comté, CNRS, Besançon, France
{paul.breugnot,christophe.lang,laurent.philippe}@univ-fcomte.fr, benedicte.herrmann@femto-st.fr

Abstract. Modern Multi-Agent System simulations may involve millions of agents that are simulated over an extended period of time in order to better catch real world emergent properties. In this context, the usage of distributed computing resources may raise single machine limits both in terms of available memory and execution time. Distributing a simulation however implies lots of complex and specific issues as the data synchronization issues that we tackle here. Based on an interface that allows to develop models independently of the distribution, we propose the definition of *synchronization modes*, some inspired from existing platforms, other providing new features such as remote interactions. Since each mode comes with its pros and cons, guidelines are provided to help developers to find the best compromise for the distributed implementation of a model or a simulation platform. The performance of each mode is discussed and evaluated using a classical epidemiological *SIR* model.

Keywords: Multi agent system · Distributed simulation · High performance computing · Data synchronization

1 Introduction

Multi-Agent System (MAS) simulation is used in various fields such as biology, epidemiology, economics, sociology, energy management or traffic simulation. In any case, simulating real world phenomena might require the microscopic simulation of millions of agents on a large time scale: for example, EURACE [9] aims at simulating the economic system at the scale of Europe, and the purpose of the ChiSIM [10] model is to simulate the propagation of an epidemic in the city of Chicago at the individual scale. Such large scale simulations usually cannot be handled on a single machine, due to available memory and execution time limitations. The distributed execution on High Performance Computing (HPC) resources can be a solution to raise those limits since the intrinsic parallelism of MAS makes them good candidates to benefit from such architectures. On the other hand, the requirement for numerous and stochastic interactions among agents or with the environment, that become remote when agents are distributed,

© The Author(s), under exclusive license to Springer Nature Switzerland AG 2022
F. Dignum et al. (Eds.): PAAMS 2022, LNAI 13616, pp. 50–62, 2022.
https://doi.org/10.1007/978-3-031-18192-4_5

raises numerous issues since agents do not have a direct access to each others' memory: the only way to distribute information is through explicit message exchanges. Solving those issues in the context of MAS simulation is especially difficult considering the fact that MAS modelers are not expected to be HPC experts.

Several platforms, such as Repast HPC [7], D-MASON [8] or FLAME [6], among others [1,2,14,16], provide solutions to issues related to agent modeling and execution on distributed platforms, in terms of communication scheme, load balancing or time synchronization. They however lack of data synchronization features to correctly manage remote interactions and the user is generally required to adapt his model to the platform, sometimes preventing the simulation of models with strong or specific constraints. The exchange of data with remote agents is indeed a critical feature that need to be solved efficiently in order to find a compromise between implementation complexity, performance, and model constraints.

This paper brings the following contributions:

- a formal definition of the data synchronization problem, with the proposition of a distribution independent interface and a generic and extensible specification of a synchronization mode concept.
- the definition and implementation of synchronization modes, unifying choices of other platforms, and introducing modes allowing remote modifications.
- a theoretical analysis of each mode, in terms of interaction rules and reproducibility levels, and a performance analysis based on an SIR model.

Following this introduction, data synchronization issues and their management within existing platforms are presented in the next section. The definition of synchronization modes and their analysis is then provided, and finally the performances of each mode are assessed using an SIR epidemiological model.

2 Data Synchronization in Distributed MAS Simulations

In a MAS simulation, allowed interactions, message exchanges or execution policies usually depend on the model definition [11]. More generally, MAS modeling techniques, supported by the simulators (NetLogo, Repast, MASON, GAMA...) imply constraints on the simulated models. Because of the distributed memory issues, distributed simulators usually constrain even more the models.

On HPC systems, the distribution of a MAS simulation consists in assigning agents and environment parts to a set of processes running on different nodes. This assignment is called *agent partitioning*. We define agents assigned to a process as *local* agents from this process. In order to allow remote interactions, *local* agents can access representations of agents executed on remote processes, that we call *distant* agents. Representations of *distant* agents are generally built according to the *local* agents perception fields, that can be considered as a geographical area of interest, or as neighbors in a graph.

In [5] authors show that different models might have different needs in terms of synchronization policy to properly run on a distributed architecture. For example, agents in a Flocking model only need to read their neighbors' positions. In consequence, it might be satisfying to read *local* agents' positions in place, and read *distant* agents' positions from a copy imported at the end of each time step. Another case is the Prey-Predator model where a predator agent might try to eat a *distant* agent, i.e. a prey executed on another process. According to the model rules, it means that (i) the prey state must be changed on the prey's origin process and (ii) it must be ensured that only one predator on all the processes will be allowed to eat this prey. In consequence, it is necessary to concurrently manage distant modifications within a time step.

Existing generic platforms supporting the distribution of models however lack support for different needs. In Repast HPC [7], *distant* agents are updated from their origin process at the end of each time step. The imported data overrides any modification performed on a *distant* agent during the time step. *Local* agents are directly accessed, and can be modified. D-MASON [8] also updates *distant* agents' states at the end of each time step. But, in order to improve reproducibility, agents read *local* agents' data from the previous time step, so that data access does not depend on the *local* or *distant* state of agents. This might however imply severe limitations and the impossibility to simulate some models. The FLAME [6] platform only allows agents to communicate through a common *message board*, updated at the end of each time step. This facilitates model distribution, since agents cannot directly access other agents' data, but concurrent modifications within the current time step are not allowed.

Other works [13,15] propose the definition of methods where agents send action requests to a *conflict resolver*, that manages concurrency by sending back action results once all requests have been received. Being able to react to negative responses is however specific to some models. It fits in particular the Influence-Reaction [12] modeling technique. Since the proposed implementations require global synchronizations before conflict resolutions, to ensure all requests are received for each agent, each agent must however wait for the execution of all others to know the result of its request, which is costly.

3 Synchronization Modes

Even if existing platforms define synchronization techniques, motivations are not always clear and proposed solutions might not fit the requirements of all models. It is then the responsibility of the user to adapt his model to the platform. For this reason we propose the synchronization mode concept based on a generic data synchronization interface.

In the following we first characterize agent interactions, then we describe the proposed interface that we use to specify synchronization modes.

3.1 Read and Write Operations

In order to provide a generic and meaningful interface to MAS modelers, describing agent interactions with *read* and *write* operations notably seems to satisfy most model requirements, even if behaviors are not directly described as such. For example, sending a message can be seen as a write operation in a buffer from the sender, and a read operation in the buffer from the receiver. In addition, the implementation of data synchronization in terms of *read* and *write* allows us to rely on existing parallel and distributed data management algorithms.

It can then be observed that a fundamental aspect of synchronization is the temporal aspect of *read*/*write* operations. An agent executed at time step T can read data from time steps T or $T-1$, and write data to time steps T or $T+1$. A *read* at time $T-1$ corresponds to an access to a *ghost* copy, while a *read* at time T means that modifications performed by *writes* at time T will be perceived. A *write* at time T means other agents performing *reads* at time T will be able to perceive the modifications during the current time step, while a *write* at time $T+1$ is only accessible at the next time step. *Write* operations can also be prohibited in some cases.

Note that each operation has to specify the target agent with which an agent interact: (i) *self*: the target agent is the agent itself, (ii) *local*: the target agent is executed on the same process as the executed agent, (iii) *distant*: the target agent is executed on another process than the executed agent.

Then, using these observations, we can illustrate the concept of synchronization modes with several propositions that support different model specificities. In the *GhostMode*, which corresponds to the RepastHPC interaction implementation, the synchronization consists in allowing *writes* only on *local* agents while *distant* agents are *read* from a *ghost* copy of the system state at the previous time step $(T-1)$. In the *GlobalGhostMode*, which corresponds to the D-MASON implementation of interactions, *local* and *distant* agents must always read other agents' data from a *ghost* copy. Finally, we define the *HardSyncMode* that allows concurrent and remote *reads* and *writes*, the strongest synchronization requirement.

Considering this, the previously introduced Flocking model might be simulated using *GhostMode* or *GlobalGhostMode*, while the *PreyPredator* model should be simulated using the *HardSyncMode*. Table 1 summarizes the temporal aspects of the proposed synchronization modes and others that will be discussed later in this section.

Table 1. Temporal aspect of interactions for different synchronization modes

	self	*local*		*distant*	
Synchronization Mode	write	read	write	read	write
GhostMode	T	T	T	$T-1$	×
GlobalGhostMode	$T+1$	$T-1$	×	$T-1$	×
HardSyncMode	T	T	T	T	T
PushGhostMode	T	T	T	$T-1$	$T+1$
PushGlobalGhostMode	$T+1$	$T-1$	$T+1$	$T-1$	$T+1$

3.2 Data Synchronization Interface

Implementing data synchronization may turn out to be difficult for a model developer. For this reason, we propose the definition of a data synchronization interface, independently of the platform specification, in order to:

1. Propose a generic interface to implement models, independently of distribution or synchronization requirements.
2. Define a common specification, to characterize existing synchronization modes and to define new ones. This allows to theoretically compare the properties of each mode, and to provide meaningful benchmarks.

This interface is based on five functions, inspired from lock mechanisms: `read(Agent agent)`, `release_read(Agent agent)`, `acquire(Agent agent)`, `release_acquire(Agent agent)` and `synchronize(Model model)`.

They allow to define protected blocks of code in which it is safe to call any existing agent method, rather that defining atomic *read/write* operations for each piece of data an agent can possibly own. In consequence, the only adaptations required from the user is to wrap instructions that access or modify agent data with the following guards:

`read(Agent agent)`, `release_read(Agent agent)` : Any data can be safely *read* from the specified agent between `read()` and `release_read()` calls. How the internal data is updated (or not), i.e. which data is actually read, depends on the implemented synchronization mode.

`acquire(Agent agent)`, `release_acquire(Agent agent)` : The `acquire()` operation gives to the calling process an exclusive access to the specified agent, so that any modification, considered as *write* operations, can be performed on the agent until `release_acquire()` is called. The actual behavior of those methods is also implementation defined, and does not require to take modifications into account.

`synchronize(Model model)` : This method is called from each process once it has finished to execute its *local* agents at the end of each time step.

Using this platform independent interface we can specify the implementation of synchronization modes. The implementation of each method then defines the properties supported by a synchronization mode, but must be provided in any case, even if some methods have no effect. Using this generic interface allows to develop a model without altering its implementation with synchronization dependent code and to transparently apply different modes on the same model.

3.3 Specification of Proposed Modes

Thus we provide some synchronization mode specifications that platform developers might implement according to their needs, independently of the simulation environment. This requires that some predefined distribution specific features, not discussed in this work, are provided:

1. Methods to query the neighbors of each *local* `Agent`. The neighbors might be *local* or *distant*, so that the agents' neighborhoods are properly preserved [5]. The neighborhood relation is model dependent (neighbors in a graph, agents in the Moore neighborhood, agents in a perception radius...).
2. Methods to query the complete list of *local* and *distant* agents on the current process within a `Model`.
3. A method to query the process on which each *distant* `Agent` is executed (for *local* agents, the method returns the current process).

Even if implementation choices are up to the developer, the behavior of each method of the interface for each mode should comply with the statements below:

GhostMode. `read()` and `acquire()` immediately return the local agent state, for both *local* and *distant* agents. The `synchronize()` method updates *distant* agents from data fetched from their origin process. In consequence, only *distant* agents are accessed from a *ghost* copy.

GlobalGhostMode. The `read()` method always returns a *ghost* copy of the agent, even if it is *local.* The `acquire()` method returns the local state of the agent, to allow an agent to update itself, but should not be called on other agents. The `synchronize()` method updates *distant* agents as in *GhostMode*, and updates the *ghost* copy of each *local* agent with its current state.

HardSyncMode. Fetching up-to-date data from distant processes at each *read* or *write* operation, and performing concurrent data modifications within the time step, including on *distant* agents, is allowed. `read()` and `acquire()` methods might hence fetch data from other processes. The `acquire()` method must ensure an exclusive access upon return, while several processes are allowed to simultaneously `read()` an agent. The release methods are used to manage locks according to the well-known Readers-Writers problem. When a *distant* agent is acquired, its complete state is imported on the current process which can perform any modification on it since the access is exclusive. The `releaseAcquire()` method then sends back the new agent state, in order to update the agent on its origin process. Such design allows users to implicitly perform any write operation on *distant* agents, without specifying any specific action or message exchange protocol. Notice that this implies that `read()` and `acquire()` methods might block even when performed on *local* agents, waiting for distant processes to release them. The `synchronize()` method is not required to perform any data update, but should act as a synchronization barrier so that it returns only when all processes have reached the `synchronize()` call.

PushGhostMode. Data access is managed as in *GhostMode* but modifications on *distant* agents are not overridden at the end of each time step but sent back to the origin process by the `synchronize()` method. A user specified conflict resolution mechanism can be implemented to handle updates received from several processes (including the process that owns the agent).

PushGlobalGhostMode. Read access and data updates are performed using a *ghost* copy, as in *GlobalGhostMode.* The acquired *local* agents can however be modified, and pushed back as in *PushGhostMode.*

It is worth noting that the final user, i.e. the MAS modeler, does not need to know anything about the implementation details once a synchronization mode has been successfully implemented within a simulation platform. From the user point of view, the only requirement is to call the functions of the proposed interface. For instance, in the *HardSyncMode*, he just has to call `acquire()` and `releaseAcquire()` to modify any agent as if the agent behavior was performed in a sequential shared memory environment. He does not even need to know whether the modified agent is *local* or *distant*. All calls and concurrency management are automatically and transparently handled in the background by the simulation platform.

3.4 Properties

Several properties can be deduced from the specification of modes, notably in terms of allowed interactions and reproducibility. Such analysis might help modelers to identify which mode can be used depending on their model requirements.

While *GhostMode* and *GlobalGhostMode* prevent write operations on *distant* agents, only the *HardSyncMode* can handle read and write operations at time T on *distant* agents. Performing *write* operations only on *local* agents, as allowed by the *GhostMode*, can however be relevant in some contexts, for example when the model is guaranteed to be distributed so that all agents at the same location are assigned to the same process, as in RepastHPC. In that case, predators in the Prey-Predator model could safely eat preys in their current location. However, such modes cannot handle the case when agents are required to perform modifications within their Moore or Von Neumann neighborhood in a grid environment for example, or when agents evolve in a continuous or even non-spatial environment. In the Prey-Predator context, this would require predators to eat *distant* preys executed on other processes, what is not allowed by *GhostMode* or *GlobalGhostMode*. Moreover, since several predators might try to simultaneously eat a same prey within the time step, the *HardSyncMode* is the only mode that can support such interactions. However, if the model rules state that predators *try* to eat preys and wait until the next time step to know if their attack was successful, as in the Influence-Reaction scheme, the model can be simulated using *PushGhostMode* or *PushGlobalGhostMode*. Also notice that the Flocking model, that can be simulated with *GhostMode* or *GlobalGhostMode*, might also be simulated using the *HardSyncMode*: in this case, the position of the *distant* agents will be read directly from the distant processes, not from a local *ghost* copy, what might be a behavior much closer to a sequential execution.

On the other hand, the reproducibility of simulations is directly influenced by the temporal aspect of interactions. This criteria notably motivated the D-MASON authors to implement a *Global Ghost* synchronization. Indeed, reproducibility levels can be defined as specified in table 2. It can be shown that each level is a necessary condition to the next level. Note that the "fixed partitioning" condition requires that a fixed count of processes is also used.

Agent interactions, and thus model results, clearly depend on agents execution order when *reads* and *writes* are performed at time T, since agents perceive

Table 2. Reproducibility levels

Level	Description
0	No reproducibility requirement
1	Results are statistically reproducible
2	Results are reproducible considering a fixed partitioning
3	Results do not depend on agents execution order
4	Results do not depend on partitioning

modifications in the current time step only for agents executed before them. In consequence, modes allowing such interactions cannot go beyond the level 2 reproducibility. On the other hand, since reads in *ghost* data, i.e. at time $T-1$, do not depend on the execution order of agents, it is possible to reach levels 3 and 4 using *Global Ghost* based modes. Notice that the *ghost* usage is however not sufficient to guarantee such reproducibility levels, since random number generation at the scale of each agent must also not depend on agents execution order or partitioning. Providing this feature is actually not trivial, and even impossible in some contexts. A solution, not discussed in this work, as yet been implemented for grid based models in the FPMAS platform that we use for the experiments.

4 Experiments

The objective of the presented experiments is to compare the synchronization mode performance, using a reference model so as to give to the model developers indications on the impacts of the chosen synchronization mode.

4.1 Experimental Settings

Experiments are based on the well known SIR epidemiological model. The advantage of this model is that it can run properly with all the synchronization modes introduced in this paper. It consists in a grid where agents randomly move and perceive other agents in their Moore neighborhood at each time step. At each time step, *Infected* agents can infect each of their *Susceptible* neighbor with a probability β, can *Recover* with a probability γ, or die with a probability μ. Model sources and more detailed information can be accessed online [4]. From such model specification, two versions of the model can be implemented:

- A read-only version, where each agent performs a Bernoulli experiment of parameter β with each of its *Infected* neighbor: if the result of at least one is positive, the agent gets *Infected.*
- A write version, where *Infected* agents directly infect their *Susceptible* neighbors with a probability β.

The read-only version can run properly with *GhostMode*, *GlobalGhostMode* and *HardSyncMode*, even if this might implicitly result in different interactions. For example, in *GhostMode*, *local* agents already *Infected* within the time step will be perceived as *Infected*, while *distant* agents *Infected* in the current time step will still be perceived *Susceptible* until the next time step. In *HardSyncMode*, *distant* agents *Infected* in the current time step will immediately be perceived as *Infected*, while in *GlobalGhostMode* all infections are only perceived at the next time step. The *write* version could run properly with *HardSyncMode*, *PushGhostMode* and *PushGlobalGhostMode*.

For the experiments we use the C++ FPMAS [3] platform, that allows to transparently distribute MAS model simulations. The SIR model is distributed using a grid based load balancing. Currently only the *GhostMode*, *GlobalGhostMode* and *HardSyncMode* are implemented but *PushGhostMode* and *PushGlobalGhostMode* could easily be implemented. While *GhostMode* and *GlobalGhostMode* are relatively trivial to implement, the *HardSyncMode* introduces a complex architecture to provide features that have not been encountered in existing platforms. In consequence, some of the *HardSyncMode* implementation details within FPMAS are provided as a contribution. The solution is based on a distributed client/server architecture. Each process is attached to a client and a server instance. Each server handles requests to its *local* agents, while the client sends requests to *distant* agents to other processes. When `read()` or `acquire()` is called on a *local* agent, the local process possibly waits for other processes to release it, while processing requests of other agents in order to ensure progress. In order to prevent deadlocks, requests are performed using non-blocking communications: while waiting for a response, the local process keeps handling incoming requests. This allows a deadlock free single thread *HardSyncMode* implementation, but other solutions based on multi-threading could be designed. The `synchronize()` method then consists in handling incoming requests until all processes have initiated the `synchronize()` method, i.e. all agents have been executed.

4.2 Results

We note that the objective here is only to provide a relative performance comparison of modes, so we do not compare the FPMAS *HardSyncMode* with the RepastHPC *GhostMode* equivalent synchronization for example.

Execution times for a SIR model instance, depending on the number of cores, are presented on Fig. 1. Experiments were run on the local computing center, on Intel Xeon 6126 processors running at 2.60GHz. Each measure is the average of 10 runs of 1000 time steps with different seeds: execution time variations are negligible. First we can observe that with the *GlobalGhostMode* the execution time of the model with $1,000,000$ agents on a 1500×1500 grid drops from 17 h in sequential to 26 min using 64 processes, what illustrates the point of using HPC resources to execute MAS simulations.

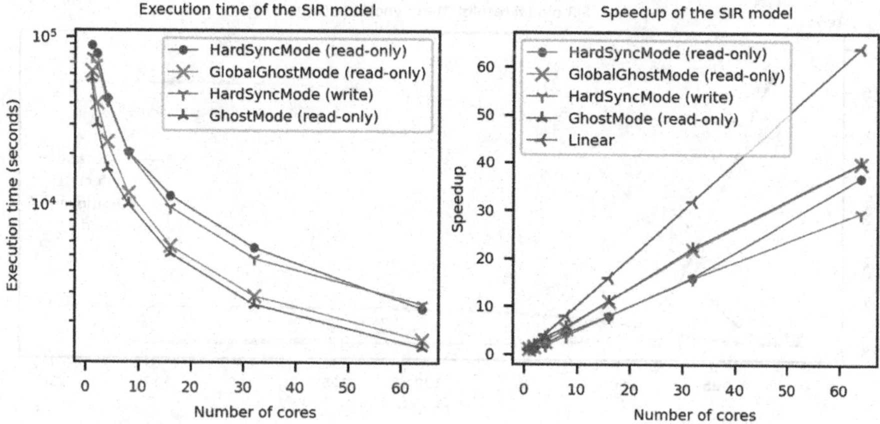

Fig. 1. Execution times (log scale) and speedups for a SIR model instance with 1,000,000 agents on a 1500 × 1500 grid, with read-only and write versions. The speedup is computed for each mode as $\frac{T_n}{T_1}$ where T_n represents the execution time with n cores.

The cost of the *GlobalGhostMode* can be explained by the required copies of all agents at the end of each time step. In comparison, the *GhostMode* only needs to perform copies on *distant* agents, with the same amount of communication. The cost of the *HardSyncMode* comes from the point to point communications that are required for each *read* or *write*. As observed on the speedup curves, such communications scales less than other modes, especially considering the fact that more cores means more *distant* agents and so more communications since the number of agent is constant. The *GhostMode* and *GlobalGhostMode* scale well because they only require well balanced collective communications.

The results of the write version of the SIR model obtained with *HardSyncMode* on 64 processes are presented on Fig. 2 and shows the consistency of a simulation performing *distant writes* with *HardSyncMode*. Even if this mode is the most costly, we ran the simulation with 7,000,000 agents and a 3000 × 3000 grid on 64 cores for 500 time steps in 3 h, which show that this mode can practically be used.

Note that the results are not limited to the chosen platform, and the relative comparison of modes should hold independently of their implementation. FPMAS indeed allows to build meaningful benchmarks, since the implementation of each mode is well optimized and the synchronization mode can be changed at the model level, without altering the read and write SIR model implementations [4], preventing implementation bias.

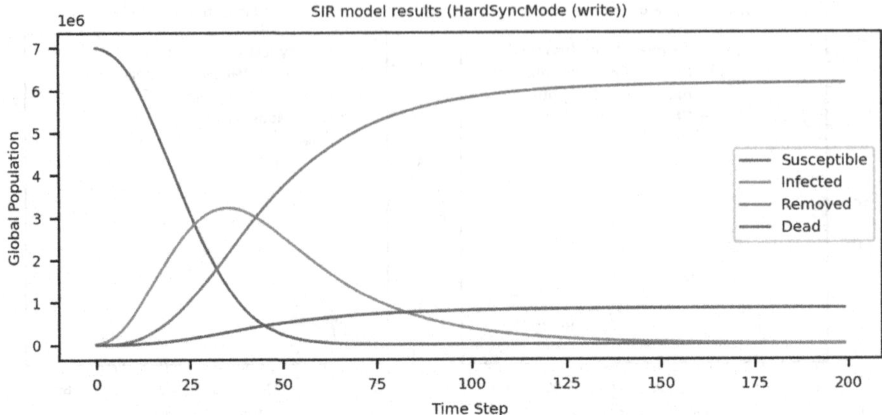

Fig. 2. Example results with 7,000,000 agents and a 3000×3000 grid on 64 processes (cropped to 200 time steps).

5 Conclusion

To address the data synchronization issue in distributed MAS simulations, several synchronization modes with different properties have been presented. The generic definition of the problem allows to define a common interface to implement models using generic operations, without considering distributed memory issues. This interface also allows to inject different synchronization modes in the same model, without changing its implementation, what is particularly useful to produce robust performance and results benchmarks. In this work, we notably focused on a theoretical analysis of proposed modes, and on their performances. It appears that even if the *GhostMode* does not provide the best properties in terms of reproducibility and does not allow remote writes, it is very efficient in terms of performance. On the other hand, the *HardSyncMode* is slower, but is currently the only mode that provides concurrent and remote *reads* and *writes* within the current time step. Finally, the *GlobalGhostMode* is relatively costly and does not allow remote writes, but it is the only mode that can guarantee reproducible results independently of the model distribution. Such considerations show how the synchronization mode used to execute a MAS simulation on HPC resources is relevant, and should depend on models and user requirements, justifying the need for platforms that propose several well defined modes.

In our future works we plan to realize a detailed experimental analysis about the model results and reproducibility, in order to study the synchronization mode impacts on model results. Distinct or specific model needs might also motivate the definition of new modes, formally specified with the generic interface.

Acknowledgments. Computations have been performed on the supercomputer facilities of the Mésocentre de calcul de Franche-Comté. FPMAS [3] and model sources [4] are accessible online thanks to permanent identifiers provided by Software Heritage.

References

1. Blythe, J., Tregubov, A.: FARM: architecture for distributed agent-based social simulations. In: Lin, D., Ishida, T., Zambonelli, F., Noda, I. (eds.) Massively Multi-Agent Systems II. pp. 96–107. Lecture Notes in Computer Science, Springer International Publishing, Cham (2019). https://doi.org/10.1007/978-3-030-20937-7_7
2. Borges, F., Gutierrez-Milla, A., Luque, E., Suppi, R.: Care HPS: a high performance simulation tool for parallel and distributed agent-based modeling. Futur. Gener. Comput. Syst. **68**, 59–73 (2017). https://doi.org/10.1016/j.future.2016.08.015
3. Breugnot, P.: FPMAS Platform v1.5.1. FEMTO-ST (2022). https://archive.softwareheritage.org/swh:1:rel:eb975b2c3c4fc42c186c51a3c339b348496f1d27
4. Breugnot, P.: FPMAS Virus Model v1.0. FEMTO-ST (2022). https://archive.softwareheritage.org/swh:1:rel:9f2e8b300e02ea0907a25725c825627227d085d7
5. Breugnot, P., Herrmann, B., Lang, C., Philippe, L.: A synchronized and dynamic distributed graph structure to allow the native distribution of multi-agent system simulations. In: 2021 29th Euromicro International Conference on Parallel, Distributed and Network-Based Processing (PDP), pp. 54–61 (2021). https://doi.org/10.1109/PDP52278.2021.00017
6. Chin, L.S., Worth, D.J., Greenough, C., Coakley, S., Holcombe, M., Kiran, M.: FLAME : an approach to the parallelisation of agent-based applications. Rutherford Appleton Laboratory Technical Reports (RAL-TR-2012-013) (2012). https://doi.org/10.5286/raltr.2012013
7. Collier, N., North, M.: Parallel agent-based simulation with repast for high performance computing. SIMULATION (2012). https://doi.org/10.1177/0037549712462620
8. Cordasco, G., Spagnuolo, C., Scarano, V.: Toward the new version of D-MASON: efficiency, effectiveness and correctness in parallel and distributed agent-based simulations. In: 2016 International Parallel and Distributed Processing Symposium Workshops, pp. 1803–1812 (2016). https://doi.org/10.1109/IPDPSW.2016.52
9. Deissenberg, C., van der Hoog, S., Dawid, H.: EURACE: a massively parallel agent-based model of the European economy. Appl. Math. Comput. **204**(2), 541–552 (2008). https://doi.org/10.1016/j.amc.2008.05.116
10. Macal, C.M., Collier, N.T., Ozik, J., Tatara, E.R., Murphy, J.T.: CHISIM: an agent-based simulation model of social interactions in a large urban area. In: 2018 Winter Simulation Conference (WSC), pp. 810–820 (2018). https://doi.org/10.1109/WSC.2018.8632409
11. Mathieu, P., Secq, Y.: Environment updating and agent scheduling policies in agent-based simulators. In: Proceedings of the 4th International Conference on Agents and Artificial Intelligence, vol. 1, pp. 170–175. SciTePress (2012). https://doi.org/10.5220/0003732301700175
12. Michel, F.: The IRM4S model: the influence/reaction principle for multiagent based simulation. In: Conference on Autonomous Agents and Multiagent Systems, pp. 1–3. AAMAS 2007, ACM, Honolulu, Hawaii (2007). https://doi.org/10.1145/1329125.1329289
13. Popov, K., Rafea, M., Holmgren, F., Brand, P., Vlassov, V., Haridi, S.: Parallel agent-based simulation on a cluster of workstations. Parallel Process. Lett. **13**(04), 629–641 (2003). https://doi.org/10.1142/S0129626403001562
14. Rubio-Campillo, X.: Pandora: a versatile agent-based modelling platform for social simulation. In: Proceedings of SIMUL, pp. 29–34 (2014). https://doi.org/10.13140/2.1.5149.4086

15. Scerri, D., Drogoul, A., Hickmott, S., Padgham, L.: An architecture for modular distributed simulation with agent-based models. In: International Conference on Autonomous Agents and Multiagent Systems, vol. 1, pp. 541–548, Toronto, Canada (2010)
16. Suryanarayanan, V., Theodoropoulos, G., Lees, M.: PDES-MAS: distributed simulation of multi-agent systems. Procedia Comput. Sci. **18**, 671–681 (2013). https://doi.org/10.1016/j.procs.2013.05.231

Co-Learning: Consensus-based Learning for Multi-Agent Systems

C. Carrascosa, J. Rincón, and M. Rebollo(✉)

VRAIn - Valencian Research Institute for Artificial Intelligence, Universitat Politècnica de València, Valencia, Spain
{carrasco,jrincon,mrebollo}@dsic.upv.es

Abstract. One of the main advancements in distributed learning may be the idea behind Google's Federated Learning (FL) algorithm. It allows a distributed deep learning process being made by different units while maintaining the privacy of the data used by each one of these units to train their model. This idea perfectly fits a Multi-Agent System, where the units learning and sharing the model are agents. FL is a centralized approach, where a server is in charge of receiving, averaging, and distributing back the models to the different units making the learning process. Based on this idea, we propose that the distributed learning process not be centralized, and all the agents have the same role in the system. We propose to use a Consensus-based Learning algorithm, which we call "Co-Learning," that uses a consensus algorithm (i) to share the models each agent is learning with its private data and (ii) to calculate the aggregated model of each agent with its local neighbors. As we are using a consensus algorithm, Co-Learning has the properties associated with this algorithm: the whole system calculates the average of the models shared by the agents with their local neighbors. The system adapts automatically to the change in the availability of the agents during its execution. Therefore, agents that fail during the execution and are not available anymore are excluded, or agents that become available during the execution are included and averaged with the rest of the participants.

Keywords: Multi-agent systems · Deep learning · Federated learning · Complex networks · Consensus

1 Introduction

The present paper focuses on developing multi-agent learning, trying to get the most out of a distributed approach by mixing the learning in each agent so that any agent takes profit not only from its own learning process but also from one of its known local neighbors. Along with this, we are interested in the privacy of the data used by each agent for its local learning. These features are, in some way, present in other approaches, mainly Federated Learning (FL).

The FL algorithm was defined by Google [1]. The main idea behind this algorithm is to take advantage of distributed learning and maintain the privacy

© The Author(s), under exclusive license to Springer Nature Switzerland AG 2022
F. Dignum et al. (Eds.): PAAMS 2022, LNAI 13616, pp. 63–75, 2022.
https://doi.org/10.1007/978-3-031-18192-4_6

of the data used by each agent in the learning process. The algorithm uses two different kinds of agents: server and client. Agents connect in a Federated-like hierarchy, with clients connected to the server. The server defines the training model and sends it to all the clients. Each agent trains with its private data and sends it back to the server. Then, the server agent aggregates all the models calculating an averaged one. This average model is sent back again to the client agents, who use it in the next training iteration. In [2], a deep analysis of the open challenges related to FL algorithms is made, where it can be underlined that, for instance, in Decentralized Distributed Learning must be studied the effect of the connection topology of the agents on the convergence rate.

However, the FL approach lacks some relevant features. First of all, it is distributed but centralized, so all the system is synced and evolves at the speed of the slowest agent. Moreover, the system is not designed to be able to adapt to fails (some agent does not answer or disappear) or even to the incorporation of new agents in the system during execution.

These features are of great importance when developing systems that must be deployed in environments with a high probability of communication failure, where there are nodes (agents) that communicates only once a day, or when they must deal with disconnection periods to save battery. This situation can be found if deploying systems in rural areas, where the connectivity is very limited, and the system may remain isolated without supervision for long time periods. These features can be obtained if, instead of using a centralized approach, a fully distributed one is used, as is the one followed by a consensus algorithm [3].

This paper presents a *Consensus-based Learning algorithm* coined *Co-Learning*, trying to take advantage of a complete decentralized approach. We analyze different network topologies to determine the structure that minimizes the communication overload, keeping the network as robust as possible under failures. Finally, an actual implementation using SPADE agents is provided [4].

SPADE is an agent platform based on Python and the XMPP (Extensible Messaging and Presence Protocol) communication protocol. This platform has been used in different areas, but especially in IoT [5]. Our implementation takes profit of the *Presence* feature of the XMPP Protocol so that it can detect when a neighbor agent decides not to go on being connected or fails its connection, not having to wait for a deadline to detect those failures. There is also some previous work in implementing a *pure* FL algorithm in *SPADE* agents, called *FLaMAS* [6].

The rest of the paper is structured as follows: a section where the Co-Learning Algorithm is presented, followed by a section where we validate this algorithm. Next, a section detailing the implementation of this algorithm in SPADE agents, including an execution example, is shown. The paper ends with some conclusions.

2 Co-Learning Algorithm

This section presents the model that supports the distributed training of the machine learning model, combined with the consensus process to average the parameters learned by the agents. An interaction topology delimits the ability of the agents to communicate and exchange information.

2.1 Consensus-based Multi-Agent Systems

A Consensus-based Multi-Agent System is defined by [3] as the Multi-Agent System where the agents agree a value x so that at iteration t, the agent a_i calculates its new value $x_i(t+1)$ according to the Eq. 1.

$$x_i(t+1) = x_i(t) + \varepsilon \sum_{j \in N_i} [x_j(t) - x_i(t)] \tag{1}$$

where N_i denotes the neighbors on node i and $\varepsilon \leq \frac{1}{\max d_i}$ is a factor bounded by the maximum degree of the network. The consensus process converges to the average of the initial values $x_i(0)$. This algorithm has been the base for different and multiple applications and other algorithms as, for instance, *Supportive Consensus* [7].

2.2 Algorithm Description

Let us define a set of N identical agents A; each one of them implements the same NN structure (same layers and neurons). The goal is to learn a global model (W, tr) with a set of weights W for a training dataset tr. All the N agents will share this global model, needing only to share the set of weights W. The training dataset is divided into N fragments of the same length. Results extrapolates to non-IID by using weighted consensus variation [8].

The set of agents are connected following a topology modeled by an undirected network $G = (A, E)$, where the nodes are the agents of set A, and the set of edges E are pairs (i, j) denoting that agent i is connected with agent j. The neighborhood of agent i is denoted with $N_i = \{j \in A : (i, j) \in E\}$

Each agent keeps a NN (W_i, tr_i), being W_i a set of weights and biases for each layer of the NN (all the agents share the same structure)

$$W_i = (W_{i,1}, \ldots, W_{i,k}) \tag{2}$$

where $W_{i,j} \in \mathbb{R}^{n,m}$ represents the weights (or the bias) learned by agent i for the layer j of its NN. Without losing generality, we can assume that the parameters of the NN can be reshaped into a conforming representation.

The *Consensus-based Learning Algorithm* or *Co-Learning* Algorithm can be described as a set of identical agents learning a model through a Deep Neural Network (DNN), where all the agents share the same DNN structure. This allows sharing the model being learned by each agent with its local neighbors and making a consensus of such model based on the Eq. 1. This model is formed by the weights matrices result of the training of the learning process (Eq. 2). This consensual model is then used for each agent in the next training. Figure 1 shows the *Co-Learning algorithm* in a network formed by 4 SPADE agents.

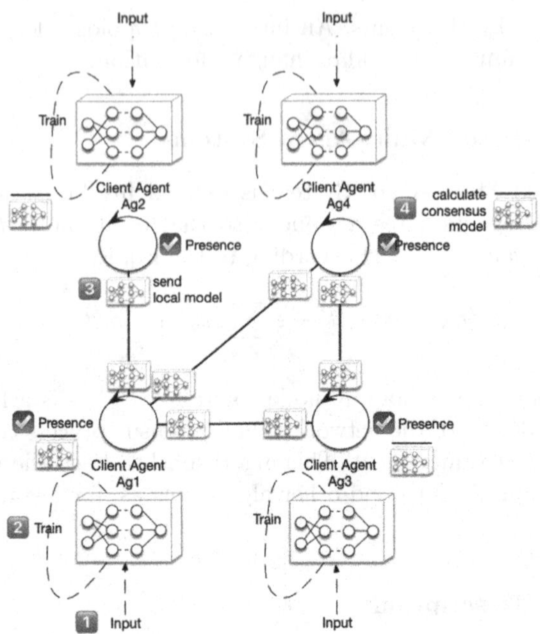

Fig. 1. Co-Learning framework description.

So, an agent a_i following the *Co-Learning* algorithm (Algorithm 1) first of all will make e epochs of training the algorithm. The result of this training is the set of k matrices at Eq. 2, and for each one of them, the next c iterations of the consensus algorithm, following the Eq. 1 are made, leading to k new matrices that will be used in the training process again.

Algorithm 1. Co-Learning Algorithm for agent a_i

while !doomsday **do**
  for $f \leftarrow 1, e$ **do**
    $W \leftarrow Train(f)$
  end for
  for $j \leftarrow 1, k$ **do**
    $X_i(0) \leftarrow W_j$
    for $t \leftarrow 1, c$ **do**
      $X_i(t+1) \leftarrow X_i(t) + \varepsilon \sum_{j \in N_i} [X_j(t) - X_i(t)]$
    end for
  end for
end while

3 Validation of Co-Learning Algorithm

Communication is critical in Co-Learning solutions. The underlying network topology does not affect the final consensus value, but it does the convergence speed. Therefore, to minimize the number of iterations needed to achieve the consensus of the weights and bias matrices, this section analyzes the performance of the process considering (i) the network topology, (ii) the network efficiency-failure tolerance-, and (iii) the effect of the network size. The analysis considers different structures for regular grids and random networks.

3.1 Convergence Analysis

The solution achieved by the consensus process is the same independently of the network topology. Nevertheless, its structure affects the performance of the algorithm. Whenever the network of agents from one connected component, the consensus process converges to the average of the initial values, the averaged trained model. Nevertheless, the topology of the communication structure G determines the convergence speed. As for actual devices, their location plays a relevant role. We use different types of spatial networks. There is some factor that we need to take into account.

The first one refers to the homogeneity of the forces between two agents. We can consider that the influence is different according to certain space orientations (anisotropic space). However, isotropic networks have been demonstrated to be more efficient [9]. Therefore, we will propose topologies in which just the distance between the agents is relevant and not their relative position.

The number of iterations to converge to steady values for all W_i is relevant to achieving an efficient performance. The size of the messages and the communication overhead is not negligible, and the connection scheme may minimize it. The number of iterations needed to reach the consensus can be bounded, and the formula is well known (see [10]).

In actual systems, failures can occur and affect the network topology. The network can be designed to be as robust as possible when it belongs to an organization or the resource location is fixed [11]. Nevertheless, when an open and flexible configuration is needed, the effect of node deletion or disconnection has to be studied.

Figure 2 depicts the network topologies studied for the interaction of G:

- **2d grid:** each agent is located in a regular grid and links with its four nearest neighbors,
- **triangular grid:** a regular grid formed by triangles,
- **Kleinberg's network:** a regular grid with additional random edges with a probability inversely proportional to the distance,
- **Random geometric graph (RGG):** agents are located at random positions and linked to all other agents inside a radius r,
- **Delaunay triangulation:** the dual graph of a Voronoi's diagram,

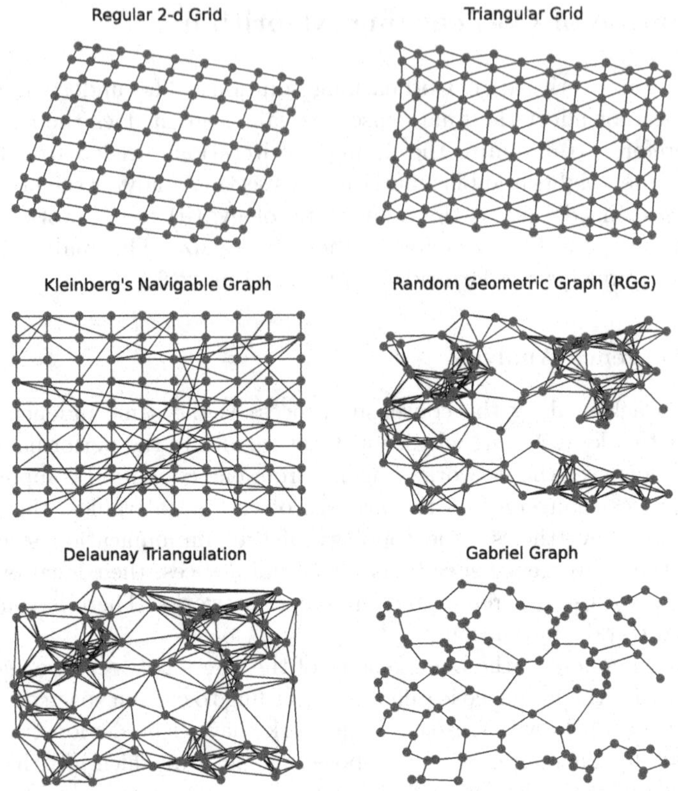

Fig. 2. Network topologies analyzed for spatial graphs.

- **Gabriel's graph:** a subgraph of the Delaunay in which two agents are connected if in the circle between them there is no other agent.

Spatial nodes usually do not follow power laws for the degree distribution and, therefore, there are no hubs responsible for quickly spreading the information Fig. 3 shows the cumulative degree distribution for each network type, varying the number of nodes. The value came from the average distribution of 1,000 different samples for each size for the random networks. All the results of this section belong to the same set of randomly-generated networks.

The distribution of the degree of the nodes and the average short path length has been studied to determine the performance of the network (see Fig. 4). Some topologies are based on regular grids. We have generated network sizes following perfect squares: 25, 36, 49, 64, 81, and 100 nodes. Regular networks and Gabriel's graph maintain a constant degree (as expected), whereas RGG and Delaunay ones increase along with the size of the network. However, path length follows the opposite direction, especially for RGG, which decreases path length. Having shortest paths improves the overall performance of the consensus algorithm and makes RGG a good candidate.

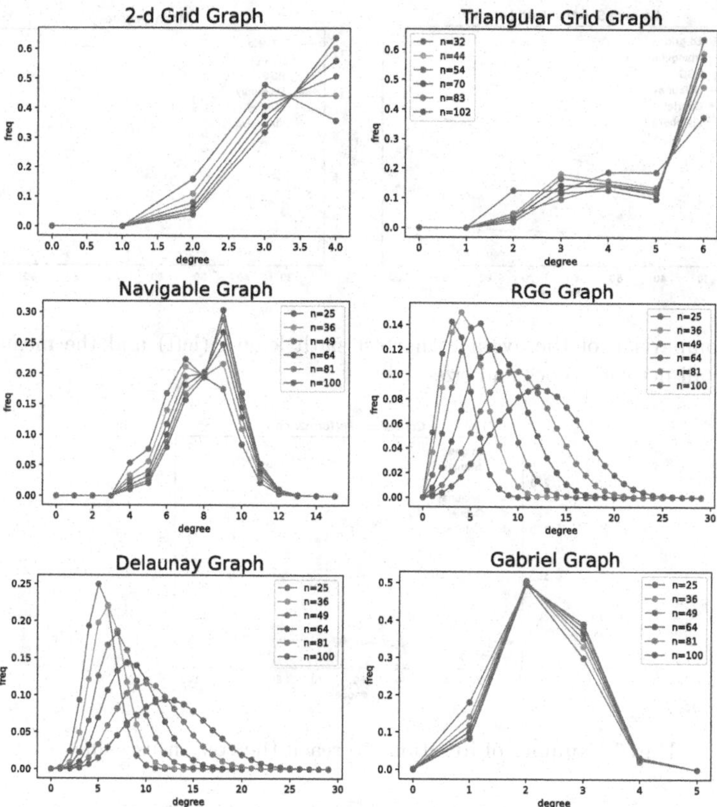

Fig. 3. Degree distribution depending on the network size. Data averaged from 1000 generated networks of each size

Another factor to study is the bounds for the number of consensus iterations until convergence. In Fig. 5, we can see that all the topologies except Gabriel's graph behave similarly, maintaining the number of iterations under 100 epochs.

We can estimate the number of messages that each method will exchange in average, and compare it with the number of messages that the federated version needs to complete the model aggregation. In general, the FL needs $2\times n$ messages. We can bound the consensus version by the number of iterations multiplied by the degree of the network. Nodes that are not connected can communicate in parallel, being the node with maximum degree the bottleneck of the process. Therefore, for the worst case, we use the maximum degree. If t denotes the number of iterations and

$$\max_i deg(i)t \leq 2n \tag{3}$$

and the co-learning process reduces the communication cost when

$$t \leq \frac{2n}{\max_i deg(i)} \tag{4}$$

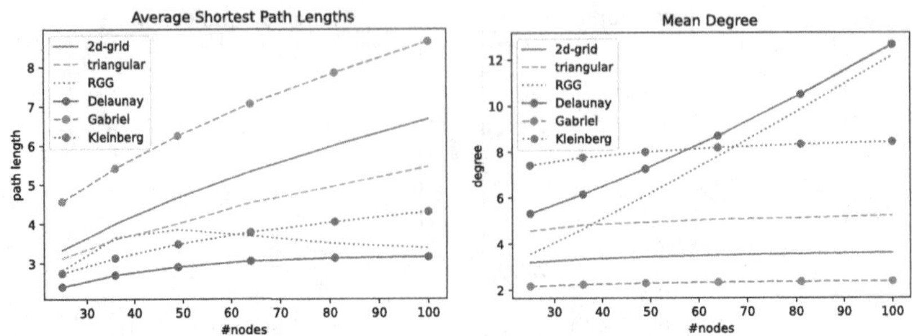

Fig. 4. Comparison of the average shortest path length (left) and the mean degree (right) for all network types and sizes

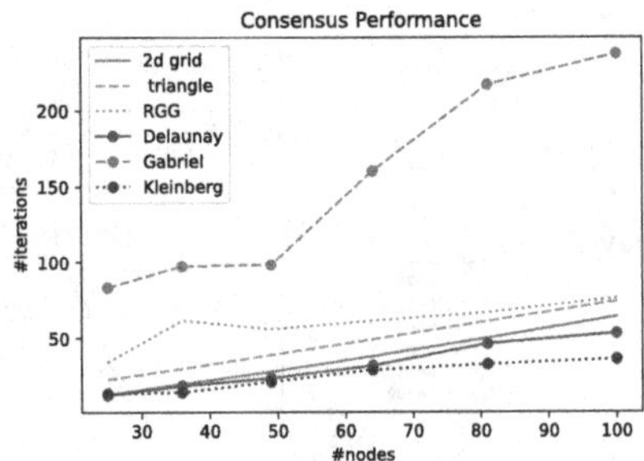

Fig. 5. Number of iterations to reach the consensus value.

3.2 Network Efficiency

The robustness of the networks is analyzed by considering random and targeted failures. A random failure affects any agent with the same probability, whereas targeted attacks simulate someone trying to sabotage the process, and it is addressed to the most vulnerable agent. In our case, targeted attacks are focused on agents with a higher degree since their disconnection may break the network into isolated pieces. Figure 6 shows the results of both cases.

The measure used to indicate the failure tolerance of the network is efficiency. Nodes are removed one by one, and the efficiency of the network is recalculated. That value is normalized, divided by the efficiency of the complete network, to compare all the cases.

Again, Gabriel's graph is the most vulnerable one. Delaunay and RGG are the most robust under random failures and the regular networks for targeted ones since the degree is more homogeneous than random topologies. Nevertheless, all the cases through similar results.

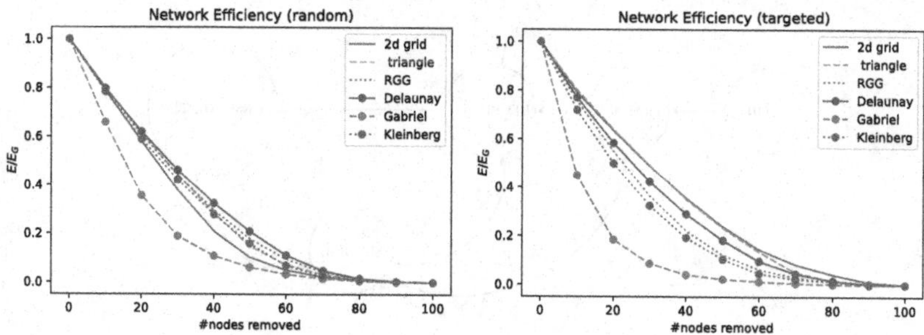

Fig. 6. Network efficiency (top) random node deletion (bottom) targeted node deletion by degree

3.3 Effect of Network Size

Finally, the last experiments show how the training dataset's loss and accuracy improve when more epochs are executed following Algorithm 1. The second iteration reaches accuracy values over 80% and passes the 90% with just five combined epochs of training and consensus (Fig. 7). Data shows the average values of 10 repetitions. Shadow area is limited by the best and the worst accuracy and loss, respectively

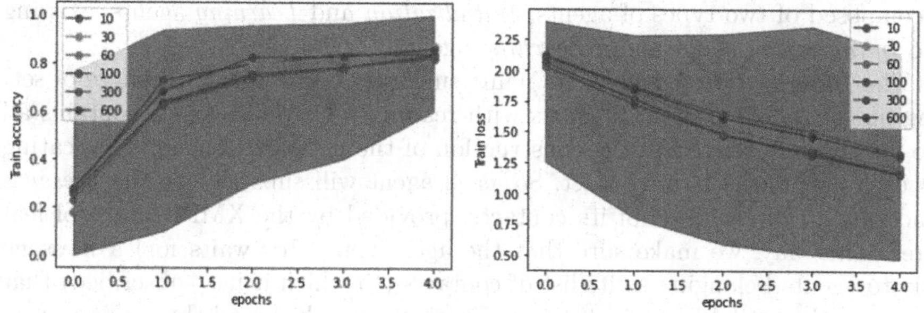

Fig. 7. Train loss and accuracy depending on the network size.

We can conclude that RGG topology improves the performance of the consensus process. The path length compensates their higher degree for the communication delay. RGG is better for random failures and good enough in case of deliberate attacks.

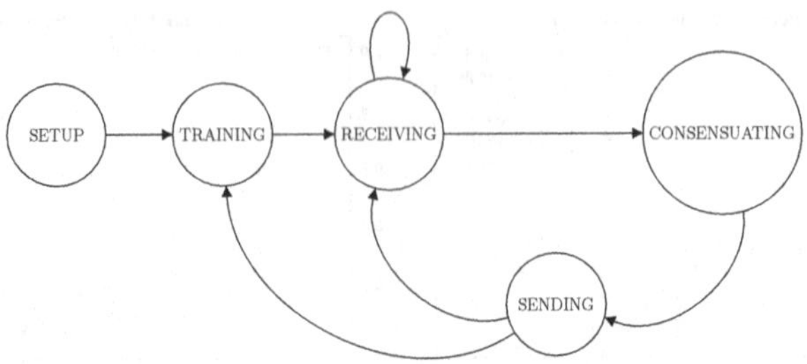

Fig. 8. FSM for the *Learning* agents in the *Co-Learning* system.

4 Execution Using SPADE Agents

This section shows a current implementation of the $Co-Learning$ algorithm using $SPADE$ agents. First, there is a description of how the algorithm has been included in an $SPADE$ agent. Next, some execution experiments using the MNIST dataset are presented.

4.1 Co-Learning in SPADE

In this section, the Consensus-based Learning algorithm implementation using a specific kind of agents, *SPADE* ones [4], is presented. Our $Co-Learning$ system is composed of two types of agents, *Initialization* and *Learning* agents, existing one *Initialization* agent and n *Learning* agents.

The *Initialization* agent, as its name suggests, is the agent in charge of setting up the whole system. It starts with reading a CSV file, which contains all the information related to the construction of the network of agents, indicating for each agent who is in contact. So, each agent will subscribe to the *presence* functionality of each one of its contacts, provided by the XMPP protocol features. This way, we make sure that the agent sends (or waits for) a message only to agents belonging to its list of contacts (to which it has subscribed) that are currently available. Once the initialization agent has read the configuration information, it sends messages to each agent. These messages will be received by the *learning* agents. The behavior of these *Learning* agents is defined as a Finite-State Machine (FSM) in *SPADE* as shown in Fig. 8.

The first state is the $SETUP$ state. In this state, the FSM that will control the agent is initialized. Then, it will go to the $TRAINING$ state, where it will train the model during e epochs. The next state is the $RECEIVING$ state, in charge of receiving two different kinds of messages: configuration messages and new training weights messages. The first one allows changing the network's structure, that is, changing the agent's neighbors. The second one is the messages sent by the agents to their neighbors during the consensus process to communicate their model. When the agent has received a message from all its active neighbors communicating their new training weights, it will pass to the *CONSENSUATING* state, where it will calculate a new aggregated model applying the consensus equation. Then, it will go to the *SENDING* state, where it will send the new model to its neighbors. While it is making c iterations of the consensus algorithm, it will go back to the *RECEIVING* state. When it has finished the c consensus iterations, it will go back to the *TRAINING* set, where it will use the new aggregated model to go on training during e epochs.

4.2 Execution Example

This section describes the different executions carried out with the SPADE multi-agent system platform, showing the validation results obtained in the experiments performed. The MINIST database [12] has been used to carry out the experiments of our *Co-Learning* system. The MNIST database comprises handwritten digits and has a training set of 60.000 examples and a test set of 10.000 examples. Each digit has been normalized and centered on a fixed-size image.

In the experiment, we have developed a Multi-Agent System formed by three agents fully connected. A Convolutional Neural Network (CNN) [13] has been designed to create a deep-learning model:

- Conv1: Conv2d(1, 10, kernel_size = (5, 5), stride = (1, 1))
- Conv2: Conv2d(10, 20, kernel_size = (5, 5), stride = (1, 1))
- Conv2_drop: Dropout2d(p = 0.5, inplace = False)
- Fc1: Linear(in_features = 320, out_features = 50, bias = True)
- Fc2: Linear(in_features = 50, out_features = 10, bias = True)

The accuracy threshold was defined during the training process, so only those models that meet the threshold would be trained. In our case, it was above 95%.

The validation process was carried out on 5,000 examples extracted from the test set. This validation was made using the models obtained during the training process. The result of this validation process can be seen in the following Confusion Matrix:

		predicted									
		1	2	3	4	5	6	7	8	9	10
actual	1	98.06	0.00	0.31	0.10	0.00	0.41	0.61	0.10	0.41	0.00
	2	0.00	98.50	0.35	0.26	0.00	0.00	0.26	0.18	0.44	0.00
	3	1.07	0.29	90.41	0.39	1.16	0.19	0.97	1.36	3.78	0.39
	4	0.00	0.00	4.46	88.32	0.00	2.08	0.00	1.58	2.87	0.69
	5	0.10	0.41	0.71	0.00	88.90	0.10	1.53	0.31	0.41	7.54
	6	0.90	0.11	0.90	3.14	0.45	89.69	1.01	0.78	2.24	0.78
	7	1.36	0.53	0.63	0.00	0.52	1.15	95.41	0.00	0.42	0.00
	8	0.19	1.17	3.02	0.00	0.39	0.00	0.00	93.39	0.10	1.75
	9	0.41	0.72	1.03	0.92	0.41	1.23	0.41	0.72	93.33	0.82
	10	1.19	0.59	0.00	0.69	0.99	0.99	0.10	1.19	0.99	93.26

A high classification percentage can be observed in the confusion matrices presented for each agent, exceeding 90% for all classes. The validation results obtained in the validation face are above 90%, and the same results were obtained in the centralized training (without multi-agent systems) and FL. The same values were obtained in the tests, considering the type of dataset.

5 Conclusions

We have presented a Consensus-based Learning algorithm that takes profit from the distributed learning (based on the idea behind Federated Learning) of sharing a model between a set of agents. This advantage is based on complementing the training of such models made by the agents individually with the aggregation of the models so that all agents may profit from the training completed by the rest of the agents. The agents share the models, so the data's privacy is maintained for the training. As we use a consensus-like algorithm for the model's aggregation, we have some other advantages as the adaptation to fails in the system (agents failing or abandoning the system) and the possibility of aggregating new agents during the execution. The paper shows how this *Co-Learning* algorithm has been implemented in *SPADE* agents. Some validation of the algorithm is shown by some test examples of the *SPADE* implementation. Additional validation, scaling the size of the system is made in simulation, allowing to study the network influence in the results that can be obtained.

RGG topology improves the performance of the convergence of consensus since the average path lengths are shorter than the rest of the networks, compensating for the excess of time for communication due to its higher degree. Finally, regular grids are more robust for targeted attacks, and RGG is better for random failures. In conclusion, we consider that RGG is the most promising topology for implementing a Co-Learning platform.

References

1. McMahan, B., Moore, E., Ramage, D., Hampson, S., y Arcas, B.A.: Communication-efficient learning of deep networks from decentralized data. In: Artificial intelligence and statistics, pp. 1273–1282. PMLR (2017)
2. Kairouz, P., et al.: Advances and open problems in federated learning. Found. Trends ML **14**(1–2), 1–210 (2021)
3. Olfati-Saber, R., Murray, R.M.: Consensus problems in networks of agents with switching topology and time-delays. IEEE TAC **49**(9), 1520–1533 (2004)
4. Palanca, J., Terrasa, A., Julian, V., Carrascosa, C.: Spade 3: supporting the new generation of multi-agent systems. IEEE Access **8**, 182537–182549 (2020)
5. Savazzi, S., Nicoli, M., Rampa, V.: Federated learning with cooperating devices: a consensus approach for massive IoT networks. IEEE Internet Things J. **7**(5), 4641–4654 (2020)
6. Rincon, J., Julian, V., Carrascosa, C.: FlaMAS: federated learning based on a spade mas. Appl. Sci. **12**(7), 1–14 (2022)

7. Palomares, A., Rebollo, M., Carrascosa, C.: Supportive consensus. PLoS ONE **15**(12), 1–30 (2020)
8. Pedroche, F., Rebollo, M., Carrascosa, C., Palomares, A.: Convergence of weighted-average consensus for undirected graphs. Int. J. Complex Syst. Sci. **4**(1), 13–16 (2014)
9. Gotesdyner, O., Gross, B., Porath, D.V.B., Havlin, S.: Percolation on spatial anisotropic networks. arXiv e-prints, pp. 1–9 (2022)
10. Chan, T.-H.H., Ning, Li.: Fast convergence for consensus in dynamic networks. ACM Trans. Algorithms **10**(3), 1–15 (2014)
11. Lyutov, A., Uygun, Y., Hütt, M.T.: Local topological features of robust supply networks. arXiv e-prints, pp. 1–14 (2021)
12. Deng, L.: The mnist database of handwritten digit images for machine learning research. IEEE Signal Process. Mag. **29**(6), 141–142 (2012)
13. Albawi, S., Mohammed, T.A., Al-Zawi, S.: Understanding of a convolutional neural network. In: 2017 International Conference on Engineering and Technology (ICET), pp. 1–6. IEEE (2017)

Multiagent Pickup and Delivery for Capacitated Agents

Evren Çilden(✉) and Faruk Polat

Middle East Technical University, 06800 Ankara, Turkey
{evren.cilden,polat}@ceng.metu.edu.tr

Abstract. In Multi-Agent Pickup and Delivery (MAPD), multiple robots continuously receive tasks to pick up packages and deliver them to predefined destinations in an automated warehouse. If the capacity of agents is increased, agents can pick up more than one item on their way, which will presumably reduce the time required to accomplish all deliveries–that is, makespan. In this paper, we propose two algorithms for MAPD with Capacities (MAPDC) that are *complete* and scalable: Token Passing with Multiple Task Assignments (TPMT) and Token Passing with Multiple Capacity (TPMC). Both of the methods are based on the Token Passing (TP) algorithm, one of the *suboptimal* and complete solutions by Ma et al. [6]. The performance of the algorithms is analyzed in terms of makespan, service time, and throughput. TPMC turns out to be more effective than TPMT at utilizing capacitated agents.

Keywords: Multiagent Pickup and Delivery (MAPD) · MAPD with Capacities (MAPDC) · Warehouse automation

1 Introduction

A current trend in logistics is automated warehouses, where robots operate to store and retrieve objects at fulfillment/distribution centers (Fig. 1). A problem originating from this real-world domain is Multi-Agent Pickup and Delivery (MAPD) [6]. The aim is to perform some delivery tasks with a fixed number of homogeneous and autonomous agents, where a new task can enter the system at any time. When an agent is assigned to a task, it moves to the pickup location, takes the item, and carries it to the delivery point, while planning non-conflicting paths with other agents.

As inventory pods allocate most of the space at automated warehouses, robots navigate through narrow paths and occasionally need to avoid collisions with other agents. Hence, MAPD is closely related to the classical NP-hard problem of multi-agent path-finding (MAPF), where each agent located in a grid environment is assigned a destination position (the robots operate in an environment by following bar-code stickers on the floor provided for discretization of the navigation space, which we can model as a grid-environment). The solver computes the location of agents at each time step so that all agents reach

© The Author(s), under exclusive license to Springer Nature Switzerland AG 2022
F. Dignum et al. (Eds.): PAAMS 2022, LNAI 13616, pp. 76–87, 2022.
https://doi.org/10.1007/978-3-031-18192-4_7

their destinations without colliding with obstacles or other agents. MAPD is the lifelong version of MAPF [6] where new tasks can enter the system at any time. Agents are assigned new targets, which better suits the domain of automated warehouses. Two interdependent concerns of MAPD, task assignment and collision-free path-finding, make the problem even more challenging than MAPF. There is a search for online and efficient solvers for MAPD that can plan for hundreds of agents.

(a) Amazon warehouse robot [9]

(b) HAI Pick System [1]

Fig. 1. Robots operating at fully automated warehouse environments.

In real life, there are cases where agents are capable of carrying multiple items (Fig. 1(b)). We can generalize MAPD for capacitated agents so that they can pick up or deliver items on their way to reduce the average time for the completion of a series of tasks. Multiple capacity was first considered by Chen et al. [1], exploring a coupled solution of task assignment and path-finding called Regret Based Marginal Cost Assignment (RMCA). Although they obtained a valuable decrease in makespan by employing capacitation to RMCA, they noted the completeness of the algorithm needs improvement [1]. Later, Tajelipirbazari et al. [10] named the capacitated variant as MAPDC and devised a solution within the declarative framework of Answer Set Programming (ASP). The algorithm guarantees optimality for makespan but fails to scale to real-world situations. In this study, we provide two complete, scalable yet suboptimal solutions to MAPDC: TPMT and TPMC.

2 Related Work

Most of the existing solutions to MAPD attack the problem sequentially by decoupling assignment and path-finding. They first assign tasks to agents to determine the pickup and put-down points they will travel to. Then they apply MAPF techniques to find a non-colliding path sequence for each agent. A classical problem that is most relevant to the task assignment aspect of MAPD is Vehicle Routing within the problem class of Multi-robot Task Allocation (MRTA) [4,7]. Under predefined constraints, it focuses on making optimal route assignments, assuming that agents do not collide. Multiagent Path Finding (MAPF) is also a well-studied problem that aims at planning a path for each agent while avoiding collisions with other agents [2]. The optimality criterion is minimizing the sum of paths of all agents. A foundational algorithm used in developing solutions to MAPF problems is A* [3], a complete and optimal algorithm that performs a best-first search on a spanning tree. CBS [8] is an optimal algorithm that keeps track of a high-level search tree of constraints by examining collisions between agents, which is shown to examine fewer states compared to A*.

After its first introduction in 2017 by Ma et al. [6], many solutions to MAPD was proposed. In decentralized solutions, agents individually calculate their paths and then fix collisions. Otherwise a central solver computes paths of all agents. Offline solvers require a priori knowledge of the task list to compute the whole path. Online algorithms provide a solution composed of computation and movement phases.

Token-Passing (TP) [6] is a decentralized online solution based on the idea of tokens. A global token stores the set of unexecuted tasks and paths of agents. As new tasks are added, unoccupied agents select the task with the closest pickup location and take over the token, in turn, to calculate their paths using the A* algorithm. Agents hold task endpoints for deadlock avoidance, which guarantees completeness for well-formed instances [6]. Token-Passing with Task Swaps (TPTS) [6] enhances task assignment of TP by allowing task transfer between agents while the previously assigned agent is on its way for pickup.

CENTRAL [6] is an online algorithm, where a centralized solver assigns tasks by the Hungarian method and calculates paths by CBS. TA-Prioritized [5] is another centralized algorithm that computes a task sequence for each agent, then plans paths by prioritized planning. Regret Based Marginal Cost Assignment (RMCA) [1] integrates task assignment and path planning to optimize the total task delivery time of agents. Different from other approaches, RMCA considers actual delivery costs instead of lower-bound estimates in path planning. RMCA is based on prioritized planning with A* and does not guarantee completeness. Chen et al. executed RMCA with capacitated agents and reported a huge enhancement in makespan [1]. Tajelipirbazari et al. [10] devised a centralized offline solution based on ASP to MAPDC.

3 Problem Description

We define MAPDC formally as:

- a set of m agents $A = \{a_1, a_2, ..., a_m\}$, where each agent has a capacity of carrying at most n items.
- an undirected connected graph $G = (V, E)$, where V is the set of the locations and E is the set of edges connecting the locations.
- a set of tasks $\mathcal{T}$, which are waiting to be executed by an agent (solver's task list). Each task $\tau_j \in \mathcal{T}$ is a tuple (s_j, g_j) of pickup location $s_j \in V$ and delivery location $g_j \in V$.

In this context, MAPD is a special case of MAPDC, where $n = 1$. In MAPDC, each agent has a set of assigned and ongoing tasks T with a size bound n, since each agent is capable of carrying at most n items. An agent is *under-capacity* when $0 \leq |T| < n$, so that the solver can assign a new task $\tau_j \in \mathcal{T}$ to the agent (i.e. $T \cup \{\tau_j\}$). If the agent's path to the location s_j is planned, the task τ_j is removed from the solver's task list $\mathcal{T}$ to avoid re-assignments. The execution of the task ends when the agent navigates to the location g_j of the task τ_j, and the task is removed from the agent's set of tasks, T.

While executing a task, the agent a_i either waits at its current position or moves to an adjacent node in a single time step ($l_i(t+1)$ is either $l_i(t)$ or $l_i(t+1) \neq l_i(t)$ where $(l_i(t), l_i(t+1)) \in E$). Agents cannot simultaneously be at the same location ($\forall a_i, a_j$ where $a_i \neq a_j$ and $\forall t : l_i(t) \neq l_j(t)$). Two agents cannot simultaneously move in opposite directions along the same edge ($\forall a_i, a_j$ where $a_i \neq a_j$, and $\forall t : l_i(t) \neq l_j(t+1)$ or $l_j(t) \neq l_i(t+1)$).

A valid solution for MAPDC completes the set of tasks in a finite number of timesteps and returns non-colliding paths of agents. For a MAPD problem to be solvable at finite steps, Ma et al. introduced the notion of *well-formedness* and stated conditions for a well-formed MAPD instance [6]. Since MAPDC is an extension of the task-assignment aspect of MAPD, the underlying constraints about path-finding are also applicable. Thus, we can infer that the constraints defined for well-formedness hold for the capacitated variation of the problem as well.

4 Method

TP algorithm, a complete and scalable solution to MAPD, is a promising candidate for devising such a solution to MAPDC. We examined possible enhancements to the TP algorithm and proposed two methods. The first algorithm is Token Passing with Multiple Task Assignments (TPMT). In this method, the agent holding the token can plan a path for up to n tasks, where n is its capacity. In the second method named Token Passing with Multiple Capacity (TPMC), every under-capacity agent holding the token can choose a task before completing its tasks to pick up items on the way.

4.1 TPMT

The pseudo-code for TPMT is available at Algorithm 1. Firstly, agents are initialized to stay at their current locations ($[loc(a_i)]$) (Line 1). New tasks introduced at the current timestep are added to the end of the task set $\mathcal{T}$ (line 3). Solver passes *token* to the next free agent that has reached the end of its path. The agent takes the control of execution after Line 4. The agent selects tasks until its capacity is full ($|T_i| = n$) or there are no available tasks among the task set such that no path of other agents ends in the pickup or delivery location of the task (lines 5 to 12). The selection criterion is finding the tasks with the start location that has the minimum h-value to the current location of the agent (line 9). For efficiency, h-values, that is, path costs from all locations to all endpoints (i.e., possible pickup and delivery locations) are pre-calculated to be used by

Algorithm 1. Token Passing with Multiple Task Assignments (TPMT)

```
Initialize token with path [loc(a_i)] for each agent a_i
while true do
    Add all new tasks, if any, to the task set 𝒯
    while agent a_i exists that requests token do
        𝒯' ← {τ_j ∈ 𝒯 | no other path in token ends in s_j or g_j}
        if 𝒯' ≠ ∅ then
            T_i ← ∅                                        ▷ empty task set of a_i
            while 𝒯' ≠ ∅ and |T_i| ≠ n do                  ▷ n: capacity of a_i
                T_i ∪ {arg min_{τ_j ∈ 𝒯'} h(loc(a_i), s_j)}
                Remove τ_j from 𝒯'
            end while
            P ← GetOrderedPoints(T_i)
            for each p ∈ P do
                Update a_i's path in token with Path1(a_i, p, token)
            end for
            for each τ ∈ T_i do
                Remove τ from 𝒯
            end for
        else if no task τ_k ∈ 𝒯 exists with g_k = loc(a_i) then
            Update a_i's path in token with path [loc(a_i)]
        else
            Update a_i's path in token with Path2(a_i, token)
        end if
    end while
end while
function GetOrderedPoints(T_i)
    Add s_1 to P                                   ▷ P is the list of ordered points
    Add g_1 to V                                   ▷ V is the list of points to visit
    for each j ≠ 1 and τ_j ∈ T_i do
        Add s_j to V
        Add (s_j, g_j) to C                        ▷ C is the list of visit constraints
    end for
    while V is not empty do
        l ← last(P)                                ▷ l is the last visited point
        v_k ← arg min_{v_k ∈ V} h(l, v_k)
        Add v_k to P
        if there exists (v_k, g_k) in C then
            Add g_k to V
            Remove (v_k, g_k) from C
        end if
        Remove v_k from V
    end while
    return P
end function
```

task allocation and A* searches. Agent a_i finds an ordered list P of endpoints for all s_j and g_j of $\tau_j \in T_i$ (Line 13). For each point $p \in P$, the agent calculates its path from $[loc(a_i)]$ to p by A* (Path1), and updates the *token* (lines 13–15). After calculating its path for all points in P, the agent removes all tasks in T_i from $\mathcal{T}$ (lines 16–18). If T_i is empty and there is no task that the agent can execute, it checks whether its location is the delivery location of another task. If so, to avoid deadlocks, updates its path to Path2 that is the path to move to an unoccupied endpoint. Otherwise, the agent plans the trivial path to stay at its final destination, $[loc(a_i)]$.

The function GetOrderedPoints(T_i) calculates the visiting order for start and goal points of tasks in T_i. The problem is a special case of the TSP on the directed graph $G_i = (V_i, E_i)$ where V_i contains the start and delivery locations of tasks in T_i. Since there is a path between any two endpoints for every well-formed MAPD problem, the graph is fully connected except for the directed edges from g_j to s_j for every task $\tau_j \in T_i$ (because agents visit the delivery location only after picking up an item). The function keeps track of the visiting constraints and the list of nodes to visit and applies the nearest neighborhood heuristic to choose the point with the minimum h-value to the last visit position. A goal location is not considered as a candidate for the next visit until its pickup location is in the ordered list of points.

4.2 TPMC

TPMT selects the first n tasks that have the nearest pickup locations to the agent at the time of decision. As the agent advances in execution, previously selected tasks can be distant to its updated position, which may have a huge negative impact on the overall makespan. TPMC method aims at making better task assignments in an online fashion by allowing under-capacity agents to choose the next task after visiting a point.

Algorithm 2 presents the outline of the TPMC method. Like TPMT, it is a decoupled algorithm based on TP [6] with the same initialization and agent selection logic. Different from TPMT, the agent keeps a list of points to visit (i.e. V_i). After taking the token, the agent counts the number of items waiting for delivery (i.e. finds the number of delivery points in V_i). If it is under-capacity, the agent decides that it can pick up another item, and if any, chooses an available task τ_j having the minimum h-value for the location pair $(loc(a_i), s_j)$ (Lines 5–8). The constraint that no other path in *token* ends in s_j or g_j is also valid for the task assignment of TPMC. The agent updates the state of the task τ_j as taken and appends s_j to its V_i (Lines 9–10). If V_i is not empty, the agent finds the point p in V_i that has the minimum h-value to its current location and updates its path in the *token* with the path calculated by A* (Lines 20–21). After path-finding, p is removed from V_i (Line 22). If p is a start point of a task τ_k, a_i adds the delivery location g_k to end of V_i (Lines 23–24). If it is a delivery point, τ_k is removed from the task list of *token* (Line 26). If V_i is empty, and if the agent is in the delivery location of a task, it calls function Path2 and updates its path to move to an unoccupied endpoint to avoid deadlocks (Line

17). Otherwise, the agent plans the trivial path to stay in its current location (Line 15).

Algorithm 2. Token Passing with Multiple Capacity (TPMC)

1: Initialize *token* with path $[loc(a_i)]$ for each agent a_i
2: **while** *true* **do**
3: Add all new tasks, if any, to the task set $\mathcal{T}$
4: **while** agent a_i exists that requests *token* **do**
5: **if** the number of goal points in $V_i < n$ **then** ▷ n is the capacity and V_i is to-Visit list of a_i
6: $\mathcal{T}' \leftarrow \{\tau_j \in \mathcal{T} \mid \tau_j$ is not taken and no other path in *token* ends in s_j or $g_j\}$
7: **if** $\mathcal{T}' \neq \emptyset$ **then**
8: $\tau_j \leftarrow \arg\min_{\tau_j \in \mathcal{T}'} \mathrm{h}(loc(a_i), s_j)$
9: Add s_j to V_i
10: Mark τ_j as taken
11: **end if**
12: **end if**
13: **if** V_i is empty **then**
14: **if** no task $\tau_k \in \mathcal{T}$ exists with $g_k = loc(a_i)$ **then**
15: Update a_i's path in *token* with path $[loc(a_i)]$
16: **else**
17: Update a_i's path in *token* with Path2(a_i, *token*)
18: **end if**
19: **else**
20: $p \leftarrow \arg\min_{v_k \in V_i} \mathrm{h}(loc(a_i), v_k)$ and no other path in *token* ends with v_k

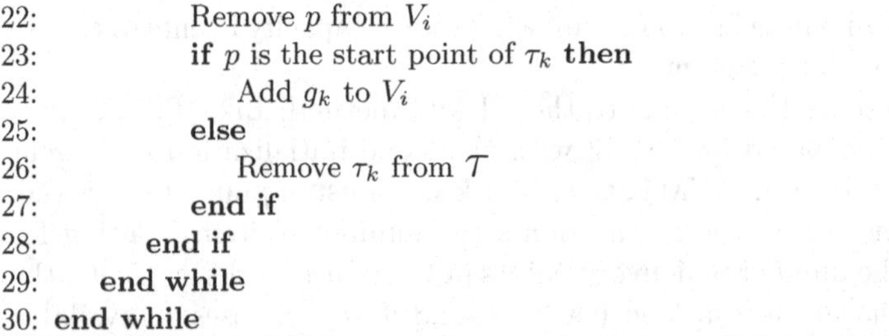

21: Update a_i's path in *token* with Path1($a_i, p, token$)
22: Remove p from V_i
23: **if** p is the start point of τ_k **then**
24: Add g_k to V_i
25: **else**
26: Remove τ_k from $\mathcal{T}$
27: **end if**
28: **end if**
29: **end while**
30: **end while**

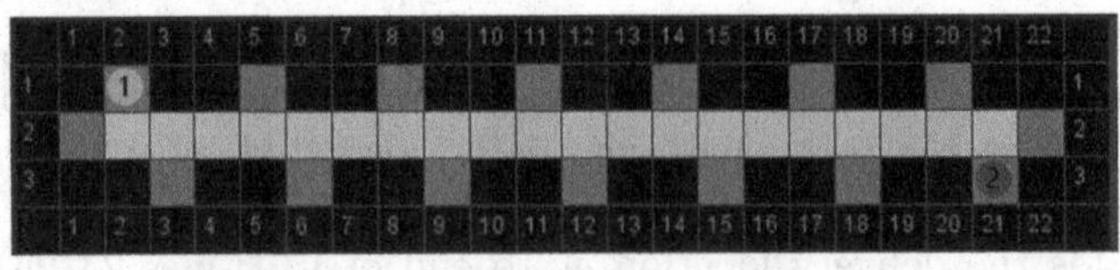

Fig. 2. Narrow domain for case studies.

Table 1. Task list for case studies

Task number	Pickup → Delivery
1	(5, 1) → (20, 1)
2	(8, 1) → (17, 1)
3	(11, 1) → (14, 1)
4	(18, 3) → (3, 3)
5	(15, 3) → (6, 3)
6	(12, 3) → (9, 3)

5 Evaluation

5.1 Case Studies

Two case studies were performed on the narrow domain (Fig. 2), where the black and gray cells are obstacles and endpoints respectively. Colored circles represent the initial locations of agents and their ids. The capacity of agents is set to 5 for both cases. The first case study examines whether the algorithms generate a valid solution for a single agent, therefore the second agent is removed from the environment. Table 1 is the list of tasks introduced at the first timestep of execution. The second case study is a simple multi-agent setting to see whether the paths planned are collision-free. The top half of the task list is introduced at the first timestep, and the rest at the following timestep. At each run, we measured the timestep at which the task list is empty and all deliveries are complete (i.e. makespan) and the average number of timesteps to complete tasks (i.e. service time).

Both TPMT and TPMC provide valid solutions for the Narrow Domain with single and double agent cases. As seen in Table 2, figures for makespan and service time of TPMT and TPMC appear to be less when compared with the single capacity algorithm TP. In the first case, the TPMT algorithm plans for the first five tasks in a row. The agent has to visit the distant pickup location of the last task separately. Instead, the TPMC algorithm assigns tasks with the closest start location whenever the agent is under-capacity, resulting in a better makespan. TPMT algorithm can make poor assignments when the start and the delivery of tasks are distant. Conversely, TPMT performs much better than TPMC in the second case study. The makespan for TPMC is the same as TP, indicating an insufficient utilization of multiple capacities. In the TPMT run, the first agent takes over the first three tasks, and the second agent takes the rest. In TPMC execution, tasks are assigned in an interleaved fashion. The first agent is under-capacity most of the time, hence greedily takes on new tasks including the fourth one. The second agent finishes earlier than first one and starts waiting. It would be much better if tasks were more evenly distributed among agents.

Table 2. Results for case studies I and II

	Case study I		Case study II	
Algorithm	Makespan	Service time	Makespan	Service time
TP	98	64	60	36
TPMT	84	44	33	25
TPMC	60	41	60	33

Table 3. Measures for TP algorithm

Agents	Tasks	Freq.	Makespan	Service time	Runtime
2	100	1	1161	508.9	0.19
5	100	1	531	196.7	2.39
10	500	1	1198	311.8	5.67
50	100	5	153	60.8	722.20
50	500	5	395	124.6	675.43

5.2 Experimental Setup

We performed an experimental evaluation to compare the efficiency and effectiveness of the two methods on the simulated warehouse environment [6], which is used as a benchmark in studies on MAPD. The sample environment consists of a 21×35 4-neighbor grid with narrow pathways. We performed experiments with various numbers of agents, capacities, and task frequencies on lists of 100 and 500 tasks. Task files were generated by randomly selecting pickup and delivery locations among the endpoints defined in the environment map file. All experiments are implemented in C++ programming language and run on a 1.80 GHz Intel Core i7-8565U laptop with 24 GB RAM.

5.3 Results

Tables 3 and 4 summarize the results of experiments. Increasing the number of agents has a huge positive impact on the makespan of all algorithms. Task frequency (number of tasks released at each timestep) seems to have a minor effect on makespan and service time for experimented cases. Even though there is a slight positive effect of capacity expansion for TPMT at the test with two agents, performance degrades with capacitation for more agents. On the other hand, for five agents, there is about 30% improvement on the makespan for TPMC. The greedy task assignment approach of TPMT is the reason for worse efficiency. Agents try to get more tasks to fill their capacity, and an agent closer to the pickup point may not have the chance to take over the task. In TPMC, an agent can visit the start point of a task τ and finish many other tasks before visiting the delivery point of τ. This may result in longer service times for some tasks. Compared to TP, the average service times of TPMC are still better for capacitated agents. As seen in Table 4, there is a trend of decrease in makespan as capacity of agents increase for TPMC. In general, TPMC better utilizes the capacity of agents than TPMT. Additionally, runtime values (in milliseconds per timestep) of TPMC are strongly preferable to TPMT. Therefore, TPMC suits better to a lifelong and real-time operation setting.

Table 4. Summary of experimental results (f.: frequency, Cap.: Capacity, S.Time: Service Time)

				TPMT			TPMC		
Agents	Task	f	Cap	Makespan	S.Time	Runtime	Makespan	S.Time	Runtime
2	100	1	1	1161	508.88	0.30	1161	509.12	0.16
			3	1186	519.23	0.93	740	319.5	0.19
			5	1031	458.19	1.16	680	285.15	0.20
5	100	1	1	531	196.7	1.66	500	190.05	0.70
			3	536	220.33	4.26	379	136.9	0.82
			5	746	357.45	33.58	341	126.25	0.92
10	500	1	1	1198	311.78	4.95	1192	308.39	2.05
			3	1603	474.37	63.40	841	168.97	2.10
			5	2414	815.61	165.66	771	134.30	1.93
50	100	5	1	153	60.82	131.77	126	47.7	19.59
			3	307	144.81	486.79	140	51.97	14.64
			5	679	312.36	494.36	126	51.96	17.16
50	500	5	1	395	124.59	97.58	353	102.62	36.64
			3	1056	479.25	1138.78	295	81.77	33.49
			5	2321	1235.74	1593.524	284	87.66	33.46

As in Ma et al. [6], we analyzed the throughput of the algorithms. Throughput is measured as the number of executed tasks within a 100-timestep window as a function of timestep t. Figure 3 visualizes the number of tasks added and executed for different types of algorithms (the number to the right of the name of the algorithm indicates the capacity). We preferred to present the throughput data for two agents and 100 tasks as the number of tasks per agent is higher, which may better reflect the long-term behavior of the system. It is apparent from the figure that TPMC is much better at utilizing capacitated agents.

Table 5 presents a comparison of TPMC algorithm with RMCA-r [1], the only scalable MAPD algorithm for capacitated agents to our knowledge. We performed experiments with 500 tasks of frequency 10 on small simulated warehouse instances of 20 and 50 agents with capacities 1, 3, and 5 respectively. Both makespan and total travel delay (total time elapsed between release and completion of all tasks) are smaller in RMCA than TPMC. This is an expected result as task assignment search is informed by actual costs in RMCA, whereas TPMC

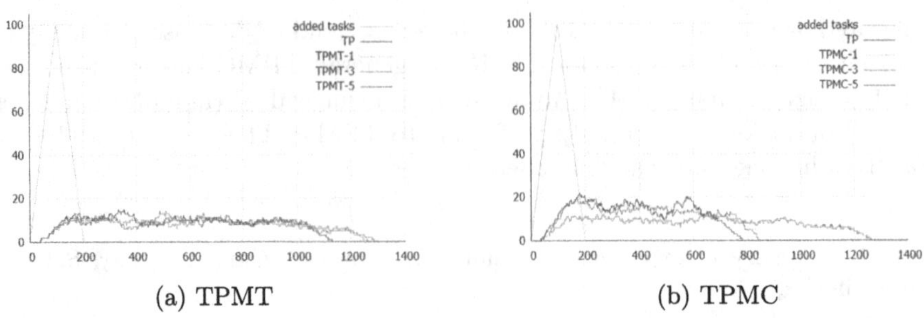

(a) TPMT (b) TPMC

Fig. 3. Results for 2 agents, 100 tasks and task frequency 1 (Timestep vs. number of tasks).

uses lower-bound estimates. RMCA-r also incorporates meta-heuristic improvement strategies, which are reported to improve solutions substantially [1]. In spite of its better performance, RMCA does not guarantee to solve all well-formed instances of MAPD and needs an improvement on completeness.

Table 5. TPMC vs. RMCA-r (Cap.: Capacity, TTD: Total Travel Delay)

		RMCA-r		TPMC	
Cap.	Agents	Makespan	TTD	Makespan	TTD
1	20	624	106290	702	136912
	50	280	38050	371	64344
3	20	322	52771	524	95060
	50	153	15851	276	46912
5	20	247	36790	423	81507
	50	129	11464	270	43091

6 Conclusion

Despite the substantial amount of related work, MAPD for capacitated agents seems an under-explored area. We believe that MAPDC solvers will have potential uses in future automated warehouse systems, as well as in automated manufacturing and sorting systems. This study introduced TPMT and TPMC methods that expanded the Token Passing algorithm [6] to make use of capacitated agents. Agents executing TPMT request the token less often. Once they obtain it, they take over as many tasks as possible and plan a visiting route to complete the tasks. In TPMC, agents plan the smallest portion of their overall route each time they take the token. Whenever under-capacity, they take over the task with the nearest pick up location. Even though the results for TPMT are encouraging for the narrow domain, evaluations on the small simulated warehouse environment suggest TPMC as a better choice for all performance measures taken into consideration. Although RMCA-r performs better than TPMC with capacitated agents, its prioritized planner needs improvement on completeness. TPMC guarantees completeness for well-formed instances of MAPD since it employs the same deadlock prevention mechanisms as TP (the proof is similar to the one given for Theorem 3 stated in [6]).

As the incorporation of capacitated agents remarkably improves the throughput of the system, MAPDC is a promising step toward highly scalable automated warehouse systems. Being a complete, efficient, and decentralized solution to MAPDC, TPMC is an encouraging method for such systems. Directions for future work include improving the solution quality of TPMC and exploring better task dispatching strategies for capacitated agents.

Acknowledgment. This work is partially supported by the Scientific and Technological Research Council of Turkey under Grant No 120E504 (Incremental Multi-Agent Path Finding).

References

1. Chen, Z., Alonso-Mora, J., Bai, X., Harabor, D.D., Stuckey, P.J.: Integrated task assignment and path planning for capacitated multi-agent pickup and delivery. IEEE Robot. Autom. Lett. **6**(3), 5816–5823 (2021)
2. Felner, A., et al.: Search-based optimal solvers for the multi-agent pathfinding problem: summary and challenges. In: SOCS (2017)
3. Knight, K.: Are many reactive agents better than a few deliberative ones? In: Bajcsy, R. (ed.) Proceedings of the 13th International Joint Conference on Artificial Intelligence. Chambéry, France, August 28 – September 3, 1993, pp. 432–437. Morgan Kaufmann (1993). http://ijcai.org/Proceedings/93-1/Papers/061.pdf
4. Korsah, G.A., Stentz, A., Dias, M.B.: A comprehensive taxonomy for multi-robot task allocation. Int. J. Robot. Res. **32**(12), 1495–1512 (2013)
5. Liu, M., Ma, H., Li, J., Koenig, S.: Task and path planning for multi-agent pickup and delivery, p. 9 (2019)
6. Ma, H., Li, J., Kumar, T.K.S., Koenig, S.: Lifelong multi-agent path finding for online pickup and delivery tasks. arXiv:1705.10868 [cs] (2017). http://arxiv.org/abs/1705.10868, arXiv: 1705.10868
7. Nunes, E., Manner, M.D., Mitiche, H., Gini, M.L.: A taxonomy for task allocation problems with temporal and ordering constraints. Robot. Auton. Syst. (2017). https://doi.org/10.1016/j.robot.2016.10.008
8. Sharon, G., Stern, R., Felner, A., Sturtevant, N.R.: Conflict-based search for optimal multi-agent pathfinding. Artif. Intell. **219**, 40–66 (2015)
9. Statt, N.: Amazon says fully automated shipping warehouses are at least a decade away (2019). https://www.theverge.com/2019/5/1/18526092/amazon-warehouse-robotics-automation-ai-10-years-away
10. Tajelipirbazari, N., et al.: Multi-agent pick and delivery with capacities: action planning vs path finding. In: Cheney, J., Perri, S. (eds.) PADL 2022. LNCS, vol. 13165, pp. 24–41. Springer, Cham (2022). https://doi.org/10.1007/978-3-030-94479-7_3

Using Institutional Purposes to Enhance Openness of Multi-Agent Systems

Rafhael R. Cunha[1,2](✉), Jomi F. Hübner[2], and Maiquel de Brito[3]

[1] Federal Institute of Education, Science and Technology of Rio Grande do Sul (IFRS), Campus Vacaria, Vacaria, Brazil

[2] Department of Automation and Systems Engineering, Federal University of Santa Catarina, Florianópolis, Brazil
rafhael.cunha@posgrad.ufsc.br, jomi.hubner@ufsc.br

[3] Control, Automation, and Computation Engineering Department, Federal University of Santa Catarina, Blumenau, Brazil
maiquel.b@ufsc.br

Abstract. In this paper, we consider a programmer who needs to develop an agent to publish information on different existing social networks. Several works in the literature allow the interaction of agents with a social network, but as far as we know, they are not focused on the interaction with several networks. Considering this problem, the paper highlights two options the programmer can take to enable the agent to interact with existing social networks and achieve its goal. The first option requires that the programmer knows the features present in the APIs used to interact with social networks, and the consequences that the functions can bring when executed in the system. The second option uses the institutional notion of *purpose* aiming to reduce the amount of previous knowledge required by the programmer. The paper aims to discuss the advantages and disadvantages of these options considering the development of open multi-agent system. A JaCaMo implementation of both options is used the help the evaluation.

Keywords: Agent programmer · Artificial institutions · Purposes

1 Introduction

We have recently witnessed a massive diffusion of social networking based on web applications that have quickly become an unprecedented cultural phenomenon [7]. Such web applications allow members to publish personal information in a semi-structured form and to define links to other members with whom they have relationships of various kinds [4]. These applications are available for both human and software agents, allowing them to enter and leave the

This study was supported by the Federal Institute of Education, Science and Technology of Rio Grande do Sul (IFRS).

© The Author(s), under exclusive license to Springer Nature Switzerland AG 2022
F. Dignum et al. (Eds.): PAAMS 2022, LNAI 13616, pp. 88–99, 2022.
https://doi.org/10.1007/978-3-031-18192-4_8

system to achieve their goals. Therefore, these applications can be considered as an open multi-agent systems (MAS).

Software agents may pursue the same goals in the different available social network systems. In this context, imagine an agent developer who needs to program the agent *Bob* whose goal is to publish information on different social networks. Existing proposals for interaction between agents and social networks [1,2,8,16] adopt ad-hoc solutions that require that the developer knows each social network and implements the necessary actions for the agent to reach its goal in these systems. The main drawback of this approach is that the developer needs to know the peculiarities of each social network application and program the agents with the necessary actions to interact with each one or, conversely each particular system needs to be programmed in a way that is compatible with the agent specifications.

Besides requiring a specific program for every different system, there are other disadvantages of current approaches. To understand them, consider that *Bob* is programmed to achieve its goal (i.e., information published) by sending a text through a method called *tweet* on the social network *Twitter*. Also consider that *Bob* has an anti-goal (i.e., a state of the system it avoids [3]) of *fake news spread*. First, suppose that new actions become available or existing ones are modified. The developer needs to know about these new methods or modifications and change Bob's program to keep it working on this system. Second, suppose that other actions produce similar effects. For example, consider that for some reason the social network *Twitter* is currently unavailable. To achieve its goal, *Bob* could publish this information on another social network (e.g., *Instagram*). However, the developer did not specify in Bob's program that a similar action performed on another social network produces similar practical effects. To handle this situation, the developer has to know the practical effects of actions and program *Bob* to act on different systems, or the different systems have to be compatible with Bob's specification. Third, suppose that the actions programmed into the agent's program bring unwanted effects to the system. For example, consider that the action *tweet* produces two effects on the system: (i) it publishes information, that is the goal of *Bob*, but (ii) it spreads fake news, that is an anti-goal of *Bob*. The developer needs to know all the effects of the action and evaluate whether or not to program the agent to perform the action to achieve the agent's goal.

Considering these limitations, we propose a solution that moves part of the programmer task to the agent, using its reasoning capabilities. For that, we instrument the system based on social concepts already proposed in the literature, which are institutions [20,21] and purposes [10,11]. Both concepts, when combined, allow the system to make explicit to the agents what are the effects in the environment of performing certain actions in the system. The agents can then relate these effects to their (anti) goals. The connection between available actions and their effects is moved from the agents program (as defined by the programmer) to the institution where they act. Possible changes in these connections, in the actions, or in their effects require changes in the institutional specification while the agents remain unchanged. Besides, the agents can move along different systems looking for satisfying their goals based on the desired effects of the available actions even if these actions are unknown a priori. In this paper, we illustrate this approach through a practical example, which supports a discussion about the advantages and disadvantages of this programming model.

This paper is organized as follows: Sect. 2 introduces the main background concepts necessary to understanding the model used in this work and its required interfaces. Section 3 illustrates how the use of artificial institutions and purposes facilitates the development of agents capable of acting in different systems. Section 4 identifies and discusses some limitations and advantages that the use of the purpose model offers for MAS programming from the agent programmer's perspective. Finally, Sect. 5 presents some conclusions about this work and suggests future works.

2 Artificial Institutions and Purposes

The essential elements of the model used in this work are *agents*, *(anti) goals*, *institutions*, and *purposes*, depicted in the Fig. 1. *Agents* are autonomous entities that can interact within a dynamic environment composed of non-autonomous elements to achieve their goals [23]. The literature presents several definitions of *goal* that are different but complementary to each other (see more in [5,13–15,18,22]). In this work, *goals* are states that agents aim to achieve. According to Aydemir, et.al [3], *anti-goal* is an undesired situation of the system. In this work, *anti-goal* represents states that agents aim to avoid for ethical reasons, particular values, prohibitions, etc. Moreover, agents can perform actions that trigger events in the MAS. *States* are formed by one or more properties that describe the characteristics of the system at some point of its execution [9].

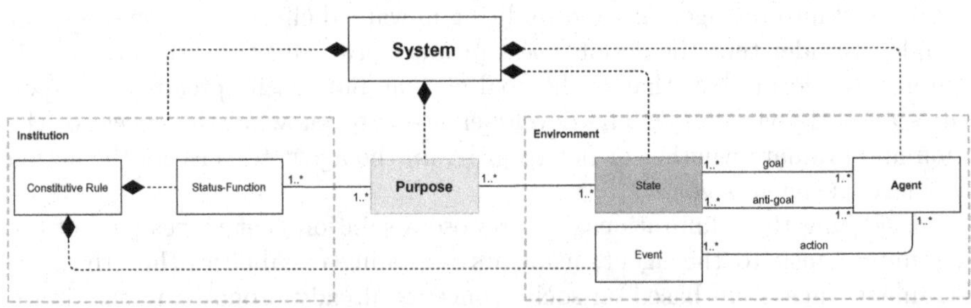

Fig. 1. Overview of the model.

Institutions provide social interpretations for the environment elements that compose the system. They are simplified here to be based on two concepts: *Status-functions* and *Constitutive rules* [20,21]. *Status-functions* are *status* that assign *functions* to the elements. These functions cannot be explained through their physical virtues. For example, the status *buyer* assigns to an agent some functions such as performing payments, taking loans, etc. *Constitutive rules* specify the assignment of status-functions to elements with the following formula: X count-as Y in C. For example, a piece of paper count-as money in a bank, where X represents the environmental element, Y the status-function, and C the context where the constitution is valid. The assignment of status-functions to environmental elements is called *constitution* and creates institutional facts, which gives rise to institutions. Artificial Institutions (or simply *institutions*) are the component of the MAS that is responsible for defining the conditions for an agent to become a *buyer*, or an action to become a *payment* [20, 21].

The functions associated with status-functions can satisfy the practical interests of agents [21, p.20]. From the institution's perspective, we call these interests as *Purposes.* From the agents' perspective, these interests are their goals or anti-goals. Then, we claim that (i) *goals and anti-goals match with the purposes of status-functions* and (ii) *goals, anti-goals and purposes point to environmental states related to the status-functions.* For example, when an agent performs an action that constitutes *tweet*, this makes possible the execution of other intermediate actions that bring the system to states such as *information published* (i.e., the agent goal) or *fake news spread* (i.e., the agent anti-goal). The intermediate actions (e.g., server receives the message, filter the message if necessary, etc.) between the constitution of the status-functions and the environmental states being reached are ignored in our proposal, since we consider that the agent is not interested in these intermediate steps.

Shortly, this model provides two relationships: (i) between purposes and status-functions and (ii) between purposes and agent goals and anti-goals. Thus, if (i) there is a constitutive rule specifying how a status-function is constituted, (ii) a purpose associated with that status-functions, and (iii) an agent has a goal or anti-goal that matches with the states pointed to by the purpose, then (iv) it is explicit how the agent should act to achieve its goal or avoid its anti-goal. In the previous example, the programmer can use these two relations in the agent code to program two queries: (i) a query to find which states the purposes point to and that match the agent goals or anti-goals and (ii) a query to find out which status-function is associated with the found purposes. Thus, for example, the agent can find that the purpose of *transmitting information* points to the *information published* state which matches the goal and that the purpose of *transmitting information* is associated with the *tweet* status-function. Therefore, if the agent constitutes *tweet*, it achieves its goal in this system.

3 Implementing a Multi-agent System with and Without the Purpose Model

This section illustrates how the use of artificial institutions and purposes facilitates the development of agents towards acting in different systems. We describe the development of a multi-agent system without using and then using the model described in Sect. 2. For this, we recall the example where *Bob* wants to achieve its goal of *information published* on different social networks. It is assumed that different programmers develop each social network and that the development of the agent has no influence on this. While the example focuses on the achievement of goals, it is important to make it clear that the model could be used to deal with anti-goals. For example, *Bob* could have a belief in a schedule that describes its anti-goals. Knowing that a certain action could bring about an anti-goal state for it, it could reason about and avoid or not the execution of the action according to its interests.

The example is implemented through the components depicted in Fig. 2. Agents are programmed in Jason [6] and the environment in CArtAgO [17]. A CArtAgO artifact encloses specific APIs and provides actions for the agents to act upon each social network. For the artificial institution, we use an implementation of the Situated Artificial Institution (SAI) model [12]. It provides means to specify status-functions and constitutive rules and to manage the constitution process. The purpose model is implemented through an ontology encapsulated in a CArtAgO artifact which is accessible to the agents. The query and persistence of data in the ontology are enabled by the MasOntology[1], a set of tools developed in CArtAgO to interact with ontologies[2]

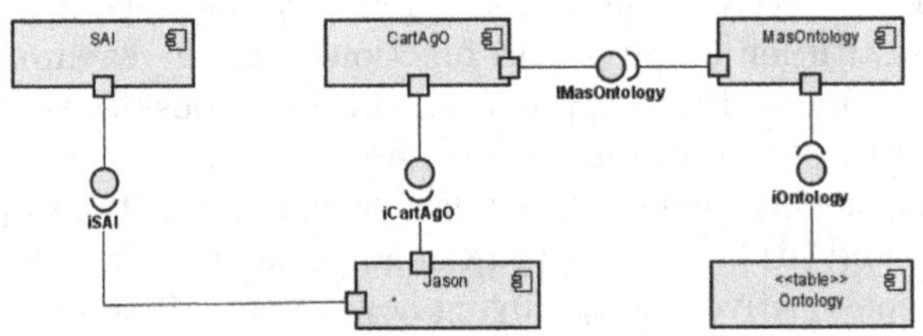

Fig. 2. Component diagram with the systems used to compose the example.

This section is organized as follows: Subsect. 3.1 describes a first implementation that does not use of the proposed model. For this implementation, the programmer needs to know all the actions that the agent must perform on each system it interacts with. Therefore, the program of the agents and the systems that it interacts with are tightly coupled. Subsection 3.2 describes a second implementation that uses the proposed model. In this implementation, the programmer does not need to know the actions that the agent should perform to interact with other systems because they can be discovered at runtime. Therefore, the program of the agents and the systems it interacts with are loosely coupled.

[1] https://github.com/smart-pucrs/MasOntology.

[2] An initial implementation of this platform can be found in https://github.com/rafhaelrc/psf_model..

3.1 Implementation Without Institutions and Purposes

In this section, we consider a scenario where there is no institution or purposes. For this reason, the connection between the available actions and the goals must be coded in the agent. The programmer should thus previously know these implementation details for all the social network systems. This program corresponds to a first alternative for moving the system from the state *S1* (where *Bob* desires to reach its goal) to the state *S2* (where *Bob* has reached its goal).

```
1 !infoPublished.
2
3 +!infoPublished : knet(Twitter)   <- sendMessageByTwitter.
4 +!infoPublished : knet(Telegram)  <- talkWithBot.
5 +!infoPublished : knet(Instagram) <- uploadAPIcture.
6 +!infoPublished : knet(Facebook)  <- uploadAMessage.
```

Listing 1.1. Bob's program.

Listing 1.1 contains part of the Bob's program. In this implementation we assume that when the agent enters different systems, it acquires the belief $knet(S)$ where $S \in \{twitter, telegram, instagram, facebook\}$ is the name of the system where the agent is currently acting. Bob's goal is specified in line 1. The plans that *Bob* may execute to achieve its goal are outlined between lines 3 and 6. The plan that *Bob* executes depends on which social network it is interacting. Consider that *Bob* starts believing in *knet(Facebook)* when it enters the *Facebook* system. The next step, *Bob* chooses which plan should be executed to achieve its goal. Looking at the available plans and their respective contexts, Bob selects the plan in line 6. Then *Bob* performs the action called `uploadAMessage`. At this point it is important to be clear that the available actions (e.g., `uploadAMessage`, `talkWithBot`, etc.) are not provided by the social network systems. Rather, they are implemented in the CArtAgO artifact that provides access to the APIs of the social networks. This action causes some consequences in the system, including switching the system to a new state where *Bob* achieves its goal of *information published.* In this example, we highlight that, to write the program of *Bob*, the programmer of *Bob* needs to know the actions and their consequences for each system in which *Bob* interacts.

3.2 Implementation with Institutions and Purposes

In this section, we consider a scenario where the social network systems include implementations of institutions and purposes. For this reason, the connection between available actions and their effects is moved from the agents to the systems where they act. The programmer does not need to know the implementation details of the social network systems. Figure 3 depicts an overview of the implementation. This program is a second alternative for moving the system from state *S1* to state *S2*.

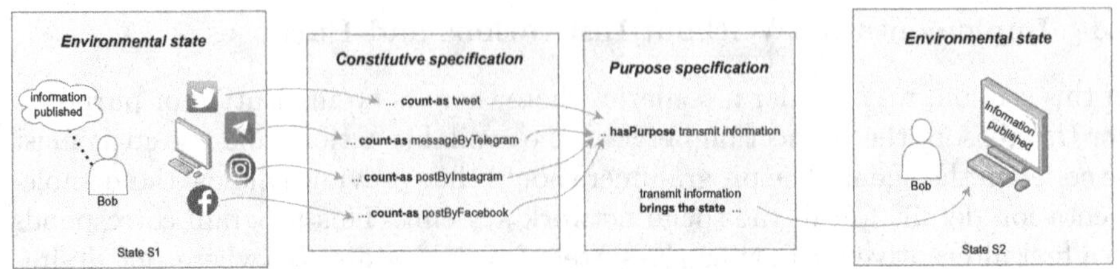

Fig. 3. Implementation overview with institutions and purpose.

In this program, we assume that (i) each system has a specification of the constitutive rules that make up the institution and (ii) each system has a purpose specification that is related with (a) the status-functions and (b) the states of the world that the purpose points to. These specifications are shown in listings 1.2, 1.3, 1.4 and 1.5. We also assume that the agent has runtime access to the institutional and purpose specifications of each system.

```
status_functions: tweet
tweet has purpose of: transmit information
transmit information brings the state information published

Constitutive_rules:
1: sendMessageByTwitter count-as tweet.
```

Listing 1.2. Twitter Institutional and Purpose Specification

```
status_functions: messageByTelegram
messageByTelegram has purpose of: transmit information
transmit information brings the state information published

Constitutive_rules:
1: talkWithBot count-as messageByTelegram.
```

Listing 1.3. Telegram Institutional and Purpose Specification

```
status_functions: postByInstagram
postByInstagram has purpose of: transmit information
transmit information brings the state information published

Constitutive_rules:
1: uploadAPicture count-as postByInstagram.
```

Listing 1.4. Instagram Institutional and Purpose Specification

```
status_functions: postByFacebook
postByFacebook has purpose of: transmit information
transmit information brings the state information published

Constitutive_rules:
1: uploadAMessage count-as postByFacebook.
```

Listing 1.5. Facebook Institutional and Purpose Specification

Listing 1.6 illustrates Bob's program. Bob's goal is specified on line 1 and does not change regardless of which system *Bob* interacts with. At this point it is important to be clear that the actions from lines 4 to 6 are available by the institutional infrastructures of the different systems in which *Bob* can interact. Each institution has a CArtAgO artifact that allows the agent to access information related to institutional specification and purposes. Each system has also a CArtAgO artifact developed by us that allows access to an API that interacts with that social network. Given Bob's program access to the institutional and constitutive specifications of each system, the programmer of *Bob* can implement it with a generic plan that helps *Bob* to achieve its goal on many systems. The plan has the following steps: (i) discover the purpose that points to the desired state (line 4), (ii) discover the status-function associated with the found purpose (line 5), (iii) discover which concrete action can constitute the status-function (line 6) and finally perform the concrete action (line 7). Figure 3 depicts, through the green arrows, the steps described in descending order (i.e., after the action is performed). As an example, consider that Bob's program should interact with the social network *Twitter* and Listing 1.2 which describes the institutional specification of purposes for this system. To do this, Bob's program identifies the plan to be executed (lines 3–7). When executing the plan, some information is discovered at runtime: First, *Bob* queries the purpose that points to the desired state. The name of the purpose is *transmit information*. Second, *Bob* queries which status-function is associated with the *transmit information* purpose. The status-functions name is *tweet*. Third, *Bob* queries what concrete action can constitute the *tweet* status-function. The action name is `sendMessageByTwitter`. Finally, *Bob* performs this action.

```
1 !infoPublished.
2
3 +!infoPublished
4      <- getPurposesOfState(infoPublished,NamePurposes);
5         getStatusFunctionsFromPurposes(NamePurposes,
              NameStatusFunction);
6         ?constitutive_rule(Action,NameStatusFunction,_,_);
7         Action.
```

Listing 1.6. Bob's program using institutions and purposes.

The difference between this implementation and the one described in Sect. 3.1 is that it uses mechanisms (i.e., institutions and purposes) that make explicit (i) the statuses that can be assigned to concrete actions when executed in the system and (ii) the intrinsic functions related to these statuses, called purposes, which describe the states that can be reached in the system related to the status-functions. The execution of the selected action (line 7) constitutes a status-function whose purposes point to environmental states desired by the agent. The advantages of this approach from the programmer's point of view are discussed in the next section.

4 Discussion About both Implementations

In this section we discuss some limitations in Bob's program from Sect. 3.1 (called from now on *Program 1*) that are overcome in Sect. 3.2 (called from now on *Program 2*). These limitations are due to the *tight coupling between the agent specification and the systems in which it operates* and can be observed from (i) the point of view of the system implementation and (ii) the abstractions necessary to develop of the system.

From the perspective of system implementation, *Program 1* requires that the programmer code all the functions that are necessary for the agent to interact with different social networks and know their consequences when executed. Or, conversely, each social network should be compatible and prepared to work with the agent. However, (i) whenever new actions are added, or existing actions are extinguished in the social network API, Bob's program must be updated; (ii) every different action that produces the same effect must be coded in the agent to be exploited in running time; (iii) if the practical effects of the action bring other consequences not foreseen or unwanted by Bob's program, the program may not function properly.

In *program 2* the limitations from the perspective of system implementation are overcome because *the connection between available actions and their effects is moved from the agents to the systems where they act.* Possible changes in these connections, in the actions, or in their effects require changes in the systems while the agents remain unchanged. This modification brings advantages to the system: (i) if new actions are added, or existing ones are modified, the agent's program remains stable as long as the changes are incorporated by the institutions (through the addition of new constitutive rules that reflect these changes); (ii) The agent can exploit any action that produces the desired effect without any additional coding since it acts based on the effects of the actions (connected to the purposed) instead of acting based on the actions themselves; (iii) if some actions bring undesired practical effects by the agent program, the program can use this information in its decision process as long as these practical effects are pointed out through the purposes specification.

From the perspective of abstractions necessary to develop the system, *Program 1* requires the programmer to know all the abstractions needed to code *Bob* to interact with different systems to achieve its goal. The connections between (i) the actions that *Bob* has to perform, (ii) their consequences on the system, and (iii) the satisfaction of bob's goal are implicit (they exist only in the mind of the programmer). If the programmer does not know any of this information, s/he may have trouble programming the agent.

In *program 2* the limitations on the perspective of abstractions needed to implement the system are overcome because the connections between the actions that *Bob* has to perform and its effects are moved to the institutional and purpose specifications respectively, allowing agents to be able to relate them to the satisfaction of its goals. So, the programmer can focus on other aspects of the agent. The programming of the other dimensions of the system (institution, purpose, etc.) is left to other programmers.

5 Conclusions and Future Work

This paper aims to discuss the advantages in programming agents for an open MAS composed of artificial institutions and purposes. From the programmer's perspective, there are some advantages to using the solution presented in this paper. The first is related to the adaptability of the developed agent to act in different systems. If the program is designed to discover which purposes match the agent's goal and then which status-functions that when constituted creates the possibility of states pointed out by the purposes, the agent's program keeps working on any system that provides this information as long as the purposes related to status-functions match to states of the environment desired by the agents. Therefore, the programmer can code the agent to interact with different systems without modifying the program whenever the agent moves to another system. Second, by externalizing the effect of actions to other appropriate concepts (i.e., institutional purposes), part of the programmer task (i.e., to code plans for each system) is delegated to the agent reasoning.

From the agents' perspective, there are some advantages of using the solution presented in this paper. One of them is the improvement in the agent's decision-making since it has more information available to help it to decide whether to achieve its goals or avoid its anti-goals. Agents can access and reason about the environmental states pointed to by the purposes and adapt themselves to different scenarios. They can (a) notice that some purposes point to environmental states that match to their interests and therefore useful to reach their goals and (b) avoid these environmental states because they are match to their anti-goals. The agent understanding about what makes its goal satisfied or what it can avoid to not satisfy anti-goals are important advances in its autonomy [19]. In this case, the agent can reason about the actions and regulative rules that govern the system. In both cases, the agent has more information while deciding whether a particular action will help it or hinder. Some advantages can be observed from an institutional point of view, which are detailed in [10].

While social networks are used to illustrate the approach, the proposal can be applied in several other scenarios. The problem presented can be generalized to the fact that (i) the agent has a goal that can be satisfied in different systems and that (ii) these systems make explicit the connections that exist between their actions and effects. From this generalization, consider the scenario where an agent needs to make a purchase on different websites. The way to solve this problem is similar to that presented in this paper, considering that (a) the programmer codes the agent to search for the actions it has to perform on each website it accesses and (b) the websites describe the actions that are available and the effects of those actions when performed. Therefore, problems that present similar characteristics can use the solution presented in this paper to enable the solution.

As future work, we plan to explore some aspects related to the proposal, such as (i) the relation between purposes and the values of the agents, (ii) discovering the learning curve for the programmer to use the purpose model, (iii) investigating additional advantages of the use of the purpose model and (iv) assess whether the design of the complete system becomes more dynamic or prolonged if it externalizes the concepts that make the necessary connections to make the program more flexible.

References

1. Abreu, J.V.F.: AgentBotSpotter: a multi-agent system for online Twitter bot detection. Ph.D. thesis, Universidade de Brasília (2021)
2. Amaral, C.J., Hübner, J.F.: Jacamo-web is on the fly: an interactive multi-agent system IDE. In: Dennis, L.A., Bordini, R.H., Lespérance, Y. (eds.) EMAS 2019. LNCS (LNAI), vol. 12058, pp. 246–255. Springer, Cham (2020). https://doi.org/10.1007/978-3-030-51417-4_13
3. Aydemir, F.B., Giorgini, P., Mylopoulos, J.: Multi-objective risk analysis with goal models. In: 2016 IEEE Tenth International Conference on Research Challenges in Information Science (RCIS), pp. 1–10. IEEE (2016)
4. Bergenti, F., Franchi, E., Poggi, A.: Enhancing social networks with agent and semantic web technologies. In: Collaboration and the Semantic Web: Social Networks, Knowledge Networks, and Knowledge Resources, pp. 83–100. IGI Global (2012)
5. Boissier, O., Bordini, R.H., Hubner, J., Ricci, A.: Multi-agent oriented programming: programming multi-agent systems using JaCaMo. MIT Press (2020)
6. Bordini, R.H., Hübner, J.F., Wooldridge, M.: Programming multi-agent systems in AgentSpeak using Jason, vol. 8. John Wiley & Sons (2007)
7. Boyd, D.M., Ellison, N.B.: Social network sites: definition, history, and scholarship. J. Comput.-Mediat. Commun. **13**(1), 210–230 (2007)
8. Calvaresi, D., Calbimonte, J.P., Dubosson, F., Najjar, A., Schumacher, M.: Social network chatbots for smoking cessation: agent and multi-agent frameworks. In: 2019 IEEE/WIC/ACM International Conference on Web Intelligence (WI), pp. 286–292. IEEE (2019)
9. Cassandras, C.G., Lafortune, S.: Introduction to discrete event systems. Springer, Cham (2008)
10. Cunha, R.R., Hübner, J.F., de Brito, M.: Coupling purposes with status-functions in artificial institutions. arXiv preprint arXiv:2105.00090 (2021)
11. Cunha, R.R., Hübner, J.F., de Brito, M.: A conceptual model for situating purposes in artificial institutions. Revista de Informática Teórica e Aplicada **29**(1), 68–80 (2022)
12. de Brito, M., Hübner, J.F., Boissier, O.: Situated artificial institutions: stability, consistency, and flexibility in the regulation of agent societies. Auton. Agent. Multi-Agent Syst. **32**(2), 219–251 (2017). https://doi.org/10.1007/s10458-017-9379-3

13. Hindriks, K.V., de Boer, F.S., van der Hoek, W., Meyer, J.-J.C.: Agent programming with declarative goals. In: Castelfranchi, C., Lespérance, Y. (eds.) ATAL 2000. LNCS (LNAI), vol. 1986, pp. 228–243. Springer, Heidelberg (2001). https://doi.org/10.1007/3-540-44631-1_16
14. Hübner, J.F., Bordini, R.H., Wooldridge, M.: Declarative goal patterns for agentspeak. In: Proceedings of the Fifth International Joint Conference on Autonomous Agents and Multiagent Systems (AAMAS 2006) (2006)
15. Nigam, V., Leite, J.: A dynamic logic programming based system for agents with declarative goals. In: Baldoni, M., Endriss, U. (eds.) DALT 2006. LNCS (LNAI), vol. 4327, pp. 174–190. Springer, Heidelberg (2006). https://doi.org/10.1007/11961536_12
16. Pérez-Marcos, J., Jiménez-Bravo, D.M., De Paz, J.F., Villarrubia González, G., López, V.F., Gil, A.B.: Multi-agent system application for music features extraction, meta-classification and context analysis. Knowl. Inf. Syst. **62**(1), 401–422 (2019). https://doi.org/10.1007/s10115-018-1319-2
17. Ricci, A., Piunti, M., Viroli, M.: Environment programming in multi-agent systems: an artifact-based perspective. Auton. Agent. Multi-Agent Syst. **23**(2), 158–192 (2011)
18. van Riemsdijk, B., van der Hoek, W., Meyer, J.J.C.: Agent programming in dribble: from beliefs to goals using plans. In: Proceedings of the Second International Joint Conference on Autonomous Agents and Multiagent Systems, pp. 393–400 (2003)
19. Rodriguez-Aguilar, J.A., Sierra, C., Arcos, J.L., Lopez-Sanchez, M., Rodriguez, I.: Towards next generation coordination infrastructures. Knowl. Eng. Rev. **30**(4), 435–453 (2015). https://doi.org/10.1017/S0269888915000090
20. Searle, J.: Making the social world: The structure of human civilization. Oxford University Press, Oxford (2010)
21. Searle, J.R.: The Construction of Social Reality. Simon and Schuster, New York (1995)
22. Winikoff, M., Padgham, L., Harland, J., Thangarajah, J.: Declarative and procedural goals in intelligent agent systems. In: International Conference on Principles of Knowledge Representation and Reasoning. Morgan Kaufman (2002)
23. Wooldridge, M.: An Introduction to Multiagent Systems. Wiley, Hoboken (2009)

Developing BDI-Based Robotic Systems with ROS2

Devis Dal Moro(✉), Marco Robol, Marco Roveri, and Paolo Giorgini

University of Trento, Via Sommarive, 9-38123 Povo, Italy
devis.dalmoro@unitn.it, marco.robol@unitn.it, marco.roveri@unitn.it, paolo.giorgini@unitn.it

Abstract. Robots are very effective in automatizing repetitive operations leveraging hard-coded control, actuation, and sensing algorithms. Current industrial automation trends demand combining low-level reactive primitives with high-level autonomy capabilities (e.g., reasoning and planning). Recent robotic reactive architectures provide capabilities to reliably sense the environment and promptly react to stimuli, but their autonomy capabilities are in an early stage and present several limitations. The BDI model has been proposed as a reference model to build autonomous agents, but it does not provide any kind of conceptual and developing framework to connect the reasoning and planning capabilities with the lower level reactive functionalities of a robotic system. In this paper, we propose an architecture supporting BDI-based solutions to develop agents with deliberation and priority aware executions of plans, and that consider deadline-aware prioritization of desires. We build our architecture on top of ROS 2 (a standard robotic framework) leveraging and extending state-of-the-art ROS planning infrastructures. We provide a novel development tool-kit that allows for the implementation of autonomous robotic systems. Finally, we show by means of a realistic industrially inspired scenario how to use the developed tool-kit.

Keywords: Real-time multi-agent systems · Planning and execution · ROS2

1 Introduction

Robots are very effective in automatizing processes and repetitive, high-precision, and mechanical operations. They are typically designed leveraging on controlling actuators and sensors with hard-coded algorithmic-based software running on dedicated hardware parts. However, in the recent I4.0 industrial revolution, robots are asked to operate in complex and evolving environments with more and more degree of autonomy to cope with problem that are difficult to predict at design time. This introduces the need of combining low-level reactive primitives (e.g., sensor management, obstacle avoidance, navigation) with more high-level capabilities, such as reasoning, autonomous deliberation, planning and communication.

© The Author(s), under exclusive license to Springer Nature Switzerland AG 2022
F. Dignum et al. (Eds.): PAAMS 2022, LNAI 13616, pp. 100–111, 2022.
https://doi.org/10.1007/978-3-031-18192-4_9

Recent reactive architectures (e.g., those provided by state-of-the-art robotic infrastructure like Robotic Operating System - ROS - [17]) provide capabilities to reliably sense the environment and promptly react to stimuli. ROS allows for the implementation of core logic software, hiding the complexity of dealing with physical installations aspects, such as, the deployment of the software in distributed and dedicated hardware parts, and dealing with communication latency. However, the functionalities that allow a robot to autonomously deliberate are still in an early stage [1–3,5,7,11,15], and they present a number of open problems. For instance, although ROSPlan [4] and PlanSys2 [13] provide planning functionalities, they are not supported by any deliberative functionalities making planning unusable in real scenarios. This is a well-known problem in the AI community, where the BDI (Belief -Desire-Intention) model [16] has been proposed as a reference model to build autonomous agents that can use their beliefs to reason about goals and elaborating plans to achieve them. The literature on BDI agents does not offer, however, any kind of conceptual and developing framework to connect the reasoning and planning capabilities with the lower level reactive functionalities of a robotic system.

In this paper, we focus on the problem of developing distributed autonomous robotic systems proposing an architecture supporting BDI-based deliberation to develop agents with (temporal) planning capabilities. The architecture provides deadline-aware prioritization of desires and it supports preemption of running plans with lower priority. The BDI agent's architecture is built on top of ROS 2 [17] leveraging on and extending the functionalities provided by PlanSys2 [13]. As result, we provide a novel tool-kit for ROS 2 that allows for the implementation of autonomous robotic systems. Then, we show by means of a realistic industrially inspired scenario how the development kit can be used.

The paper is organized as follows. Section 2 presents the baseline, including PDDL planning, and the PlanSys2 ROS2 planning system. Section 3 presents the architecture and the development tool-kit. In Sect. 4, the previously presented architecture is demonstrated within a robotic simulated industrially inspired scenario. Section 5 presents the related work. Finally, Sect. 6 concludes and discusses future work.

2 Background

In this work we build on i) a temporal planning infrastructure; ii) and the PlanSys2 ROS2 robotic planning infrastructure. In the rest of this section we summarize the main concepts of these two components.

PDDL Based Temporal Planning. [10] is a framework for i) modeling the behavior of agents considering that actions might not be instantaneous and last some known amount of time, ii) generate time-triggered plans (i.e., sequences of actions where each action is associated with the time instant at which the action shall be scheduled, and the respective duration) for achieving a goal. Time-triggered plans allow to represent multiple actions active at the same time, thus capturing the case where e.g. two different actions are executed in parallel by e.g. two different agents or the case where a single agent executes two actions in parallel by leveraging two different actuators to perform a task. These are our minimal requirements to represent the possible activities of the agents, and are supported by the PDDL version 2.1 [10]. The AI planning community also considered richer formalisms like e.g. PDDL 3.1 [12] that complements PDDL 2.1 with constraints, preferences, and other features. These features will be nice to have in the framework we will describe later on, but, as far as our knowledge is concerned, there are no tools that support all the features of PDDL 3.1 (in particular constraints, preferences and durative actions).

The **ROS2 Planning System** (PlanSys2 in short) [13] is the reference open-source framework for symbolic temporal planning within the ROS2 [17] infrastructure, which in turn is a de facto standard in robotic software development. PlanSys2 incorporates novel approaches for the execution of time-triggered tasks on robots working in demanding environments (also considering real-time constraints at communication and execution level). It supports several features, but the most important ones for our purpose are i) optimized execution, based on Behavior Trees [14] (a mathematical model suitable for formal verification, important in several critical applications), of plans through an actions auction protocol; ii) integrated support for temporal planning systems, in particular of the POPF [6] and Temporal Fast Downward [9] symbolic planners which supports PDDL 2.1 and are able to generate time-triggered temporal plans minimizing a given cost function; iii) multi-robot planning capabilities. Finally, it has a growing community of users and developers.

3 A Multi-agent Robotic RT-BDI Architecture

This section presents a framework for the development of Multi-Agent Real-Time BDI (MA-RT-BDI) systems for robotic architecture based on ROS2. The framework includes: i) an architecture built on top of the ROS2 robotic platform, that leverages the BDI model [16] to provides autonomous behavior with planning capabilities; and ii) a development tool-kit to support the implementation of autonomous robotic systems based on ROS2, adopting the proposed architecture.

Current robotic solutions, including ROS2, provides a multi-layer architecture to support efficient communication protocols to share data and allow remote control of robots. However, such systems have strong limitations when they are adopted in open environments, where a limited initial knowledge and a partial observability of events demand robots a proactive behavior to allow them taking decisions in autonomy. To address this, we present an architecture that provides the following features: i) autonomous behavior based on the BDI-model ii) multi-agent iii) planning capabilities iv) deadline-aware desire prioritization v) preemption of running plans with lower priority vi) distributed and vii) implemented over ROS2 nodes, topics and services. Being based on ROS2, the architecture can be straightforwardly adopted into robotic systems and deployed on a single machine or on several machines connected through a network.

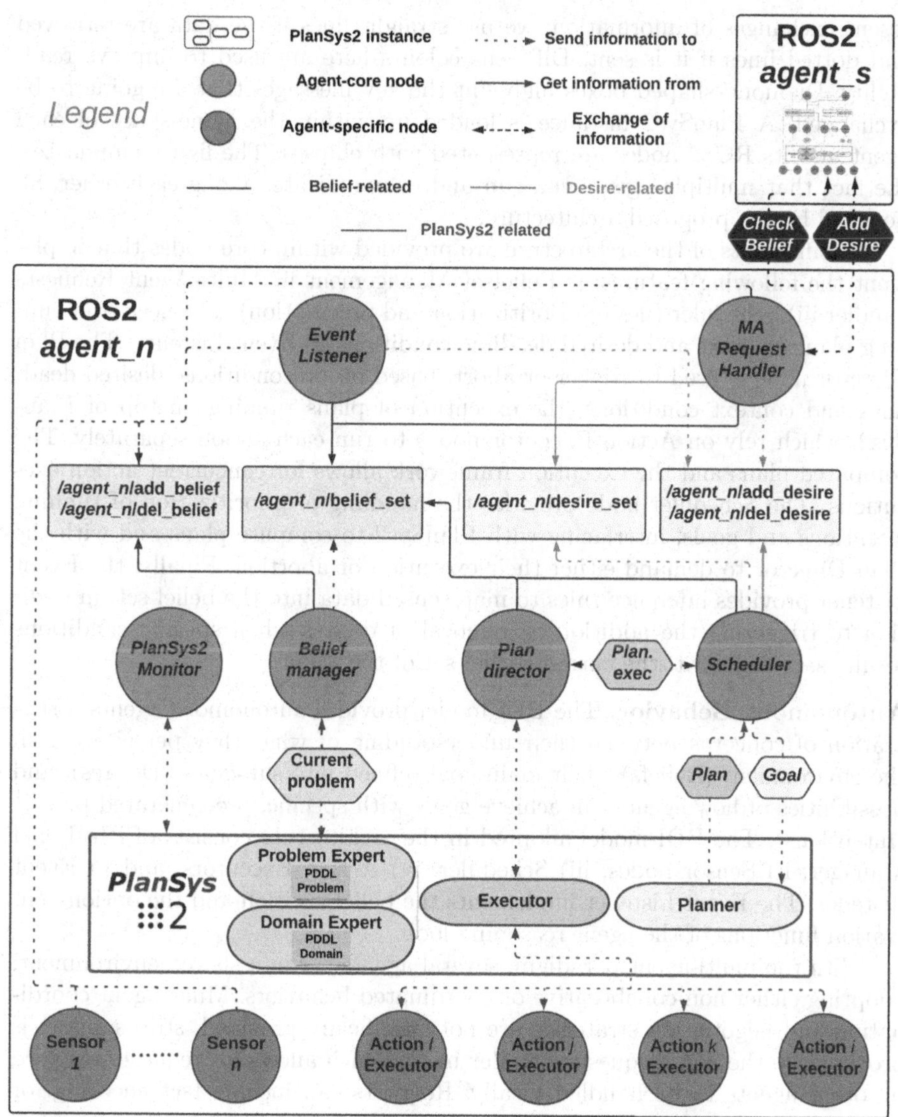

Fig. 1. The proposed multi-agent BDI robotic architecture.

Figure 1 depicts the proposed architecture. Rectangles stand for one or more ROS2 topics (i.e., communication channels), while circles represent ROS2 nodes encapsulating the core functionalities of the agent. By using different colours for them, we aim to distinguish core nodes (green) from agent-specific ones (teal). The former group is fixed in terms of composition and just the behavior of its component might be tuned, while the latter varies in number and inner logic depending on the specific sensing and acting skills of the agent. All arrows represent exchanges of information: we use straight lines if the data are retrieved and dotted lines if it is sent. Different colours here are used to improve readability. Diamond-shaped boxes highlight the key messages that are going to be exchanged. A PlanSys2 instance is loaded up within the name-space of each agent and its ROS2 nodes are represented with ellipses. The figure emphasizes the fact that multiple agents can run and communicate among each other, all powered by the proposed architecture.

Specific parts of the architecture are provided within core nodes that implement the following features: i) Beliefset Management ii) Multi-Agent Requests handler iii) Scheduler (desire prioritization and preemption) iv) Check over running plan's context and desired deadline conditions v) Event Listener. The Plan Director node is used to trigger or abort, based on preconditions, desired deadlines and context conditions, the execution of plans running on top of PlanSys2, which rely on Action Executor nodes to run each action separately. The computed plans and the execution framework allows for concurrent action executions. The Scheduler node provides the handling of prioritization of running intentions and goals, interfacing with PlanSys2 to compute plans and with the Plan Director to demand either their execution or abortion. Finally, the Event Listener provides inference rules to map sensed data into the belief set, in addition to triggering the addition or removal of desires when specific conditions results satisfied w.r.t. the current belief set of the agent.

Autonomous Behavior. The BDI model provides autonomous agents a separation of concerns between their understanding of what they perceived from the environment (Beliefs), their main goal refined into sub-goals (Desires), and possibilities of how agents can achieve goals with specific, pre-generated plans.[1] (Intentions). The BDI-model adopted in the architecture consists of i) a Belief Manager, ii) Sensor nodes, iii) Scheduler, iv) Action Executors, and v) Event Listener. The Event Listener implements the belief revision and the option generation functions of the agent reasoning loop.

With the multi-agent paradigm, several agents act in a shared environment, adopting either non-collaborative or coordinated behaviors. Multi-agent coordination and negotiation strategies are not specifically provided, still, support is provided by the MA Requests Handler node, which allows for requests received by other agents to be handled locally. Requests can include fact checking, or submission of belief or desires. Decision of accepting or rejecting the request is enforced by means of agent-specific static policies. Once a desire is accepted, a priority is associated, which may have the effect of postponing its execution at a later time, or completely missing the deadline associated to the request.

Planning Capabilities. Planning capabilities are provided by PlanSys2. A Monitoring node has been defined to control its running status. The Belief Manager takes care of synchronizing the knowledge of the agent with the Problem Expert of the planning system, by encoding it into the PDDL problem initial status. A one-to-one mapping is applied between beliefs and PDDL instances,

[1] In our setting, plans are automatically generated through the invocation of a planner.

predicates and functions. In addition, the Scheduler invokes directly the planner to verify whether desires are achievable, and how.

Scheduling and Execution. The Scheduler provides two main features: i) pursuing of desires to be fulfilled based on their respective priority and deadline, ii) aborting plans in execution. The Plan Director triggers, aborts and monitors the execution of plans. Additional features include: plan failure management with rollback functionalities, along with deadline and context condition monitoring.

Deadline-aware prioritization is supported by the Scheduler, who decides which desire to pursue, based first on priorities and secondly on the deadline, adopting an Earliest Deadline First (in the case of desires with the same priority). Before demanding the execution, preconditions are taken into consideration too.

Additionally, it can also force the interruption of a running scheduled plan so to handle a newcomer desire with a higher priority or with the same and a shorter deadline, for which a plan to fulfill such new desire can be scheduled. Differently from a preemption mechanism, the interruption mechanism implemented in our architecture does not suspend and then resume the execution from where it was left. Once the plan is aborted, the desire it was supposed to fulfill is put back in the desire set, from where it may be picked up again later. When the preempted desire is considered again in a following rescheduling operation, a new plan might be computed and selected for execution. Note that this new plan might differ from the former one, given the relevant environment has changed.

The events for which a plan gets aborted includes i) an explicit request by the Scheduler if the desire is fulfilled during execution (e.g. sensors might detect that part of the goals are already fulfilled while running the plan), or ii) if there is a desire with higher priority than the one currently executing that can be fulfilled. However, the latter is an optional configuration (option PREEMPT), for which preemption is applied to the running plan in the case of upcoming higher priority desires. New plans are periodically computed for each pending desire and one might be selected to run, after aborting the plan currently in execution. Otherwise, Scheduler would wait for the termination, successful or failing, of the currently executing plan, even if higher priority ones are present in the desire set. Additionally, in both cases there is an upper bound to the number of times for which plan computation for a desire is unsuccessful. When reached, the desire is discarded.

The Plan Director node triggers and aborts the execution of a plan on behalf of a request by the Scheduler, forwarding it to the Executor node of PlanSys2. Moreover, it processes its progress feedback and publishes it in a topic, so that the Scheduler has a feed of the currently running plan too. Furthermore, the Plan Director monitors over the context conditions and requests the plan abortion in case they are not satisfied anymore. This happens also in the case deadlines are missed by a multiplication factor with respect to the desire deadline. For example, given the default factor 2, when the duration the plan is taking goes over 2 times the desire deadline, it is automatically aborted. Plan execution can fail also at the PlanSys2 level in the case of unsatisfied run-time requirements or failed action executions. The Scheduler, which is notified about plan failures, discards a desire after a given number of failing plan executions to fulfill it.

A basic rollback feature is provided by the Plan Director aborting function. This consists of restoring the status of the belief set by pushing or deleting a few given declared values. Limitations consist in the possibility of incurring in an inconsistent belief set, due to the difficulty of writing sound rollback rules that can be valid for any plan failure situation. This feature should be used in simulated scenarios, but in real ones a dedicated set of sensors and an exhaustive set of belief revision rules enforced by the Event Listener should suffice.

3.1 Development Tool-Kit

The development tool-kit provided includes interfaces for the definition of BDI messages, sensors, and actions. Furthermore, a python module has been included to offer a straightforward and ready-to-use agent's launch description generator.

Both sensors and actions are basically ROS2 nodes. The former extends the `rclcpp::Node` class, while the latter is built on top of the one provided by PlanSys2 for developing action executors, i.e., `plansys2::ActionExecutorClient`. The sensor interface, given a statically defined belief prototype, acts at run-time processing periodically or aperiodically raw-level data, presumably retrieved from ROS2 topics, into "valid" belief items that can be easily exploited to update the belief set, i.e., the current perception the agent has of the environment. A periodic method for sensing can be easily enabled, enforcing the logic provided by the user, but it's not necessary, e.g., the API call for sensing can be called within one or more subscription callbacks. This is not true in the case of Action Executor, where a periodic method has to be developed, implementing the logic behind a "step-execution" of the action and returning the relative progress made. Here, we mainly want to hide the complexities related to the setup and API calls that need to be made to correctly communicate with the PlanSys2 Executor, while providing a very lean way to exploit the communication APIs and interact with other agents to consult or update their belief or desire sets. Additionally, methods are provided to monitor the fulfillment of a desire that was previously pushed to a "collaborator" agent.

Finally, the provided tool-kit aims to facilitate the bring-up of an agent, by hiding the loading definition of a PlanSys2 instance linked to the provided PDDL domain for the agent and all the core nodes properly set up w.r.t. the configured behavior. Indeed, many parameters can be overridden to comply better with domain-specific requirements, tuning the behavior of the core nodes of the agent. For instance, one might want to force the abortion of a plan execution as soon as the deadline is reached, regardless of the desire being fulfilled, or explicitly select the aforementioned preemptive mechanism. They are supposed to be used also to select the files to initialize at startup the belief and desire set, as well as the rules enforced by the Event Listener and to identify the group of agents which are allowed to ask for a factual check or an update to the agent's belief or desire set. In summary, the tool-kit provides a compact way to define all of the above and easily attach sensor and action nodes to the agent definition.

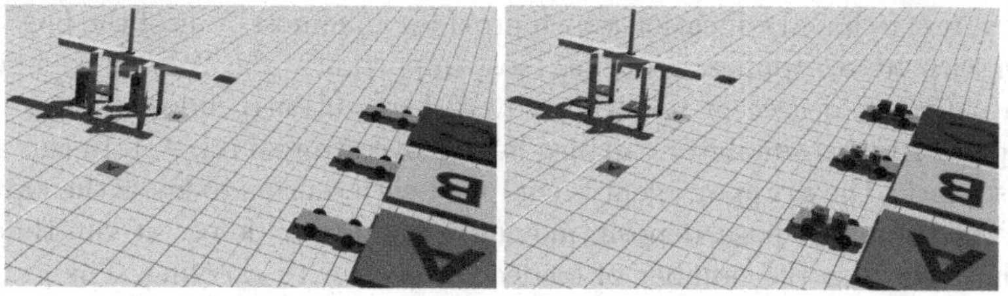

Fig. 2. Initial situation depicted on the left, while the goal one is on the right.

4 Demonstration of the MA-RT-BDI Architecture

In order to demonstrate the capabilities of the proposed architecture, we implemented our architecture on top of the PlanSys2 ROS2 infrastructure, and we deployed it in a realistic scenario inspired by industrial applications, although simulated. In particular, the considered scenario is a paradigmatic instance of a typical logistic problem. There are multiple deposit areas, and there are several agents each aiming to specific activities that range from sorting and carrying operations to get boxes from their initial stacks to specific destination deposits. The specific scenario consists of a deposit with three different stacks (named `1`, `2`, and `3`) each composed of boxes of possibly different types (e.g., `A`, `B`, and `C`), and three loading areas (one for each type of the boxes, i.e., `A`, `B`, and `C`). The loading areas are positioned on a straight line. There are three destination areas one for each type of box (also named with the same name of the boxes). These destination areas are positioned in front of the respective loading area but at a far distance. In this specific demonstrative scenario we considered two kind of agents. We have a robotic agent equipped with a `gripper` and a `carrier` robotic agent that can carry up two boxes and can move between locations. The `gripper` robotic agent can move between the stacks following a rail track with the concurrent capability of shifting the y-position of its gripper arm across its transversal bridge. This agent can grasp the box on top of the stack, and can load it on top of another stack or on a moving vehicle. The scenario considers one `gripper` robotic agent and three `carrier` agents. A `carrier` agent is needed to move boxes from loading area to corresponding destination area. Each `carrier` agent is assigned to a particular loading and destination, and it can move back and forth between these two locations. Figure 2 shows the pictorial representation of this scenario. In this specific scenario we require the `gripper` to sort the boxes. The boxes are initially randomly stacked in the three stacks. The `gripper` can move the boxes one by one on top of the `carrier` which is able to deliver them to the right deposit. To achieve this, the `gripper` could ask a `carrier` to come into the right place for loading the box. Once the `carrier` has been loaded, it can move back to the assigned deposits to deliver the boxes.

We designed this scenario within the Webots[2] simulation environment (see for instance Fig. 2). Webots is a free and open-source 3D robot simulator used in

[2] https://cyberbotics.com/.

industry, research and education which provides an almost "out of the box" integration with ROS2 applications, and most importantly the Webots simulations have a sufficient degree of fidelity w.r.t. real executions (indeed, the controls developed with this simulator can also be deployed to real robots). In this simulation scenario, the `gripper` agent is equipped with sensors to know the `carrier` agents' position (i.e. base/deposit/moving), while they detect at run-time not only that, but also the number of loaded boxes they're carrying. The `gripper` agent can move between stackbases and loading areas, pickup and putdown boxes and finally call carriers to come to their loading base. `carrier` can move and unload boxes. Low-level implementations of all the actions, but the one to request a `carrier` to come to its base, has been developed through the Webots ROS2 driver interface[3] to enable the triggering from within ROS2. The `gripper` action to request a `carrier` to come to its base has been implemented through the API provided by the ROS2 framework described in this paper to push to the specific `carrier` a new desire to do so (carriers are designed to accept them). The sensing (e.g., GPS) from the carriers, the gripper arm and all the boxes is continuously made available to ROS2 leveraging the Webots ROS2 driver. This sensing data is then processed by the sensors proposed within our architecture to become "valid" belief items that can be used to update the belief set of the agent. Further inference is then performed by rules (specified programmatically) within the event listener of both types of agents (e.g., if the carrier is loaded with 2 boxes, it considers itself `fully_loaded`). The latter is used also to make the carrier agents self-submit the desire of unloading the boxes to the deposit, when they're "fully loaded". The gripper is provided at the start with the desire to put the boxes on top of the "right" carrier, so to get the rest of the demo started. To complete the scenario, additional static information regarding the environment is also provided at the start, to initialize the belief set of each agent. The framework, its documentation, and the demonstrative scenario are available at https://github.com/devis12/ROS2-BDI.

We showcase two different demonstrative runs on top of the scenario described above. The first is a simple, successful execution: all boxes are sorted and moved to the right deposit without any unexpected event occurring. The second is a small variation, where the `carrier` for boxes of type `C` moves to the destination location before being fully loaded. In this case, the `gripper` when attempting to load the last box of `C` in the respective `carrier` detects that the `carrier` is not there, the execution of its plan fails, it re-plans from this situation generating a plan requiring the carrier to come back to base, and then continue with the new plan to achieve the overall desire to move all the boxes to their respective destination. This last scenario shows that with our framework, when something does not go as expected and the plan execution fails, the agent might be able to use its updated knowledge of the world to find a new plan and eventually fulfill its initial desire, or receive a new desire to be fulfilled (e.g., the `carrier` to come back to base). The video showing our proposed framework at work on these two scenarios is available at https://youtu.be/zB2HvCR5H9E.

[3] https://github.com/cyberbotics/webots_ros2.

5 Related Work

In the literature there have been several works that addressed the problem of designing complex and intelligent autonomous architectures for the robotic setting, mostly focusing on specific contexts [2,7,11]. More recently, it was proposed a preliminary integration of BDI concepts in the ROS2 framework [1]. This work inspired the design of our architecture. Many of the concepts we adopted were introduced firstly here. However, this preliminary work, differently from our, was not addressing the problem of the autonomous deliberation nor the problem of autonomous re/planning to answer to contingencies and/or new emerging desires. In [1], all the BDI elements were manually specified and pre-loaded in the architecture, the focus was on defining the messages to be exchanged among the different components and on the real-time (re-)scheduling of the intentions. As far as the robotic setting is concerned, noticeable related works are CogniTAO [5], CORTEX [3], SkiROS2 [15], ROSPlan [4] (for ROS1), and its successor PlanSys2 [13] (for ROS2). CogniTAO [5] implements a BDI model in the ROS architecture. However, differently from our approach, where the BDI model is completely integrated within ROS together with the deliberation ability (not supported by CogniTAO), the execution of the agent paradigm is delegated to the TAO machine (which is logically separated from the other ROS-related components). CORTEX is a cognitive centralized robotics architecture built on top of an ad-hoc communication framework, while we rely on ROS2. In CORTEX there is a centralized common knowledge base for the group of agents that use it as a communication mean. Similarly to our approach, CORTEX includes a deliberation capacities, but differently from us, the planning is centralized, the actions of the different agents are instantaneous, and thus it is not possible to have overlapping action executions by the different agents (a feature needed in several realistic applications). Last, in the framework it is not possible to integrate concepts like real-time scheduling, which are supported by our framework through ROS2. SkiROS2 is another platform to create complex robotic behaviors through composition of skills delivered in modular software blocks, while maintaining a centralized semantic database to manage environmental knowledge based on OWL ontologies. Even if it offers an integration point for PDDL task planning, it lacks support for temporal planning and interactions among different agents. Finally, ROSPlan first, and PlanSys2 later cannot be considered real BDI infrastructures. They focused on integrating deliberation capabilities based on (temporal) planning, and respective plan execution in the single agent robotic setting. While in ROSPlan the plans are generated and executed with internal ad-hoc representations, in PlanSys2 the generated plans are transformed into Behavior Trees [14]. Other important features provided by PlanSys2 w.r.t. ROSPlan are i) the ability to build incrementally the deliberation model thus being modular, ii) an auction mechanism for delivering actions to action performers, thus enabling for targeting multi-robot/agent executions. Moreover, these frameworks lack of several BDI capabilities like e.g. detection-reaction, high-level deliberation and multi-agent interaction mechanisms, local re-planning, automatic generation of new desires, that come directly "out of the box" with the BDI model. Nonetheless, PlanSys2 was the baseline on top of which we have built our Multi-Agent Robotic BDI Architecture.

6 Conclusions and Future Work

In this work, we proposed a distributed architecture powering robotics agents with autonomous behavior through the means offered by the widely accepted and increasingly used ROS2 robotic infrastructure and PlanSys2 planning system. To improve the intuitiveness of the design and adaptability of every agent, the reasoning flow is strongly based on the BDI model which has been decomposed into modular, decoupled, event-based processes, in compliance with the standard pattern of development of the target platform. The developed architecture comes packed with a provided toolkit guiding the user toward the definition of agents' specific detection and operating skills and behavior. A validating use case is presented working as proof of concept and model to inspire and facilitate the development of new solutions powered by the framework. Even if we consider the delivered and open-to-use framework based on the proposed architecture a promising tool, ready for powering up real world applications, enhancing the definition, flexibility of the robotic agents, as well as the degree of interaction and cooperation among them, it should be noted that there are still some limitations and several directions of further improvement to address them that are subject to future work. The reasoning cycle needs to be enriched with additional functionalities, e.g. store multiple plans to choose among in response to emerging new desires; to make the scheduling and execution of all the core and domain-specific behavior more computational aware, leaning toward a greater degree of real-time compliance as for instance discussed in [19]. To improve the deliberation and execution capabilities of the proposed framework we plan to extend its use by integrating forms of online planning and execution along the lines discussed in [8,18], i.e., have a more tight integration of the deliberation and execution activities. Moreover, we will address some limitations of existing planning systems by allowing the use of planning systems able to optimize the solution plans w.r.t. a given objective functions specified as part of a desire. We will also consider the integration of advanced meta-reasoning to evaluate whether to trigger specific new behaviors (e.g., self-submission of desire to fulfill precondition or context condition of a pending desire) which at the moment are defined statically (for the sake of simplicity of the development) at design time. Finally, we will study also mechanisms to identify and handle deadlock scenarios, thus moving the responsibility of avoiding deadlock scenarios from the agent designer to the deliberation reasoning, e.g., by employing the rules enforced by the Event Listener and/or other means offered by the toolkit (e.g., rollback belief after an execution abortion) to tackle the issue in a context-specific manner.

References

1. Alzetta, F., Giorgini, P.: Towards a real-time BDI model for ROS 2. In: WOA. CEUR Workshop Proceedings, vol. 2404, pp. 1–7. CEUR-WS.org (2019)
2. van Breemen, A., Crucq, K., Krose, B., Nuttin, M., Porta, J., Demeester, E.: A user-interface robot for ambient intelligent environments. In: Proceedings of the 1st International Workshop on Advances in Service Robotics, (ASER) (2003)
3. Bustos, P., Manso, L.J., Bandera, A., Rubio, J.P.B., García-Varea, I., Martínez-Gómez, J.: The CORTEX cognitive robotics architecture: use cases. Cogn. Syst. Res. **55**, 107–123 (2019)
4. Cashmore, M., et al.: ROSPlan: planning in the robot operating system. In: ICAPS 2015, pp. 333–341. AAAI Press (2015)
5. CogniTAO-Team: CogniTAO (BDI). http://wiki.ros.org/decision_making/Tutorials/CogniTAO
6. Coles, A.J., Coles, A., Fox, M., Long, D.: Forward-chaining partial-order planning. In: ICAPS 2010, pp. 42–49. AAAI (2010)
7. Duffy, B.R., Collier, R., O'Hare, G.M., Rooney, C., O'Donoghue, R.: Social robotics: reality and virtuality in agent-based robotics. In: Bar-Ilan Symposium on the Foundations of Artificial Intelligence: Bridging theory and practice (BISFAI-99), Ramat Gan, Israel, 23–25 June 1999 (1999)
8. Elboher, A., Shperberg, S.S., Shimony, S.E.: Metareasoning for interleaved planning and execution. In: SOCS, pp. 167–169. AAAI Press (2021)
9. Eyerich, P., Mattmüller, R., Röger, G.: Using the context-enhanced additive heuristic for temporal and numeric planning. In: Towards Service Robots for Everyday Environments - Recent Advances in Designing Service Robots for Complex Tasks in Everyday Environments. Springer Tracts in Advanced Robotics, vol. 76, pp. 49–64. Springer, Berlin (2012). https://doi.org/10.1007/978-3-642-25116-0_6
10. Fox, M., Long, D.: PDDL2.1: an extension to PDDL for expressing temporal planning domains. J. Artif. Intell. Res. **20**, 61–124 (2003)
11. Gottifredi, S., Tucat, M., Corbata, D., García, A.J., Simari, G.R.: A BDI architecture for high level robot deliberation. Inteligencia Artif. **14**(46), 74–83 (2010)
12. Helmert, M.: Changes in PDDL 3.1 (2008), unpublished summary from the IPC 2008. https://ipc08.icaps-conference.org/deterministic/
13. Martín, F., Clavero, J.G., Matellán, V., Rodríguez, F.J.: Plansys2: a planning system framework for ROS2. In: IROS, pp. 9742–9749. IEEE (2021)
14. Marzinotto, A., Colledanchise, M., Smith, C., Ögren, P.: Towards a unified behavior trees framework for robot control, pp. 5420–5427. IEEE (2014)
15. Polydoros, A.S., Großmann, B., Rovida, F., Nalpantidis, L., Krüger, V.: Accurate and versatile automation of industrial kitting operations with SkiROS. In: Alboul, L., Damian, D., Aitken, J.M.M. (eds.) TAROS 2016. LNCS (LNAI), vol. 9716, pp. 255–268. Springer, Cham (2016). https://doi.org/10.1007/978-3-319-40379-3_26
16. Rao, A.S., Georgeff, M.P.: Modeling rational agents within a BDI-architecture. In: KR, pp. 473–484. Morgan Kaufmann (1991)
17. ROS2 - Robot Operating System version 2 (2022). https://docs.ros.org
18. Shperberg, S.S., Coles, A., Karpas, E., Ruml, W., Shimony, S.E.: Situated temporal planning using deadline-aware metareasoning. In: ICAPS, pp. 340–348. AAAI Press (2021)
19. Traldi, A., Bruschetti, F., Robol, M., Roveri, M., Giorgini, P.: Real-time BDI agents: a model and its implementation. In: Press, A. (ed.) IJCAI 2022 (2022)

Combining Multiagent Reinforcement Learning and Search Method for Drone Delivery on a Non-grid Graph

Shiyao Ding[1(✉)], Hideki Aoyama[2], and Donghui Lin[1]

[1] Kyoto University, Kyoto-shi, Kyoto 606-8501, Japan
dingshiyao0217@gmail.com
[2] Panasonic Holdings Corporation, 1006, Oaza Kadoma, Kadoma-shi, Osaka 571-8501, Japan
aoyama.hideki@jp.panasonic.com

Abstract. With the high development of online commerce, drone delivery has shown a potential to reduce logistical costs. Multiple drone delivery can be formulated as a multiagent path finding (MAPF) problem which is used to identify a group of collision-free paths for multiple agents. However, most prior work on MAPF has studied on grid graphs, which is not proper for drone delivery problem. We study here a non-grid MAPF problem for drone delivery. Some algorithms for solving grid MAPF can also be applied to this new problem, which can be categorized into two types: search-based methods and dynamic programming methods. However, the challenges created by non-grid features, such as a large state/action space, impede the application of either of these two methods. We therefore propose a novel approach that combines a search method and a dynamic programming method which can accelerate the learning process. The experimental results show our proposed method to be more effective than some existing algorithms.

Keywords: Multiagent path finding · Drone delivery · Multiagent reinforcement learning

1 Introduction

The applications of drones to the logistics sector are being increasingly scrutinized [3,5,6]. They are anticipated to be an efficient solution to the ever-increasing demand for deliveries in response to the growth of online commerce. The delivery problems are usually formulated as vehicle routing problem (VRP). The objective of VRP is to achieve the most cost-effective round trip for all the delivery destinations, given a set of moving vehicles with limited capacity. Although some work formulated drone delivery problem as VRP [3], avoiding collisions is not addressed. This issue cannot be ignored in the drone delivery problem, since the drone flight paths are usually too narrow to allow multiple

© The Author(s), under exclusive license to Springer Nature Switzerland AG 2022
F. Dignum et al. (Eds.): PAAMS 2022, LNAI 13616, pp. 112–126, 2022.
https://doi.org/10.1007/978-3-031-18192-4_10

drones to pass each other. In this paper we formulate this challenge as a multiagent path finding (MAPF) problem, in which the goal is to search for a group of collision-free optimal paths while optimizing a team goal (e.g., minimizing the summation of all drones' moving times) [16,23,24].

MAPF problem has been intensively studied [4,9,15], in which finding optimal solutions for MAPF is NP-hard [25]. Many algorithms have been proposed for MAPF using various scales of agents, variants in problem setting, and by adding different constraints. However, most current MAPF research assumes that agents move on a 4-connected grid graph [20,23,24]. Time is discretized, and each agent can take five actions: up, down, right, left, or wait in single time steps [7], arriving at the next node after choosing an action. Since each edge has the same length, and all the agents move at the same time, they will always occupy a node. However, this assumption hinders the application of MAPF to the drone delivery scenario in this paper. Since, in the environment of drone delivery, each node can connect with any number of neighboring nodes in any direction, and in which drones can stay on edges, which does not correspond to a grid map.

Specifically, MAPF methods can be broadly divided into two general types: search methods and dynamic programming methods. Search methods treat MAPF as a single-stage decision problem, in which it is modeled as a decision tree whose nodes represent path information such as agents' locations or collisions. The solving pathfinding problem then switches to the search for a node-transition trajectory in the decision tree. The main drawbacks are with scalability and robustness: the computing time increases exponentially with rising numbers of agents or collisions, and it requires a re-search once small changes are made, such as in obstacle or goal positions. The other type consists of dynamic programming (DP) methods that treat MAPF as a multi-stage decision problem by extending MAPF along a discrete-time line. The goal is thus to learn a strategy that will allow agents to optimize their actions at each step. Multiagent reinforcement learning (MARL), a classical DP method, has been applied to MAPF in numerous studies. The main drawback is that it has low effectiveness if all agents need to learn together from zero.

Moreover, the object we consider in this paper is based on a non-grid graph, which creates two challenges: 1) the action space is large if all the nodes can be occupied rather than allowing only five actions on the grid graph; and 2) the state space is large if the agents can remain on edges rather than exclusively on nodes. Also, some existing MAPF methods are designed for grid maps, preventing them from being directly applied to non-grid graphs.

We therefore propose a novel algorithm called multiagent reinforcement learning with search algorithm (MARL-SA) that combines MARL and a search algorithm. In MARL-SA, one part of the agents' pathfinding process is solved using the search method, and the remaining part of the agents' processes is then further trained using MARL. Since not all agents are required to learn together from zero, this can accelerate the learning process. We then evaluate the MARL-SA algorithm under various experimental settings by comparing it with both a search-based method and the MARL method. The experimental results reveal our MARL-SA method to have greater effectiveness than the baseline algorithms.

2 Model

2.1 Problem Definition

In this paper, we define drone delivery problem as a non-grid MAPF as follows. As shown in Fig. 1, the map that the drones move over is an undirected graph with the following two constraints: 1) two drones cannot move in the opposite direction along the same edge; 2) multiple drones cannot occupy the same node. In each step, each drone occupying a node chooses one of its neighbor nodes to move and the drone staying on the edge can only move forward. The game is over when all the drones arrive at their goals or the maximum step length of one episode is reached. The drones move in a decentralized way on a non-grid graph and the goal is to search a collision-free path with the minimum moving cost on the graph.

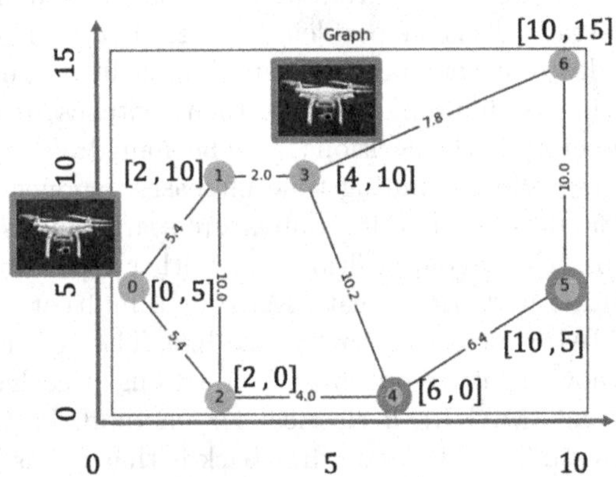

Fig. 1. Formulate drone delivery problem as a Dec-MDP.

2.2 Formulate Problem as Dec-MDP

The non-grid MAPF problem has two features: distributed agents and discrete-time dynamics. We therefore formulate this problem as a decentralized Markov decision processes (Dec-MDP), in which the drones are regarded as agents. Dec-MDP is a classical model for formulating the discrete time decision process with distributed agents [8].

In a Dec-MDP, each agent takes its own action based on its local observation. Then, an immediate reward can be obtained, depending on the results from all the agents' actions. Specifically, we use a tuple $< \mathcal{N}, \mathcal{S}, \mathcal{A}^i, \mathcal{O}^i, \mathcal{T}, r^i >$ to represent the Dec-MDP, where $\mathcal{N} = \{1, ..., |\mathcal{N}|\}$ is the set of agents, $\mathcal{S}$ is the state set of the environment, $\mathcal{A}^i$ is the agent i's action set. We can then have a joint action $\mathbf{a} = a^1 \times ... \times a^{|\mathcal{N}|}$, $\mathcal{O}^i$ is the agent i's observation set, $\mathcal{T}$ is the state transition function which represents the probability to transfer the next state s' under current state s and joint action $\mathbf{a}$, r^i is the reward function for agent i whose value $r^i(s, \mathbf{a}, s')$ depends on the joint action $\mathbf{a}$ under state s. Then, formulating the non-grid MAPF problem as a Dec-MDP is then stated as follows.

Observation: We regard each drone as an agent. Each agent observes the state from its own viewpoint, which includes two parts: 1) its own position, 2) the positions of other agents. Thus, an observation is denoted by

$$o^i[t] = \left[\ l^i[t],\ l^{-i}[t]\ \right],$$

where $l^i[t]$ is the agent i's current position at step t, $l^{-i}[t]$ is the all agents current positions beside agent i.

State: We can have a state consisting of all agents' positions which is defined by $s[t] = \left[l^1[t], ..., l^{|\mathcal{N}|}[t]\ \right]$.

Action: For observation $o^i[t]$, each agent will decide one node to move. This is regarded as an action a^i. Then, a joint action can be obtained by collecting all the agents' actions,

$$\mathbf{a}[t] = (a^1[t], ..., a^{|\mathcal{N}|}[t]), \tag{1}$$

where $\mathbf{a}[t] \in \mathcal{A}^1 \times ... \times \mathcal{A}^{|\mathcal{N}|}$.

Policy: Each agent has its own policy function $\pi^i : \mathcal{O}^i \times \mathcal{A}^i \rightarrow [0, 1]$ to chose an action a^i under its own observation o^i.

Reward Function: For each state transition $(s[t], \mathbf{a}[t], s[t+1])$, we can obtain an immediate cost $c^i(s[t], \mathbf{a}[t], s[t+1])$ for each agent i at step t. A drone moving/waiting one step corresponds to one unit of time cost, making it easy to calculate the summation of time cost from all the drones during the whole episode; this is defined as the team cost. If the moving cost to the node is less than one unit time cost, we take it as a unit time cost. We then set the minimization of the team cost $\sum_i c^i(s[t], \mathbf{a}[t], s[t+1])$ from all drones as the immediate cost. In Dec-MDP, the objective is always to set the goal of maximizing the reward summation, thus we take the additive inverse of cost as the immediate team reward, i.e., $r[t] = -\sum_i c^i(s[t], \mathbf{a}[t], s[t+1])$ at step t. Moreover, we set $r[t] = 1$ if the drone gets its goal and $r[t] = -1$ if there is a collision. In this way, we try to maximize the reward, which corresponds to minimizing the costs of moving time.

Objective Function: Given a certain period h with T steps, i.e., $h = [s[1], \mathbf{a}[1], s[2], \mathbf{a}[2], ..., s[T], \mathbf{a}[T], s[T+1]]$. The objective is to identify several policies $(\pi^1, ..., \pi^{|\mathcal{N}|})$ for all agents to maximize the sum $R(h)$ of team rewards during the total period h which is defined as

$$R(h) = \sum_{t=1}^{T} \gamma^{t-1} \sum_i r^i(s[t], \mathbf{a}[t], s[t+1]), \tag{2}$$

where γ is a discount factor to denote the importance of the rewards obtained in the future. This means that all drones need to cooperate in decision-making instead of considering only their own interests.

3 Related Work

The methods of solving MAPF can be classified into two types: search methods and dynamic programming methods. Search methods, which have a very long research history, treat MAPF as a static problem which does not extend to spreading along a discrete-time line. They plan paths based on certain search rules for designing paths for each agent, such as A* and conflict based search (CBS) [19]. However, the search space increases exponentially with every added agent. Then, the problem of MAPF can be spread to a discrete-time decision problem in which it is possible to optimize the decision at each step. Correspondingly, dynamic programming methods are proposed to guide agents make optimal actions at each step.

3.1 Search Methods

Many search methods have been studied in the single-agent pathfinding problem, such as breadth-first search, the Floyd-Warshall Algorithm and the A^* algorithm. They can be readily extended to MAPF problems by converting the single agent state space to a joint state space that consists of individual agent states. However, it suffers from the dimension curse: the joint state space grows exponentially with every added agent. Several search methods have thus been proposed that decouple MAPF to several sub-problems. Optimal reciprocal collision avoidance (ORCA) [23] solves each agent's individual path and then adjusts the paths to prevent collisions. It can guarantee local collision-free motion for a large number of agents. Sharon et al. [19] proposed a two-level algorithm called CBS where the high-level search is to detect collisions from all agents paths by constructing a constraint tree whose nodes consist of constraints on time and location for a single agent. Low-level searching is then used to find paths for all agents under the constraints from high-level.

3.2 Dynamic Programming Methods

The above search methods are mostly based on traditional shortest-path solving methods that can be regarded as static programming methods. The search space is usually huge if the number of agents is large, and thus a high time cost is incurred to solve it. More recently, MARL as a DP method has been used for MAPF, which trains agents by interaction with the environment in a trial-and-error way. This is a classical DP method that has been examined in many studies [17,18]. Any single RL method such as DQN [13] and DDPG [10] can be directly applied to it by regarding it as a single agent problem. However, it suffers the dimension problem, since the state space increases with the number of agents.

In [1] it assumes a continuous action space and trains a value-network to evaluate each state value, which is called deep V-learning. It can then generate a path to its goal by choosing an action that can convert the state with maximized value. Since MAPF is based on a cooperation setting, many cooperative MARL algorithms can be applied to MAPF. They usually correspond to a framework of centralized learning and decentralized execution, such as MADDPG [11], VDN [21] and Q-MIX [14]. Sartoretti et al. propose a MARL method combining with imitation learning (IL) called PRIMAL [16]. Each agent shares a common neural network that is trained by MARL to perform a decentralized execution and IL with an expert centralized planner to train agents to exhibit coordination. However, the above methods are usually based on a grid graph to design methods that cannot be directly applied to a non-grid graph. The MARL algorithm would usually cost more time than search method, and it is also difficult to cope with a large map while training a neural network. MARL algorithms usually have a low efficiency if all agents learn from zero. This prompted us to examine a strategy for combining search methods and MARL methods and to propose a new framework for solving MAPF on a non-grid graph.

4 Algorithm

Although MARL as a classical DP method can be used for MAPF. It is usually both difficult and ineffective to make all agents learn by sharing a neural network with initial random parameters, especially for large numbers of agents. However, although it can work if all agents follow the same search method, there is a high risk of converging on a sub-optimal solution. We therefore combine these two kinds of methods to propose a novel MARL algorithm called multiagent reinforcement learning with search algorithm (MARL-SA). The main idea of MARL-SA method is to designate one agent as the learning agent and make the other agents follow the search method initially. It includes search module and MARL module, illustrated as follows.

4.1 The Search Module

In the search module, a dynamic-decoupled search method is employed that consists of two parts. The first part is called the *shortest path*, and is used to calculate each agent's shortest path without taking other agents into consideration. Note that, as shown on the left of Fig. 2, the inputs of the shortest part are the graph information and its own starting point and goal. The output therefore consists of evaluation values for each node $short(V) = [vs_1, ..., vs_{|V|}]$ based on the shortest path ($V = \{v_1, ..., v_i, ..., v_{|V|}\}$ is the set of nodes on the graph).

The shortest-path algorithm can be any single agent's shortest-path algorithm. In this paper we calculate it using the Warshall-Floyd algorithm. The second part is called *collision avoidance on the nearest edge*, where, as shown in the middle part of Fig. 2, the inputs are the results $short(V)$ from part 1) and information on drones on the nearest edges. The output is therefore

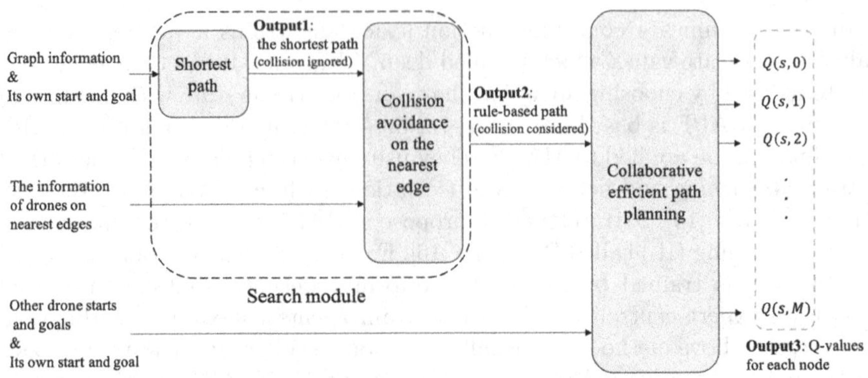

Fig. 2. The framework of MARL-SA algorithm.

the learning agent's path solved according to the following rule, denoted as $coll(V) = [vc_1, ..., vc_{|V|}]$. The specific calculation of $coll(V)$ is denoted as follows. $vc_i = 0$, if node v_i is in the shortest path. $vc_i = -1$, if v_i is the node that does not connect with the current node. $vc_i = cost_i/\beta$, if v_i is the node that connects with the current node, but is not on the shortest path, where $cost_i$ is the additional cost compared with the shortest path. β is a large number to make the value of vc_i less than 1. This is because a large reward value would make the learning process unstable.

At each step, we run the two parts sequentially. Each agent can move to its goal to avoid collisions by choosing the node with the maximum evaluation value, i.e., $\text{argmax}_{i \in V} vc_i$. We therefore call the above parts the search module.

- part 1) Shortest path: the inputs are the graph information and its own starting point and goal. The output is the shortest path (without considering the other agents' information), solved by the shortest pathfinding algorithm;
- part 2) Collision avoidance on the nearest edge: the inputs are the shortest path, solved from the shortest path part and the information from drones on the nearest edges. The output is the learning agent's path solved by a rule that belongs to the dynamic-decoupled method.

4.2 The MARL Module

The above search module, when applied, can usually find collision-free paths. However, it may only find suboptimal paths and cannot improve its performance by iteration. We therefore further take the output from the search module as one of the inputs to the MARL module to cause it to learn cooperative behavior and thus more closely approach optimal paths.

In MARL, $Q^i : \mathcal{O}^i \times \mathcal{A}^i \rightarrow \mathbb{R}^i$ is used to denote the expectation of the discounted sum of agent i's rewards that will be obtained in the future after choosing action a^i given observation o^i. Specifically, Q^i does not only depend on its own policy but also depends on the other agents' policies.

When several optimal policies $(\pi^{1*}, ..., \pi^{|\mathcal{N}|*})$ that can maximize the $R(h) = \sum_i r^i(s[t], \mathbf{a}[t], s[t+1])$ are given, it is called the optimal Q-value, defined as $Q^{i*}(o^i, a^i) = \mathbb{E}_{\pi^{1*},...,\pi^{|\mathcal{N}|*}}\left[R(h)|o^i[1] = o^i, a^i[1] = a^i\right]$, where "$|o^i[1] = o^i, a^i[1] = a^i$" means the initial state and the action of agent i is fixed at observation o^i and a^i, respectively. Our aim is to train each agent to adopt a decentralized strategy that causes it to act cooperatively. We therefore want to identify a couple of the policies $(\pi^{1*}, ..., \pi^{\mathcal{N}*})$ for all agents to maximize the sum of team rewards during the total period h.

If each agent were trained by its individual reward, it would result in selfish behavior. For instance, an agent can arrive at its goal by following the shortest path, but it might block another agent; this results in a low team reward. We therefore use the team reward to train them which is the inverse number of summation costs. We also assume all the drone types are same, then they can share one same neural network. For drone delivery, for instance, all the drones are assumed to be identical, which means that the results are the same after any drone takes the same actions under the same set of conditions. We called collaborative efficient path planning as part 3), illustrated as follows.

- part 3) Collaborative efficient path planning, which is a deep Q-network (DQN). Although we have defined the agent i's observation i's observation $o^i[t] = [\ l^i[t],\ l^{-i}[t]\ ]$, taking it as the input of DQN may result in low efficiency. This is because it includes only the location information of agents, meaning that the map information is not used effectively. We therefore take τ^i as the input, which comprises three parts: 1) the values of $coll(V) = [vc_1, ..., vc_{|V|}]$, 2) the learning agent's own start node and goal node which are represented in a one-hot way; and 3) all the drone starting nodes and goal nodes. This is because the value of $coll(V)$ is calculated using the heuristic shortest path method, which has used both the agent location information and the map information. The output is Q-values for all the nodes. Finally, the learning agent chooses actions using an ϵ-greedy policy based on the Q-value solved using the above learning module.

4.3 The Training Process

We adopt a round-based training method to train the decentralized strategy network, as shown in Fig. 3. In the first round, the other non-learning agents (the agents beside learning agent 1) follow a search module (parts 1 and 2). Only agent 1 follows a MARL module (parts 1, 2 and 3) for learning. After accomplishing the first round of training, the other agents copy the learning result from agent 1 and keep the parameters unchanged, with only agent 1 learning to update its parameters. Similarly, after accomplishing the second round of training, the above process is repeated.

Our goal is to discover the optimal Q^1 (1 is the No. of learning agent) that can maximize the sum $R(h)$ of the team rewards over a period h. A reply memory D is used to store the tuple of $(\tau^1[1], a^1[1], r[1], \tau^1[2], ..., \tau^1[T], a^1[T], r[T], \tau^1[T+1])$, where τ^1 includes all agent starts, goals, and its output from search module. We then randomly sample the tuples from D to train $Q^1(\tau^1, a^1)$ with the aim of minimizing the following loss function:

$$\mathcal{L}(\theta) = \sum_{k \in D} \left[\left(y_k - Q^1(\tau^1, a^1; \theta) \right) \right] \tag{3}$$

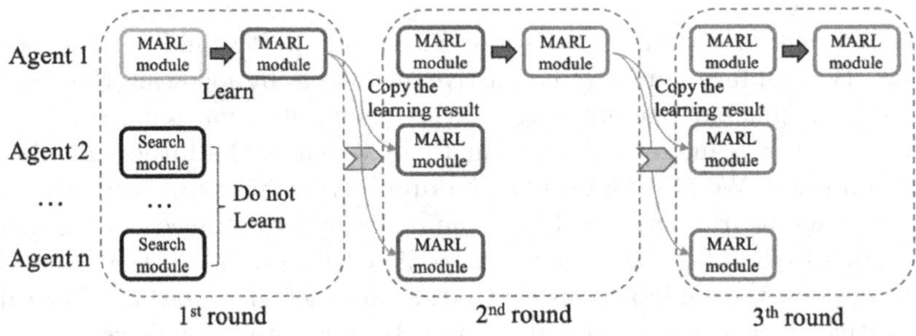

Fig. 3. The learning process of MARL-SA algorithm.

where k is the sample index and $y_k = r_k + \gamma \max_{a^1} Q(\tau^1, a^1; \theta)$ is the target, θ is the set of the network parameters.

5 Evaluation

5.1 Evaluation Settings

In this section, we run several experiments to evaluate MARL-SA method against other baseline algorithms on four maps with 9, 18, 20 and 43 nodes, as shown in Fig. 4.

The maps whose name include "near-grid" are created randomly in a format closed to grid map. The maps whose name include "aoba" are created based on real road information in Aoba district, Kanagawa, Japan. The last numbers of the map names represent the node numbers. Without losing generality, at each episode we randomly generate tasks for each map. Each task has different starts and goals for agents. To simulate the dynamic environment characteristic of drone delivery, we make the agent disappear once it has arrived at its goal; this can change the number of the agents. Further, the starting points and goals of the agents change dynamically in each episode. One episode will terminate if either of the following cases happens: 1) all agents have arrived at their goals, or 2) a collision occurs. Since the action set of an agent is all the nodes of the map, we let it stay on the current node if one drone chooses a non-neighboring node. Correspondingly, when an agent waits once, the cost is one unit of time. To achieve cooperative behavior, a team reward is utilized, which is the summation of individual rewards from all the agents. All the algorithms were implemented

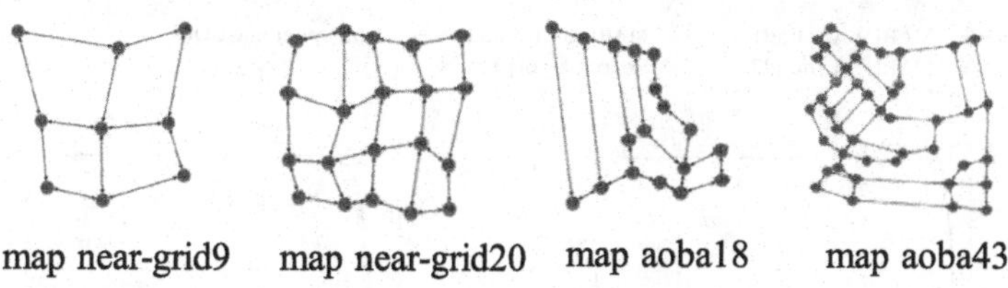

Fig. 4. Four non-grid maps used for evaluation.

in Python 3, and the experiments were conducted on an Apple computer running macOS-Catalina 10.15.7 with an Intel Core i7 CPU and 32 GB of memory.

In MARL-SA method, we designate one drone as the learning agent and make the other agents simply follow the search module which is illustrated in 4.1. The learning agent follows the MARL module which is a DQN network whose input layer size is equal to $|o_i|+2|V|+|V|^2$ and its output layer size is equal to the node number on the map. The size of the hidden layer is equal to the output layer, and the activation function of the layer is the ReLU function. We implemented the neural network using PyTorch 2.0. We set the same hyper-parameters for all the RL based algorithms with $\gamma=0.9$.

5.2 Evaluation Results

Proposed Method by Round Training. We first confirm the practicality of MARL-SA method by round training. We take three rounds to train the agents, with each round consisting of 30,000 episodes. In the first round, we designate one agent as the learning agent, based on a DQN network. The other agents adopt a search method which characterizes them as non-learning agents. In the second round, the non-learning agents copy the results of trained DQN network from the learning agent. Although non-learning agents use a DQN to carry out decision-making, the parameters of the neural network will not be updated during training. Only the learning agent continues to train the DQN network. Similarly, in the third round, the non-learning agents continue to copy the learning results from the learning agent in the previous round.

We run it on various maps shown in Fig. 4. with three agents and run three rounds, consisting of 90,000 episodes. We repeat each experiment three times and take the average as the final result. In round 1, the learning agent begins to learn from a neural network with initial random parameters. The learning agent can learn effectively given the condition that the two other non-learning agents follow a search method. In Fig. 5, we can see that the rate of reaching the goal has closely risen to 100% after finishing the first round. In Fig. 6, it is clear that the costed distances on arriving at goals decrease with each training round (the distance is the sum of moving costs). Figure 5 and 6, when taken together, show that paths with smaller distances to goals can be learned, although the goal rate has risen to 100% in both round 2 and 3. This means that the agent's performance can be improved by training in rounds.

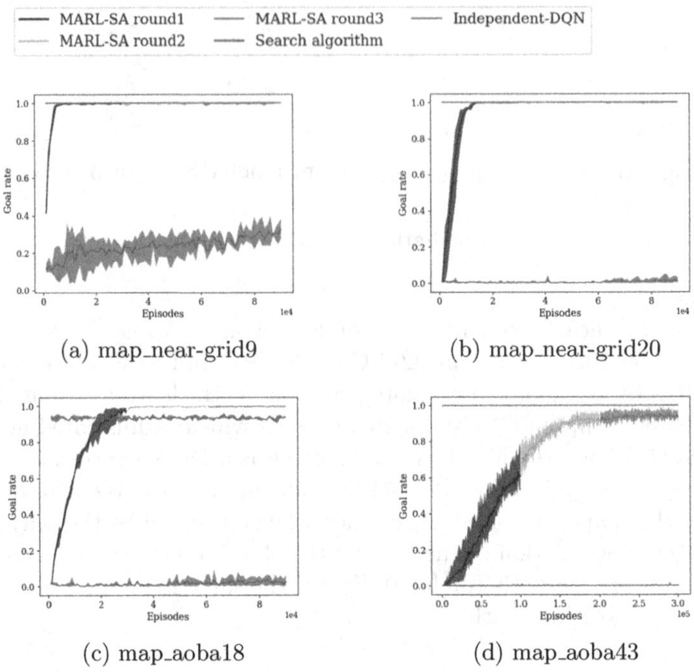

(a) map_near-grid9 (b) map_near-grid20

(c) map_aoba18 (d) map_aoba43

Fig. 5. Compare the performances of MARL-SA algorithm with other baseline algorithms on various maps in goal arriving rate.

Comparison with Baselines. In this part we analyze the MARL-SA method by comparing with the search method which is based on the search module in Fig. 2, and the independent-DQN method [22] which trains independent action-value functions for each agent using DQN. We compare them using various maps that have different sizes and shapes. As for the map_near-grid9, we run the MARL-SA method for three rounds, and the numbers of episodes in each round change to fit the size of the map. We can see in Fig. 5(a) that when all the agents share one DQN, they are slow to learn during the training period, since its effectiveness is poor due to having all the agents learn at the same time. Figures 5(a) and 6(a) show that the search method gives a better performance than independent DQN, since it can ensure that each agent arrives at its goal. The final result shows that the search method has the same goal arrival rate as that learned using the MARL-SA method. However, our MARL-SA method achieves better performance than the search method, since it requires shorter distances to reach the goals, as can be seen in Fig. 6(a). The sum cost of one episode using the search method is around 27, whereas the moving distance to the goals in one episode of MARL-SA method corresponds to around 18, showing a reduction of around 30% in moving costs. Our proposed MARL-SA appears to have the optimal performance in terms of minimizing the sum of all agents' moving costs.

We also tested the performances using a larger map (map_aoba18, map_near-grid20, map_aoba43) with 18, 20, and 43 nodes respectively. The performance of the independent-DQN method decreases with growing map size. This is because the larger the map, the more dynamic the learning process. The independent-DQN method cannot learn better than a search method with a map that has nine nodes. This means that the larger the map, the less effective the independent DQN method.

The search method can usually obtain a 100% goal rate, however it cannot guarantee it. For instance, it achieves a goal rate around 95% on the map_aoba18. Although the search method can maintain a better performance than independent-DQN, it costs more distance-wise to arrive at the goals than the MARL-SA method. For instance, let us compare the results of map_aoba18 and map_near-grid20, which have similar numbers of nodes. Figure 6 (b) shows that the performance of the search method is equally as good as that of MARL-SA on map_near-grid20. However, its performance on map_aoba18 is lower than that of MARL-SA, as shown in Fig. 6 (c). This is because the search method usually learns up to a sub-optimal solution that is close to the optimal solution on map_near-grid20 where the edge costs usually have similar values. On map_aoba18, where edge costs have a high variance, large differences can be seen between sub-optimal solutions and optimal solutions. In summary, the MARL-SA method maintains a better performance than other existing methods, even when scaling up to larger maps.

6 Discussion

6.1 The MARL-SA Position in MAPF Solutions

In this paper, we classify MAPF solutions into search methods and dynamic programming methods. However, in most previous studies, they have been classified into coupled, decoupled and their mixed methods [16]. 1) Coupled methods: the multiagent problem is treated as a single-agent problem, such as a standard A algorithm. However, this method suffers from exponentially increasing complexity with each increment in the number of agents. 2) Decoupled methods calculate each agent's shortest path individually and then adjust the results to prevent collisions. However, this method is at risk of leading to suboptimal solutions. 3) Mixed coupled and decoupled methods: these combine coupled and decoupled methods that can learn the complex behaviors of agents.

We then reposition MARL-SA method to the decoupled method category. In this paper, we focus on proposing a new learning framework that combines a search method and the MARL method. Thus, MARL-SA can also be extended to the coupled methods or the mixed coupled-decoupled methods. Beside improving the learning efficiency and optimality, the another advantage of MARL-SA is that it can cope with a strong dynamic feature: the number of drones is uncertain, in that some drones will dynamically join or leave the drone delivery network. When applying some traditional MAPF algorithms, it is necessary to re-search the paths of all the agents due to the alteration of agent number. This is usually

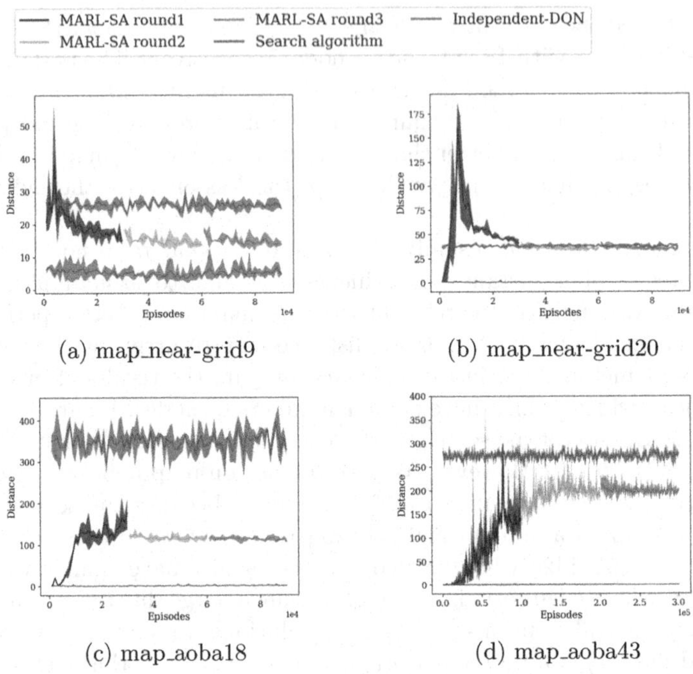

(a) map_near-grid9 (b) map_near-grid20

(c) map_aoba18 (d) map_aoba43

Fig. 6. Compare the performances of MARL-SA algorithm with other baseline algorithms on various maps in distances to goal.

impractical in real-world scenarios, since the computation time of re-search may cause a huge latency. Thus, our proposed MARL-SA is more practical in the realistic scenario of drone delivery where the drone number can dynamically change according to the user delivery requests.

6.2 Learning Agent Selection in MARL-SA

Each agent shares the same policy network when all of them adopt a learning-based method, so no differences result from choosing any particular agent as the learning agent. The only differences between agents are their starting points and goals; however, these dynamically change at the initial step of each episode, with the result that such changes will eliminate any differences among agents. We can therefore treat all the agents as a homogeneous whole.

The only task is therefore to decide on the number of learning agents. Since the non-learning agents will adopt a static search method, the result will be a stable environment for learning agents. It is obvious that the more non-learning agents are, the more stable the environment for learning agents will become, thus learning agents will achieve a higher learning efficiency. However, the policy that the learning agent learns is based on other learning policies, meaning that the learning agent tries to learn a best response policy to the other non-learning policies. Too many non-learning agents may narrow the policy space for learning agents, which readily leads to sub-optimal policies being learned. Deciding the number of learning agents is therefore a trade-off problem between learning efficiency and learning optimality.

7 Conclusion

In this paper, we studied a drone delivery problem which is formulated as a non-grid MAPF. Most existing work can not be used for efficiently solving this problem, since they are usually designed based on grid-maps, such as in studies [2,12,16], in which encoding on a grid graph is necessary and cannot be used in our non-grid cases. We propose a novel MARL-SA algorithm, formulated by importing a search method into MARL, in which only one agent learns and the other agents follow. The MARL-SA method achieves a faster learning process than with traditional independent-DQN, in which all agents learn together from zero. Through the evaluations, the results show our approach to achieve significantly greater rewards than some baseline algorithms. As for the future work, the evaluations with more number of agents and bigger size of map are considered to be done.

Acknowledgment. This research was supported by a joint research of Non-Grid Pathfinding Optimization in Continuous Time and Space from Panasonic Holdings Corporation.

References

1. Chen, Y.F., Liu, M., Everett, M., How, J.P.: Decentralized non-communicating multiagent collision avoidance with deep reinforcement learning. In: 2017 IEEE International Conference on Robotics and Automation (ICRA), pp. 285–292. IEEE (2017)
2. Damani, M., Luo, Z., Wenzel, E., Sartoretti, G.: Primal 2: pathfinding via reinforcement and imitation multi-agent learning-lifelong. IEEE Robot. Autom. Lett. **6**(2), 2666–2673 (2021)
3. Dorling, K., Heinrichs, J., Messier, G.G., Magierowski, S.: Vehicle routing problems for drone delivery. IEEE Trans. Syst. Man Cybern.: Syst. **47**(1), 70–85 (2016)
4. Felner, A., et al.: Search-based optimal solvers for the multiagent pathfinding problem: summary and challenges. In: Tenth Annual Symposium on Combinatorial Search (2017)
5. Frachtenberg, E.: Practical drone delivery. Computer **52**(12), 53–57 (2019)
6. Jones, T.: International commercial drone regulation and drone delivery services. Technical report RAND Santa Monica, CA, USA (2017)
7. Kaduri, O., Boyarski, E., Stern, R.: Algorithm selection for optimal multi-agent pathfinding. In: Proceedings of the International Conference on Automated Planning and Scheduling, vol. 30, pp. 161–165 (2020)
8. Lee, J.: Optimization of a modular drone delivery system. In: 2017 Annual IEEE International Systems Conference (SysCon), pp. 1–8. IEEE (2017)

9. Li, J., Tinka, A., Kiesel, S., Durham, J.W., Kumar, T.S., Koenig, S.: Lifelong multi-agent path finding in large-scale warehouses. In: AAMAS, pp. 1898–1900 (2020)
10. Lillicrap, T.P., et al.: Continuous control with deep reinforcement learning. arXiv preprint arXiv:1509.02971 (2015)
11. Lowe, R., Wu, Y., Tamar, A., Harb, J., Abbeel, P., Mordatch, I.: Multiagent actor-critic for mixed cooperative-competitive environments. arXiv preprint arXiv:1706.02275 (2017)
12. Ma, Z., Luo, Y., Ma, H.: Distributed heuristic multi-agent path finding with communication. In: 2021 IEEE International Conference on Robotics and Automation (ICRA), pp. 8699–8705. IEEE (2021)
13. Mnih, V., et al.: Human-level control through deep reinforcement learning. Nature **518**(7540), 529–533 (2015)
14. Rashid, T., Samvelyan, M., Schroeder, C., Farquhar, G., Foerster, J., Whiteson, S.: Qmix: Monotonic value function factorisation for deep multi-agent reinforcement learning. In: International Conference on Machine Learning, pp. 4295–4304. PMLR (2018)
15. Salzman, O., Stern, R.: Research challenges and opportunities in multi-agent path finding and multi-agent pickup and delivery problems. In: Proceedings of the 19th International Conference on Autonomous Agents and MultiAgent Systems, pp. 1711–1715 (2020)
16. Sartoretti, G., et al.: Primal: pathfinding via reinforcement and imitation multi-agent learning. IEEE Robot. Autom. Lett. **4**(3), 2378–2385 (2019)
17. Sartoretti, G., Shi, Y., Paivine, W., Travers, M., Choset, H.: Distributed learning for the decentralized control of articulated mobile robots. In: 2018 IEEE International Conference on Robotics and Automation (ICRA), pp. 3789–3794. IEEE (2018)
18. Sartoretti, G., Wu, Y., Paivine, W., Kumar, T.K.S., Koenig, S., Choset, H.: Distributed reinforcement learning for multi-robot decentralized collective construction. In: Correll, N., Schwager, M., Otte, M. (eds.) Distributed Autonomous Robotic Systems. SPAR, vol. 9, pp. 35–49. Springer, Cham (2019). https://doi.org/10.1007/978-3-030-05816-6_3
19. Sharon, G., Stern, R., Felner, A., Sturtevant, N.R.: Conflict-based search for optimal multi-agent pathfinding. Artif. Intell. **219**, 40–66 (2015)
20. Stern, R., et al.: Multi-agent pathfinding: definitions, variants, and benchmarks. In: Twelfth Annual Symposium on Combinatorial Search (2019)
21. Sunehag, P., et al.: Value-decomposition networks for cooperative multi-agent learning. arXiv preprint arXiv:1706.05296 (2017)
22. Tampuu, A., et al.: Multiagent cooperation and competition with deep reinforcement learning. PLoS ONE **12**(4), e0172395 (2017)
23. Van Den Berg, J., Guy, S.J., Lin, M., Manocha, D.: Reciprocal n-body collision avoidance. In: Robotics research, vol. 70, pp. 3–19. Springer, Heidelberg (2011)
24. Wagner, G., Choset, H.: Subdimensional expansion for multirobot path planning. Artif. Intell. **219**, 1–24 (2015)
25. Yu, J., LaValle, S.M.: Structure and intractability of optimal multi-robot path planning on graphs. In: Twenty-Seventh AAAI Conference on Artificial Intelligence (2013)

Hierarchical Collaborative Hyper-Parameter Tuning

Ahmad Esmaeili(✉), Zahra Ghorrati, and Eric T. Matson

Department of Computer and Information Technology, Purdue University, West Lafayette, IN 47907, USA
{aesmaei,zghorrat,ematson}@purdue.edu

Abstract. Hyper-parameter Tuning is among the most critical stages in building machine learning solutions. This paper demonstrates how multi-agent systems can be utilized to develop a distributed technique for determining near-optimal values for any arbitrary set of hyper-parameters in a machine learning model. The proposed method employs a distributedly formed hierarchical agent-based architecture for the cooperative searching procedure of tuning hyper-parameter values. The presented generic model is used to develop a guided randomized agent-based tuning technique, and its behavior is investigated in both machine learning and global function optimization applications. According the empirical results, the proposed model outperformed both of its underlying randomized tuning strategies in terms of classification error and function evaluations, notably in higher number of dimensions.

Keywords: Multi-agent systems · Distributed machine learning · Hyper-parameter tuning

1 Introduction

Almost all Machine Learning (ML) algorithms comprise a set of hyper-parameters that control their learning experience and the quality of their resulting models. The number of hidden units, the learning rate, the mini-batch sizes, etc. of a neural network; the kernel parameters and regularization penalty amount of a support vector machine; and maximum depth, samples split criteria, and the number of used features of a decision tree are few examples of hyper-parameters that need to be adjusted for the aforementioned learning methods. Numerous research studies have been devoted to hyper-parameter tuning in the machine learning literature. In the most straight forward manual approach an expert knowledge is used to identify and evaluate a set of potential values in the hyper-parameter search space. Accessing the expert knowledge and generating reproducible results are among the primary difficulties in using the manual searching technique [4], especially knowing that different datasets will likely require different set of hyper-parameter values for a specific learning model [14].

© The Author(s), under exclusive license to Springer Nature Switzerland AG 2022
F. Dignum et al. (Eds.): PAAMS 2022, LNAI 13616, pp. 127–139, 2022.
https://doi.org/10.1007/978-3-031-18192-4_11

Let $\Lambda = \{\lambda\}$ and $\mathcal{X} = \{\mathcal{X}^{(train)}, \mathcal{X}^{(valid)}\}$ respectively denote the set of all possible hyper-parameter value vectors and the data set split into training and validation sets. The learning algorithm with hyper-parameter values vector λ is a function that maps training datasets to model $\mathcal{M}$, i.e. $\mathcal{M} = \mathcal{A}_\lambda(\mathcal{X}^{(train)})$, and the hyper-parameter optimization problem can be formally written as [4]:

$$\lambda^{(*)} = \arg\min_{\lambda \in \Lambda} \mathbb{E}_{x \sim \mathcal{G}_x} \left[\mathcal{L}\left(x; \mathcal{A}_\lambda(\mathcal{X}^{(train)})\right) \right] \tag{1}$$

where $\mathcal{G}_x$ is the grand truth distribution, $\mathcal{L}(x; \mathcal{M})$ is the expected loss of applying learning model $\mathcal{M}$ over i.i.d. samples x, and $\mathbb{E}_{x \sim \mathcal{G}_x} \left[\mathcal{L}\left(x; \mathcal{A}_\lambda(\mathcal{X}^{(train)})\right) \right]$ is the generalization error of algorithm $\mathcal{A}_\lambda$. Estimating the generalization error using the cross-validation technique [5], the above-mentioned optimization problem can be rewritten as:

$$\lambda^{(*)} \approx \arg\min_{\lambda \in \Lambda} \operatorname*{mean}_{x \in \mathcal{X}^{(valid)}} \mathcal{L}\left(x; \mathcal{A}_\lambda(\mathcal{X}^{(train)})\right) \equiv \arg\min_{\lambda \in \Lambda} \Psi(\lambda) \tag{2}$$

where $\Psi(\lambda)$ is called hyper-parameter response function [4].

There are a broad range of methods that address this problem using global optimization techniques. Grid search [12,17], random search [4], Bayesian optimization [9,15,16], and evolutionary and population-based optimization [1,7,21] are among the widely used class of approaches that are studied extensively in the literature. In grid search, for instance, every combination of predetermined set of values in each hyper-parameter is examined and the best point, i.e. the one that minimizes the loss, is selected. Assuming $\mathcal{V}_j$ and k denote the set of candidate values for the hyper-parameter $\lambda_j^{(i)} \in \lambda^{(i)}$ and the number of hyper-parameter to configure, respectively, the number of trials that grid search evaluates is $T = \Pi_{j=1}^{k} |\mathcal{V}_j|$, which clearly indicates the curse of dimensionality because of the exponential growth of joint-values with the increase in the number of hyper-parameters [3].

When applied to machine learning and data mining, Multi-Agent Systems (MAS) and agent-based technologies offer various benefits, such as scalability, facilitating the autonomy and distributedness of learning resources, and supporting strategic and collaborative learning models, to name a few [8,20]. Collaborative and agent-based methods to tune the hyper-parameters of a machine learning model has previously studied in the literature. Among the noteworthy contributions, the research reported in [2] proposes a surrogate-based collaborative tuning method that incorporates the gained experience from previous experiments. The collaboration in this model is basically through simultaneous tuning of same hyper-parameter sets over multiple datasets and using the obtained information about the optimized hyper-parameter values in all subsequent tuning problems. In [22], a distributed and collaborative system called Auto-Tuned Models (ATM) is proposed to automate hyper-parameter tuning and classification model selection procedures. ATM uses Conditional Parameter Tree (CPT) to represent the hyper-parameter search space in which the root is learning method and the children of the root are hyper-parameters. During model selection, different tunable subsets of hyper-parameter nodes in CPT are selected and assigned to a cluster of workers to tune. Koch et al. [13] has introduced a derivative-free hyper-parameter optimization framework called Autotune. This framework is composed of a hybrid and extendible set of solvers that concurrently run various searching methods, and a potentially distributed set of workers for evaluating objective functions and providing feedback to the solvers. Autotune uses an iterative process during which the solver manager exchanges all the points that have been evaluated with the solvers to generate new sets of points to evaluate. Iranfar et al. [10] have proposed a Mutli-Agent Reinforcement Learning (MARL)-based technique to optimize the hyper-parameters of deep convolutional neural networks. In their work, the design-space is split into sub-spaces by devoting each agent to tuning the hyper-parameters of a single network layer using Q-learning. In [18] Parker-Holder et al. introduce Population-Based Bandit (PB2) algorithm that utilizes a probabilistic model to efficiently guide the searching operation of hyper-parameters in Reinforcement Learning. In PB2, a population of agents are trained in parallel, and periodically observing their performance, the network weights of an under-performing agent is replaced with the ones of a better performing agent, and its hyper-parameters are tuned using Bayesian optimization.

Our paper presents a distributed agent-based collaborative optimization model that can be used to solve problems related to ML hyper-parameter tuning as well as generic function optimization. In the suggested method, in which each terminal agent focuses on sub-optimizing based on a single hyper-parameter, and the high-level agents are responsible for aggregating sub-optimal results and facilitating subordinates' collaborations. Thanks to the intrinsic autonomy of the agents in a MAS, each agent in the proposed model can flexibly utilize a different searching/optimization procedure to locate optima. Notwithstanding, for the sake of experiments, we have developed a guided random-based searching approach for all terminal agents, and have applied set theoretic operations as the aggregation techniques in hight-level agents. The suggested agent-based modeling of the problem enables the tuning process to be carried out based on multiple metrics and be easily implemented over not only parallel processing units in a single machine, but also multiple heterogeneous devices connected by a network.

The remainder of this paper is organized as follows: Sect. 2 presents the details of the proposed agent-based method, Sect. 3 discusses the performance of the proposed model and presents empirical results from applying it to ML hyper-parameter tuning and function optimization use cases, and at the end, Sect. 4 concludes the paper and provides future work suggestions.

2 Methodology

This section provides the details of the proposed agent-based hyper-parameter tuning approach. The first part presents the general algorithms for building the initial multi-agent structure and using it for tuning the hyper-parameters, and the second part uses the presented foundations to develop a guided randomized optimization and hyper-parameter tuning method.

2.1 Agent-Based Hyper-Parameter Tuning

The agents in our proposed model are basically the solvers that are specialized in tuning a specific subset of hyper-parameters. Because of the hierarchical representation of the model, we have two sets of agents: (1) *internals*, which have subordinates and mainly focus on aggregating results and directing information; (2) *terminals*, which do not have any child agents, and implement a single hyper-parameter tuning algorithm based on the provided information. Throughout this paper, we use notation $\mathcal{T}_\lambda^l$ to refer to the agent(tuner) that is at level l of the hierarchy and specialized in tuning hyper-parameter set λ.

The placement of agents in the hierarchy is determined by the hyper-parameter sets that they tune. Let $\lambda = \{\lambda_1, \lambda_2, \ldots, \lambda_n\}$ be the set of n hyper-parameters used by ML algorithm $\mathcal{A}_\lambda$. We assume $\lambda = \lambda_o \cup \lambda_f$, where λ_o is the sets of objective hyper-parameters we try to tune, and λ_f denote the set of hyper-parameters we intend to keep their values fixed. We form the hierarchy of the agents by recursively dividing λ_o into *primary* hyper-parameter subsets, $\hat{\lambda}_o$, and assigning each, together with its *complement*, $\hat{\lambda}'_o = \lambda_o - \hat{\lambda}_o$, to an agent. The recursive division is based on the maximum number of parallel connections, $c > 1$, the agents can handle and continues until the hyper-parameter set is no longer divisible, i.e. $|\hat{\lambda}_o| = 1$, where $|\ldots|$ denotes the set cardinality operator. Figure 1 illustrates an example structure built for $\lambda_o = \{\lambda_1, \lambda_2, \lambda_3, \lambda_4, \lambda_5\}$ and $c = 2$. In this figure, green and orange highlighters are used to distinguish the primary and complementary hyper-parameters at each node respectively. Moreover, for the sake of brevity, we have used the indexes as the label of the nodes.

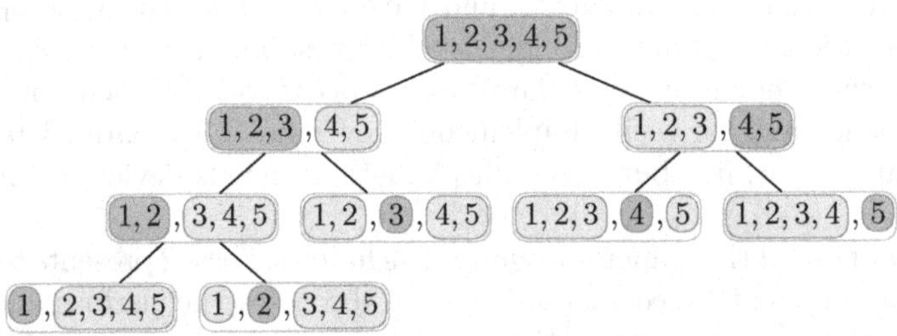

Fig. 1. Hierarchical structure built for $\lambda_o = \{\lambda_1, \lambda_2, \lambda_3, \lambda_4, \lambda_5\}$, where the primary and complementary hyper-parameters of each node are respectively highlighted in green and orange, and the labels are the indexes of λ_i (Color figure online)

The proposed tuning technique is a two-phase process: (1) distributedly forming the hierarchical multi-agent system, and (2) iteratively tuning the hyper-parameters through the cooperation between the agents, both presented in Algorithm 1. Building the hierarchy is initiated when the root agent receives a tuning query made based on a user's request. Such query is characterized by tuple

$$\langle \mathcal{A}_\lambda, \{\hat{\lambda}_o, \hat{\lambda}'_o, \lambda_f\}, \mathcal{V}, \{\mathcal{X}^{(train)}, \mathcal{X}^{(valid)}\}, \mathcal{L}\rangle \tag{3}$$

where $\mathcal{V} = \{(\lambda_i, v_i)\}; |\mathcal{V}| \geq |\lambda_f|$ denotes the set containing hyper-parameter values, and all remaining notations are defined as in Eq. 1. It is clear that in the very first query given to the root agent, we have: $\hat{\lambda}_o = \lambda_o \subseteq \lambda$ and $\hat{\lambda}'_o = \emptyset$.

The function and variable names in Algorithms 1 are chosen to be self-explanatory, and additional comments are provided as needed. Additionally, some of the important parts are described as follows: function PREPARERESOURCES in line 3 prepares the agent, in terms of data and computation resources it will need for training, validating, and tuning the ML algorithm it represents; function SPAWNORCONNECT in line 8 creates a subordinate agent, by either creating a new agent or connecting to an existing idle one, to represent algorithm $\mathcal{A}_\lambda$ and expected loss function $\mathcal{L}$; PREPAREFEEDBACK function in line 17 works on providing guidance to subordinate agents about their next move; and finally, function SHOULDSTOP in line 34, which is run by the root agent, determines when to stop based on a set of specified criteria, such as number of iterations, quality of improvements, etc. In the proposed model, the agents have flexible autonomy; at the same time that they are committed to follow the directions of their superior agents in the hierarchy and provide a specific format of responses, they can implement their own independent tuning algorithm. Moreover, using the feedback received from their parents, the terminal nodes have better control on handling defined and hidden constraints of the hyper-parameters.

There are various factors that determine the computational complexity of the entire process: (1) the tuning algorithm that each terminal agent uses and (2) the hierarchical structure of the MAS. Let n denote the total number of hyper-parameters that we initially intend to tune and $t_i(n)$ be the temporal cost of the tuning algorithm run by terminal agent $\mathcal{T}_i$. Due to the recursive division of the objective hyper-parameters at each node of the hierarchy, and assuming that the parallelization budget of each agent equals c, it can be easily shown that the height of formed structure is $\lceil \log_c n \rceil$. Since the agents run in parallel, the formation of the structure has the worst case time complexity of $\mathcal{O}(\log_c n)$. Assume the maximum number of iterations before reaching the stopping criteria is denoted by $\mathcal{I}$, and the temporal cost of result aggregation process be $g(n)$. After building the hierarchy, the time complexity of running all aggregations for each iteration will be $\mathcal{O}(g(n) \log_c n)$, because of the parallel execution of the agents. Finally, recalling the fact that all actual tuning algorithms are conducted by the terminal agents and we have n number of such agents in the structure, the time complexity of the model will be $\mathcal{O}(\mathcal{I} \times \max(g(n) \log_c n, t_1(n), t_2(n), \ldots, t_n(n))) = \mathcal{O}(\max(g(n) \log_c n, t_1(n), t_2(n), \ldots, t_n(n)))$. The space complexity, on the other hand, will depend on the number of agents created and the space complexity of tuning and aggregation algorithms. In the worst case, the hierarchical structure is full, and the total number of agents will be $\mathcal{N} = \sum_{j=1}^{\log_c n} c^j = \frac{1-nc}{1-c}$. Among all the agents, the internal ones will use a fixed amount of space for internal hourse keeping operations. Therefore, assuming $t'_i(n)$ and $g'(n)$ to be

Algorithm 1: Distributed formation of the hierarchical agent-based hyper-parameter tuning structure, and the iterated hierarchical tuning of the hyper-parameters.

```
Function START(⟨A_λ, {λ̂_o, λ̂'_o, λ_f}, V, {X^(train), X^(valid)}, L⟩, c):
    if |λ̂_o| = 1 then                                    ▷ agent is terminal
        R ←PREPARERESOURCES(⟨{λ̂_o, λ̂'_o, λ_f}, {X^(train), X^(valid)}⟩)
        INFORM(Parent, R)                                 ▷ informs the parent agent
    else                                                  ▷ agent is internal (|λ̂_o| > 1)
        k ← min(c, |λ̂_o|, MyBudget)                       ▷ the number of children
        for i ← 1 to k do
            T_i ← SPAWNORCONNECT(A_λ, L)
            λ̂_{o_i} ←DIVIDE(λ̂_o, i, k)                    ▷ the i^th unique devision
            λ̂'_{o_i} ← (λ̂_o − λ̂_{o_i}) ∪ λ̂'_o
            R_i ←ASK(T_i, START,
                    ⟨A_λ, {λ̂_{o_i}, λ̂'_{o_i}, λ_f}, V, {X^(train), X^(valid)}, L⟩, c)
        end
        R ←AGGREGATE({R_i}_i)                             ▷ combines children's answers
        if Parent ≠ ∅ then
            INFORM(Parent, R)
        else
            F ← PREPAREFEEDBACK(R, V)
            TUNE(F)                                       ▷ initiates the tuning process
        end
    end
end
Function TUNE(F):
    if Children = ∅ then
        R^(*) ←RUNTUNINGALGORITHM(F)                      ▷ single-agent tuning
        INFORM(Parent, R^(*))
    else
        foreach T_i ∈ Children do
            R_i^(*) ←ASK(T_i, TUNE, F_i)
        end
        R^(*) ←AGGREGATERESULTS({R_i^(*)}_i)              ▷ combines results
        if Parent ≠ ∅ then                                ▷ non-root internal agent
            INFORM(Parent, R^(*))
        else
            if SHOULDSTOP(StopCriteria)≠ True then
                F ← PREPAREFEEDBACK(R^(*))
                TUNE(F)                                   ▷ initiates next tuning iteration
            else
                PREPAREREPORT(R^(*))                      ▷ reports final result
            end
        end
    end
end
```

the space cost of terminal agent $\mathcal{T}_i$'s tuning algorithm and the result aggregation procedure, respectively, the time complexity of the proposed model will be $\mathcal{O}(\max(n.g'(n), t_1'(n), t_2'(n), \ldots, t_n'(n)))$.

2.2 Guided Randomized Agent-Based Tuning Algorithm

This section presents a multi-level randomized tuning technique – we refer to it as Guided Randomized Agent-based Tuning (GRAT) – not only to demonstrate how the generic model can be used in practice, but also to empirically analyze its performance and behavior.

Terminal agents' tuning strategy and internal agents' aggregation and feedback preparation techniques are the most important things to specify designing any tuning process based on the previously presented general model. The tuning strategy that we propose in this section is based on the randomized searching method that is widely used in practice. We have chosen this approach as the base strategy because of its broad usage as a baseline method in the literature and its natural parallelization capabilities. Furthermore, we assume that all terminal agents are homogeneous in the sense that they implement the same tuning algorithm.

For the sake of clarity, we explain the used aggregation and feedback preparation operations before delving into the details of the used tuning strategy. According to line 24 of Algorithm 1, each terminal agent returns optimal result it finds for each hyper-parameter. Let such result defined as $\mathcal{R}_i^{(*)} = \{(\lambda_j, \mathcal{V}_j^{(*)}, \Psi_j^{(*)})\}$, where $\Psi_j^{(*)}$ denotes the response function value of sub-optimal hyper-parameter values $\mathcal{V}_j^{(*)}$ tuned by terminal agent $\mathcal{T}_j$. Receiving all the sub-optimal value sets from the subordinates, the inner agents of GRAT then aggregates the results by simply applying set union operator $\bigcup_{\mathcal{T}_i \in Children} \mathcal{R}_i^{(*)}$.

The bottom-up aggregation process continues until the results reach the root node, where the feedback for the next iteration is prepared. Let $\{(\lambda_i, \mathcal{V}_i^{(*)}, \Psi_i^{(*)}); 1 \leq i \leq n\}$ be the set of all results merged and received by the root node. For each objective hyper-parameter $\lambda_i \in \hat{\lambda}_o$ in a minimization task, the root agent assigns the sub-optimal values corresponding the minimum response function value, $\Psi_j^{(*)}$, of all the ones found by the terminal agents representing other hyper-parameters, $j \neq i$. That is:

$$\text{PREPAREFEEDBACK}(\{(\lambda_i, \mathcal{V}_i^{(*)}, \Psi_i^{(*)})\}) = \left\{ (\lambda_i, \mathcal{V}_j); j = \underset{1 \leq j \neq i \leq n}{\arg\min} \Psi_j^{(*)} \right\} \quad (4)$$

The feedback will be split and propagated recursively until it reaches the terminal agents. Let $\mathcal{F}_i = \mathcal{V}_j$ be the feedback received by agent $\mathcal{T}_i$. Starting from the location specified by $\mathcal{F}_i$, the agent follows the steps in Algorithm 2 to locate a hyper-parameter values that yield $\Psi(\lambda)$ that is relatively lower than the one for the starting values. To do the search, GRAT divides the domain of real-value $\hat{\lambda}_o = \lambda_i$ into a pre-specified number of slots, η_i, and uniformly chooses a value in each. For the remaining hyper-parameters, it chooses either the same value specified by $\mathcal{F}_i$ or a new one depending on a weight factor, $\omega_i \in \mathbb{Z}^+$, and whether the hyper-parameter belongs to $\hat{\lambda}'_o$ or λ_f.

Algorithm 2: Guided Randomized Agent-based Tuning (GRAT) process.

```
1  Function RunTuningAlgorithm(𝓕 = 𝒱_i):
2      𝒱[0] ← 𝒱_i
3      for s ← 1 to s = η do
4          𝒱[s](λ_i) ← UniformRand(λ_i, η, s)
5          forall λ_k ∈ λ − λ_i do
6              if λ_k ∈ λ̂_o then
7                  𝒱[s](λ_k) ← WeightedRand(λ_k, ω)
8              else
9                  𝒱[s](λ_k) ← 𝒱(λ_f)
10             end
11         end
12     end
13     𝒱^(*) ← arg min_{0≤j≤η} Ψ(𝒱[j])
14     return {(λ_i, 𝒱^(*), Ψ(𝒱^(*)))}
15 end
```

Similar to the previous algorithms, the functions' and variables' names are chosen to be self-explanatory. Function UniformRand in line 4 chooses a random value in the sth slot based on the uniform distribution. In case the domain of λ_i is discrete, e.g. in nominal type hyper-parameters, the function samples the values without replacement. In our implementation for function WeightedRand in line 7, we assume similar η slots for the real type hyper-parameters and choose the current value $\mathcal{V}[0](\lambda_k)$ with weight ω or a value in other slots with weight 1. In such formulation, the probabilities of choosing the value of the feedback set and a random value in any other slots will be $\frac{\omega}{\omega+(\eta-1)}$ and $\frac{1}{\omega+(\eta-1)}$ respectively. Depending on the improvements, the root agent might adjusts the weight through iterations to induce exploration in agents' searching process. Figure 2 provides a toy example to briefly demonstrate 3 iterations of GRAT.

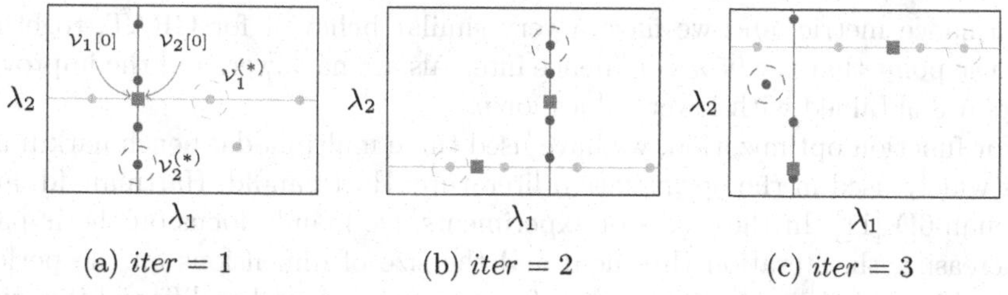

Fig. 2. A toy example demonstrating 3 iteration of running GRAT on two hyper-parameters λ_1, and λ_2 using red and blue terminal agents respectively. In this example, we have assumed $\eta = 4$ (Color figure online)

3 Results and Discussion

This section presents the empirical results of using GRAT for both hyper-parameter tuning and function optimization use cases. In all of the experiments, we have assumed that $c = 2$ and agents' *budget* $= \infty$. We have assessed the behavior of our model based on different metrics and compared the results with the ones from normal and latine hyper-cube randomized methods. To make the comparisons fair, in all experimental settings, we have fixed the total number of evaluations for both randomized methods to $c \times \eta \times \mathcal{I}$. All experiments have been carried out on a desktop with Intel Core-i5 @ 1.6GHz CPU and 16 GB RAM running Ubuntu 20.04 OS and Python 3.7. Additionally, all the used ML resources are from scikit-learn library [19], and the results reported in both ML and function optimization experiments are averaged over 100 trials.

In ML hyper-parameter tuning use case, we have chosen C-Support Vector Classification(SVC) [6] and Logistic Regression (LR) algorithms on two synthetic datasets of size 100 with 2 classes and 20 features, both generated by scikit-learn's make_classification tool [19]. The ML experiments focuses on studying the behavior of GRAT at different number of randomized points that terminal agents are allowed to evaluate, i.e. η. For SVC we have set $\lambda_1 = C \sim logUniform(10^{-2}, 10^{13}), \lambda_2 = \gamma \sim Uniform(0, 1), \lambda_3 = kernel \in \{poly, linear, rbf, sigmoid\}, \mathcal{I} = 15$. Similarly, for LR we have $\lambda_1 = C \sim logUniform(10^{-2}, 10^{13}), \lambda_2 = solver \in \{newtoncg, linear, lbfgs, liblinear\}, \mathcal{I} = 5$, where C and *solver* are respectively the inverse of regularization strength and LR's optimization algorithm. In all of the experiments, we have used 5-fold cross validation with stratified sampling as the model evaluation method. Figure 3 depicts the results obtained in each classification task, along side the average value of the last best iteration count – any increase in the iteration count beyond this value has not improved the performance. In SVC, we have used mean squared error (MSE) to measure the performance and as it can be seen, GRAT has outperformed the other two methods in almost all η values, while the model evaluation counts for all methods is the same. Furthermore, with an increase in η, we observe a decrease the number of iterations needed to find the improved performance. LR also uses MSE as the performance metric, and we have a very similar behavior for GRAT, together with the point that the 95% confidence intervals are narrower, and the improved values are obtained with lower values for η.

For function optimization, we have used three multi-modal benchmark functions widely used in the optimization literature: Hartman-3d, Hartman-4d, and Hartman-6D [11]. In these sets of experiments, we mainly focus on the impact of increasing the iteration threshold and the size of dimensions on the performance. Figure 4 illustrates the average function values found at different iteration thresholds. In all of the experiments, we have fixed the value of η to 10. As it can be seen in, the average function values that have been found by GRAT are less (better) than the other two methods – this is a minimization problem. Furthermore, a careful look at the plots reveal that the improvements of the results are significantly more when the number of dimension, i.e. the number of the parameters that we optimize, increases from 3 to 4 and then to 6.

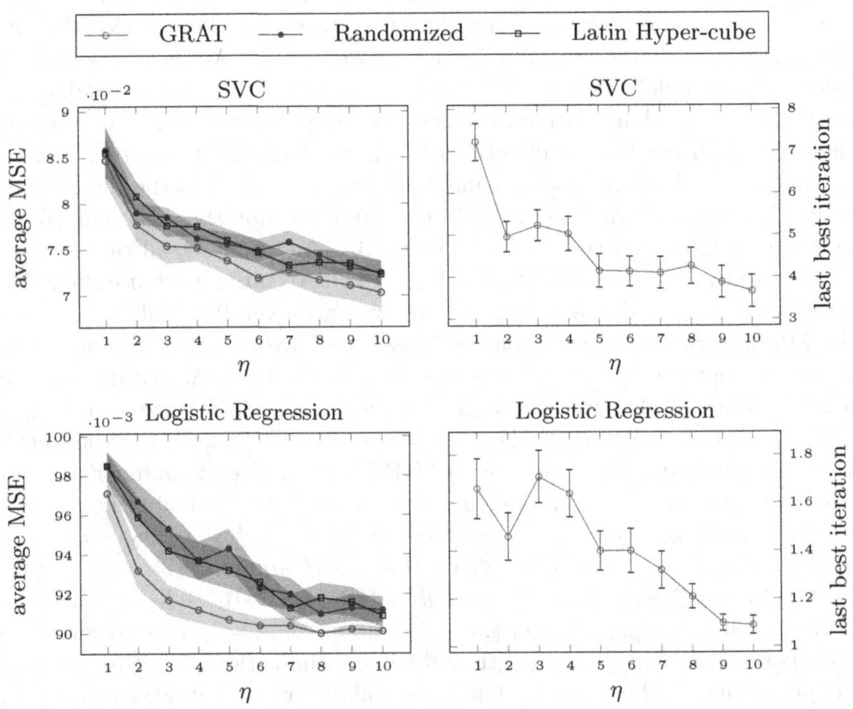

Fig. 3. Average performance of SVC (first row) and Logistic Regression (second row) classifiers on two synthetic classification datasets based on mean squared error and the last best iteration number. The color bands on the left column plots represent 95% confidence interval, and the error bars on the right column plots are calculated based on the standard error

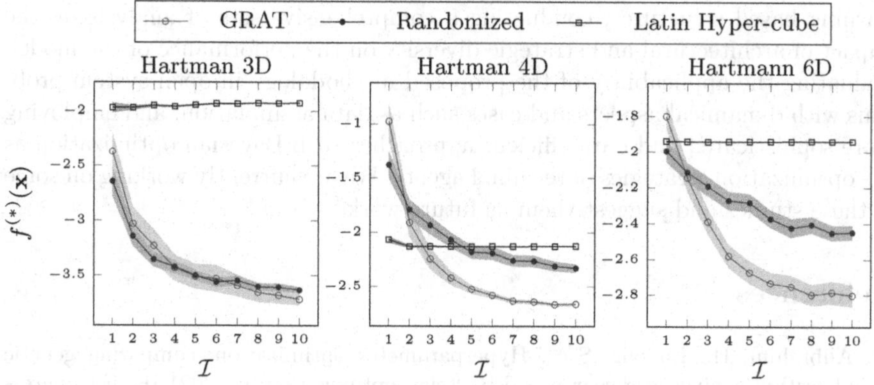

Fig. 4. Optimal function value, $f^{(*)}(\mathbf{x})$, vs iteration threshold $\mathcal{I}$, averaged over 100 different experiments. The plots include 95% confidence interval bands of the results

It is worth noting that the goal in these sets of experiments are not to compete with the state-of-art hyper-parameter tuning and function optimization methods but to demonstrate how our proposed model can be used to develop distributed tuning/optimization techniques and how effective it is in comparison to the baseline methods. We believe our core model is capable of providing competitive results provided with more sophisticated and carefully chosen tuning strategies and corresponding configurations.

4 Conclusion

In this paper we presented a hierarchical multi-agent based model for machine learning hyper-parameter tuning and function optimization. The presented model includes a two-phase procedure to distributively form the hierarchical structure and collaboratively tune/optimize the hyper-parameters. Using its flexible configuration, our proposed generic approach supports the development of solutions that comprise diverse sets of tuning strategies, computational resources, and cooperation techniques, and we successfully showed how it can be used in practice for both ML hyper-parameter tuning and global function optimization tasks. For the sake of evaluation, this paper presented analytical discussion on the computational complexities and implemented a basic guided randomized agent based tuning technique, called GRAT. The empirical results, obtained from both ML classification and multi-modal function optimization use cases, showed the success of the suggested collaborative model in improving the performance of the underlying tuning strategies, especially in higher dimension problems.

This paper provided the foundations and a basic implementation for a novel agent-based distributed hyper-parameter tuning model. Despite its demonstrated success in small size problems, the research can be extended in various directions such as investigating its behavior and performance in large scaled deep learning based structures, conducting a comprehensive sets of analysis on the impact of architectural and strategic diversity on the performance of the model, evaluating the applicability of the proposed methodology in open system problems with dynamical aspects and cases such as data assimilation, and employing more sophisticated and data-efficient approaches such Bayesian optimization as the optimization strategies of terminal agents. We are currently working on some of these studies and suggest them as future work.

References

1. Alibrahim, H., Ludwig, S.A.: Hyperparameter optimization: comparing genetic algorithm against grid search and Bayesian optimization. In: 2021 IEEE Congress on Evolutionary Computation (CEC), pp. 1551–1559 (2021)
2. Bardenet, R., Brendel, M., Kégl, B., Sebag, M.: Collaborative hyperparameter tuning. In: International Conference on Machine Learning, pp. 199–207. PMLR (2013)
3. Bellman, R.E.: Adaptive Control Processes. Princeton University Press (1961)
4. Bergstra, J., Bengio, Y.: Random search for hyper-parameter optimization. J. Mach. Learn. Res. **13**(2) (2012)
5. Bischl, B., Mersmann, O., Trautmann, H., Weihs, C.: Resampling methods for meta-model validation with recommendations for evolutionary computation. Evol. Comput. **20**(2), 249–275 (2012)
6. Chang, C.C., Lin, C.J.: LIBSVM: a library for support vector machines. ACM Trans. Intell. Syst. Technol. (TIST) **2**(3), 1–27 (2011)
7. Esmaeili, A., Mozayani, N.: Adjusting the parameters of radial basis function networks using particle swarm optimization. In: 2009 IEEE International Conference on Computational Intelligence for Measurement Systems and Applications, pp. 179–181. IEEE (2009)
8. Esmaeili, A., Gallagher, J.C., Springer, J.A., Matson, E.T.: HAMLET: a hierarchical agent-based machine learning platform. ACM Trans. Auton. Adapt. Syst. **16** (2022). http://orcid.org/10.1145/3530191
9. Feurer, M., Hutter, F.: Hyperparameter optimization. In: Hutter, F., Kotthoff, L., Vanschoren, J. (eds.) Automated Machine Learning. TSSCML, pp. 3–33. Springer, Cham (2019). https://doi.org/10.1007/978-3-030-05318-5_1
10. Iranfar, A., Zapater, M., Atienza, D.: Multi-agent reinforcement learning for hyperparameter optimization of convolutional neural networks. IEEE Trans. Comput.-Aided Des. Integr. Circuits Syst. **41**, 1034–1047 (2021)
11. Jamil, M., Yang, X.S.: A literature survey of benchmark functions for global optimisation problems. Int. J. Math. Model. Numer. Optimisation **4**(2), 150 (2013). https://doi.org/10.1504/ijmmno.2013.055204
12. John, G.H.: Cross-validated C4.5: using error estimation for automatic parameter selection. Technical report (1994)
13. Koch, P., Golovidov, O., Gardner, S., Wujek, B., Griffin, J., Xu, Y.: Autotune: a derivative-free optimization framework for hyperparameter tuning. In: Proceedings of the 24th ACM SIGKDD International Conference on Knowledge Discovery & Data Mining, pp. 443–452 (2018)
14. Kohavi, R., John, G.H.: Automatic parameter selection by minimizing estimated error. In: Machine Learning Proceedings 1995, pp. 304–312. Elsevier (1995)

15. Močkus, J.: On Bayesian methods for seeking the extremum. In: Marchuk, G.I. (ed.) Optimization Techniques 1974. LNCS, vol. 27, pp. 400–404. Springer, Heidelberg (1975). https://doi.org/10.1007/3-540-07165-2_55
16. Mockus, J.: Bayesian Approach to Global Optimization: Theory and Applications, vol. 37. Springer, Heidelberg (2012)
17. Montgomery, D.C.: Design and Analysis of Experiments. Wiley, Hoboken (2017)
18. Parker-Holder, J., Nguyen, V., Roberts, S.J.: Provably efficient online hyperparameter optimization with population-based bandits. In: Advances in Neural Information Processing Systems, vol. 33, pp. 17200–17211 (2020)
19. Pedregosa, F., et al.: Scikit-learn: machine learning in Python. J. Mach. Learn. Res. **12**, 2825–2830 (2011)
20. Ryzko, D.: Modern Big Data Architectures: A Multi-agent Systems Perspective. Wiley, Hoboken (2020)
21. Simon, D.: Evolutionary Optimization Algorithms. Wiley, Hoboken (2013)
22. Swearingen, T., Drevo, W., Cyphers, B., Cuesta-Infante, A., Ross, A., Veeramachaneni, K.: ATM: a distributed, collaborative, scalable system for automated machine learning. In: 2017 IEEE International Conference on Big Data (Big Data), pp. 151–162. IEEE (2017)

Towards the Combination of Model Checking and Runtime Verification on Multi-agent Systems

Angelo Ferrando[1(✉)] and Vadim Malvone[2(✉)]

[1] University of Genova, Genova, Italy
angelo.ferrando@unige.it
[2] Télécom Paris, Paris, France
vadim.malvone@telecom-paris.fr

Abstract. Multi-Agent Systems (MAS) are notoriously complex and hard to verify. In fact, it is not trivial to model a MAS, and even when a model is built, it is not always possible to verify, in a formal way, that it is actually behaving as we expect. Usually, it is relevant to know whether an agent is capable of fulfilling its own goals. One possible way to check this is through Model Checking. Specifically, by verifying Alternating-time Temporal Logic (ATL) properties, where the notion of strategies for achieving goals can be described. Unfortunately, the resulting model checking problem is not decidable in general. In this paper, we present a verification procedure based on combining Model Checking and Runtime Verification, where sub-models of the MAS model belonging to decidable fragments are verified by a model checker, and runtime monitors are used to verify the rest. We present our technique and show experimental results.

Keywords: Model checking · Runtime verification · Strategic reasoning

1 Introduction

Intelligent systems, such as Multi-Agent Systems (MAS), can be seen as a set of intelligent entities capable of proactively decide how to act to fulfill their own goals. These entities, called generally agents, are notoriously autonomous, *i.e.*, they do not expect input from a user to act, and social, *i.e.*, they usually communicate amongst each other to achieve common goals.

Software systems are not easy to trust in general. Because of this, we need verification techniques to verify that such systems behave as expected. More specifically, in the case of MAS, it is relevant to know whether the agents are capable of achieving their own goals, by themselves or by collaborating with other agents by forming a coalition. This is usually referred to as the process of finding a strategy for the agent(s).

A well-known formalism for reasoning about strategic behaviours in MAS is Alternating-time Temporal Logic (ATL) [1]. Before verifying ATL specifications, two questions need to be answered: (i) *does each agent know everything about the system?* (ii) *does the property require the agent to have memory of the system?* The first question

© The Author(s), under exclusive license to Springer Nature Switzerland AG 2022
F. Dignum et al. (Eds.): PAAMS 2022, LNAI 13616, pp. 140–152, 2022.
https://doi.org/10.1007/978-3-031-18192-4_12

concerns the model of the MAS. If each agent can distinguish each state of the model, then we have *perfect information*; otherwise, we have *imperfect information*. The second question concerns the ATL property. If the property can be verified without the need for the agent to remember which states of the model have been visited before, then we have *imperfect recall*; otherwise, we have *perfect recall*.

The model checking problem for ATL giving a generic MAS is known to be undecidable. This is due to the fact that the model checking problem for ATL specifications under imperfect information and perfect recall has been proved to be undecidable [12]. Nonetheless, decidable fragments exist. Indeed, model checking ATL under perfect information is PTIME-complete [1], while under imperfect information and imperfect recall is PSPACE [23]. Unfortunately, MAS usually have imperfect information, and when memory is needed to achieve the goals, the resulting model checking problem becomes undecidable. Given the relevance of the imperfect information setting, even partial solutions to the problem are useful.

Given an ATL formula φ and a model of MAS M, our procedure extracts all the sub-models of M with perfect information that satisfy a sub-formula of φ. Then, runtime monitors are used to check if the remaining part of φ can be satisfied at execution time. If this is the case, we conclude at runtime the satisfaction of φ for the corresponding system execution. Note that, this does not imply that the system satisfies φ, indeed future executions may violate φ. The formal result over φ only concerns the current execution, and how it has behaved in it. However, we will present preservation results on the initial model checking problem of φ on the model of the system M, as well.

Related Work. Several approaches for the verification of specifications in ATL and ATL^* under imperfect information and perfect recall have been recently put forward. In one line, restrictions are made on how information is shared amongst the agents, so as to retain decidability [10,11]. In a related line, interactions amongst agents are limited to public actions only [6,7]. These approaches are markedly different from ours as they seek to identify classes for which verification is decidable. Instead, we consider the whole class of iCGS and define a general verification procedure. In this sense, existing approaches to approximate ATL model checking under imperfect information and perfect recall have either focused on an approximation to perfect information [5,8] or developed notions of bounded recall [4].

Differently from these works, we introduce, for the first time, a technique that couples model checking and runtime verification to provide results. Furthermore, we always concludes with a result. Note that the problem is undecidable in general, thus the result might be inconclusive (but it is always returned). When the result is inconclusive for the whole formula, we present sub-results to give at least the maximum information about the satisfaction/violation of the formula under exam.

Runtime Verification (RV) has never been used before in a strategic context, where monitors check whether a coalition of agents satisfies a strategic property. This can be obtained by combining Model Checking on MAS with RV. The combination of Model Checking with RV is not new [17]; even though focused only on LTL. Instead, in here, we focus on strategic properties, such as ATL^*. Because of this, our work is closer in spirit to [17]; in fact, we use RV to support Model Checking in verifying at runtime what the model checker could not at static time. Finally, in [14], a demonstration paper presenting the tool deriving by this work may be found. Specifically, in this paper we present the theoretical foundations and experimental results behind the tool.

2 Preliminaries

In this section we recall some preliminary notions. Given a set U, $\overline{U}$ denotes its complement. We denote the length of a tuple v as $|v|$, and its i-th element as v_i. For $i \leq |v|$, let $v_{\geq i}$ be the suffix $v_i, \ldots, v_{|v|}$ of v starting at v_i and $v_{\leq i}$ the prefix $v_1, \ldots, v_i$ of v. We denote with $v \cdot w$ the concatenation of the tuples v and w.

2.1 Models for Multi-agent Systems

We start by giving a formal model for Multi-agent Systems by means of concurrent game structures with imperfect information [1,18].

Definition 1. *A* concurrent game structure with imperfect information (iCGS) *is a tuple* $M = \langle Ag, AP, S, s_I, \{Act_i\}_{i \in Ag}, \{\sim_i\}_{i \in Ag}, d, \delta, V\rangle$ *such that:* $Ag = \{1, \ldots, m\}$ *is a nonempty finite set of agents (or players);* AP *is a nonempty finite set of atomic propositions (atoms);* $S \neq \emptyset$ *is a finite set of* states, *with* initial state $s_I \in S$*; for every* $i \in Ag$*,* Act_i *is a nonempty finite set of* actions *where* $Act = \bigcup_{i \in Ag} Act_i$ *is the set of all actions and* $ACT = \prod_{i \in Ag} Act_i$ *is the set of all joint actions; for every* $i \in Ag$*,* $\sim_i$ *is a relation of* indistinguishability *between states, that is, given states* $s, s' \in S$*,* $s \sim_i s'$ *iff* s *and* s' *are observationally indistinguishable for agent* i*; the* protocol function $d : Ag \times S \to (2^{Act} \setminus \emptyset)$ *defines the availability of actions so that for every* $i \in Ag$*,* $s \in S$*, (i)* $d(i, s) \subseteq Act_i$ *and (ii)* $s \sim_i s'$ *implies* $d(i, s) = d(i, s')$*; the* (deterministic) transition function $\delta : S \times ACT \to S$ *assigns a successor state* $s' = \delta(s, \vec{a})$ *to each state* $s \in S$*, for every joint action* $\vec{a} \in ACT$ *such that* $a_i \in d(i, s)$ *for every* $i \in Ag$*, that is,* $\vec{a}$ *is* enabled *at* s*; and* $V : S \to 2^{AP}$ *is the* labelling function.

By Definition 1 an iCGS describes the interactions of a group Ag of agents, starting from the initial state $s_I \in S$, according to the transition function δ. The latter is constrained by the availability of actions to agents, as specified by the protocol function d. Furthermore, we assume that every agent i has imperfect information of the exact state of the system; so in any state s, i considers epistemically possible all states s' that are i-indistinguishable from s [13]. When every $\sim_i$ is the identity relation, *i.e.*, $s \sim_i s'$ iff $s = s'$, we obtain a standard CGS with perfect information [1]. Given a set $\Gamma \subseteq Ag$ of agents and a joint action $\vec{a} \in ACT$, let $\vec{a}_\Gamma$ and $\vec{a}_{\overline{\Gamma}}$ be two tuples comprising only of actions for the agents in Γ and $\overline{\Gamma}$, respectively. A history $h \in S^+$ is a finite (non-empty) sequence of states. The indistinguishability relations are extended to histories in a synchronous, point-wise way, *i.e.*, histories $h, h' \in S^+$ are *indistinguishable* for agent $i \in Ag$, or $h \sim_i h'$, iff (i) $|h| = |h'|$ and (ii) for all $j \leq |h|$, $h_j \sim_i h'_j$.

2.2 Syntax

To reason about the strategic abilities of agents in iCGS with imperfect information, we use Alternating-time Temporal Logic ATL^* [1].

Definition 2. *State (φ) and path (ψ) formulas in ATL^* are defined as follows, where $q \in AP$ and $\Gamma \subseteq Ag$:*

$$\varphi ::= q \mid \neg\varphi \mid \varphi \wedge \varphi \mid \langle\langle\Gamma\rangle\rangle\psi$$
$$\psi ::= \varphi \mid \neg\psi \mid \psi \wedge \psi \mid X\psi \mid (\psi U \psi)$$

Formulas in ATL^* are all and only the state formulas.

As customary, a formula $\langle\langle\Gamma\rangle\rangle\Phi$ is read as "the agents in coalition Γ have a strategy to achieve Φ". The meaning of linear-time operators *next* X and *until* U is standard [2]. Operators $[\![\Gamma]\!]$, *release* R, *finally* F, and *globally* G can be introduced as usual. Formulas in the ATL fragment of ATL^* are obtained from Definition 2 by restricting path formulas ψ as follows (where φ is a state formula and R is the *release* operator):

$$\psi ::= X\varphi \mid (\varphi U \varphi) \mid (\varphi R \varphi)$$

We will also consider the syntax of ATL* in negation normal form (NNF):

$$\varphi ::= q \mid \neg q \mid \varphi \wedge \varphi \mid \varphi \vee \varphi \mid \langle\langle\Gamma\rangle\rangle\psi \mid [\![\Gamma]\!]\psi$$
$$\psi ::= \varphi \mid \psi \wedge \psi \mid \psi \vee \psi \mid X\psi \mid (\psi U \psi) \mid (\psi R \psi)$$

where $q \in AP$ and $\Gamma \subseteq Ag$.

2.3 Semantics

When giving a semantics to ATL^* formulas we assume agents are endowed with *uniform strategies* [18], *i.e.*, they perform the same action whenever they have the same information.

Definition 3. *A* uniform strategy *for agent $i \in Ag$ is a function $\sigma_i : S^+ \to Act_i$ such that for all histories $h, h' \in S^+$, (i) $\sigma_i(h) \in d(i, last(h))$; and (ii) $h \sim_i h'$ implies $\sigma_i(h) = \sigma_i(h')$.*

By Definition 3 any strategy for agent i has to return actions that are enabled for i. Also, whenever two histories are indistinguishable for i, then the same action is returned. Notice that, for the case of CGS (perfect information), condition (ii) is satisfied by any strategy σ. Furthermore, we obtain memoryless (or imperfect recall) strategies by considering the domain of σ_i in S, *i.e.*, $\sigma_i : S \to Act_i$.

Given an iCGS M, a *path* $p \in S^\omega$ is an infinite sequence $s_1 s_2 \ldots$ of states. Given a joint strategy $\sigma_\Gamma = \{\sigma_i \mid i \in \Gamma\}$, comprising of one strategy for each agent in coalition Γ, a path p is *σ_Γ-compatible* iff for every $j \geq 1$, $p_{j+1} = \delta(p_j, \vec{a})$ for some joint action $\vec{a}$ such that for every $i \in \Gamma$, $a_i = \sigma_i(p_{\leq j})$, and for every $i \in \overline{\Gamma}$, $a_i \in d(i, p_j)$. Let $out(s, \sigma_\Gamma)$ be the set of all σ_Γ-compatible paths from s.

Definition 4. *The satisfaction relation $\models$ for an iCGS M, state $s \in S$, path $p \in S^\omega$, atom $q \in AP$, and ATL^* formula ϕ is defined as follows (clauses for Boolean connectives are immediate and thus omitted):*

$(M, s) \models q$ iff $q \in V(s)$
$(M, s) \models \langle\langle \Gamma \rangle\rangle \psi$ iff for some σ_Γ, for all $p \in out(s, \sigma_\Gamma)$, $(M, p) \models \psi$
$(M, p) \models \varphi$ iff $(M, p_1) \models \varphi$
$(M, p) \models X\psi$ iff $(M, p_{\geq 2}) \models \psi$
$(M, p) \models \psi U \psi'$ iff for some $k \geq 1$, $(M, p_{\geq k}) \models \psi'$, and for all $1 \leq j < k \Rightarrow (M, p_{\geq j}) \models \psi$

We say that formula ϕ is *true* in an iCGS M, or $M \models \phi$, iff $(M, s_I) \models \phi$.

Definition 5. *Given an iCGS M and a formula ϕ, the model checking problem concerns determining whether $M \models \phi$.*

Since the semantics provided in Definition 4 is the standard interpretation of ATL^* [1, 18], it is well known that model checking ATL, *a fortiori* ATL^*, against iCGS with imperfect information and perfect recall is undecidable [12]. In the rest of the paper we develop methods to obtain partial solutions to this by using Runtime Verification (RV).

2.4 Runtime Verification and Monitors

The standard formalism to specify formal properties in RV is Linear Temporal Logic (LTL) [21]. The syntax and semantics of LTL is the same of ATL^* (Definition 2–4), with state formulas $\varphi ::= q$ (*i.e.*, no strategic operators are allowed).

Definition 6 (Monitor). *Let M be an iCGS and ψ be an LTL property. Then, a monitor for ψ is a function $Mon_\psi^M : S^+ \rightarrow \mathbb{B}_3$, where $\mathbb{B}_3 = \{\top, \bot, ?\}$:*

$$Mon_\psi^M(h) = \begin{cases} \top & \forall_{p \in S^\omega} \ (M, h \cdot p) \models \psi \\ \bot & \forall_{p \in S^\omega} \ (M, h \cdot p) \not\models \psi \\ ? & otherwise. \end{cases}$$

where the path p is a valid continuation of the history h in M.

Intuitively, a monitor returns $\top$ if all continuations of h satisfy ψ; $\bot$ if all continuations of h violate ψ; ? otherwise. The first two outcomes are standard representations of satisfaction and violation, while the third is specific to RV. In more detail, it denotes when the monitor cannot conclude any verdict yet. This is closely related to the fact that RV is applied while the system is still running, and not all information about it are available. For instance, a property might be currently satisfied (resp., violated) by the system, but violated (resp., satisfied) in the (still unknown) future. The monitor can only safely conclude any of the two final verdicts ($\top$ or $\bot$) if it is sure such verdict will never change. The addition of the third outcome symbol ? helps the monitor to represent its uncertainty w.r.t. the current system execution.

2.5 Negative and Positive Sub-models

Now, we recall two definitions of sub-models and some preservation results, defined in [15], that we will use in our verification procedure.

Definition 7 (Negative and Positive sub-models). *Given an iCGS* $M = \langle Ag, AP, S, s_I, \{Act_i\}_{i \in Ag}, \{\sim_i\}_{i \in Ag}, d, \delta, V \rangle$, *we denote with* $M' = \langle Ag, AP, S', s_I, \{Act_i\}_{i \in Ag}, \{\sim'_i\}_{i \in Ag}, d', \delta', V' \rangle$ *a negative sub-model of* M, *formally* $M' \subseteq M$, *such that:* $S' = S^\star \cup \{s_t\}$, *where* $S^\star \subseteq S$ *and* $s_I \in S^\star$; $\sim'_i$ *is defined as the corresponding* $\sim_i$ *restricted to* $S^\star$; *the protocol function is defined as* $d'(i,s) = d(i,s)$, *for every* $s \in S^\star$ *and* $d'(i, s_t) = Act_i$, *for all* $i \in Ag$; *given a transition* $\delta(s, \vec{a}) = s'$, *if* $s, s' \in S^\star$ *then* $\delta'(s, \vec{a}) = \delta(s, \vec{a}) = s'$ *else if* $s' \in S \setminus S^\star$ *and* $s \in S'$ *then* $\delta'(s, \vec{a}) = s_t$; *for all* $s \in S^\star$, $V'(s) = V(s)$ *and* $V'(s_t) = \emptyset$. *Furthermore, we denote with* $M^* = \langle Ag, AP, S', s_I, \{Act_i\}_{i \in Ag}, \{\sim'_i\}_{i \in Ag}, d', \delta', V^* \rangle$ *a positive sub-model of* M, *formally* $M^* \subseteq M$, *such that:* $V^*(s) = V(s)$ *and* $V^*(s_t) = AP$.

The intuition behind the above sub-models is to remove the imperfect information by replacing each state involved in $\sim$ with a sink state s_t that under (resp., over) approximates the verification of ATL formulas in negative (resp., positive) sub-models. We conclude this part by recalling two preservation results presented in [15].

Lemma 1. *Given a model* M, *a negative (resp., positive) sub-model with perfect information* M' *(resp.,* M^**) of* M, *and a formula* φ *of the form* $\varphi = \langle\langle A \rangle\rangle \psi$ *(or* $[\![A]\!]\psi$*) for some* $A \subseteq Ag$. *For any* $s \in S' \setminus \{s_t\}$, *we have that:*

$$M', s \models \varphi \Rightarrow M, s \models \varphi \qquad\qquad M^*, s \not\models \varphi \Rightarrow M, s \not\models \varphi$$

3 Our Procedure

In this section, we provide a procedure to handle games with imperfect information and perfect recall strategies, a problem in general undecidable. The overall model checking procedure is described in Algorithm 1. It takes in input a model M, a formula φ, and a trace h (denoting an execution of the system) and calls the function $Preprocessing()$ to generate the NNF of φ and to replace all negated atoms with new positive atoms inside M and φ. After that, it calls the function $FindSub\text{-}models()$ to generate all the positive and negative sub-models that represent all the possible sub-models with perfect information of M. Then, there is a while loop (lines 4–7) that for each candidate checks the sub-formulas true on the sub-models via $CheckSub\text{-}formulas()$ and returns a result via $RuntimeVerification()$. For additional details on $Preprocessing()$, $FindSub\text{-}models()$, and $CheckSub\text{-}formulas()$ see [15].

Now, we focus on the last step, the procedure $RuntimeVerification()$. It is performed at runtime, directly on the actual system. In previous steps, the sub-models satisfying (resp., violating) sub-properties φ' of φ are generated, and listed into the set $result$. In Algorithm 2, we report the procedure performing runtime verification on the system. Such algorithm gets in input the model M, an ATL property φ to verify, an execution trace h of events observed by executing the system, and the set $result$ containing the sub-properties of φ that have been checked on sub-models of M. First, in lines 2–3, M and φ are updated according to the atoms listed in $result$. This step is used to identify in M and φ which sub-formulas have already been verified through $CheckSub\text{-}formulas()$. The two resulting functions are not reported for space constraints, but their full description can be found in [15]. Note that, $UpdateFormula()$

Algorithm 1. $ModelCheckingProcedure\ (M, \varphi, h)$

1: $Preprocessing(M, \varphi)$;
2: $candidates = FindSub\text{-}models(M, \varphi)$;
3: $finalresult = \emptyset$;
4: **while** $candidates$ is not empty **do**
5: extract $\langle M_n, M_p \rangle$ from $candidates$;
6: $result = CheckSub\text{-}formulas(\langle M_n, M_p \rangle, \varphi)$;
7: $finalresult = RuntimeVerification(M, \varphi, h, result) \cup finalresult$;
8: **return** $finalresult$;

produces two new ATL formulas (ψ_n, ψ_p), which correspond to the updated version of φ for the negative and positive sub-models, respectively. Once ψ_n and ψ_p have been generated, they need to be converted into their corresponding LTL representation to be verified at runtime. This translation is obtained by removing the strategic operators, while leaving the temporal ones (and the atoms). The resulting two new LTL properties φ_n and φ_p are so obtained (lines 4–5). Finally, by having these two LTL properties, the algorithm proceeds generating (using the standard LTL monitor generation algorithm [3]) the corresponding monitors $Mon_{\varphi_n}^{M'}$ and $Mon_{\varphi_p}^{M'}$. Such monitors are then used by Algorithm 2 to check φ_n and φ_p over an execution trace h given in input. The latter consists in a trace observed by executing the system modelled by M' (so, the actual system). Analysing h the monitor can conclude the satisfaction (resp., violation) of the LTL property under analysis (w.r.t. the model M'). However, only certain results can actually be considered valid. Specifically, when $Mon_{\varphi_n}^{M'}(h) = \top$, or when $Mon_{\varphi_p}^{M'}(h) = \bot$. The other cases, which may include the inconclusive verdict (?), are considered undefined, since nothing can be concluded at runtime. The reason why the conditions in lines 8–9 are enough to conclude $\top$ and $\bot$ directly follow from the following lemmas. The rest of the algorithm is only for storing how the sub-formulas have been verified, whether at runtime (*i.e.*, stored in φ_{rv}), at static time (*i.e.*, stored in φ_{mc}), or not at all (*i.e.*, stored in φ_{unchk}).

We present the preservations results to provide the correctness of our algorithm.

Lemma 2. *Given a model M and a formula φ, for any history h of M starting in s_I, we have that:*

$$Mon_{\varphi_{LTL}}(h) = \top \implies M, s_I \models \varphi_{Ag}$$
$$Mon_{\varphi_{LTL}}(h) = \bot \implies M, s_I \not\models \varphi_{\emptyset}$$

where φ_{LTL} is the variant of φ where all strategic operators are removed, φ_{Ag} is the variant of φ where all strategic operators are converted into $\langle\langle Ag \rangle\rangle$, $\varphi_{\emptyset}$ is the variant of φ where all strategic operators are converted into $\langle\langle \emptyset \rangle\rangle$.

Due to the limited space, the proof is omitted. It can be found in [16]. However, it is important to evaluate in depth the meaning of the lemma presented above.

Remark 1. Lemma 2 shows a preservation result from RV to ATL* model checking that needs to be discussed. If our monitor returns true we have two possibilities: (1)

Algorithm 2. $RuntimeVerification\ (M, \varphi, h, result)$

$k = ?$;
$M' = UpdateModel(M, result)$;
$\langle \psi_n, \psi_p \rangle = UpdateFormula(\varphi, result)$;
$\varphi_n = FromATLtoLTL(\psi_n, n)$;
$\varphi_p = FromATLtoLTL(\psi_p, p)$;
$Mon^{M'}_{\varphi_p} = GenerateMonitor(\varphi_p)$;
$Mon^{M'}_{\varphi_n} = GenerateMonitor(\varphi_n)$;
if $Mon^{M'}_{\varphi_n}(h) = \top$ **then** $k = \top$;
if $Mon^{M'}_{\varphi_p}(h) = \bot$ **then** $k = \bot$;
$\varphi_{unchk} = \emptyset$;
for $\varphi' \in \varphi_{rv}$ **do**
    $Mon^{M'}_{\varphi'} = GenerateMonitor(\varphi')$;
    if $Mon^{M'}_{\varphi'}(h) = ?$ **then** $\varphi_{rv} = \varphi_{rv} \setminus \varphi'$; $\varphi_{unchk} = \varphi_{unchk} \cup \varphi'$;
return $\langle k, \varphi_{mc}, \varphi_{rv}, \varphi_{unchk} \rangle$;

the procedure found a negative sub-model in which the original formula φ is satisfied then it can conclude the verification procedure by using RV only by checking that the atom representing φ holds in the initial state of the history h given in input; (2) a sub-formula φ' is satisfied in a negative sub-model and at runtime the formula φ_{Ag} holds on the history h given in input. While case (1) gives a preservation result for the formula φ given in input, case (2) checks formula φ_{Ag} instead of φ. That is, it substitutes Ag as coalition for all the strategic operators of φ but the ones in φ'. So, our procedure approximates the truth value by considering the case in which all the agents in the game collaborate to achieve the objectives not satisfied in the model checking phase. That is, while in [5,8] the approximation is given in terms of information, in [4] is given in terms of memory of strategies, and in [15] the approximation is given by generalizing the logic, here we give results by approximating the coalitions. So, the main limitation of our approach concerns this aspect. Furthermore, we recall that our procedure produces always results, even partial. This aspect is strongly relevant in concrete scenario in which there is the necessity to have some sort of verification results. For example, in the context of swarm robots [19], with our procedure we can verify macro properties such as "the system works properly" since we are able to guarantee fully collaboration between agents because this property is relevant and desirable for each agent in the game. The same reasoning described above, can be applied in a complementary way for the case of positive sub-models and the falsity.

Theorem 1. *Algorithm 1 terminates in double-exponential time. Moreover, Algorithm 1 is sound: if the value returned is different from ?, then $M \models \varphi$ iff $k = \top$.*

Due to the limited space, the proof is omitted (see [16] for details).

4 Our Tool

The algorithms presented previously have been implemented in Java[1]. The resulting tool implementing Algorithm 1 allows to extract all sub-models with perfect information that satisfy a strategic objective from a model given in input. The extracted sub-models, along with the corresponding sub-formulas, are then used by the tool to generate and execute the corresponding monitors over a system execution (Algorithm 2). In more detail, as shown in Fig. 1, the tool expects a model in input formatted as a Json file. This file is then parsed, and an internal representation of the model is generated. After that, the verification of a sub-model against a sub-formula is achieved by translating the sub-model into its equivalent ISPL (Interpreted Systems Programming Language) program, which then is verified by using the model checker MCMAS[2] [20]. This corresponds to the verification steps performed in $CheckSub\text{-}formulas()$ (*i.e.*, where static verification through MCMAS is used). For each sub-model that satisfies this verification step, the tool produces a corresponding tuple; which contains the information needed by Algorithm 2 to complete the verification at runtime. The entire manipulation, from parsing the model formatted in Json, to translating the latter to its equivalent ISPL program, has been performed by extending an existent Java library [9]; the rest of the tool derives directly from the algorithms presented in this paper. The monitors are obtained using LamaConv [22], which is a Java library capable of translating expressions in temporal logic into equivalent automata and generating monitors out of these automata. For generating monitors, LamaConv uses the algorithm presented in [3].

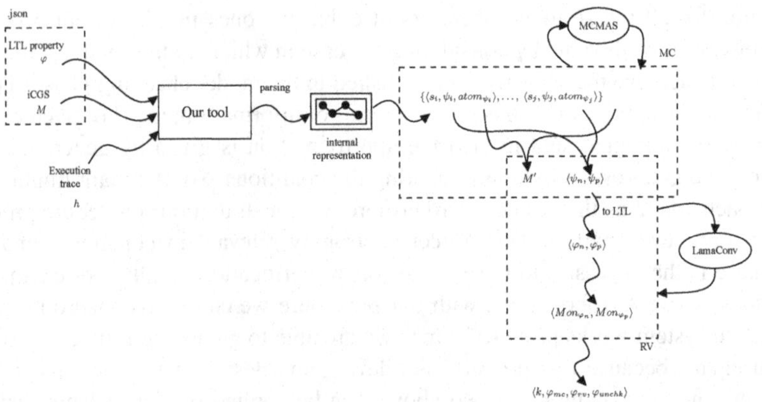

Fig. 1. Overview of the implemented tool

[1] The tool can be found at https://github.com/AngeloFerrando/StrategyRV.

[2] https://vas.doc.ic.ac.uk/software/mcmas/.

4.1 Experiments

We tested our tool on a large set of automatically and randomly generated iCGSs. The objective of these experiments was to show how many times our algorithm returned a conclusive verdict. For each model, we ran our procedure and counted the number of times a solution was returned. Note that, our approach concludes in any case, but since the general problem is undecidable, the result might be inconclusive (*i.e.*, ?). In Fig. 2, we report our results by varying the percentage of imperfect information (x axis) inside the iCGSs, from 0% (perfect information, *i.e.*, all states are distinguishable for all agents), to 100% (no information, *i.e.*, no state is distinguishable for any agent). For each percentage selected, we generated 10000 random iCGSs and counted the number of times our algorithm returned with a conclusive result (*i.e.*, $\top$ or $\bot$). As it can be seen in Fig. 2, our tool concludes with a conclusive result more than 80% of times. We do not observe any relevant difference amongst the different percentage of information used in the experiments. This is due to the random nature of the iCGSs used. Moreover, the results we obtained depend on the topology of the iCGSs, so it is very hard to precisely quantify the success rate. However, the results obtained by our experiments using our procedure are encouraging. Unfortunately, no benchmark of existing iCGSs exists, thus these results may vary on more realistic scenarios. Nonetheless, considering the large set of iCGSs we experimented on, we do not expect substantial differences.

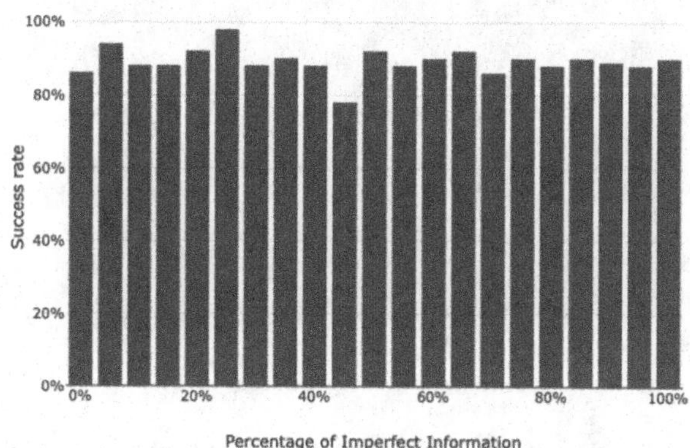

Fig. 2. Success rate of our tool when applied to a set of randomly generated iCGSs

Other than testing our tool w.r.t. the success rate over a random set of iCGSs, we evaluated the execution time as well. Specifically, we were much interested in analysing how such execution time is divided between $CheckSub\text{-}formulas()$ and Algorithm 2. *I.e.*, how much time is spent on verifying the models statically (through model checking), and how much is spent on verifying the temporal properties (through runtime verification). Figure 3 reports the results we obtained on the same set of randomly generated ICGSs used in Fig. 2. The results we obtained are intriguing, indeed we can note a variation in the percentage of time spent on the two phases (y-axis) moving from low percentages to high percentages of imperfect information in the iCGSs (x-axis). When the iCGS is close to have perfect information (low percentages on x-axis), we may observe that most of the execution time is spent on performing static verification ($\sim$70%), which corresponds to $CheckSub\text{-}formulas()$. On the other hand, when imperfect information grows inside the iCGS (high percentage on x-axis), we may observe that most of the execution time is spent on performing runtime verification ($\sim$90% in occurrence of absence of information). This behaviour is determined by the number of candidates extracted by the $FindSub\text{-}models()$ function. When the iCGS has perfect information, such function only extracts a single candidate (*i.e.*, the entire model), since $FindSub\text{-}models()$ generates only one tuple. Such single candidate can be of non-negligible size, and the resulting static verification, time consuming; while the subsequent runtime verification is only performed once on the remaining temporal parts of the property to verify. On the other hand, when the iCGS has imperfect information, $FindSub\text{-}models()$ returns a set of candidates that can grow exponentially w.r.t. the number of states of the iCGS. Nonetheless, such candidates are small in size, since $FindSub\text{-}models()$ splits the iCGS into multiple smaller iCGSs with perfect information. Thus, the static verification step is applied on small iCGSs and require less execution time; while the runtime verification step is called for each candidate (so an exponential number of times) and is only influenced by the size of the temporal property to verify.

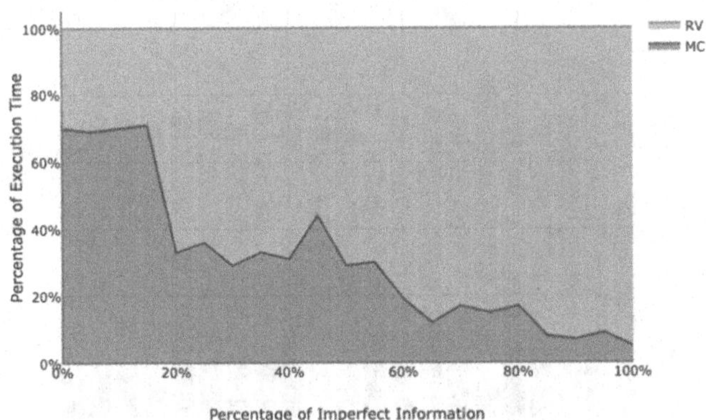

Fig. 3. How the execution time of our tool when applied to randomly generated iCGSs is divided

In conclusion, it is important to emphasise that, even though the monitor synthesis is computationally hard (*i.e.*, $2EXPTIME$), the resulting runtime verification process is polynomial in the size of the history analysed. Naturally, the actual running complexity of a monitor depends on the formalism used to describe the formal property. In this work, monitors are synthesised from LTL properties. Since LTL properties are translated into Moore machines [3], the time complexity w.r.t. the length of the analysed trace is linear. This can be understood intuitively by noticing that the Moore machine so generated has finite size, and it does not change at runtime.

5 Conclusions and Future Work

The work presented in this paper follows a standard combined approach of formal verification techniques, where the objective is to get the best of both. We considered the model checking problem of MAS using strategic properties that is undecidable in general, and showed how runtime verification can help by verifying part of the properties at execution time. The resulting procedure has been presented both on a theoretical (theorems and algorithms) and a practical level (prototype implementation). Note that this is the first attempt of combining model checking and runtime verification to verify strategic properties on MAS. Thus, even though our solution might not be optimal, it is a milestone for the corresponding lines of research. Additional works will be done to improve the technique and, above all, its implementation. For instance, we are planning to extend this work by considering a more predictive flavour.

References

1. Alur, R., Henzinger, T., Kupferman, O.: Alternating-time temporal logic. J. ACM **49**(5), 672–713 (2002)
2. Baier, C., Katoen, J.P.: Principles of Model Checking (2008)
3. Bauer, A., Leucker, M., Schallhart, C.: Runtime verification for LTL and TLTL. ACM Trans. Softw. Eng. Methodol. **20**(4), 14:1–14:64 (2011)
4. Belardinelli, F., Lomuscio, A., Malvone, V.: Approximating perfect recall when model checking strategic abilities. In: KR, pp. 435–444 (2018)
5. Belardinelli, F., Lomuscio, A., Malvone, V.: An abstraction-based method for verifying strategic properties in multi-agent systems with imperfect information. In: AAAI (2019)
6. Belardinelli, F., Lomuscio, A., Murano, A., Rubin, S.: Verification of multi-agent systems with imperfect information and public actions. In: AAMAS 2017, pp. 1268–1276 (2017)
7. Belardinelli, F., Lomuscio, A., Murano, A., Rubin, S.: Verification of multi-agent systems with public actions against strategy logic. Artif. Intell. **285**, 103302 (2020)
8. Belardinelli, F., Malvone, V.: A three-valued approach to strategic abilities under imperfect information. In: KR, pp. 89–98 (2020)
9. Belardinelli, F., Malvone, V., Slimani, A.: A Tool for Verifying Strategic Properties in MAS with Imperfect Information (2020). https://github.com/VadimMalvone/A-Tool-for-Verifying-Strategic-Properties-in-MAS-with-Imperfect-Information
10. Berthon, R., Maubert, B., Murano, A.: Decidability results for ATL* with imperfect information and perfect recall. In: AAMAS (2017)
11. Berthon, R., Maubert, B., Murano, A., Rubin, S., Vardi, M.Y.: Strategy logic with imperfect information. ACM Trans. Comput. Log. **22**(1), 5:1–5:51 (2021)
12. Dima, C., Tiplea, F.: Model-checking ATL under imperfect information and perfect recall semantics is undecidable. CoRR abs/1102.4225 (2011)
13. Fagin, R., Halpern, J., Moses, Y., Vardi, M.: Reasoning About Knowledge. MIT, Cambridge (1995)
14. Ferrando, A., Malvone, V.: Strategy RV: a tool to approximate ATL model checking under imperfect information and perfect recall. In: AAMAS (2021)
15. Ferrando, A., Malvone, V.: Towards the verification of strategic properties in multi-agent systems with imperfect information. CoRR abs/2112.13621 (2021)
16. Ferrando, A., Malvone, V.: Towards the combination of model checking and runtime verification on multi-agent systems. CoRR abs/2202.09344 (2022)

17. Hinrichs, T.L., Sistla, A.P., Zuck, L.D.: Model check what you can, runtime verify the rest. In: Voronkov, A., Korovina, M.V. (eds.) HOWARD-60, pp. 234–244. EasyChair (2014)
18. Jamroga, W., van der Hoek, W.: Agents that know how to play. Fund. Inf. **62**, 1–35 (2004)
19. Kouvaros, P., Lomuscio, A.: Parameterised verification for multi-agent systems. Artif. Intell. **234**, 152–189 (2016)
20. Lomuscio, A., Raimondi, F.: Model checking knowledge, strategies, and games in multi-agent systems. In: AAMAS, pp. 161–168 (2006)
21. Pnueli, A.: The temporal logic of programs. In: SFCS, pp. 46–57 (1977)
22. Scheffel, T., Schmitz, M., et al.: LamaConv- logics and automata converter library (2016)
23. Schobbens, P.: Alternating-time logic with imperfect recall. ENTCS **85**(2), 82–93 (2004)

Explaining Semantic Reasoning Using Argumentation

Carlos Eduardo A. Ferreira[1], Alison R. Panisson[1(✉)], Débora C. Engelmann[2,4], Renata Vieira[3], Viviana Mascardi[4], and Rafael H. Bordini[2]

[1] Department of Computing, UFSC, Florianópolis, Brazil
alison.panisson@ufsc.br

[2] School of Technology, PUCRS, Porto Alegre, Brazil
debora.engelmann@edu.pucrs.br, rafael.bordini@pucrs.br

[3] CIDEHUS, University of Évora, Evora, Portugal
renatav@uevora.pt

[4] DIBRIS, University of Genoa, Genoa, Italy
viviana.mascardi@unige.it

Abstract. Multi-Agent Systems (MAS) are popular because they provide a paradigm that naturally meets the current demand to design and implement distributed intelligent systems. When developing a multi-agent application, it is common to use ontologies to provide the domain-specific knowledge and vocabulary necessary for agents to achieve the system goals. In this paper, we propose an approach in which agents can query semantic reasoners and use the received inferences to build explanations for such reasoning. Also, thanks to an internal representation of inference rules used to build explanations, in the form of argumentation schemes, agents are able to reason and make decisions based on the answers from the semantic reasoner. Furthermore, agents can communicate the built explanation to other agents and humans, using computational or natural language representations of arguments. Our approach paves the way towards multi-agent systems able to provide explanations from the reasoning carried out by semantic reasoners.

Keywords: Argumentation schemes · Multi-agent systems · Semantic reasoning · Explainability

1 Introduction

Explainability is pointed out as an essential characteristic in artificial intelligence applications, because it provides users with the necessary information for them to effectively understand, trust, and manage such applications [20]. The need for explaining a decision/reasoning/action was discussed as early as the 1970s, starting with the development of expert systems and the need for those systems to explain their decisions [1]. Nowadays, explainability becomes an essential

© The Author(s), under exclusive license to Springer Nature Switzerland AG 2022
F. Dignum et al. (Eds.): PAAMS 2022, LNAI 13616, pp. 153–165, 2022.
https://doi.org/10.1007/978-3-031-18192-4_13

characteristic in MAS [40], given that MAS are one of the most powerful paradigms to implement complex distributed systems powered by artificial intelligence techniques.

Ontologies are known for empowering the execution of semantic reasoners, providing functionalities such as *consistency checking* [36]. Also, ontologies make it possible to share a common understanding of the structure of information among people and software agents as well as to reuse domain knowledge [17]. Integrating semantic reasoners and ontologies with agents enhances the knowledge representation features and reasoning capabilities of MAS applications [14]. Indeed, one notable possibility resulting from the use of ontologies in MAS is the capability of software agents to infer new knowledge based on logic rules [25] that can be applied by semantic reasoners. In this context, although semantic reasoners provide the computational steps (logic rules, concepts, etc.) used during inferences for an answer (i.e., query answering systems), they are not user-friendly explanations, and it would be difficult for users to understand those answers provided by semantic reasoners. Thus, in this paper, we propose an approach in which software agents are able to query semantic reasoners to obtain the answer, containing the trace of computational steps used for a particular inference, then they are able to translate those computational steps to explanations that can be communicated to software agents and humans, using computational and natural language representations of arguments. Our approach is based on the idea that inference rules, used by semantic reasoners to provide answers to queries, can be internally represented and stored by agents as argumentation schemes used to instantiate arguments based on the argumentation-based framework in [28,31].

The contributions of this work are: (i) we propose an approach that enables agents to query semantic reasoners and explain the received answer to other software agents or human users, as illustrated in Fig. 1; (ii) our approach allows the automatic translation of inference rules from answers received when querying semantic reasoners into argumentation schemes written in an Agent Oriented Programming Language (AOPL) (arrow 1 in Fig. 1). Translating those inferences into argumentation schemes, like those proposed by [39], bring us two main benefits. First, agents can store in their belief bases the argumentation schemes extracted from the answers obtained from the semantic reasoner and use them to instantiate arguments they can use for reasoning and communication (arrow 2 in Fig. 1). Second, using natural language templates for those argumentation schemes (arrows 3 and 4 in Fig. 1), agents can translate computational arguments into natural language arguments, using them to build natural language explanations for human users; and (iii) we describe a real-world multi-agent application for bed allocation in hospitals, exemplifying our approach based on what we have developed for that application.

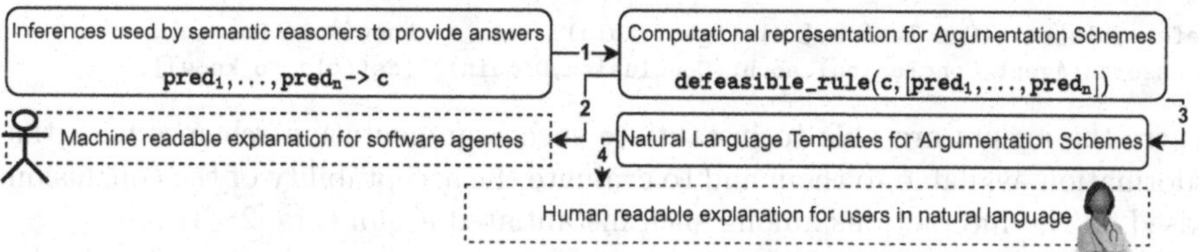

Fig. 1. Our approach for explaining semantic reasoning

2 Background

2.1 Agent Oriented Programming Languages

Among the many AOPLs and platforms, such as Jason, Jadex, Jack, AgentFactory, 2APL, GOAL, Golog, and MetateM, as discussed in [3], we chose the Jason platform [4] to implement our work. Jason provides excellent conceptual/theoretical support; it extends the AgentSpeak language, an abstract logic-based AOPL introduced by Rao [32], which is one of the best-known languages inspired by the Beliefs, Desires, Intentions (BDI) architecture. Besides specifying BDI agents with well-defined mental attitudes, the Jason platform has some other features that are particularly interesting for our work, for example, strong negation, belief annotations, and (customisable) speech-act based communication.

2.2 Argumentation Schemes

Argumentation schemes represent reasoning/argument patterns normally found in daily conversation, as well as in specific argumentation, as scientific argumentation (scientific reports, discourses, etc.) [39]. Argumentation schemes provide a very elegant manner to represent and analyse these common argument patterns that are naturally found in the construction of reasoning.

For example, the *Argument from role to know in MAS* (*role to know* for short) from [28,31] is represented as follows:

> "Agent *ag* is currently playing a role *R* (its position) that implies knowing things in a certain subject domain *S* containing proposition *A* **(Major Premise)**. *ag* asserts that *A* (in domain *S*) is true (or false) **(Minor Premise)**. *A* is true (or false) **(Conclusion)**".

In order to allow agents to instantiate arguments from argumentation schemes, Panisson and colleagues [26–28,31] have proposed a framework to represent argumentation schemes in Jason multi-agent platform using defeasible inference rules. For example, the argumentation scheme *role to know* is represented in Jason as follows[1]:

[1] Note that argumentation schemes are modelled as agents beliefs, and the annotation `[as(as_name)]` is used to distinguish argumentation schemes from other beliefs.

```
defeasible_rule(Conclusion,[role(Agent,Role), role_to_know(Role,Domain),
  asserts(Agent,Conclusion),about(Conclusion,Domain)])[as(role_to_know)].
```

where the agents are able to instantiate such argumentation schemes with the information available to them and to evaluate the acceptability of the conclusion based on the interactions among such instantiated arguments [28,31].

For example, imagine that an agent `ag` knows that `john` (another agent in the system) is playing the role of `doctor`—`role(john, doctor)`. Further, `ag` knows that doctors know about cancer—`role_to_know(doctor, cancer)`. Therefore, if `john` asserts that *"smoking causes cancer"*—`asserts(john, causes(smoking, cancer))`, and given that causes of cancer are a subject matter related to cancer—`about(causes(smoking, cancer), cancer)`, `ag` is able to instantiate the argumentation scheme *role to know*, which allows `ag` to conclude that smoking causes cancer—`causes(smoking, cancer)`, based on the unification function {`Agent` ↦ `john`, `Role` ↦ `doctor`, `Domain` ↦ `cancer`, `Conclusion` ↦ `causes(smoking, cancer)`}.

Further, argumentation schemes combined with natural language templates can be used for translating arguments from a computational representation to natural language representation [29]. For example, the natural language template for the argumentation scheme `role_to_know` is as follows:

⟨"<`Agent`> is a <`Role`>, and <`Role`>s know about <`Domain`>. <`Agent`> asserts <`Conclusion`>, therefore we should believe that <`Conclusion`>".⟩$_{[\texttt{as(role\_to\_know)}]}$

using the same unification function {`Agent` ↦ `john`, `Role` ↦ `doctor`, `Domain` ↦ `cancer`, `Conclusion` ↦ `causes(smoking, cancer)`}, it is possible to build the following natural language argument:

⟨"`john` is a `doctor`, and `doctors` know about `cancer`. `john` asserts `smoking causes cancer`, therefore we should believe that `smoking causes cancer`".⟩$_{[\texttt{as(role\_to\_know)}]}$

2.3 OWL Ontologies

An ontology is an explicit and formal specification of a shared conceptualisation consisting of concepts or classes, relationships, instances, attributes, axioms, restrictions, rules, and events [18,38]. Currently, ontologies are used in projects of several domains: Internet of Things (IoT) [22], smart cities [6], higher education [37], among others. A standard for representing ontologies that is widely used both in academia and industry is the OWL (Ontology Web Language), based on formal logic. OWL is based on description logic and has an inference mechanism based on this logic developed in the context of the global Semantic Web project and graphical editors for the creation of ontologies [38].

When developing an ontology, Semantic Web Rule Language (SWRL) [25] can be used to model more sophisticated inferences, and they are specified in the following format: $\texttt{pre}_1, \ldots, \texttt{pre}_n - > \texttt{conc}$, with $\texttt{pre}_1, \ldots, \texttt{pre}_n$ the n premises of the rule, and `conc` the conclusion of the rule.

3 Scenario

In this paper, we use a scenario of bed allocation in hospitals, based on the work reported in [8,10–12], in order to exemplify how we have built our approach for explaining semantic reasoning using argumentation. Bed allocation is a challenge hospitals face since hospital beds are scarce, and when poorly managed, it can generate long lines and chaos in emergency rooms [19]. The large number of constraints that need to be considered during the allocation process makes this process difficult for humans to perform. Considering that MAS can be powered by different artificial intelligence techniques, they are suitable to deal with complex problems like bed allocation in hospitals. Thanks to recent developments, MAS are equipped with communication in natural language [9,10] and ontological reasoning [14].

Below, we have an example of dialogue that occurs in the multi-agent application developed, in which a human operator tries to allocate a patient named `patient2` to the bed `101b`; however, bed `101b` is considered unsuitable for that patient given the hospital rules modelled in the domain-specific ontology of that application. Thus, the agent (software agent) responsible to assist the bed allocation in the multi-agent application opens a dialogue with the human operator to inform that bed is not suitable for that patient, later explaining why it is not suitable:

- **Assistant**: Your bed allocation plan has flaws. Bed `101b` is unsuitable for `patient2`.
- **Operator**: Why do you think bed `101b` is unsuitable for **patient2**?
- **Assistant**: Because patient `patient1` is of care `semi-Intensive-Care` and occupies bed `101a`. So bed `101a` is of care `semi-Intensive-Care`. Bed **101a** is in bedroom `101` and it is of care `semi-Intensive-Care`. So bedroom `101` is of care `semi-Intensive-Care`. Bed **101b** is in bedroom `101` and bedroom `101` is of care `semi-Intensive-Care`. So bed `101b` is of care `semi-Intensive-Care`. Patient `patient2` is of care `minimal-Care` and bed `101b` is of care `semi-Intensive-Care` that is different from `minimal-Care`. So bed `101b` is unsuitable for patient `patient2`.
- **Operator**: And how about bed 103a? Is it suitable?
- **Assistant**: No, it isn't.
- **Operator**: Why?
- **Assistant**: Because patient `patient3` is of care `intensive-Care` and occupies bed `103b`. So bed `103b` is of care `intensive-Care`. Bed `103b` is in bedroom `103` and is of care `intensive-Care`. So bedroom `103` is of care `intensive-Care`. Bed `103a` is in bedroom `103` and bedroom `103` is of care `intensive-Care`. So bed `103a` is of care `intensive-Care`. Patient `patient2` is of care `minimal-Care` and bed `103a` is of care `intensive-Care` that is different from `minimal-Care`. So bed `103a` is unsuitable for patient `patient2`.

This dialogue in natural language is resulting from the approach we will present in this paper, combined with other technologies: (i) Dial4JaCa[2] [10],

[2] https://github.com/smart-pucrs/Dial4JaCa.

which allows the integration between chatbot technologies and MAS, and it is used to identify users' intentions and to extract entities from natural language inputs as well as to provide responses to users in natural language; and (ii) an interface between MAS and ontologies [14], which allows extending the agents' belief bases with semantic technologies. While Dial4JaCa represents an important component in the multi-agent application developed, which provides an interactive interface with human users, in this work we are going to focus only on the the components necessary to present our approach, namely the interface between ontologies and MAS.

4 Querying Ontologies

In a series of papers, Freitas and colleagues [13–15] developed an approach to interface OWL ontologies and MAS using CArtAgO artifacts [33]. Using the proposed approach, agents are able to store, access, and query domain-specific OWL ontologies. The infrastructure proposed by [14] has been used in different applications as evidenced by [30,35], and it provides an elegant architecture for engineering intelligent systems based on the MAS paradigm.

While agents are able to query OWL ontologies using the approach developed in [14], the interface does not provide explanations for queries, or even traces of computational steps used by the semantic reasoner to reach that particular conclusion. Even though an agent would have access to answers from semantic reasoners, queries result from complex reasoning executed over domain-specific inference rules, modelled using SWRL rules [25], and those inferences would not be easily understood by software agents in their original form[3].

We have extended the approach presented by [14] to process the traces of computational steps (including the application of inference rules) used by semantics reasoners during queries to OWL ontologies. Then, using our approach to translate those answers into an agent-oriented programming representation, agents are able not only to understand and manipulate that information but also to build explanations from external semantic reasoning.

5 Translating SWRL Rules into Argumentation Schemes

Our approach for building explanations for answers from semantic reasoners is based on the idea that agents are able to internally model and store inference rules returned by semantic reasoners (when providing an answer for a query) using argumentation schemes like those presented in Sect. 2.2, which are processed by agents using the framework presented in [28,31]. Then, using templates in natural language for argumentation schemes, also introduced in Sect. 2.2, agents build natural language explanations for those answers.

First, we provide an approach for agents to query semantic reasoners, obtaining the answer for the queries in the format of traces of computational steps

[3] Frequently, they are not easily understood even by users of those technologies.

Table 1. Correspondence between answers from semantic reasoners and an AOPL representation

Answer from the Semantic Reasoner	Representation in AOPL
101b is-in 101	`is_in("101b","101")`
DifferentIndividuals: Intensive-Care, Minimal-Care, Semi-Intensive-Care	`isDifferentFrom("Intensive-Care","Minimal-Care")` `isDifferentFrom("Intensive-Care","Semi-Intensive-Care")` `isDifferentFrom("Minimal-Care","Semi-Intensive-Care")`
101a is-in 101	`is_in("101a","101")`
Patient2 is-care Minimal-Care	`is_care("Patient2","Minimal-Care")`
101b **Type** Hospital_Bed	`hospital_Bed("101b")`
Hospital_Bed(?B1r), Bedroom(?Br), is-in(?B1r,?Br), bed-is-care(?B1r,?C1r) -> bedroom-is-care (?Br,?C1r)	`defeasible_rule(bedroom_is_care(Br,C1r), [hospital_Bed(B1r),bedroom(Br),is_in(B1r,Br), bed_is_care(B1r,C1r)])[as(<schemeName>)]`
101a **Type** Hospital_Bed	`hospital_Bed("101a")`
Patient(?P2r), Hospital_Bed(?B2r), is-care(?P2r,?C2r), bed-is-care(?B2r,?C1r), **DifferentFrom**(?C1r,?C2r) -> is-unsuitable-for(?B2r,?P2r)	`defeasible_rule(is_unsuitable_for(B2r,P2r)[patient(P2r), hospital_Bed(B2r),is_care(P2r,C2r),bed_is_care(B2r,C1r), differentFrom(C1r,C2r)])[as(<schemeName>)]`
101 **Type** Bedroom	`bedroom("101")`
Hospital_Bed(?B2r), Bedroom(?Br), is-in(?B2r,?Br), bedroom-is-care(?Br,?C1r) -> bed-is-care(?B2r,?C1r)	`defeasible_rule(bed_is_care(B2r,C1r), [hospital_Bed(B2r),bedroom(Br),is_in(B2r,Br), bedroom_is_care(Br,C1r)])[as(<schemeName>)]`
Patient1 occupy-one 101a	`occupy_one("Patient1","101a")`
Patient1 is-care Semi-Intensive-Care	`is_care("Patient1","Semi-Intensive-Care")`
Patient2 **Type** Patient	`patient("Patient2")`
Patient(?P1r), is-care(?P1r,?C1r), Hospital_Bed(?B1r), occupy-one(?P1r,?BIr) -> bed-is-care(?BIr,?C1r)	`defeasible_rule(bed_is_care(B1r,C1r), [patient(P1r),is_care(P1r,C1r),hospital_Bed(B1r), occupy_one(P1r,B1r)])[as(<schemeName>)]`
Patient1 **Type** Patient	`patient("Patient1")`

(including concepts, classes and inference rules) used by the semantic reasoner to infer that particular query. We implemented our approach using a CArtAgO artifact [34], using the OWL API[4] (a Java API for creating, manipulating and serializing OWL Ontologies) as a basis for querying ontologies in conjunction with Openllet[5] (an open-source OWL DL reasoner for Java) to extract the answers about inferences made based on SWRL rules.

Through the CArtAgO artifact developed, we provide agents with an operation called `getExplanation` that receives as a parameter the string corresponding to the `objectProperty` (e.g. `"is-unsuitable-for"`) that relates the individuals, and the predicate corresponding to the query (e.g. `is_unsuitable_for ("101b","patient2")`). Then, the artifact executes the query to the semantic reasoner, and provides the answer to agents in the following format:

```
explanationTerms(rules(RulesList),assertions(AList),classInfo(CInfoList))
```

To build this internal representation based on the data returned for OWL API and Openllet we created a class that converts each axiom to an AOPL

[4] https://github.com/owlcs/owlapi.
[5] https://github.com/Galigator/openllet.

representation. An example of this process is shown in Table 1, based on the answer received by the assistant agent from the running scenario presented in Sect. 3. Also, our approach translates the inference rules returned into an answer to the format of argumentation schemes. This representation allows agents to build arguments from the reasoning patterns extracted from the answers, being able to reason, understand and communicate arguments instantiated from these argumentation schemes using the argumentation-based framework presented in [31].

We also created an internal action named `unifyRule` that receives as parameters the rule list and the assertion list that we identified with the logical variables `RulesList` and `AList`, respectively, in the `explanationTerms` internal representation introduced above. It allows agents to unify terms in argumentation schemes based on the assertions received in the answer provided by our interface. That is, the unification function is obtained from `RulesList`, `AList`, and `CInfoList`. This process provides agents with the set of arguments extracted from the answer, which we call here an *argumentation-based explanation*. With an internal representation of those reasoning patterns, agents are able to build and communicate explanations represented in a computational representation for arguments, which is useful when the system requires agents to provide explanations to other software agents.

In order to provide explanations to human users, agents use natural language templates for argumentation schemes [29] to translate those arguments to natural language arguments, then using those arguments to build and provide natural language explanations to human users.

Continuing our example, below, we demonstrate 1 of the 40 domain-specific rules[6] modelled by experts in order to establish the reasoning pattern necessary to bed allocation in the multi-agent application described in Sect. 3. These rules are used by the semantic reasoner to provide the answer used by the assistant agents when building the explanation from our running scenario.

Argumentation Scheme for Unsuitable Beds (AS4UB): "Patient `P` is of care `C1` (**premise**). Bed `B` is of care care `C2` (**premise**). Care `C1` is different of care `C2` (**premise**). Bed `B` is unsuitable for patient `P` (**conclusion**)".

This argumentation scheme is extracted from the below SWRL rule available in the ontology used in the multi-agent application.

```
Patient(?P), Hospital_Bed(?B), is-care(?P,?C1), bed-is-care(?B,?C2),
DifferentFrom(?C1,?C2) -> is-unsuitable-for(?B,?P)
```

When the assistant agent queries the semantic reasoners, asking if a particular bed `101b` is unsuitable for the patient `patient2` – `is_unsuitable_for(101b, patient2)` – looking for validating the operator allocation, the semantic reasoner

[6] All rules are available at https://github.com/DeboraEngelmann/explaining-ontological-reasoning/blob/main/base_rules.md.

will answer that query with the trace of computational steps used to make the inference. From the answer provided by the semantic reasoner, our approach automatically translates the inference rules contained in that answer to argumentation schemes, according the representation required by the argumentation-based framework from [31], i.e., using defeasible inference rules represented by the predicate `defeasible_rule(Conclusion,Premises)`, in which `Conclusion` represents the conclusion of the rule, and `Premises` the set of premises used in the body of that particular rule. For example, the argumentation scheme presented in this section is internally represented by agents as follows:

```
defeasible_rule(is_unsuitable_for(B,P),  [patient(P), hospital_Bed(B),
is_care(P,C1), bed_is_care(B,C2), differentFrom(C1,C2)])[as(as4ub)]
```

Thus, when agents need to communicate an explanation to another software agent, for example, to explain why bed `101b` is unsuitable to patient `patient2`, according to our running scenario, they are going to build an explanation using the computational representation for arguments introduced in Sect. 2.2, using the argumentation-based framework [28,31].

```
explanation(is_unsuitable_for(101b,patient2),
[defeasible_rule(bed_is_care(101a,semi-intensive-care),[...])[as(as4bc1)],
defeasible_rule(bedroom_is_care(101,semi-intensive-care),[...])[as(as4br)],
defeasible_rule(bed_is_care(101b,semi-intensive-care),[...])[as(as4bc2)],
defeasible_rule(is_unsuitable_for(101b,patient2), [patient(patient2),
  hospital_Bed(101b), is_care(patient2,minimal-care),
  bed_is_care(101b,semi-intensive-care),
  differentFrom(minimal-care,semi-intensive-care)])[as(as4ub)]])}
```

To build the explanation presented above[7], agents query their belief base for the predicate they are interested to provide an explanation for, using `argument(Q, Arg)` with `Q` the queried predicate, and `Arg` a free variable that will unify with the argument supporting `Q`. This query uses the argumentation-based framework [31], which looks for argumentation schemes that infer that particular queried information, using the information available to the agent to instantiate argumentation schemes, building an argument that supports the queried information. In our scenario, `Arg` unifies with the set of arguments (or chained/complex argument) presented above, supporting `is_unsuitable_for(101b,patient2)`.

When it is necessary to communicate with human users, agents are able to build natural language explanations, translating the computational representation of arguments to natural language arguments, using natural language templates for argumentation schemes, as we describe in the next section.

5.1 Translating Arguments to Natural Language Explanations

When agents need to communicate an explanation in natural language, they use the plan `+!translateToNaturalLanguage` that implements how agents translate argu-

[7] We omitted the premises of argumentation schemes we did not present in this paper. All argumentation schemes are available in the GitHub repository.

ments from a computational representation to natural language, then aggregating those natural language arguments into an explanation. As it can be observed in Sect. 3, an explanation might be a sequence of arguments (also considered as a chained/complex argument). Thus `+!translateToNaturalLanguage` receives a list of one or more arguments (each one of those arguments are instances of an argumentation scheme), and then it translates each computational argument to a corresponding natural language argument, recovering the natural language template to the argumentation scheme used to instantiate that particular argument and returning its natural language representation.

6 Related Work and Conclusions

Explainablility has become a central topic in AI, and the literature of MAS exploring explainability has significantly increased in the last few year, mostly of it focusing on the health domain [2,5,7,16,21]. Also, interesting work exploring the integration of ontologies and MAS has been developed, for example, AgentSpeakDL [24], and CooL-AgentSpeak [23].

While our approach is inspired by much of these works, to the best of our knowledge, our approach is the first to propose that intelligent agents are able to explain the reasoning executed externally by semantic reasoners. Also, our approach is the first to propose an internal representation for SWRL rules using argumentation schemes in MAS, which allows agents to understand and manipulate those reasoning patterns that were only processed by semantic reasoners at the ontology level.

In this paper, we proposed an approach in which agents are able to build explanations based on answers received from semantic reasoners about their queries. Explanations can be communicated to both software agents and human users, using a computational or a natural language representation for explanations, respectively.

Our approach is based on the idea that inference rules contained in answers obtained from queries to semantic reasoners can be translated into argumentation schemes that agents are able to understand and manipulate using the argumentation-based framework from [28,31]. Thus, agents can instantiate arguments from argumentation schemes, using them for reasoning and communication. Furthermore, using natural language templates for argumentation schemes, agents are able to translate the computational representation of arguments into natural language arguments. Thus, they are able not only to build explanations for other software agents but also for human users.

Combining the approach presented in this work with other technologies used for human-agent interactions [10] allowed us to achieve the natural language dialogue presented in Sect. 3, which is part of a real-world multi-agent application (under development) that aims to help human operators in the process of bed allocation in hospitals.

Acknowledgements. This research was partially funded by CNPq and CAPES.

References

1. Akata, Z., et al.: A research agenda for hybrid intelligence: augmenting human intellect with collaborative, adaptive, responsible, and explainable artificial intelligence. Computer **53**(8), 18–28 (2020)
2. Baskar, J., Janols, R., Guerrero, E., Nieves, J.C., Lindgren, H.: A multipurpose goal model for personalised digital coaching. In: Montagna, S., Abreu, P.H., Giroux, S., Schumacher, M.I. (eds.) A2HC/AHEALTH 2017. LNCS (LNAI), vol. 10685, pp. 94–116. Springer, Cham (2017). https://doi.org/10.1007/978-3-319-70887-4_6
3. Bordini, R.H., Dastani, M., Dix, J., Seghrouchni, A.E.F.: Multi-Agent Programming: Languages, Tools and Applications. Springer, Heidelberg (2009)
4. Bordini, R.H., Hübner, J.F., Wooldridge, M.: Programming Multi-Agent Systems in AgentSpeak using Jason. Wiley, Hoboken (2007)
5. Cheng, C.Y., Qian, X., Tseng, S.H., Fu, L.C.: Recommendation dialogue system through pragmatic argumentation. In: 2017 26th IEEE International Symposium on Robot and Human Interactive Communication, pp. 335–340. IEEE (2017)
6. De Nicola, A., Villani, M.L.: Smart city ontologies and their applications: a systematic literature review. Sustainability **13**(10), 5578 (2021)
7. Donadello, I., Dragoni, M., Eccher, C.: Explaining reasoning algorithms with persuasiveness: a case study for a behavioural change system. In: Proceedings of the 35th Annual ACM Symposium on Applied Computing, pp. 646–653 (2020)
8. Engelmann, D., Couto, J., Gabriel, V., Vieira, R., Bordini, R.: Towards an ontology to support decision-making in hospital bed allocation. In: Proceedings of 31st International Conference on Software Engineering & Knowledge Engineering, pp. 71–74 (2019)
9. Engelmann, D., et al.: Dial4JaCa – a demonstration. In: Dignum, F., Corchado, J.M., De La Prieta, F. (eds.) PAAMS 2021. LNCS (LNAI), vol. 12946, pp. 346–350. Springer, Cham (2021). https://doi.org/10.1007/978-3-030-85739-4_29
10. Engelmann, D., et al.: Dial4JaCa – a communication interface between multi-agent systems and chatbots. In: Dignum, F., Corchado, J.M., De La Prieta, F. (eds.) PAAMS 2021. LNCS (LNAI), vol. 12946, pp. 77–88. Springer, Cham (2021). https://doi.org/10.1007/978-3-030-85739-4_7
11. Engelmann, D.C., Cezar, L.D., Panisson, A.R., Bordini, R.H.: A conversational agent to support hospital bed allocation. In: Britto, A., Valdivia Delgado, K. (eds.) BRACIS 2021. LNCS (LNAI), vol. 13073, pp. 3–17. Springer, Cham (2021). https://doi.org/10.1007/978-3-030-91702-9_1
12. Engelmann, D.C.: An interactive agent to support hospital bed allocation based on plan validation. Dissertation, PUCRS (2019)
13. Freitas, A., Panisson, A.R., Hilgert, L., Meneguzzi, F., Vieira, R., Bordini, R.H.: Integrating ontologies with multi-agent systems through CArtAgO artifacts. In: 2015 IEEE/WIC/ACM International Joint Conferences on Web Intelligence (WI) and Intelligent Agent Technologies (IAT) (2015)
14. Freitas, A., Panisson, A.R., Hilgert, L., Meneguzzi, F., Vieira, R., Bordini, R.H.: Applying ontologies to the development and execution of multi-agent systems. In: Web Intelligence, vol. 15, pp. 291–302. IOS Press (2017)
15. Freitas, A., Schmidt, D., Panisson, A., Bordini, R.H., Meneguzzi, F., Vieira, R.: Applying ontologies and agent technologies to generate ambient intelligence applications. In: Koch, F., Meneguzzi, F., Lakkaraju, K. (eds.) AVSA CARE 2014. CCIS, vol. 498, pp. 22–33. Springer, Cham (2014). https://doi.org/10.1007/978-3-662-46241-6_3

16. Grando, A., Moss, L., Bel-Enguix, G., Jiménez-López, M.D., Kinsella, J.: Argumentation-based dialogue systems for medical training. In: Neustein, A., Markowitz, J. (eds.) Where Humans Meet Machines, pp. 213–232. Springer, New York (2013). https://doi.org/10.1007/978-1-4614-6934-6_10
17. Gruber, T.R.: A translation approach to portable ontology specifications. Knowl. Acquis. **5**(2), 199–220 (1993)
18. Gruber, T.R.: Toward principles for the design of ontologies used for knowledge sharing? Int. J. Hum. Comput. Stud. **43**(5), 907–928 (1995)
19. da Silveira Grübler, M., da Costa, C.A., Righi, R., Rigo, S., Chiwiacowsky, L.: A hospital bed allocation hybrid model based on situation awareness. Comput. Inform. Nurs. **36**, 249–255 (2018)
20. Gunning, D., Stefik, M., Choi, J., Miller, T., Stumpf, S., Yang, G.Z.: XAI-explainable artificial intelligence. Sci. Robot. **4**(37) (2019)
21. Kökciyan, N., et al.: A collaborative decision support tool for managing chronic conditions. In: MedInfo, pp. 644–648 (2019)
22. Li, W., Tropea, G., Abid, A., Detti, A., Le Gall, F.: Review of standard ontologies for the web of things. In: 2019 Global IoT Summit (GIoTS), pp. 1–6 (2019)
23. Mascardi, V., Ancona, D., Bordini, R.H., Ricci, A.: CooL-AgentSpeak: enhancing AgentSpeak-DL agents with plan exchange and ontology services. In: 2011 IEEE/WIC/ACM International Conferences on Web Intelligence and Intelligent Agent Technology, vol. 2, pp. 109–116. IEEE (2011)
24. Moreira, Á.F., Vieira, R., Bordini, R.H., Hübner, J.F.: Agent-oriented programming with underlying ontological reasoning. In: Baldoni, M., Endriss, U., Omicini, A., Torroni, P. (eds.) DALT 2005. LNCS (LNAI), vol. 3904, pp. 155–170. Springer, Heidelberg (2006). https://doi.org/10.1007/11691792_10
25. O'Connor, M.: The semantic web rule (2009)
26. Panisson, A.R., Bordini, R.H.: Knowledge representation for argumentation in agent-oriented programming languages. In: 2016 Brazilian Conference on Intelligent Systems, BRACIS (2016)
27. Panisson, A.R., Bordini, R.H.: Uttering only what is needed: enthymemes in multi-agent systems. In: Proceedings of the 16th Conference on Autonomous Agents and MultiAgent Systems, pp. 1670–1672. International Foundation for Autonomous Agents and Multiagent Systems (2017)
28. Panisson, A.R., Bordini, R.H.: Towards a computational model of argumentation schemes in agent-oriented programming languages. In: International Joint Conference on Web Intelligence and Intelligent Agent Technology (WI-IAT) (2020)
29. Panisson, A.R., Engelmann, D.C., Bordini, R.H.: Engineering explainable agents: an argumentation-based approach. In: Alechina, N., Baldoni, M., Logan, B. (eds.) EMAS 2021. LNCS, vol. 13190, pp. 273–291. Springer, Cham (2021). https://doi.org/10.1007/978-3-030-97457-2_16
30. Panisson, A.R., et al.: Arguing about task reallocation using ontological information in multi-agent systems. In: 12th International Workshop on Argumentation in Multiagent Systems, vol. 108 (2015)
31. Panisson, A.R., McBurney, P., Bordini, R.H.: A computational model of argumentation schemes for multi-agent systems. Argument Comput. 1–39 (2021)
32. Rao, A.S.: AgentSpeak(L): BDI agents speak out in a logical computable language. In: Van de Velde, W., Perram, J.W. (eds.) MAAMAW 1996. LNCS, vol. 1038, pp. 42–55. Springer, Heidelberg (1996). https://doi.org/10.1007/BFb0031845
33. Ricci, A., Piunti, M., Viroli, M.: Environment programming in multi-agent systems: an artifact-based perspective. Auton. Agent. Multi-Agent Syst. **23**(2), 158–192 (2011)

34. Ricci, A., Viroli, M., Omicini, A.: CArtAgO: an infrastructure for engineering computational environments in MAS. In: Weyns, D., Parunak, H.V.D., Michel, F. (eds.) 3rd International Workshop "Environments for Multi-Agent Systems" (E4MAS), pp. 102–119 (2006)
35. Schmidt, D., Panisson, A.R., Freitas, A., Bordini, R.H., Meneguzzi, F., Vieira, R.: An ontology-based mobile application for task managing in collaborative groups. In: Florida Artificial Intelligence Research Society Conference (2016)
36. Sirin, E., Parsia, B., Grau, B.C., Kalyanpur, A., Katz, Y.: Pellet: a practical OWL-DL reasoner. J. Web Semant. **5**(2), 51–53 (2007)
37. Tapia-Leon, M., Rivera, A.C., Chicaiza, J., Luján-Mora, S.: Application of ontologies in higher education: a systematic mapping study. In: 2018 IEEE Global Engineering Education Conference (EDUCON), pp. 1344–1353 (2018)
38. Vieira, R., Abdalla, D.S., Silva, D.M., Santana, M.R.: Web Semântica: Ontologias, Lógica de Descrição e Inferência, pp. 127–167. SBC (2005)
39. Walton, D., Reed, C., Macagno, F.: Argumentation Schemes. Cambridge University Press, Cambridge (2008)
40. Wooldridge, M.: An Introduction to Multiagent Systems. Wiley, Hoboken (2009)

How to Solve a Classification Problem Using a Cooperative Tiling Multi-agent System?

Thibault Fourez[1,2(✉)], Nicolas Verstaevel[1], Frédéric Migeon[1], Frédéric Schettini[2], and Frédéric Amblard[1]

[1] Institut de Recherche en Informatique de Toulouse, Université de Toulouse, CNRS, Toulouse INP, UT3, UT1, Toulouse, France
{thibault.fourez,nicolas.verstaevel,frederic.migeon, frederic.amblard}@irit.fr

[2] Citec Ingénieurs Conseil, Geneva, Switzerland
frederic.schettini@citec.ch

Abstract. Adaptive Multi-Agent Systems (AMAS) transform dynamic problems into problems of local cooperation between agents. We present *smapy*, an ensemble based AMAS implementation for mobility prediction, whose agents are provided with machine learning models in addition to their cooperation rules. With a detailed methodology, we propose a framework to transform a classification problem into a cooperative tiling of the input variable space. We show that it is possible to use linear classifiers for online non-linear classification on three benchmark toy problems chosen for their different levels of linear separability, if they are integrated in a cooperative Multi-Agent structure. The results obtained show a significant improvement of the performance of linear classifiers in non-linear contexts in terms of classification accuracy and decision boundaries, thanks to the cooperative approach.

Keywords: Adaptative multi-agent system · Ensemble learning · Non-linear classification

1 Introduction

Supervised classification problems have been extensively addressed using machine learning algorithms called classifiers. These problems are generally not linearly separable (i.e. the point clouds of the different classes are not separable by hyperplanes). Moreover, in so-called dynamic problems, new classes appear and disappear and the behavior of individuals evolves in time and space (e.g. management of smart cities and the appearance of new transport modes and behavior). Dynamic problems are often associated with ambient environments in which new devices may appear or disappear dynamically [12,16]. Many classifiers are themselves composed of multiple linear classifiers (i.e. whose decision function is a linear combination of input variables) that they aggregate.

© The Author(s), under exclusive license to Springer Nature Switzerland AG 2022
F. Dignum et al. (Eds.): PAAMS 2022, LNAI 13616, pp. 166–178, 2022.
https://doi.org/10.1007/978-3-031-18192-4_14

After positioning *smapy* with respect to machine learning techniques for classifier aggregation in Sect. 2, we detail its operation in Sect. 3. In Sect. 4.2, we show that our MAS is able, thanks to a space exploration by four types of linear classifiers and cooperation rules, to linear toy classification problems with different levels of linear separability from the literature. **We show through this experiment that it is possible to transform a classification problem into a cooperation problem** through the exploration of the space of input variables. The results presented in Sect. 5 are discussed in Sect. 6.

The main contributions of this paper are:

- *Smapy*, an ensemble Multi-Agent System (MAS) for online non-linear classification based on the AMAS framework
- An experiment on three two-dimensional problems from literature to evaluate the performance of our MAS for different levels of linear separability

2 Related Work

In this section, we situate our approach among other machine learning methods based on aggregation of classifiers. After presenting their advantages and weaknesses, we show that the AMAS approach is a constructivist and ensemble learning method. We then detail how our approach meets the objectives of **online** solving of **dynamic problems** through cooperative tiling of the input variable space.

2.1 Aggregation of Classifiers

Many non-linear classifiers aggregate several linear classifiers. We distinguish two types of aggregation: connectionist and ensemble approaches. We also present self-constructing algorithms in classifier aggregation.

Connectionism. The connectionist approach can be illustrated by a serial electrical circuit. The input data passes successively through a chain of classifiers and the decision function of the global classifier is a composition of the decision functions of the internal classifiers. In supervised learning, the information on the output goes back up the chain of classifiers in the opposite direction.

The connectionist approach is associated with artificial neural networks (ANN) in which the information of the output data is fed back through the gradient back-propagation algorithm [18]. The neurons composing the network can be seen as internal classifiers. A network is usually composed of several layers (multi-layer perceptron). The multiplication of these layers is at the origin of deep learning.

The main limitation of the connectionist approach is the need for a large number of observations to optimize the weights associated with each internal classifier. In dynamic problems where the behavior of individuals evolves over time, new data are generally not available in sufficient number to update the learning model.

Ensemble. The ensemble approach is similar to a parallel electrical circuit. The input data passes through several classifiers in parallel, and the output of the decision function is an aggregation of the outputs of the decision functions of each classifier.

Bagging is a learning technique combining the use of bootstraps and the aggregation of prediction models. The assumption of bagging, inspired by the law of large numbers, is that averaging the predictions of several independent models reduces the variance and thus the error of the global prediction. The Random Forest algorithm [2] uses binary decision trees by adding a random draw of the input variables to be considered for each intermediate model.

Unlike bagging, boosting algorithms build a model sequentially from so-called weak models. At each step, the bad points predicted by the previous model are given a higher weight when training the current model. Adaptive Boosting (AdaBoost) [19] uses binary decision trees with a single node and a single input variable. In Gradient Boosting [11] and eXtreme Gradient Boosting (XGBoost) [5], the weights of the points are no longer incremented but a cost function minimized by gradient descent allows to aggregate intermediate models to the global model.

Constructivism. In self-constructing aggregation approach, the graph of internal classifiers (connectionist or ensemble) does not have a fixed structure. This structure is built during the learning process and can evolve over time. When changes to the classifier graph are made by the classifiers themselves, the system is self-organizing.

Algorithms such as self-constructing neural networks [4] lie at the intersection of connectionism and constructivism, because the structure of the layers of neurons is built incrementally.

Context-aware learning is a constructivist and almost ensemble approach. In ELLSA [8], the Context agents can be seen as linear classifiers (although they can only predict one class) with cooperative rules.

The constructivist approach allows us to design self-organizing non-linear classifiers suitable for solving dynamic problems. In this paper, we propose an ensemble context-based learning MAS. In the following paragraphs, we situate our contribution in the field of adaptative MAS.

2.2 Multi-agent Systems

Multi-agent systems (MAS) are systems involving autonomous entities called agents, capable of communicating in a common environment in which each has its own perceptions and knowledge [10]. Each agent acts locally to get closer to its objectives using its own skills.

Problem solving by MAS is the search for a balance in the interactions between agents. It is not the sum of the individual abilities of the agents, but rather the product of their interactions, which leads to the emergence of new resolution abilities. This phenomenon of emergence is regularly invoked to justify the use of MAS for the collective resolution of dynamic and complex problems.

Self-organization. Self-organization is the capacity of a system to dynamically modify its internal structure without external intervention [14]. Self-organization is said to be strong when the modifications are not the consequence of a centralized decision. In the framework of MAS, the agents can modify the global function of the system by acting on their local environment.

The theory of adaptive multi-agent systems (AMAS) [3] proposes a cooperative approach to interactions between agents. The design criteria presented for these interactions guarantee a satisfactory, but not necessarily optimal, result in the resolution of the problem at hand (functional adequacy theorem).

Context Learning. Context learning consists in exploring the space defined by the input variables of the model using cooperating agents. The AMAS for context learning (AMAS4CL) approach is based on the AMAS theory and more particularly on the Self-Adaptive Context Learning (SACL) [1] paradigm to define the rules of cooperation between agents and proposes a structure composed of several types of agents to explore the space of the problem variables. Algorithms based on the SACL approach are used to solve various problems such as learning by demonstration [21] or Inverse Kinematics [9] in robotics and optimization of the operation of a heat pump [1]. SACL architectures are typically composed of three types of agents:

- Context agents that define hypercubes of the input variable space. When a new point belongs to one of these zones, the corresponding Context agent is said to be activated and proposes a system decision according to its own knowledge
- The Percept agents which retrieve the values of the input variables (sensors) at each iteration and transmit them to the Context agents
- The Head agent which receives the proposals of the activated Context agents and sends them feedbacks from oracle

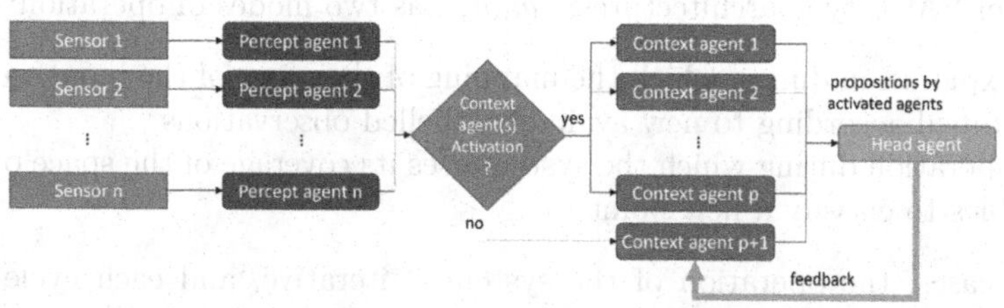

Fig. 1. Cooperative operation of a SACL architecture in exploration phase

A context learning MAS has two modes of operation: exploration (learning) which consists in tiling the input variable space by instantiating and arranging the Context agents thanks to the feedback from the Head agent, and exploitation (prediction) which consists in taking a decision without updating the system.

The functioning of this architecture is presented in Fig. 1 for the cooperative case in the exploration phase (i.e., the optimal functioning case). When the behavior of the system is not optimal with respect to the user's objectives, the situation is said to be non-cooperative (NCS). The system must adapt to maximize the cooperation between agents to return to the cooperative state. In Context Learning, this cooperation is expressed in the sizes (i.e., the dimensions of the hypercubes), positions and knowledge of the Context agents.

The SACL approach is adapted to dynamic problems (i.e. the system adapts to changes in the distribution of the input data over time) and supports online learning. Moreover, the position and size of the agents in the space of the input variables provide additional information about the phenomenon under study and a geometric interpretation.

3 Smapy

In our contribution, we provide each Context agent with an internal machine learning model, linear or not, with the only requirement to support online learning. Each internal model is trained on the points that have activated the corresponding Context agent and thus constitutes a local modeling (in the sense of the space of input variables) of the underlying function of the problem to solve. This context learning MAS, *smapy*, has been implemented in python for the industrial needs of the research project.

The structure of our MAS theoretically allows to integrate smapy instances in a Context agent in a recursive way, like Holonic Multi-Agent Systems (HMAS) [17]. However, unlike HMAS, such a Context agent would not be composed of sub-agents of lower autonomy, but of a smapy instance independent of the global smapy instance.

3.1 General Principle

Like other SACL type architectures, *smapy* has two modes of operation:

- The exploration during which the mapping of the space of the input variables is modified according to new available labelled observations
- The operation during which the system uses its coverage of the space of input variables to classify a new point

In both cases, the operation of the system is iterative, and each cycle starts with a new observation. During the exploration, the activated Context agents update their internal model with the last observation after they have proposed an output class to the Head agent and received feedback (positive or not). The feedback received by a Context agent allows it to update its perception of itself within the collective through a performance metric explained in the Sect. 3.3. It also allows him to know if he has a non-cooperative behavior with respect to the objective of the system and, if necessary, to act on itself or its neighbors to return to a cooperative state (c.f. Sect. 3.4).

3.2 Agents

In this section, we present the three types of agents involved in our SACL architecture, whose relationships have been described in Fig. 1.

Percept. The p Percept agents collect the values of the p input variables of each new observation and pass them to the Context agents. They also store the observed extrema for each variable.

Context. A Context agent l defines a hypercube in the p-dimensional space of input variables. For each dimension j, it has two parameters $r_{l,j,0}^t$ and $r_{l,j,1}^t$ that define the lower and upper bounds of an activation interval at iteration t. The agent can compute at any time $v_l(T)$, the volume of its activation hypercube at iteration T, according to the following formula:

$$v_l(T) = \prod_{j=1}^{p} (r_{l,j,1}^t - r_{l,j,0}^t) \tag{1}$$

The Context agent also has a confidence level $c_l(T)$ at iteration T, depending on its history $\mathcal{H}_l^T$ (set of its activation cycles since its creation), its class proposals $\hat{y}_l^t$t for observations y^t on this history, and two external parameters F_+ and F_- that respectively weight the positive and negative feedbacks of the agent Head:

$$c_l(T) = \sum_{t \in \mathcal{H}_l^T} (F_+ * \Vdash_{\hat{y}_l^t = y^t} - F_- * \Vdash_{\hat{y}_l^t \neq y^t}) \tag{2}$$

From its two terms, we define the score $s_l(T)$ of a Context agent at iteration T using a normalization function N_c which is an external parameter of *smapy*:

$$s_l(T) = N_c \circ c_l(T) \tag{3}$$

Finally, the Context agent has an internal classification model learned from the observations that activated it. The python implementation of *smapy* makes it possible to use models in the *scikit-learn* fashion if they support online learning to adapt the agent to new observations. For the rest of this paper, we define several properties of Context agents:

Definition 1 (Expansion/retraction). *A Context agent expands (resp. retracts) by a factor α when it increases (resp. decreases) its boundaries to multiply its volume by $1 + \alpha$ (resp. $1 - \alpha$).*

Definition 2 (Push). *A Context agent l_1 pushes a Context agent l_2 when l_2 retracts so that the previous intersection of l_1 and l_2 is completely outside l_2 (and thus contained only within l_1).*

Definition 3 (Absorption). *A Context agent l_1 absorbs a Context agent l_2 when l_1 expands to completely contain the area covered by l_2 and the agent l_2 is destroyed.*

Definition 4 (Point exclusion). *A Context agent l_1 excludes an observation y when l_1 retracts so that y ends up outside l_1. Point exclusion is controlled by an external Boolean parameter E.*

Definition 5 (Overlapping index). *The overlapping index o_{l_1,l_2} is the ratio of the volume of the intersection of two Context agents l_1 and l_2 to the minimum of the volumes of these agents:*

$$o_{l_1,l_2} = o_{l_2,l_1} = \frac{v_{l_1 \cap l_2}}{\min(v_{l_1}, v_{l_2})} \tag{4}$$

Head. The Head agent supervises the cooperation of the Context agents. At each iteration, it selects the class proposed by the activated Context agent with the highest score (and proceeds by majority vote in case of a tie) and sends feedbacks to all the agents activated during the exploration phase (c.f. Sect. 3.3). The Head agent can also create new Context agents in case of system incompetence (c.f. Sect. 3.4).

3.3 Feedback

When the Context agents are activated, they propose a prediction to the Head agent. The latter selects the prediction of the agent with the highest score. During the exploration phase (learning), the Head agent sends feedbacks to the Context agents which have proposed a prediction:

- If the prediction is good (with respect to the label of the new point), then the confidence of the context agent increases by F_+ and it expands by a factor α (external parameter)
- If the prediction is bad, then the confidence of the context agent decreases by F_-. If point exclusion is allowed (i.e., E is true), then the context agent excludes the new point. Otherwise, the Context agent's local model is fine-tuned with the new point (in the sense of online learning), and it retracts by a factor α

3.4 Non-cooperative Situations

The objective of AMAS is to transform the initial problem into a problem of cooperation between agents. Non-cooperative situations (NCS) are states during which the behavior of the system must evolve to reach the goal set by the user. In context learning, this results in the rearrangement of the Context agents to improve the tiling of the input variable space. In this section, we present and schematize in Fig. 2 the three types of NCS that can occur during the operation of *smapy* and their resolution.

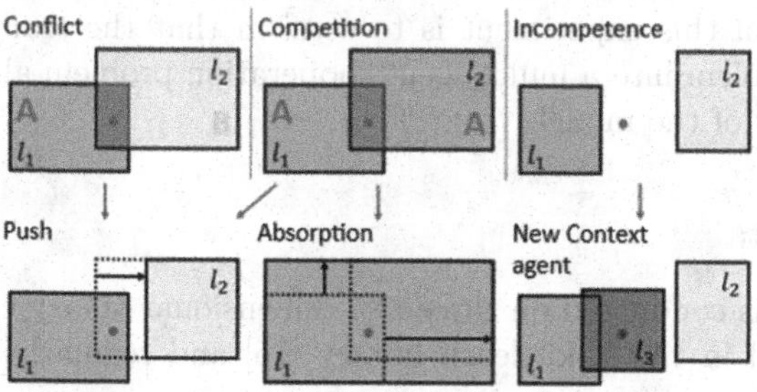

Fig. 2. Schematic of NCS (top row) and their resolution (bottom row) for Context agents l_1, l_2 and l_3 predicting classes A and B

Incompetence. Incompetence occurs when no Context agent has been activated:

- Exploration: a new Context agent is created around the new point and any NCS generated are resolved. The initial radius of the new agent is controlled by an external parameter R
- Exploitation: the closest Context agent to the new point (in the sense of the Euclidean distance between the point and the agent's boundary) proposes its prediction

Competition. Competition occurs during the exploration phase when two activated Context agents propose the same prediction (in this case, the same class):

- If an overlapping threshold is defined through the external parameter O, and if the overlapping index of the two agents is greater than this threshold, the agent with the higher score absorbs the other
- Otherwise, the Context agent with the higher score pushes the other agent

Conflict. Conflict occurs during the exploration phase when two activated Context agents propose different predictions. The agent with the higher score then pushes the other agent.

4 Comparison of Linear Classifiers Alone with Context Learning Approach

In this section, we present the experiment of comparing four types of linear classifiers and instances of *smapy* with these same models inside Context agents. The linear classifiers used in this paper are:

- Logistic regression (ridge [13], LASSO [20] or ElasticNet [22])
- Linear Support Vector Machine (SVM) [7]
- Passive Agressive algorithms [6] (PA-I and PA-II)

The motivation of this experiment is to confirm that the transformation of a classification problem into a multi-agent cooperation problem allows to improve the performances of the model.

4.1 Input Data

The experiment is conducted on three two-dimensional binary classification toy datasets included in the scikit-learn library [15] and regularly used for model comparison purposes:

- Moons: Two interleaved point clouds explained by the two variables (`noise=0.3`)
- Circles: A circular point cloud embedded in another ring-shaped cloud (`noise=0.2`, `factor=0.5`)
- Linearly separable: Two point clouds with a linear boundary explained by only one of the two variables

Each data set contains 100 points. They are centered and reduced using the scikit-learn `StandardScaler` model before learning.

4.2 Experimental Protocol

Table 1. List of value grids for the search of optimal combinations of parameters of the studied linear models (scikit-learn implementation)

Parameter	Grid of values		
Logit & Linear SVM			
`alpha`	0.0001	0.001	0.01
`penalty`	l_1	l_2	ElasticNet
PA-I & PA-II			
`C`	0.5	1.0	2.0

Table 2. List of value grids for finding the optimal combinations *smapy* parameters

Parameter	Grid of values		
R	0.1	0.2	0.5
O	0.2	0.5	
E	False	True	
N_c	Sigmoid		
α	0.0	0.1	0.2
F_+	1.0		
F_-	0.5	1.0	2.0

Step 1. First, we search for the optimal combination of parameters for each of the four linear classifiers among a grid of parameters presented in the Table 1 using a five-fold cross validation.

Step 2. Once these combinations are obtained, we search for the optimal combination of *smapy* parameters for each linear classifier among a grid of parameters presented in the Table 2 with a five-fold cross validation. The Context agents of the *smapy* instances have as internal model the corresponding linear model, trained with the parameters of its previously obtained optimal combination.

This protocol is repeated for each dataset to obtain 12 *smapy* instances and 12 corresponding linear classifier instances, all of which have been optimized by cross-validation. The optimized *smapy* instances are then compared with the linear classifiers using two evaluation metrics:

- Classification accuracy (multi-class) averaged over the five iterations of cross-validation (step 1 for linear models, step 2 for *smapy*)
- Decision boundaries of the models (linear or *smapy*) trained with the best parameter combinations obtained by cross-validation

5 Results

In this section, we present comparative results between linear classifiers alone and *smapy* instances according to the two metrics introduced previously (Sect. 4.2).

5.1 Classification Accuracy

Table 3. Comparison of the classification accuracies obtained for each classifier alone or inside *smapy*

	Moons		Circles		Linearly separable	
	Alone	MAS	Alone	MAS	Alone	MAS
Logit	0.83	**0.89**	0.49	**0.83**	**0.92**	0.91
Linear SVM	0.86	**0.89**	0.53	**0.83**	0.90	**0.91**
PA-I	0.82	**0.89**	0.53	**0.83**	0.89	**0.90**
PA-II	0.84	**0.87**	0.53	**0.83**	**0.89**	**0.89**

Table 3 shows no significant difference in accuracy after switching to MAS with the dataset *Linearly separable*. The linear classifiers already achieve a high score despite the noise in the data.

For the other two datasets, we observe an improvement of the accuracy with the *smapy* instances. In particular, we observe a ∼30% improvement for the dataset *Circles*, for which the linear classifiers alone give a result close to chance (50%). The poor performance of these classifiers is explained by the low linear separability of the dataset. However, we see that the integration of these classifiers in an SMA allows to approach the quadratic boundary of the dataset.

The accuracies obtained on the dataset *Moons* (intermediate case in terms of linear separability) are slightly better with the MAS approach, but the linear classifiers alone allow to obtain satisfactory scores.

5.2 Decision Boundaries

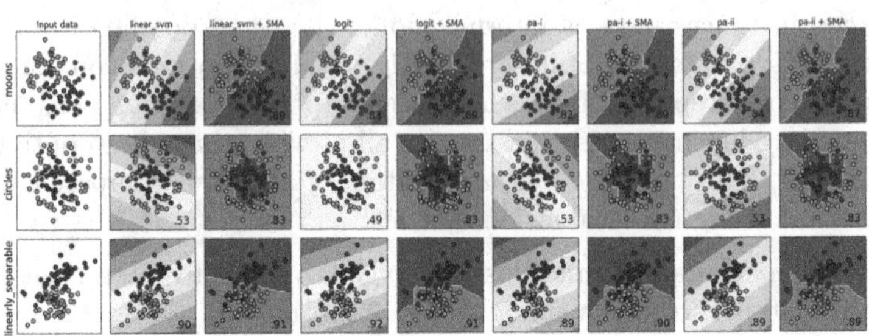

Fig. 3. Decision boundaries and classification accuracy obtained for each dataset (rows) and for each linear classifier alone or in a *smapy* instance (columns)

Figure 3 shows that linear classifiers alone give linear boundaries that are suitable for the classification problem for the datasets *Moons* and *Linearly separable.* The MAS approach on these two datasets reproduces this linear behavior in the boundaries.

On the other hand, with the dataset *Circles*, the linear models alone are unable to separate the two enclosed point clouds, contrary to the MAS approach.

6 Discussion

Using a MAS approach, the initial classification problem is solved locally at the Context agent level. Thus, even if the agents have linear internal classifiers, they have positioned and sized each other in such a way as to locally approximate a non-linear boundary thanks to the cooperation rules presented in the Sect. 3.

However, the Context agents may have over-specialized locally by observing homogeneous groups of individuals (in the sense of the class). The point exclusion mechanism, although often selected by cross validation, tends to reinforce this over-specialization by excluding new class points from agents' activation zones.

Nevertheless, the ideal behavior sought for *smapy* is to build Context agents that cover homogeneous areas of the explored input variable space, notably for reasons of explicability. There is therefore a trade-off between the geometric interpretability of the layout of the Context agents and the generalization of the system to dynamic problems in which new classes may appear.

7 Conclusion

Our contribution lies at the intersection of the constructivist SACL pattern and ensemble learning methods. Our contribution provides each Context agent with an internal supervised classification model, as well as rules for cooperation with other agents. By choosing linear models for the Context agents, we show that it is possible to simplify a non-linear classification problem by transforming it into a local cooperation problem within a context learning MAS. Our experimental methodology allows us to observe a significant improvement of the classification accuracy on non linearly separable datasets.

The next step is the use of *smapy* for dynamic real-world problems such as smart city management with the guarantee of an interpretable prediction compared to other state-of-the-art algorithms.

Our main research direction on *smapy* is the possibility to use different algorithms in the internal models of the Context agents. The idea is to exploit the strengths and weaknesses of different known algorithms to optimize prediction quality at specific locations in the space where certain models perform best.

Finally, improvements in the operating rules of *smapy* are needed to avoid over-specialization of the Context agents while maintaining the explicability and stability of the system. For this purpose, the "severity" of the NCS correction mechanisms could evolve according to the convergence of the agents' layout towards a supposedly optimal layout.

Acknowledgements. We thank the National Association for Research and Technology (ANRT) for the CIFRE funding of the thesis project in partnership with the Institut de Recherche en Informatique de Toulouse (IRIT) and the company Citec Ingénieurs Conseil. We also thank all the reviewers for their help and advice.

References

1. Boes, J., Nigon, J., Verstaevel, N., Gleizes, M.-P., Migeon, F.: The self-adaptive context learning pattern: overview and proposal. In: Christiansen, H., Stojanovic, I., Papadopoulos, G.A. (eds.) CONTEXT 2015. LNCS (LNAI), vol. 9405, pp. 91–104. Springer, Cham (2015). https://doi.org/10.1007/978-3-319-25591-0_7
2. Breiman, L.: Random forests. Mach. Learn. **45**(1), 5–32 (2001)
3. Capera, D., Georgé, J.P., Gleizes, M.P., Glize, P.: The AMAS theory for complex problem solving based on self-organizing cooperative agents. In: Proceedings of the Twelfth IEEE International Workshops on Enabling Technologies: Infrastructure for Collaborative Enterprises, WET ICE 2003, pp. 383–388. IEEE (2003)
4. do Carmo Nicoletti, M., Bertini, J.R., Elizondo, D., Franco, L., Jerez, J.M.: Constructive neural network algorithms for feedforward architectures suitable for classification tasks. In: Franco, L., Elizondo, D.A., Jerez, J.M. (eds.) Constructive Neural Networks. SCI, vol. 258, pp. 1–23. Springer, Heidelberg (2009). https://doi.org/10.1007/978-3-642-04512-7_1
5. Chen, T., Guestrin, C.: XGBoost: a scalable tree boosting system. In: Proceedings of the 22nd ACM SIGKDD International Conference on Knowledge Discovery and Data Mining, pp. 785–794 (2016)
6. Crammer, K., Dekel, O., Keshet, J., Shalev-Shwartz, S., Singer, Y.: Online passive aggressive algorithms. J. Mach. Learn. Res. **7**, 551–585 (2006)
7. Cristianini, N., Shawe-Taylor, J., et al.: An Introduction to Support Vector Machines and Other Kernel-Based Learning Methods. Cambridge University Press, Cambridge (2000)

8. Dato, B.: Lifelong learning by endogenous feedback, application to a robotic system. Ph.D. thesis, Université Toulouse 3-Paul Sabatier (2021)
9. Dato, B., Gleizes, M.P., Migeon, F.: Cooperative neighborhood learning: application to robotic inverse model. In: 13th International Conference on Agents and Artificial Intelligence (ICAART 2021) (2021)
10. Ferber, J., Weiss, G.: Multi-agent Systems: An Introduction to Distributed Artificial Intelligence, vol. 1. Addison-Wesley Reading (1999)
11. Friedman, J.H.: Stochastic gradient boosting. Comput. Stat. Data Anal. **38**(4), 367–378 (2002)
12. Guivarch, V., Camps, V., Péninou, A., Stuker, S.: Dynamic filtering of useless data in an adaptive multi-agent system: evaluation in the ambient domain. In: Demazeau, Y., Ishida, T., Corchado, J.M., Bajo, J. (eds.) PAAMS 2013. LNCS (LNAI), vol. 7879, pp. 110–121. Springer, Heidelberg (2013). https://doi.org/10.1007/978-3-642-38073-0_10
13. Hoerl, A.E., Kennard, R.W.: Ridge regression: biased estimation for nonorthogonal problems. Technometrics **12**(1), 55–67 (1970)
14. Di Marzo Serugendo, G., Gleizes, M.P., Karageorgos, A.: History and definitions. In: Di Marzo Serugendo, G., Gleizes, M.P., Karageorgos, A. (eds.) Self-organising Software. Natural Computing Series, pp. 33–74. Springer, Heidelberg (2011). https://doi.org/10.1007/978-3-642-17348-6_3
15. Pedregosa, F., et al.: Scikit-learn: machine learning in Python. J. Mach. Learn. Res. **12**, 2825–2830 (2011)
16. Perles, A., Crasnier, F., Georgé, J.-P.: AMAK - a framework for developing robust and open adaptive multi-agent systems. In: Bajo, J., et al. (eds.) PAAMS 2018. CCIS, vol. 887, pp. 468–479. Springer, Cham (2018). https://doi.org/10.1007/978-3-319-94779-2_40
17. Rodriguez, S., Hilaire, V., Gaud, N., Galland, S., Koukam, A.: Holonic multi-agent systems. In: Di Marzo Serugendo, G., Gleizes, M.P., Karageorgos, A. (eds.) Self-organising Software. NCS, pp. 251–279. Springer, Heidelberg (2011). https://doi.org/10.1007/978-3-642-17348-6_11
18. Rumelhart, D.E., Hinton, G.E., Williams, R.J.: Learning representations by back-propagating errors. Nature **323**(6088), 533–536 (1986)
19. Schapire, R., Freund, Y., et al.: A decision-theoretic generalization of on-line learning and an application to boosting. In: Second European Conference on Computational Learning Theory, pp. 23–37 (1995)
20. Tibshirani, R.: Regression shrinkage and selection via the lasso. J. Roy. Stat. Soc.: Ser. B (Methodol.) **58**(1), 267–288 (1996)
21. Verstaevel, N., Régis, C., Gleizes, M.P., Robert, F.: Principles and experimentations of self-organizing embedded agents allowing learning from demonstration in ambient robotic. Procedia Comput. Sci. **52**, 194–201 (2015)
22. Zou, H., Hastie, T.: Regularization and variable selection via the elastic net. J. R. Stat. Soc.: Ser. B (Stat. Methodol.) **67**(2), 301–320 (2005)

Multi-agent Learning of Numerical Methods for Hyperbolic PDEs with Factored Dec-MDP

Yiwei Fu[1(✉)], Dheeraj S.K. Kapilavai[1], and Elliot Way[2]

[1] GE Research, 12309 Niskayuna, NY, USA
{yiwei.fu,kapilava}@ge.com
[2] Binghamton University, Binghamton, NY 13902, USA

Abstract. Factored decentralized Markov decision process (Dec-MDP) is a framework for modeling sequential decision making problems in multi-agent systems. In this paper, we formalize the learning of numerical methods for hyperbolic partial differential equations (PDEs), specifically the Weighted Essentially Non-Oscillatory (WENO) scheme, as a factored Dec-MDP problem. We show that different reward formulations lead to either reinforcement learning (RL) or behavior cloning, and a homogeneous policy could be learned for all agents under the RL formulation with a policy gradient algorithm. Because the trained agents only act on their local observations, the multi-agent system can be used as a general numerical method for hyperbolic PDEs and generalize to different spatial discretizations, episode lengths, dimensions, and even equation types.

Keywords: Decentralized markov decision process · Multi-agent system · Numerical method · Partial differential equation

1 Introduction

Numerical methods such as the finite difference method (FDM), finite element method (FEM), and finite-volume method (FVM) were designed on grids of data points to approximate the solutions of partial differential equations (PDEs) numerically. Specifically, hyperbolic PDEs are often used in real-world applications, especially in the field of fluid dynamics for modeling the motion of viscous fluids with high Reynolds numbers, multiphase flows, water waves, etc. Often, simulations of these physical processes exploit the numerical fluxes of some conserved quantities from finite differences between two elements, and time integration is used to determine the next state. This kind of incremental computation in time is similar to a Markov Decision Process (MDP), where the next state is determined only by the current state, and actions provided by the numerical method. Since numerical computations happen at all grid points simultaneously, this can be viewed as a multi-agent system where each agent only has partial knowledge of the state, modeled by a decentralized MDP (Dec-MDP) [4].

© The Author(s), under exclusive license to Springer Nature Switzerland AG 2022
F. Dignum et al. (Eds.): PAAMS 2022, LNAI 13616, pp. 179–190, 2022.
https://doi.org/10.1007/978-3-031-18192-4_15

The reason that a Dec-MDP is the proper framework for modeling numerical methods can be justified from two perspectives. On one hand, if we let a single agent act on the entire physical space, which often has at least hundreds of discretized locations and requires multiple actions at each location, the number of action dimensions would be huge, with each one being continuous. Such large continuous action space quickly becomes impossible to deal with. Even with the most recent advances in deep Reinforcement Learning (RL), DQN [10] and all of its follow-ups are only able to handle large observation spaces, while the action spaces remain small discrete ones. Many Deep RL applications in robotics and control [7] do handle continuous action spaces, but they usually have less than ten dimensions, because there are simply not that many degrees of freedom in one robot. Besides, learning a numerical method with a single agent is not generalizable: any changes in spatial discretization require retraining.

On the other hand, existing numerical schemes cannot be treated as multiple independent agents acting alone at their respective locations. PDEs that describe some underlying processes must have physics that propagates from one location to the other, so if the action at one location changes, the state at another location would be different even if the action at that location stays the same. This causes the non-stationary issue in a multi-agent environment [23]. Therefore, to properly model numerical methods, a Dec-MDP framework has to be used to account for the effects of other agents.

Specifically in this paper, we focus on learning Weighted Essentially Non-Oscillatory (WENO) [8,18], a state-of-the-art numerical scheme with a uniform high order of accuracy in flux reconstruction. The main idea of WENO is to form a weighted combination of several local reconstructions based on different stencils and use it as the final WENO reconstruction. The combination coefficients (weights) depend on the linear weights and smooth indicators [24]. Later we will highlight the insight that these weights can be viewed as actions of agents.

In the field of multi-agent systems, it is well known that optimally solving a Decentralized Partially Observable Markov Decision Process (Dec-POMDP) is NEXP-complete [3]. Although Dec-POMDP is a more generalized formulation of Dec-MDP, with the latter being the jointly fully observable version of the former, Dec-MDP is still NEXP-complete. In our previous work [22], a policy gradient algorithm called Backpropagation Through Time and Space (BPTTS) is proposed to solve the multi-agent reinforcement learning problem for numerical methods with recurrent neural networks (RNNs). Here we use BPTTS to solve a factored Dec-MDP problem, and show that automatic differentiation is possible for the RL formulation to learn a generalizable numerical scheme.

In this paper, we introduce the fundamentals of both Dec-MDPs and numerical methods. Then, the key insight that the learning of numerical methods can be modeled as a factored Dec-MDP is drawn. We analyzed different reward formulations which lead to either RL or behavior cloning. A policy gradient algorithm, BPTTS [22], is used to solve the homogeneous multi-agent RL problem. We show that the learned policy can generate numerical solutions for hyperbolic PDEs comparable to WENO methods, and can generalize to different grid discretizations, initial conditions, dimensions, and equations. This practical application of using a factored Dec-MDP framework to solve hyperbolic PDEs is novel, and could potentially have real impacts on both industry and academia.

2 Related Work

In the field of numerical analysis, there are two distinct classes of methods: mesh-based methods and meshfree methods. The comparison of these two is beyond the scope of this paper, but usually they are incompatible, thus so are the machine learning approaches that try to learn them. For example, the WENO method [18] used in this paper is a mesh-based method; while on the other hand, the popular Physics Informed Neural Network (PINN) [15] and their descendants are meshfree: they directly use neural networks to approximate the solutions, gradients, or operators of PDEs. Since both the spatial and temporal coordinates are explicit in PINN inputs, modern deep learning architectures which handle spatial or temporal information implicitly, like Convolutional Neural Networks (CNNs), Recurrent Neural Networks (RNNs), etc., are not directly applicable. As a result, PINNs often resort to fully-connected neural networks.

Among numerous papers at the intersection of machine learning and mesh-based numerical methods, the setup in Wang et al. [21] resembles that of this paper most closely. Although they are also trying to learn a high-order numerical scheme for hyperbolic PDEs, they treat this inherently multi-agent problem as multiple independent single-agents. This will lead to a sub-optimal solution at best because for each agent the environment becomes non-stationary: the actions taken by one agent will affect the rewards of other agents and the state evolution at other locations. This invalidates the stationary Markovian assumption that the individual reward and current state should depend only on the previous state and actions taken. There exist some other papers that claim to have used multi-agent RL to discover closure models in simulations of turbulent flows [2,11]. However, they are not formulated under a truly decentralized framework because of the use of replay buffers. When sampling different state-action pairs inside a replay buffer, the temporal correlations are broken, therefore the effects of other agents' actions over time on one agent's current state are lost, again leading to a non-stationary environment. To sum up, solutions to these multi-agent systems must be consistent both spatially and temporally.

In the field of multi-agent systems, there have been some previous papers on factored Dec-POMDPs, which is close to the formulation in this paper. Oliehoek et al. [12] exploit the locality of interactions between agents in a factored Dec-POMDP and formulated decomposable value functions. This leads to a single framework based on collaborative graphical Bayesian games and is solved by heuristic policy search. However, this approach is only tested on a simple factored Firefighting problem (FFP) with three agents. Later on, this was extended to deal with more agents [13] by using a factored forward-sweep policy computation that tackles the stages of the problem one by one, but the action space for each agent remains the same (two discrete choices). Pajarinen et al. [14] propose an expectation-maximization based optimization for factored infinite-horizon Dec-POMDP and kept the complexity tractable by factored approximations. They apply the algorithm to the same FFP with a maximum of 10 agents. Messias et al. [9] convert a factored Dec-POMDP to a centralized Multi-agent POMDP by allowing inter-agent communications. Amato et al. [1] model macro-actions as options in a factored Dec-POMDP model to model systems where coordination decisions only occur at the level of deciding which macro-actions to execute. They have demonstrated that near-optimal solutions can be generated for longer horizons and larger state spaces than previous Dec-POMDP methods.

3 Background

In this section, we introduce the background of both factored Dec-MDP for modeling multi-agent systems, and weighted essentially nonoscillatory (WENO) scheme, a high-order accurate numerical scheme for hyperbolic PDEs.

3.1 Factored Dec-MDP

Before defining the multi-agent framework used in this paper, factored Dec-MDP, it is helpful to first introduce Dec-POMDP and Dec-MDP, because factored Dec-MDP is a special case of Dec-MDP, who is a special case of Dec-POMDP [4].

Definition 1. ***Dec-POMDP:*** *A Dec-POMDP for n agents is defined as a tuple $\langle \mathcal{S}, \mathcal{A}, \mathcal{P}, \Omega, \mathcal{O}, \mathcal{R} \rangle$ where:*

- *$\mathcal{S}$ is a finite set of system states;*
- *$\mathcal{A} = \langle \mathcal{A}_1, \ldots, \mathcal{A}_n \rangle$ is a set of joint actions; $\mathcal{A}_i$ is the set of actions a_i that can be executed by agent $\mathcal{A}g_i$;*
- *$\mathcal{P} = \mathcal{S} \times \mathcal{A} \times \mathcal{S} \rightarrow [0,1]$ is a transition function; $\mathcal{P}(s, a, s')$ is the probability of the outcome state s' when the agents execute the joint action a from s;*
- *$\Omega = \Omega_1 \times \Omega_2 \times \cdots \times \Omega_n$ is a finite set of observations, where Ω_i is $\mathcal{A}g_i$'s set of observations;*
- *$\mathcal{O} = \mathcal{S} \times \mathcal{A} \times \mathcal{S} \times \Omega \rightarrow [0,1]$ is the observation function; $\mathcal{O}(s, a, s', o = \langle o_1, \ldots, o_n \rangle)$ is the probability that each agent $\mathcal{A}g_i$ observes o_i when they execute the joint action a from state s and the system moves to state s'*
- *$\mathcal{R}$ is a reward function; $\mathcal{R}(s, a, s')$ is the reward the system obtains when the agents execute joint action a from state s and the system moves to state s'.*

Definition 2. ***Dec-MDP:*** *A Dec-MDP is a special case of Dec-POMDP where the system state is jointly observable, i.e.:*

- *If $\mathcal{O}(s, a, s', o = \langle o_1, ..., o_n \rangle) > 0$, then $Pr(s' | \langle o_1, ..., o_n \rangle) = 1$.*

Note that joint observability does not entail local observability. For each individual agent, the full system state is still partially observable.

Definition 3. ***Factored Dec-MDP:*** *A factored Dec-MDP is a Dec-MDP where the state of the system $\mathcal{S} = \mathcal{X}_1 \times \mathcal{X}_2 \times \cdots \times \mathcal{X}_{|\mathcal{X}|}$ has $|\mathcal{X}|$ components and is spanned by $\mathcal{X} = \{\mathcal{X}_1, \mathcal{X}_2, \cdots, \mathcal{X}_{|\mathcal{X}|}\}$.*

Like factored Dec-POMDP in [12], the reward function of factored Dec-MDP can often be compactly represented by exploiting *additive separability*, meaning that the total reward can be decomposed into the sum of local reward functions $R = R^1 + \cdots + R^p$. The local reward functions are often defined over a smaller number of state and action variables and the scope of them is smaller.

3.2 Hyperbolic PDEs and WENO Scheme

Conservation laws in many branches of classical physics, such as fluid dynamics and electrodynamics, are often described by hyperbolic PDEs. The finite-difference grid is often used when dealing with such equations. The goal is to evolve a vector of conserved quantities $u \in \mathbb{R}^d$ on a uniform N-point discretization $D_N = \{x_1, x_2, \ldots, x_j, \ldots, x_N\}$ for hyperbolic PDE of the form:

$$\frac{\partial u}{\partial t} + \frac{\partial}{\partial x} f(u) = 0 \tag{1}$$

where $f(u)$ are fluxes of each quantity in u that are exchanged at the interface $x_{j\pm\frac{1}{2}}$ of each cell, $I_j = [x_{j-\frac{1}{2}}, x_{j+\frac{1}{2}}]$. The initial conditions, $u(x_j, 0)$ at all locations at the beginning of the simulation, along with boundary conditions, $u(x_1, t)$ and $u(x_N, t)$ at all times, are required to specify the PDE. Then, the method of lines [17] is used to convert the PDE to an ordinary differential equation (ODE), where the spatial derivative is approximated by the finite differences:

$$\frac{du_j(t)}{dt} = -\frac{1}{\Delta x}(\hat{f}_{j+\frac{1}{2}} - \hat{f}_{j-\frac{1}{2}}) \tag{2}$$

with u_j being the approximation to the point value $u(x_j, t)$ and $\hat{f}_{j\pm\frac{1}{2}}$ being the numerical fluxes computed at the interfaces using cell values. A high-order finite difference scheme boils down to

- using a high-order time integration scheme (e.g., a high-order Runge-Kutta method);
- using the finite difference in Eq. (2) to approximate the derivative of the flux to a high order.

WENO scheme [18] is one high-order scheme. A WENO scheme of order r can achieve a $2r-1$ order spatially accurate construction of $\hat{f}_{j+\frac{1}{2}}$ by using the stencil S_j with $2r-1$ points around $u(x_j, t)$. Specifically, it computes $\hat{f}_{j+\frac{1}{2}}$ as a convex combination of polynomials defined on r small stencils inside S_j:

$$\hat{f}_{j+\frac{1}{2}} = \sum_{k=0}^{r-1} \omega_k \hat{f}_{k,j+\frac{1}{2}} \quad \text{with} \quad \sum_{k=0}^{r-1} \omega_k = 1 \tag{3}$$

where $\hat{f}_{k,j+\frac{1}{2}}$ is the polynomial reconstruction of the k-th small stencil. For example, for a 2-nd order WENO scheme at location x_j, the stencil is:

$$S_j = \{x_{j-1}, x_j, x_{j+1}\} \tag{4}$$

and the 2 small stencils are $\{x_{j-1}, x_j\}$, $\{x_j, x_{j+1}\}$ respectively.

To choose these convex weights ω_k and ensure they sum up to 1, WENO scheme computes the following:

$$\omega_k = \frac{\alpha_k}{\sum_{m=1}^{r} \alpha_m} \quad \text{with} \quad \alpha_k = \frac{d_k}{(\varepsilon + \beta_k)^2} \tag{5}$$

where d_k is a pre-computed optimal coefficient determined by a smoothness indicator β_k, and ϵ is a small positive number to avoid the denominator becoming zero. In smooth regions, these weights are designed to produce higher-order approximations. At discontinuities, WENO can select the single best small stencil to avoid discontinuities as far as possible by setting the one ω_k corresponding to that small stencil to be 1, and all other weights to be 0. Since the core of WENO scheme is actually an approximation procedure not directly related to hyperbolic PDEs or finite difference methods, it can also be generalized and applied to other types of schemes (finite volume, compact schemes, residual distribution schemes, limiters for the discontinuous Galerkin schemes, etc.), or to different fields [19].

4 Problem Formulation and Analysis

With the background information provided in Sect. 3, here we draw the connection between numerical methods and factored Dec-MDP, and provide some analysis on the reward formulations.

4.1 Numerical Methods as Multi-agent Systems

Because of the difficulty of translating a PDE into a computable model, the design of numerical schemes often requires substantial efforts by domain experts. If the discovery of numerical schemes can be automated, it could potentially have huge impacts on many applications. We make the key connection here that WENO scheme works exactly like a collaborative multi-agent system.

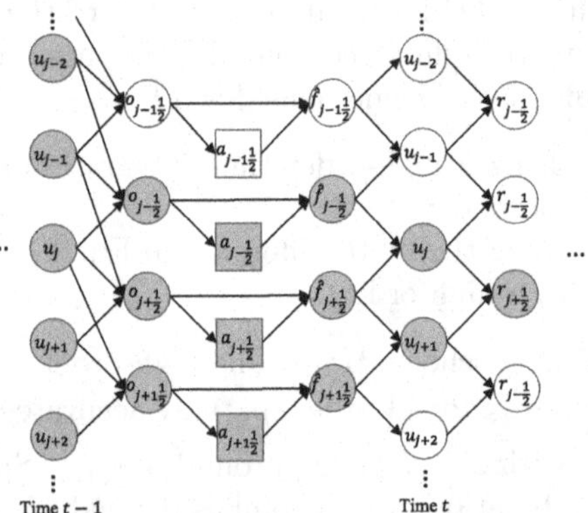

Fig. 1. The dynamics of the numerical scheme over two steps. The scope of $r_{j+\frac{1}{2}}$, illustrated by shading, increases when going back in time

To formulate the learning of numerical methods for hyperbolic PDEs as a factored Dec-MDP problem, we can start with the discretization of the physical space in Equation (1), which is precisely factoring the entire system state $\mathcal{S} \equiv u$ into n components $u_1 \times u_2 \cdots \times u_n$ as in Definition 3. From Equation (3) to (5), we can see that for WENO scheme at a certain location, it is essentially doing a local observation on the stencil and then coming up with the weights to recompute the fluxes. This process is exactly an agent taking an action a after observing a state, with the action being the weights ω_k in Equation (3). Then, the PDE (or environment) uses Equation (2) to integrate the system to the next state, which defines a deterministic transition function. This system state is Markovian and the next set of agents' actions only depends on the next state, because WENO scheme does not keep track of the history. Furthermore, since the joint observation for all agents fully covers the entire physical space, the system state is jointly observable, but not locally fully observable. Therefore, the learning of WENO schemes can be properly modeled as a factored Dec-MDP problem.

In order to learn WENO scheme, the immediate reward (the details of which will be discussed in Sect. 4.2) is defined at interface $j + \frac{1}{2}$ as the average of the error in its two adjacent cells. An error of 0 means that our agents have learned actions similar to WENO actions so that the PDE system state evolves to the same one. Following the definition of scope in [12], we can draw the dynamics of the numerical scheme in Fig. 1 and observe that the scope increases when going back in time. This should make sense from both the multi-agent system perspective and the physics perspective: the action of an agent at a certain time and space would affect the observations of other agents at a later time, or the physics would propagate from one location to another. This is precisely the reason that a multi-agent system should not be modeled as multiple independent single agents as in [21]. It should be noted that as with our previous work [22], Lax-Friedrichs flux splitting [6] was used to ensure numerical stability and avoid entropy-violating solutions, which makes the flux reconstruction slightly different by splitting them into plus and minus terms, but the main idea still holds.

4.2 Analysis of Different Reward Formulations

Among components of the factored Dec-MDP, the transition function and observation function are already determined by physics, so the only moving piece is the reward function. We formalize the reward at interface $j + \frac{1}{2}$ as follows:

$$r^t_{j+\frac{1}{2}} = -\frac{|u^t_j - ref^t_j| + |u^t_{j+1} - ref^t_{j+1}|}{2} \tag{6}$$

where u^t_j is factored state u_j at time t, and ref^t_j is a reference state at the same location j and time t computed by some existing numerical methods like WENO. Maximizing this reward will lead to the agents trying to evolve the state to be as close to the reference state as possible. Because the system immediate reward at time t is the summation of $r^t_{j+\frac{1}{2}}$ in Eq. (6) at all interfaces, $r^t = \sum_j r^t_{j+\frac{1}{2}} = -\sum_j |u^t_j - ref^t_j|$ (with a small caveat that the boundary conditions needed to be computed according to the physics), we can further analyze the reward function with integration from Eq. (2) and (3) as follows:

$$\begin{aligned} r_t &= -\sum_j |u_j^t - ref_j^t| = -\sum_j |u_j^{t-1} - \frac{\Delta t}{\Delta x}(\hat{f}_{j+\frac{1}{2}} - \hat{f}_{j-\frac{1}{2}}) - ref_j^t| \\ &= -\sum_j |u_j^{t-1} - \frac{\Delta t}{\Delta x}\sum_{k=0}^{r-1}(a_{k,j+\frac{1}{2}}\hat{f}_{k,j+\frac{1}{2}} - a_{k,j-\frac{1}{2}}\hat{f}_{k,j-\frac{1}{2}}) - ref_j^t| \end{aligned} \tag{7}$$

There are different choices of reference states, and different reward functions can be combined. However, reward engineering is beyond the scope of this paper, here we analyze 3 simple reward formulations for the PDE environment:

1. *RL-WENO* (Markovian WENO agent-based simulation rewards): the reference state is calculated from u^{t-1} with the standard WENO scheme following the computational graph in Fig. 1. This reward is Markovian because the actions of the standard WENO actions depend only on the most recent state. This reward leads to a *reinforcement learning* problem. Equation (7) becomes $r_t = -\frac{\Delta t}{\Delta x}\sum_j \sum_{k=0}^{r-1} |(a_{k,j+\frac{1}{2}} - \omega_{k,j+\frac{1}{2}})\hat{f}_{k,j+\frac{1}{2}} - (a_{k,j-\frac{1}{2}} - \omega_{k,j-\frac{1}{2}})\hat{f}_{k,j-\frac{1}{2}})|$, with ω_k being the actions taken by the WENO scheme at u_k^{t-1}.
2. *BC-WENO* (Non-Markovian fixed WENO solution rewards): the reference state is pre-calculated by running a WENO scheme from an initial condition all the way till the end. This reward is non-Markovian because the reference state is fixed and does not depend on the current system state. This fixed expert trajectory leads to *behavior cloning* and is a *supervised learning* problem. Equation (7) becomes $r_t = -\frac{\Delta t}{\Delta x}\sum_j \sum_{k=0}^{r-1} |a_{k,j+\frac{1}{2}}\hat{f}_{k,j+\frac{1}{2}} - C_{k,j+\frac{1}{2}}^t - a_{k,j-\frac{1}{2}}\hat{f}_{k,j-\frac{1}{2}} + C_{k,j-\frac{1}{2}}^t|$, with $C_{k,j+\frac{1}{2}}^t$ and $C_{k,j-\frac{1}{2}}^t$ being constants predetermined by the reference state trajectory.
3. *BC-analytical* (Non-Markovian fixed analytical solution rewards): similar to *BC-WENO*, but the reference trajectory is pre-calculated by using the analytical solution to the PDE. Of course, this requires the existence of such analytical solutions to begin with. This reward also leads to *behavior cloning*. The reward structure is similar to *BC-WENO*, but with different constants calculated by the analytical solution.

With the reward function defined and exploiting the fact that all state transitions are differentiable in this PDE environment, we could train a policy gradient algorithm (such as BPTTS [22]) for this homogeneous multi-agent system to learn numerical methods. The policy is parameterized by a fully connected neural network (NN) whose weights are shared by all agents. During training, gradients flow back in time and space following the shaded routes as illustrated in Fig. 1 and an RNN-like computational graph is created. However, this recurrent structure is not used once the agents are trained, because in a factored Dec-MDP, each agent's actions only depend on its immediate observations. This leads to incredible generalizability for the multi-agent system: they can be applied to different spatial and/or temporal discretizations, as shown in Sect. 5.

Although the performance of agents in *RL-WENO* is upper-bounded by the WENO scheme (so is *BC-WENO*), i.e., the best learning results would be $a_{k,j+\frac{1}{2}} = \omega_{k,j+\frac{1}{2}}$ or the agents take actions exactly like WENO schemes leading to the maximum reward of 0, the RL formulation provides a straightforward framework for the agents to learn. This is also the reward used in our previous work [22]. *BC-WENO* and *BC-analytical* not only suffer from the distributional drift problem in behavior cloning [16], but also have an obvious local minimum where $a_{k,j+\frac{1}{2}}\hat{f}_{k,j+\frac{1}{2}} = a_{k,j-\frac{1}{2}}\hat{f}_{k,j-\frac{1}{2}}$ since $C^t_{k,j+\frac{1}{2}}, C^t_{k,j-\frac{1}{2}}$ are just constants. This could potentially make gradient descent difficult, as shown in Sect. 5.

5 Experiment Results

In this section, we introduce the Euler equations as an example of hyperbolic PDEs, and compare the training on the 3 different reward formulations proposed in Sect. 4.2. We then show that the trained system of *RL-WENO* agents can generalize to different spatial discretizations and temporal lengths, initial conditions (ICs), equations, and even 2D Euler equations.

5.1 Euler Equations and Training Setup

The Euler equations describe the conservation of mass, momentum, and energy for fluids. They are given by:

$$\mathcal{U}_t + [\mathbf{F}(\mathcal{U})]_x = 0 \quad \text{with} \quad \mathcal{U} = \begin{pmatrix} \rho \\ \rho u \\ \rho E \end{pmatrix} \quad \mathbf{F}(\mathcal{U}) = \begin{pmatrix} \rho u \\ \rho u u + p \\ \rho u E + u p \end{pmatrix} \tag{8}$$

where ρ is the density, u is the velocity, p is the pressure and E is the total energy. E is calculated by internal energy, e, and kinetic energy as $E = e + \frac{1}{2}u^2$. The equations are closed by the addition of an equation of state, a common choice of which is the gamma-law given by $p = \rho e(\gamma - 1)$ where $\gamma = 1.4$.

Following the training setup in [22], we trained a system of agents to learn the order $r = 2$ WENO schemes on the Sod initial condition [20]. During training, the space is discretized into $N = 128$ points, i.e., the factored Dec-MDP has a system state $\mathcal{S}$ of 128 factors, resulting in a state of the shape $(3, 128)$ for the 3 equations. For agents trying to learn the $r = 2$ WENO scheme, the system observation space has a shape of $(3, 129, 2, 3)$: 3 equations, 129 agents for each equation, 2 plus and minus fluxes (because of Lax-Friedrichs flux splitting mentioned in Sect. 4.1) and 3 points in each stencil. The corresponding action space shape is $(3, 129, 2, 2)$: the first three dimensions are the same as the observation space, and the last is the 2 weights (actions) on the small stencils as given in Eq. 3. Each component of the observation and action space is continuous.

During training, the system is evolved to 1,000 timesteps of 0.0001 s seconds for a total of 0.1 s for each episode, and a total of 10,000 episodes. The policy network for each agent is a 2-layer NN with 64 neurons each and ReLU activation. An Adam optimizer [5] with a learning rate of 0.0003 is used to train the policy gradient algorithm. The training takes about 2 days on a 2.2 GHz CPU (GPU was tried but turned out to be slower because most of the computations are in the environment, not during NN training). Once trained, the system of agents can perform inference at a similar speed as standard WENO schemes.

5.2 Results and Discussions

The same multi-agent system is trained with the 3 reward formulations described in Sect. 4.2 and their total rewards during training are shown in Fig. 2. The agents are not able to learn under either *BC-WENO* or *BC-analytical* reward formulation (potentially trapped in a local minimum), but in contrast, *RL-WENO* is successful. In fact, when we train agents on $r \geq 3$ schemes, *BC-WENO* and *BC-analytical* would lead to gradient explosion immediately and the simulation has to be terminated. This is not to prove that they cannot be learned, but merely to show that behavior cloning can be difficult to train in this multi-agent system. Trained *RL-WENO* agents are used for the rest of this section.

We then show the generalizability of the trained *RL-WENO* agents in Table 1. They were tested on different initial conditions (ICs) and evolved to longer timesteps, as detailed in [22]. Because in this factored Dec-MDP formulation each agent only acts on its local observations, when the spatial discretization changes we can simply add more trained agents. As shown in Table 1, the agents have learned the standard WENO agents' policy and the system is able to perform almost exactly like the state-of-the-art WENO numerical scheme for solving Euler equations.

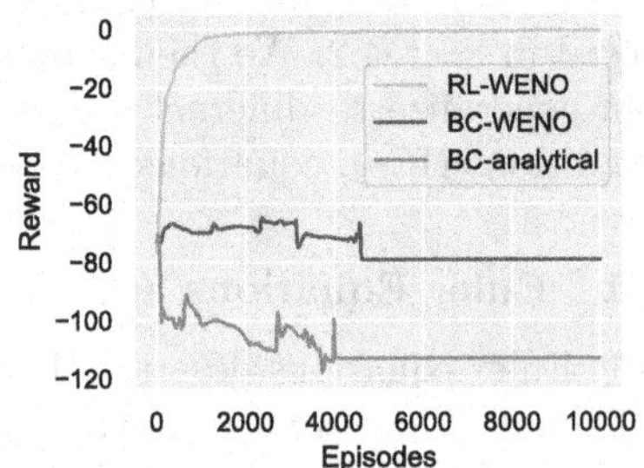

Fig. 2. Reward during training for different reward formulations

Table 1. Comparison of trained *RL-WENO* agents' and standard WENO agents' L2 error with the analytical solution for Euler equations on different ICs

IC	Sod		Sod2		Lax		Sonic rarefaction	
N	**RL-WENO**	**WENO**	**RL-WENO**	**WENO**	**RL-WENO**	**WENO**	**RL-WENO**	**WENO**
64	0.0707	0.0707	0.0628	0.0628	0.5275	0.5280	2.1192	2.1183
128	0.0420	0.0420	0.0407	0.0407	0.4109	0.4110	1.2401	1.2402
256	0.0278	0.0278	0.0267	0.0267	0.2411	0.2411	0.7867	0.7866
512	0.0218	0.0218	0.0183	0.0183	0.2232	0.2233	0.5531	0.5532

Furthermore, we show that the *RL-WENO* agents trained on 1D Euler Equations can be applied to solving a different hyperbolic PDE, Burger's Equation, as shown in Fig. 3a. The agents behave exactly like the standard WENO scheme and generate solutions close to the true analytical solution. The same agents can also be applied to solving 2D Euler equations as shown in Fig. 3b by acting on both dimensions. These results show that the agents have truly learned the physics and the multi-agent system can perform new tasks.

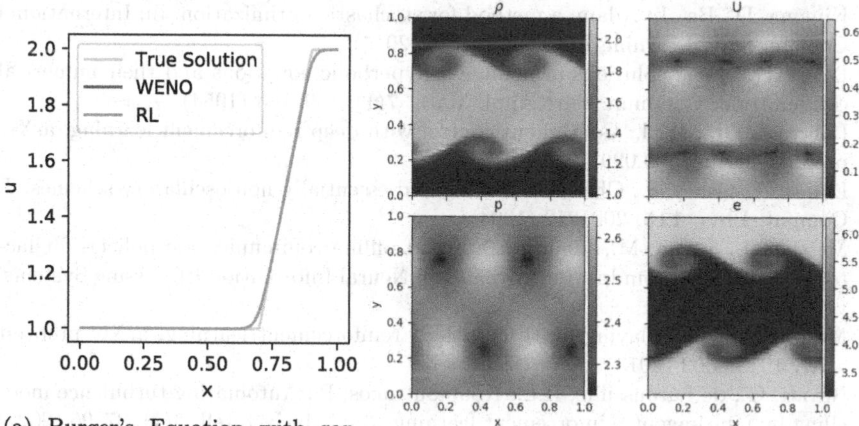

(a) Burger's Equation with rarefaction initial condition, evolved to 0.2s.

(b) 2D Euler Equations with Kelvin-Helmholtz initial condition, evolved to 2.0s.

Fig. 3. Testing *RL-WENO* agents on different equation and different dimension

6 Conclusion

In this paper, we introduced both factored Dec-MDP and numerical methods and formulated the learning of WENO scheme as a multi-agent learning problem. We analyzed different reward formulations, which lead to reinforcement learning (RL) or behavior cloning. We experimentally tested these formulations and showed that the agents could learn a policy under the RL formulation using a policy gradient algorithm. Because of the flexibility provided by this factored Dec-MDP framework, the trained agents can be applied to different spatial discretizations, episode lengths, and even equations. This paper aims to bridge the gap between the domains of scientific computing and multi-agent systems. There are many future directions for this work, including but not limited to learning new numerical schemes that go beyond imitating existing methods by automatically discovering better ones.

References

1. Amato, C., Konidaris, G.D., Kaelbling, L.P.: Planning with macro-actions in decentralized pomdps (2014)
2. Bae, H.J., Koumoutsakos, P.: Scientific multi-agent reinforcement learning for wall-models of turbulent flows. Nat. Commun. **13**(1), 1–9 (2022)
3. Bernstein, D.S., Givan, R., Immerman, N., Zilberstein, S.: The complexity of decentralized control of markov decision processes. Math. Oper. Res. **27**(4), 819–840 (2002)
4. Beynier, A., Charpillet, F., Szer, D., Mouaddib, A.I.: Dec-mdp/pomdp. In: Markov Decision Processes in Artificial Intelligence, pp. 277–318 (2013)

5. Kingma, D., Ba, J.: Adam: a method for stochastic optimization. In: International Conference on Learning Representations (2014)
6. Lax, P.D.: Weak solutions of nonlinear hyperbolic equations and their numerical computation. Commun. Pure Appl. Math. **7**(1), 159–193 (1954)
7. Lillicrap, T.P., et al.: Continuous control with deep reinforcement learning. arXiv preprint arXiv:1509.02971 (2015)
8. Liu, X.D., Osher, S., Chan, T.F.: Weighted essentially non-oscillatory schemes. J. Comput. Phys. **115**, 200–212 (1994)
9. Messias, J., Spaan, M., Lima, P.: Efficient offline communication policies for factored multiagent pomdps. In: Advances in Neural Information Processing Systems, vol. 24 (2011)
10. Mnih, V., et al.: Playing atari with deep reinforcement learning. arXiv preprint arXiv:1312.5602 (2013)
11. Novati, G., de Laroussilhe, H.L., Koumoutsakos, P.: Automating turbulence modelling by multi-agent reinforcement learning. Nat. Mach. Intell. **3**(1), 87–96 (2021)
12. Oliehoek, F.A., Spaan, M.T., Vlassis, N., Whiteson, S.: Exploiting locality of interaction in factored dec-pomdps. In: International Joint Conference on Autonomous Agents and Multi-Agent Systems, pp. 517–524 (2008)
13. Oliehoek, F.A., Whiteson, S., Spaan, M.T., et al.: Approximate solutions for factored dec-pomdps with many agents. In: AAMAS, pp. 563–570 (2013)
14. Pajarinen, J.K., Peltonen, J.T.: Efficient planning for factored infinite-horizon dec-pomdps. In: Twenty-Second International Joint Conference on Artificial Intelligence (2011)
15. Raissi, M., Perdikaris, P., Karniadakis, G.E.: Physics-informed neural networks: a deep learning framework for solving forward and inverse problems involving nonlinear partial differential equations. J. Comput. Phys. **378**, 686–707 (2019)
16. Ross, S.: Interactive learning for sequential decisions and predictions. Ph.D. thesis, Carnegie Mellon University (2013)
17. Schiesser, W.E.: The numerical method of lines: integration of partial differential equations. Elsevier (2012)
18. Shu, C.-W.: Essentially non-oscillatory and weighted essentially non-oscillatory schemes for hyperbolic conservation laws. In: Quarteroni, A. (ed.) Advanced Numerical Approximation of Nonlinear Hyperbolic Equations. LNM, vol. 1697, pp. 325–432. Springer, Heidelberg (1998). https://doi.org/10.1007/BFb0096355
19. Shu, C.W.: High order weighted essentially nonoscillatory schemes for convection dominated problems. SIAM Rev. **51**(1), 82–126 (2009)
20. Sod, G.A.: A survey of several finite difference methods for systems of nonlinear hyperbolic conservation laws. J. Comput. Phys. **27**(1), 1–31 (1978)
21. Wang, Y., Shen, Z., Long, Z., Dong, B.: Learning to discretize: solving 1d scalar conservation laws via deep reinforcement learning. arXiv preprint arXiv:1905.11079 (2019)
22. Way, E., Kapilavai, D.S., Fu, Y., Yu, L.: Backpropagation through time and space: learning numerical methods with multi-agent reinforcement learning. arXiv preprint arXiv:2203.08937 (2022)
23. Zhang, K., Yang, Z., Başar, T.: Multi-agent reinforcement learning: a selective overview of theories and algorithms. In: Handbook of Reinforcement Learning and Control, pp. 321–384 (2021)
24. Zhang, Y.T., Shu, C.W.: Eno and weno schemes. In: Handbook of Numerical Analysis, vol. 17, pp. 103–122. Elsevier (2016)

Multi-agent-based Structural Reconstruction of Dynamic Topologies for Urban Lighting

Félix Furger[1], Carole Bernon[1], Jean-Pierre Georgé[1(✉)], Nazim Pigenet[2], and Paul Valiere[2]

[1] IRIT, Université de Toulouse, CNRS, Toulouse INP, UT3, Toulouse, France
{felix.furger,carole.bernon,jean-pierre.george}@irit.fr
[2] Kawantech, Toulouse, France
{nazim.pigenet,paul.valiere}@kawantech.com
https://www.irit.fr/, https://www.kawantech.com/

Abstract. Until humanity succeeds in massively producing clean energy to satisfy its inexhaustible needs, one of its biggest challenges is to save and use its resources as efficiently as possible. With outdoor lighting being responsible for 2% of worldwide electricity consumption, smart urban lighting has recently gained a lot of attention in this respect. As an integrated part of smart cities, smart urban lighting rests on the analysis of sensed data to tackle highly dynamical problems. This sensed data shapes a representation of the environment in which the smart system will have to perform. To reduce problem complexity, distributed solutions commonly apply local lighting policies and therefore benefit from the knowledge of the geographical positioning of the relevant streetlights in the environment. In this paper, we propose an adaptive multi-agent approach that aims at ensuring the robustness and coherence through time of the smart system's environment representation. Our approach leverages real time series data returned by streetlight sensors informing on vehicles and pedestrians traffic. We exploit this data to perform a structural reconstruction of the streetlight "fleet" topology without any *a priori* knowledge about its internal structure. We then ensure its correctness through time by handling internal structure changes in order to continuously provide a coherent foundation for the smart lighting system to perform upon.

Keywords: Multi-agent systems · Self-adaptation · Structural network reconstruction · Smart lighting · Smart cities

1 Introduction

To combat the upcoming environmental crisis, our biggest challenge probably still resides in saving and using our resources as efficiently as possible. With outdoor lighting being responsible for 2% of worldwide electricity consumption, smart urban lighting recently gained some attention in this respect [15].

© The Author(s), under exclusive license to Springer Nature Switzerland AG 2022
F. Dignum et al. (Eds.): PAAMS 2022, LNAI 13616, pp. 191–202, 2022.
https://doi.org/10.1007/978-3-031-18192-4_16

Smart Cities and Smart Lighting. Recent breakthroughs in light emitting diodes (LEDs) offered smart urban lighting the means it was lacking. Not only do LEDs offer long lifetime and low energy consumption compared to traditional streetlight technologies but they also provide much easier control opportunities [9]. First solutions benefited from the implementation of light sensors within the streetlights to strictly limit urban light use to low natural light situations. As an integrated part of smart cities however, smart urban lighting state of the art solutions nowadays rest on the analysis of more complex and informative sensed data [11] to adapt the light to different users: motion detectors can generate data informing about urban users' trajectories, their speed and their type (vehicle, cyclist or pedestrian). Moreover, in order to fully profit from such highly informative data and reduce problem complexity, an increasing number of distributed solutions focus on applying local context-aware lighting policies [9].

These solutions therefore benefit from the knowledge of the geographical positioning of the relevant streetlights in the environment. More specifically, in the already existing smart lighting solution that this research is aiming to support, each streetlight is not only capable of detecting the presence of a user in the street but also of communicating any relevant information to its nearest neighbors. This communication allows streetlights to preemptively light up before they even detect any user activity, in an effort to guarantee their comfort and safety.

To ensure fluid communication however, every streetlight needs to be aware of the identity, positioning and distance of its relevant neighbors. This requires a precise manual configuration at the time when the technology is deployed, which is hardly realistic considering how streetlights are deployed and maintained in practice. Moreover, if the neighborhood happens to change (failure, street works...) or if the sensors are moved or reset, this cumbersome configuration step has to be repeated. We therefore propose an automatic solution capable of determining each streetlight's local neighborhood.

Multi-agent Systems (MAS) are a decentralized approach, based on self-organisation mechanisms, where the calculation task is distributed over agents which are virtual or physical autonomous entities (more complete definitions of an "agent" are given in [12] and [5]). Each agent has only a local point of view of the problem it is solving, corresponding to a local goal. This particularity enables to easily distribute calculation tasks in the resolution process and consequently reduces computational costs. That is why multi-agent approaches are preferred where centralized approaches have limited flexibility and scalability.

Multi-Agent Systems are used in a wide variety of real-world application domains: optimization algorithms [3], power systems [8], complex networks and IoT [6], smart manufacturing [1], multi-robot systems [13].

We propose to adopt the Adaptive Multi-Agent Systems (AMAS) [2] theory where cooperation [7] is the engine that drives the behavior of an agent and the emergence of a global functionality.

2 Real-World and Simulated Environment

The research is conducted using both simulation software and real world data collected from already deployed streetlight smart sensors.

Kara Sensors. *Kara* is a smart urban lighting technology deployed in more than 40 cities across France and developed by Kawantech (www.kawantech.com). Their technology already guarantees a minimum energy saving of 55% on a LED streetlight since they ensure that streetlights fully light up only when user presence is detected. The system consists of an optical sensor such as a low definition camera combined with a calculator unit and is directly mounted into each individual streetlight. The smart system uses real time informative data about moving entities in the urban environment to monitor the streetlight's light level. Moreover, the solution implements a variety of telecommunication technologies such as Wi-Fi, LoRaWAN or DASH7. DASH7 ensures communication between *Karas* in order for streetlights to exchange information and potentially preemptively light up before they even detect any user activity.

In the scope of this paper, which objective is for each streetlight to be able to determine its local neighborhood, we leverage *Kara's* real time capabilities to inform about the presence of moving entities in the street, their positional tracking within the embedded camera's field of view as well as their speed and all associated timestamps.

Environment Simulation with GAMA. GAMA is a free, open-source simulation software designed for spatially explicit agent-based simulations development [4]. We use it to simulate the university campus in which the *Kara* technology is currently being deployed, as well as to generate and simulate various fictional urban lighting topologies. Fig. 1 shows such a fictional topology example in which simulated users can navigate and streetlights inform about real time user traffic just as if they were equipped with *Kara* sensors.

3 Objective and Methods

The objective of the research is to develop a solution that would lead each streetlight to identify and position its nearest neighbors without any prior knowledge of their identity. By taking advantage of time series data observed by *Kara* sensors, not only would the solution perform structural reconstruction of each streetlight's local neighbors topology but also continuously ensure its coherence through time. Motivated by the fact that the knowledge of each streetlight's neighborhood is the very foundation of the smart lighting system's functioning, the solution would aim at improving overall robustness through a more generic approach. It would therefore handle dynamic internal structure changes within local topologies, as well as estimate distances and relative positions between streetlights through time. Because of the dynamic and distributed nature of the problem, we tackle it with an Adaptive Multi-Agent System approach.

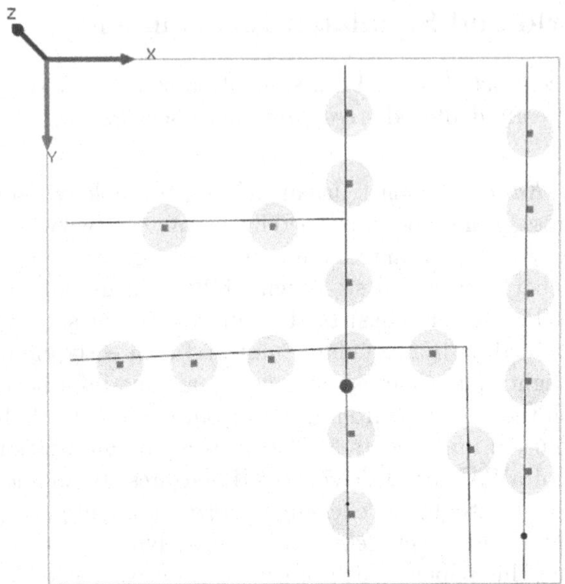

Fig. 1. Example of a fictional but realistic urban lighting topology simulation in GAMA. Yellow squares representing streetlights are positioned alongside traffic axes represented by black lines. Black, green and red circles respectively represent pedestrians, bikes and motorised vehicles (Color figure online)

3.1 Agent Modelling and Formalisation

We define an agent as an independent entity corresponding to a streetlight on which a *Kara* sensor has been mounted. An agent can therefore acquire data about user traffic happening in the street where it is located, and communicate its observations to other agents. The criticality of an agent is defined by how far an agent is from its local goal. In order to maintain a low level of criticality, each agent has to accurately identify and position its nearest neighbors in the environment. By comparing their respective sequences of observations and quantifying their correlation, two agents can gather knowledge about the likelihood of them being neighbours as well as, if applicable, their relative positioning in the neighborhood (distance and direction).

An agent is able to detect user activity in the street where it is located and can store this information in its local memory, hence forming time series data referred as O, an array of observations:

$$O = (o_1, o_2, o_3, ..., o_n) \qquad \text{with } o_i = (s_i, \overrightarrow{v_i}, t_i) \qquad i \in [1, n] \tag{1}$$

where s_i is the user's speed and $\overrightarrow{v_i}$ its average direction at t_i, the associated timestamp. An observation o_i is removed from the internal memory of the agent after a given time Δ_t. The agent also holds a list of contacts $C = (c_1, c_2, c_3, ..., c_p)$, representing other agents with whom communication is possible. The agent is able to send its observations O to its contacts at any time as well as to receive its contacts' observations. With every contact c_k, the agent associates three values $conf_k$, $dist_k$ and $\overrightarrow{dir_k}$ where:

- $conf_k$ is the confidence with which the agent assumes c_k to be part of its neighborhood,
- $dist_k$ is the estimated distance between the agent and c_k,
- $\overrightarrow{dir_k}$ is the estimated direction in which c_k is situated relatively to the agent.

If $conf_k$ happens to become greater than an empirically determined threshold δ_{conf}, the agent considers c_k as a neighbor situated at a distance $dist_k$ in the direction $\overrightarrow{dir_k}$. The objective of the agent is to accurately estimate these three values for every contact in order to correctly reconstruct its neighborhood's topology. For the specific estimation of $dist_k$, the agent uses an additional *exploration* distance λ_k, as well as a memory of optimal estimated distances Λ_k.

3.2 Local Neighborhood Discrimination

In order to understand the topology of its neighborhood and discriminate neighbors from simple contacts, the agent compares its observations with its contacts' observations through communication. This comparison enables the agent to update $conf_k$, $dist_k$, λ_k and $\overrightarrow{dir_k}$ associated with the involved contact c_k.

***Ghost* Observations.** When an agent receives observations $O_k = (o_{k_1}, o_{k_2}, o_{k_3}, ..., o_{k_m})$ with $o_{k_i} = (s_{k_i}, \overrightarrow{v_{ki}}, t_{k_i})$ as defined in Eq. (1) from a contact c_k, four arrays G_1, G_2, G_3 and G_4 referred as *ghost* observations are computed as follows:

$$G_j = (g_{j_1}, g_{j_2}, g_{j_3}, ..., g_{j_m}) \quad j \in [1, 4]$$
$$\text{with } g_{j_i} = (\tau_{j_i}, \overrightarrow{v_{k_i}}) \quad i \in [1, m] \quad \text{where } \tau_{j_i} = t_{k_i} - \frac{d_j}{s_{k_i}} \tag{2}$$

$$\begin{aligned} \text{and } d_1 &= dist_k \\ d_2 &= \lambda_k - \Delta_\lambda \\ d_3 &= \lambda_k \\ d_4 &= \lambda_k + \Delta_\lambda \qquad \text{with } \Delta_\lambda \text{ a given small distance.} \end{aligned}$$

G_j therefore represents the observations the agent should have made if c_k is indeed a neighbor and if the distance d_j between them is accurate.

***Paired* Observations.** Each G_j is then compared to the actual agent's observations $O = (o_1, o_2, o_3, ..., o_n)$ as defined in Eq. (1). This comparison is performed to determine which distance d_j ensures the best correlation between the agent's observations O and its contact's observations O_k. The objective is therefore to converge with steps of size Δ_λ towards the real distance, if it only exists, after several communication rounds. Four arrays P_1, P_2, P_3 and P_4 referred as *paired* observations are then computed from G_1, G_2, G_3, G_4 and O as follows:

$$P_j = (p_{j_1}, p_{j_2}, p_{j_3}, ..., p_{j_m}) \quad j \in [1,4] \quad \text{with } p_{j_i} = (g_{j_i}, \omega_{j_i}) \quad i \in [1,m] \tag{3}$$

where $\omega_{j_i} \in O = (o_1, o_2, o_3, ..., o_n)$ is the agent's observation for which $|\tau_{j_i} - t_l|_{l \in [1,n]}$ is minimum, τ_{j_i} being the timestamp of the current *ghost* observation g_{j_i} and t_l the timestamp of o_l for $l \in [1,n]$. This results in every *ghost* observation $g_{j_i} \in G_j$ being matched with the temporally closest agent's observation $\omega_{j_i} \in O$. Not every $o_i \in O$ is however necessarily matched with a *ghost* observation and several *ghost* observations can be matched with the same agent's observation.

Each array of *paired* observations P_j is then used to compute three scores referred as $match_j$, gap_j and $rate_j$.

Match. This score corresponds to the proportion of observations that have successfully been paired with a *ghost* observation out of all observations. We note $match_j = \frac{N_j}{n}$ with N_j the number of observations in O that have been paired with a *ghost* observation in G_j and n the overall number of observations in O. We consider $match_A$ better than $match_B$ if $match_A > match_B$.

Gap. This score corresponds to the average absolute time difference between a *ghost* observation's timestamp and its associated observation's timestamp.

$$gap_j = \frac{1}{m} \sum_{i=1}^{m} |\tau_{j_i} - t_{j_i}| \tag{4}$$

with τ_{j_i} the timestamp of g_{j_i} and t_{j_i} the timestamp of the associated ω_{j_i}, for $i \in [1,m]$ and m the number of *paired* observations in P_j. We consider gap_A better than gap_B if $gap_A < gap_B$.

Rate. This score corresponds to the proportion of *paired* observations for which the absolute time difference between the *ghost* observation's timestamp and its associated observation's timestamp is less than or equal to δ_t, a given tolerance threshold, out of all *paired* observations. We note $rate_j = \frac{M_j}{m}$ with M_j the number of *paired* observations in P_j for which $|\tau_{j_i} - t_{j_i}| < \delta_t$ and m the overall number of *paired* observations in P_j. We consider $rate_A$ better than $rate_B$ if $rate_A > rate_B$.

The *paired* observations P_{best} is chosen out of P_1, P_2, P_3 and P_4 resulting in the best *rate*, *match* and *gap*, by this order of priority. This represents the criticality of the agent whose goal is thus to improve it by modifying its position as described in the following.

Confidence Update. The confidence $conf_k$ with which the agent assumes c_k to be part of its neighborhood holds a gliding average of the S most recent *rates* the agent evaluated. The current $rate_{best}$ resulting from P_{best} is therefore used to update $conf_k$ as follows:

$$conf_k \leftarrow conf_k - \frac{conf_k - rate_{best}}{S} \quad (5)$$

Moreover, if $conf_k$ becomes greater than the threshold δ_{conf} then c_k is now considered as a neighbor by the agent. The contrary leads c_k to be considered as a regular contact.

Direction Update. The estimated direction $\overrightarrow{dir_k}$ in which c_k is situated relatively to the agent holds a gliding average of the S most recent relevant directions the agent evaluated. Are considered relevant the users directions in the *paired* observations in P_{best} for which $|\tau_{best_i} - t_{best_i}| < \delta_t$ for $i \in [1, n]$. The average direction $\overrightarrow{\mu_{best}}$ resulting from these relevant users directions is therefore used to update $\overrightarrow{dir_k}$ as follows:

$$\overrightarrow{dir_k} \leftarrow \overrightarrow{dir_k} - \frac{\overrightarrow{dir_k} - \overrightarrow{\mu_{best}}}{S} \quad (6)$$

Distance Update. The *exploration* distance λ_k previously used to compute the *ghost* observations G_2, G_3 and G_4 is simply the most recent best evaluated distance d_{best} from which P_{best} is originated. This distance d_{best} is therefore used to update λ_k as follows: $\lambda_k \leftarrow d_{best}$.

Moreover, if $rate_{best} > 0$, d_{best} is saved in the optimal estimated distances memory Λ_k. The update of the estimated distance $dist_k$ between the agent and c_k then requires to sample a random value λ_{sp} from this optimal estimated distances memory Λ_k. This sampled distance λ_{sp} is then used to update $dist_k$ as follows: $dist_k \leftarrow dist_k + sgn(\lambda_{sp} - dist_k) \cdot \Delta_{dist}$ where sgn is the sign function and Δ_{dist} a given small distance.

Although the *exploration* distance λ_k is quite sensitive to dynamic noise and can quickly deviate from the real distance between the agent and c_k, $dist_k$ is at all time converging with steps of size Δ_{dist} towards one of the most optimal estimated distances stored in Λ_k. We therefore consider λ_k as a good tool to ensure exploration and $dist_k$ as the most relevant and robust estimated distance between the agent and c_k.

3.3 Evaluation Metrics

We use a number of metrics to evaluate our topology reconstruction performance. Three criteria are taken into account:

- the correctness of the neighbors discrimination,
- the accuracy of the estimated distances between the agent and its neighbors,
- the accuracy of the estimated directions in which the neighbors are situated relatively to the agent.

Neighbors Discrimination. For a given agent with N true neighbors and N_e estimated neighbors, we name P_T the number of true positives and P_F the number of false positives within the estimated neighbors. We use these basic quantities to build two standard metrics referred as R_{TP} (true positive rate) and *Precision* [10] as follows: $R_{TP} = \frac{P_T}{N}$ and $Precision = \frac{P_T}{P_T+P_F} = \frac{P_T}{N_e}$

Distances Estimation Error. For a given agent with N true neighbors, the local distances estimation error is the average absolute difference between the estimated distances and the real ones, for all N neighbors.

Directions Estimation Error. For a given agent with N true neighbors, the local directions estimation error is the average absolute difference between the estimated angles and the real ones, for all N neighbors.

4 Results and Discussion

Confidence Threshold Determination. For the solution to function once deployed, there is no strict need for the streetlights to be able to discriminate neighbors from regular contacts in a binary way. Indeed, since each streetlight associates a neighbor confidence score with each one of its contacts, such a score can be used in a flexible manner to infer a variety of different lighting policies depending on the specific needs of the user. However, for the metrics to accurately evaluate the reconstruction performance of the solution, it is necessary to perform a binary discrimination between estimated neighbors and regular contacts. We thus provide the agents with a confidence threshold δ_{conf}, whose role is to ensure such a discrimination during the performance evaluation task only.

For a given network whose structure is to be reconstructed, Fig. 2 exhaustively shows all confidence scores within the agent population after a simulated period of 48 h (in the following, all durations are simulated). In this example, we see that true neighbors have been given significantly higher confidence scores by the system than regular contacts.

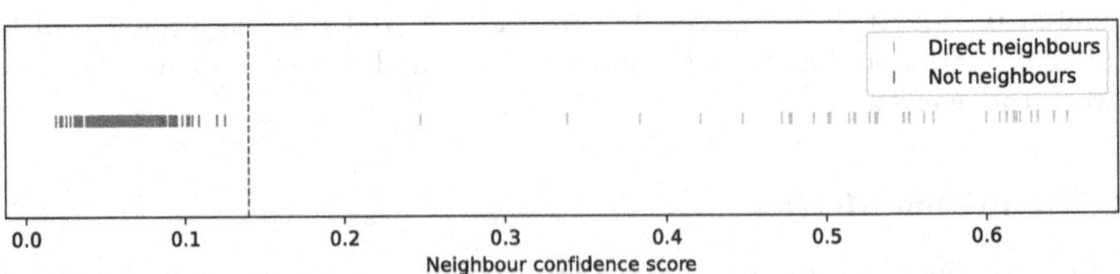

Fig. 2. Exhaustive confidence score distribution within the agent population after a simulated period of 48 h for a realistic topology. Green lines represent confidence scores associated with agents that have been validated as neighbors by humans (true neighbors) whereas red ones represent those that are not. Indirect neighbors (*i.e.* a direct neighbor is situated between them and the agent) are not displayed. The empirically chosen threshold δ_{conf} is represented in blue. High confidence is correlated with true neighborhood. (Color figure online)

Confidence score therefore appears to be a good tool to whether or not consider a contact as a neighbor. Empirically, we choose $\delta_{conf} = 0.14$ since this value appears to accurately discriminate neighbors from regular contacts.

In the scope of the neighbors discrimination evaluation task in this simulated environment, we can therefore consider any contact with a confidence score higher than 0.14 as an estimated neighbor, the contrary leading it to be considered as a regular contact.

Global Reconstruction Performance (Simulation). To validate the global reconstruction performance of our solution in a simulated environment, we run multiple simulations on the same fictional urban lighting topology, shown in Fig. 1. In Fig. 3, we demonstrate that with the chosen threshold $\delta_{conf} = 0.14$, both our neighbors discrimination metrics R_{TP} (true positive rate) and $Precision$ quickly increase and exceed 0.9 after a simulated period of 2–3 hours. $Precision$ tends to reach a rate of 1 after 2 h, which means that every estimated neighbor is indeed an actual neighbor. However, it takes about a day for the system to fill the gap between an R_{TP} of 0.95 and an R_{TP} of 1. This shows that even if 5% of the true neighbors seem harder to identify, the system eventually discriminates them correctly after some time. Moreover, we show that once the system converges, it is not impacted by dynamic noise and durably maintains both a $Precision$ and an R_{TP} of 1. This points out the absence of false positives, as well as an exhaustive identification of all true neighbors.

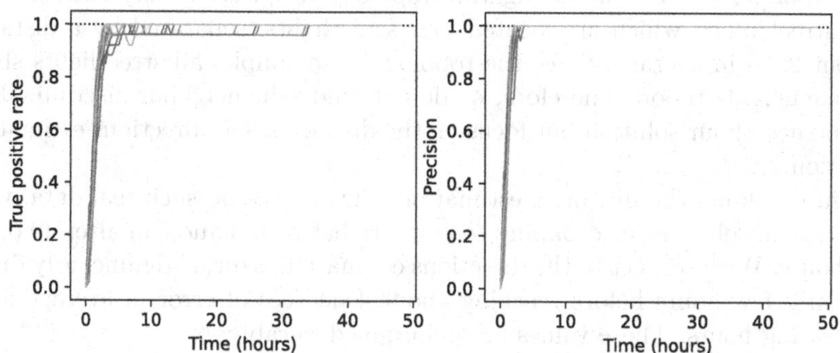

Fig. 3. Evolution through time of R_{TP} (true positive rate, on the left) and $Precision$ (on the right) for 15 simulation runs on the same fictional urban lighting topology. An R_{TP} of 1 indicates that all true neighbors are identified by the system and a $Precision$ rate of 1 indicates that all estimated neighbors are true neighbors (*i.e.* true positives)

In addition, Fig. 4 clearly shows the distances estimation convergence, with an average absolute error smaller than 1 m after 12 simulated hours. The system then reaches an average minimum distances estimation error of about 30 cm (streetlights are usually situated at a distance between 15 and 35 m from each others). With regard to the directions estimation error, it also significantly drops in the first few hours, before reaching 1 degree of error in average after about 7 h. These low error values are maintained durably.

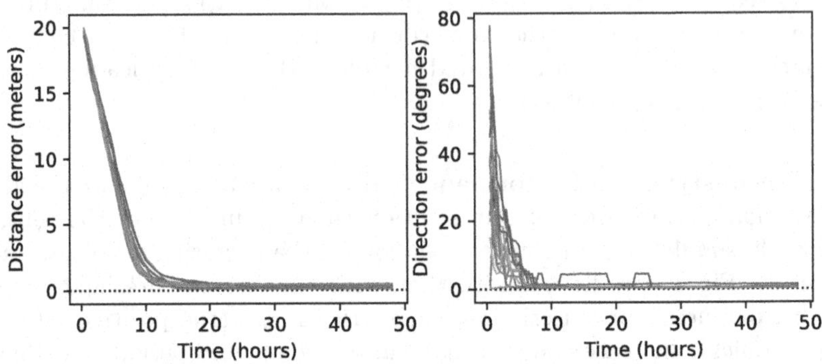

Fig. 4. Evolution through time of absolute distances estimation error (on the left) and absolute directions estimation error (on the right) for 15 simulation runs on the same fictional urban lighting topology

Global Reconstruction Performance (Real World). To test the global reconstruction performance of our solution in a real world situation, we ran experiments on real data collected by *Kara* sensors on two different occasions in the same street. The urban lighting topology in question only consists of a single street along which are located four streetlights, separated by a distance of about 28 m in average. Since the topology is so simple, all streetlights share the same neighborhood. Therefore, we do not study the neighbor discrimination performance of our solution but focus on the distances and directions estimation evaluation.

Figure 5 shows the distances estimation convergence on such real data, with an average absolute error dropping somewhere between 3 and 5 m after 40 operating hours. With respect to the directions estimation error, it significantly drops in the first few hours before reaching about 4 degrees of error in average after 14 operating hours. These values are maintained durably.

Discussion. We demonstrate that our solution performs particularly well in the case of a simulated urban lighting topology, with close to perfect neighbors discrimination evaluation rates and negligible absolute distances and directions estimation errors after a few simulated hours. Because the studied topology is sufficiently varied and realistic, these results suggest that the solution would perform well on a grand variety of urban lighting topologies. However, further simulations are needed to explore more specific topologies as well as scaling-up.

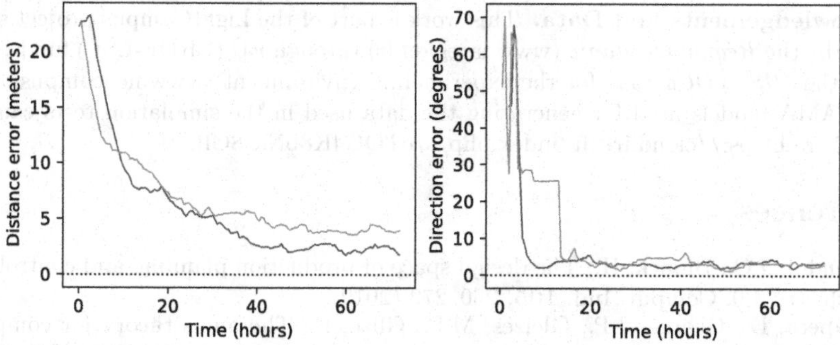

Fig. 5. Evolution through time of absolute distances estimation error (on the left) and absolute directions estimation error (on the right) on two real world data sets

It is noteworthy that the agents only communicate the events they perceive, and have no other information about their position nor do they sense the other agents, as is the case in multi-robot topology reconstruction research [14].

When we test our solution in a real world situation, although the system still converges, results are not as accurate as in a simulated environment, especially in terms of distances estimation. While simulated user traffic may not be as realistic as real user traffic, simulated *Kara* sensors certainly collect more accurate data about a simulated world than real *Kara* sensors do about the real one. In this respect, uncertainties about the users detection timestamps, their speed as well as their positional tracking in the real world are elements possibly explaining the difference between our system's performance in a simulated and a real environment. In addition, we did not test our system's neighbors discrimination performance in a real world situation as *Kara* sensors are still being installed on a larger scale.

5 Conclusion

In order to reduce computational costs as well as problem complexity, smart urban lighting solutions commonly aim to adopt distributed approaches, implementing local lighting policies within autonomous streetlights. In some cases, the possibility for streetlights to exchange information offers opportunities for more flexible and relevant lighting policies.

Motivated by the fact that the effectiveness of such local lighting policies highly depends on the quality of each streetlight's environmental representation, we proposed, implemented and evaluated a solution that enables each streetlight to continuously identify and position its nearest neighbors. We demonstrate the performance of our solution when embedded in simulated environments and obtain encouraging results when tested in a real world situation.

As *Kara* sensors are currently being deployed on the campus of our university, we will be able to upscale real-world testing in the following months.

Acknowledgements and Data. This work is part of the LightCampus project supported by the *Région Occitanie* (www.laregion.fr) through EU (ERDF-ESF) funds. We thank the *GIS neOCampus* for the experimental environment (www.neocampus.org). The GAMA models used for generating the data used in the simulation tests can be found here https://cloud.irit.fr/index.php/s/cTQG4K8bNsn8CIi.

References

1. Bendul, J.C., Blunck, H.: The design space of production planning and control for industry 4.0. Comput. Ind. **105**, 260–272 (2019)
2. Capera, D., Georgé, J.P., Gleizes, M.P., Glize, P.: The amas theory for complex problem solving based on self-organizing cooperative agents. In: WET ICE 2003. Proceedings. Twelfth IEEE International Workshops on Enabling Technologies: Infrastructure for Collaborative Enterprises, 2003. IEEE (2003)
3. Couellan, N., Jan, S., Jorquera, T., Georgé, J.P.: Self-adaptive support vector machine: a multi-agent optimization perspective. Expert Syst. Appl. **42**(9), 4284–4298 (2015)
4. Drogoul, A., et al.: GAMA: a spatially explicit, multi-level, agent-based modeling and simulation platform. In: Demazeau, Y., Ishida, T., Corchado, J.M., Bajo, J. (eds.) PAAMS 2013. LNCS (LNAI), vol. 7879, pp. 271–274. Springer, Heidelberg (2013). https://doi.org/10.1007/978-3-642-38073-0_25
5. Ferber, J., Weiss, G.: Multi-Agent Systems: An Introduction to Distributed Artificial Intelligence, vol. 1. Addison-Wesley Reading, Boston (1999)
6. Fortino, G., Russo, W., Savaglio, C., Shen, W., Zhou, M.: Agent-oriented cooperative smart objects: from IoT system design to implementation. IEEE Trans. Syst. Man Cybern. Syst. **48**(11), 1939–1956 (2017)
7. Georgé, J.P., Gleizes, M.P., Camps, V.: Cooperation. In: Serugendo, G.D.M., Gleizes, M.P., Karageorgos, A. (eds.) Self-organising Software. Natural Computing Series book series (NCS), Springer, Heidelberg (2011). https://doi.org/10.1007/978-3-642-17348-6_9
8. González-Briones, A., De La Prieta, F., Mohamad, M.S., Omatu, S., Corchado, J.M.: Multi-agent systems applications in energy optimization problems: a state-of-the-art review. Energies **11**(8), 1928 (2018)
9. Juntunen, E., Sarjanoja, E.M., Eskeli, J., Pihlajaniemi, H., Österlund, T.: Smart and dynamic route lighting control based on movement tracking. Build. Environ. **142**, 472–483 (2018). https://doi.org/10.1016/j.buildenv.2018.06.048
10. Ma, C., Chen, H.S., Lai, Y.C., Zhang, H.F.: Statistical inference approach to structural reconstruction of complex networks from binary time series. Phys. Rev. E **97**(2) (2018). https://doi.org/10.1103/PhysRevE.97.022301
11. Paz, J.F.D., Bajo, J., Rodríguez, S., Villarrubia, G., Corchado, J.M.: Intelligent system for lighting control in smart cities. Inf. Sci. **372**, 241–255 (2016)
12. Wooldridge, M., Jennings, N.R.: Intelligent agents: theory and practice. Knowl. Eng. Rev. **10**(2), 115–152 (1995)
13. Yan, Z., Jouandeau, N., Cherif, A.A.: A survey and analysis of multi-robot coordination. Int. J. Adv. Rob. Syst. **10**(12), 399 (2013)
14. Yi, S., Luo, W., Sycara, K.: Distributed topology correction for flexible connectivity maintenance in multi-robot systems. In: Proceedings of (ICRA) International Conference on Robotics and Automation (2021)
15. Zissis, G.: Energy consumption and environmental and economic impact of lighting: the current situation. In: Handbook of Advanced Lighting Technology, pp. 1–13. Springer, Heidelberg (2016). https://doi.org/10.1007/978-3-319-00295-8_40-1

Control Your Virtual Agent in its Daily-activities for Long Periods

Lysa Gramoli[1,2(✉)], Jérémy Lacoche[1], Anthony Foulonneau[1], Valérie Gouranton[2], and Bruno Arnaldi[2]

[1] Orange, Rennes, France
{jeremy.lacoche,anthony.foulonneau}@orange.com
[2] Univ Rennes, INSA Rennes, Inria, CNRS, Irisa, Rennes, France
lysa.gramoli@irisa.fr, {valerie.gouranton,bruno.arnaldi}@irisa.fr

Abstract. Simulating human behavior through virtual agents is a key feature to improve the credibility of virtual environments (VE). For many use cases, such as daily activities data generation, having a good ratio between the agent's control and autonomy is required to impose specific activities while letting the agent be autonomous. This is why we propose a model allowing a user to configure the level of the agent's decision-making autonomy according to their requirements. Our model, based on a BDI architecture, combines control constraints given by the user, an internal model simulating human daily needs for autonomy, and a scheduling process to create an activity plan considering these two parts. Using a calendar, the activities that must be performed in the required time can be given by the user. In addition, the user can indicate whether interruptions can happen during the activity calendar to apply an effect induced by the internal model. The plan generated by our model can be executed in the VE by an animated agent in real-time. To show that our model manages well the ratio between control and autonomy, we use a 3D home environment to compare the results with the input parameters.

Keywords: Autonomous agent · Daily activity model · Scheduling · Control over the agent's decision-making autonomy

1 Introduction

Reproducing human behavior through virtual agents is an essential feature to improve the usefulness of virtual environments (VE). To increase the credibility of agent's behaviors, some human processes can be simulated such as human needs, decision-making, or preferences. With such features, a virtual agent can reason and adapt its behavior according to the situation and its internal state. As a result, it becomes more autonomous in its decision-making process as per the definition of autonomy provided by Avradinis et al. [3].

© The Author(s), under exclusive license to Springer Nature Switzerland AG 2022
F. Dignum et al. (Eds.): PAAMS 2022, LNAI 13616, pp. 203–216, 2022.
https://doi.org/10.1007/978-3-031-18192-4_17

In this paper, we particularly focus on an agent model allowing the generation of daily routines in indoor environments. Such a model could be useful for virtual environment developers and researchers using simulations to generate new databases. Indeed, it could integrate and improve existing simulators allowing the generation of data for "indoor inhabitant understanding" based for example on computer vision as in VirtualHome [17] or on data from connected objects such as OpenSHS [1]. In such use cases, they may want to impose specific activities to execute in the VE while maintaining an agent autonomous process outside these periods. Therefore, a model adjusting the degree of autonomy and being able to execute activities in a VE is required to generate accurate, diversified and credible datasets. To go further, Suggesting a way to interrupt specified activities is also important to make the generated behaviour more credible.

However, being able to modify the agent's level of decision-making autonomy with the same model is quite rare in the literature. Current approaches are based either on agents reacting to the situation but facing the challenge of respecting strong constraints, or agents being able to plan but facing the challenge of adapting to the situation. Yet, it is important for us to ensure that the activities required by the user are performed on time with the correct duration, regardless of what the agent was doing before.

To address this issue, we propose a model adjusting the degree of agent's decision-making autonomy according to the user's will. Our model, based on a BDI architecture [21], combines an internal state model simulating human daily needs, a module giving the user's constraints through a calendar, a scheduler guiding the decision-making according the both previous parts, and an execution process performing activities in a VE. Moreover, an interruption mechanism is also introduced in the scheduler so that the agent can interrupt, delay or shorten activities indicated by the user. To demonstrate our model, we propose to simulate daily routines in a 3D house environment which could be adapted to our identified use cases, shown in Fig. 1. As our model is oriented towards decision making and activity execution, work focusing on the production of verbal agents is not covered in this paper. The paper is organized as follows. In Sect. 2, we propose some related work. In Sect. 3, we explain our model and its main process implied in the management of autonomy. Finally, the Sects. 4 and 5, are used for the results and the conclusion.

Fig. 1. Global view of the 3D simulator and the agent performing activities

2 Related Work

Approaches to simulate human behavior can be divided into many classes such as reactive-based methods, plan-based methods and learning-based methods.

Regarding reactive-based methods, the agent chooses and executes the most appropriate action according to the current context. They are particularly well suited to dynamic environments and multi-agent issues. One well-known action-based method is Beliefs-Desires-Intentions (BDI) [21]. In BDI, a perception system interpreting the state of the world is modeled through beliefs, the choice of possible goals is modelled through desires, and the choice of predefined sequences of actions to satisfy these goals is done by intentions. In this category, we can also find action selection mechanisms such as the work of De Sevin and Thalmann [19] and MAGE [3] where the level of motivations (or needs) is used to select activities. These approaches stay limited on the control over the agent's decision-making since the activities are chosen in reaction to the VE or the agent's internal state including motivation or needs.

In contrast to reactive-based methods, other approaches use plan-based methods. In this case, the agent sets up a plan according to the current context and constraints. Among the best known methods, we can find Hierarchical Tasks Network (HTN) [8], STRIPS [7] or meta-heuristics such as Genetic algorithms [5]. This category is interesting to schedule activities and to control the agent's choices. However, they have some limitations regarding the reactivity to the change of the environment and the internal state. In our case, only using a scheduler is not sufficient because we want to simulate the agent's internal state for its autonomy as well as interruptions when they cannot be satisfied otherwise.

Finally, recent approaches use learning-based systems to simulate daily activities, such as LIDA [13], the work of Jang et al. [9] or rules-based approaches like Soar and ACT-R models [10]. In the work of Jang et al. a double Deep Q-Network (DQN) structure is used to find the most appropriate goals according to the agent's needs, the input real data and the time. For the Rules-Based approaches, they use memory systems and explicit rules to construct the decision-making process. All these approaches are promising, but they are limited in terms of the behavior extensibility and control, due to their nature.

The three category described above provide autonomous agents which are free to make their own decisions during all the simulation. However, these solutions are not really focused on the problematic of offering different level of autonomy. Thus, the control that we can have over them is insufficient for our case. Therefore, it would be more relevant for us to get close to approaches combining several categories such as the work of de Silva [20] where BDI and HTN are mixed even though our problematic is not still addressed in their work. There is also the work of Azvine et al. [4] where an intelligent assistant is proposed to help the user with communication, information and time management. This multi-agent system includes reactive scheduling methods to manage various level of time constraints. Thus, a good ratio between control and autonomy can be reached with this system. However, it is difficult to use it in our context, since the proposed model is a user-oriented approach and the use cases are distinct.

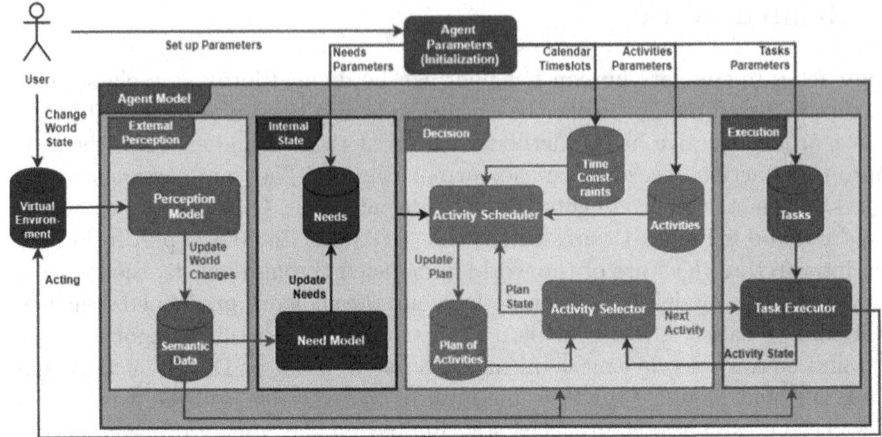

Fig. 2. Our proposed agent model

In addition, this model does not execute actions in a 3D environment. Other approaches also started to address our problematic This is the case of SMACH [2,18] and the work of Ordoñez [15]. For SMACH, the choice of activities is based on probabilities. Consequently, strong constraints have not formal guarantees of being kept. For the work of Ordoñez, the algorithm is run on a user-defined time windows. Unfortunately, this model does not consider the internal state and the effects of activities occurring in another time window. Finally, for both papers, activities are not executed in a 3D Simulator. This is thus limiting for our use cases since the visual aspects are essentials if we want to simulate sensors (cameras or connected objects). This is why, we propose a model allowing the user to adjust the level of decision-making autonomy and allowing to perform activities in a 3D virtual environment.

3 Agent Model Description

3.1 Global Model Structure

Our model structure is inspired from the BDI models [21] where some adjustments were made to consider our requirements regarding the management of the agent's autonomy. BDI was chosen because of its compatibility with our requirements and for its intuitive approach of the human decision model. Our proposed model is configured to adapt the level of decision-making autonomy according to the user's will and to execute activities in the VE. Using a calendar, the user can give activities that must be performed in the required time. Moreover, interruptions can be allowed to interrupt these activities. In this paper, an activity is a concrete formulation of the way to satisfy a goal or a need. For example, if the agent wants to improve its hygiene, then "Showering" can be an activity. Figure 2 shows the global structure made of the following processes:

Agent Parameters: It manages the initial parameters. A calendar can be given in input to provide activities that must be performed. The user is also able to configure activities, needs and tasks.

Internal State Model: It can be related to desires in BDI. However, its name differs because it could include other cognitive factors than desires. For now, it is used to update the urgency of needs. Needs are inspired by human needs defined in the Maslow's theory of needs [12]. They can be physiological such as hunger or they can be more elaborated like self-esteem. More details are given in Sect. 3.2.

Decision-Making Model: At the heart of the decision-making, it can be related to intentions in the BDI process. However, our model does not retrieve predefined plan according to the situation but it builds the plan of activities during the simulation. Our model adjusts the agent's autonomy to respect the user's constraints while producing autonomous behaviours through the internal state. Our scheduler is designed to be able to reschedule at any time, so it is compatible with dynamic environments. More details are given in Sect. 3.3.

Task Execution Model: This model executes the selected activity in the VE by executing the related sequences of tasks. A task is made of basic actions and animations that can be executed in the VE. For instance, a task can be "Getting dry" for the activity "Showering". This model receives from the decision-making model the activity to perform. In exchange, the activity state is returned. More details are given in Sect. 3.4

External Perception Model: This model can be related to Beliefs in BDI, since all the useful data from the VE are stored in its semantics database. It is used to filter activities according to their available resources and to provide the semantics needed to make the execution possible in the VE.

3.2 Agent Internal State

The internal state model provides essential information about the agent's internal conditions. This information will be then used in the decision-making model for autonomy phases and interruptions. For now, only needs are described here, but other factors such as preferences or emotions could be included.

According to the Maslow's pyramid of needs [12], needs are ordered according to their level of urgency: basic but imperative needs are distinguished from more elaborate needs, which are more complex but less urgent to satisfy. To integrate this approach in our work, a value Pyra $\in \{1, \ldots, 5\}$ is assigned to each need, where 1 corresponds to basic needs and 5 to the most elaborate needs. For this paper, we explain our function-based approach evolving through the time, as in the work of De Sevin and Thalmann [19]. However, the process to calculate needs urgency can be made with other approaches as in the work of Jang et al. [9] where a fuzzy-logic approach is used. For now, The computation of the level of urgency called P_{Need} is made of 3 steps:

(1) Need threshold Initialization Th_{Need}: this threshold is used to determine when a need becomes urgent to satisfy. Each threshold has a default val $\text{Th}_d \in (0, 1)$ modifiable by the user (in this paper, the default is set to 0.5). At this step, preferences could be used to deviate the threshold from this default value, and thus modifying the time when the need becomes urgent.

(2) Need intensity $i(t)$: Each need has an intensity value evolving through time as shown in Eq. 1. This evolution is modelled as the second half of a parabola bounded in $[0, 1]$, similar to the Need Manager of the work by De Sevin and Thalmann [19]. The start $i(t) = 0$ occurs for $t = t_{\text{start}}$, and the maximum $i(t) = 1$ occurs for $t = t_{\text{end}}$. These two parameters allow us to control the evolution of needs intensity over long periods. Each need has its own $[t_{\text{start}}, t_{\text{end}}]$ interval that can be set in two ways:

- **Specific hours**: they are set so that intensity starts and peaks at specific times. i.e. we can constrain hunger to start at 12 p.m. and peak at 13 p.m.
- **Periods of time**: they are set so that intensity peaks at varying intervals. For example, to simulate the toilet need, which is not constrained by specific hours, we can set time slots for its intensity at regular intervals of 3 h.

In both cases, real data could be used to configure these time slots, such in the work of Jang et al. [9]. The user can configure them through the agent parameters process. When the intensity reaches its maximum, it stays at this value until the need is satisfied. After this, its intensity decreases by the value given by the activity satisfying it.

$$i(t) = \left(\frac{t - t_{\text{start}}}{t_{\text{end}} - t_{\text{start}}} \right)^2 \tag{1}$$

(3) Need priority P_{Need}: the need priority grows in $[-1, 1]$ proportionally to need intensity, considering $Pyra$ and Th_{Need} as shown in Eq. 2.

$$P_{Need} = \frac{i(t) - \text{Th}_{\text{Need}}}{\text{Pyra} \cdot (1 - \text{Th}_{\text{Need}})} \tag{2}$$

This priority could also depend on the satisfaction of another need. For instance, if the agent drinks, then toilet need could evolve faster.

3.3 Decision-Making Model

The decision-Making model is the main process to control the level of the agent's decision-making autonomy according to the user's constraints. Two main process, called activity scheduler and activity selector, are described here.

The Activity Selector retrieves the activities of the plan and runs the scheduler to produce a new plan when there is no more activity to perform. In the latter case, the activity selector relays the start and end times of the plan to the scheduler. The last executed activity and the one starting just after the plan are also given. These activities surrounding the plan are either calendar activities or special activities only serving to delimit the plan. Thus, the activities calendar are included with the right times while leaving autonomy between them. The activity selector also transfers the selected activity to the task executor and gets its status back.

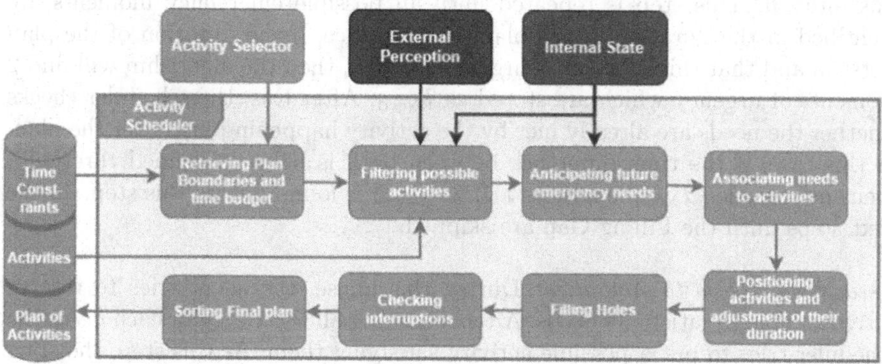

Fig. 3. Main Steps of the activity scheduler

The Activity Scheduler is inspired by the principle of reactive schedulers proposed in particular by the work of Azvine et al. [4]. This process can be relaunched if necessary, making our model compatible with dynamic VE. It has several functions summarized in Fig. 3:

Retrieving Plan Boundaries and Time Budget: This step corresponds to the moment when the agent defines the duration of its free time in relation to the activities already scheduled. The agent will then prepare a plan of activities to be carried out during this free time Concretely, The scheduler retrieves the plan period given by the activity selector. This period is converted into a time budget that must be respected to avoid trimming the future activities of the calendar. The last activity executed and the activity being just after the plan are stored to be considered. They will define what we call the boundaries of the plan. If there is no activity in the calendar after the period, then a special activity called "Activity Boundaries" with a duration of 0 is given by the activity selector to indicate the end of the plan. If the time budget is too short to put any activity, all the next steps until the checking interruption are skipped.

Filtering Possible Activities: During this step, the agent identifies what activity is possible or not during his free time. Activities having a minimum duration exceeding the time budget or reaching its maximum occurrence are excluded. The perception model is also used to exclude activities using unavailable resources. If no activity is found, all the next steps until the Filling Gap are skipped.

Anticipating Future Emergency Needs: In this step, the agent will anticipate its needs for the duration of its free time. To do this, the scheduler identifies the future moments when the needs become urgent. This forecast is limited to the period of the plan. First, the scheduler retrieves the level of urgency of each need at the current time. Then, for each time step, the scheduler launches the process calculating the level of urgency described in the previous Sect. 3.2. The scheduler thus gets the interval of urgency. A time called T_{Need} is retrieved randomly inside this interval. This step is repeated until all possible emergency moments are identified in the duration of the plan. For instance, if the duration of the plan lasts 7 h and that thirst becomes urgent every 3 h, then the algorithm will find 2 moments of urgency which are stored as T_{Need}. After this, the scheduler checks whether the needs are already met by the activity happening just after the plan. In this case, if the time difference between both is below a defined threshold, then the regarded T_{Need} is removed. If no T_{Need} is found during this step, all the next steps until the Filling Gap are skipped.

Associating Needs to Activities: During this phase, the agent tries to reserve activities able to satisfy its needs. After retrieving all the T_{Need} for each need, the scheduler tries to put a possible activity satisfying them. At this step, the start time of the activity is positioned at each occurrence of T_{Need} with its minimum duration. The scheduler starts by placing the activities on the T_{Need} closest in time. When an activity is placed, the minimum duration of this activity is removed from the remaining time budget. This step ends when the time budget is exhausted, in this case all the next T_{Need} are removed, or when all the T_{Need} have been associated to activities. Due to this setting, activities cannot be performed at the same time. For instance, if we have T_{Need} occurring at 1 p.m. for thirst and another at 2 p.m. for hunger, then the scheduler firstly places drinking activity at 1 p.m. and then eating activity at 2 p.m. if the time budget is not exceeded.

Positioning Activities and Adjustment of their Duration: At this step, The agent adapts the duration and the beginning of the activities, in order to be ready at the end of its free time. The scheduler adjusts the start time and duration of each activity so that they are close to their related T_{Need}. It also ensures that the start and end times do not exceed the time window. To do this, the scheduler first goes through the list of T_{Need} in reverse chronological order to temporally shift the activities having their end times arriving either outside of the plan boundaries, or after the start of another activity. Then, the scheduler performs a second run of this list, but in chronological order to shift the activities that have their start time beginning before the start of the plan or before the end of another activity. With these two round trips, activities are sure to start and end within the plan without overlapping with other placed activities. After this, starting with the activity closest in time, the duration of each activity are extended either until its maximum duration or the start of the next activity if the maximum is larger.

Filling Gaps: At this stage, The agent also schedules activities outside of its needs to keep busy. Concretely, time gaps where no activities are scheduled can appear. Here, gaps are considered as moments when the agent has no constraints coming from the user or its internal state. Therefore, these are periods when the agent can wait if the duration is short or can entertain itself. We thus use activities linked to entertaining or waiting to fill gaps. Of course, these activities can be configured by the user. Concretely, we use activities such as "Watching TV", "Computing", "Waiting" and so on.

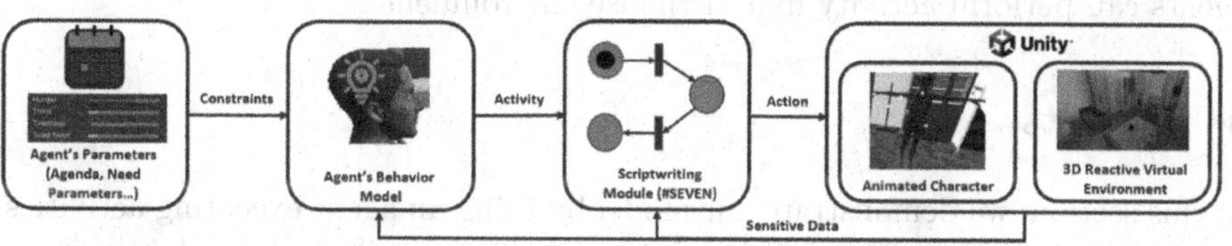

Fig. 4. Global Architecture of the implementation

Checking Interruptions: Sometimes, the agent will also have to interrupt its scheduled activities to satisfy its urgent needs. This is the case when needs could not be satisfied during the plan period. To solve this, the user can indicate whether a need may interrupt a calendar activity when it is urgent. In the same way, it can also indicate what calendar activity can be interruptible. During this step, the scheduler takes the activity situated just after the plan and verifies if this activity is interruptible. In addition, it checks if this activity has a sufficient duration to support a reduction equal to the duration of the interruption. If these conditions are reached, the scheduler checks whether a need that may interrupt and being urgent at the beginning of the plan has a moment of satisfaction in the plan. If it does not, the scheduler creates an interruption. A random moment is retrieved between the start and the end of the interruptible activity. Depending on this moment value, the interruption can starts before, after or during the interruptible activity, without exceeding the initial duration of this activity.

3.4 Task Execution Model

This model executes the current activity in the VE by launching the associated sequence of predefined tasks, containing animations or moves. It communicates with the activity selector to retrieve the activity to perform and returns its status. The perception model is also used to retrieve the needed semantics of the 3D environment so as to correctly perform the activities. For instance, the objects like the door to open or the book to take are given by the perception model. Of course, the user can modify objects used by tasks, as long as the object type and semantics are respected.

For this model, we use existing approaches specialized in the tasks execution. Among them, we can mention petri nets [16], finite state machines [11] or behavior trees [14]. These approaches allow to go from a state to another via transitions triggering actuators (animations, movements...) while respecting the conditions given by sensors (object state, agent's location...). For our use case, petri-nets were used because some tasks sequences were already provided in this form, but the other approaches can be well integrated instead. The duration of these sequences is automatically synchronized with the activity duration to respect the allocated time. The animation times are also considered in the calculation of the tasks to respect this duration. Figure 1 shows our use case where agents can perform activity in a 3D house environment.

4 Results

In this section, we demonstrate our model by using an agent executing activities in a 3D virtual house. Figure 4 shows the global structure of our implementation that produced the results explained below. To execute tasks in the VE, we use a Petri-Net based scripting module called #SEVEN [6]. *Unity Engine*[1] is used to represent the VE where an animated character as well a 3D reactive environment were imported. This 3D reactive environment mainly contains the 3D virtual house, the semantic data and the algorithm allowing the relationship between the semantic and our behavior model.

More than 20 daily activities were implemented and animated as well as 8 needs to represent the agent's internal states. Some example of activities and needs can be seen in the figures and tables of this part. All the simulations last 8 simulated days. For these simulations, needs and activities were configured

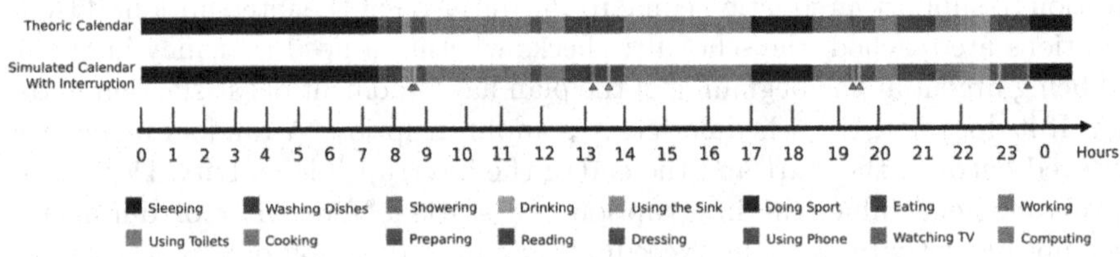

Fig. 5. Comparison between theoretic and simulated timelines for a same day with a strict calendar

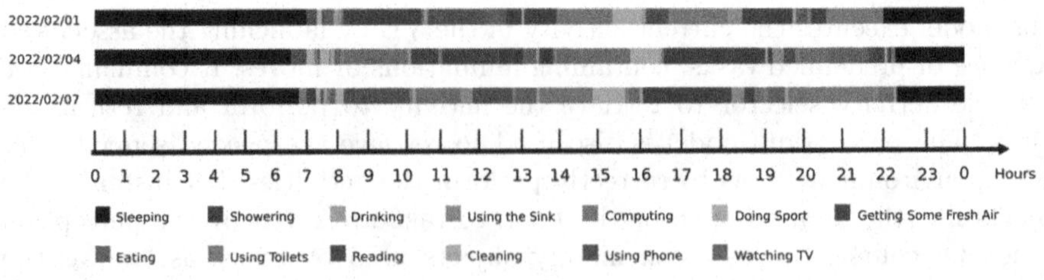

Fig. 6. Timelines of three separated days without theoretic calendar

[1] *Unity Engine*, official website: https://unity.com/.

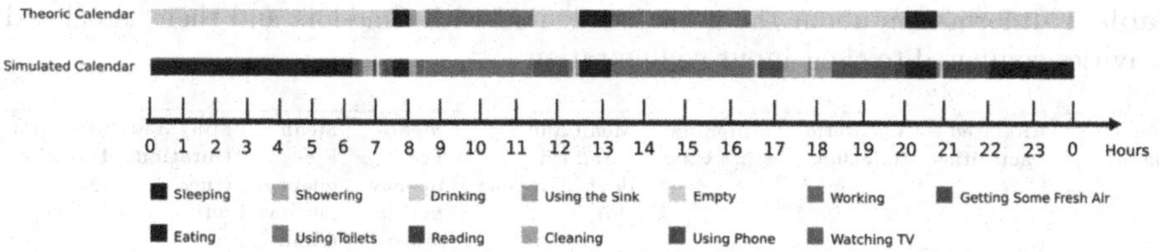

Fig. 7. Comparison between theoretic and simulated timelines for a same day with a moderate calendar

as detailed in Tables 1 and 2 for all these simulations. This section presents results showing the different level of control that the user can have over the agent's decision-making autonomy. Validation is done first on a specific day, then over the long term by analysing several days to obtain quantitative results. The numbers of activities and needs are for illustrative purposes. The user can thus add as many as necessary without impacting the model working. A video of our use case can be viewed at the following link: https://youtu.be/v8GxXCAAV1k

The first result presents the case where the user provides a calendar with no free time. To illustrate it, Fig. 5 compares timelines between a day coming from a theoretic calendar without free time with the results obtained after the simulation of this day. Here, thirst and toilets needs have been authorized to interrupt the calendar. Some calendar activities such as Using Phone, Reading are interruptible. These results show that calendar activities are performed on time and with the right duration. Interruptions are indicated by blue triangles for thirst and yellow triangles for toilets. Thus, the agent is able to interrupt a calendar activity to satisfy its needs allowed to interrupt.

Tables 1 and 2 and the Fig. 6 show the result of a simulation without calendar. They summarize information about satisfaction of needs according to the initial parameters. We can see that needs are satisfied when they are urgent since the average satisfaction over 8 days is globally in the bracket between the beginning of the emergency and its maximum urgency. A better accuracy is also observed when time slots are used rather than periods. Moreover, the frequencies are respected since differences come from the sleep period which approximately takes 8 h. Indeed, in the simulated case, sleep was not allowed to be interrupted, so the nightly satisfaction could not be reached. For the Fig. 6, we can conclude that the periodic satisfaction of needs creates a routine having small variations due to the variety of possible activities and the number of occurrences per day. For instance, eating is made three times per day around the same periods. This variation is interesting to produce more credible behavior.

Figure 7 compares timelines between a day coming from a theoretic calendar containing free times with the results of the same day simulation. Here, the agent must manage its free time in order to be ready for the next required activity. As seen in this timeline, the agent schedules accurately its activities during its free time while taking into account the satisfaction of its needs. The difference between the simulated and the theoretical for the calendar activities is again of

Table 1. Information about the needs configured with timeslots and their associated activities compared to their input configuration

Need name	Related activities	Theoretic time slot	Min/Max start time slot	Mean and standard deviation time slot	Mean Frequency per day (theoretic)	Mean Frequency per day (simulated)	Min/Max Duration (theoretic)	Min/Max Duration (simulated)
Hungry	Eating	[7 a.m., 9.30 a.m.]	7.19 a.m./7.48 a.m	7.34 a.m. ± 0 h 11 m	3	3.0	0 h 10 m/1 h	0 h 10 m/1 h
		[12 p.m., 1.30 p.m.]	12.04 p.m./1.12 p.m	12.36 p.m.± 0 h 27 m				
		[7 p.m., 9 p.m.]	7.04 p.m./8.47 p.m	7.53 p.m. ± 0 h 37 m				
Tiredness	Sleeping	[10 p.m., 12 a.m.]	10.08 p.m./10.40 p.m	10.24 p.m. ± 0 h 12 m	1	1.0	8 h/11 h	8 h/11 h

Table 2. Information about the needs configured with period and their associated activities compared to their input configuration

Need name	Related activities	Theoretic periods	Min/Max gap between 2 satisfactions (except night)	Mean and standard deviation between 2 satisfactions	Mean Frequency per day (theoretic)	Mean Frequency per day (simulated)	Min/Max Duration (theoretic)	Min/Max Duration (simulated)
Thirst	Drinking	Every 3 h (urgency 2 h 05 m)	2 h 13 m/3 h 41 m	2 h 57 m ± 0 h 26 m	8	5.75	0 h 01 m/0 h 05 m	0 h 01 m/0 h 05 m
Hygiene	Showering Using the Sink	Every 6 h (urgency 4 h 02 m)	4 h 25 m/6 h 40 m	5 h 29 m ± 0 h 45 m	4	3.0	0 h 15 m/1 h 0 h 05 m/0 h 20 m	0 h 15 m/0 h 35 m 0 h 05 m/0 h 20 m
Sport	Doing Sport	Every 48 h (urgency 33 h 56 m)	34 h 57 m/37 h 22 m	36 h 10 m ± 1 h 12 m	0.5	0.50	0 h 15 m/2 h	0 h 15 m/0 h 38 m

the same order as the strict calendar, proving that the agent respects the strong constraints. We can also see that there is no redundancy when the calendar activities satisfy needs and are positioned close to the times when these needs are urgent. This is the case with hunger for instance, where the "Eating" calendar activity happens when hunger becomes urgent. The planner also considers the calendar activities to satisfy the agent's needs.

These results show that the agent performs activities in the VE while respecting its input constraints and its needs. We can thus consider that our model is able to adjust the level of autonomy according to the user's configurations and the agent's internal state. The autonomous part satisfies the needs when they become urgent and respects the schedule given by the user, allowing a good ratio between control and autonomy.

5 Conclusion

We presented a model allowing the user to configure the level of the agent's decision-making autonomy. With our model, combining BDI architecture and scheduling processes, either the user can leave the agent totally autonomous during the simulation, or the activities to perform can be fully or partially controlled by users through a calendar. Interruption can also be used to satisfy the urgent needs of the agent if the calendar is too restrained. In addition, all activities are performed in a 3D virtual environment through animations and movements. Thus, our model is ready to use for data generation: if virtual sensors or simulated cameras are included in the VE, then users could retrieve information about the agent's activities to generate data.

In future work, we will evaluate this model for activity detection with virtual sensors of a smart house. Some experiments will be also made to compare our simulated data with real data. Moreover, the internal state can also be enriched by other cognitive methods such as preferences or emotions. Similarly, perception can be improved to manage resources in addition to activity filtering. We also plan to produce concrete examples showing the management of dynamic VE. After this, our goal would be to extend this model for multi-agent systems.

References

1. Alshammari, N., Alshammari, T., Sedky, M., Champion, J., Bauer, C.: OpenSHS: open smart home simulator. Sensors **17**(5), 1003 (2017)
2. Amouroux, É., Huraux, T., Sempé, F., Sabouret, N., Haradji, Y.: SMACH: agent-based simulation investigation on human activities and household electrical consumption. In: Filipe, J., Fred, A. (eds.) ICAART 2013. CCIS, vol. 449, pp. 194–210. Springer, Heidelberg (2014). https://doi.org/10.1007/978-3-662-44440-5_12
3. Avradinis, N., Panayiotopoulos, T., Anastassakis, G.: Behavior believability in virtual worlds: agents acting when they need to. SpringerPlus **2**(1), 1–11 (2013). https://doi.org/10.1186/2193-1801-2-246
4. Azvine, B., Djian, D., Tsui, K.C., Wobcke, W.: The intelligent assistant: an overview. In: Intelligent Systems and Soft Computing, pp. 215–238 (2000)
5. Charypar, D., Nagel, K.: Generating complete all-day activity plans with genetic algorithms. Transportation **32**(4), 369–397 (2005)
6. Claude, G., Gouranton, V., Berthelot, R.B., Arnaldi, B.: Short Paper: #SEVEN, a sensor effector based scenarios model for driving collaborative virtual environment, p. 5 (2014)
7. Fikes, R.E., Nilsson, N.J.: Strips: a new approach to the application of theorem proving to problem solving. Artif. Intell. **2**(3–4), 189–208 (1971)
8. Georgievski, I., Aiello, M.: An overview of hierarchical task network planning. arXiv preprint arXiv:1403.7426 (2014)

9. Jang, H., Hao, S., Chu, P.M., Sharma, P.K., Sung, Y., Cho, K.: Deep Q-network-based multi-criteria decision-making framework for virtual simulation environment. Neural Comput. Appl. **33**, 10657–10671 (2020)
10. Laird, J.E.: An analysis and comparison of act-r and soar. arXiv preprint arXiv:2201.09305 (2022)
11. Lee, D., Yannakakis, M.: Principles and methods of testing finite state machines-a survey. Proc. IEEE **84**(8), 1090–1123 (1996)
12. Maslow, A.H.: A theory of human motivation. Psychol. Rev. **50**(4), 370 (1943)
13. McCall, R.J., Franklin, S., Faghihi, U., Snaider, J., Kugele, S.: Artificial motivation for cognitive software agents. J. Artif. Gener. Intell. **11**(1), 38–69 (2020)
14. Miller, D.: Hierarchical task network prototyping in Unity3D, p. 124 (2016)
15. Ordóñez Medina, S.A.: Personalized multi-activity scheduling of flexible activities. Arbeitsberichte Verkehrs-und Raumplanung 1099 (2015)
16. Peterson, J.L.: Petri nets. ACM Comput. Surv. (CSUR) **9**(3), 223–252 (1977)
17. Puig, X., Ra, K., Boben, M., Li, J., Wang, T., Fidler, S., Torralba, A.: Virtualhome: simulating household activities via programs. In: Proceedings of the IEEE Conference on Computer Vision and Pattern Recognition, pp. 8494–8502 (2018)
18. Reynaud, Q., Haradji, Y., Sempé, F., Sabouret, N.: Using time use surveys in multi agent based simulations of human activity. In: ICAART, no. 1, pp. 67–77 (2017)
19. de Sevin, E., Thalmann, D.: A motivational model of action selection for virtual humans. In: International 2005 Computer Graphics, pp. 213–220. IEEE, Stony Brook (2005)
20. de Silva, L.: BDI agent reasoning with guidance from HTN recipes. In: Proceedings of the 16th Conference on Autonomous Agents and MultiAgent Systems. pp. 759–767. International Foundation for Autonomous Agents and Multiagent Systems, Richland (2017)
21. Silva, L.d., Meneguzzi, F., Logan, B.: BDI agent architectures: a survey. In: Proceedings of the Twenty-Ninth International Joint Conference on Artificial Intelligence, Yokohama, Japan, pp. 4914–4921 (2020)

Multi-Agent Task Allocation Techniques for Harvest Team Formation

Helen Harman(✉) and Elizabeth I. Sklar

Lincoln Institute for Agri-food Technology, University of Lincoln, Lincoln, UK
{hharman,esklar}@lincoln.ac.uk

Abstract. With increasing demands for soft fruit and shortages of seasonal workers, farms are seeking innovative solutions for efficiently managing their workforce. The harvesting workforce is typically organised by farm managers who assign workers to the fields that are ready to be harvested. They aim to minimise staff time (and costs) and distribute work fairly, whilst still picking all ripe fruit within the fields that need to be harvested. This paper posits that this problem can be addressed using multi-criteria, multi-agent task allocation techniques. The work presented compares the application of Genetic Algorithms (GAs) vs auction-based approaches to the challenge of assigning workers with various skill sets to fields with various estimated yields. These approaches are evaluated alongside a previously suggested method and the teams that were manually created by a farm manager during the 2021 harvesting season. Results indicate that the GA approach produces more efficient team allocations than the alternatives assessed.

Keywords: Multi-agent system · Applied AI · Harvest management

1 Introduction

Seasonal workers are frequently employed on farms to pick ripe soft fruit (e.g. strawberries, raspberries, cherries and blackberries) during the harvesting season. These workers are usually managed by harvest managers, who make daily decisions about which fields should be picked and which workers to assign to each of those fields. This process typically involves an awkward manual process of juggling spreadsheets produced from different software systems and can be quite time consuming, particularly at the height of the season when there are hundreds of workers available, with varying skills and levels of experience. As there is an increasing demand for soft fruits and shortages in seasonal workers [6,20,28], farms are requiring more innovative solutions for managing their workforce. Having sufficient labour and effectively managing the workforce will help ensure all ripe fruit is harvested. If this is not achieved, unharvested ripe produce will rot in the field. This situation results in food waste and a loss of investment for the grower [5].

© The Author(s), under exclusive license to Springer Nature Switzerland AG 2022
F. Dignum et al. (Eds.): PAAMS 2022, LNAI 13616, pp. 217–228, 2022.
https://doi.org/10.1007/978-3-031-18192-4_18

A range of strategies to address the labour shortage issue are being explored. This includes the introduction of robotic devices to assist with harvesting and crop-care tasks [3,20,21,34,35]. In contrast, our research investigates practical applications of *Artificial Intelligence (AI)* for managing the harvesting workforce, drawing on literature from *Multi-Agent Task Allocation* (MATA). Our approach can be implemented *now*, before a newfangled robotic workforce is ready to be deployed, and can also manage a hybrid human-robot workforce in the future.

MATA methods seek to distribute a set of tasks fairly amongst a set of agents. Our previous MATA work [12], showed that variations of Round Robin (RR) could be adapted to the problem of assigning workers (agents) to fields (tasks). This paper investigates applying Genetic Algorithms (GAs), Ordered Single Item (OSI) auctions and Sequential Single Item (SSI) auctions to this problem. GAs take a population-based approach, inspired by natural selection, they progressively adapt the suitability of the individuals for their environment. In contrast, OSI and SSI are auction-based methods, in which bidders bid for items and the bidder that places the best bid (according to the auctioneer) is assigned the item being bid on. To apply these approaches to our application domain, we define a fitness function that incorporates the farm's desire to minimise staff time (due to the shortages of labour) and balance workload amongst workers. If the workload is unbalanced, some workers would have very few fruits to pick while others would spend too long working. If these discrepancies are large, then the workforce can become disgruntled—as pickers are typically paid by the volume they pick, those with few fruits to pick earn less. Since workers are usually free to leave one farm and move to another, the farm managers would like to keep their workers happy so that their workforce remains intact during the season.

The GA, OSI and SSI methods introduced in this paper are evaluated on real-world data provided by a commercial fruit farm during their 2021 harvesting season. This paper also compares these approaches to the method proposed in [12] and the teams that were manually created by farm managers. This paper is organised as follows. Section 2 highlights related work in the literature on MATA. Section 3 describes our approach to allocating human workers to teams. Section 4 explains the experiments we conducted, within a real-world scenario, in order to evaluate the impact of our approach. Section 5 presents and analyses our experimental results. Finally, we close (Sect. 6) with a summary of our contributions and directions for future work.

2 Background

A key challenge in multi-agent and multi-robot systems is to decide which *tasks* should be assigned to which agents so that the overall execution of a *mission* (set of tasks to be executed within a particular overall timeframe) is *efficient*: resources are used effectively, so that time and energy are not wasted and, often, some reward is maximised. Many different types of *task allocation* mechanisms have been explored within the multi-agent systems (MAS) and multi-robot systems (MRS) communities, generally addressing what are referred to as *MATA* or *multi-robot task allocation (MRTA)* problems.

An effective approach to MATA is the use of Genetic Algorithms (GA) [16]. GAs aim to minimise (or maximise) a fitness function by *evolving* a set of possible solutions—the population. A solution is represented as a "chromosome", (usually) a vector of values referred to as genes. To evolve the population, i.e. to create a new generation, the strongest (i.e. fittest) individuals are selected to survive and to be adapted. Various methods for representing a solution exist. For instance, the Traveling Salesman Problem (TSP) has been represented as a binary string, where each city is represented by a binary number and the order they appear in a chromosome is the order in which they are visited. As large problems require lengthy strings and many infeasible routes could be generated, often approaches use integer strings [22, 29]. The fitness function for the TSP calculates the duration and distance associated with visiting each city in the sequence a chromosome represents.

A selection strategy is chosen to retain the most promising individuals and/or maintain diversity (by selecting a mixture of low- and high-ranked individuals). A wide range of methods have been proposed and evaluated within literature [2, 10, 17]. This includes truncation selection, where the best (least/most fit) individuals are selected; tournament selection, where the best individual from a random subset of population is selected, and fitness proportionate selection, where the probability of an individual being selected is based on their fitness. The two most common types of adaptation (also known as "reproduction operators" [15]) are crossover and mutation. Single-point crossover combines two individuals by randomly choosing a gene and swapping all genes that fall after this gene with the genes of the other individual. Researchers have also investigated multi-point crossover in which the crossing over starts/stops at multiple genes. In mutation, a gene's value is changed; for example, a binary gene can be changed from 0 to 1 or vice versa, or an integer gene could be changed to a different, randomly selected, value.

Multi-objective algorithms (MOA) aim to minimise (or maximise) multiple fitness functions (or objectives) [4, 8, 19]. Often MOA attempt to find the solutions that appear on the *pareto front* (i.e. a set of possible good solutions—depending on which objective is preferred). Nevertheless, as we intend our system to determine automatically which fields pickers will be assigned to, our approach must be able to return a single solution. In our work, this is performed by finding the weighted sum of the two objectives. This approach has been taken in prior work, such as [11], in which a path length is combined with the path smoothness (amount of rotation) to plan a robot's route.

Auction-based approaches to MATA are often controlled by a centralised auction manager. The auction manager announces item(s) to the bidders, the bidders place a value on the item(s), and the auction manager decides which bidders should be rewarded which item(s). Auctions usually repeat in "rounds" until all items have been allocated. Auctions take into account both the self-interests of individual bidders as well as group goal(s) represented by the auction manager—hence their popularity in multi-agent systems, which seek to balance both sets of, potentially conflicting, goals.

An *Sequential Single-Item (SSI)* auction [18] is a particularly popular method. In SSI, several tasks are announced to bidders at one time. Each bidder, responds with a bid representing the value (utility) of the task to them, incorporating cost to execute and potential reward. The auction manager then determines the winner by picking the bidder with the best (lowest/highest) bid for any task. SSI has been a popular choice for multi-robot task allocation, and many variants have been studied (e.g. [14,23–25,32,33]).

GAs have been applied to a wide range of domains. This includes deciding where to apply nitrates to soil [27], allocating jobs to high-performance computer resources [9], assigning search and rescue tasks after natural disasters [26] and finding appropriate learning experiences for students [37]. Likewise, auctions have been applied to many domains, including allocating harvesting tasks to agents within a single field [13], controlling traffic [30], managing ambulance dispatch [31] and planning the routes of heterogeneous robots [38]. The objective of our work is to automate the process of managing the workforce of a large commercial fruit farm. This workforce could consist of humans and/or robotic workers. Specifically, we investigate applying GAs, OSI and SSI to the complex problem of assigning workers to fields.

3 Approach

On a daily basis, farm managers decide which fields should be picked based on yield estimates and customer demand. They assign workers to "teams", each of which will harvest in one or more of the selected fields. The aim of our work is to decide which workers should be assigned to which field(s), saving farm managers from having to undertake this time-consuming job. This section introduces the problem and the fitness function, and then explains how GAs and auction-based approaches can each be applied to the problem.

To help address labour shortages and reduce farm expenditures, *staff time* (the total time worked by all staff each day) must be minimised. However, the solution with the minimum staff time has an unevenly distributed workload: the quickest worker is assigned to the field with the highest estimated yield, the second fastest to the field with the second highest estimated yield and so on. Each field has a single worker, except the field with lowest estimated yield, which all remaining workers are assigned to. This is problematic for two reasons. First, a worker picking alone will not manage to harvest the whole field—they will tire and/or run out of allowable time[1]. Since soft fruit must be harvested within a specific timeframe, unpicked fruit could spoil. Second, workers picking the field with the lowest yield would have relatively little work, and thus lower earnings. To prevent these problems, our approach also aims to minimise *execution time*—a proxy for evenness (and thus fairness), calculated as the duration of time between when the first picker starts work and when the last picker stops work on a given day. Our method assumes that enough pickers are available so that all ripe fruit can be harvested each day.

[1] Labour regulations restrict the number of hours per day a worker can work.

3.1 Problem Description

For each date within the picking season, the farm manager selects a set of fields (F) that require harvesting by the workers (W) who are available on that date. Each of the fields has an *estimated yield.* In our approach, groups of fields that are picked by the same team of workers are treated as one field (i.e. their estimated yields are summed). Our aim is to assign each worker ($w \in W$) to a field ($f \in F$), so that staff time and execution time are minimised. A solution is only valid if each worker is assigned to exactly one field (or group of fields) and no fields have zero workers.

Each of the workers has a set of skills, indicating how quickly they can pick each type of fruit. Their picking speed (in grams per second) is computed using data that is already produced by commercial fruit farms. This data is recorded so that a farm can pay the pickers by piece-rate (i.e. by the amount of fruit they pick). When a worker's picking speed is unknown for a particular type of fruit (e.g. they have not picked that type of fruit before), a picking speed of 1 is used. This is lower than the speed of any picker with experience.

3.2 Solution Fitness

We have developed a single fitness function that reflects and combines the two factors we aim to minimise: staff time and execution time. To calculate this we first need to introduce how to estimate the time it takes to pick a field. This section details the components of our fitness function.

The **estimated picking time** (*ept*) is calculated for each field ($f \in F$) selected for picking on a particular date (d), assuming it is picked by a specific team of workers ($f.W$). It is calculated by dividing the *estimated yield* (for field f on date d) by the sum of the picking speeds ($w.ps$) for the workers assigned to that field (Eq. 1). If a field has no workers, the *ept* of that field is infinity.

$$ept(f) = \begin{cases} \frac{f.estimated\_yield}{\sum_{w \in f.W} w.ps(f.\text{fruit})}, & \text{if } |f.W| \geq 1 \\ \infty, & \text{otherwise} \end{cases} \tag{1}$$

The first factor we aim to minimise is the average *ept* of workers (*eptw*), representing *staff time.* This is calculated by summing the time all workers spend picking and dividing this by the number of workers. This is shown in Eq. 2, in which W is the set of all workers available on the date being scheduled.

$$eptw(F, W) = \frac{\sum_{f \in F}(ept(f) \times |f.W|)}{|W|} \tag{2}$$

Equation 3 calculates the second factor we aim to minimise: the average *ept* of the fields (*eptf*), which represents the *execution time.* The *ept* of the fields is summed and then this is divided by the number of fields.

$$eptf(F) = \frac{\sum_{f \in F} ept(f)}{|F|} \tag{3}$$

The weighted sum of *eptw* and *eptf* is calculated to find the fitness of a solution. Raw staff time (sum of the *ept* of workers) and execution time (maximum of the *ept* of fields) are not combined because staff time is a much greater value than execution time and is likely to undergo larger changes when the workers are rearranged. This would result in staff time being more dominant, whereas, *eptw* and *eptf* are of similar scale and can be balanced against each other. The fitness function is shown in Eq. 4. In Sect. 5.2, we discuss the results for different values of the linear weighting factor (α).

$$fitness(F, W, k) = (eptw(F, W) * \alpha) + (eptf(F) * (1 - \alpha)) \tag{4}$$

3.3 GA Approach

Our approach is implemented using the Jenetics library [39]. After creating the initial population, the following steps are repeated until the termination criteria has been reached (the best fitness remains unaltered for 5 generations):

1. Select survivors.
2. Select individuals for adaptation.
3. Adapt to create offspring (using mutation and single-point crossover).
4. Combine survivors and offspring to form new generation. 60% of the new generation contains the offspring and 40% is formed of the survivors. This represents a 60:40 exploration:exploitation ratio.

For our problem, the size of a chromosome is equal to the number of workers ($|W|$), with each gene representing which field each worker is assigned to. A gene is an integer value in the range 0 to $|F| - 1$. An example, for a problem with 5 workers and 3 fields, is shown in Fig. 1.

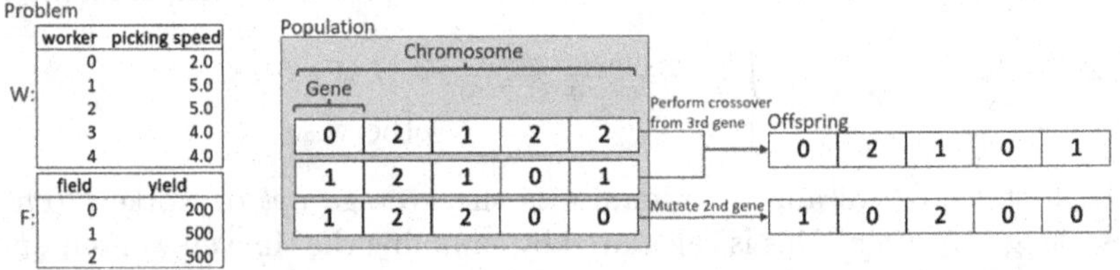

Fig. 1. Example population representing 3 possible solutions for assigning 5 workers to 3 fields. For the first chromosome, the first worker is assigned to field 0; the second, fourth and fifth to field 2, and the third to field 1. The offspring on the top right shows the result when single-point crossover (from 3rd gene) is performed on the top two chromosomes. The fitness of the original chromosomes are (top down) 71.28, 74.54 and 63.33; the offspring have fitness (top down) of 59.26 and 60.51. In this case, crossover and mutation have produced individuals who are stronger (have a lower fitness) than those in the original population. This example assumes that there is a single type of fruit; multiple types of fruit are used in our experiments.

3.4 Auction Approach

Typically, in auction methods, an auction manager advertises items (e.g. tasks) to the agents. The agents bid on these items and the auction manger decides which bid wins, and thus which agent is assigned the items(s) they have bid on. For our problem domain, it is the fields that bid on the workers. Each agent (field) aims to minimise its own *ept* (the individual's goal); whereas, the auction manager aims to minimise the *fitness* (the team's goal). Thus, the cost of a bid is the field's *ept* if it were to be assigned the worker being bid on. The auction manager replaces the *ept* of this field when calculating the fitness (Eqs. 2, 3 and 4) with the bid's cost. We have implemented two auction-based approaches.

- *Ordered Single Item (OSI)* : Workers are sorted slowest first, and one worker at a time is advertised to the fields. The auction manager assigns the field whose bid produces the lowest *fitness* the worker being bid on.
- *Sequential Single Item (SSI)* : All unassigned workers are advertised to all fields and each field responds with a bid for the worker that results in the lowest *ept* (i.e. for the worker that has the quickest picking speed for the type of fruit the field contains). As with OSI, the auction manager assigns the field whose bid produces the lowest *fitness* the worker the field bid on.

To handle tiebreaks, if two bids have an equally low fitness, then the winner is the field that has the fewest agents. If the fields also have the same number of agents, the field with the highest yield wins. This guarantees that each field will be assigned at least one worker (if $|W| \geq |F|$).

4 Experiments

Our experiments are designed to evaluate the effectiveness, for managing a harvest workforce, of our GA approach compared to two auction-based approaches: OSI and SSI. First, we evaluate the impact changing the linear weighting factor (α) has on the execution time and staff time. Then we compare the methods to the RR variant proposed in [12] and the actual teams created by farm mangers.

4.1 Data

A commercial fruit farm provided us with data during their 2021 harvesting season, which involved 182 picking days. This data was for strawberry, raspberry, cherry, and blackberry fields, a total of 30 fields. Note, this data has been used within our previous work [12], and thus processing this real-world data is not novel here. The following was provided incrementally during the 2021 season:

- **Estimated yield :** A spreadsheet containing an approximate volume of ripe fruit for each field the farm plans to pick on the morrow.
- **Worker list :** A list of available workers.
- **Recorded picking data :** The amount of fruit picked so far by each picker. This data is used to calculate the picking speeds of the workers, and to extract the actual teams (that were manually created by farm managers).

4.2 Metrics

To evaluate our proposed approaches, for each picking day, we calculate *staff time*—the sum of the *ept* of all workers across all fields, and *execution time*—the maximum *ept* of the fields. For determining the significance of our results, we applied statistical testing and factor analysis, where appropriate. A Shapiro-Wilk test [36] was performed to check if each sample is normally distributed. For all samples there is 95% chance that the sample is normally distributed, thus ANalysis Of VAriance (ANOVA) tests [1,7] were performed (for which the F test statistics are reported). The significance of results is indicated by p, the probability of the results occurring randomly. All plots show mean; the error bars indicate the standard deviation.

To tune our GA, we ran experiments to choose amongst 8 different selectors, 15 initial population sizes, 10 mutation probabilities and 15 crossover probabilities. The setup we found produced the lowest fitness is used for the experiments presented here: truncation selection, population size of 1500, crossover probability of 0.9 and mutation probability of 0.0 (i.e., no mutation). Our GA approach was ran 5 times. The result of the run that produced the lowest fitness is shown here since this is for the team that would be recommended to farm managers. OSI, SSI and the RR variant [12] are deterministic, and thus were ran once.

5 Results

5.1 Trade-off Between Staff Time and Execution Time

As mentioned in Sect. 3, only taking into account staff time causes the workload to be unbalanced. Our results, shown in Fig. 2, demonstrate this. When $\alpha = 1.0$ (the point at the top left of the plots), the lowest staff time was achieved; however, this also resulted in the highest execution time. As α was decreased, execution time decreased and staff time increased.

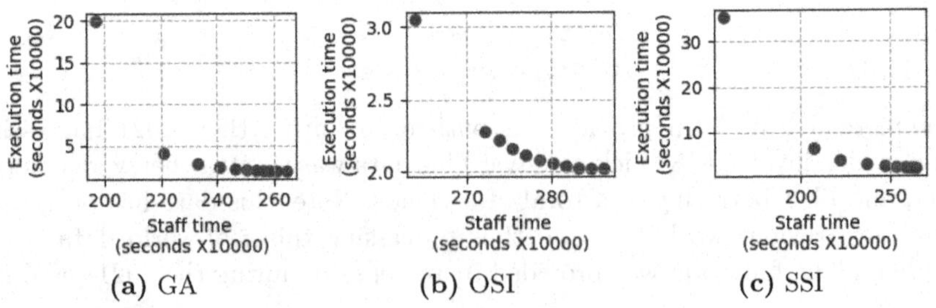

Fig. 2. Scatter plots showing the trade-off between the two criteria: staff time and execution time. The data points in purple indicate the results used in the comparison shown in Fig. 3. Note the different x and y axis ranges

5.2 Comparison to Alternative Approaches

The results for comparing our GA, OSI and SSI approaches with $\alpha = 0.5$ to the RR variations proposed in [12] (i.e. RR3) and to the teams manually created by farm managers (Actual) are shown in Fig. 3.

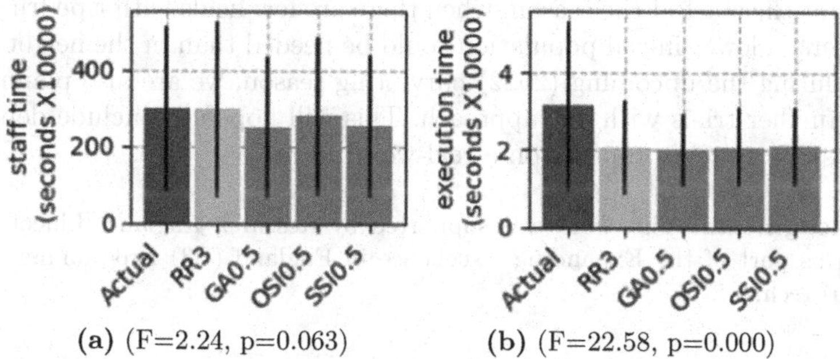

(a) (F=2.24, p=0.063) (b) (F=22.58, p=0.000)

Fig. 3. The estimated staff time (left) and execution time (right) for the Actual teams, the RR3 approach proposed in [12], and the GA, OSI and SSI approaches described in this paper for $\alpha = 0.5$. The sample size is equal to the number of picking days. (Note, that Actual uses the actual picking days and actual yield; whereas, the remaining approaches use the estimated data.)

Our GA approach achieved the lowest staff time and execution time. SSI achieved the second lowest staff time and OSI had the second lowest execution time. The difference in staff time is not statistically significant, but the difference in execution time is. Nevertheless, based on the mean staff times, if all workers were paid the UK hourly minimum wage (of £9.50), employing the teams proposed by our GA approach could save the farm an average of £1229.72 per day. The downside of the GA approach is that, for these experiments, it took longer to run than the other approaches. Often there is a trade-off between run-time and solution quality. Within our application domain, when picking has finished for the day, farm managers send us the data required to created the team allocations for the following day. Thus far, all approaches we have tested would produce a result within a timely manner; we therefore, focus on which created the most efficient team allocations. In future experimentation, the farm managers' opinions on the run-time of our approach will be gathered.

6 Summary and Future Work

This paper explored applying Genetic Algorithms (GAs), Ordered Single Item (OSI) auctions and Sequential Single Item (SSI) auctions to the problem of allocating workers to the fields selected for harvesting. We proposed a fitness function that combines minimising the average staff time of workers with minimising the average execution time of the fields. Minimising staff time causes the workload to become unevenly distributed, and this execution time must also be considered. Our experiments compared our GA, OSI and SSI approach to the Round Robin (RR) variant proposed in [12] and the teams manually created by farm managers during the 2021 harvesting season. The resulting staff time and execution time of the GA approach was less than the alternatives.

During future work, we will explore the seasonal variation in our results. For instance, at the start of the season, when there are few fields with ripe fruits and few workers, a lower initial population could be needed than in the height of the season. During the upcoming (2022) harvesting season, we are also planning to perform further trials with our approach. This will hopefully include deploying the teams our system proposes on a real-world farm.

Acknowledgments. This work was supported by Research England [Lincoln Agri-Robotics] as part of the Expanding Excellence in England (E3) Programme and by Ceres Agri-tech.

References

1. Anscombe, F.: The validity of comparative experiments. J. Roy. Stat. Soc. Ser. A (General) **111**(3), 181–211 (1948)
2. Blickle, T., Thiele, L.: A comparison of selection schemes used in evolutionary algorithms. Evol. Comput. **4**(4), 361–394 (1996). https://doi.org/10.1162/evco.1996.4.4.361
3. Das, G., Cielniak, G., From, P., Hanheide, M.: Discrete event simulations for scalability analysis of robotic in-field logistics in agriculture-a case study. In: IEEE International Conference on Robotics and Automation, Workshop on Robotic Vision and Action in Agriculture (2018)
4. Deb, K., Jain, H.: An evolutionary many-objective optimization algorithm using reference-point-based nondominated sorting approach, part i: Solving problems with box constraints. IEEE Trans. Evol. Comput. **18**(4), 577–601 (2014). https://doi.org/10.1109/TEVC.2013.2281535
5. Doward, J., Baldassari, V.: Red Alert: UK farmers warn of soft fruit shortage. The Guardian (2018)
6. Duckett, T., Pearson, S., Blackmore, S., Grieve, B., Smith, M.: Agricultural Robotics White Paper: The Future of Robotic Agriculture (2018). www.ukras.org/wp-content/uploads/2018/10/UK_RAS_wp_Agri_web-res_single.pdf. Accessed 10 Mar 2020)
7. Fisher, R.A.: Statistical methods for research workers (1925)
8. Fonseca, C.M., Fleming, P.J.: Genetic algorithms for multiobjective optimization: formulation discussion and generalization. In: Proceedings of the 5th International Conference on Genetic Algorithms, pp. 416–423. Morgan Kaufmann Publishers Inc., San Francisco (1993)
9. Gabaldon, E., Lerida, J.L., Guirado, F., Planes, J.: Multi-criteria genetic algorithm applied to scheduling in multi-cluster environments. J. Simul. **9**(4), 287–295 (2015). https://doi.org/10.1057/jos.2014.41
10. Goldberg, D.E., Deb, K.: A comparative analysis of selection schemes used in genetic algorithms. In: Foundations of Genetic Algorithms, vol. 1, pp. 69–93. Elsevier (1991). https://doi.org/10.1016/B978-0-08-050684-5.50008-2

11. Hao, K., Zhao, J., Yu, K., Li, C., Wang, C.: Path planning of mobile robots based on a multi-population migration genetic algorithm. Sensors **20**(20) (2020). https://doi.org/10.3390/s20205873
12. Harman, H., Sklar, E.: Multi-agent task allocation for fruit picker team formation. In: Proceedings of the 21th International Conference on Autonomous Agents and MultiAgent Systems, AAMAS 2022, International Foundation for Autonomous Agents and Multiagent Systems (2022)
13. Harman, H., Sklar, E.I.: A practical application of market-based mechanisms for allocating harvesting tasks. In: Dignum, F., Corchado, J.M., De La Prieta, F. (eds.) PAAMS 2021. LNCS (LNAI), vol. 12946, pp. 114–126. Springer, Cham (2021). https://doi.org/10.1007/978-3-030-85739-4_10
14. Heap, B., Pagnucco, M.: Repeated sequential single-cluster auctions with dynamic tasks for multi-robot task allocation with pickup and delivery. In: Klusch, M., Thimm, M., Paprzycki, M. (eds.) MATES 2013. LNCS (LNAI), vol. 8076, pp. 87–100. Springer, Heidelberg (2013). https://doi.org/10.1007/978-3-642-40776-5_10
15. Holland, J.H.: Adaptation in natural and artificial systems: an introductory analysis with applications to biology, control, and artificial intelligence. University of Michigan Press (1975)
16. Holland, J.H.: Genetic algorithms. Sci. Am. **267**(1), 66–73 (1992). https://www.jstor.org/stable/24939139
17. Katoch, S., Chauhan, S.S., Kumar, V.: A review on genetic algorithm: past, present, and future. Multimedia Tools Appl. **80**(5), 8091–8126 (2020). https://doi.org/10.1007/s11042-020-10139-6
18. Koenig, S., et al.: The power of sequential single-item auctions for agent coordination. In: Proceedings of AAAI, vol. 2 (2006)
19. Konak, A., Coit, D.W., Smith, A.E.: Multi-objective optimization using genetic algorithms: a tutorial. Reliabil. Eng. Syst. Safety **91**(9), 992–1007 (2006). https://doi.org/10.1016/j.ress.2005.11.018
20. Kootstra, G., Wang, X., Blok, P.M., Hemming, J., Van Henten, E.: Selective harvesting robotics: current research, trends, and future directions. Curr. Rob. Rep. **2**, 95–104 (2021)
21. Kurtser, P., Edan, Y.: Planning the sequence of tasks for harvesting robots. Rob. Auton. Syst. **131** (2020)
22. Larranaga, P., Kuijpers, C.M.H., Murga, R.H., Inza, I., Dizdarevic, S.: Genetic algorithms for the travelling salesman problem: a review of representations and operators. Artif. Intell. Rev. **13**(2), 129–170 (1999). https://doi.org/10.1023/A:1006529012972
23. McIntire, M., Nunes, E., Gini, M.: Iterated multi-robot auctions for precedence-constrained task scheduling. In: AAMAS 2016 - Proceedings of the 2016 International Conference on Autonomous Agents and Multiagent Systems, pp. 1078–1086. International Foundation for Autonomous Agents and Multiagent Systems (IFAAMAS) (2016)
24. Nunes, E., Gini, M.: Multi-robot auctions for allocation of tasks with temporal constraints. In: Proceedings of the Twenty-Ninth AAAI Conference on Artificial Intelligence, AAAI 2015, pp. 2110–2216. AAAI Press (2015). https://dl.acm.org/doi/10.5555/2886521.2886614
25. Nunes, E., McIntire, M., Gini, M.: Decentralized allocation of tasks with temporal and precedence constraints to a team of robots. In: 2016 IEEE International Conference on Simulation, Modeling, and Programming for Autonomous Robots (SIMPAR), pp. 197–202 (2016)

26. Pallin, M., Rashid, J., Ögren, P.: A decentralized asynchronous collaborative genetic algorithm for heterogeneous multi-agent search and rescue problems. In: 2021 IEEE International Symposium on Safety, Security, and Rescue Robotics (SSRR), pp. 1–8 (2021). https://doi.org/10.1109/SSRR53300.2021.9597856
27. Peerlinck, A., Sheppard, J., Pastorino, J., Maxwell, B.: Optimal design of experiments for precision agriculture using a genetic algorithm. In: 2019 IEEE Congress on Evolutionary Computation (CEC), pp. 1838–1845 (2019). https://doi.org/10.1109/CEC.2019.8790267
28. Pelham, J.: The Impact of Brexit on the UK Soft Fruit Industry. British Summer Fruits, London (2017)
29. Potvin, J.Y.: Genetic algorithms for the traveling salesman problem. Ann. Oper. Res. **63**(3), 337–370 (1996). https://doi.org/10.1007/BF02125403
30. Raphael, J., Sklar, E.I.: Towards dynamic coalition formation for intelligent traffic management. In: Belardinelli, F., Argente, E. (eds.) EUMAS/AT -2017. LNCS (LNAI), vol. 10767, pp. 400–414. Springer, Cham (2018). https://doi.org/10.1007/978-3-030-01713-2_28
31. Schneider, E., et al.: The Application of Market-based Multi-Robot Task Allocation to Ambulance Dispatch. arxiv.org/abs/2003.05550 (2020)
32. Schneider, E., Sklar, E.I., Parsons, S.: Evaluating multi-robot teamwork in parameterised environments. In: Proceedings of the 17th Towards Autonomous Robotic Systems (TAROS) Conference, pp. 301–313 (2016)
33. Schneider, E., Sklar, E.I., Parsons, S., Özgelen, A.T.: Auction-based task allocation for multi-robot teams in dynamic environments. In: Dixon, C., Tuyls, K. (eds.) TAROS 2015. LNCS (LNAI), vol. 9287, pp. 246–257. Springer, Cham (2015). https://doi.org/10.1007/978-3-319-22416-9_29
34. Seyyedhasani, H., Peng, C., Jang, W.J., Vougioukas, S.G.: Collaboration of human pickers and crop-transporting robots during harvesting - part i: model and simulator development. Comput. Electron. Agric. **172**, 105324 (2020)
35. Shamshiri, R.R., Hameed, I.A., Karkee, M., Weltzien, C.: Robotic harvesting of fruiting vegetables: a simulation approach in V-REP, ROS and MATLAB. In: Proceedings in Automation in Agriculture-Securing Food Supplies for Future Generations (2018)
36. Shapiro, S.S., Wilk, M.B.: An analysis of variance test for normality (complete samples). Biometrika **52**(3/4) (1965)
37. Sklar, E.I.: CEL: a framework for enabling an internet learning community. Ph.D. thesis, Brandeis University (2000)
38. Sullivan, N., Grainger, S., Cazzolato, B.: Sequential single-item auction improvements for heterogeneous multi-robot routing. Rob. Auton. Syst. **115**, 130–142 (2019). https://doi.org/10.1016/j.robot.2019.02.016
39. Wilhelmstötter, F.: Jenetics (2022). http://jenetics.io/. Accessed 21 Mar 2022

Study of Heterogeneous User Behavior in Crowd Evacuation in Presence of Wheelchair Users

John Hata[1], Haoxiang Yu[2], Vaskar Raychoudhury[1(✉)], Snehanshu Saha[3], and Huy Tran Quang[1]

[1] Miami University, Oxford, USA
{hatajm,tranquh}@miamioh.edu, vaskar@ieee.org

[2] University of Texas at Austin, Austin, USA
hxyu@utexas.edu

[3] BITS Pilani K.K. Birla Goa Campus, Sancoale, India
snehanshu.saha@ieee.org

Abstract. Crowd modeling is an area of study of increasing importance for understanding the dynamics of a crowd in an environment. Evacuation modeling focuses on how humans evacuate these environments as well as the intricacies and outcomes of the evacuation. Previous evacuation models do not take into account how human populations are physically heterogeneous as well as how the presence of wheelchair users affects an evacuation. In order to address the aforementioned open challenges, in this research, we propose a novel model to study the effect of wheelchair users in evacuation modeling. Our model is developed as an agent-based panic model and is built using the Unity gaming platform and includes speed, mass, and radius as the agent attributes. From the agent-based panic model, it was observed that larger wheelchair populations increased evacuation times while a larger number of and width of doorways decreased the evacuation times. Of the agent attributes in the panic model, speed had a negative correlation while mass and radius both had positive correlations with evacuation time. The findings from this study suggest that future crowd models may benefit in accuracy by using heterogeneous populations.

Keywords: Crowd modeling · Evacuation · User behavior · Wheelchair users

1 Introduction

Addressing emergency evacuation of mobility-impaired individuals, especially wheelchair users is an important problem to study. While extensive research has been developed with regard to modeling massive crowds, individual movements, the behavior of pedestrians, evacuation scenarios, and other scenarios related to everyday pedestrian movement [3,4,16,19,20], there is hardly any focus on

© The Author(s), under exclusive license to Springer Nature Switzerland AG 2022
F. Dignum et al. (Eds.): PAAMS 2022, LNAI 13616, pp. 229–241, 2022.
https://doi.org/10.1007/978-3-031-18192-4_19

evacuation modeling of a heterogeneous crowd involving pedestrian as well as wheelchair users. Crowd models deepen our understanding of how crowds behave under different conditions and help uncover the intricacies of pedestrian behavior in response to their environment, as well as how the environment can be shaped to combat factors that inhibit pedestrian movement. A specific yet important scenario to consider is an evacuation in response to an emergency. In an evacuation scenario, pedestrians exhibit behaviors in response to the emergency at hand in order to avoid injury and evacuate the premises. Modeling and simulating evacuations allow for a preemptive analysis of how a crowd might behave in an environment given an emergency situation.

Current research in evacuation modeling focuses on the mathematical modeling of pedestrians without taking into account that pedestrians are not homogeneous in their physical characteristics. The differences in these characteristics may cause a discrepancy in how specific pedestrians are and are not able to evacuate in a timely manner, this is a significant concern for wheelchair users, who may not be as mobile or agile as pedestrians who can walk and run to the exit. This information enhances evacuation preparedness through building design and event planning, plausibly leading to a greater number of lives saved in the event of a catastrophic emergency.

Agent-based pedestrian models have been used to model crowd dynamics by taking a bottom-up approach. In agent-based models, individual agent behaviors result in the recreation of larger, realistic crowd phenomena. Currently, there are only a few studies covering heterogeneous aspects of agents in crowd dynamics. This has been due to previous works focusing on the optimization of agent-based simulations for extremely large crowds [15], or not considering heterogeneity among pedestrians in crowds due to homogenizing psychological behaviors, such as those related to panic and high stress [13]. Recent empirical studies [10] [9] have revealed some affects of physical heterogeneity in corridors and bottlenecks, but this has not yet been further explored in the domain of simulation modeling.

In this paper, we have proposed a novel crowd evacuation model in order to measure the effects of heterogeneous mobility parameters on an evacuation. The model comprises an agent-based simulation of both walking and wheelchair-using agents evacuating a room under the effects of panic. The results of the model is intended to contribute additional information that may assist in the improvement of present and construction of future crowd and evacuation models. A crucial difference between the proposed model and previous works is that some previous works had gathered empirical data and derived behaviors from that in order to build their model. The proposed model will use behaviors seen in previous works, but the pedestrian characteristics will be generated to observe the effect of a heterogeneous population. The model is developed using a multi-platform game engine, named Unity, that allows for the development of two and three dimensional games as well as experiences and simulations. Our model has the following unique contributions:

- We capture how crowd behaviors are affected by heterogeneous agent attributes by considering wheelchair users for the first time.

- Our model demonstrates how environmental parameters affect crowd evacuation. Especially the agent parameters have a low, but statistically significant correlation with evacuation time.
- Extensive simulation results show that larger percentages of wheelchair users result in a lower rate and deviation of evacuation and larger doorways lead to an increase in rate and deviation of evacuation.

2 Related Works

This research has drawn motivations from three different albeit related research domains - *pedestrian behavior modeling*, *crowd dynamics analysis*, and *evacuation modeling*. We will briefly discuss those in relation to our problem.

Computer simulations [7] allow the *modeling of pedestrian behavior* and pedestrian models help simulate and predict movement behavior of both individuals and crowds. Zheng et al. [20] have found several common approaches to modeling individual pedestrians and their behaviors including (1) Cellular Automata, (2) Agent-based model, (3) Social Force model, (4) Lattice Gas model, (5) Fluid Dynamics model, (6) Game Theory, and (7) Animal-based Experimentation. Agent-based models simulate virtual, autonomous agents that organize and move using rule-based interactions [11]. Each agent possesses its own, typically simplified, attributes that fuel actions based on heuristics rather than strict logic. For our purpose, agent-based model appears to be most appropriate. Existing surveys describe a concise overview of pedestrian models over the past decade [3,4]. *Crowd dynamics*, the macroscopic approach to pedestrian behavior modeling focuses on behaviors and outcomes of the crowd as a whole instead of individual behaviors. Crowd behaviors are defined as spontaneous phenomena that emerge from the interaction among the crowd and the environment and are divided into several categories, such as collective intelligence, crowd turbulence, the faster-is-slower effect, the freezing-by-heating effect, panic, and self-organisation [14]. We focus on 'panic' which is simply defined as the "breakdown of ordered, cooperative behavior of individuals due to anxious reactions to a certain event." Crowd dynamics information can be used for better building design and accommodations, a review of expected behaviors for economic planning, and emergency evacuation planning for extreme scenarios. *Evacuation modeling* is the focus on ensuring the safety and comfort of people in hazardous scenarios through crowd management. Given its importance, works vary from microscopic and macroscopic approaches as well as different implementations, which include agent-based, cellular automata, and social force. Researchers have also studied different other aspects of crowd modeling such as, crowd safety [19], crowd merging [17], and property of very large crowd [8].

Geoerg, Paul et al. carried out a series of movement studies in order to address the need for empirical data relating to pedestrian safety through corridors and bottlenecks [10]. This study featured a 10 percent population of wheelchair users within the greater pedestrian population. Movement speeds of pedestrians with no wheelchair users present were consistent with previous works, but with the introduction of wheelchair users non-disabled participants adjusted their movement speeds to accommodate, resulting in a difference in overall movement speed.

3 Our Proposed Agent-Based Panic Model Involving Wheelchair Users

In order to explore the effects of a heterogeneous pedestrian model, an agent-based approach was chosen. Agent-based models (ABMs) allow for the implementation of individual behaviors to combine and form larger group behaviors [11].

3.1 Agent Attributes

In order to portray realistic behaviors of the pedestrians, distinct behaviors were chosen to reconstruct a simulation of a panicked crowd. Important considerations involve attributes that focus on decision-making and interaction-based behaviors. The main attributes chosen to be implemented are:

- Field of View (FoV): This encompasses how large or wide an area a person is able to visualize. The range of FoV is 100° outwards towards the ears, 60° inwards towards the nose, 60° upwards, and 75° downward [18].
- Herding: It is the tendency of pedestrians to subconsciously form groups when moving in similar directions. Even in a room with multiple exits pedestrians would not necessarily divide themselves equally amongst the exits to evacuate. A lack of visibility and unfamiliarity with the environment, and panic- can cause phenomena of social contagion where pedestrians will group together and follow others whom they believe know the best way to evacuate [12]. In our model we assume that all exits will not be used equally and pedestrians will tend to increasingly group (herd) at specific exits.
- Physical Attributes and Ability: We have considered a model with heterogeneous population of *agents-who-can-walk* (walking agents) and *agents-who-use-wheelchair* (wheelchair agents) with realistic attribute values calibrated using recent empirical data [5,6]. The specific attributes in the proposed model are (a) Mass, (b) Radius, (c) Max. velocity, and (d) Wheelchair use.

These attributes were chosen due to a combination of use in previous models as well as their foundational importance to crowd behavior within a panicked crowd. For this model, agents are assumed to not fall over or become injured during the evacuation process; collisions are inelastic.

3.2 Agent Model

We have chosen Unity game engine [2] as the platform to develop our evacuation model because of flexibility and open access. Unity uses GameObjects to represent different entities such as pedestrians. Pedestrian GameObjects can be fitted with RigidBody components and Colliders for collision handling and various scripts to control their motion. Other GameObjects can be added to the Scene in various shapes and positions in order to represent walls and obstacles. Pedestrians are separated between walking agents and wheelchair-user agents. The environments are built to be large square or rectangular spaces (known as *NavMesh*) in order to house a large number of agents with the number and size of the exits depending on the current experiment. In order to calculate agent paths and to assign those paths to individual agents in the NavMesh, one managerial GameObject is used. This guarantees that no agent will be motionless as the simulation begins. The Manager will recalculate all agent paths each time update is called and while it is not currently calculating paths. Once all paths are calculated, the Manager updates the agents' current paths to their targets.

3.3 Agent Behavior Logic

Agents are assumed to be in a panicked state. We have implemented three types of agent behaviors as explained below.

- **Agent Instantiating:** At the start of the simulation, pedestrians are generated within an indoor environment, distributed randomly, and without intersecting. Knowing how many agents, and how many of those agents will be wheelchair users, we use the following logic. Select a point inside the simulation environment for each wheelchair-user agent and place it with a random orientation. If the point collides with other agents or the environment re-select a point.
- **Agent Decision-making:** The goal of agent decision-making is to decide on the fastest escape from the room. Agents are able to use their FoV to pursue the closest visible exit or they follow another agent if no exit is within sight. If no exits or other peers to follow, the agent will move and rotate while attempting to locate either of the two to pursue.
- **Agent Updating:** Each update call of the panic model attempts to accomplish several actions; agent paths must be calculated and assigned accordingly, agent data must be recorded and stored, and agents must be removed from the scene when necessary.

4 Experimental Setup

Our proposed model is constructed using Unity Version 2020.1.8f1 running on the Windows 10 operating system. Data from the experiments was collected as text files and later processed for analysis. The hardware used to simulate our model includes a AMD Ryzen 9 3950X 16-Core 3.5 GHz CPU, an NVidia RTX3070 GPU, and 64Gb of DDR4 3200 RAM.

4.1 Agent Parameters

Agent attributes are selected based on empirical data obtained from the Anthropometric Reference Data for Children and Adults: the United States, 2015–2018,

Table 1. Parameters for agents

Walking agent		
Parameter	Min value	Max value
Radius	14.6 cm	16.4 cm
Mass	60 kg	80 kg
Speed	3.0 m/s	6.0 m/s
Wheelchair-using agent		
Parameter	Min value	Max value
Radius	25.4 cm	25.4 cm
Mass	66.8 kg	107.2 kg
Speed	2.0 m/s	3.6 m/s

Table 2. Simulation parameters in terms of number of doors, the width of the doorways, and the percentage of wheelchair users

Parameters	Doors	1	2	3
Width (meters)				
1		0-50%	0-50%	0-50%
2		0-50%	0-50%	0-50%
3		0-50%	0-50%	0-50%

and human running performance data collected and analyzed by Emig et al. [6] [5]. Attributes for both wheelchair using and walking agents are chosen randomly and uniformly within the ranges seen in Table 1.

The human running data from Emig, et al. is based on marathon running data as the best available option for a panic scenario and provides a benchmark for the range of speeds present in a population. Similarly, radius and mass are based on waist circumference and weight data Table 1. Agent attributes are further differentiated between wheelchair and non-wheelchair users through radius, mass, and speed. Wheelchair radii are consistent across all wheelchair users under the assumption that the models used are similar. Wheelchair agent masses range from an additional 6.8 kg to 27 kg assuming the potential for a mix of powered and manual wheelchair users which vary in weight depending on brand and weight carrying capacity [1].

4.2 Environmental Parameters

The environment dimensions are 33× 59 m, roughly double the dimensions of a standard basketball court. The number of exits and size of the exits vary per parameter set. For each combination of number of exits and width, the total population percentage of wheelchair users changes from 0, 10, 25, and to 50 %.

4.3 Performance Metrics

The following metrics are used to evaluate the proposed model.

- **Evacuation Rate (ER)**: Measures the number of agents exiting the environment per second. Both the average ER and the standard deviation is evaluated in order to capture the effects of environmental parameters on ER.

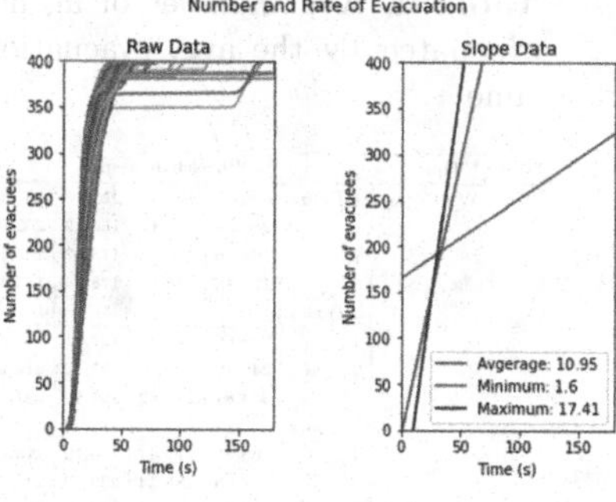

Fig. 1. Number and Rate (as visualized given the solution to each function) of Evacuation for 1-meter-wide Doorway with 10% Wheelchair Users.

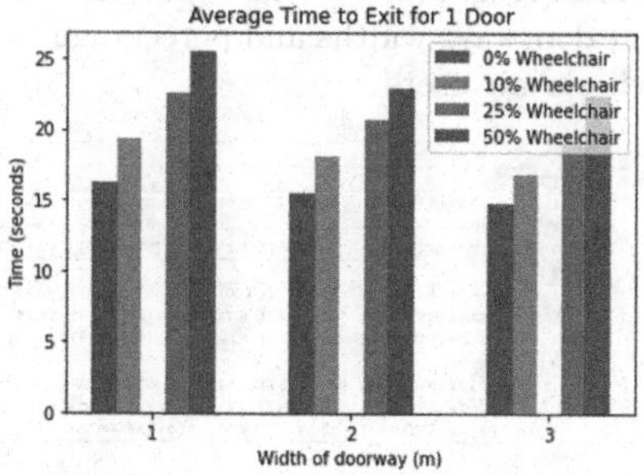

Fig. 2. Avg. time to evacuate through one doorway of varying width with varying number of wheelchair users

- **Average Time to Evacuate**: The average time in seconds for an agent to evacuate the environment per parameter set. This generalized metric will summarize the effects of the environment parameters for an agent.
- **Correlation Coefficient Attribute Versus Time Evacuated**: The correlation coefficient for each agent attribute versus time evacuated is measured in order to understand the effects of each agent attribute on exit time.
- **Rate * Time**: Multiplying the average ER by the average time evacuated results in the average number of agents evacuated by the average time. This metric is examined to find further consistencies and differences that ER and time do not.
- **Rate per Door**: This metric is defined as the average rate of evacuation while accounting for the number of doors in the environment. This value examines how the rate per door changes across parameter sets.

5 Performance Evaluation and Results

The panic model was run with 400 agents for 200 iterations per parameter set, totaling 7200 simulations conducted for data collection. Data for each iteration consisted of agent positions and velocities at each time step, as well as each agent attribute. The simulation data was recorded at each time step and reset once all agents had left the environment. Runs were capped at 180 s in order to provide for reasonable exit time. More detailed results pertaining to the Figs. 1 to 4 can be found here[1].

5.1 Rate of Evacuation

The last time step that each agent existed within the simulation was recorded. The time steps are then plotted to find the rate of agents evacuating the envi-

[1] Complete Figures: https://bit.ly/37Bwv4y More results: https://bit.ly/3FyGu73.

Table 3. Avg. evacuation rates for different doorways widths and percentage of wheelchair users

Avg. evacuation rates		% Wheelchair users			
Door Width (m)	1 Door	0	10	25	50
	1	17.54 (STD 3.65)	10.95 (STD 2.64)	7.39 (STD 2.63)	7.95 (STD 2.51)
	2	10.86 (STD 6.83)	9.98 (STD 4.60)	8.63 (STD 3.75)	8.5 (STD 3.34)
	3	12.15 (STD 6.53)	10.47 (STD 5.29)	9.29 (STD 4.28)	8.18 (STD 3.50)
	2 Doors				
	1	19.94 (STD 7.11)	9.88 (STD 4.60)	6.75 (STD 4.17)	6.17 (STD 3.23)
	2	23.28 (STD 9.68)	17.91 (STD 8.71)	13.90 (STD 4.91)	13.28 (STD 3.31)
	3	25.08 (STD 10.92)	22.30 (STD 9.69)	16.90 (STD 8.01)	16.02 (STD 4.71)
	3 Doors				
	1	22.71 (STD 6.89)	15.30 (STD 7.02)	7.63 (STD 4.75)	6.24 (STD 3.50)
	2	28.78 (STD 5.71)	26.22 (STD 4.81)	18.12 (STD 3.59)	15.61 (STD 2.04)
	3	35.42 (STD 7.95)	32.32 (STD 7.99)	27.21 (STD 6.08)	22.08 (STD 3.04)

Table 4. Avg. number of agents evacuated by the avg. evacuation time

Rate * Time		% Wheelchair users			
Door Width (m)	1 Door	0	10	25	50
	1	285.55	212.10	166.72	202.88
	2	168.76	180.34	178.47	195.16
	3	179.46	176.11	178.74	183.40
	2 Doors				
	1	246.66	164.11	127.91	130.37
	2	249.10	211.52	195.16	219.25
	3	254.81	234.82	207.19	237.74
	3 Doors				
	1	263.21	217.41	136.12	128.67
	2	283.63	285.54	233.39	244.61
	3	303.90	290.23	275.09	275.78

Table 5. Evacuation rate of the agents w.r.to the number of doors

Rate Per Door		% Wheelchair Users			
Door Width (m)	1 Door	0	10	25	50
	1	17.54	10.95	7.39	7.95
	2	10.86	9.98	8.63	8.50
	3	12.15	10.47	9.29	8.18
	2 Doors				
	1	9.97	4.94	3.38	3.09
	2	11.64	8.96	6.95	6.64
	3	12.54	11.15	8.45	8.01
	3 Doors				
	1	7.57	5.10	2.54	2.08
	2	9.26	8.74	6.04	5.20
	3	11.81	10.77	9.07	7.36

Table 6. T values for each attribute correlation. The T Table value used (1.972) was based on the 200 samples per correlation with a 0.05 probability.

T Values												
	1 Door				2 Door				3 Door			
1 Meter	0	10	25	50	0	10	25	50	0	10	25	50
Speed	3.479	3.633	4.104	4.104	4.588	2.427	2.723	3.022	4.264	2.135	1.990	1.701
Mass	0.000	1.845	2.872	3.326	0.141	0.563	1.557	1.845	0.000	0.563	0.846	0.987
Radius	0.987	2.575	3.326	3.633	1.414	0.987	1.845	2.135	1.272	0.987	1.129	1.129
2 Meter												
Speed	1.990	2.723	3.479	3.633	3.326	2.872	3.789	4.425	3.789	3.173	3.633	3.789
Mass	0.000	1.557	2.723	3.022	0.000	1.272	2.427	3.173	0.000	1.129	2.281	2.723
Radius	0.281	1.990	3.173	3.326	0.563	1.557	2.872	3.633	0.846	1.557	2.723	3.022
3 Meter												
Speed	1.845	2.575	3.326	3.173	2.723	3.022	3.479	4.588	3.326	2.872	3.789	4.588
Mass	0.000	1.557	2.723	2.575	0.000	1.414	2.427	3.633	0.000	1.414	2.575	3.633
Radius	0.141	1.990	3.022	2.872	0.422	1.845	2.723	3.946	0.704	1.845	3.022	3.946

ronment. Both scatter plots of the time steps and rates, measured in the number of agents evacuated per second, are found through linear regression can be seen in Fig. 1. The rates themselves allow for the direct examination of the effects of each parameter set. Average, minimum, and maximum rates for each parameter set are shown to more clearly describe these effects.

Figure 1 showcases the rEvac (Rate of Evacuation) for each set of environmental parameters. The left plot of each sub figure shows the raw number of agents that have evacuated while the right plot shows the minimum, maximum, and average slopes found through linear regression. The slopes show the exact rEvac in agents per second. Evacuation rates as labeled in Tables 3, 4, and 5. show how the rEvac changes per environment parameter set. For the 1-door-environment, rEvac decreases as a larger wheelchair user population are introduced and generally increases as the door width increases. The standard deviation of each rate for 1 door gives insight into how each parameter set affects the variance; the variance lowers as more wheelchair users are introduced, and raises as the width of the door increases. The rEvac for the 1-meter-door width is significantly higher than its peers due to how the agents are colliding. The most likely cause of this, based on speculation from observing the animation of the model, is from agents pushing other agents through the door in combination with agents forming a collective stream towards the exit. As many agents attempt to run to the only door in the environment they create pressure by pushing and jettisoning the agents already within the doorway through to the exit. This effect is likely mitigated as the size and number of exits increase, which may reduce and even eliminate the amount of pressure created by the pushing crowd.

For the 2-door-environment in Tables 3, 4, and 5, rEvac follows a similar trend to the previous environment, but showcases nearly double the average evacuation rate in Table 3 as might be expected when the number of available exits doubles as well. rEvac decreases with the introduction of more wheelchair users, and increases as the size of the doors increases. The standard deviation follows a similar trend as the wheelchair user population increases and the width of the doorways increase. For the 3-door-environment, rEvac and standard deviations continue the previous trends of decreasing the rEvac for higher wheelchair populations and increasing the evacuation rate for larger door widths. Overall, the evacuation rates are higher than the previous cases while the standard deviations are lower. The visible trends across environmental parameters can be summarized as: evacuation rates increase with wheelchair user population as well as with larger exits, variance in evacuation rates is higher with an increased wheelchair population and larger exits.

Figure 2 displays the average time to evacuate for each parameter set. The trends seen across environment parameters showcase similar results to the analysis of evacuation rate.Evacuation times generally decrease as the width of doors increase, and increase as the percentage of wheelchair users increases. The changes to average evacuation time are consistent with changes in rEvac and consistent across environment parameter sets. A greater number of exits decreases the average evacuation time, larger exits decrease the average evacuation time, and a larger wheelchair population increases the evacuation time.

5.2 Agent Attribute Distribution Versus Exit Time

Scatter plots of specific agent attributes versus when said agent exited the environment were used in order to determine the existence of correlations. These scatter plots were then analyzed using linear regression to confirm the correlation as well as the impact each attribute has on evacuation time. Figures are organized by attribute then by percentage of wheelchair users present, which can be partially seen by the gap within an attribute range.

Figure 3 shows the distribution of agent attributes versus the time evacuated along with the corresponding correlation coefficients. The correlation coefficients are also visualised in Fig. 3 in order to show trends across environment parameters. The figure also visualize the correlation coefficients to show trends across environment parameters.Across all coefficient trends, speed has a negative correlation with evacuation time that further decreases as the wheelchair user population increases. Mass and radius are nearly identical across all environment parameter sets, showing a positive correlation with evacuation time that increases as the wheelchair user population increases. It is important to note that

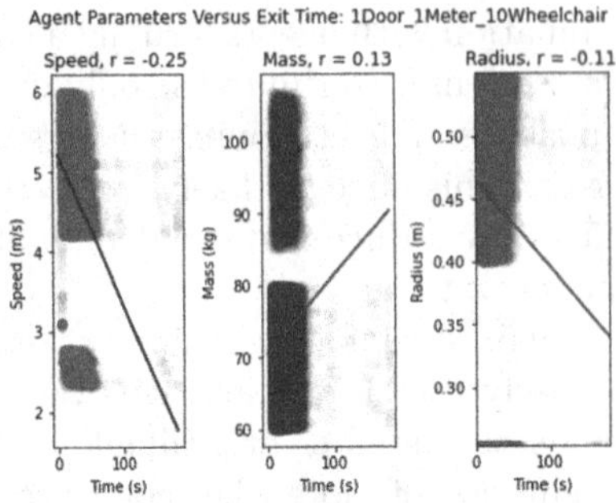

Fig. 3. Agent Parameters vs Exit Time for 1-meter-wide One Doorway with 10% Wheelchair Users

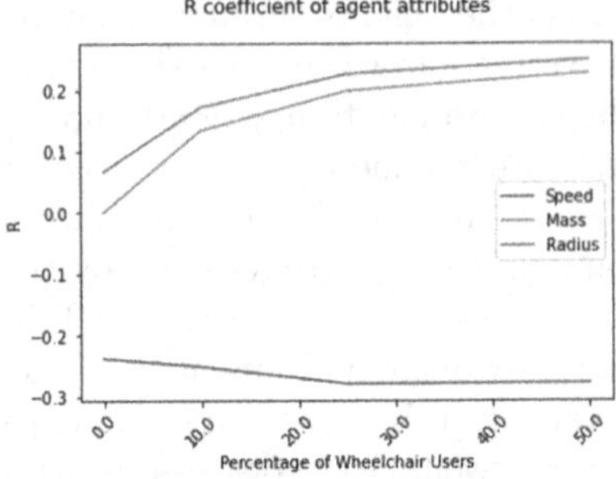

Fig. 4. Agent Parameters vs Exit Time for 1-meter-wide one doorway

despite the correlations staying consistently positive or negative across environment parameter sets, the correlation values themselves show a weak correlation for all attributes, ranging between 0.0 to 0.3. These results may indicate that the specific attribute values used may not significantly affect evacuation time or do not vary enough to create a significant difference in an evacuation, however both previous metrics in evacuation rate as well as average time to evacuate show that these slight correlations affect the overall evacuation speed.

5.3 Correlation Coefficient Trend

Figure 4 visualizes the correlation coefficients of agent attributes versus the exit time in order to show trends across environment parameters. Across all coefficient trends, speed has a negative correlation with evacuation time that further decreases as the wheelchair user population increases. Mass and radius are nearly identical across all environment parameter sets, showing a positive correlation with evacuation time that increases as the wheelchair user population increases. It is important to note that despite the correlations staying consistently positive or negative across environment parameter sets, the correlation values themselves show a weak correlation for all attributes, ranging between 0.0 to 0.3. These indicate that the specific attribute values studied have weak correlations with the time an agent evacuates. The statistical significance of these correlations will be further discussed separately.

- **Rate * Time:** Examining the average rate multiplied by the evacuation time finds the average number of agents exited by the average time. The number of agents across door width stays generally consistent, with the exception being for the 1 m width doorways. In all cases for 1 m doorways, the average number of agents is considerably higher than both 2 and 3 m doorways. This is likely caused by a combination of agents organizing into a stream in order to pass through the smaller doorway with other agents pushing from behind. This additional pressure from agent collisions forces the agents through the doorway at a quicker rate. The wider doorways allow for a wider spread of agents and reduces the occurrence of agent collisions creating additional forward pressure.

- **Rate Per Door:** Examining the average rate while accounting for the number of doors shows that the rate stays approximately consistent across parameter combinations. The rate decreases as the wheelchair population increases as well as when the door widths are increased. The rate for the singular 1 m doorway is still significantly elevated compared to 2 and 3 m doorways in other cases.
- **T test of correlations:** A t-test was used in order to determine the statistical significance of the correlations. The T value was calculated using $T = \frac{r\sqrt{n-2}}{\sqrt{1-r^2}}$, where n is 200 samples, and r is the correlation coefficient. Table 6 shows the t-test values for each correlation based on the data from 200 samples of each parameter set. Values that are colored gray indicate a probability less than 0.05, and that we can reject the null hypothesis and that the correlation is statistically significant. Values that are bold are greater than the T table value and therefore we retain the null hypothesis. Across all parameter sets, the speed attribute correlation is the most consistently statistically significant. Mass and radius are consistently statistically significant for wheelchair populations at 25 and 50% with 2 and 3-meter doorways. One-meter doorways show similar statistical significance for 1-door, but no statistical significance for mass and only one instance for radius.
- **Validation:** The model is internally validated by the consistency of the results. The behaviors used to represent the panicked state were previously described by Helbing et al. [14]. External validity is difficult due to the ethics of purposefully creating a panicked evacuation scenario. Further complications lie in the absence of any previous models that consider the presence of wheelchair users within the crowd.

6 Conclusion and Future Works

In this paper we present a novel evacuation model to address both the gaps in heterogeneous-population evacuation modeling as well as the lack of models that include wheelchair users. Our model shows agents behaving in such a way as to exit as fast as possible regardless of their peers. The goal of our model was to determine the effects of the heterogeneous agent parameters while considering wheelchair users within the crowd. The major findings of the model shows (1) agent parameters have a low, but statistically significant correlation with evacuation time, (2) larger percentages of wheelchair users result in a lower rate and deviation of evacuation, and (3) larger doorways lead to an increase in rate and deviation of evacuation. In future we plan to extend our model to include different types of environments such as stairways, pillars, accessibility ramps, and other expected occurrences that may effect an evacuation. Other agent attributes such as endurance, strength, etc. may also be considered to find more significant correlations with desired metrics.

References

1. 1800wheelchair. https://1800Wheelchair.com. Accessed 08 May 2022
2. Unity. https://unity.com/. Accessed 08 May 2022
3. Bellomo, N., Clarke, D., Gibelli, L., Townsend, P., Vreugdenhil, B.: Human behaviours in evacuation crowd dynamics: from modelling to "big data" toward crisis management. Phy. Life Rev. **18**, 1–21 (2016)
4. Duives, D.C., Daamen, W., Hoogendoorn, S.P.: State-of-the-art crowd motion simulation models. Transp. Res. Part C: Emerg. Technol. **37**, 193–209 (2013) https://doi.org/10.1016/j.trc.2013.02.005, www.sciencedirect.com/science/article/pii/S0968090X13000351
5. Emig, T., Peltonen, J.: Human running performance from real-world big data. Nat. Commun. **11**(1), 1–9 (2020)
6. Fryar, C.D., Gu, Q., Ogden, C.L.: Anthropometric reference data for children and adults: United states, 2007–2010. Vital and health statistics. Series 11, Data from the National Health Survey **252**, 1–48 (2012)
7. Gaud, N., Galland, S., Gechter, F., Hilaire, V., Koukam, A.: Holonic multilevel simulation of complex systems: application to real-time pedestrians simulation in virtual urban environment. Simul. Model. Pract. Theory **16**, 1659–1676 (2008). https://doi.org/10.1016/j.simpat.2008.08.015
8. Gayathri, H., Aparna, P., Verma, A.: A review of studies on understanding crowd dynamics in the context of crowd safety in mass religious gatherings. Int. J. Disaster Risk Reduction **25**, 82–91 (2017)
9. Geoerg, P., Schumann, J., Holl, S., Boltes, M., Hofmann, A.: The influence of individual impairments in crowd dynamics. Fire Mater. **45**(4), 529–542 (2019)
10. Geoerg, P., Schumann, J., Holl, S., Hofmann, A.: The influence of wheelchair users on movement in a bottleneck and a corridor. Journal of Advanced Transportation **2019** (2019)
11. Goldstone, R.L., Janssen, M.A.: Computational models of collective behavior. Trends Cogn. Sci. **9**(9), 424–430 (2005). https://doi.org/10.1016/j.tics.2005.07.009, https://www.sciencedirect.com/science/article/abs/pii/S1364661305002147
12. Helbing, D., Buzna, L., Johansson, A., Werner, T.: Self-organized pedestrian crowd dynamics: experiments, simulations, and design solutions. Transp. Sci. **39**(1), 1–24 (2005). https://doi.org/10.1287/trsc.1040.0108, https://pubsonline.informs.org/doi/abs/10.1287/trsc.1040.0108
13. Helbing, D., Farkas, I., Vicsek, T.: Simulating dynamical features of escape panic. Nature **407**(6803), 487–490 (2000)
14. Helbing, D., Johansson, A.: Pedestrian, crowd and evacuation dynamics. In: Encyclopedia of Complexity and Systems Science (2009)
15. Kountouriotis, V., Thomopoulos, S.C., Papelis, Y.: An agent-based crowd behaviour model for real time crowd behaviour simulation. Pattern Recogn. Lett. **44**, 30–38 (2014)
16. Papadimitriou, E., Yannis, G., Golias, J.: A critical assessment of pedestrian behaviour models. Transp. Res. Part F: Traffic Psychol. Behav. **12**(3), 242–255 (2009). https://doi.org/10.1016/j.trf.2008.12.004, https://www.sciencedirect.com/science/article/abs/pii/S1369847808001046
17. Shi, X., Ye, Z., Shiwakoti, N., Tang, D., Wang, C., Wang, W.: Empirical investigation on safety constraints of merging pedestrian crowd through macroscopic and microscopic analysis. Accid. Anal. Prev. **95**, 405–416 (2016)
18. Spector, R.H.: Visual fields (1990). https://www.ncbi.nlm.nih.gov/books/NBK220

19. Vermuyten, H., Beliën, J., De Boeck, L., Reniers, G., Wauters, T.: A review of optimisation models for pedestrian evacuation and design problems. Saf. Sci. **87**, 167–178 (2016)
20. Zheng, X., Zhong, T., Liu, M.: Modeling crowd evacuation of a building based on seven methodological approaches. Build. Environ. **44**(3), 437–445 (2009)

Agent-Based Modelling and Simulation of Decision-Making in Flying Ad-Hoc Networks

Philipp Helle(✉), Sergio Feo-Arenis, Carsten Strobel, and Kevin Shortt

Airbus Central Research and Technology, Munich, Germany
{philipp.helle,sergio.feo,carsten.strobel,kevin.shortt}@airbus.com

Abstract. At Airbus, an architecture for an ad-hoc network amongst flying platforms, e.g., commercial aircraft, satellites, high altitude platforms, has been developed. Since centralized decision-making for building the network topology becomes impracticable in ad-hoc networks with many mobile participants, the network architecture is based on a decentralized collaborative decision-making process. Agent-based modelling and simulation was used to support the design of the overall ad-hoc network architecture, its core decision-making algorithm, and the required hardware for laser communication. This paper describes the implementation, evaluation, and results of these activities using the agent-based modelling and simulation tool Repast Simphony.

Keywords: ABM · FANET · ConOps · Repast

1 Introduction

Vehicular Ad-hoc Networks (VANETs) [1] are a specific subclass of Mobile Ad-hoc Networks (MANETs) [2] - wireless mobile nodes that cooperatively form a network without infrastructure - where moving vehicles act as either a node, or a router to exchange messages between vehicles, or an access point.

At Airbus Central R&T (CRT), a novel architecture for a Flying Ad Hoc Network (FANET), a special kind of VANET, has been developed that effectively extends the reach of traditional, high capacity optical fiber networks. A FANET is classically defined as one airborne networking domain characterized by a wireless ad-hoc network of flying platforms connected via wireless communication links [3]. While FANET are typically associated with groups of UAVs, the CRT FANET encompasses networks of a variety of different flying elements such as commercial aircraft, satellites, high-altitude pseudo-satellites (HAPS), and other such platforms.

A number of different technology bricks needed to be developed to enable the CRT FANET:

- Hardware for Free-space Optical Communication (FSO) on the ground and on board the flying platforms

© The Author(s), under exclusive license to Springer Nature Switzerland AG 2022
F. Dignum et al. (Eds.): PAAMS 2022, LNAI 13616, pp. 242–253, 2022.
https://doi.org/10.1007/978-3-031-18192-4_20

- Network management software that manages the flow of traffic through the established network connections
- A Concept of Operations (ConOps) that defines how the overall network operates, i.e., how the network manifests itself amongst the multitude of moving nodes.

It is the latter point from which the notion of a ConOps Agent algorithm is derived, which is the focus of this paper. It is important to note that in contrast to more traditional network simulations [7], the ConOps Agent modelling and simulation activities described here are not at the network level, i.e., focused on the protocol, routing, data rates and such but on the overall FANET system level, in particular on the establishment of the physical topology of the network.

To support the design of the ConOps Agent algorithm as well as the design of the hardware, the agents involved in the network were modelled using Agent-based Modeling (ABM) and evaluated in an ABM tool.

The questions that shall be answered by this model are:

- Does the ConOps Agent algorithm achieve the goal of building a stable network in the sky?
- How many aircraft and how many ground stations are required to achieve what level of connectivity?
- How many directed terminals with what fields of regard are required on an aircraft, and where should they be installed?

This document is structured as follows: Section 2 provides an overview of the CRT FANET project and describes the main elements of the system. Furthermore, it provides a brief explanation of the decentralized ConOps Agent algorithm. Section 3 provides background about ABM and explains how the system was modelled and what data has been used for the simulation. Furthermore, it provides a description of the evaluation method and the simulation results. Section 4 provides some final conclusions.

2 Motivation

To provide context for the ABM application described in this paper, this section provides some background about the overall CRT FANET architecture and the ConOps Agent algorithm that was implemented in Repast Simphony.

2.1 System Overview

Figure 1 shows the overall system concept that was the target for the project. The key idea behind the system is the ability to ensure seamless, ubiquitous connectivity to a flying, or even orbiting, platform with capacity mirroring that of terrestrial backbone networks.

Not only should the links provide backbone network capacity, they should also function within the overall network architecture the same way as fixed fiber

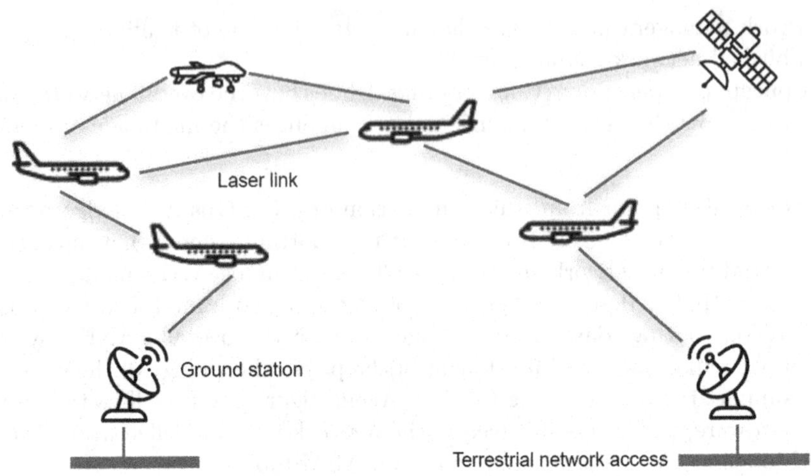

Fig. 1. System concept overview

links. That is to say, from the perspective of the Network Operations Center (NOC), the hybrid links to various platforms should appear like any other fiber link in the network. Factors such as laser link pointing, acquisition, and tracking, cloud cover, aircraft position determination etc. should be autonomous enough to require as little human intervention as possible.

2.2 ConOps Agent Algorithm

For traditional wired networks, the network topology is determined by the physical cables connecting network nodes and is generally mostly static. If nodes are mobile, the topology is dynamic and is implicitly determined by the environment, the transmission ranges - affected by the transmission power - and the node movement. In networks that utilize steerable directional communication links, such as FSO links, a topology must be explicitly determined and managed as nodes move. Nodes have a finite number of terminals for building network links and, therefore, a finite number of directly connected neighbors. Each directional FSO terminal must be commanded to point at its intended neighbor, who also must point one of its terminals back.

A major difference in the control strategy compared to similar FANET concepts such as Loon by Google [12], which is built on a centralized control algorithm for establishing the network topology, is the fact that the CRT FANET is built upon the principle of decentralized collaborative decision-making. This means that each node computes and executes its own actions based on local information and communication with nearby nodes without relying on a central controller.

This decision, with which neighboring node to form a connection, is at the heart of the ConOps Agent - the component that hosts the ConOps logic. At its core, the logic follows the basic steps of collecting pertinent information about neighboring nodes, prioritizing those nodes based on a given set of desired goals, and then using that prioritized list to engage in a negotiation with those neighboring nodes in order to form a mutually agreed set of network links. A more detailed description of the ConOps Agent algorithm as well as a description of the design decisions made during its conception can be found in a related publication [6]. The ConOps Agent will be implemented by software on controller hardware to command some actuators, e.g. the FSO terminal, and provide network management information.

3 Agent-Based Modelling and Simulation

This chapter describes the concept of Agent-based Modeling (ABM) that was used to model, simulate, and evaluate the ConOps Agent described in the previous section.

In ABM, a system is modelled as a collection of autonomous decision-making entities called agents. Each agent individually assesses its situation based on inputs it receives, makes decisions on the basis of a set of rules, and acts according to that decision. Franklin and Graesser collected a variety of definitions for the term *agent* from different sources and distilled them into the following essential definition: "An autonomous agent is a system situated within and a part of an environment that senses that environment and acts on it, over time, in pursuit of its own agenda and so as to effect what it senses in the future." [5] According to Macal and North, "the single most important defining characteristic of an agent is its capability to act autonomously, that is, to act on its own without external direction in response to situations it encounters" [8]. This precisely fits the design of the ConOps Agent algorithm, where each network node takes decisions autonomously based on local information and collaborates with its neighbors.

A wide range of ABM tools exist. North et al. provide an overview in [9]. The choice for the ABM tool for the work presented here fell on Repast Simphony [4], which "is an agent-based modelling toolkit and cross-platform Java-based modelling system [..]. Repast supports the development of extremely flexible models of interacting agents for use on workstations and computing clusters. Repast Simphony models can be developed in several forms including the ReLogo dialect of Logo, point-and-click statecharts, Groovy, or Java, all of which can be fluidly interleaved." [10].

The reason for choosing Repast Symphony were:

- It is a free open-source tool.
- It has existing interfaces and visualizations for Geographic Information System (GIS), i.e., maps and geographical data.
- It runs on different platforms.
- It provides a Graphical User Interface (GUI) for controlling the simulation, which allows non-ABM experts to use the model.

- It is based on the Java programming language, which is already in use by the project team, and allows for the use of the Java libraries ecosystem.

Especially the last point, where Repast differs from tools using their own Domain-Specific Language (DSL) such as GAMA [11], was a major reason for choosing Repast.

3.1 Implementation and Usage

The overall implementation of the CRT FANET model is written in Java. Classes to load the necessary data for the simulation context were implemented. The static positions of base stations, together with time series containing aircraft positions and speeds and cloud data are loaded at the start of the simulation to be replayed sequentially and thus provide environment inputs for the simulated agents. The behavior of agents (network nodes) is also modelled by using a variety of Java objects. Network nodes have a dedicated class that encapsulates the node's state, composed of its position and the status of its terminals. Dedicated classes to encapsulate data related to other elements of the simulation such as geometric constraints for terminals and links were also implemented. The network node class additionally implements the logic related to identifying potential candidates for connection and performing link negotiation. Finally, specializations of the node class were implemented to provide behavior variants corresponding to different node types such as aircraft, base stations, and satellites.

Flight Data. Other mobile networking simulations use some sort of mobility model to determine the movements of nodes in a simulation. To evaluate the efficiency of the ConOps Agent in the real world, the simulation in this work uses previously collected flight path data to model the movements of aircraft in the network. Another reason for choosing the aircraft networking scenario is that it represents the most dynamic use case for the overall system. The data used for the evaluation is based on Automatic Dependent Surveillance - Broadcast (ADS-B) data recorded on Tuesday, January 14th, 2020 for 24 h starting from midnight to simulate aircraft movement on a typical day. Since the time resolution in the simulation is finer than the recorded flight path data, geodesic interpolation for coordinates together with linear interpolation for other flight parameters are used to obtain the expected positions of aircraft between position samples in the data set.

Cloud Data. In order to evaluate the impact of clouds on the performance of the system, we included volumetric cloud data. The data set was obtained from fusing satellite observations and ground imaging sensors through numerical weather prediction models to achieve a 3D model of cloud occlusion fraction. During simulation, agents can query the environment to retrieve the maximum cloud fraction for the voxels traversed by the line joining a pair of geographic coordinates. This process is used to approximate the probability of a directed link (in this case assumed to be a laser) being occluded by clouds, which in turn can be fed as an input to the ConOps Agent algorithm.

Simulation Execution. Once the simulation is progressing, either stepwise or continuously, aircraft are added to the simulation based on the loaded aircraft position data and displayed on the map along with laser communication links between base stations and aircraft as shown by Fig. 2.

An aircraft is green, if it has a network path to the ground, i.e., if the current network topology contains a path from that node to a base station, and red otherwise. Base stations are considered to have a permanent path to the ground. A link is marked blue, if established, green if agreed, gray if initiated, and black if terminated. A link is in the initiated state, when one node has made the decision to establish a link to the other one and starts the link negotiation by sending a link request to the other partner. In reality, this process would be facilitated over something such as an omni-directional Radio Frequency (RF) link. A link is in the agreed state when the recipient of the link request responds positively and both nodes start to command their selected terminals in the correct direction. A link is established when both terminals are pointing in the right direction and data can be transferred between them. A link is terminated when it is blocked by clouds, the nodes move out of range of each other, or when one link participant makes the conscious decision to terminate the link.

Figure 3 shows a zoomed portion of the map to show the coloring of the link edges more clearly.

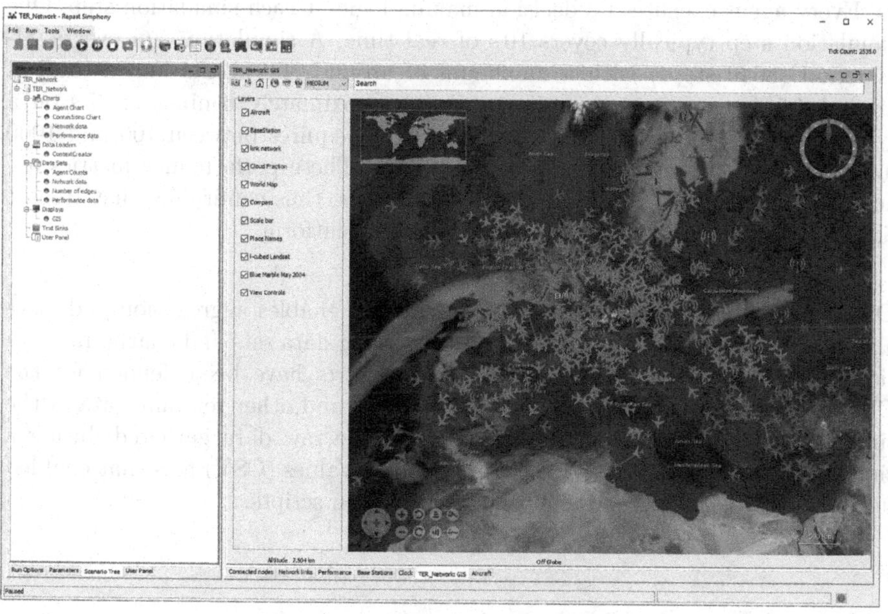

Fig. 2. Running simulation

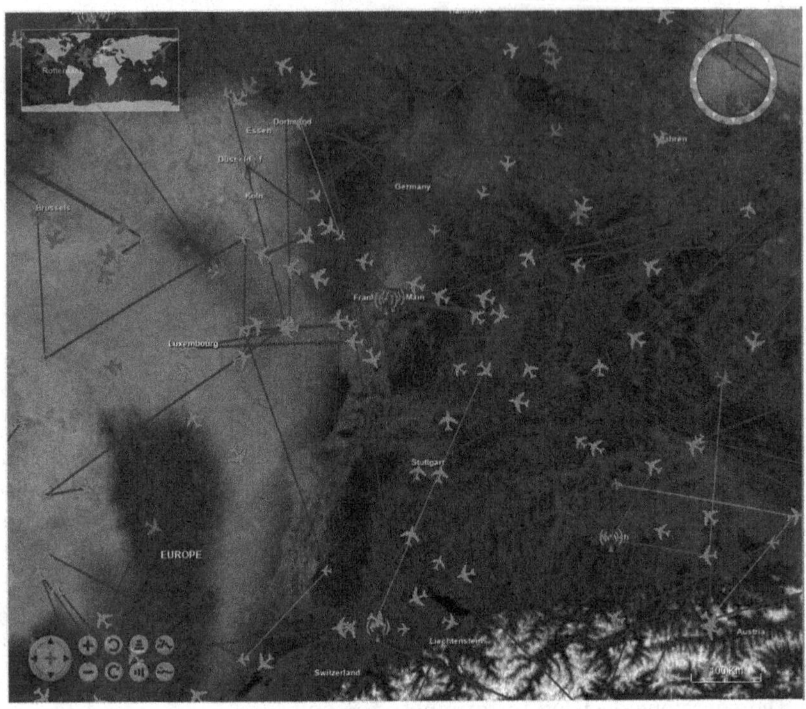

Fig. 3. Simulation details

Every agent executes its decision-making logic at each simulation step. One simulation step typically covers 10 s of real time. A simulation run over a 24-h period (8640 steps) with a maximum of around 800 agents and a total of around 4.5M agent step executions takes approximately 6 min and 35 s on a typical laptop computer. Each simulation step requires between 100 and 1000 ms depending on the number of active agents. These performance metrics are acceptable for quickly iterating algorithm designs, thus confirming that Repast Simphony was a good choice for the simulation platform.

Data Visualization and Processing. Repast enables aggregation and visualization of simulation data during run-time using data sets and charts. In addition to the main GIS map display, several charts have been defined for the CRT FANET simulation to monitor key metrics and other relevant data of the simulation during run-time. Additionally, all the raw data gathered during a simulation run was stored as Comma-separated Values (CSV) files that enabled further post-processing and analysis using Python scripts.

3.2 Evaluation Method

In order to evaluate the performance of the ConOps Agent algorithm and to answer the initial questions set out in the introduction, several performance indicators were measured and analyzed:

Ground Connectedness. The number of aircraft with a path of established links to any ground station.

Link duration. The distribution of the link duration, i.e., the distribution of the time elapsed between the establishment and interruption of a link.

Distribution of link angles. The distribution of the geometric angles (azimuth and elevation) of the established links over time.

Distribution of link distances. The distribution of the distance between terminals of established links over time.

Whereas ground connectedness and link duration are metrics that are relevant to assess the performance of the ConOps Agent algorithm, the distribution of link angles and link distances are relevant for designing the system hardware, e.g., the required range and field of regard of the laser terminals.

The presented evaluation is based on a configuration with three terminals per aircraft, of which two are installed *on the underside* of the aircraft, i.e., field of regard restricted to 360° azimuth and elevation between 1° and -90°. In order to illustrate the effectiveness of the ConOps Agent to select neighboring nodes for connection, we compare it to a link selection algorithm that randomly selects a neighboring node.

3.3 Evaluation Results

Connectedness and Link Duration. In order to compare the scenarios, we evaluate the amount of time over the simulated period in which connectedness exceeds ratios of 50%, 80% and 90%. Additionally, we observe the correlation between the number of aircraft and the level of ground connectedness. The closest fit is achieved by using a logarithmic regression, which we will use to estimate the number of aircraft required to attain a given level of ground connectedness.

50% connectedness is attained only after around 4:00 until shortly before midnight. An 80% connectedness level is achieved between 5:30 and 21:30 approximately, and a 90% connectedness only between 11:00 and 14:45. According to the regression analysis, the number of aircraft required for the 80% and 90% are 440 and 600 respectively, as depicted by Fig. 5.

The random algorithm fails to achieve 50% connectivity through most of the simulated time period. As expected, the connectedness is strongly correlated with the number of aircraft flying. Low connectedness at night when the sky is less densely populated is negligible regarding achieving the overall goals of the FANET. Backhauling support as well as increased passenger connectivity are mostly required during daytime.

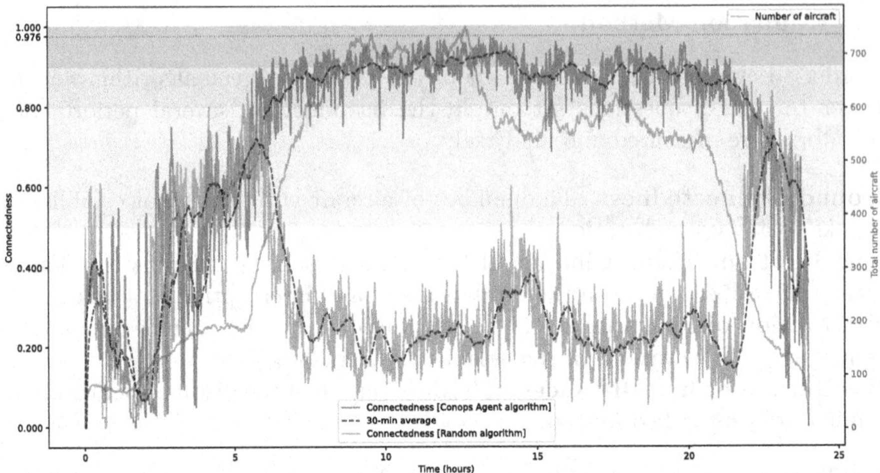

Fig. 4. Comparison of connectivity over time

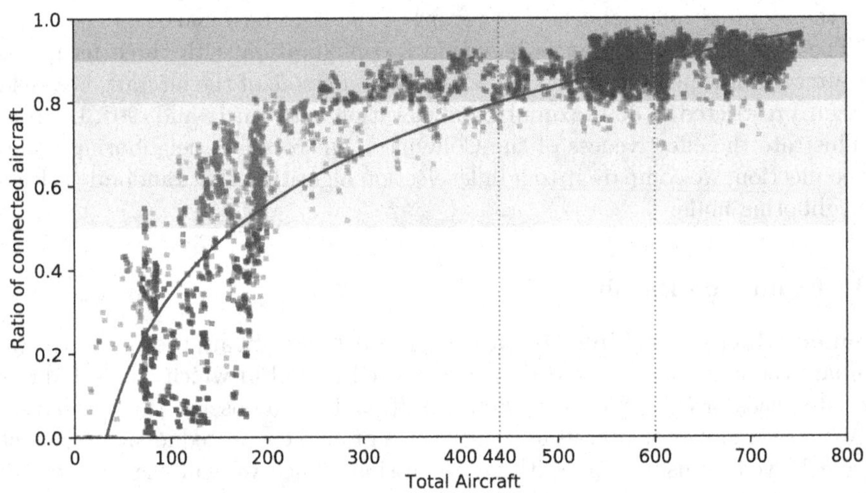

Fig. 5. Connectivity ratio vs. number of aircraft

In order to estimate the stability of the network topology, we compare the distribution of link durations. As Fig. 6 depicts, the ConOps Agent achieves significantly higher link durations than the random algorithm. Median link duration for the random algorithm is 420 s (i.e. 7 min) compared to 590 s (i.e. approximately 10 min) for the ConOps Agent algorithm.

Link Angles and Distances. In order to support the physical design of FSO terminals, we investigated the geometric configuration of the directed links as established by the ConOps Agent. We distinguished between different link types:

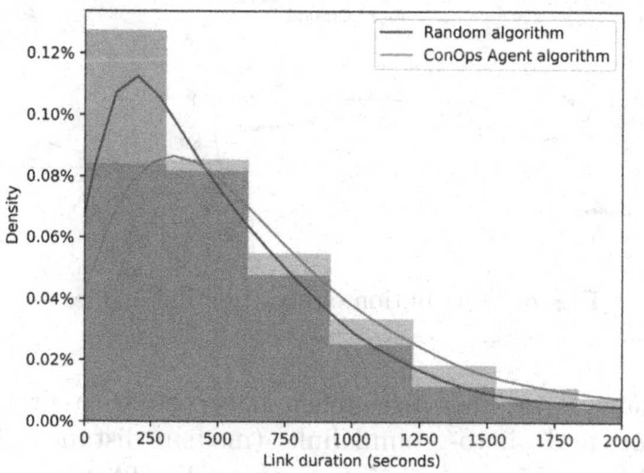

Fig. 6. Comparison of link duration

air-to-air (between aircraft), air-to-ground (from an aircraft to a base station) and ground-to-air (from a base station to an aircraft). We then analyzed the distribution of link angles for each link type relative to the local coordinate system of the aircraft. Here, the azimuth is assumed to be 0° towards the direction of flight and positive in the clockwise direction while the elevation is assumed to be 0° towards the horizon and positive in the zenith direction. Figures 7 and 8 show the resulting distribution.

It is shown that most air-to-air links are established at small angles close to the horizon in elevation but very often pointed close to the forward and aft directions in azimuth. Here, it is suggested for engineers to look for locations above the aircraft's fuselage but close to the nose and tail while air-to-ground links usually point down at shallow angles (smaller than 10°) and often looking aft, which suggests the need for locations below the aircraft's fuselage close to the tail and clear of potential occlusions by the engines. For base stations, azimuth is more or less evenly distributed while elevations are concentrated at shallow angles close to 5°. In this case, the suggestion is to find locations for base stations in elevated places without occlusions at the indicated elevation angles.

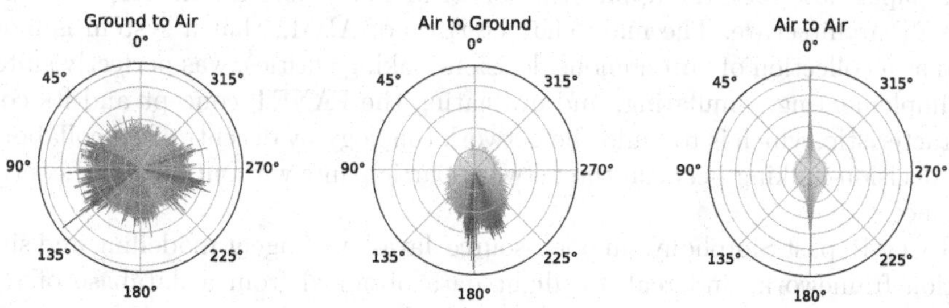

Fig. 7. Distribution of azimuth link angles

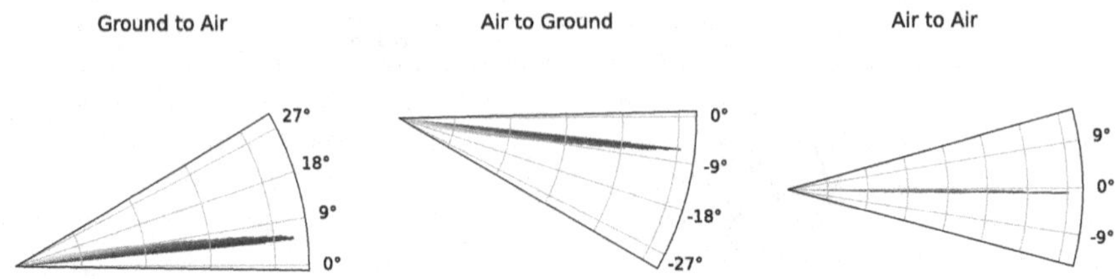

Fig. 8. Distribution of elevation link angles

For link distances, we also distinguish between air-to-air (with a median distance of 65 km) and air-to-ground links (median distance of 172 km). The figures extracted from this analysis (as shown on Fig. 9) were communicated to the FSO designers in order to guide the decisions about the range, and thus of the required power of the terminals.

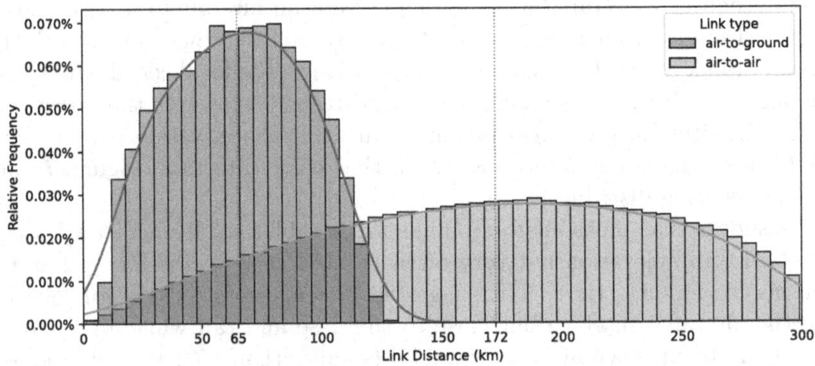

Fig. 9. Distribution of link distances

4 Conclusion

This paper described the application of ABM to support the development of a FANET architecture. The main characteristic of ABM,, that a system is modelled as a collection of autonomous decision-making entities, was perfectly suited for implementing, simulating, and evaluating the FANET concept and its core characteristic, which is to build the network topology by decentralized collaborative decision-making between the network participants without a central control instance.

Using Repast Simphony, an open-source Java-based agent modelling and simulation framework, and realistic flight data obtained from a database of real flights, it was shown that a significant number of aircraft over the European sky can be connected with this FANET concept. The results from the ABM simulation were used to validate the overall concept and the decision-making ConOps

Agent algorithm and delivered valuable inputs for developing the hardware that is required for the FANET concept. The ABM simulation, which can easily be parametrized to reflect different assumptions and implementation possibilities, is in active use for discussing different implementation scenarios.

Acknowledgement. The authors wish to thank the project partner Reuniwatt SAS, in particular Olivier Liandrat, for providing the volumetric cloud data used in the presented work.

References

1. Anwer, M.S., Guy, C.: A survey of VANET technologies. J. Emerg. Trends Comput. Inf. Sci. **5**(9), 661–671 (2014)
2. Chlamtac, I., Conti, M., Liu, J.J.N.: Mobile ad hoc networking: imperatives and challenges. Ad Hoc Netw. **1**(1), 13–64 (2003)
3. Chriki, A., Touati, H., Snoussi, H., Kamoun, F.: FANET: communication, mobility models and security issues. Comput. Netw. **163**, 106877 (2019)
4. Collier, N.: Repast: an extensible framework for agent simulation. Univ. Chicago's Soc. Sci. Res. **36**, 2003 (2003)
5. Franklin, S., Graesser, A.: Is it an agent, or just a program?: a taxonomy for autonomous agents. In: Müller, J.P., Wooldridge, M.J., Jennings, N.R. (eds.) Intelligent Agents III Agent Theories, Architectures, and Languages. ATAL 1996. Lecture Notes in Computer Science, vol. 1193, pp. 21–35. Springer, Heidelberg (1996). https://doi.org/10.1007/BFb0013570
6. Helle, P., Feo, S., Shortt, K., Strobel, C.: Decentralized Collaborative Decision-Making for Topology Building in Mobile Ad-Hoc Networks In: Proceedings of the 13th International Conference on Ubiquitous and Future Networks (ICUFN 2022) (2022, to appear)
7. Kurkowski, S., Camp, T., Colagrosso, M.: MANET simulation studies: the incredibles. ACM SIGMOBILE Mob. Comput. Commun. Rev. **9**(4), 50–61 (2005)
8. Macal, C.M., North, M.J.: Tutorial on agent-based modelling and simulation. J. Simul. **4**(3), 151–162 (2010). https://doi.org/10.1057/jos.2010.3
9. North, M.J., et al.: Complex adaptive systems modeling with repast simphony. Complex Adapt. Syst. Model. **1**(1), 3 (2013)
10. Repast project: repast simphony reference manual (2021). https://repast.github.io/docs/RepastReference/RepastReference.html. Accessed 8 Apr 2022
11. Taillandier, P., et al.: Building, composing and experimenting complex spatial models with the gama platform. GeoInformatica **23**(2), 299–322 (2019)
12. Teller, E., Patrick, W.G.: Balloon clumping to provide bandwidth requested in advance. US Patent 9,826,407, 21 November 2017

Deep RL Reward Function Design for Lane-Free Autonomous Driving

Athanasia Karalakou(✉), Dimitrios Troullinos, Georgios Chalkiadakis, and Markos Papageorgiou

Technical University of Crete, 73100 Chania, Greece
akaralakou@isc.tuc.gr, {dtroullinos,markos}@dssl.tuc.gr, gehalk@intelligence.tuc.gr

Abstract. In this paper we present an application of Deep Reinforcement Learning to lane-free traffic, where vehicles do not adhere to the notion of lanes, but are rather able to be located at any lateral position within the road boundaries. This constitutes an entirely different problem domain for autonomous driving compared to lane-based traffic, as vehicles consider the actual two dimensional space available, and their decision making needs to adapt to this concept. We also consider that each vehicle wishes to maintain a (different) desired speed, therefore creating many situations where vehicles need to perform overtaking, and react appropriately to the behaviour of others. As such, in this work, we design a Reinforcement Learning agent for the problem at hand, considering different components of reward functions tied to the environment at various levels of information. Finally, we examine the effectiveness of our approach using the Deep Deterministic Policy Gradient algorithm.

Keywords: Deep reinforcement learning · Lane-free traffic · Autonomous driving

1 Introduction

Applications of Reinforcement Learning (RL) in the field of autonomous driving are gaining momentum in recent years [1] due to advancements in Deep RL [2,11], giving rise to novel techniques [1,4]. Another important reason for this momentum is an increasing interest towards autonomous vehicles (AVs), as the current and projected technological advancements in the automotive industry can enable such methodologies in the real-world [7,8].

As a result, novel traffic flow research endeavours have already emerged, such as *TrafficFluid* [12], which primarily targets traffic environments with 100% penetration rate of AVs (no human drivers). *TrafficFluid* examines traffic environments with two fundamental principles, namely: (i) *Lane-free* vehicle movement,

The research leading to these results has received funding from the European Research Council under the European Union's Horizon 2020 Research and Innovation programme/ ERC Grant Agreement n. [833915], project TrafficFluid.

© The Author(s), under exclusive license to Springer Nature Switzerland AG 2022
F. Dignum et al. (Eds.): PAAMS 2022, LNAI 13616, pp. 254–266, 2022.
https://doi.org/10.1007/978-3-031-18192-4_21

meaning that AVs under this paradigm do not consider lane-keeping, but are rather free to be located anywhere laterally;and (ii) *Nudging*, where vehicles may adjust their behavior so as to assist vehicles in their rear that attempt overtake.

In the context of lane-free driving, multiple vehicle movement strategies have already been proposed [6,12,15,17]. To the best of our knowledge, so far there is no work that tackles the problem with RL techniques, while there is an abundance of (Deep) RL applications for conventional (lane-based) traffic environments [1,4,8]. In this work, we view the problem of designing an RL agent that learns a vehicle movement strategy in lane-free traffic environments. Specifically, we examine the Deep Deterministic Policy Gradient (DDPG) algorithm, which was designed to handle continuous action domains.

The reward design is crucial and determines the overall efficiency of the resulting policy [8]. Given the nature of the algorithms, their ability to properly learn only with delayed rewards and obtain a (near) optimal policy is uncertain, so we propose a set of different reward components, ranging from delayed rewards to more elaborate and therefore more informative regarding the problem's objectives. The learning objectives in our environment are twofold, and include safety, i.e., collision avoidance among vehicles, and that our agent is able to maintain a desired speed of choice.

2 Background and Related Work

This section presents the theoretical background of the Deep Deterministic Policy Gradient algorithm that we utilised, as well as related work tied to lane-free environments.

2.1 Deep Deterministic Policy Gradient

Deep Deterministic Policy Gradient (DDPG) [10] is an off-policy, actor-critic, deep reinforcement learning algorithm based on the Deterministic Policy Gradient (DPG) [10], developed specifically for continuous action domains.

It uses experience replay and target networks, as in DQN [11], solving the issues of network learning stability. The target networks are two separate networks which are copies of the actor and critic network and track the learned networks with soft target updates.

The update for the critic is given by the standard DQN [11] update by taking targets $y_t = r_t + \gamma Q(s_{t+1}, \mu(s_{t+1}; \theta^{\mu-}); \theta^{Q-})$, where $Q(s, a; \theta^{Q-})$ and $\mu(s; \theta^{\mu-})$ refer to the target networks for the critic and actor respectively. The actor network is updated according to the sampled policy gradient, as stated in the Deterministic Policy Gradient Theorem [10].

2.2 Related Work

Under the lane-free traffic paradigm, multiple vehicle movement strategies [6, 12,15,17] have already been proposed, with approaches stemming from Control

Theory, Optimal Control and Multi-agent decision making. In more detail, [12] introduces a lane-free vehicle movement strategy based on heuristic rules that involve the notion of "forces" being applied to vehicles, in the sense that vehicles "push" one another so as to overtake, or in general to react appropriately. Now, [17] introduces a policy for lane-free vehicles based on optimal control methods, and more specifically *model predictive control*, where each vehicle optimizes its behavior for a specified future horizon, considering the trajectories of nearby vehicles as well. Furthermore, [6] designs a two-dimensional cruise controller for lane-free traffic, with more emphasis on Control Theory. Finally, [15] tackles the problem with the use of the max-plus algorithm, and constructs a dynamic graph structure of the vehicles, considering communication among vehicles as well. In this work, we introduce an alternative movement strategy based on Deep RL, providing various configurations for the reward function.

3 Our Approach

In this section we first present in detail the lane-free traffic environment we consider, and then the various aspects of the MDP formulation, specifically the State Representation, and Action Space, along with the different components proposed for the Reward Function Design.

3.1 The Lane-Free Traffic Environment

As a training environment, we consider a ring-road traffic scenario populated with multiple automated vehicles applying the lane-free driving behavior, as outlined in [12]. Our agent is a vehicle that adopts the proposed MDP formulation, learning a policy through observation of the environment. The observational capabilities of our agent includes the position (x, y), speed (v_x, v_y) of nearby vehicles and its own. Both the position and speed are observed as 2-dimensional vectors, consisting of the associated longitudinal (x axis) and lateral (y axis) values. All the observable vehicles share the same dimensions and movement dynamics. Each vehicle selects randomly a desired speed v_d, within a specified range ($[v_{d,min}, v_{d,max}]$), and this information can also be monitored. Our agent controls 2 (continuous) variables, namely the longitudinal and lateral acceleration values (a_x, a_y), and determines the acceleration/deceleration through a_x, and left/right steering through a_y. Figure 1 illustrates the traffic environment. The examined ring-road scenario is emulated through a highway, by having vehicles reaching the end-point reenter the highway appropriately. Vehicles' observations are adjusted accordingly, so that they observe a ring-road, e.g., vehicles towards the end of the highway observe vehicles in front, located after the highway's starting point.

As mentioned, other vehicles follow the lane-free vehicle movement strategy in [12], which does not involve learning, i.e., other agents follow a deterministic behavior w.r.t. their own surroundings. In addition, we disable nudging [12] for other vehicles—since when enabled, other vehicles move aside whenever we attempt an overtake maneuver, effectively easing the environment of our RL agent and leading it to learn an unrealistically aggressive driving policy.

Fig. 1. Snapshot of the Lane-Free traffic environment

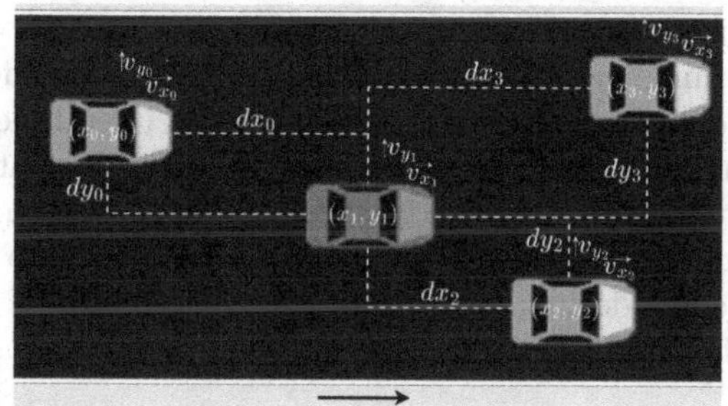

Fig. 2. Observed information of surrounding vehicles

3.2 State Representation

The state space describes the environment and must contain sufficient information for choosing the appropriate action. Thus, our observation space contains information about both the state of the agent in the environment and the surrounding vehicles. More specifically, regarding the state of the agent, it was deemed necessary to store its lateral position y, as well as both its longitudinal and lateral speed v_x, v_y. On the other hand, as far as the environment and the surrounding vehicles are concerned, matters are more complicated, due to the nature of our problem. In particular, in lane-based environments, the state space can be defined in a more straightforward manner, as an agent can be trained by utilizing information about the front and back vehicles on its lane, and the position of its previous vehicle on the adjacent lanes, in case it handles lane-changing movement as well. By contrast, in a lane-free environment, we need a more extensive set of information that depicts our environment in its entirety, as the number of surrounding vehicles in the 2D space we consider varies.

Our state needs to include information about a predefined number of vehicles, so only the n closest vehicles are considered in the state space, while 'placeholder' vehicles appearing far away may be included in the event that the number of vehicle is lower than n. This is necessary since the MDP formulation does not handle state vectors with variable size.

We store information about the speed of the surrounding vehicles, both longitudinal and lateral. Additionally, intending to have a sufficient state representation, we include information regarding the longitudinal (dx) and lateral (dy) distances of the agent among our car's center and the cars within an at most d meters' (longitudinal) distance—as shown in Fig. 2. Finally, the state space of our experiments contains our agent's desired speed v_d.

3.3 Action Space

In this work, the primary objective is to find an optimal policy that generates the appropriate high-level driving behavior for the agent to move efficiently in a lane-free environment. Hence, our action space consists of two principal actions: one concerning the car's longitudinal movement by addressing braking and accelerating commands; and one relevant to the lateral movement through acceleration commands for acceleration towards the left or right direction. Since the DDPG method, which we used in this work, is developed on to environments with continuous action spaces, we formed our action space into a vector $\mathbf{a} \in \mathbb{R}^2$, coinciding with the two desired types of actions: a longitudinal acceleration and a lateral acceleration.

3.4 Reward Function Design

Finding an appropriate reward function for this problem is quite arduous due to the novel traffic environment. In particular, most of the related work in the literature on RL techniques for traffic is typically based on the existence of driving lanes, which constitutes a different problem altogether. For this reason, a reward function was constructed specifically for lane-free environments.

Several components of reward functions were investigated to explore their mechanism of influence, as well as to find the most effective form. Before presenting the various components, we first determine the agent's objectives within the lane-free traffic environment.

The designed reward function should combine the two objectives of our problem, that is, maintaining the desired speed v_d and avoiding collisions with other vehicles. All of the presented reward components attempt to tackle these two objectives. Some are more targeted only towards the end goal, and do not provide the agent with information for intermediate states, i.e., delayed rewards, while others are more elaborate and informative, and consequently tend to better guide the agent towards the aforementioned goals. Naturally, the more informative rewards aid in the learning process, and for the baseline algorithms examined, we also observe a strong influence in the results.

Longitudinal Target. Regarding the desired speed objective, we utilize a linear function that focuses on maintaining the desired speed. In detail, the function is linear with respect to the current longitudinal speed v_x and calculates a reward based on the the deviation from the desired speed v_d of the agent at that specific time-step. To achieve this, the following mathematical formula is used:

$$c_x = \frac{|v_x - v_d|}{v_d} \tag{1}$$

It is evident that this function tends to be minimized at 0 whenever we approach the respective goal. As such, the form of the total reward r_t is a reciprocal function that contains a weighted form of c_x in the denominator. That being the case, we determined that our evaluation function should reverse this, so we select a reciprocal form $(1/x)$, and we put c_x as a denominator.

$$r_t = \frac{\epsilon_r}{\epsilon_r + w_x \cdot c_x} \tag{2}$$

where r_t is the total reward at any time-step t, while ϵ_r is a parameter that allows the reward to be maximized at 1 whenever c_x tends to 0. We choose a small value for ϵ_r, specifically $\epsilon_r = 0.1$, so as to make the minimum reward be close to 0 when c_x is maximized.

Overtake Motivation Term. In our preliminary experiments, we determined that our agent tends to stuck behind slower vehicles, as it is deemed a"safer" action. However, this behavior is not ideal, as it usually leads to a greater deviation from the desired speed. To address this particular problem, we created a function that motivates the agent to overtake its surrounding vehicles.

In detail, a positive reward $c_{overtake}$ is attributed whenever our agent overtakes one of its neighboring vehicle. However, this reward is received only in cases that there are no collisions.

$$r_{t,o} = \begin{cases} r_t + c_{overtake} & \text{if agent does not collide \& overtakes a vehicle;} \\ r_t & \text{otherwise} \end{cases} \tag{3}$$

Collision Avoidance Term. During the experimental evaluation of the aforementioned methods, we noticed that even though a significant number of collisions seemed to be averted, there were still some occurring that our agent did not manage to avoid. Based on that, the next logical step was to incorporate the collisions into our reward function. In this light, we examined numerous components, with the first being a "simpler" reward, by incorporating the training objective directly into the reward, aiming to "punish" the agent whenever a collision occurs.

This is exclusively based on the collisions between our agent and its surrounding vehicles. Specifically, a negative reward $c_{collide}$ is received whenever a collision occurs. Essentially, provided with a reward r_t according to one of the aforementioned forms, the reward $r_{t,c}$ that the agent receives is calculated as:

$$r_{t,c} = \begin{cases} r_t + c_{collide} & \text{if agent is involved in a collision;} \\ r_t & \text{otherwise} \end{cases} \quad (4)$$

However, this imposes the issue of delayed rewards, as our agent only receives a negative reward due to a collision with another vehicle. Especially in our domain of interest, our agent can be in many situations where a collision is inevitable, even many time-steps before the collision actually occurs, depending on the speed of our agent, along with the speed deviation and distance from the colliding vehicle.

Potential Fields. To tackle the problem above, we also employ an alternative, more informative reward component, one that "quantifies" the danger of collision among two vehicles. The use of ellipsoid fields has been already utilized for lane-free autonomous driving as a measurement of collision danger with other vehicles [15,17]. Provided with a pair of vehicles, the form of the ellipsoid functions calculates a utility that evaluates the danger of collision, taking into account the longitudinal and lateral distances, along with the respective longitudinal and lateral speeds of the vehicles and their deviations, adopted from [15].

Given our agent and a neighboring vehicle j, with longitudinal and lateral distance dx_j, dy_j, and longitudinal and lateral speed deviation $dv_{x,j}, dv_{y,j}$, the form of the ellipsoid functions is as follows: $u_j = E_c(dx_j, dy_j) + E_b(dx_j, dy_j, dv_{x,j}, dv_{y,j})$. Both $E_c(dx_j, dy_j)$ and $E_b(dx_j, dy_j, dv_{x,j}, dv_{y,j})$ contain an ellipsoid function and capture a critical and broad region respectively. Essentially, the critical region is based only on the distance of the two vehicles, while the broader region stretches appropriately according to the speed deviations, so as to properly inform on the danger of collision from a greater distance, and consequently the agent has more time to respond appropriately. The interested reader may refer to [15] for more information on these functions.

Table 1. Hyper-parameters for RL algorithms

Parameter	Value	Parameter	Value
Optimizer	Adam	Learning rate α	0.001
Mini-Batch size	64	Actor Act. Function	ReLU(Hidden), TanH(Output)
Discount factor γ	0.98	Critic Act. Function	ReLU(Hidden), Linear(Output)
Replay Memory size	100000	Actor layer size	256,128,2
Soft update parameter	0.001	Critic layer size	256,128,1
Training episodes N	625	Noise process	Ornstein-Uhlenbeck

Moreover, we also need to accumulate the corresponding values for all neighboring agents, i.e., $u_t = \sum_j u_j$ for each neighboring vehicle j within our state observation at a given time-step t. Finally, to bound the associated reward, we have $c_{fields} = \min\{u_t, 1\}$. We know that each ellipsoid function is bounded within $[0, m_u]$, where m_u is a tuning parameter. As such, each utility u_j is bounded within $[0, 2m_u]$. Therefore, m is set accordingly ($m_u = 0.5$), so as to normalize each u_j values to $[0, 1]$. Thus, the reward $r_{t,fields}$ is adjusted according to r_t in Eq. 2 so as to incorporate this new component, and is calculated as:

$$r_{t,fields} = \frac{\epsilon_r}{\epsilon_r + w_x \cdot c_x + w_f \cdot c_{fields}} \tag{5}$$

Notice that $r_{t,fields} = r_t$ whenever there is no captured danger with neighboring vehicles, i.e., the ellipsoid functions for each neighbor j returns $u_j = 0$.

All-Components Reward Function. To further improve our agent's performance, we combine all of the previous components in a single reward function $r_{t,all}$, that contains $r_{t,fields}$ (Eq. 5) and the additional terms for overtake (Eq. 3) and collision avoidance (Eq. 4).

Table 2. Simulation Parameters

Parameter	Value	Parameter	Value
Highway length	500 m	Vehicles' length	3.5 m
Highway width	10.2 m	Vehicles' width	1.8 m
Types of vehicles	2	Num. of vehicles	35
Agent's length	3.2 m	Time-Interval	0.25 s
Agent's width	1.6 m	Execution time	200 s

4 Experimental Evaluation

In this section we present our experimental results via a comparative study of the different reward functions that we propose, aiming to showcase trade-offs between the two objectives.

4.1 RL Algorithm and Simulation Setup

DDPG was the prevalent choice for testing the proposed design, as it tackles continuous action domains. DQN (and popular variants) were also examined with a discretized action domain, but exhibited inferior performance. The hyperparameters used in our implementation are provided in Table 1. We empirically examined different parameter tunings, and selected the ones that provide the best overall results.

We train and evaluate our method on a lane-free extension of the Flow [16] simulation tool, as described in [15]. Moreover, to facilitate our experiments, we utilized the Keras-RL library [13]. The Keras-RL framework implements

Table 3. Parameter choices related to MDP formulation

Parameter	Value	Parameter	Value
agent's desired speed v_d	$20\,m/s$	w_x	0.65
other vehicles' desired speed	$[18-22]\,m/s$	$c_{overtake}$	2
num. of vehicles in state n	5	$c_{collide}$	-2.5
longitudinal observation distance d	80	w_f	1

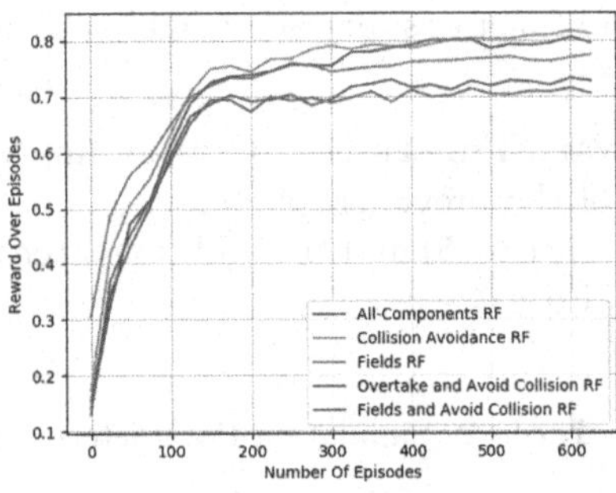

Fig. 3. Reward over time for different reward functions

some of the most widely used deep reinforcement learning algorithms in Python and seamlessly integrates with Tensorflow and Keras. However, technical adjustments and modifications were necessary to make this library compatible with our problem and environment. Furthermore, the proposed lane-free driving behavior decision-making model was tested in the highway scenario as specified in Sec. 3.1 with the specified parameter choices of Table 2, whereas in Table 3, we provide the parameter settings related to the MDP formulation.

4.2 Results and Analysis

As discussed in Sect. 3.4, we proposed several reward components. Their effectiveness is evaluated based on three metrics. These are: the average reward value, the speed deviation from the desired speed (for each step, we measure the deviation of the current longitudinal speed from the desired one $(v_x - v_d)$, in m/s), and the average number of collisions. All results are averaged from 10 runs.

In Figs. 3, 4 and 5 we demonstrate our agent's average reward, speed deviation, and the number of collisions respectively. In each of these figures, there are five curves that depict the performance of the proposed reward functions. Specifically, in each examined reward function, the Longitudinal Target reward Sect. 3.4 is combined with an associated component to tackle the collision avoidance objective. We refer to the reward associated with the Collision Avoidance Term (Eq. 4) as 'Collision Avoidance Reward Functions', while the addition of the overtaking motivation in that specific reward function, (Eq. 3), is labeled as 'Overtake and Avoid Collision Reward Function'. Furthermore, the use of the fields (Eq. 5) for that objective is labeled as 'Fields Reward Function' and 'Fields and Avoid Collision Reward Function' when combined with the Collision Avoidance Term. Finally, the assembly of all components in a single reward function (see Sect. 3.4) is referred to as 'All-Components Reward Function'. All of the aforementioned functions demonstrate how the agent's policy has improved over time.

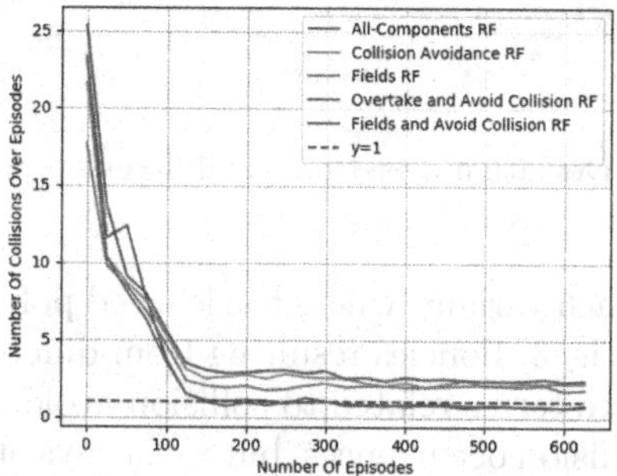

Fig. 4. Collisions over time for different reward functions

Table 4. Comparing the different Collision related components

Function	Coll.	Overtake & Coll.	Fields	Fields & Coll.	All-Components
Collisions	2.26	2.29	1.76	0.72	0.64
Speed Dev. (m/s)	−0.13	−0.05	−0.32	−0.69	−0.61

As evident in Figs. 4 and 5, the 'Collision Avoidance Reward Function' manages to maintain a longitudinal speed close to the desired one. Yet, it does not manage to decrease the number of collisions sufficiently. Moreover, the addition of the overtaking component, in 'Overtake and Avoid Collision Reward Function', achieves a longitudinal speed slightly closer to the desired one, while the collision number is still relatively high. On the contrary, the 'Fields Reward Function' exhibits a similar behavior to the previous mentioned reward functions, with a slight improvement on collision occurrences. Finally, both the 'Fields and Avoid Collisions Reward Function' and the 'All-Components Reward Function' perform slightly worse in terms of speed deviations. However, they obtain significantly better results in terms of collision avoidance, therefore balancing the two objectives much better. On closer inspection though, the 'All-Components Reward Function' manages to maintain a smaller speed deviation and number of collisions, thus making it the prevalent choice for a more effective policy overall.

To further demonstrate this point, we present in Table 4 a detailed comparison between these 5 reward functions. The reported results are averaged from

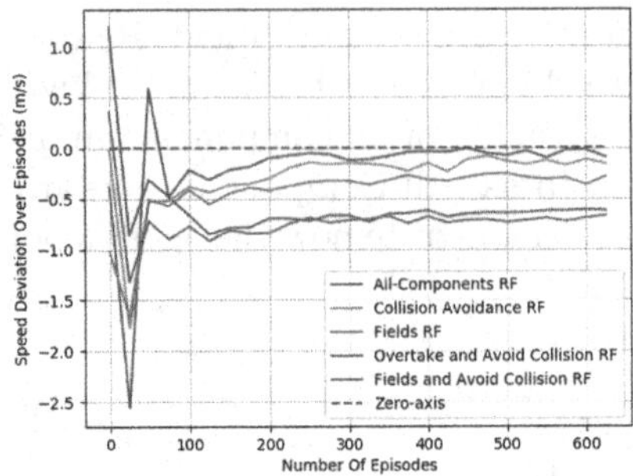

Fig. 5. Speed Deviation over time for different reward functions

the last 50 episodes of each variant, where the learned policy has converged in all cases, as noticeable in Fig. 3. Policies resulting from different parameter tunings that give more priority to terms related to collision avoidance ($c_{collide}, w_f$) do in fact further decrease collision occurrences, but we always observed a very simplistic behavior where the learned agent just follows the speed of a slower moving vehicle in front, i.e., is too defensive and never attempts overtake. Therefore, such policies were neglected.

Evidently, higher rewards do not coincide with fewer collisions, meaning that the reward metric should not be taken at face value, as we compare different reward functions. This is particularly noticeable in the case of the 'All-Components Reward Function' and the 'Fields and Avoid Collisions Reward Function', where there is a reduced reward over episodes, but when observing each objective, they clearly exhibit the best performance (cf. Figs. 4, 5 and Table 4). This is expected, since the examined reward functions have different forms. In Table 4 we also observe the effect of the 'Overtake' component. Its influence in the final policy is apparent only when combined with 'Fields and Avoid Collisions Reward Function', i.e., forming the 'All-Components Reward Function'.[1]

Finally, we must point out that a slight deviation from the desired speed in our experiments is to be expected. Maintaining the desired speed throughout an episode is not realistic. Throughout our experiments, it is obvious that the two objectives are countering each other since a vehicle operating with slower speed is more conservative, while a vehicle wishing to maintain higher speed than its neighbors needs to overtake in a safe manner, and consequently has to learn a more complex policy that performs such an elaborate maneuvering.

5 Conclusions and Future Work

In this work, we formulated the problem of single agent autonomous driving in a lane-free traffic environment, and introduced a set of reward functions at var-

[1] Videos showcasing a trained agent with 'All-Components Reward Function' can be found at: https://bit.ly/3O0LjJW.

ious levels of information in order to tackle the two objectives, namely collision avoidance and targeting a specific speed of interest. Moreover, we evaluated our formulation and compared the proposed reward functions, utilizing a popular Deep RL algorithm, DDPG. In future work, we plan on examining different RL algorithms, such as NAF [5], PPO [14], other noteworthy advancements from the Deep RL literature [2], and also methods that do not necessarily involve learning, such as Monte-Carlo tree search (MCTS) [3]. Finally, it would be interesting to utilize Deep RL to explicitly tackle multi-objective problems [9].

References

1. Aradi, S.: Survey of deep reinforcement learning for motion planning of autonomous vehicles. IEEE Trans. Intell. Transp. Syst. **23**(2), 740–759 (2022)
2. Badia, A.P., et al.: Agent57: outperforming the Atari human benchmark. In: Proceedings of the 37th International Conference on Machine Learning, PMLR, vol. 119, pp. 507–517 (2020)
3. Coulom, R.: Efficient selectivity and backup operators in Monte-Carlo tree search. In: van den Herik, H.J., Ciancarini, P., Donkers, H.H.L.M.J. (eds.) CG 2006. LNCS, vol. 4630, pp. 72–83. Springer, Heidelberg (2007). https://doi.org/10.1007/978-3-540-75538-8_7
4. Di, X., Shi, R.: A survey on autonomous vehicle control in the era of mixed-autonomy: From physics-based to AI-guided driving policy learning. Transp. Res. Part C: Emerg. Technol. 125(4), 103008 (2021)
5. Gu, S., Lillicrap, T., Sutskever, I., Levine, S.: Continuous deep Q-learning with model-based acceleration. In: Proceedings of The 33rd International Conference on Machine Learning, PMLR, vol. 48, pp. 2829–2838 (2016)
6. Karafyllis, I., Theodosis, D., Papageorgiou, M.: Two-dimensional cruise control of autonomous vehicles on lane-free roads. In: 60th IEEE conference on Decision and Control (CDC2021), pp. 2683–2689 (2021)
7. Kendall, A., et al.: Learning to drive in a day. In: 2019 International Conference on Robotics and Automation (ICRA), pp. 8248–8254 (2019)
8. Kiran, B.R., et al.: Deep reinforcement learning for autonomous driving: a survey. IEEE Trans. Intell. Transp. Syst. **PP**(99), 1–18 (2021)
9. Li, C., Czarnecki, K.: Urban driving with multi-objective deep reinforcement learning. In: Proceedings of the 18th International Conference on Autonomous Agents and MultiAgent Systems, pp. 359–367. AAMAS 2019 (2019)
10. Lillicrap, T.P., et al.: Continuous control with deep reinforcement learning. In: Proceedings of the 4th International Conference on Learning Representations, ICLR (2016)
11. Mnih, V., et al.: Playing atari with deep reinforcement learning (2013)
12. Papageorgiou, M., Mountakis, K.S., Karafyllis, I., Papamichail, I., Wang, Y.: Lane-free artificial-fluid concept for vehicular traffic. Proc. IEEE **109**(2), 114–121 (2021)
13. Plappert, M.: keras-RL. https://github.com/keras-rl/keras-rl (2016)
14. Schulman, J., Wolski, F., Dhariwal, P., Radford, A., Klimov, O.: Proximal policy optimization algorithms. arXiv preprint arXiv:1707.06347 (2017)
15. Troullinos, D., Chalkiadakis, G., Papamichail, I., Papageorgiou, M.: Collaborative multiagent decision making for lane-free autonomous driving. In: Proceedings of AAMAS-2020, pp. 1335–1343 (2021)

16. Wu, C., Kreidieh, A.R., Parvate, K., Vinitsky, E., Bayen, A.M.: Flow: a modular learning framework for mixed autonomy traffic. IEEE Trans. Robot. **38**, 1–17 (2021)
17. Yanumula, V.K., Typaldos, P., Troullinos, D., Malekzadeh, M., Papamichail, I., Papageorgiou, M.: Optimal path planning for connected and automated vehicles in lane-free traffic. In: 2021 IEEE International Intelligent Transportation Systems Conference (ITSC), pp. 3545–3552 (2021)

An Emotion-Inspired Anomaly Detection Approach for Cyber-Physical Systems Resilience

Eskandar Kouicem(✉), Clément Raïevsky, and Michel Occello

Université Grenoble Alpes, Grenoble INP, LCIS, 26000 Valence, France
{eskandar.kouicem,clement.raievsky,michel.occello}@univ-grenoble-alpes.fr

Abstract. Nowadays, cyber-physical systems (CPS) are becoming ubiquitous in various application domains. The variety of design and implementation methodologies utilized for cyber-physical systems, as well as the dynamic interaction of its components, make the resilience of these systems a major challenge. We aim to increase the resilience of these systems in a decentralized way by leveraging knowledge of the social sciences and humanities (SSH) and especially emotional processes. Both individual decision-making processes and social coordinating mechanisms are based on emotional inspiration. Our hypotheses and studies on resilience approaches, cyber-physical systems and emotional processes allowed us to choose the multi-agent paradigm. In this paper, we present the results of our research on resilience, which includes an emotion-inspired anomaly detection approach for improving CPS resilience. This approach is integrated into an agent architecture, compared to the literature, and validated through the development of proof-of-concept scenarios. The experimental results prove its advantages in terms of resilience properties.

Keywords: Anomaly detection · Resilience · Cyber-physical systems · Agent architecture · Multi-agent systems · Artificial emotions

1 Introduction

Almost all complex systems are controlled by computers that interact with the real world. These interactions are not done through a touch screen, mouse or keyboard, but also through direct actions in the physical world. These systems are made of interconnected subsystems, at least some of which interact directly with the physical world, which is why we call them "*cyber-physical systems*".

The development of interoperability protocols, lower hardware costs, and the simplicity with which a variety of hardware components can be connected provide designers with a wide number of configurations and combinations of components over which they may not have complete control. Furthermore, most of these systems are designed to be "open". As a result, the system's designers will be unable to anticipate all possible scenarios. This concerns the systems'

© The Author(s), under exclusive license to Springer Nature Switzerland AG 2022
F. Dignum et al. (Eds.): PAAMS 2022, LNAI 13616, pp. 267–279, 2022.
https://doi.org/10.1007/978-3-031-18192-4_22

resilience, or its ability to detect, manage, and adapt to specific or unusual situations that the designers may not have anticipated [22].

In previous works [12,13], we draw on knowledge from the human and social sciences, particularly emotional processes, to design an agent architecture that improves the resilience of cyber-physical systems. In this architecture, we have integrated processes for detecting abnormal situations. The main objective of this paper is to present our anomaly detection approach used in this architecture.

In this paper, Sect. 2 defines resilience and classify relevant work on anomaly detection for CPSs resilience, as well as a position within that work; Sect. 3 presents the emotion-inspired anomaly detection approach and the R-ECM architecture (R: Resilience, E: Emotional processes, C: CPS and M: MAS); Sect. 4 demonstrates the viability of the proposed approach; Sect. 5 presents our conclusions and relevant future directions.

2 Related Work

In this section, we define resilience and provide a classification of anomaly detection approaches that address it.

2.1 Resilience

Resilience is studied by researchers from various fields. In psychology, resilience is defined as a person's or a group's ability to grow and project themselves into the future overcoming destabilizing events, tough living conditions, and often severe trauma [19]. Resilience in systems engineering refers to how quickly a system bounces following an incident that causes its degradation. It is defined by the computer networking community as a combination of reliability and tolerance. Resilience is defined by the IT community as the continuity of service delivery and the availability of functionality [20]. For our work, we have adopted the definition of Woods [22], from the resilience engineering field: "Resilience is the ability to recognise and adapt to handle unanticipated perturbations that call into question the model of competence, and demand a shift of processes, strategies and coordination."

Resilience in artificial systems should be distinguished from robustness, which is closely related to it. Because of its design, a robust system can "resist" to abnormal situations by maintaining its performance without affecting its functionality. A resilient system, on the other hand, can *detect* abnormal situations and adapt its operations to keep its critical functions [14]. So robustness does not allow the system to adapt its behavior, but resilience does.

2.2 Anomaly Detection for CPS Resilience

Anomalies and faulty components must be detected in order to preserve the system's resilience and provide correct operation. A study of existing detection approaches for resilience yielded the following four categories, in the Table 1.

Table 1. Classification of detection approaches for CPS resilience.

Category	Keywords	Application areas	Features	Examples
Redundancy based	Additional information sources, Triple Modular Redundancy (TMR).	Avionics, automotive ECUs, VANETs.	Reliability and multiplying components.	[2]
Monitoring based/ dependability based	Machine learning, Signal Temporal Logic	CPS.	The normal behavior of the system needs to be planned in advance.	[9, 11]
Statistical model based	Gaussian models, histograms, machine learning, data mining, deep learning.	CPS, Iot, time series...	Simplicity, suitable for time series and used in CPS.	[6, 15]
Signature based	Intrusion detection, functional footprint.	Malware detection, IoT.	Efficient (few false positives), requires accurate signature parameters.	[8, 10]

In [2], authors use redundancy to merge data from different sensors and simultaneously calculate trust values for the information sources in VANETs.

Falcone *et al.* [9] explains how to improve resilience using in-the-field runtime approaches. Autonomic monitors use sensor data to observe, analyze, and plan before taking action to detect anomalies. They respond to failures by using redundancy or variants. In [11], authors build a signal temporal logic (STL) formula using the data that represents the system's usual behavior. Abnormal traces are those that do not conform to the formula.

Statistical models are used to detect anomalies in [6, 15]. These approaches, which use K-means, clustering, machine learning, and deep learning to find anomalies in time series, are effective. The nature of statistical model used is determined by the time series' complexity.

A signature-based approach is used by [10]. This approach efficiently detects intrusions with a low amount of false positives, but it requires a well parameterized signature. Machine learning can help to reinforce it [8].

According to our classification, many centralised or redundancy-based approaches require reliable communication and may face the "Single point of failure" problem. The designer of monitoring-based approaches must anticipate all the situations that the system will face during its normal operation. Since most CPSs are designed to be "open", he will not be able to anticipate all possible scenarios when a component is added or removed.

To avoid these issues, we use incremental processes which can rely on component collaboration to detect anomalies. A component initiates anomaly detection, following which the same component or other components, depending on the situation, trigger other processes. In our approach, perceived data is represented as time series. Due to the benefits of simplicity and speed, we have chosen to use a basic statistical model in our detection approach to process this type of data. To improve its efficiency, we combined it with a signature-based detection approach.

3 The Proposed Approach

As mentioned previously, anomaly detection is a series of incremental processes in our approach.

To begin, we apply a basic statistical model to find anomalies in the sensor's data (out-of-domain values, strange sequences, or long repetitions of similar data). This choice depends on the simplicity and quickness with which this statistical model provides results, as well as the fact that it is not resource expensive. At first, each sensor elicits this process on its own, then correlates it with other sensors. A *perception grid* is used in this process. "A situation has no significance within itself; each individual has their own perception grid that determines whether the situation is good or bad [1]". In other words, sensor's perceptions are interpreted differently depending on its environment model. If the agent has interpreted a perception as anomaly, the result of this process is "a doubt". It refers to the occurrence of a situation which triggers the emotional episode in emotional processes. In case of doubt, the sensor must continue its perception functions, so it will increase its sampling frequency and remain more vigilant by ignoring any doubtful perception. This is known as "the arousal" in emotional processes.

Then, if there's any doubt, it move on to the next process. The sensor's interpretations will be based on the perceived data history and its *episodic memory*, rather than the environment model. In cognitive psychology, episodic memory is the mechanism through which a person recalls past experiences along with their context (date, location, and emotional state) [21]. This memory is used to store the normal and abnormal situations that the sensor encounters. This allows the sensor to learn its operating signatures. In emotional processes, this process refers to "the appraisal" of the situation. In psychology, appraisal is the process of extracting emotions from evaluations of events that produce specific reactions in different persons [18].

Finally, if the appraisal does not validate the doubt, the detection will be assisted by the system's similar sensors. If the situation is confirmed as abnormal by their appraisal, the other sensors lower their tolerance thresholds and communicate the result of the appraisal as a confirmation or rejection to the sensor which first detected the anomaly. This sensor's episodic memory is improved by creating an episode that reflects the negotiation result, and then its tolerance thresholds and perception grid are updated. The sensor will better preserve the system's functions with this upgrade by identifying and isolating the disturbance faster in the case of a similar situation in the future. In this process, some of the system's operating parameters have been changed, resulting in a change in readiness to act, which refers to the activation of a behavioural script in the emotional processes (but not its realization) with the goal of changing the individual's relationship with his environment and focusing his attention on more important things.

In order to integrate these processes to the components of a CPS, we chose the multi-agent paradigm. This choice is justified by the fact that MAS is built to accommodate for the distributed nature of CPSs. It's especially well-suited to various resilience-related issues, such as the "single point of failure". The agent's autonomy distinguishes our approach from those based on redundancy or centralization, which are frequently used in resilience approaches [7,17]. Agent-centered design is also interesting for our approach because of its ability to integrate knowledge from SSH such as emotions.

After a study of agent architectures, we chose to integrate our decision-making processes in a layered agent architecture to organize them [16]. This architecture integrates reactive architectures' simplicity, low algorithmic complexity, and fault tolerance [5] with more cognitive architectures' capacity to exploit non-local information, learning capabilities, and social interactions [3]. However, managing the interactions between the different layers to achieve the intended behavior is a challenge in this type of architecture.

The decomposition of cognitive processes into layers allows us to implement simple, perception-related, emotion eliciting mechanisms in a reactive layer while allowing higher level cognitive processes, potentially based on symbolic information and reasoning, to unfold without interrupting processes supporting critical functions [4].

Figure 1 illustrates the R-ECM architecture, which integrates emotional processes (in blue) that allow CPSs to become more resilient [13].

This architecture is divided into two parts: on the left, which is made of the agent's processes and behaviors, on the right, which is made of the agent's knowledge. It is also important to note that the layers are finite-state machines with the following functions: The reactive layer (RL): ensures reliable behavior on short time scales by interacting with the environment, perceiving data, and utilizing a perception grid (PG) to recognize major events and potentially abnormal situations before transmitting the data to the proactive layer; The proactive-deliberative layer (PDL): works on a longer time scale and is used to initiate specific behaviors like evaluating the reactive layer or the other agents' doubt (*the appraisal*). It takes decisions according to its data, its knowledge, its action plans and the episodic memory (M); The social layer (SL): uses social relations knowledge (SR) to communicate with other system agents, as well as the diffusion and negotiation of detected situations.

The *message exchange protocol* is used to communicate between the layers and the agents. The actions in the R-ECM architecture are not always triggered by a perception. The proactive-deliberative layer can also initiate actions in response to internal decisions, while the social layer can initiate actions in response to a message from another agent. The functions and interactions of the layers are illustrated in Fig. 3. In our previous work [13], we well explained the functioning of the architecture and its layers.

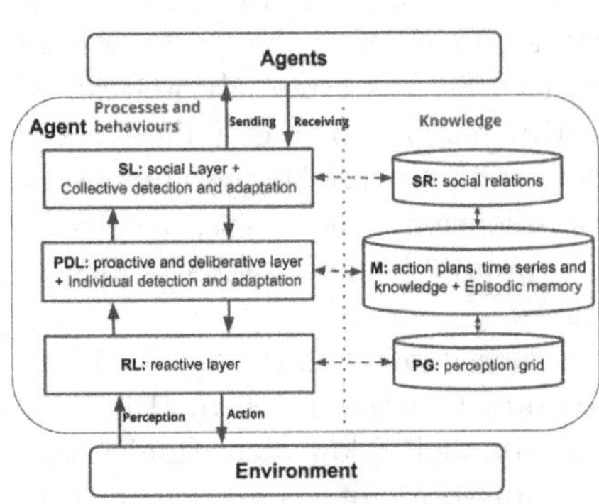

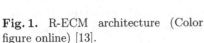

Fig. 1. R-ECM architecture (Color figure online) [13].

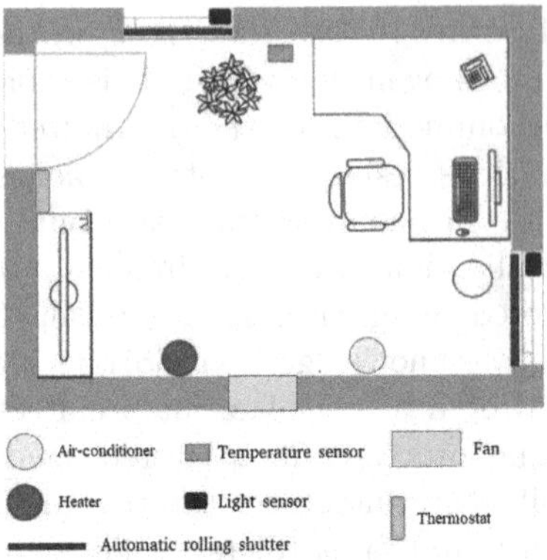

Fig. 2. Components in a room.

4 Experiments

One of the main goals of this paper is to show how our detection approach and the R-ECM architecture work, as well as the added value provided by decisions made about the layered agent architecture on the one hand, and processes, knowledge, and behaviors on the other. We also want to validate our choice to combine a simple statistical model, a perception grid, an episodic memory, and a collective detection for detecting anomalies.

4.1 System Description

To demonstrate the functionality of the processes and the agent architecture, we used a building temperature control system "CPS_{btc}" (see Fig. 2). In CPS_{btc}, the components (sensors and actuators) are implemented as R-ECM agents, which can communicate via messages, have some autonomy, and store their own data. We use T_i as a name of room i temperature sensor, Ac_i and He_i for air-conditioner and heater. In our multi-agent system, we'll have several groups of agents, each one made of agents from the same room. In our system, another sort of agent organization is taken into account: the organization of similar neighboring agents. Layers, agents and the environment are implemented as Java Threads that work permanently.

4.2 Measures of Resilience

We used several quantitative measurements to evaluate our approach. Our assessment measures are mainly based on the resilience features mentioned in [13] which are: critical functions preservation, reactivity in terms of anomaly detection, anomaly sensitivity and the impact of the approach on system resources.

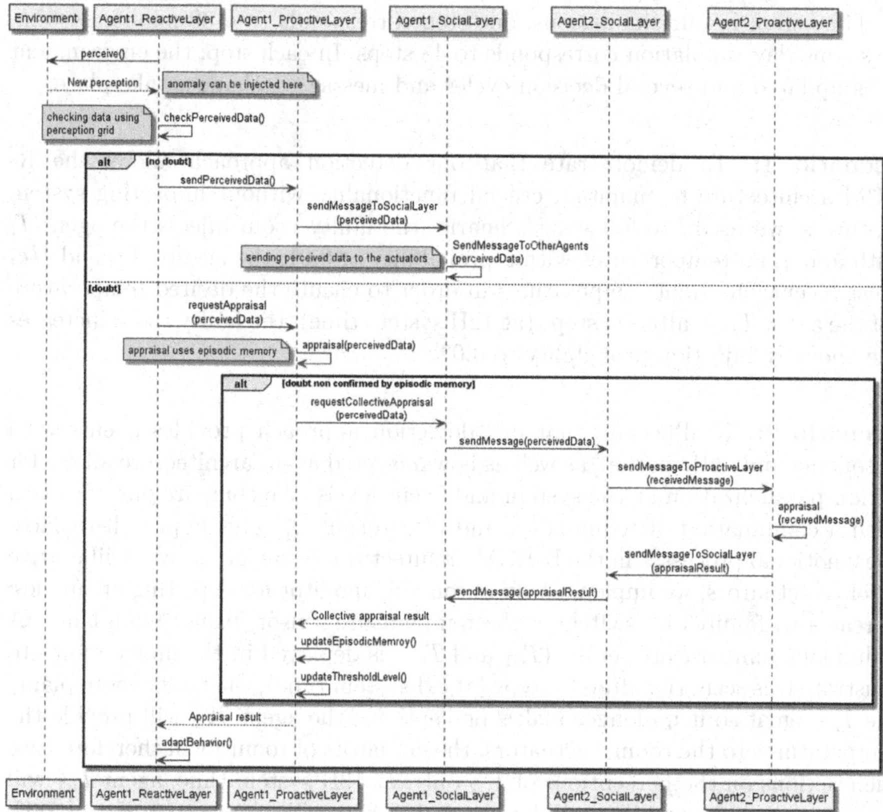

Fig. 3. The functioning of the anomaly detection in R-ECM.

According to these features, we chose to log following measures in the simulations: perceived temperature (for CPS_{btc}), number of exchanged messages, CPU usage, memory usage (RAM), and anomaly detection delay.

4.3 Scenario Description

Before describing the scenarios, we first define some notions that concern our simulations:

- A faulty room: a room with faulty or abnormal behavior.
- Anomaly injection: an action made by a faulty room, it can send an abnormal value in response to a reactive layer perception.
- Abnormal value: a temperature value that has a significant deviation from the current temperatures.
- Anomaly injection probability: a value between 0 and 1. This value is used by the faulty room to decide whether it injects an anomaly or not.

- Time step: in our simulations, one step corresponds to a 30-minute system, so one-day simulation corresponds to 48 steps. In each step, the environment is updated and several decision cycles and message exchanges take place.

Scenario 1: To demonstrate that our detection approach allows the R-ECM architecture to maintain crucial functionality without impacting system resources, we used the following scenario: the faulty room injects the agent T_i with abnormal temperatures with a probability of 0.01; the agents Ac_i and He_i must receive the right temperatures in order to ensure the desired temperature (of the agent Th_i); after 24 steps (at 12H system time), the faulty room increases the anomaly injection probability to 0.02.

Scenario 2: To illustrate that our detection approach provides agents with autonomy and anticipation, as well as how a layered agent architecture allows for action parallelization at the system and agent levels. We compare our approach with a combination of redundancy and monitoring [9]. This approach replaces the emotional processes in the R-ECM architecture. In the proactive-deliberative layer of actuators, we implement an autonomic monitor for detecting anomalies; it reacts to failures by switching the temperature sensor, using redundancy. A redundant temperature sensor ($T_{i.1}$ and $T_{i.2}$) is deployed in the faulty rooms to illustrate this scenario: after 10 steps (at 5H system time), the faulty room plants the $T_{i.1}$ agent so it no longer makes perceptions; the agent $T_{i.2}$ will provide the temperatures to the room's actuators; the actuators of room i will therefore base their actions on the perceptions of $T_{i.2}$ only; at 12H system time, agent $T_{i.1}$ will be restarted and anomalies will be injected to agent $T_{i.2}$ between 14H and 18H.

4.4 Results and Evaluation

In simulations with 3 rooms (27 agents for scenario 1 and 28 agents for scenario 2) we obtained the following results: For scenario 1 with our approach, we got three injected anomalies, the first one injected at 5:00, detected by the reactive layer at the same step and confirmed by other agents two steps later. The time needed to get the confirmation from all agents is 850 ms (the anomaly detection delay). The second one injected at 08:00, detected by reactive layer and confirmed by the episodic memory in the same step. The time needed to get the confirmation from episodic memory is 156 ms. The third injection at 22:00, detected by the reactive layer at the same step and confirmed by other agents two steps later. The time needed to get the confirmation from from all agents is 950 ms.

For scenario 2 with our approach, an anomaly was injected at 15:00, detected by the reactive layer one step later and confirmed by other agents two steps later. The time needed to get the confirmation from all agents is 859 ms. With the autonomic monitoring approach, two anomalies were injected. The first one injected at 14:00, detected by the monitor one step later. The time needed to detect this anomaly is 549 ms. The second one injected at 16:00, detected by the monitor one step later. The time needed to detect this anomaly is 398 ms. We conclude that the collective detection is slower than appraisal and autonomic monitoring. But the appraisal using episodic memory is still faster than autonomic monitoring in term of the anomaly detection delay.

In Figs. 4 and 5, we see that injecting anomalies did not impact the operation of the system using our approach and autonomic monitoring. The agents using both approaches were able to maintain the desired temperature (20 °C) when they detect the anomalies.

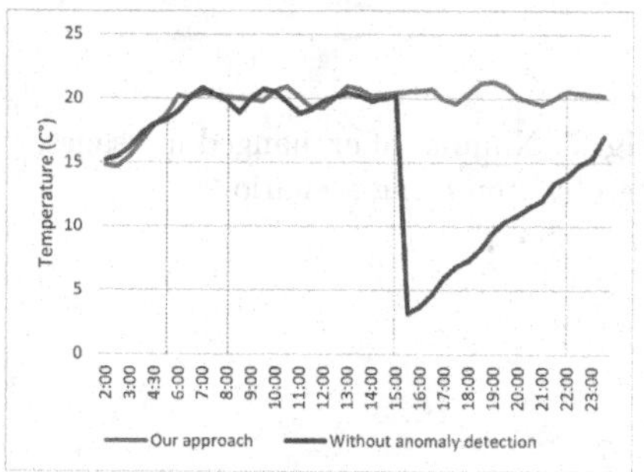

Fig. 4. Perceived temperature in faulty room using scenario 1.

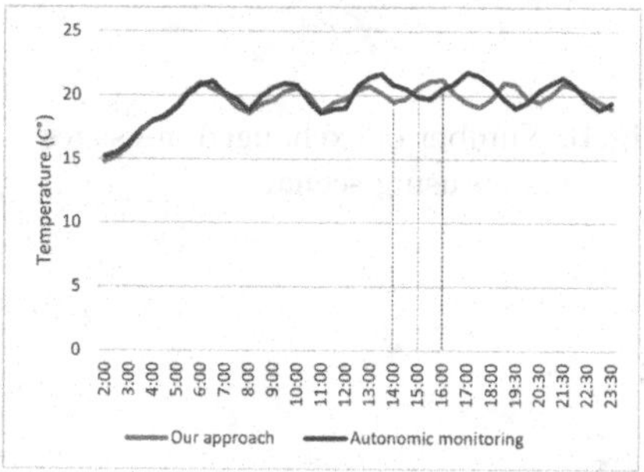

Fig. 5. Perceived temperature in faulty room using scenario 2.

We can see in scenario 1 (Fig. 6) that the first anomaly between 04:00 and 05:00 has increased the amount of exchanged messages, which is justified by the fact that the appraisal requires more message exchange than normal system operation. Because the reply was so quick due to episodic memory, the second anomaly at 08:00 did not increase the amount of messages exchanged. The third anomaly at 22:00 has increased the number of exchanged messages.

When anomalies are injected in both approaches, there are some gaps in scenario 2 (Fig. 7), but the gaps in our approach are more significant because the layers and agents exchange messages once they have a doubt about a perception. We conclude that our approach has very little effect on the amount of exchanged messages.

In Fig. 8, when the simulation was launched (before 10:00), the execution time of the steps was longer than in the end. So the anomalies occurrences impact the running time but not a lot compared to the simulations without processes. In Fig. 9, there the running time is close for both approaches. Because of the incremental processes, there is a big difference (30 cycles) between our approach and simulations without anomaly detection (see Fig. 10). Same comment for Fig. 11, we just add that there is a big gap when an agent is faulty. In our approach, the incremental processes for detecting anomalies are integrated in sensors but this is not the case for autonomic monitoring.

In Fig. 12 and 13, we measured the time spent by the processor in the simulations. As we can see, our approach had no significant impact on CPU time. We note that the autonomic monitoring approach is more CPU-intensive. In Figs. 14

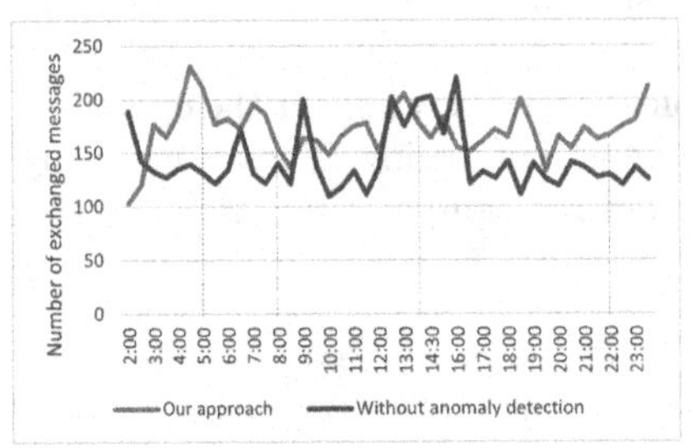

Fig. 6. Number of exchanged messages step by step using scenario 1.

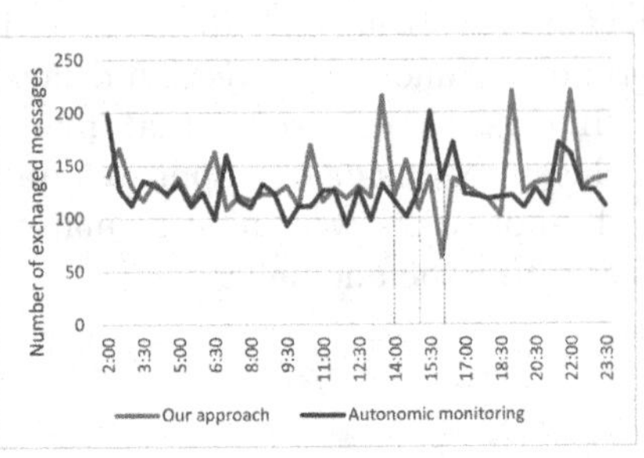

Fig. 7. Number of exchanged messages step by step using scenario 2.

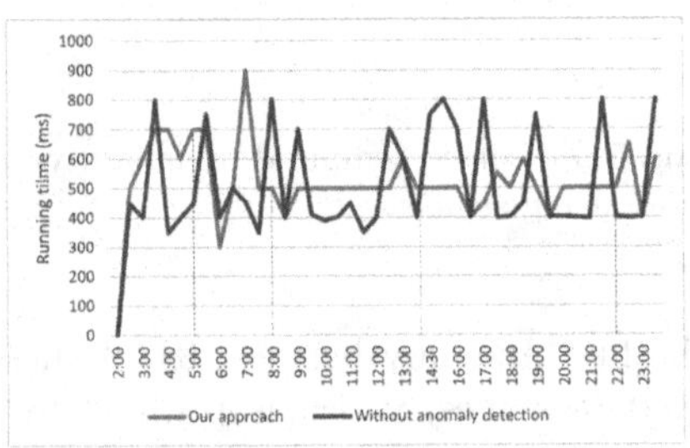

Fig. 8. Simulation running time step by step using scenario 1.

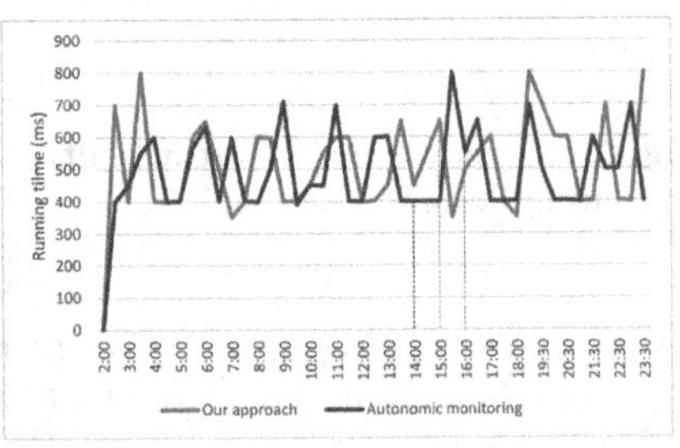

Fig. 9. Simulation running time step by step using scenario 2.

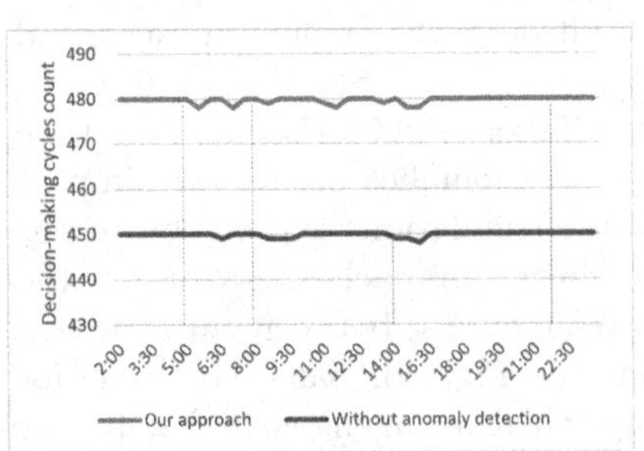

Fig. 10. Decision-making cycles count step by step using scenario 1.

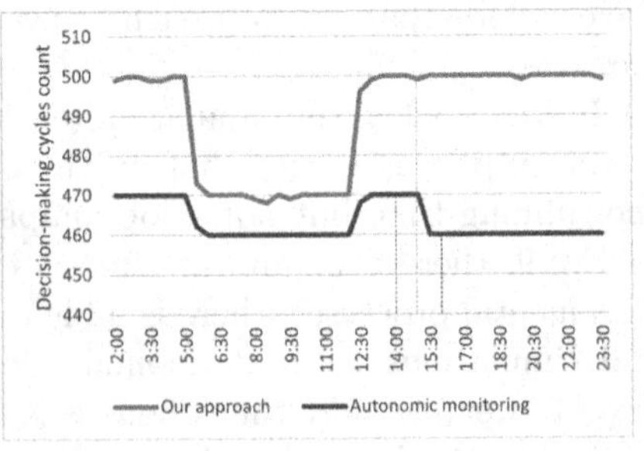

Fig. 11. Decision-making cycles count step by step using scenario 2.

and 15, we measured the used memory (RAM) in each step of the simulation. We have drawn the same conclusion as the CPU time. But we note that the the autonomic monitoring approach saves a little bit of memory.

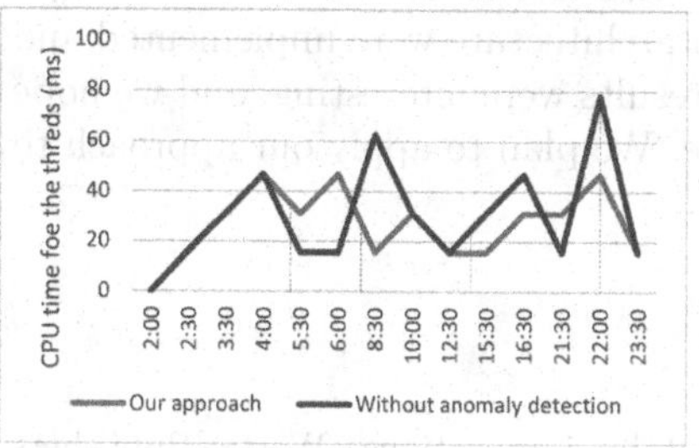

Fig. 12. CPU time using scenario 1.

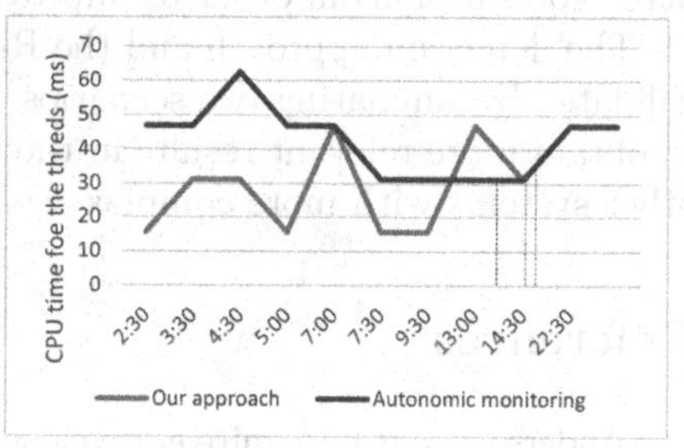

Fig. 13. CPU time using scenario 2.

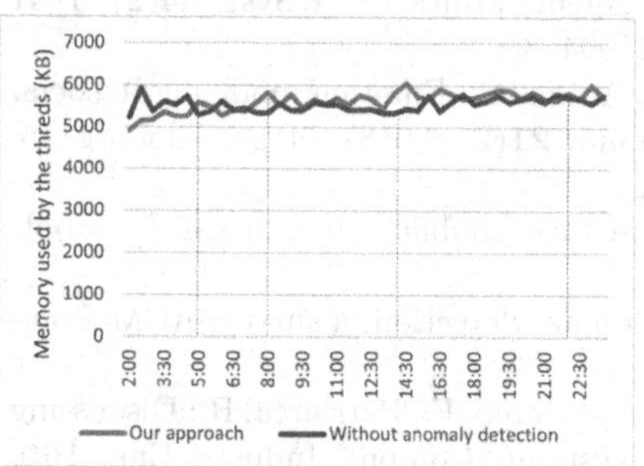

Fig. 14. Used memory (RAM) using scenario 1.

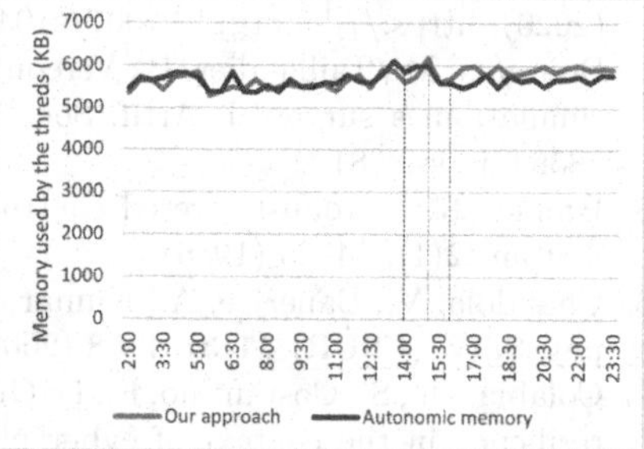

Fig. 15. Used memory (RAM) using scenario 2.

5 Conclusions and Perspectives

In this paper, we presented our anomaly detection approach, which is inspired by emotional processes, for improving the resilience of cyber-physical systems. We discussed some resilience definitions as well as our position in relation to resilience-related approaches.

In order to detect abnormal situations, we integrate individual and collective emotion-inspired processes into an agent architecture. For detecting abnormal situations, our approach includes a statistical model, a perception grid, an episodic memory, and a collective detection mechanism. Individual detection processes have an impact on the system's control group, triggering a collective detection to affirm or reject a suspicious situation. The agent's knowledge (perception grid and episodic memory) and behavior are affected by a confirmed situation (sampling frequency and tolerance thresholds). This architecture also includes processes for adapting individual and collective behavior in response to detected situations in order to improve the resilience of CPSs.

The detection approach and the R-ECM architecture were implemented and validated by simulating two scenarios. The results were interesting, and we hope to obtain more relevant results in the future. We plan to apply our approach to other systems with more complex scenarios.

References

1. Anderson, J.R.: Cognitive psychology and its implications. Worth Publishers (2000)
2. Bißmeyer, N., Mauthofer, S., Bayarou, K.M., Kargl, F.: Assessment of node trustworthiness in VANETs using data plausibility checks with particle filters. In: 2012 IEEE Vehicular Networking Conference (VNC), pp. 78–85. IEEE (2012)
3. Bordini, R.H., El Fallah Seghrouchni, A., Hindriks, K., Logan, B., Ricci, A.: Agent programming in the cognitive era. Auton. Agent. Multi-Agent Syst. **34**(2), 1–31 (2020). https://doi.org/10.1007/s10458-020-09453-y
4. Bourgais, M., Taillandier, P., Vercouter, L., Adam, C.: Emotion modeling in social simulation: a survey. J. Artif. Soc. Soc. Simul. **21**(2) (2018). https://doi.org/10.18564/jasss.3681
5. Brooks, R.: A robust layered control system for a mobile robot. IEEE J. Robot. Autom. **2**(1), 14–23 (1986)
6. Chandola, V., Banerjee, A., Kumar, V.: Anomaly detection: a survey. ACM Comput. Surv. (CSUR) **41**(3), 1–58 (2009)
7. Colabianchi, S., Costantino, F., Di Gravio, G., Nonino, F., Patriarca, R.: Discussing resilience in the context of cyber physical systems. Comput. Industr. Eng. **160**, 107534 (2021)
8. David, O.E., Netanyahu, N.S.: DeepSign: deep learning for automatic malware signature generation and classification. In: 2015 International Joint Conference on Neural Networks (IJCNN), pp. 1–8. IEEE (2015)
9. Falcone, Y., Mariani, L., Rollet, A., Saha, S.: Runtime failure prevention and reaction. In: Bartocci, E., Falcone, Y. (eds.) Lectures on Runtime Verification. LNCS, vol. 10457, pp. 103–134. Springer, Cham (2018). https://doi.org/10.1007/978-3-319-75632-5_4
10. Fauri, D., Dos Santos, D.R., Costante, E., den Hartog, J., Etalle, S., Tonetta, S.: From system specification to anomaly detection (and back). In: Proceedings of the 2017 Workshop on Cyber-Physical Systems Security and PrivaCy, pp. 13–24 (2017)
11. Jones, A., Kong, Z., Belta, C.: Anomaly detection in cyber-physical systems: a formal methods approach. In: 53rd IEEE Conference on Decision and Control, pp. 848–853. IEEE (2014)
12. Kouicem, E., Raïevsky, C., Occello, M.: Towards a cyber-physical systems resilience approach based on artificial emotions and multi-agent systems. In: Proceedings of the 12th International Conference on Agents and Artificial Intelligence (ICAART 2020), vol. 1, pp. 327–334 (2020)

13. Kouicem, E., Raïevsky, C., Occello, M.: Emotional processes for cyber-physical systems resilience. In: 2021 IEEE International Conference on Systems, Man, and Cybernetics (SMC), pp. 333–338. IEEE (2021)
14. Linkov, I., Kott, A.: Fundamental concepts of cyber resilience: introduction and overview. In: Kott, A., Linkov, I. (eds.) Cyber Resilience of Systems and Networks. RSD, pp. 1–25. Springer, Cham (2019). https://doi.org/10.1007/978-3-319-77492-3_1
15. Malhotra, P., et al.: Long short term memory networks for anomaly detection in time series. In: Proceedings, vol. 89, pp. 89–94 (2015)
16. Müller, J.P., Pischel, M.: The agent architecture inteRRaP: concept and application (1993)
17. Ratasich, D., Khalid, F., Geissler, F., Grosu, R., Shafique, M., Bartocci, E.: A roadmap toward the resilient internet of things for cyber-physical systems. IEEE Access **7**, 13260–13283 (2019)
18. Scherer, K.R., Schorr, A., Johnstone, T.: Appraisal processes in emotion: theory, methods, research. Oxford University Press (2001)
19. Sisto, A., Vicinanza, F., Campanozzi, L.L., Ricci, G., Tartaglini, D., Tambone, V.: Towards a transversal definition of psychological resilience: a literature review. Medicina **55**(11), 745 (2019)
20. Trivedi, K.S., Kim, D.S., Ghosh, R.: Resilience in computer systems and networks. In: Proceedings of the 2009 International Conference on Computer-Aided Design, pp. 74–77. ACM (2009)
21. Tulving, E., et al.: Episodic and semantic memory. Organ. Mem. **1**, 381–403 (1972)
22. Woods, D.D.: Essential characteristics of resilience. In: Resilience engineering, pp. 21–34. CRC Press (2017)

Bundle Allocation with Conflicting Preferences Represented as Weighted Directed Acyclic Graphs

Application to Orbit Slot Ownership

Sara Maqrot(✉), Stéphanie Roussel(✉), Gauthier Picard, and Cédric Pralet

ONERA/DTIS, Université de Toulouse, 2 Avenue Edouard Belin, 31055 Toulouse Cedex 4, France

{sara.maqrot,stephanie.roussel,gauthier.picard,cedric.pralet}@onera.fr

Abstract. We introduce resource allocation techniques for a problem where (i) the agents express requests for obtaining item bundles as compact edge-weighted directed acyclic graphs (each path in such graphs is a bundle whose valuation is the sum of the weights of the traversed edges), and (ii) the agents do not bid on the exact same items but may bid on conflicting items, that cannot be both assigned. This setting is motivated by real applications such as Earth observation slot allocation, virtual network functions, or multi-agent path finding. We study several allocation techniques and analyze their performances on an orbit slot ownership allocation problem.

Keywords: Path allocation · Fairness · Constraint optimization · Satellite constellation

1 Introduction

Imagine the following scenario. The operator of an Earth Observation Satellite Constellation X has to attribute ownership of some orbit portions to clients. Each client has some points of interest (POI) she wishes to acquire at some frequency, e.g. capture L'Aquila city every 2 h for 6 months. Since several satellites may capture the very same point on Earth around the requested observation times, several bundles are specified by each client, which valuate differently depending on the quality of the sequence of orbit slot, e.g. proximity to the dates or acquisition angles. Moreover, several clients may be interested in very close POIs, resulting in overlapping orbit slots that cannot be simultaneously allocated to the corresponding clients. This situation can be captured by the model we propose in this paper. We consider a problem of allocation of bundles of indivisible items constrained by item chaining (to allocate to each agent a chain of successive items) and conflicting items. The first constraint is captured by an edge-weighted directed acyclic graph (DAG), with a source node and a sink

© The Author(s), under exclusive license to Springer Nature Switzerland AG 2022
F. Dignum et al. (Eds.): PAAMS 2022, LNAI 13616, pp. 280–293, 2022.
https://doi.org/10.1007/978-3-031-18192-4_23

node, representing all the valid bundles (i.e. paths) of items for an agent, where the quality of a bundle is represented by additive edge weights. The second constraint expresses that conflicting items cannot be allocated at the same time and has to be handled so that each agent obtains one conflict-free path in her graph. Such a setting occurs in application domains such as network function virtualization (NFV) where users request to allocate directed graphs of services into a shared networked infrastructure [17], or in Earth observation using a constellation of satellites, where users demand the ownership of some repetitive orbit slots (without overlapping with other users' slots) to implement periodic observation requests [10,15], as illustrated before. In such settings, beside the additive edge weights, other criteria can be considered to guide the allocation process, especially when constellation users are stakeholders expecting allocations to be fair or proportional to their investment.

Related Work. Literature contains some work related to allocation of goods structured as graphs. In fair division of graph, the objective is to divide a graph of items between several agents, with additive utilities attached to nodes [2,7]. These works provide interesting properties to find envy-free or Pareto-optimal allocations, in an efficient manner in some specific graph structures, e.g. paths, trees, stars. However, in our problem, (i) agents do not compete for the very same set of items, (ii) the graph is directed to compose paths from a start time to an end time, (iii) even by mapping our problem to a graph division one and by regrouping conflicting items into composite items, it is highly improbable that the resulting graph is acyclic. Here, graphs are used to express preferences, and not the goods to allocate. In short, our work does not fall into the existing graph fair division frameworks, or cannot benefit from theoretical results on path-shaped or star-shaped graphs. Another related work is path auctions [5,8,18], where agents bid for paths in a graph where each edge is owned by an agent. The goal is to assign paths to agents by the means of auctions, and optionally to keep some privacy for the edge owners. In the case of a utilitarian objective function for the winner determination problem, without price privacy, this falls into the Vickrey-Clarke-Groves framework, and thus guarantees some efficient and *strategyproof* mechanisms. But, here again, agents bid on the very same set of nodes and edges. In the transportation domain, investigations on very similar structures, that is flow networks, provide techniques for fair maximum flow in multi-source and multi-sink networks [11]. While the techniques used are very similar to ours (linear programming), the maximum flow objective is very different from path utility maximization. Besides, [6] worked on multiple shortest path problems based on deconflicting techniques. While the problem displays similar characteristics, once again the agents evolve on the very same graphs, and the objective is focused on minimizing path length and minimizing conflicting paths, without fairness desiderata. In congestion games, agents are allocated paths so that delay incurred by crossing paths are minimized. The more agents are allocated the same nodes, the more delay is attached to their paths [13,14]. In our work, we don't consider delay but incompatibilities. Even if they could be modeled as non linear $\{0, \infty\}$ functions, in our problem some path allocations are unfeasible, contrarily to congestion games. Besides, using congestion game solution methods as in [14] may result in unfair Nash equilibria, because of numerous unfeasible paths[1]. More generally, another classical approach to fair allocation of indivisible goods is *round-robin*, which is almost envy-free [3]. This is notably one favored technique to allocate virtual network functions in network function virtualization infrastructures [16], or to schedule tasks. We will use it as a competitor for our techniques.

Contributions. This paper introduces and presents a model for such scenarios, under the prism of optimality and fairness, which captures any application where agents express preferences as edge-weighted DAGs and where there exist conflicts between some nodes of these DAGs. We show that this allocation problem is NP-hard. We describe and assess several algorithms on data coming from simulated satellite constellations and requests, with respect to utilitarian optimality, computation time, and fairness.

2 Problem Model

We study allocation problems, as illustrated in Fig. 1, where agents' valuations of item bundles are represented as edge-weighted DAGs and some conflicts exists between nodes of these graphs. An allocation consists in choosing one full path in each graph, so that selected paths do not conflict with each other.

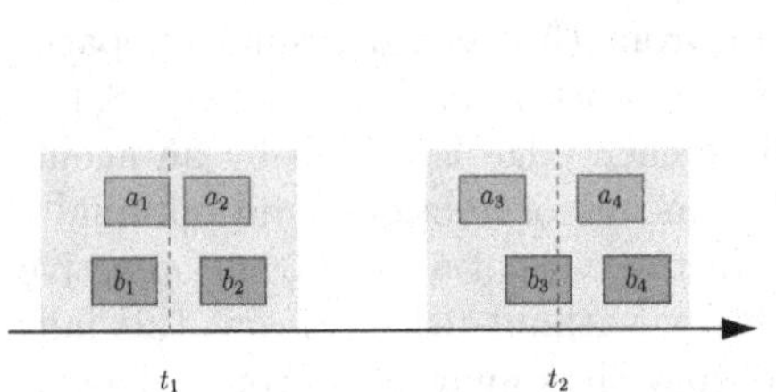

Fig. 1. An orbit slot allocation problem with 2 agents (a in red, b in blue) requesting slots around 2 requested observation times (t_1 and t_2), tolerance windows around each plot (in gray), and with 2 opportunities for each date (a_1,...,a_4,b_1,...,b_4). (Color figure online)

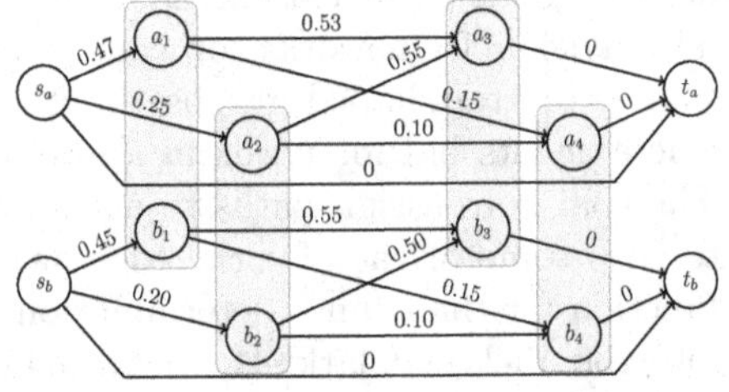

Fig. 2. Sample users' bundle valuations (or preferences) represented as DAGs. Conflicts are represented as gray hypernodes.

---

[1] A Nash equilibrium is an allocation in which the modification of a path for a single agent does not improve its associated utility.

Definition 1. *A problem of* path allocation in multiple conflicting edge-weighted directed acyclic graphs *(PADAG) is a tuple $\langle \mathcal{A}, \mathcal{G}, \mu, \mathcal{C}\rangle$, where $\mathcal{A} = \{1, \ldots, n\}$ is a set of* agents*; $\mathcal{G} = \{g_1, \ldots, g_m\}$ is a set of edge-weighted DAGs, where each $g \in \mathcal{G}$ is a triple $\langle V_g, E_g, u_g\rangle$ that represents some preferences over some items in V_g, with connections between items in $E_g \subset V_g \times V_g$, weighted using utility function $u_g : V_g \times V_g \to \mathbb{R}$; we also assume that V_g contains two specific nodes, the source s_g and the sink t_g, and that E_g contains an edge from s_g to t_g labeled by utility 0 (useful to deal with cases where no bundle of items can be selected in g); $\mu : \mathcal{G} \to \mathcal{A}$ maps each graph g in $\mathcal{G}$ to its owner a in $\mathcal{A}$; $\mathcal{C} \subseteq \{(v, v') | (v, v') \in V_g \times V_{g'}, g, g' \in \mathcal{G}^2, \mu(g) \neq \mu(g')\}$ is a set of conflicts between pairs of items from two distinct graphs in $\mathcal{G}$ from two distinct agents.*

For each graph g and each set of edges $X \subseteq E_g$, the utility of X for g is defined by $u_g(X) = \sum_{e \in X} u_g(e)$, which means that edge valuations are considered as additive in this paper. As a result, each path from s_g to t_g in a graph g is evaluated by summing the utilities of the traversed edges, and each DAG represents in a compact manner a set of valuations for bundles of items, as in combinatorial auctions. Also, we denote by $\mathcal{G}_a = \mu^{-1}(a)$ the set of graphs owned by agent a, and the utility of a set of edges X for agent a is defined by $u_a(X) = \sum_{g \in \mu^{-1}(a)} u_g(X \cap E_g)$.

Definition 2. *An* allocation *is a function π that associates, with each graph $g \in \mathcal{G}$, one path $\pi(g)$ from s_g to t_g in g. Formally, $\pi(g)$ can be represented as a set of nodes in V_g. Indeed, as DAGs are manipulated, it is easy to reconstruct the edges successively traversed by the path from this set. By extension, the allocation for agent a is given by $\pi(a) = \cup_{g \in \mu^{-1}(a)} \pi(g)$.*

By convention, we denote by $u(\pi(g)) = u_{\mu(g)}(\pi(g))$ (resp. $u(\pi(a)) = u_a(\pi(a))$), the utility of graph g (resp. agent a) for allocation π. Last, the global utility obtained with allocation π is given by $u(\pi) = \sum_{g \in \mathcal{G}} u(\pi(g))$ (or equivalently $u(\pi) = \sum_{a \in \mathcal{A}} u(\pi(a))$).

Definition 3. *An allocation π is* valid *if for each pair of distinct graphs g and g' there is no conflict between nodes in the resulting paths, i.e. $(\pi(g) \times \pi(g')) \cap \mathcal{C} = \emptyset$.*

Example 1. Figure 1 and Fig. 2 respectively illustrate an orbit slot allocation problem and a PADAG for this problem. While the best paths for agent a and b are $\{s_a, a_1, a_3, t_a\}$ and $\{s_b, b_1, b_3, t_b\}$ respectively, both valued at 1, they cannot both have these paths due to node conflicts, e.g. between a_1 and b_1. A valid allocation could be $\pi_{\mathsf{ex}} = \{a \mapsto \{s_a, a_2, a_4, t_a\}, b \mapsto \{s_b, b_1, b_3, t_b\}\}$ with global utility $u(\pi_{\mathsf{ex}}) = u(\pi_{\mathsf{ex}}(a)) + u(\pi_{\mathsf{ex}}(b)) = 0.35 + 1.0 = 1.35$.

The problems we consider in this paper are (i) *how to compute an optimal (utilitarian) allocation* π that maximizes $u(\pi)$, and (ii) *how to compute an optimal fair allocation* π, by the way of a leximin optimization, *i.e.* maximizing the ordered utility vector $(\Lambda_1, \ldots, \Lambda_n)$ containing one component per agent. Formally, given the set of agents $\mathcal{A} = \{1, \ldots, n\}$, vector $(\Lambda_1, \ldots, \Lambda_n)$ is a sorted version of vector $(u(\pi(1)), \ldots, u(\pi(n)))$, where $\forall i \leq j, \Lambda_i \leq \Lambda_j$ holds. Note that leximin-based fair allocations allow to favor agents that are the less satisfied.

Proposition 1. *Determining whether there exists a valid allocation* π *such that utilitarian evaluation* $u(\pi)$ *is greater than or equal to a given value is NP-complete.*

Proof. First, the problem is NP since $u(\pi)$ is computable in polynomial time. Then, there exists a polynomial reduction of 3-SAT (which is NP-complete) to our problem. Basically, in a 3-SAT formula, each clause over propositional variables x, y, z can be represented as a weighted DAG g where (1) the set of nodes is $V_g = \{x, \neg x, y, \neg y, z, \neg z, s_g, t_g\}$, (2) the set of paths from s_g to t_g in g corresponds to the set of truth-values for x, y, z that satisfy the clause (decision diagram representation), (3) the weight of every edge is set to 0 except for edges $s_g \rightarrow n$ where $n \neq t_g$ that have weight $1/m$, with m the number of clauses in the 3-SAT formula. Last, for every propositional variable x, we can add one conflict (n, n') for each pair of nodes labeled by literals x and $\neg x$ in two distinct graphs. Then, as one path is selected in each graph and as there are m graphs, determining whether there exists a valid allocation π such that $u(\pi) \geq 1$ is equivalent to finding a solution that satisfies all the clauses, hence the NP-completeness result given that all operations used in the transformation are polynomial. □

Proposition 2. *It is NP-complete to decide whether there exists a valid allocation whose leximin evaluation is greater than or equal to a given utility vector. The proposition holds even if there is a unique graph per agent.*

Proof. In the general case, it suffices to consider a problem involving a unique agent owning all the graphs, and to use the result of the previous proposition. If there is a unique graph per agent, it suffices to use the exact same 3-SAT encoding as before but to replace weights $1/m$ by weights 1. Then, it is possible to show that there exists a valid allocation whose leximin evaluation is greater than or equal to $(1, 1, \ldots, 1)$ iff there exists a solution for the 3-SAT problem. Plus, the leximin evaluation of an allocation π can be computed in polynomial time, hence the NP-completeness result. □

3 Path Allocation Schemes

We propose here several allocation schemes for PADAGs. Some of them are based on integer linear programming (ILP) and mixed integer linear programming (MILP), so we first introduce decision variables and constraints for these models. For any DAG $g = \langle V_g, E_g, u_g \rangle$, we define binary variables $x_e \in \{0, 1\}$, for any $e \in E_g$, stating whether edge e is selected in the path defining the solution bundle. We also use auxiliary binary variables β_v stating whether node v is selected in solution path $\pi(g)$, i.e. $\beta_v = 1$ if $v \in \pi(g)$, 0 otherwise. For any node v in V_g, we denote by $\mathsf{In}(v)$ (resp. $\mathsf{Out}(v)$) its set of incoming (resp. outcoming) edges. In all ILP models introduced thereafter, we impose constraints (1)–(3) to define all the possible paths, (4)–(5) to account for item selection conflicts, and

(6) to ensure that sources and sinks are selected.

$$\sum_{e \in \mathsf{In}(v)} x_e = \sum_{e \in \mathsf{Out}(v)} x_e, \quad \forall g \in \mathcal{G}, \forall v \in V_g \setminus \{s_g, t_g\} \tag{1}$$

$$\sum_{e \in \mathsf{Out}(s_g)} x_e = 1, \quad \forall g \in \mathcal{G} \tag{2}$$

$$\sum_{e \in \mathsf{In}(t_g)} x_e = 1, \quad \forall g \in \mathcal{G} \tag{3}$$

$$\sum_{e \in \mathsf{In}(v)} x_e = \beta_v, \quad \forall g \in \mathcal{G}, \forall v \in V_g \setminus \{s_g, t_g\} \tag{4}$$

$$\sum_{v \in c} \beta_v \leq 1, \quad \forall c \in \mathcal{C} \tag{5}$$

$$\beta_{s_g} = \beta_{t_g} = 1, \quad \forall g \in \mathcal{G} \tag{6}$$

3.1 Utilitarian Allocation (util)

The classical approach to allocation is the utilitarian one. It consists in finding the allocation that maximizes the sum of utilities of all selected paths. This corresponds to solving the integer linear program $P_{\mathsf{util}}(\langle \mathcal{A}, \mathcal{G}, \mu, \mathcal{C} \rangle)$ given below:

$$\max \quad \sum_{a \in \mathcal{A}} \sum_{g \in \mathcal{G}_a} \sum_{e \in E_g} u_g(e) \cdot x_e \tag{7}$$

$$\text{s.t.} \quad (1), (2), (3), (4), (5), (6)$$

$$x_e \in \{0, 1\}, \quad \forall a \in \mathcal{A}, \forall g \in \mathcal{G}_a, \forall e \in E_g \tag{8}$$

The resulting allocation π is decoded from the β_v variables. Formally, for all $g \in \mathcal{G}$, $\pi(g) = \{v \in V_g \mid \beta_v = 1\}$.

Example 2. In Fig. 2, the utilitarian allocation is $\pi_{\mathsf{util}} = \{a \mapsto \{s_a, a_2, a_3, t_a\}, b \mapsto \{s_b, b_1, b_4, t_b\}\}$, with utility $u(\pi_{\mathsf{util}}) = u(\pi_{\mathsf{util}}(a)) + u(\pi_{\mathsf{util}}(b)) = 0.80 + 0.60 = 1.40$.

3.2 Leximin Allocation (lex)

Beyond utilitarianism, one way to implement fair allocation and Pareto-optimality is to consider the *leximin* rule that selects, among all possible allocations, an allocation leading to the best utility profiles wrt the leximin order [12]. More precisely, let $z = [z_1, \ldots, z_n]$ be the utility vector where each component $z_a \in [0, Z_a]$ represents the utility for agent $a \in \mathcal{A}$. Z_a denotes here the best utility value for user a considered alone, i.e. for the mono-agent problem where the best path can be chosen for each graph $g \in \mathcal{G}_a$. In leximin optimization, the objective is to lexicographically maximize vector $\Lambda = [\Lambda_1, \ldots, \Lambda_n]$ obtained after ordering $[z_1, \ldots, z_n]$ following an increasing order. Such a leximin rule can be implemented through a sequence of ILP [9]. We adapt here such a procedure to the specific case of PADAGs. Suppose we have already optimized over the first $K - 1$ components $[\Lambda_1, \ldots, \Lambda_{K-1}]$ of Λ, for $K \in [1..n]$. Then, one can use the

Algorithm 1: Leximin algorithm

Data: A PADAG problem $\langle \mathcal{A}, \mathcal{G}, \mu, \mathcal{C} \rangle$
Result: A leximin-optimal path allocation π
for $K = 1$ *to* $|\mathcal{A}|$ **do**
  $(\lambda^*, sol) \leftarrow$ solve $P_{\text{lex}}(\langle \mathcal{A}, \mathcal{G}, \mu, \mathcal{C} \rangle, K, [\Lambda_1, \ldots, \Lambda_{K-1}])$
  $\Lambda_K \leftarrow \lambda^*$
for $g \in \mathcal{G}$ **do** $\pi(g) \leftarrow \{v \in V_g \mid sol(\beta_v) = 1\}$
return π

MILP presented thereafter to optimize the Kth component Λ_K of the leximin profile of z. In this model, λ represents the utility obtained at level K in Λ, with $\lambda \in [\Lambda_{K-1}, \max_{a \in \mathcal{A}} Z_a]$ and by convention $\Lambda_0 = 0$. y_{ak} is a binary variable equal to 1 if agent $a \in \mathcal{A}$ plays the role of the agent associated with level $k \in [1..K-1]$ in $[\Lambda_1, \ldots, \Lambda_{K-1}]$, 0 otherwise. The optimization of Λ_K can be performed using program $P_{\text{lex}}(\langle \mathcal{A}, \mathcal{G}, \mu, \mathcal{C} \rangle, K, [\Lambda_1, \ldots, \Lambda_{K-1}])$ given below:

$$\max \quad \lambda \tag{9}$$

$$\text{s.t.} \quad (1), (2), (3), (4), (5), (6)$$

$$z_a = \sum_{g \in \mathcal{G}_a} \sum_{e \in E_g} u_g(e) \cdot x_e, \quad \forall a \in \mathcal{A} \tag{10}$$

$$\sum_{a \in \mathcal{A}} y_{ak} = 1, \quad \forall k \in [1..K-1] \tag{11}$$

$$\sum_{k \in [1..K-1]} y_{ak} \leq 1, \quad \forall a \in \mathcal{A} \tag{12}$$

$$\lambda \leq z_a + M \sum_{k \in [1..K-1]} y_{ak}, \quad \forall a \in \mathcal{A} \tag{13}$$

$$z_a \geq \sum_{k \in [1..K-1]} \Lambda_k \cdot y_{ak}, \quad \forall a \in \mathcal{A} \tag{14}$$

In Constraint 13, $M = \max_{a \in \mathcal{A}} Z_a$ is used to ignore agents associated with levels strictly lower than K when optimizing λ (big-M formulation). Constraint 14 ensures that the utility obtained for the agent associated with level $k \in [1..K-1]$ must not be less than Λ_k. To implement the leximin rule, it then suffices to solve a sequence of P_{lex} problems for $K \in \mathcal{A}$ to optimize the value of each component of the utility profile.

Example 3. For the example in Fig. 2, the leximin-optimal allocation is $\pi_{\text{lex}} = \{a \mapsto \{s_a, a_1, a_4, t_a\}, b \mapsto \{s_b, b_2, b_3, t_b\}\}$, with utility vector $(u(\pi_{\text{lex}}(a)), u(\pi_{\text{lex}}(b))) = (0.62, 0.70)$ and global utility $u(\pi_{\text{lex}}) = 0.62 + 0.70 = 1.32$.

3.3 Approximated Leximin Allocation (a-lex)

This previous model implements an exact leximin rule, and thus enforces fairness in the resulting allocation, but may not scale well when increasing the number

Algorithm 2: Approximated leximin algorithm

Data: A PADAG problem $\langle \mathcal{A}, \mathcal{G}, \mu, \mathcal{C} \rangle$
Result: An iterated maximin-optimal allocation π

1 $\Delta \leftarrow [-1, \ldots, -1]$
2 **for** $K = 1$ *to* $|\mathcal{A}|$ **do**
3 $\quad (\delta^*, sol) \leftarrow$ solve $P_{\text{a-lex}}(\langle \mathcal{A}, \mathcal{G}, \mu, \mathcal{C} \rangle, \Delta)$
4 $\quad S \leftarrow \mathop{\mathbf{argmin}}\limits_{a \in \mathcal{A} \mid \Delta_a = -1} \sum_{g \in \mathcal{G}_a} \sum_{e \in E_g} u_g(e) sol(x_e)$
5 $\quad \hat{a} \leftarrow$ choose an agent a in S
6 $\quad \Delta_{\hat{a}} \leftarrow \delta^*$
7 **for** $g \in \mathcal{G}$ **do** $\pi(g) \leftarrow \{v \in V_g \mid sol(\beta_v) = 1\}$
8 **return** π

of agents and edges. This is why we provide an approximate version of the computation of the leximin, based on an iterated maximin scheme. Basically, this approach considers at each step a minimum utility $\Delta_a \geq 0$ for some agents and maximizes the worst utility among the remaining agents, for which we arbitrarily assume $\Delta_a = -1$. The problem to solve, referred to as $P_{\text{a-lex}}(\langle \mathcal{A}, \mathcal{G}, \mu, \mathcal{C} \rangle, \Delta)$, is the following one:

$$\max \ \delta \tag{15}$$

$$\text{s.t.} \ (1), (2), (3), (4), (5), (6)$$

$$\delta \leq \sum_{g \in \mathcal{G}_a} \sum_{e \in E_g} u_g(e) x_e, \quad \forall a \in \mathcal{A} \mid \Delta_a = -1 \tag{16}$$

$$\sum_{g \in \mathcal{G}_a} \sum_{e \in E_g} u_g(e) x_e \geq \Delta_a, \quad \forall a \in \mathcal{A} \mid \Delta_a \neq -1 \tag{17}$$

The solution method then consists in optimizing in an iterated manner, as for leximin. As sketched in Algorithm 2, at each iteration (one per agent), $P_{\text{a-lex}}$ is solved, one worst agent $\hat{a}$ is determined, and its minimum utility $\Delta_{\hat{a}}$ is fixed. The main difference with P_{lex} is that at each iteration, in $P_{\text{a-lex}}$, the position of an agent in the order is implicitly determined once for all, while in P_{lex} the order can be revised at each iteration. Moreover, if any equality occurs at line 5 to determine the worst agent (case $|S| > 1$), one may rely on some heuristic or arbitrary choice. Thus, $P_{\text{a-lex}}$ is an approximation of P_{lex} that contains fewer variables and constraints.

Example 4. The approximated leximin allocation for the example in Fig. 2 is $\pi_{\text{a-lex}} = \{a \mapsto \{s_a, a_1, a_4, t_a\}, b \mapsto \{s_b, b_2, b_3, t_b\}\}$, with utility vector $(u(\pi_{\text{a-lex}}(a)), u(\pi_{\text{a-lex}}(b))) = (0.62, 0.70)$ and global utility $u(\pi_{\text{a-lex}}) = 0.62 + 0.70 = 1.32$. This is the same as π_{lex} since there are only two agents and no equality between the worst utilities.

3.4 Greedy Allocation (greedy)

For very fast decisions, iterated maximin might still be too slow. In such cases, a greedy approach can provide valid allocations quickly. The main idea of greedy path allocation is to iterate over the set of graphs. At each step, one graph g^* that has the best utility path is selected, this path is chosen as $\pi(g^*)$, and all nodes in the other graphs that are in conflict with nodes in $\pi(g^*)$ are deactivated. Graph g^* is then removed, and the process continues until there is no more graph to consider. This process ensures that constraints (1), (2), (3), (4), (5), (6) are met. Determining the best path in a DAG g is linear time $\mathcal{O}(|E_g| + |V_g|)$ [4]. Obviously, greedy is equivalent to utilitarian when there is no conflict between graphs. Indeed, greedy will return the best path for each graph, which is the best utilitarian solution in such settings. Moreover, this greedy approach results in a Nash equilibrium where no agent might be able to improve its utility without a negative impact on other agents. This is equivalent to the *Nashify* procedure from [14] in the context of congestion games, with only one turn. We will see in the experiments that this equilibrium is far from being fair.

Example 5. The greedy allocation for the example in Fig. 2 is $\pi_{\mathsf{greedy}} = \{a \mapsto \{s_a, a_1, a_3, t_a\}, b \mapsto \{s_b, b_2, b_4, t_b\}\}$, with global utility $u(\pi_{\mathsf{greedy}}) = u(\pi_{\mathsf{greedy}}(a)) + u(\pi_{\mathsf{greedy}}(b)) = 1.0 + 0.3 = 1.3$ and utility vector $(1.0, 0.3)$.

3.5 Round-Robin Allocations (p-rr and n-rr)

One fast approach to fair allocation of indivisible goods is *round-robin*. It consists in making each agent choose in turn (in a predefined fixed order) one item (depending on her preferences) until there is no more item to allocate. It is polynomial in the number of agents and items. In our case, one may consider two kinds of items to allocate: paths (noted p-rr) or nodes (noted n-rr). In the case of paths, each agent selects at her turn her best feasible path, given the already allocated nodes (to prevent conflicts). This process operates similarly to greedy, but alternates between users to balance utilities. In the case of nodes, each agent incrementally builds the path associated with each of her graphs, by choosing in turn her next best feasible node until either it reaches the sink or there is no more feasible node to choose (dead-end path). In the latter case, the agent is allocated the 0-utility source-to-sink path and looses the previously chosen nodes. In both approaches, constraints (1–6) are met since considered paths are all feasible. Note that p-rr results in a Nash equilibrium where each agent has been allocated the best path given the other allocations. This is not true for n-rr, since some nodes left by some agent falling in a dead-end may have prevented some other agents to find a better solution.

Example 6. The path-round-robin allocation $\pi_{\mathsf{p\text{-}rr}}$ for the example in Fig. 2 is equivalent to π_{greedy}, since a chooses $\{s_a, a_1, a_3, t_a\}$ and then b chooses $\{s_b, b_2, b_4, t_b\}\}$. The node-round-robin allocation $\pi_{\mathsf{n\text{-}rr}}$ is also equivalent to π_{greedy} because a first chooses a_1, then b chooses b_2 (only feasible option), then a chooses a_3 (best option), and finally b chooses b_4 (only feasible option).

4 Experimental Evaluation

In this section, we evaluate the different allocation methods proposed when applied to orbit slot allocation problems encoded as PADAGs. We present the experimental setup and analyze some results obtained on synthetic instances.

We consider a Low-Earth Orbit constellation (500 km altitude) composed of n_p regularly-spaced orbital planes having a 60-degree inclination, with $n_p \in \{2, 4, 8, 16\}$ and 2 regularly spaced satellites over each orbital plane. To generate PADAG instances, we randomly generate requests for 4 agents wishing to obtain orbit slot ownerships to implement some repetitive ground acquisitions of Points Of Interest (POIs) belonging to the same area. POIs are randomly selected within an extracted subset from [1]. All the agents have the same template for a request r: getting an observation every day at 8:00 + δ_r, 12:00 + δ_r, and 16:00 + δ_r, with a tolerance of 1 h around each Requested Observation Time (ROT), and uniform random time shift $\delta_r \in [-2\,\text{h}, 2\,\text{h}]$ for all ROTs of the same request. For each POI and for each ROT, the orbit slots over which orbit ownership can be claimed for performing observations are determined thanks to a space mechanics toolbox, based on the assumption that a satellite is relevant for a POI as soon as its elevation above the horizon is greater than 15°. Incompatible time slots are those which overlaps while belonging to the same satellite.

We then encode these requests and orbit slots into PADAGs. Each request is mapped to a graph, in which nodes (except source and sink) are orbit slots for capturing a POI at some ROT, and edges link two such consecutive orbit slots to answer the request. For instance, Fig. 2 represents two requests from two users (a and b), with two ROTs, each having two possible orbit slots per ROT per user (e.g. for user a, a_1 and a_2 for the first ROT, a_3 and a_4 for the second one). For simplicity, we only consider utilities attached to the slots, and not to the transitions between slots. We study a *linear* utility function, which is linear in the distance between the middle τ of the allocated slot and the ROT (utility linearly decreasing from 1 when τ is exactly on the ROT to 0 when τ reaches the bounds of the tolerance window). We normalize each utility wrt the maximum utility that can be achieved for each graph individually. We consider 2 requests per agent, and a horizon of 365 days resulting in DAGs having 1095 layers (1095 ROTs). This setting results in DAGs having the following properties on average:

n_p	2	4	8	16
DAG width	3.08	5.41	10.05	19.38
conflicts	26798.80	45636.06	82971.20	158180.20
slot duration (s)	603.28	600.10	599.87	598.75

Solvers are coded in Java 1.8 and executed on 20-core Intel(R) Xeon(R) CPU E5-2660 v3 @ 2.60 GHz, 62 GB RAM, Ubuntu 18.04.5 LTS. Utilitarian, leximin and approximated leximin make use of the Java API of IBM CPLEX 20.1 (with 10 min timeout). We ran 30 instances of randomly generated PADAGs and plot the average with [0.05, 0.95] confidence.

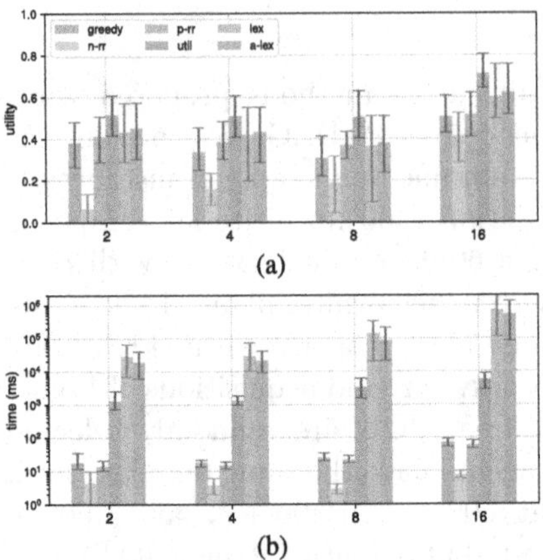

Fig. 3. Average overall utility (top) and computation time (bottom) obtained by each algorithm for each constellation size.

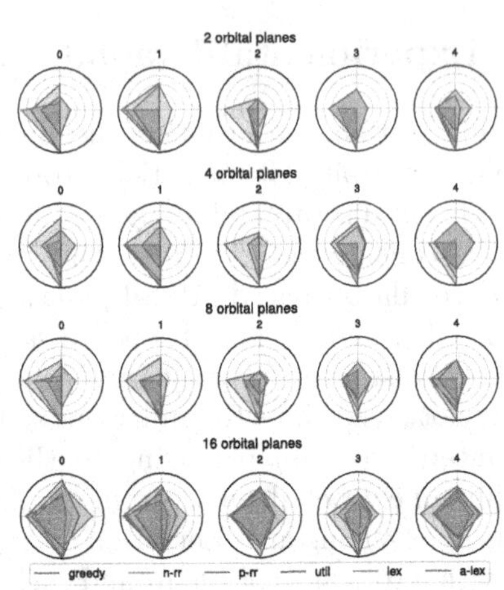

Fig. 4. Utility profiles (in leximin order) for the first 5 instances for each constellation size and each algorithm (south: best utility over all agents; west: second best utility; north: third best utility; east: worst utility).

Figure 3a shows the average normalized global utility for each algorithm and constellation size (expressed in number of orbital planes). Normalized global utility is the mean graph utility, thus between 0 and 1. Obviously util provides the optimal utilitarian allocation. In second position, a-lex provides good allocations at almost 85% of the optimal value on average. Interestingly, lex performs equivalently to a-lex (gap less than 5% on average). Indeed, a-lex provides slightly better allocations from the utilitarian point of view, at the expense of fairness approximation. Round-robin approaches really differ in utility. While p-rr provides allocations at almost 71% of the optimal, n-rr results in low-utility allocations, at almost 10% of the optimal on smaller constellations. In fact, in such settings, there are few feasible paths for each request. Thus, for most of the requests, the myopic incremental building of paths results in dead-ends, and thus on 0-utility allocations; while, by considering another agent order, the allocations could have been better. Finally, greedy behaves slightly worse than p-rr, at almost 68% of the optimal value on average. On larger instances, where many paths exist to answer each request, greedy performs even better. More generally, larger constellation problems are easier to solve from the utilitarian point-of-view for non-optimal algorithms, since there are more options to avoid conflicts, even if the number of conflicts is higher.

To analyze the fairness of the resulting allocations, Fig. 4 provides the utility profiles obtained for the first 5 instances for each algorithm. greedy, by principle, seeks to first allocate the highest utility paths, resulting in unfair allocations where only the first 2 or 3 users are served, while most of the time the fourth user has no request fulfilled. Round-robin approaches are fairer than greedy and often fulfill requests for more users. util results in profiles with the larger surface, but the fourth user is often neglected. Finally, lex and a-lex behave almost identically (their profiles are superimposed), showing that the a-lex approximation is sufficient to output fair allocations. Let's note that with growing constellations, since there is more and more options to serve users, all the algorithms tend to result in fairer allocations. Still, lex and a-lex are the best choices here, and the round-robin competitors output unsatisfactory allocations.

Figure 3b shows the average computation time in milliseconds for each algorithm and each constellation size. As expected (by design), greedy, p-rr and n-rr are the fastest. n-rr which does not even perform shortest path operations is the fastest by far, but results in very bad and not-so-fair allocations. greedy and p-rr are very fast, but are based on multiple max path search in DAGs. p-rr still quickly provides quite good utilitarian and fair allocations. util, based on a single ILP solving, is 100 times slower than the fastest algorithms. Then, lex and a-lex are up to two orders of magnitude slower than util on the largest constellations. This is due to the multiple calls ($|\mathcal{A}|$) to the MILP solver on large problems. a-lex is 2 to 3 times faster than lex since it solves smaller MILPs, while resulting in allocations that are as fair as lex's ones.

5 Conclusion

In this paper, we proposed the PADAG model, a novel allocation problem where agents express their preferences over bundles of items as edge-weighted DAGs. We introduced and analyzed several solution methods (utilitarian, leximin, approximate leximin, greedy) against the round-robin allocations, from the utilitarianism and fairness perspectives. We evaluated these methods on large randomly generated instances of orbit slot allocation problems. On large constellations, approximate leximin constitutes a good trade-off between utilitarian optimality, leximin optimality and computation time. It is equivalent to exact leximin on most instances, while improving computation times.

We identify several tracks for future investigations. First, we would like to investigate other solution methods to solve larger PADAGs and specific topologies (stars, chains, etc.). Second, since PADAGs are strongly constrained by conflicts, we aim to explore min-conflict heuristics to improve our algorithms. Finally, we believe PADAGs have great potential to be used in a variety of domains, and we thus aim to evaluate the proposed techniques on problems coming from other application fields, like the NFV domain where function chains are modeled as graphs, and incompatibilities control the access to nodes or multi-agent path finding domain (path preferences are modeled as graphs, and incompatibilities impose that two agents cannot occupy the same position at the same time).

References

1. OpenStreetMap Points of Interest (on French Territory) (2021). www.data.gouv.fr/fr/datasets/points-dinterets-openstreetmap/. Accessed 30 Aug 2021
2. Bouveret, S., Cechlárová, K., Elkind, E., Igarashi, A., Peters, D.: Fair division of a graph. In: Sierra, C. (ed.) Proceedings of the Twenty-Sixth International Joint Conference on Artificial Intelligence, IJCAI 2017, Melbourne, Australia, August 19–25, 2017, pp. 135–141. ijcai.org (2017). https://doi.org/10.24963/ijcai.2017/20
3. Caragiannis, I., Kurokawa, D., Moulin, H., Procaccia, A.D., Shah, N., Wang, J.: The unreasonable fairness of maximum Nash welfare. In: Proceedings of the 2016 ACM Conference on Economics and Computation, pp. 305–322. EC 2016, Association for Computing Machinery, New York, NY, USA (2016). https://doi.org/10.1145/2940716.2940726
4. Cormen, T.H., Leiserson, C.E., Rivest, R.L., Stein, C.: Introduction to Algorithms, 2nd edn. The MIT Press, Cambridge (2001)
5. Du, Y., Sami, R., Shi, Y.: Path auctions with multiple edge ownership. Theor. Comput. Sci. **411**(1), 293–300 (2010). https://doi.org/10.1016/j.tcs.2009.09.032
6. Hughes, M.S., Lunday, B.J., Weir, J.D., Hopkinson, K.M.: The multiple shortest path problem with path deconfliction. Eur. J. Oper. Res. **292**(3), 818–829 (2021). https://doi.org/10.1016/j.ejor.2020.11.033
7. Igarashi, A., Peters, D.: Pareto-optimal allocation of indivisible goods with connectivity constraints. In: The Thirty-Third AAAI Conference on Artificial Intelligence, AAAI 2019, pp. 2045–2052. AAAI Press (2019). https://doi.org/10.1609/aaai.v33i01.33012045
8. Immorlica, N., Karger, D.R., Nikolova, E., Sami, R.: First-price path auctions. In: Riedl, J., Kearns, M.J., Reiter, M.K. (eds.) Proceedings 6th ACM Conference on Electronic Commerce (EC-2005), Vancouver, BC, Canada, 5–8 June 2005, pp. 203–212. ACM (2005). https://doi.org/10.1145/1064009.1064031
9. Kurokawa, D., Procaccia, A.D., Shah, N.: Leximin allocations in the real world. ACM Trans. Econ. Comput. **6**(3–4) (2018). https://doi.org/10.1145/3274641
10. Lemaître, M., Verfaillie, G., Fargier, H., Lang, J., Bataille, N., Lachiver, J.M.: Equitable allocation of earth observing satellites resources. In: 5th ONERA-DLR Aerospace Symposium (ODAS 2003) (2003)
11. Megiddo, N.: Optimal flows in networks with multiple sources and sinks. Math. Program. **7**(1), 97–107 (1974). https://doi.org/10.1007/BF01585506
12. Moulin, H.: Fair Division and Collective Welfare. MIT Press, Cambridge (2003)
13. Nisan, N., Roughgarden, T., Tardos, E., Vazirani, V.V.: Algorithmic Game Theory. Cambridge University Press, New York (2007)
14. Panagopoulou, P.N., Spirakis, P.G.: Algorithms for pure Nash equilibria in weighted congestion games. ACM J. Exp. Algorithmics **11**, 2.7-es (2007)
15. Picard, G.: Auction-based and distributed optimization approaches for scheduling observations in satellite constellations with exclusive orbit portions. In: International Conference on Autonomous Agents and Multiagent Systems (AAMAS-22). IFAAMAS (2022)
16. Riera, J.F., Escalona, E., Batallé, J., Grasa, E., García-Espín, J.A.: Virtual network function scheduling: Concept and challenges. In: 2014 International Conference on Smart Communications in Network Technologies (SaCoNeT), pp. 1–5 (2014). https://doi.org/10.1109/SaCoNeT.2014.6867768

17. Yang, S., Li, F., Trajanovski, S., Yahyapour, R., Fu, X.: Recent advances of resource allocation in network function virtualization. IEEE Trans. Parallel Distrib. Syst. **32**(2), 295–314 (2021). https://doi.org/10.1109/TPDS.2020.3017001
18. Zhang, L., Chen, H., Wu, J., Wang, C., Xie, J.: False-name-proof mechanisms for path auctions in social networks. In: ECAI 2016. Frontiers in Artificial Intelligence and Applications, vol. 285, pp. 1485–1492. IOS Press (2016). https://doi.org/10.3233/978-1-61499-672-9-1485

Shifting Reward Assignment for Learning Coordinated Behavior in Time-Limited Ordered Tasks

Yoshihiro Oguni(✉), Yuki Miyashita, and Toshiharu Sugawara(✉)

Department of Computer Science and Communications Engineering, Waseda University, Tokyo 1698555, Japan
{y.oguni,y.miyashita}@isl.waseda.ac.jp, sugawara@waseda.jp

Abstract. We propose a variable reward scheme in decentralized multi-agent deep reinforcement learning for a sequential task consisting of a number of subtasks which can be completed when all subtasks are executed in a certain order before a deadline by agents with different capabilities. Developments in computer science and robotics are drawing attention to multi-agent systems for complex tasks. However, coordinated behavior among agents requires sophistication and is highly dependent on the structures of tasks and environments; thus, it is preferable to individually learn appropriate coordination depending on specific tasks. This study focuses on the learning of a sequential task by cooperative agents from a practical perspective. In such tasks, agents must learn both efficiency for their own subtasks and coordinated behavior for other agents because the former provides more chances for the subsequent agents to learn, while the latter facilitates the execution of subsequent subtasks. Our proposed reward scheme enables agents to learn these behaviors in a balanced manner. We then experimentally show that agents in the proposed reward scheme can achieve more efficient task execution compared to baseline methods based on static reward schemes. We also analyzed the learned coordinated behavior to see the reasons of efficiency.

Keywords: Multi-agent reinforcement learning · Sequential tasks · Variable reward scheme

1 Introduction

Multi-agent systems have attracted attention because sophisticated services in the real world are often realized through distributed cooperation and coordination among multiple intelligent agents. However, appropriate coordinated behavior is diverse and highly dependent on many factors such as task structures, environmental structures, and other agents' behaviors, which may also vary through their learning. Therefore, designing and implementing systems that consider possible coordination in advance is almost impossible.

Meanwhile, *deep reinforcement learning* (DRL) is known to be able to learn appropriate actions even for problems involving a large number of states and

© The Author(s), under exclusive license to Springer Nature Switzerland AG 2022
F. Dignum et al. (Eds.): PAAMS 2022, LNAI 13616, pp. 294–306, 2022.
https://doi.org/10.1007/978-3-031-18192-4_24

action patterns, such as video games [7,13]. Thus, *multi-agent deep reinforcement learning* (MADRL), in which several agents capable of DRL operate in an environment, have been studied to improve overall efficiency, and such methods have successfully learned a certain level of cooperative and coordinated behavior. However, how rewards should be provided to agents remains unclear because the performance is greatly affected not only by agent's efficient execution of their own subtasks, but also by coordinated behavior that facilitates other agents' subtasks. Thus, agents with MADRL must learn such balanced activities by appropriately providing rewards to each agent, although identifying which behaviors have actually been effective for coordinated actions is typically difficult.

In this study, we consider a sequential task with a specific time limit performed by multiple robots (agents). For example, on a building construction site, different moving robots, each of which is responsible for some labor such as carrying materials, placing and fixing them, and painting them, must execute their own subtasks in a certain order within a limited time. Such collaborative work on the part of multiple agents can be envisioned in a variety of practical situations. From the viewpoint of the agent responsible for the first subtask, the completion of the task depends on the success or failure of the subsequent agents, and the rewards obtained arrive much later, often once an agent is already working on another task. In contrast, the agents responsible for the latter subtasks cannot even have a chance to execute their subtask until the agents responsible for the former have been trained sufficiently. Therefore, actions that contribute to the success or failure of a task depend not only on the efficiency of their own subtasks, but also on the efficiency gains from coordinated behavior that enhance the collaborating actions. Thus, these actions need to be reinforced together.

Several studies have been conducted on reward schemes to facilitate the learning of cooperative behavior in MADRL. For example, in the credit assignment problem [1,14], rewards are allocated in a rational way according to the contribution of individual agents, but the sequential task cannot be accomplished if any subtask is missing, in which case the final team reward falls to zero. Some studies have addressed the cooperative/adversarial problem by adjusting agents' reward assignments [3,10]. However, in the ordered task targeted in this study, the efficiency of each agent's own subtask must be balanced with cooperative/coordinated behavior for other agents that execute their respective tasks before and after that of a given agent. For example, if an agent can improve the overall success rate by prioritizing the learning of cooperative behaviors over its own subtasks, it should to do so.

To address these issues, Miyashita et al. [6] proposed a reward scheme based on learning efficient and balanced behaviors for tasks each of which consist of two sequential subtasks with a time limit. They first showed that agents could not learn any effective behavior by simply giving a reward only when a task was completed. Then, they proposed a reward scheme in which the reward allocation was divided into two parts and the ratio of these allocated rewards were gradually varied and showed that agents were able to perform their own subtasks efficiently along with the cooperative behavior to facilitate the performance of other agents, while simultaneously making the converged reward assignment consistent with the original objective, i.e., simply giving the rewards only when a task was finished. However, they focused on simple sequential tasks consisting of only two subtasks, and it remains unclear whether their scheme would work as well and what issues would exist for more complex sequential tasks.

Therefore, we extend their study to apply to sequential tasks with a more complex structure such as longer sequence and partially ordered sequence of subtasks. We then experimentally show that agents trained with the proposed method can both increase the efficiency of their own subtasks and acquire cooperative behavior for other cooperative agents even for such complex tasks. We also analyze the difference in efficiency and learned behavior compared to the cases where only a final team reward is given only when a task is completed or where a reward is divided into two parts with a fixed ratio. We then present an investigation of the learned behaviors to see why the agents achieved the efficiency they did.

2 Related Work

In reinforcement learning (RL), the scheme of rewards to be given to agents must be designed for improved success in problem solving, but determining an appropriate reward scheme for a variety of tasks is challenging. Thus, many studies have been conducted on this issue. Ng, Harada, and Russell [8] showed a method to promote learning by providing additional rewards and at the same time learn converged behavior with no difference from the original objective. Moreover, the same authors proposed a method to generate a reward function from example behaviors [9], although they considered only single-agent learning.

Many studies have also been conducted on MADRL in which agents individually learn coordinated and cooperative behavior. Tampuu et al. [10] demonstrated that two agents can acquire continuous pong behavior through training in a pong game using MADRL based on *deep Q-networks* (DQN). Furthermore, by fixing the reward for missed balls and varying the reward for winning balls, they have confirmed that agents can change the degree of their cooperative behavior by measuring the number of consecutive rallies. Diallo, Sugiyama, and Sugawara [2] also showed that two agents were able to successfully learn cooperative behavior in doubles pong games. Meanwhile, Du et al. [3] proposed a hybrid reward scheme in which a team reward given by the environment was fixed, and agents learned their intrinsic reward functions via meta-learning. Then, by learning intrinsic reward functions to promote cooperative behaviors, they succeeded in acquiring cooperative behavior that could not be obtained only with a team reward. However, because agents only learned intrinsic rewards to maximize the team rewards they acquired, the authors' method cannot simply be applied to sequential tasks involving temporal differences in behavior, as in our problem.

A number of studies have been conducted on multi-agent (deep) RL to facilitate learning in multi-agent systems, partially ignoring decentralization. For example, Tan [11] showed that in table-based Q-learning, learning speed was increased by utilizing the vision and experience of other agents and sharing Q-tables among agents. Lowe et al. [5] proposed the *multi-agent deep deterministic policy gradient* (MADDPG) as a type of MADRL with actor-critic learning using a centralized critic during training and a decentralized execution using the copies of the network during testing. Fortster et al. [4] introduced communication between agents and proposed the *differentiable inter-agent learning* (DIAL), a method to update policy by finding the gradient including the communication channel. It improved the system's performance because agents could use information unavailable in the distributed environment during training. Therefore, while it was effective for synchronous or closely related actions, its implementation was not obvious when there is a delay in the evaluation of agents' actions as in our target problem. Meanwhile, we aim to improve the overall performance of the system by training agents to perform their own tasks efficiently and simultaneously by learning cooperative behavior together, while retaining the advantages of distributed learning by devising a specialized reward scheme.

3 Problem Description

3.1 Agent and Environment

Let $A = \{1, \ldots, n\}$ be the set of n agents. We introduce discrete time whose unit is *step*. Agents can move to one of the neighboring nodes in a grid environment $V = E \times E$, in one step, but two agents cannot remain at a single node. There are m types of materials, their storage areas are in V, and K tasks that are scattered in V (E, m, and $K \in \mathbb{Z}_+$, where $\mathbb{Z}_+$ is the set of positive integers). Agent $i \in A$ has an observable range O_i whose size is $S \times S$ ($S \in \mathbb{Z}_+$, an odd number) and whose center is itself. Agent i also has a capability denoted by c_l ($1 \leq l \leq L$) and is called c_l-class agents. We denote the set of c_l-class agents by C_l and assume that $A = C_1 \cup \cdots \cup C_L$ is a disjoint union. An example environment is shown in Fig. 1, where dark gray nodes represent tasks, white nodes with different shapes are agents with different capabilities (four capabilities in Fig. 1), and blue and green squares are material storage areas (with $m = 2$).

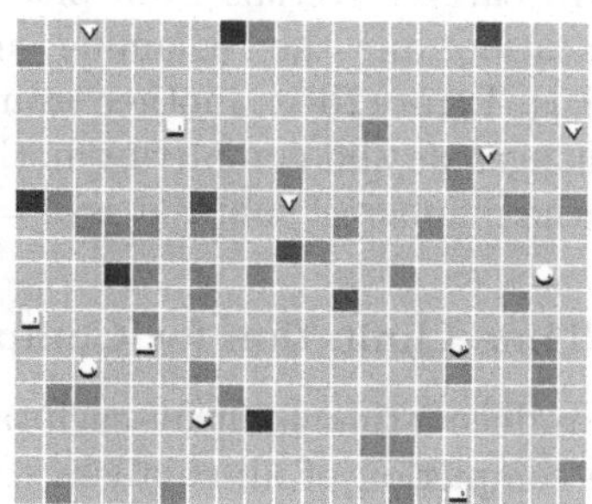

Fig. 1. Example of environment. (Color figure online)

3.2 Task Structure

The task set is denoted by $\mathcal{T} = \{T_1, \ldots, T_K\}$. Task $T_k \in \mathcal{T}$ can be described by an ordered set of subtasks $T_k = \{\tau_k^1, \ldots, \tau_k^L\}$, where τ_k^l is the l-th subtask by using the capability c_l. Then, by introducing a partial order $\prec$ between subtasks in $\{\tau_k^1, \ldots, \tau_k^L\}$, all *predecessors* $P_k^l = \{\tau_k^j \mid \tau_k^j \prec \tau_k^l\}$ must be completed before the execution of τ_k^l. We assume that $\prec$ is well-defined for $\mathcal{T}$, i.e., $\forall T_k \in \mathcal{T}$ can be completed if all subtasks can be executed according to this order. If $P_k^l = \varnothing$, τ_k^l can be executed first. We also assume $\forall T_k = \{\tau_k^1, \ldots, \tau_k^L\}$ is sorted consistently; i.e., if $\tau_k^l \prec \tau_k^{l'}$, then $l < l'$. Note that T_k is often denoted as T without subscript if no confusion. An agent can execute another subtask without waiting for the current task to finish.

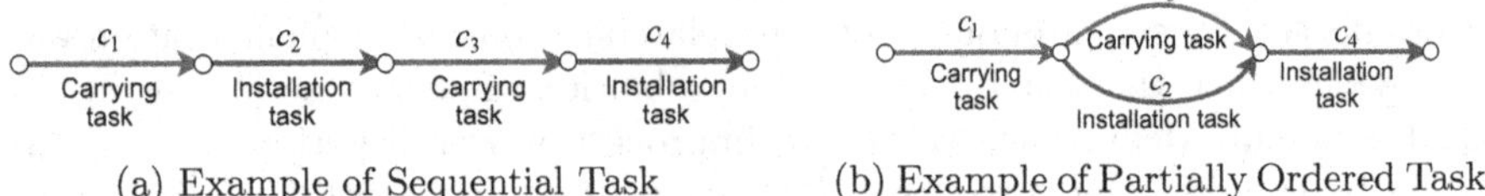

Fig. 2. Examples of Task Structure.

Example tasks are shown in Fig. 2 based on the envisioned practical robotic work process at a construction site. Figure 2a shows a task consisting of four subtasks that must start sequentially, where τ^1 and τ^3 are tasks requiring an agent to carry materials from one of the corresponding storage areas to the task location, and the remaining subtask requires them to install the carried materials. Figure 2b is another example in which the order of τ^2 and τ^3 are interchangeable and completing both τ^2 and τ^3 is required to start τ^4. In both tasks, the number of subtasks is $L = 4$.

3.3 Time Limitation for Completing Each Task

We introduce a time limit for each task from the initiation of one of its subtasks to the completion of all subtasks to prevent cooperative work from being left unattended for a long period of time in the middle of the work by assuming the actual work that the construction robots need to complete in a certain period of time, such as temporary fixing and gluing. For this purpose, we set a time limit of $w > 0$, i.e., any task T should be completed until $t_T^s + w$, where t_T^s is the time when an agent has started the first subtask in T. Moreover, to eliminate large delays in starting a middle subtask, we gradually extend the time limit of starting each subtask; i.e., when agents completed j subtasks in T, the next subtask must be started by $t_T^s + j\omega$, where $j = 1, \ldots, L-1$. and $\omega = w/(L-1)$. If agents cannot meet these time limits, the execution of *task* is considered as a failure and T returns to the initial state at the same node.

4 Proposed Method

4.1 Shifting Two-Stage Reward Assignment

We assume that the goal of the system is to complete as many tasks $T \in \mathcal{T}$ as possible. Upon completion of each task, a *team reward* $r(> 0)$ is given to each agent involved in the executions of the associated subtasks. However, as shown in experiments, team rewards alone do not enable agents to learn behavior sufficient to complete tasks, especially cooperative behaviors. Thus, we propose the *shifting two-stage reward assignment* (S2RA) to enable all agents to learn to balance between actions for their own subtasks and cooperation with other agents. Specifically, agent i receives an *individual reward* of $r_1(t) \geq 0$ when it completes a subtask that it can execute at time t, and then receives *residual reward* $r_2(t) \geq 0$ when the task (thus, all involved subtasks) was completed, where we assume that $r_1(t) + r_2(t) = r$. Initially, $r_1(0)$ is set a large proportion of r (e.g., r or $0.5r$), and $r_1(t)$ gradually decreases with t, and finally $r_1(t) = 0$ (so $r_2(t) = r$). We call time t when $r_1(t)$ becomes 0 the *reward boundary time*, and denote it by $B_r \in \mathbb{Z}_+$. Therefore, i receives only the first reward $r_1(t)$ if it reaches the time limit without completing the task, even if i has completed the responsible subtask, and i receives no reward after B_r in this case.

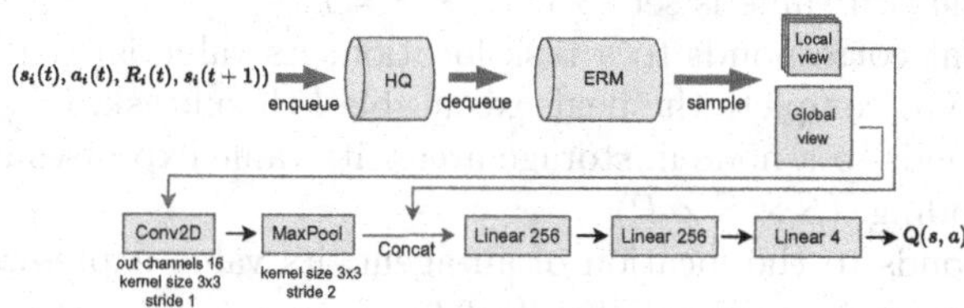

Fig. 3. Structure of double deep Q-Network.

4.2 Modified Experience Replay

Because the rewards are divided into two stages in S2RA, the true reward for each action is determined after some delay. Therefore, before registering the experience in each agent's *experience replay memory* (ERM), we introduce to each agent a *holding queue* (HQ) whose size is equal to or larger than w, to temporarily store the experience data until the actual reward is available.

More specifically, let $s_i(t)$ be the state observed by agent $i \in A$ at time t, $a_i(t)$ be the action chosen by i, and $R_i(t)$ be the immediate reward that i received. Moreover, let $s_i(t)$ be transited to $s_i(t+1)$. The tuple $(s_i(t), a_i(t), R_i(t), s_i(t+1), o_i(t))$ is first stored in the HQ in i. Here, $o_i(t)$ is the optional data associated with this action and if i executed its own subtask, $R_i(t) = r_1(t)$ and in this case, $o_i(t)$ contains the information of the involved task T such as its coordinates; otherwise, $R_i(t) = 0$ and $o_i(t) = \varnothing$. If T is completed at time t' and the team reward r has arrived, the corresponding reward $R_i(t)$ in HQ is modified to $R_i(t) = r_1(t) + r_2(t') = r$. An experience data sample is added to HQ for every step, and data overflowing from HQ is registered in ERM after removing $o_i(t)$.

4.3 Structure of Network and Input Structure

In the proposed approach, agents have their own double deep Q-network (DDQN) [12] (performing decentralized training) to autonomously learn Q-values. The structures of the input and DDQN are shown in Fig. 3. Two types of observations, *global view* and *local view*, are used as input for an environmental state. A global view of agent i at t is the matrix whose size is $E \times E$ and which expresses trajectory, i.e., the current location of i in this matrix is 1 and its past locations at $t - h$ as δ^h (where $0 < \delta < 1$ and $0 < h < H$ for the trajectory length $H \in \mathbb{Z}_+$), by assuming that i's current location in the environment can be known (if an agent stays in the same place more than once, only the larger number is used).

Meanwhile, a local view consists of a $S \times S \times (2L + P + 2)$ tensor that reflects the observable range size S and expresses the following local information.

- If the element corresponds to a task location in which subtask τ^l is not complete at t, the l-th value is set to 1. $(S \times S \times L)$
- If the element corresponds to a task location, its value is $t_T^s + (l - 1)\omega - t$, i.e., the time to complete the next executable l-th subtask. $(S \times S \times 1)$
- If it corresponds to a node in storage areas, its value expresses its type using one-hot encoding. $(S \times S \times P)$
- If it corresponds to the location of an agent, its value expresses the agent's class using one-hot encoding. $(S \times S \times L)$
- If it corresponds to the location of the agent that carries a material, its value is 1. $(S \times S \times 1)$

Note that elements that correspond to outside of V and elements that are not specified above are filled with 0.

As shown in Fig. 3, the global view is fed to the convolutional neural network (CNN). Then, its output and the local view are fed to the multi-layer perceptron. The final output is Q-value $Q(a, s)$ for action a at state s.

5 Experimental Evaluation and Discussion

5.1 Experimental Setting

We set the environment size as $E = 20$ and the observable size as $S = 7$. Then, we used two types of task structures shown in Fig. 2, in which subtasks τ^1 and τ^3 are to carry type-1 and 2 materials ($m = 2$) and subtasks τ^2 and τ^4 are those of installing them. Therefore, we call c_1- and c_3-class agents as *carrier agents* and c_2- and c_3-class agents as *installation agents*. Four material storage locations for each type of materials and $K = 40$ tasks were scattered randomly in V. Then, twelve agents are initially placed in V, so that they did not overlap with each other (see Fig. 1). Agents can move up, down, left, and right. To simplify the experiments, installation agents can complete their subtasks when they reach the locations where the corresponding subtasks are ready to be executed. Similarly, carrier agents with no material can load a material when they reach one of the

Table 1. Parameters for DDQN

Parameter	Value
Discount factor	0.99
Training frequency	4 step
gradient steps	1
Batch size	32
Update interval for target network	800 step
Size of ERM	120000

Table 2. Parameters for Adam

Parameter	Value
Learning rate α	10^{-5}
Exp. decay rate for:	
the 1st moment β_1	0.9
the 2nd moment β_2	0.999

storage nodes of their materials and can drop off their carried materials when they reach their designated location ready to unload. We set $|C_1| = |C_3| = 4$ and $|C_2| = |C_4| = 2$ because carrying subtasks are time-consuming in transporting materials to task locations. When a task has been completed, it is eliminated and another task appears somewhere in V to maintain the number of incomplete tasks K. The time limit for each task is $W = 16$; because $L = 4$, $\omega = 5$. We also set $\delta = 0.9$ and $H = 1000$ for parameters of trajectory.

The parameter values for DDQN are listed in Table 1. We used ε-greedy strategy with linear decay, i.e., the value of ε linearly decreased from 1 to 0.05 until $t = 2,000,000$ and then was subsequently fixed to $\varepsilon = 0.05$. The length of one episode was 1,000 steps. We used the Adam optimizer, whose parameter values are listed in Table 2. We set team reward as $r = 1$, individual rewards as $r_1(0) = 1$ ($r_2(0) = 0$) and the reward boundary time B_r to 4000 episodes ($t = 4,000,000$); thus, $r_1(t)$ was linearly inclined until 4000 episodes. The experimental results shown below are acquired during 1 episode with $\varepsilon = 0$ without learning after each episode.

We compare the results to those with three static reward assignments (RA), RA1, RA2 and RA3, where $r_1 = 0$ and $r_2 = 1$ in RA1, $r_1 = 1$ and $r_2 = 0$ in RA2, and $r_1 = r_2 = 0.5$ in RA3. RA1 was the natural and intuitive reward assignment because only a team reward is provided after a task is completed. RA2 was set on the opposite spectrum, with the assumption that efficient execution of each subtask should increase overall efficiency. RA3 aimed to enable agents to learn both the efficient executions of their own subtasks and the completions of the tasks. Note that agents had the proposed ERM with HQ when RA3 was used.

5.2 Performance Evaluation

We conducted experiments using the sequential tasks (Fig. 2a) in Experiment 1 (Exp. 1) and the partially ordered tasks (Fig. 2b) in Exp. 2 once for each. In Fig. 4 we plotted the moving average of 200 episodes of the number of completed tasks per episode until 20,000 episodes in Exp. 1 and 30,000 episodes in Exp. 2.

This figure clearly indicates that the proposed S2RA outperformed the other reward assignments RA1, RA2, and RA3. First the results of RA1 show that

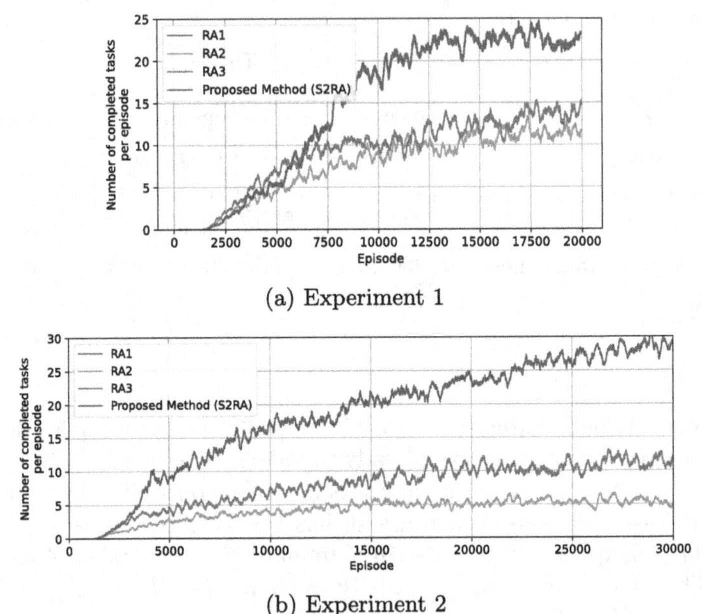

(a) Experiment 1

(b) Experiment 2

Fig. 4. Result: Number of Completed Tasks Per Episode. (Color figure online)

learning did not progress only with the final team rewards in Exps. 1 and 2 and the number of completed tasks was almost zero throughout all steps. (This may be difficult to observe from the figure.) This occurred because all agents except the c_4-class agents were not rewarded for executing their own subtasks, and as a result, all agents remained in random actions. The agents in C_4 that executed the last subtasks could receive the reward $r = r_1(t) + r_2(t)$ immediately, but fundamentally did not have the chances to learn. Therefore, we can say that learning was difficult for agents only from team rewards.

Meanwhile, in RA2 (orange line in Fig. 4), which only provided only individual rewards regardless of the success or failure of tasks, agents were able to complete more tasks than that in RA1, but fewer tasks were still completed. Agents learned only the actions for their own subtasks. Therefore, the subsequent agents did have chances to learn, which increased the number of tasks completed, but could not complete the subtasks within the time limit. Moreover, agents concentrated only on their subtasks and were not interested in the actions of the subsequent agents, which did not produce cooperative behavior. This phenomenon suggested that careful attention to subsequent agents must be incorporated into agents' behaviors.

In RA3, agents were able to receive individual rewards and residual rewards and could learn some degree of coordinated behaviors as well as behaviors for their own subtasks to enhance the completion of tasks. However, the performance was limited because their learned behavior was insufficient to execute tasks efficiently. In contrast, with the proposed reward scheme S2RA, agents were able to execute the sequential tasks with better efficiency, In this scheme, individual rewards $r_1(t)$ became 0 after 4000 episodes, but Fig. 4 indicates that the performance continued to improve subsequently. Thus, we conclude that agents were able to learn that both behaviors were essential to receive team rewards until 4000 episodes, and then continued to learn to receive more rewards.

Comparing the results of two experiments, learning was slightly slower in Exp. 2. This is due to the ambiguity in the order (i.e., *or* condition), which made learning somewhat difficult. However, even in this case, the proposed scheme achieved good performance.

Table 3. Appearance rate of Agent(s) for next Subtask(s) within O_i.

Agent class	Reward scheme	Appearance rate (Env. 1)	Appearance rate (Env. 2)
c_1	S2RA (proposed)	81.3%	84.5%
	RA3	24.6%	14.8%
c_2	S2RA (proposed)	96.7%	98.6%
	RA3	61.7%	55.1%
c_3	S2RA (proposed)	97.5%	95.8%
	RA3	72.5%	55.8%

5.3 Analysis of Cooperative Behaviors for Subsequent Agents

To understand the use of cooperative behaviors to improve performance, we analyzed the condition in which the success rate of task completion reached a high level before the time limit. Then, we found that if agent i executed its own subtask when the agents that were responsible for the subsequent subtasks were in its observable range, the success rate for task completion within the time limit was quite high. For example, in Exp. 1, when agents executed their own subtask after the agents responsible for the subsequent tasks appeared in i's observable range O_i, the success rates of the next subtasks during the last 100 episodes were 46.82% in S2RA and 32.78% in RA3, whereas they dropped to 0.84% in S2RA and 0.39% in RA3 when not in the observable range.

Therefore, we counted the number of times that when each agent i performed a task, the agents responsible for the subsequent subtasks appeared or did not appear in its range of observation O_i. The appearance rates for each agent class are listed in Table 3. Because in Exp. 2, c_1-class agents have two subsequent subtasks belonging to two different classes, we counted only the case that both agents in these classes were in O_i. Note that because the c_4-class agents had no subsequent subtasks, their data are not shown in this table.

Table 3 indicates the quite different learned behaviors of agents in S2RA and RA3; that is, because the appearance rate of agents in S2RA was high, agents seemed to almost always wait for subsequent agent(s) to enter O_i before they executed their own subtask. This *wait* action seemed to be a kind of cooperative behavior to facilitate the subsequent subtasks but was not superficially beneficial for agents belonging c_1-, c_2-, and c_3-classes because it reduced the number of completions of their subtasks. Of course, the system's objective is to complete as many tasks as possible, but in RA1, i.e., simply giving the reward when a task was completed did not perform well to learn efficient executions.

Although agents in the RA3 scheme also learned the *wait* action for cooperation, the appearance rate, which also indicates of occurrence of the cooperative behavior of agents was low in both experiments. In particular, the appearance rate of c_1-class agents in RA3, especially in Exp. 2, was much lower than others because c_1-class agents could receive a reward of 0.5 even if they ignored the subsequent subtasks and c_1 agents were required to wait for two agents belonging to c_2 and c_3 classes in Exp. 2. Note that we only show the results of RA3 because RA1 and RA2 showed poorer performance.

5.4 Discussion

Our experimental results clearly indicate that agents in S2RA exhibited better performance than those of agents in other static reward schemes, RA1, RA3, and RA3. The proposed S2RA allows agents to focus on training their own subtasks in the early stages of learning to deal with sparse reward problems as in our tasks, as shown in Fig. 2, while at the same time giving the subsequent agents chances to train. After that, $r_2(t)$ gradually increased and the learning process shifted to one, in which cooperative behavior was also considered to complete all the subtasks by facilitating other agents' subtasks. Finally, all agents were able to obtain both behaviors in a balanced manner.

Another important benefit of S2RA is that because only the team rewards are given to the involved agents for task completion, the converged reward assignment is *consistent* with the original objective of the tasks; this feature is preferable for practical applications. In contrast, Fig. 4 suggests that learning speed of agents in S2RA is not fast enough probably because progress of learning is different depending on the order of executions of subtasks. Finally, we observed that the strategy of dividing agents into groups with different functions and always having them move together as groups could not be used or was inefficient in our target tasks. This was because our task contained carrying subtasks in which agents were required to move between storage areas and unloaded nodes. Movement as a group seems to have been quite wasteful, especially for c_2- and c_4-class agents.

6 Conclusion

We have proposed a reward allocation method, S2RA, for sequentially or partially ordered tasks which consist of a number of subtasks that should be executed in a certain order by agents with different capabilities, to learn efficient behaviors by decentralized MADRL. Agents are required to learn behaviors both for their own subtasks and cooperative behavior to facilitate other cooperative agents. S2RA provides the rewards in two stages, including both individual rewards received when agents complete the execution of subtasks for which they are responsible and residual rewards received when all subtasks are completed. Then, individual rewards are gradually reduced to enhance the coordinated behaviors. Our experimental results indicate that agents were able to learn balanced behaviors in S2RA.

One issue in S2RA is learning speed; this is because the appropriate speed of varying the ratio of shifting individual rewards to residual rewards may depend on the sequence length of subtasks owing to the variation in the progress of learning among agents. Thus, we plan to study agents that autonomously determine their speed according to their learning progress in future work.

References

1. Chang, Y.H., Ho, T., Kaelbling, L.P.: All learning is local: multi-agent learning in global reward games. In: Proceedings of the 16th International Conference on Neural Information Processing Systems, pp. 807–814. NIPS2003, MIT Press, Cambridge, MA, USA (2003)
2. Diallo, E.A.O., Sugiyama, A., Sugawara, T.: Learning to coordinate with deep reinforcement learning in doubles pong game. In: 2017 16th IEEE International Conference on Machine Learning and Applications (ICMLA), pp. 14–19. IEEE (2017)
3. Du, Y., Han, L., Fang, M., Liu, J., Dai, T., Tao, D.: LIIR: Learning individual intrinsic reward in multi-agent reinforcement learning. In: Wallach, H., Larochelle, H., Beygelzimer, A., d'Alché-Buc, F., Fox, E., Garnett, R. (eds.) Advances in Neural Information Processing Systems, vol. 32. Curran Associates Inc. (2019)
4. Foerster, J.N., Assael, Y.M., de Freitas, N., Whiteson, S.: Learning to communicate with deep multi-agent reinforcement learning. In: Proceedings of the 30th International Conference on Neural Information Processing Systems, pp. 2145–2153. NIPS2016, Curran Associates Inc., Red Hook, NY, USA (2016)
5. Lowe, R., Wu, Y., Tamar, A., Harb, J., Abbeel, P., Mordatch, I.: Multi-agent actor-critic for mixed cooperative-competitive environments. In: Proceedings of the 31st International Conference on Neural Information Processing Systems, pp. 6382–6393. NIPS2017, Curran Associates Inc., Red Hook, NY, USA (2017)
6. Miyashita, Y., Sugawara, T.: Coordinated behavior for sequential cooperative task using two-stage reward assignment with decay. In: Yang, H., Pasupa, K., Leung, A.C.-S., Kwok, J.T., Chan, J.H., King, I. (eds.) ICONIP 2020. LNCS, vol. 12533, pp. 257–269. Springer, Cham (2020). https://doi.org/10.1007/978-3-030-63833-7_22
7. Mnih, V., et al.: Playing atari with deep reinforcement learning. arXiv preprint arXiv:1312.5602 (2013)
8. Ng, A.Y., Harada, D., Russell, S.J.: Policy invariance under reward transformations: theory and application to reward shaping. In: Proceedings of the 16th International Conference on Machine Learning, pp. 278–287 (1999)
9. Ng, A.Y., Russell, S.J.: Algorithms for inverse reinforcement learning. In: Proceedings of the 17th International Conference on Machine Learning, pp. 663–670 (2000)

10. Tampuu, A., et al.: Multiagent cooperation and competition with deep reinforcement learning. PLoS ONE **12**(4), e0172395 (2017)
11. Tan, M.: Multi-agent reinforcement learning: independent vs. cooperative agents. In: Proceedings of the Tenth International Conference on Machine Learning, pp. 330–337 (1993)
12. Van Hasselt, H., Guez, A., Silver, D.: Deep reinforcement learning with double Q-learning. In: Proceedings of the AAAI Conference on Artificial Intelligence, vol. 30 (2016)
13. Vinyals, O., et al.: Grandmaster level in StarCraft II using multi-agent reinforcement learning. Nature **575**(7782), 350–354 (2019)
14. Zhou, M., Liu, Z., Sui, P., Li, Y., Chung, Y.Y.: Learning implicit credit assignment for cooperative multi-agent reinforcement learning. In: Advance in Neural Information Processing Systems, vol. 33, pp. 11853–11864. Curran Associates Inc., (2020)

Mitigating Fairness and Efficiency Tradeoff in Vehicle-Dispatch Problems

Masato Ota[1], Yuko Sakurai[2(✉)], Mingyu Guo[3], and Itsuki Noda[4]

[1] Information Services International-Dentsu Ltd., Tokyo, Japan
[2] Nagoya Institute of Technology, Nagoya, Japan
sakurai@nitech.ac.jp
[3] The University of Adelaide, Adelaide, Australia
mingyu.guo@adelaide.edu.au
[4] Hokkaido University, Sapporo, Japan
i.noda@ist.hokudai.ac.jp

Abstract. We propose a fair-assignment algorithm between vehicles and passengers to mitigate the efficiency and fairness tradeoff for on-demand ride-hailing platforms. Ride-hailing platforms connect passengers and drivers in real time. While most studies focused on developing an optimally efficient assignment method for maximizing the profit of the platform, optimal efficiency may lead to profit inequality for drivers. Therefore, fair-assignment algorithms have begun to attract attention from artificial-intelligence researchers. While a fair-assignment algorithm based on max-min fairness, which is a representative concept of fairness, has been proposed, profit inequality among drivers still remains when assignments are made multiple times. To address such inequality, we develop a fair-assignment algorithm called the priority assignment algorithm $PA(k)$ to give priority to drivers with low cumulative profit then generate an optimally efficient assignment for the remaining drivers and passengers. We also develop a method of dynamically determining the number of priorities at each assignment. We experimentally demonstrated that $PA(k)$ outperforms the existing fair assignment algorithms in both efficiency and fairness in the case of excess supply by using a real-world dataset.

Keywords: On-demand vehicle-dispatch algorithm · Fairness · Efficiency

1 Introduction

Ride-hailing platforms provide a service that matches passengers with vehicles on demand via websites and mobile apps. The market for ride-hailing services throughout the world has continued to grow. Although ride-hailing platforms took a hard hit due to the COVID-19 pandemic, these platforms have quickly adapted by introducing new services such as on-demand delivery for stay-at-home orders. The need for such new on-demand delivery services is expected

© The Author(s), under exclusive license to Springer Nature Switzerland AG 2022
F. Dignum et al. (Eds.): PAAMS 2022, LNAI 13616, pp. 307–319, 2022.
https://doi.org/10.1007/978-3-031-18192-4_25

to continue expanding. Thus, the vehicle-dispatch problem for ride-hailing platforms is an important issue from the industrial and academic perspectives. We investigated the tradeoff between efficiency and fairness in ride-hailing platforms.

Traditionally, the vehicle-dispatch problem for ride-hailing platforms has been formalized as an optimization problem that maximizes the profit obtained by the platform. Even if we focus on studies addressing the vehicle-dispatch problem, various research results have been published with the purpose of obtaining an optimally efficient matching (i.e., assignment) between drivers and passengers [3,4]. For example, Zhang *et al.* (2017) formulated the vehicle-dispatch problem as a combinatorial optimization problem with the goal of maximizing the total success rate of orders. Methods based on reinforcement learning have also been explored [2]. Xu *et al.* (2018) proposed a reinforcement-learning method with which the decision of assigning a request to a vehicle is determined by solving the centralized optimization problem of optimizing the global profit. Newer methods formalize the vehicle-dispatch problem by using the multi-agent reinforcement-learning approach, with which agents share a centralized judge that rates their actions and updates their policies [6,11]. The most recent approach formalizes the vehicle-dispatch problem by using the multi-agent reinforcement learning method, where agents share a centralized judge that rates their actions and updates their policies [6,11]. A stable matching model was proposed when drivers and passengers have particular preferences for each other to maximize the total profit and minimize the number of blocking pairs under known identical independent distributions (KIIDs) [10].

Studies that considered fairness among drivers, using a fairness criterion defined in economics or game theory [1], have attracted much attention in artificial-intelligence research fields. For example, Suhr *et al.* (2019) proposed a fairness criterion based on the idea that all drivers should receive profits proportional to the amount of time they are active on the platform [8]. Lesmana *et al.* (2019) developed a fair-assignment algorithm called REASSIGN based on max-min fairness [5]. Max-min fairness is a common fair criterion. In computational experiments, the authors showed that REASSIGN also increased the worst-off driver's revenue over 6 times that of an optimally efficient assignment for a single-round assignment. Nand *et al.* (2020) introduced existence probability, which captures the potential acceptance rate for each pair of a driver and request type, and developed a flexible assignment algorithm that balances fairness and profit when there is over-demand under KIIDs [7]. There exit various tradeoff in the vehicle-dispatch problem. For example, to capture the tradeoff between the waiting time and assignment quality, Wang and Bei (2022) proposed a driver-request real-time assignment model, in which both drivers and riding requests arrive in an online fashion, and the model is allowed to make driver-request assignments at any time [9].

We develop a fair-assignment algorithm called priority-assignment algorithm ($PA(k)$) that increases the lowest global revenue of a driver. While Lesmana *et al.* (2019) developed REASSIGN based on max-min fairness as mentioned above, we experimentally found that when we consider a multiple-round assignment setting in which assignments are sequentially generated in a time horizon, REASSIGN may not always improve the worst-off driver's revenue in the end. In the case of excess supply where the number of available drivers exceeds the number of valid requests, once a driver is placed lowest in terms of historical utility, she may never again be assigned to any other request.

To overcome this issue, $PA(k)$ gives priority to the lowest k drivers in terms of historical utility. Each driver, from the lowest to the k-th lowest, selects the request that maximizes her immediate trip utility among all existing requests. After completing this procedure, we determine the optimally efficient assignment for the remaining drivers and requests. Theoretical analysis of $PA(k)$ shows that the reduction in its efficiency from the optimally efficient assignment is not larger than the max-min fairness assignment in the worst case. In $PA(k)$, the number of priorities affects efficiency. Thus, we dynamically determine the number of priorities by considering the difference between the increase and decrease in drivers' profits.

We finally evaluate the performance of $PA(k)$ by comparing it with other fair-assignment algorithms by using a New York City taxi dataset. We use the Gini coefficient, which is a common metric in economics to measure the inequality among nations, companies, and so on. Our proposed algorithm mitigates the efficiency-fairness tradeoff compared with the other algorithms when the number of drivers exceeds the number of requests.

2 Preliminaries

We now present the problem setting considered in this paper. On the basis of several studies on the vehicle-dispatch problem, we model the problem as a bipartite graph in which one side is for drivers and the other is for requests from passengers.

We consider a multi-time assignment problem. We divide the time horizon (e.g., one day) into T short periods (e.g., 30 seconds) in advance. We denote the time index as $t \in \{1, \ldots, T\}$. We collect the requests during one period then determine an assignment between the available drivers and collected requests. We eventually evaluate the global profit and fairness obtained by serving requests in a time horizon.

Let us define $G_t = (D_t \cup C_t, E_t)$ as a bipartite graph at each time t. Let D_t ($|D_t| = m_t$) be the set of available drivers (vehicles) at t and C_t ($|C_t| = n_t$) be the set of collected passengers' requests at t. Let $E_t \subseteq \{\{d_i, c_j\} : d_i \in D_t, c_j \in C_t\}$ be the set of edges. We put no restriction on the structure of the graph, that is, the graph is not always a complete bipartite graph. If driver d_i cannot serve request c_j because of the inability to satisfy a specific assignment constraint such as driver type or number of available seats (e.g., [5,7]), there does not exist an edge between d_i and c_j. Furthermore, we define D ($|D| = m$) and C ($|C| = n$) as the set of available drivers and collected requests in a finite time horizon, respectively. We also assume a single-ride setting. When a d_i is assigned to a c_j, d_i is unavailable while serving c_j and becomes available again after completing

c_j. Regarding a cancellation condition created by the passenger, we assume that a passenger will withdraw her c_j if she has not been assigned to any driver for a predetermined number of consecutive times.

We define two utilities: *historical utility* $h_t(d_i)$ and *immediate trip utility* $w_t(\{d_i, c_j\})$. For simplicity, we denote $w_t(d_i, c_j) = w_t(\{d_i, c_j\})$. The $w_t(d_i, c_j)$ is the trip utility at t that d_i receives by serving c_j. $h_t(d_i)$ indicates the accumulated trip utilities that d_i has obtained by serving the assigned requests until the previous time $t-1$.

Vehicle-dispatch problem instance $\mathcal{I}_t$ consists of a setting at each t with $G_t = (D_t \cup C_t, E_t)$, a set of historical utilities $\{h_t(d_i)\}_{d_i \in D_t}$, and a set of immediate trip utilities $\{w_t(d_i, c_j)\}_{\{d_i, c_j\} \in E_t}$. For this instance, the goal of a ride-hailing platform at t is to generate a matching (i.e., assignment) M_t satisfying two conditions: (1) each driver $d_i \in D_t$ is assigned to at most one request and (2) each request $c_j \in C_t$ is assigned to at most one driver. Let us define $\mathcal{M}_t$ as the set of all feasible assignments. The efficiency of a platform when M_t is generated is as follows. We assume that $\forall \{d_i, c_j\} \notin M_t$, $w_t(d_i, c_j) = 0$, where

$$G(M_t) = \sum_{d_i \in D_t} h_t(d_i) + \sum_{\{d_i, c_j\} \in M_t} w_t(d_i, c_j). \tag{1}$$

From the definition of $G(M_t)$, we define an assignment that maximizes the sum of immediate trip utilities $w_t(\{d_i, c_j\})$ as an optimally efficient assignment. In afterwards, we denote it briefly by an optimal assignment.

Definition 1. For vehicle-dispatch problem instance $\mathcal{I}_t$, an optimally efficient assignment (optimal assignment) $M_{t,OPT}$ satisfies

$$\max_{M_t \in \mathcal{M}_t} \sum_{\{d_i, c_j\} \in M_t} w_t(d_i, c_j). \tag{2}$$

As discussed in Sect. 1, various fairness criteria for ride-hailing platforms have been studied. Which fairness criterion to apply in determining an assignment is important for platforms, drivers, and passengers because it directly affects them. If low profit for drivers or inconvenience for passengers increases due to introducing a fairness criterion, no one would want to use such a platform. Max-min fairness has been widely used in many applications [5].

Definition 2. For vehicle-dispatch problem instance $\mathcal{I}_t$, a max-min fair assignment $M_{t,MF}$ satisfies

$$\max_{M' \in \mathcal{M}_t} \min_{d_i \in D_t} \{h_t(d_i) + w_t(d_i, c_j)\}. \tag{3}$$

Max-min fairness maximizes the least $h_t(d_i) + w_t(d_i, c_j)$ for all available drivers.

Example 1. Let us assume there exist 4 drivers and 3 requests at t as shown in Fig. 1. The value on the left side of d_i represents historical utility $h_t(d_i)$, and that on an edge represents the immediate trip utility $w_t(d_i, c_j)$. In this

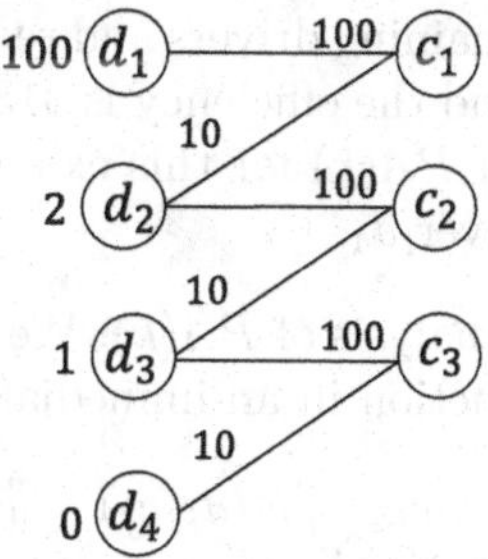

Fig. 1. Example of vehicle-dispatch problem instance

case, we have four possible matching results: $\{\{d_1, c_1\}, \{d_2, c_2\}, \{d_3, c_3\}\}$ with $200 + 102 + 101 + 0 = 403$, $\{\{d_1, c_1\}, \{d_2, c_2\}, \{d_4, c_3\}\}$ with $200 + 102 + 1 + 10 = 313$, $\{\{d_1, c_1\}, \{d_3, c_2\}, \{d_4, c_3\}\}$ with $200 + 2 + 11 + 10 = 223$, and $\{\{d_2, c_1\}, \{d_3, c_2\}, \{d_4, c_3\}\}$ with $100 + 12 + 11 + 10 = 133$. No request goes to d_4 in the first result, no request goes to d_3 in the second result, and so on.

The optimal assignment is obtained by $M_{t,OPT} = \{\{d_1, c_1\}, \{d_2, c_2\}, \{d_3, c_3\}\}$ with $G(M_{t,OPT}) = 403$. For max-min fair assignment, we obtain $M_{t,MF} = \{\{d_2, c_1\}, \{d_3, c_2\}, \{d_4, c_3\}\}$ with $G(M_{t,MF}) = 133$. This result is obtained as follows. The least $h_t(d_i) + w_t(d_i, c_j)$ in each matching result is 0, 2, 0 and 10, respectively. Thus, we determine $\{\{d_2, c_1\}, \{d_3, c_2\}, \{d_4, c_3\}\}$ as max-min fair assignment $M_{t,MF}$ because the highest value among 0, 2, 0 and 10 is 10.

3 Proposed Algorithm: *PA*(*k*)

In this section, we present $PA(k)$. The main idea with $PA(k)$ is to give priority to the worst vehicle with the lowest historical utility then assign the best request to that vehicle.

3.1 *PA*(*k*) Algorithm

The procedure of $PA(k)$ for drivers with the lowest k historical utilities is defined as follows:

1. Determine a priority list of available drivers in accordance with the increasing order of historical utility. If there exist multiple drivers with the same historical utility, determine the order randomly. From the worst-off driver to the k-th lowest driver in respect of historical utility, each driver is assigned to her best request, which provides the highest immediate trip utility among all available requests.
2. For the remaining drivers and requests, we determine an optimal assignment.

Example 2. Let us consider how $PA(k)$ works when we set $k = 1$ for the example in Fig. 1. It first selects d_4 and assigns c_3 to this driver. Next, it determines the optimal assignment for the remaining drivers and requests. As a result, it outputs $\{\{d_1, c_1\}, \{d_2, c_2\}, \{d_4, c_3\}\}$, and the efficiency is 313. Compared with the results in Example 1, the efficiency of $PA(k)$ for this example is better than $M_{t,MF}$ in still selecting the worst-off driver d_4.

We conduct a theoretical analysis of $PA(k)$. We first introduce the notations to indicate the maximum reduction in an immediate trip utility among drivers.

$$\delta = \max_{d_i \in D_t} \max_{c_j, c_{j'} \in C_t} |w_t(d_i, c_j) - w_t(d_i, c_{j'})| \tag{4}$$

Theorem 1. *For vehicle-dispatch problem instance $\mathcal{I}_t$, compared with the optimal assignment $G(M_{t,OPT})$, $G(M_{t,PA(k)})$ does not decrease more than k times the maximum immediate trip utility difference for the same request among all requests. Mathematically,*

$$G(M_{t,PA(k)}) \geq G(M_{t,OPT}) - k \times \delta. \tag{5}$$

Proof. For simplicity, we show the proof when $k = 1$, i.e., $PA(1)$. $PA(1)$ first assigns the worst-off driver with the lowest historical utility to the best request for her. Let such a driver be d_i. We assume that c_j is assigned to d_i in an optimal assignment and $c_{j'}$ is assigned to her in $PA(1)$. We also assume that $c_{j'}$ is assigned to $d_{i'}$ in an optimal assignment and c_j is assigned to her in $PA(1)$. Under these assumptions, we have the following inequality.

$$\begin{aligned} G(M_{t,PA(1)}) &\geq G(M_{t,OPT}) - \{w_t(d_i, c_j) + w_t(d_{i'}, c_{j'})\} \\ &\quad + \{w_t(d_i, c_{j'}) + w_t(d_{i'}, c_j)\} && (6) \\ &= G(M_{t,OPT}) + \{w_t(d_i, c_{j'}) - w_t(d_i, c_j)\} \\ &\quad - \{w_t(d_{i'}, c_{j'}) - w_t(d_{i'}, c_j)\} && (7) \\ &\geq G(M_{t,OPT}) - \delta. && (8) \end{aligned}$$

In (7), $w_t(d_i, c_{j'}) - w_t(d_i, c_j)$ indicates the increase in profit for d_i by changing from an optimal assignment to PA(1). However, $w_t(d_{i'}, c_{j'}) - w_t(d_{i'}, c_j)$ indicates the reduction in profit for $d_{i'}$ by changing from an optimal assignment to $PA(1)$. In $PA(1)$, the sum of profits among the other drivers except d_i is not lower than $G(M_{t,OPT}) - \{w_t(d_{i'}, c_{j'}) - w_t(d_{i'}, c_j)\}$, because $PA(1)$ generates an optimal assignment among all possible assignments for the other drivers except d_i. Furthermore, $\{w_t(d_{i'}, c_{j'}) - w_t(d_{i'}, c_j)\} \leq \delta$ holds.

In a similar manner, we give the proof for $PA(k)$ and we obtain at most $k \times \delta$ as a reduction from $G(M_{t,OPT})$ to $G(M_{t,PA(k)})$. □

Theorem 2. *For vehicle-dispatch problem setting $\mathcal{I}_t$, compared with the optimal assignment $G(M_{t,OPT})$, max-min fair assignment $G(M_{t,MF})$ does not decrease more than n_t times the maximum immediate trip utility difference for the same request among all requests. Mathematically,*

$$G(M_{t,MF}) \geq G(M_{t,OPT}) - \min\{m_t - 1, n_t\} \times \delta. \tag{9}$$

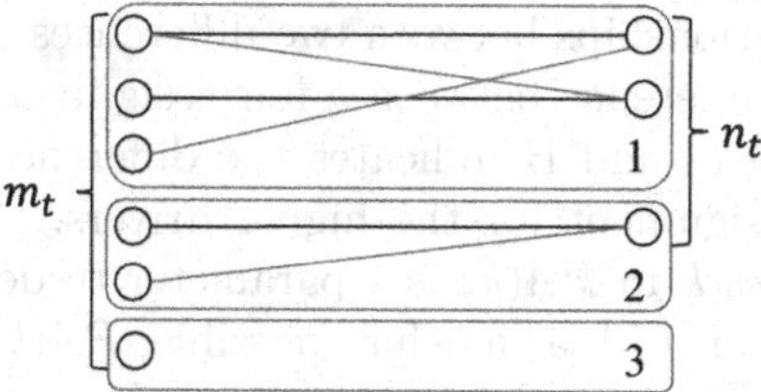

Fig. 2. Change from optimal assignment (black line) to max-min fair assignment (blue line)

Proof. We first consider when $m_t \leq n_t$. When we change from an optimal assignment to max-min fair assignment, at least one driver who has the lowest historical utility increase her immediate trip utility. Thus, we obtain $G(M_{t,OPT}) - G(M_{t,MF}) \leq (m_t - 1)\delta$.

We then consider when $m_t > n_t$. We divide the drivers and requests into groups so that the drivers whose requests are swapped by changing from an optimal assignment to max-min fair assignment belong to the identical group. Figure 2 shows such an example in which the drivers and requests are divided into three groups. We obtain the following facts from this figure. First, in each group, at most one driver has no assignment. Next, in each group, at least one driver increases her immediate trip utility for max-min fair assignment. Finally, the number of groups in which more than one driver join is at most n_t. From these facts, when we assume that the number of groups in which more than one driver join is l, the number of drivers who belong to these groups is at most n_t+l. Among at most n_t+l drivers, the number of drivers whose immediate trip utility is reduced by changing an optimal assignment to max-min fair assignment is at most n_t because at least one driver in each group reduces her immediate trip utility. As a result, we obtain (9). □

From these two theorems, we prove that the efficiency obtained with $PA(k)$ is not lower than the efficiency obtained by max-min fair assignment. The number k in $PA(k)$ indicate the degree of fairness. When we set $k = 0$, it implies the optimal assignment. In other word, we do not consider fairness in an allocation. When we set $k = \min\{m_t, n_t\}$, it implies the fairest assignment, but the efficiency is the worst. Also, it becomes equivalent to worst-off driver first (WODF) discussed in a previous study [8].

We have to determine k in $PA(k)$ as the number of priorities to give drivers. While it is simple to always fix k, it is desirable to determine k at each t depending on the relationships between efficiency and fairness. Thus, we develop a method of dynamically determining k in $PA(k)$ to give drivers at each t. Figure 3 shows an ascending order of driver profit earned by lowest to highest drivers for an optimal assignment (blue line) and fair assignment (red line). While a fair-assignment algorithm such as $PA(k)$ increases the profit for the lower drivers from an optimal assignment, it reduces the profit for the higher drivers. We focus on the relationships between the profits for lower and higher drivers.

We consider the relationships between two differences denoted as L and H in Fig. 3. L indicated the difference between a fair assignment and optimal assignment for the lower drivers and H indicates the difference between an optimal assignment and fair assignment for the higher drivers. Intuitively, our idea is that number of priorities k in $PA(k)$ is a parameter to determine how much of H moves to L. If we shift H to L as much as possible, $PA(k)$ generates the fairest assignment for $PA(k)$ by setting $k = \min\{m_t, n_t\}$. However, if we shift all of L to H, $PA(k)$ generates an optimal assignment by setting $k = 0$.

3.2 Method of Dynamically Determining k

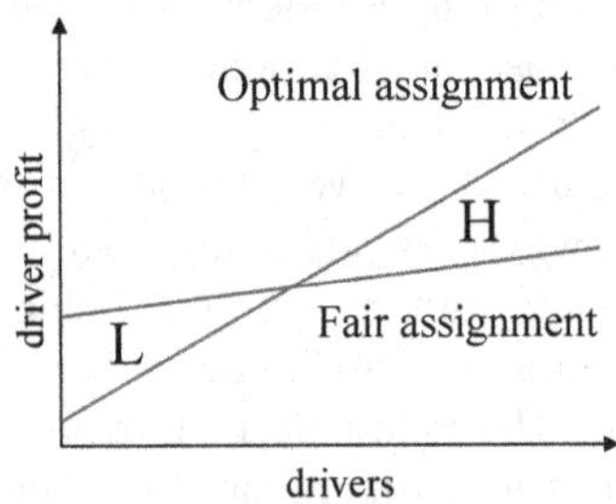

Fig. 3. Relationships between optimal assignment and fair assignment

We define several notations. Let $M_t^{\leq k}$ and $M_t^{>k}$ be matching results from 1-st to k-th lowest drivers and $k+1$-st to $|M_t|$-th lowest drivers in terms of historical utility, respectively. Here, $|M_t|$ is the number of pairs in M_t. Let W denote the average immediate travel utility for the k drivers from 1. Mathematically, we define $M_t^{\leq k}$ and $M_t^{>k}$ as follows.

$$W_{\leq k}(M_t) = \frac{1}{k} \sum_{\{d_i, c_j\} \in M_t^{\leq k}} w_t(d_i, c_j) \tag{10}$$

$$W_{>k}(M_t) = \frac{1}{\min\{m_t, n_t\} - k} \sum_{\{d_i, c_j\} \in M_t^{>k}} w_t(d_i, c_j) \tag{11}$$

When we apply $PA(k)$, i.e., $M_t = M_{t,PA(k)}$, $W_{\leq k}(M_t)$ is the average immediate travel utility among the k drivers who obtain the best request among all remaining available requests and $W_{>k}(M_t)$ is the average immediate travel utility for the other drivers whose assignments are determined on the basis of the optimal assignment rule. Let L denote $W_{\leq k}(M_{t,PA(k)}) - W_{\leq k}(M_{t,OPT})$ and H denote $W_{>k}(M_{t,OPT}) - W_{>k}(M_{t,PA(k)})$.

We are ready to give the formulation to dynamically determine k.

$$k = \arg \max_{k' \leq \min\{m_t, n_t\}} \{\lambda L - (1-\lambda)H\}, \text{where } \lambda \in [0.5, 1] \tag{12}$$

Here, λ indicates the parameter to prioritize efficiency or fairness. A ride-hailing platform prefers efficiency to fairness when λ is small and vice versa when λ is large. While λ is determined in advance, k is dynamically determined depending on λ. We call $PA(k)$ that dynamically determines k on the basis of Formulation (12) with λ as $DPA_\lambda(k)$.

4 Experimental Results

We experimentally evaluated the obtained global efficiency and fairness of the algorithm discussed in this paper. All problem instances were solved using a workstation equipped with an Intel Xeon Gold 6148 (27.5M Cache, 2.40 GHz, 20-Core) with 384-GiB DDR4, 2666-MHz RDIMM (ECC), and CentOS 7.5.

4.1 Experimental Setup

Algorithms: We compared the performances of the following algorithms: an optimal assignment, WODF ($PA(\min\{m_t, n_t\})$), REASSIGN, and different versions of $PA(k)$: $PA(1)$, $DPA_{0.5}(k)$, $DPA_{0.7}(k)$, and $DPA_{0.9}(k)$. Note that we run REASSIGN released by the authors and set a fairness threshold that outputs an optimally fair assignment.
Real-World Dataset: We solved the vehicle-dispatch problem by using a publicly available dataset of yellow taxi trips in New York City for 5 days in July 2013[1]. This dataset contains the times and locations of trip origins and destinations, fares, and trip distances for all requests served by the taxis. We selected a 4-hour horizon from 8:00 to 12:00, which includes the peak morning hours. The number of zones is 66. The average trip distances in March and April 2018 were 1.72 and 1.75 miles with standard deviations of 1.36 and 1.37, respectively. We set 15.534 mph as the speed of the taxies. The initial location of each taxi was randomly chosen from 7 major initial places.
Trip Utility (Profit): There are various methods of calculating an immediate trip utility on the basis of the length of the trip or the shortest trip time. We define the fare per minute R/S required to complete the entire trip as the trip utility, where R represents the fare required to serve a request and S represents the entire trip distance. The S consists of pickup distance and travel distance required by a passenger, i.e., the distance a driver runs to pick up a passenger. This definition indicates that a nearer passenger or request with a longer trip distance means more profit to a driver.
Parameters: We set the number of assignment rounds, $T = 240$. In more detail, we collect the requests within one minute and then determine an assignment. We also assumed that a passenger would withdraw her request if she had been assigned to no driver 5 times in a row. We set the number of requests, $m = 2,000$ and $m = 3,500$. When $m = 2,000$, which is excess demand, the number of valid requests exceeds the number of available drivers for the most assignment rounds.

[1] https://www1.nyc.gov/site/tlc/about/tlc-trip-record-data.page.

When $m = 3,500$, which is excess supply, the number of available drivers exceeds the number of valid requests for the most assignment rounds. For $DPA_\lambda(k)$, we set $\lambda = 0.5, 0.7$, and 0.9.

Table 1. Comparison among algorithms in real-world dataset when $m = 2,000$

Algorithm	Global revenue	Minimum profit	Gini coefficient
Optimal	\$55,3880.75	\$184.5	0.0489
WODF	-4.58%	+21.76%	0.0238
REASSIGN	-0.20%	+7.76%	0.0448
$PA(1)$	-0.12%	+4.69%	0.0475
$DPA_{0.5}(k)$	0.00%	+0.00%	0.0489
$DPA_{0.7}(k)$	-0.48%	+6.68%	0.0403
$DPA_{0.9}(k)$	-0.51%	+3.25 %	0.0413

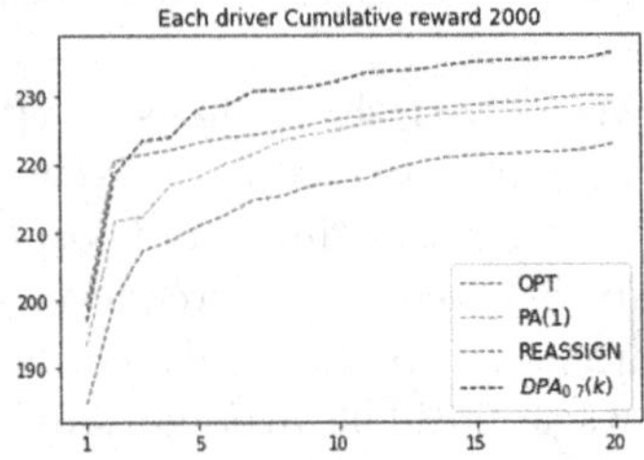

Fig. 4. Average global profit for 20 lowest drivers $m = 2,000$

Evaluation Metrics: We evaluate the global profit, minimum global profit among drivers, and Gini coefficient. The Gini coefficient ranges from 0 to 1, with 0 representing perfect equality and 1 representing perfect inequality. While the global profit indicates efficiency, the minimum global profit and Gini coefficient indicate fairness. A desirable algorithm increases the minimum global profit and Gini coefficient while only slightly decreasing the global profit.

4.2 Experimental Results

Table 1 shows the average results when $m = 2,000$, i.e., excess demand. Regarding the average global profit and the average minimum profit among all drivers, we set the actual value for an optimal assignment and ratio of increase/decrease against an optimal assignment for the other algorithms. WODF improved the minimum profit by about 21%. The issue we pointed out in the Introduction that REASSIGN may not always improve the worst-off driver's revenue in the end

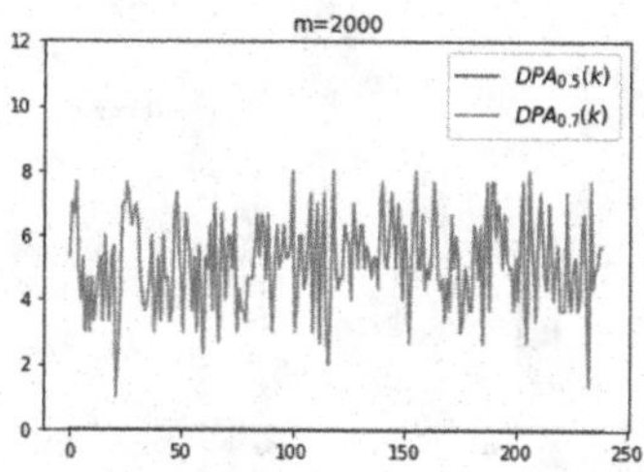

Fig. 5. Average number of priorities k, $m = 2,000$

did not occur in this setting. The balance between global profits and the minimum profits is the best. However, $DPA_{0.7}(k)$ outperforms REASSIGN in terms of the Gini coefficient. Figure 4 shows an ascending order from the lowest to the 20-th lowest global profit. While REASSIGN improved the lowest global profit, $DPA_{0.7}(k)$ improved the others. Figure 5 shows how $DPA_{\lambda}(k)$ determines k for 240 assignment rounds when we set $\lambda = 0.5, 0.7$. $DPA_{0.5}(k)$ generated the same result as an optimal assignment because no priority was given at each round. It shows that $DPA_{\lambda}(k)$ flexibly can determine k depending on the number of available drivers.

Table 2. Comparison among algorithms in real-world dataset when $m = 3,500$

Algorithm	Global profit	Minimum profit	Gini coefficient
Optimal	\$90,2519.04	\$151.16	0.0544
WODF	–5.48%	+18.30%	0.0277
REASSIGN	–0.30%	+7.93%	0.0524
$PA(1)$	–0.09%	+13.67%	0.0521
$DPA_{0.5}(k)$	0.00%	–1.28%	0.0546
$DPA_{0.7}(k)$	–0.36%	+14.88%	0.0481
$DPA_{0.9}(k)$	–0.38%	+15.65 %	0.0481

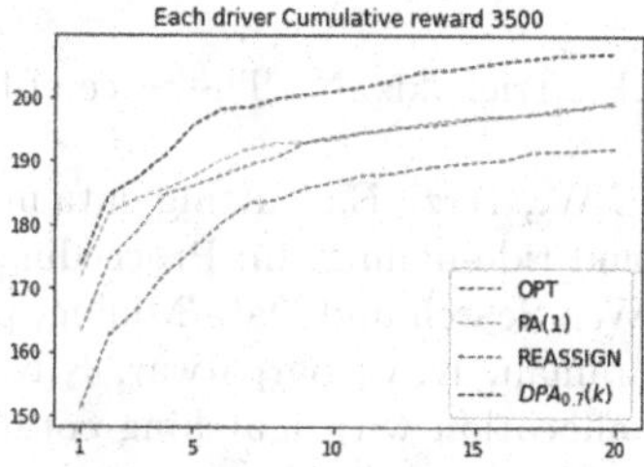

Fig. 6. Average global profit for 20 lowest drivers $m = 3,500$

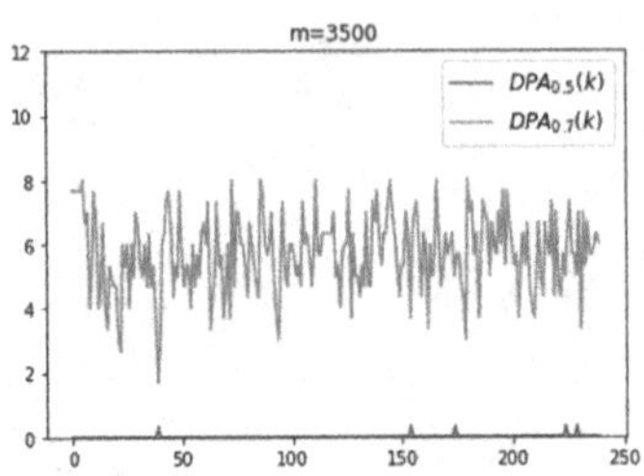

Fig. 7. Average number of priorities k, $m = 3,500$

Table 2 shows the comparison results when $m = 3,500$, i.e., excess supply. In this setting, $PA(1)$ outperforms REASSIGN. Furthermore, $DPA_{0.7}(k)$ improved about twice as much as REASSIGN with respect to the increase of minimum profit while keeping the decrease in global profit within 0.06%. Figure 6 shows that $DPA_{0.7}(k)$ improved the 20-th lowest global profits. Figure 7 shows $DPA_{\lambda}(k)$ is suitable in adjusting k when $m = 2,000$.

5 Conclusions

We developed a fair assignment algorithm called $PA(k)$ to improve the revenue inequality among drivers for the vehicle-dispatch problem in ride-hailing platforms. With $PA(k)$, we prioritize the drivers with low revenue when determining an assignment. We also developed a method of flexibly determining the number of priorities k. We experimentally showed that $PA(k)$ performed the best in terms of the mitigating the tradeoff between efficiency and fairness in the case of excess supply.

Future work will involve investigating another fairness criterion when we consider the preferences of drivers and passengers and integrating a reinforcement learning technique.

Acknowledgments. This work was partially supported by JSPS KAKENHI Grant Numbers JP18H03301, JP17KK0008 and JP18H03299.

References

1. Bertsimas, D., Farias, V.F., Trichakis, N.: The price of fairness. Oper. Res. **59**(1), 17–31 (2011)
2. Chaudhari, H.A., Byers, J.W., Terzi, E.: Putting data in the driver's seat: optimizing earnings for on-demand ride-hailing. In: Proceedings of the 11th ACM International Conference on Web Search and Data Mining, pp. 90–98 (2018)
3. Dickerson, J.P., Sankararaman, K.A., Sarpatwar, K.K., Srinivasan, A., Wu, K., Xu, P.: Online resource allocation with matching constraints. In: Proceedings of the 18th International Conference on Autonomous Agents and MultiAgent Systems (AAMAS-2019), pp. 1681–1689 (2019)

4. Dickerson, J.P., Sankararaman, K.A., Srinivasan, A., Xu, P.: Allocation problems in ride-sharing platforms: online matching with offline reusable resources. In: Proceedings of the 32nd AAAI Conference on Artificial Intelligence (AAAI-2018), pp. 1007–1014 (2018)
5. Lesmana, N.S., Zhang, X., Bei, X.: Balancing efficiency and fairness in on-demand ridesourcing. In: Advances in Neural Information Processing Systems 32, pp. 5309–5319 (2019)
6. Li, M., et al.: Efficient ridesharing order dispatching with mean field multi-agent reinforcement learning. In: Proceeding of the World Wide Web Conference 2019 (WWW-2019), pp. 983–994 (2019)
7. Nanda, V., Xu, P., Sankararaman, K.A., Dickerson, J.P., Srinivasan, A.: Balancing the tradeoff between profit and fairness in rideshare platforms during high-demand hours. In: Proceedings of AAAI-2020, pp. 2210–2217 (2020)
8. Sühr, T., Biega, A.J., Zehlike, M., Gummadi, K.P., Chakraborty, A.: Two-sided fairness for repeated matchings in two-sided markets: 2A case study of a ride-hailing platform. In: Proceedings of the 25th ACM SIGKDD International Conference on Knowledge Discovery & Data Mining (KDD-2019), pp. 3082–3092 (2019)
9. Wang, H., Bei, X.: Real-time driver-request assignment in ridesourcing. In: Proceedings of AAAI-2022 (2022)
10. Zhao, B., Xu, P., Shi, Y., Tong, Y., Zhou, Z., Zeng, Y.: Preference-aware task assignment in on-demand taxi dispatching: an online stable matching approach. In: Proceedings of AAAI-2019, pp. 2245–2252 (2019)
11. Zhou, M., et al.: Multi-agent reinforcement learning for order-dispatching via order-vehicle distribution matching. In: Proceedings of the 28th ACM International Conference on Information and Knowledge Management (CIKM-2019), pp. 2645–2653 (2019)

A Flexible Agent Architecture in SPADE

J. Palanca, J.A Rincon, C. Carrascosa, V. Julian(✉), and A. Terrasa

Valencian Research Institute for Artificial Intelligence (VRAIN),
Universitat Politècnica de València, Camí de Vera s/n, 46022 Valencia, Spain
{jpalanca,jrincon,carrasco,vinglada,aterrasa}@dsic.upv.es

Abstract. For some years now, multi-agent systems have demonstrated their potential to be used as a base technology to address the development of distributed, intelligent and autonomous systems. However, existing agent platforms still require a higher degree of flexibility in order to effectively combine decision-making processes into the same system. In this context, the main goal of this paper is to improve flexibility in the development of behavior-based agents, by means of introducing the Flexible Agent Architecture (FAA). The FAA defines agents in such a way that each agent may integrate and combine different types of reasoning processes (for example, procedural-based and BDI processes) as behaviors. This definition remarkably empowers the global behavior of the agent, by allowing it to combine different, more or less deliberative techniques in its decision making process, in a transparent and flexible way. In addition, the paper presents a full implementation of the proposal in a real agent middleware called SPADE.

Keywords: Artificial intelligence · Multi-agent systems · BDI agents

1 Introduction

Multi-agent systems have been used for the last decades in a multitude of problems where the difficulty lays in the lack of a centralized solution and the need for an intelligent decision making. In that period of time, we have gone from a slight decline in agent technology due to the high expectations of the 90s, to a renewed interest related to the emergence of new, clearly distributed domains such as autonomous cars or drones [17], [13], Internet of Things (IoT) [15], [2], Smart Cities [8], [6], Smart Grids [9] [4], or Cyber Physical Systems [3], [5], where addressing the automation and interconnection of intelligent devices is necessary. In all these domains, agent technology is highly appropriate since it facilitates the emergence of social behaviors or collective intelligence. With regard to the evolution of tools and frameworks for the development of multi-agent systems, new approaches have continued to appear over the last years. In [11], a recent, comprehensive analysis of existing platforms for the development of multi-agent systems is presented. This work concludes with the necessity of being aware of the existing approaches in order to select the framework which best fits each scientific need, as well as encouraging new theoretical and practical developments in the area.

© The Author(s), under exclusive license to Springer Nature Switzerland AG 2022
F. Dignum et al. (Eds.): PAAMS 2022, LNAI 13616, pp. 320–331, 2022.
https://doi.org/10.1007/978-3-031-18192-4_26

According to this, in the opinion of the authors of this paper, one of the key aspects which still needs to improve in order to fit the requirements of the aforementioned new domains is agent architectures. There are many different types of agent architectures, and normally they are oriented towards a particular domain or problem type where they are best suited. In this context, the work presented in this paper extends the functionality of an existing behavior-based architecture by incorporating Belief, Desire and Intention (BDI) reasoning capabilities, with the general goal of achieving a hybrid architecture which may be applied to a wide variety of current domains, especially the ones mentioned above.

The classical computational model of a BDI agent [7] is event-driven, and so, a BDI agent reacts to events (such as changes in the environment or in its own beliefs), then it adopts a plan as one of its intentions and finally, from the set of active intentions, the agent decides its next action. Although this is a very powerful computational model, in complex and dynamic environments, it may not always be the best option for all scenarios. For example, there are limitations related to the ability to respond in time to some unexpected, urgent events which may jeopardize the system's integrity; on the other hand, there are also limitations about how to implement or integrate certain types of complex tasks (as image processing, for example) directly in the BDI cycle.

In order to overcome these limitations, this paper introduces the Flexible Agent Architecture (FAA), which proposes the integration of behaviors of different types, specifically including BDI behaviors, in the same agent. In this way, a multi-agent system would be able to include pure reactive or deliberative agents, or even hybrid ones. This architecture has been implemented in the SPADE agent platform, which is a middleware for creating behavior-based, multi-agent applications that has been recently redesigned from scratch for his version 3, trying to conform to the challenges that agent platforms will be expected to face in the near future. One of the main features of *SPADE* is its flexibility, which facilitates the addition of new features to agents as needed. As a result of the work presented in this paper, SPADE now features the possibility of integrating several different types of behaviors (tasks) in the same agent, with some of them incorporating a BDI reasoning cycle based on *AgentSpeak* [12].

The paper also includes a case study, which makes use of the proposed architecture, where two robotic arms must coordinate in order to move items throughout the manufacturing process in the context of a factory. This example is presented to illustrate how the new features available for *SPADE* agents allow them to mix middle and long-term planning tasks with direct perception and control actions in the context of a realistic (although simulated) environment.

The rest of the paper is structured as follows. Section 2 proposes the Flexible Agent Architecture and explains how it has been implemented in the middleware SPADE. Section 3 presents a case study where a multi-agent system implemented in SPADE and following the FAA has been used to solve a simplified version of the World Blocks problem in the context of a real robotics environment. Finally, Sect. 4 includes the conclusions of the paper.

2 Flexible Agent Architecture

This section presents the Flexible Agent Architecture (FAA), an architecture which intends to favor the development of *flexible* multi-agent systems, allowing to combine all kinds of agents, from purely reactive or reflex to purely deliberative ones, and including hybrid ones. The section first introduces the definition of the architecture, and then describes how it has been introduced to the SPADE 3 middleware.

2.1 Definition of the Architecture

The Flexible Agent Architecture is founded on the idea behind the behavior-based control [10], which defines a set of distributed, interacting modules, called behaviors, that collectively achieve the desired agent behavior. The idea is taken from the area of robotics where behaviors are control modules that cluster sets of constraints in order to achieve and maintain a goal [1].

Sometimes, behavior-based architectures have been confused with reactive architectures, since historically, reactive architectures have been designed by including different reactive behaviors structured in layers, and where intelligence emerges from the activation or deactivation of the outputs between the different layers. However, behavior-based architectures are conceptually more capable, since they remove some of the limitations of reactive systems. In particular, there are no restrictions about maintaining an internal representation of the environment (a traditional trait of deliberative architectures) or designing arbitrarily complex behaviors. Among other considerations, this implies that the internal state of the agent, including the world representation, may be distributed among the different behaviors. Thus, compared to reactive architectures, here behaviors not only distribute inputs and outputs, but also the internal state and the decision making process of the agent, and some of these behaviors may be deliberative, maintaining a state and a world representation. All this greatly increases the flexibility of this type of architectures.

Taking this idea into account, the FAA proposes a behavior-based architecture in which each agent in the multi-agent system is internally defined as a set of behaviors, with each behavior being either procedural or logic-based (as for example, following the BDI model), and all of them sharing a common internal state and a world representation. On the one hand, this proposal favors the combination of multiple types of reasoning processes in the same agent, including, but not limited to, reflex, reactive, repetitive and logic-based processes. And, on the other hand, it overcomes some significant difficulties of pure logic-based agents, such as expressing some sorts of algorithms (e.g., neural networks or genetic algorithms) or including reflex answers apart from its reasoning cycle. As a result, the multi-agent system may include agents of multiple types, from reactive (even reflex) agents to pure deliberative agents, and any sort of hybrid ones.

Some existing agent platforms such as SPADE (or JADE) have been designed to be behavior-based, in the sense that agents are developed by implementing one or several behaviors, each of them following some pre-defined execution pattern (one-shot, cyclic, etc.) So, the implementation of the FAA in SPADE has mainly involved including BDI behaviors to agents, as described below.

2.2 Implementation in SPADE 3

As expressed above, the Flexible Agent Architecture offers a versatile framework that facilitates the development of multi-agent systems where each agent may require reactive or deliberative capabilities, or both. A version of this architecture has been implemented as an extension to the SPADE 3 middleware[1], and it is shown in Fig. 1.

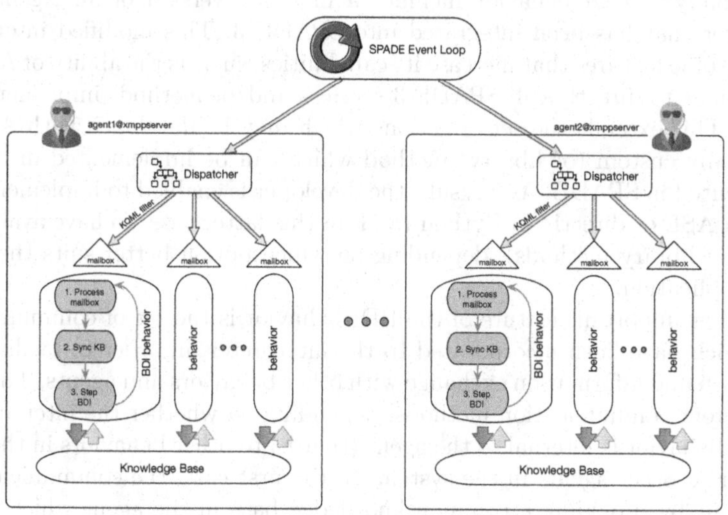

Fig. 1. Flexible agent architecture in SPADE 3.

As shown in the figure, each SPADE process may contain multiple agents, all of them internally managed by an *event loop*, which is a Python tool for scheduling and executing asynchronous functions. Each agent internally consists of a dispatcher and the set of behaviors which have been created by the agent. The dispatcher is in charge of keeping alive the connection between the agent and the XMPP server, as well as sending and receiving messages. The received messages are distributed to the particular behavior(s) to which they are addressed, using a series of filters or templates that are associated with each behavior (e.g. all messages with a particular sender and performative). Then, each message is stored in the mailbox of the designated behaviors until it is read. On the other

[1] https://github.com/javipalanca/spade_bdi.

hand, from this viewpoint, each behavior is a task which can be independently scheduled and executed by the process event loop, in a non-preemptive way.

This extension incorporates a new type of behavior based on the BDI paradigm, called *BDIBehaviour*, which can be adopted by any agent with deliberative requirements. The new BDI behavior type is automatically managed by SPADE, and so the developer does not have to intervene to program, or to keep track of, its BDI life-cycle. Any SPADE agent which wants to use the BDI behavior has to create it first by providing the name of a file written in AgentSpeak format which contains the behavior's code. When the agent starts the behavior, it initiates a cyclic execution pattern in which SPADE runs its *BDI cycle* step by step, as it is further described below. This cyclic execution is carried out indefinitely, and concurrently with any other behaviors that the agent may create. Although the behavior is automatically executed by SPADE, the agent still has some control over its execution, by pausing or resuming it at any time.

Internally, a BDI behavior includes a modified version of an AgentSpeak interpreter that has been integrated into SPADE 3. This modified interpreter includes some features that increase its capabilities, such as the ability of AgentSpeak actions to directly call SPADE 3 services and/or methods implemented in Python. This extends the set of actions which may be developed with AgentSpeak to any custom (or library) method which can be implemented in Python and executed in SPADE. As a result, the developer is enabled to implement each action in ASL or directly in Python (and, in this latter case, to have available a vast set of library methods), depending on which option better suits the needs of the application.

Another important feature of the BDI behavior is the set of communication skills which have been incorporated to the interpreter, in order to facilitate its integration and information exchange with other behaviors and agents. There are two different communication methods, depending on whether the interaction of the BDI behavior is internal to the agent (that is, to other behaviors in the same agent) or to other agents in the system. In the first case, the communication is carried out by providing a common knowledge base in the agent which all the behaviors share. By means of this knowledge base, the concept of *belief* in the BDI behavior has been extended outside the AgentSpeak interpreter, allowing any of the agent's behaviors to access, insert and erase beliefs. Thus, the set of beliefs are global to the agent, and the modification of beliefs (by any behavior) produces the corresponding events in the interpreter, ensuring a consistent response in terms of the ASL language. On the other hand, the communication of the BDI behavior with other agents (and their behaviors, BDI or not) is performed by directly using the SPADE 3 communication facilities. Such facilities have been incorporated to the interpreter, enabling a transparent communication between the BDI behaviors of any two SPADE agents by using the natural ASL syntax. This communication has been carried out using KQML messages, as this communication language is the source of AgentSpeak communication [16]. KQML implements the key concept of *performative*, that allows the sender to influence the receiver in different ways according to the *speech act theory* [14].

In conclusion, the implementation of this flexible architecture in SPADE 3 allows for a consistent integration of both BDI and non-BDI behaviors in any SPADE agent. The integration is twofold. On the one hand, non-BDI behaviors (implemented in Python) can access the BDI knowledge base by reading and modifying beliefs and objectives; in the latter case, the modifications produce the same effect as if they were performed inside the BDI reasoning process. On the other hand, BDI behaviors (expressed in AgentSpeak language) may call actions implemented in Python, which enable them to access the rest of behaviors of the agent as well as the agent's context outside BDI, that is, the agent's global information which is not represented as beliefs or objectives.

3 Case Study

This section presents an example of how the proposed Flexible Agent Architecture may be used for situations where applying deliberative an non-deliberative tasks is an advantage. In particular, the section introduces a multi-agent system in the context of a factory where different robot arms collaborate to move items throughout the manufacturing process. The application has been designed as a simplified version of the typical Blocks World problem, and the environment has been created by means of an external 3D simulator.

The multi-agent system has been designed from the viewpoint of different, collaborating behaviors, and then implemented in a version of SPADE enhanced with the FAA, as described earlier in the paper. As a result, inside each agent, the reasoning tasks have been implemented as a BDI behavior (in AgentSpeak) while other tasks related to the perception of the environment or the operation of the robot arms have been implemented (in Python) by using other types of behaviors, according to their needs. This type of architecture is particularly useful in some robotics applications (like the one presented here) where the perception, reasoning and action steps are performed independently, and even implemented with different languages and/or tools.

The following subsections separately describe the details of the case study, the simulated environment and the implementation of the multi-agent system in SPADE. Then, a final subsection presents some discussion about the development process and the resulting system.

As commented above, from the viewpoint of the application, the case study is a simplified version of the Blocks World problem, but operating in a realistic (although simulated) robotic environment.

The environment is composed of three adjacent tables (labeled A, B, and C) and two robotic arms (*arm_1* and *arm_2*) which can pick up objects by means of a gripper. The two arms are facing each other, and each one is fixed to one of the two outer tables (tables A and C), while the third table (B) is placed at the center, between them. Each arm can reach the extent of its own table and the central table in order to pick up or release objects, but not the other arm's table. Therefore, in order to move objects from table A to C (or vice-versa), the two arms need to coordinate in order to use Table B as an exchange point.

The multi-agent system operating on this environment will have the general goal of moving a cube placed somewhere in Table A to Table C. To achieve this goal, the application agents will need to interact with the environment in order to perceive the images of the cameras located at the gripper of each arm (subjective cameras), grip the cube, move it to a particular destination, etc. The next subsection further explains the details of the environment and how to interact with it.

The environment has been built by using a 3D simulation tool called PyBullet[2]. In the simulation environment, the two robotic arms which the multi-agent system will need to control are real, commercial robots called Panda arms[3]. Panda arms feature 7 degrees of freedom, which gives agents the ability of performing complex actions and ensures a more realistic interaction with the environment. In particular, agents will interact with the Panda arms by sending commands to the PyBullet server such as "move arm to a coordinate", "open/-close gripper", "take image from the arm's camera", etc.

Figure 2 presents a diagram of the case study architecture, depicting the application agents and the PyBullet server. As it can be seen in the figure, a decentralized application is proposed, where there are two SPADE agents, each one controlling one robotic arm, and each one executed in a separate process, while a third computer runs the PyBullet server. The separation between the physical simulation and the agents enables the application to interact with either the simulated or a real environment without changing the code executed by the agents. The two agents can coordinate with each other (in order to achieve the goal of moving the cube) by means of the inter-agent communication service of SPADE (which internally uses the XMPP protocol), while the communication with the PyBullet server is direct by calling the corresponding API functions.

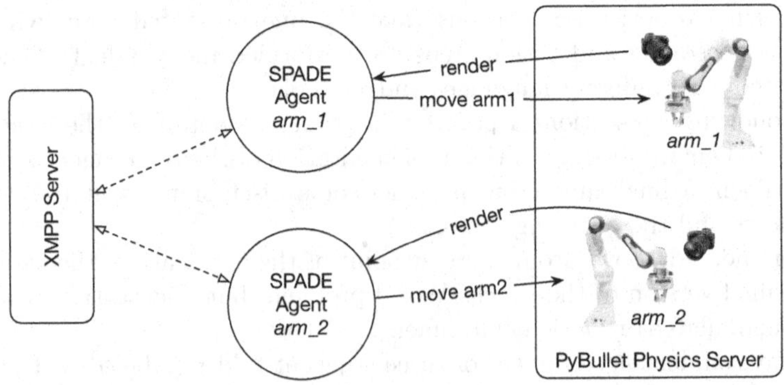

Fig. 2. Architecture of the case study. Dotted lines denote message exchange using the SPADE communication services while solid lines denote API function calls to the PyBullet server.

[2] https://pybullet.org/wordpress/.
[3] https://www.generationrobots.com/en/403317-panda-robotic-arm.html.

The multi-agent system implemented in SPADE for the example consists of two agents with BDI reasoning capabilities, each one controlling one of the Panda arms and communicating with each other in order to achieve their common goal of moving an object (cube) from Table A to Table C. Each agent is named after the arm each it is controlling, that is, *arm_1* and *arm_2*.

Internally, each agent has been designed with two main behaviors: a BDI behavior in charge of making the high-level decisions of the agent and a FSM (Finite State Machine) behavior which interacts with the (simulated) environment. These two behaviors interact with each other by sharing beliefs in the agent's knowledge base. Figure 3 presents a schematic view of both behaviors, which are now described.

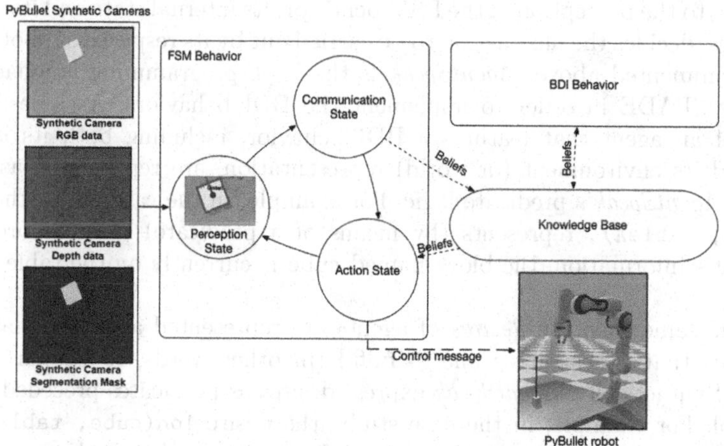

Fig. 3. Diagram of the two behaviors inside each of the SPADE agents, including their interactions with each other and with the environment.

3.1 Interaction (FSM) Behavior

The *Interaction* behavior is a FSM behavior composed of three states, called Perception, Communication and Action. The Perception state interacts with the PyBullet API in order to retrieve images from the camera located at the end of the arm's effectors (gripper). In particular, the PyBullet server returns three types of images from the camera (a segmented image, a raw image and a depth image), from which the agent then extracts relevant information of the environment, such as contour detection, shapes, segmentation, etc. An example of this segmentation process carried out by the Perception state can be seen in the left side of Fig. 3. The figure also shows how the agent uses the images in order to determine the position of the object's centroid and its outline, which enables it to delimit the location of the cube. Then, it transforms all that data into the precise location of the cube within the table under the camera.

Once the perception is complete, the Communication state then transforms the significant information about the environment (basically, the cube's location) to a format which is appropriate to be processed by the BDI behavior, and writes that information as *beliefs* in the agent's knowledge base. The BDI behavior, as described below, reasons about it and decides which is the next action to be taken by the arm. That decision, also written as beliefs in the common knowledge base, is read by the Action state, which then interacts with the PyBullet server in order to send the next command, exactly as if it was a real Panda arm.

3.2 Deliberation (BDI) Behavior

The *Deliberation* behavior is a BDI behavior including a set of plans which, according to the perception of the FSM behavior, its internal state and its current objectives, decides the next action to be carried out by its respective robotic arm.

As commented above, *AgentSpeak* is the logic programming language provided by SPADE in order to implement the BDI behaviors. As a result, the beliefs of an agent that features a BDI behavior, including both its internal state and its environment (or world) representation, are represented as predicates in *AgentSpeak*'s predicate logic. For example, in the case study, the belief `on(cube, tableA).` represents (by means of a predicate) that, according to the agent's information, the block named `cube` is currently on the table named `tableA`.

In the same way, the *desires* of agents are represented as goals, that is, as predicates that the agents want to fulfill (in other words, to be part of the beliefs). Syntactically, *AgentSpeak* express desires as predicates preceded by the ! symbol. For example, in the case study, the desire `!on(cube, tableB).` in one of the agents would mean that one of the agent's goals is to have the block named `cube` on the table named `tableB`.

Finally, *AgentSpeak* allows for the definition of plans to answer events happening to the agent, as for example events related to achieve new goals. Thus, the *intentions* of agents are defined by the plans which are instanced to react to those events. For example, the following code shows a subset of the implemented plans for one of the SPADE agents (specifically, agent *arm_1*) to define the decision making of the agent about putting a cube in an specific position in the environment. The presented code is general enough for moving different cubes across the tables in the environment, although for the sake of simplicity, the environment only includes a single cube which needs to be moved from table A to C, or vice-versa, as stated above.

```
...
// ****************************************************
// Plans to achieve that Obj1 (the cube to be moved) is
// on Obj2 (a table or another cube)
// ****************************************************
// Goal reached
+!on(Obj1, Obj2) : on(Obj1, Obj2).

// Tries to clear the cube and move Obj1 over Obj2
 +!on(Obj1, Obj2)
```

```
11 <-
12     !clear(Obj1);
13     !clear(Obj2);
14     !move(Obj1, Obj2).
15
16 // Plan fired when cube is not available for agent arm_1
17 +!on(Obj1, Obj2) : not(clear(Obj1)) & not(on(Obj1, _))
18 <-
19     .send(arm_2, achieve, on(Obj1, tableB));
20     .wait(3000).
21
22 // *************************************************
23 // Plans to achieve the movement of Obj1 over Obj2
24 // *************************************************
25 // the movement can be done
26 +!move(Obj1, Obj2) : clear(Obj1) & clear(Obj2)
27 <-
28     -on(Obj1, _);
29     +next_action(move, Obj1, Obj2).
30     // invokes the action in the FSM behavior
31 // the arm must clear the cube before moving
32 +!move(Obj1, Obj2)
33 <-
34     !clear(Obj1);
35     !clear(Obj2);
36     !move(Obj1, Obj2).
37
38 ...
```

The first three plans (lines 7 to 20) manage the triggering of the goal of placing a cube on top of a table (or another cube), represented by the goal `!on(Obj1, Obj2)`. The first plan is fired when the object `Obj1` is already in the desired position. In the second plan, the agent *arm_1* triggers the plan which moves the object (`!move( Obj1, Obj2)` in line 14), once both `Obj1` and `Obj2` are *clear*, that is, there is no other object atop of them. The plans associated to the goal `!clear()` try to make the cube/table directly accessible to the arm. For the sake of simplicity, since in this particular example there is a single cube, both the cube and the tables will always be clear, and so these plans have been omitted from the code above. The third plan is triggered when agent *arm_1* detects that the cube is not on any of the tables under its reach. In this case, the plan executes an external action (`.send()` in line 19), which sends the other agent (*arm_2*) a message containing a request to move the object to the shared table (`tableB`).

The next lines include the ASL code of the goal `!move(Obj1, Obj2)` (lines 26 to 36), which tries to make the specific movement of a cube. In the first plan, the precondition first confirms that the movement is viable (both the cube and the destination table are clear) and then the body of the plan adds a special belief called `next_action` to the agent's knowledge base. This belief is the way in which the *Deliberation* behavior tells the *Interaction* behavior which is the next action to be sent to the arm; in this case, to move object `Obj1` to the coordinates of `Obj2`. As explained in Sect. 3.1, the state called *Action* within the *Interaction* behavior is in charge of performing the required transformations from objects to coordinates and then to send the specific orders to the Panda arm in order to execute the action. The second plan is triggered when the agent tries to move the object but either the object or the destination (or both) are not clear. This situation may occur in the shared table, but only if the environment includes more than one cube; in this case, even if one of the agents thinks that it has already left the table (or a cube) accessible (*clear*), the other agent may have made a movement that invalidates this condition. It is for this reason that the former agent needs to invoke the goal `clear` again.

4 Conclusions

Behavior-based architectures for multi-agent systems are suitable in environments with dynamic and significant changes, where typical requirements include fast and constant response, a high level of adaptability, and maintaining a state of the environment which allows agents to learn from the past. For these reasons, among others, behavior-based architectures are currently the most used ones to address the development of multi-agent systems. With the idea of contributing to their improvement, this paper introduces the Flexible Agent Architecture. In essence, the FAA features the integration of BDI reasoning capabilities as a new behavior of an agent, providing the agent with total versatility regarding the type of reasoning at its disposal, which may effectively combine all sorts of cognitive and reactive procedures.

This new FAA has been implemented and tested using the SPADE platform. SPADE employs a behavior-based agent architecture in order to define the decision-making process of the agents. With the work presented in this paper, designers can make use of a BDI-based behavior based on the *AgentSpeak* BDI model in order to enhance the way the agent can carry out its deliberative reasoning process. As a result of this incorporation, it is possible to develop from purely reactive agents (implemented with fast reactive behaviors), deliberative agents (implemented with a BDI behavior), or even hybrid agents (implemented with a mix of reactive and a BDI behaviors). Thus, this has boosted the possibilities of using SPADE to develop multi-agent applications which can be used in several different domains.

The paper also includes a case of study where this new Flexible Architecture has been applied to develop an actual multi-agent system in SPADE. The system controls a simplified factory scenario in which two robotic arms need to coordinate in order to detect and move blocks. The environment has been simulated by means of a realistic 3D simulator which allows for a quick transfer from the simulation to reality. The presented multi-agent system is intentionally simple in order to illustrate the facility with which a BDI reasoning cycle can be integrated with other agent processes in a completely parallel manner; however, it could easily be extended to solve a much more challenging problem in the same scenario, thanks to the capabilities of the BDI reasoning model.

Lastly, the authors would like to underline that the work presented here is freely available to download and to be used in PyPI[4], and its sources available in GitHub[5].

[4] https://pypi.org/project/spade-bdi/.
[5] https://github.com/javipalanca/spade_bdi.

References

1. Arkin, R.C., et al.: Behavior-based robotics. MIT Press (1998)
2. Belkhala, S., Benhadou, S., Boukhdir, K., Medromi, H.: Smart parking architecture based on multi agent system. Int. J. Adv. Comput. Sci. Appl. **10**, 378–382 (2019)
3. Calvaresi, D., Marinoni, M., Sturm, A., Schumacher, M., Buttazzo, G.: The challenge of real-time multi-agent systems for enabling IoT and CPS. In: Proceedings of the International Conference on Web Intelligence, pp. 356–364 (2017)
4. Cao, J., Bu, Z., Wang, Y., Yang, H., Jiang, J., Li, H.J.: Detecting prosumer-community groups in smart grids from the multiagent perspective. IEEE Trans. Syst. Man Cybern. Syst. **49**(8), 1652–1664 (2019)
5. Chang, K.C., Chu, K.C., Wang, H.C., Lin, Y.C., Pan, J.S.: Agent-based middleware framework using distributed CPS for improving resource utilization in smart city. Future Gener. Comput. Syst. **108**, 445–453 (2020)
6. Fortino, G., Fotia, L., Messina, F., Rosaci, D., Sarné, G.M.: A meritocratic trust-based group formation in an IoT environment for smart cities. Futur. Gener. Comput. Syst. **108**, 34–45 (2020)
7. Georgeff, M.P., et al.: An abstract architecture for rational agents. In: Principles of Knowledge Representation and Reasoning, pp. 439–449 (1992)
8. Guastella, D.A., Camps, V., Gleizes, M.P.: Multi-agent systems for estimating missing information in smart cities. In: ICAART (2), pp. 214–223 (2019)
9. Howell, S., Rezgui, Y., Hippolyte, J.L., Jayan, B., Li, H.: Towards the next generation of smart grids: semantic and holonic multi-agent management of distributed energy resources. Renew. Sustain. Energy Rev. **77**, 193–214 (2017)
10. Michaud, F., Nicolescu, M.: Behavior-based systems. In: Siciliano, B., Khatib, O. (eds.) Springer Handbook of Robotics, pp. 307–328. Springer, Heidelberg (2016). https://doi.org/10.1007/978-3-540-30301-5_39
11. Pal, C.V., Leon, F., Paprzycki, M., Ganzha, M.: A review of platforms for the development of agent systems. arXiv preprint arXiv:2007.08961 (2020)
12. Rao, A.S.: AgentSpeak(L): BDI agents speak out in a logical computable language. In: Van de Velde, W., Perram, J.W. (eds.) MAAMAW 1996. LNCS, vol. 1038, pp. 42–55. Springer, Heidelberg (1996). https://doi.org/10.1007/BFb0031845
13. Schaefer, M., Vokřínek, J., Pinotti, D., Tango, F.: Multi-agent traffic simulation for development and validation of autonomic car-to-car systems. In: McCluskey, T.L., Kotsialos, A., Müller, J.P., Klügl, F., Rana, O., Schumann, R. (eds.) Autonomic Road Transport Support Systems. AS, pp. 165–180. Springer, Cham (2016). https://doi.org/10.1007/978-3-319-25808-9_10
14. Searle, J.R., et al.: Speech act theory and pragmatics, 1st Edn., vol. 10. Springer, Dordrecht (1980). https://doi.org/10.1007/978-94-009-8964-1
15. Suganuma, T., Oide, T., Kitagami, S., Sugawara, K., Shiratori, N.: Multiagent-based flexible edge computing architecture for IoT. IEEE Netw. **32**(1), 16–23 (2018)
16. Vieira, R., Moreira, Á.F., Wooldridge, M., Bordini, R.H.: On the formal semantics of speech-act based communication in an agent-oriented programming language. J. Artif. Intell. Res. **29**, 221–267 (2007)
17. Yasin, J.N., Mohamed, S.A.S., Haghbayan, M.-H., Heikkonen, J., Tenhunen, H., Plosila, J.: Navigation of autonomous swarm of drones using translational coordinates. In: Demazeau, Y., Holvoet, T., Corchado, J.M., Costantini, S. (eds.) PAAMS 2020. LNCS (LNAI), vol. 12092, pp. 353–362. Springer, Cham (2020). https://doi.org/10.1007/978-3-030-49778-1_28

Informative Communication of Robot Plans

Michele Persiani(✉) and Thomas Hellström

Umeå University, Umeå, Sweden

michelep@cs.umu.se, thomas.hellstrom@umu.se

Abstract. When a robot is asked to verbalize its plan it can do it in many ways. For example, a seemingly natural strategy is incremental, where the robot verbalizes its planned actions in plan order. However, an important aspect of this type of strategy is that it misses considerations on what is effectively informative to communicate, because not considering what the user knows prior to explanations. In this paper we propose a verbalization strategy to communicate robot plans informatively, by measuring the information gain that verbalizations have against a second-order theory of mind of the user capturing his prior knowledge on the robot. As shown in our experiments, this strategy allows to understand the robot's goal much quicker than by using strategies such as increasing or decreasing plan order. In addition, following our formulation we hint to what is informative and why when a robot communicates its plan.

Keywords: Plan verbalization · Human-robot interaction · Bayesian network · Mirror agent model

1 Introduction

With its ever-growing advancements, Artificial Intelligence (AI) is proving to be a promising partner in our lives. In envisioning this relationship, AI agents should support us by being able to perform their assigned tasks both efficiently and accurately, but, on top of that, a crucial aspect for this relationship to be successful is the degree by which agents are able to make themselves understood by their human users, either through explanations, or by behavior that is interpretable from the human perspective [6].

An interpretable behavior is a behavior that is expected by the user, because fulfilling his expectations about the agent [2,3]. Once implemented in a model, these expectations describes how the user is modeling the agent, therefore informing the agent about how it is being perceived and explained. It follows that behaviors fitting this expectations model are intrinsically explainable and therefore should not require additional explanations; however, other types behaviors could require explanations. This is because, while fulfilling other relevant properties such as being optimal, do not fit the user's expectations, and thus result

© The Author(s), under exclusive license to Springer Nature Switzerland AG 2022
F. Dignum et al. (Eds.): PAAMS 2022, LNAI 13616, pp. 332–344, 2022.
https://doi.org/10.1007/978-3-031-18192-4_27

being uninterpretable. It becomes therefore crucial to complement such behavior with explanations targeting its alignment with the user's expectation model, such that it becomes interpretable in it [3].

A relevant measure of the explanation process is its degree of *informativeness*, that is the amount of information that explanations transfer to the explainee [9]. To be informative, explanations can leverage the user's expectation model on the agent when computing what to communicate and how: given that many candidate verbalizations are possible to communicate, the agent has to determine which one is most informative, in the sense that it increases by a largest amount the user's understanding of the agent. We see the process of explanation as having a complementary role with respect to interpretable behavior, and explanations and interpretable behavior have the same objective of keeping the agent model P_R, and the expectations that the user has about the agent P_R^H, as similar as possible. This is because, when aligned, this alignment signals that the agent is being understood because fitting the expectations.

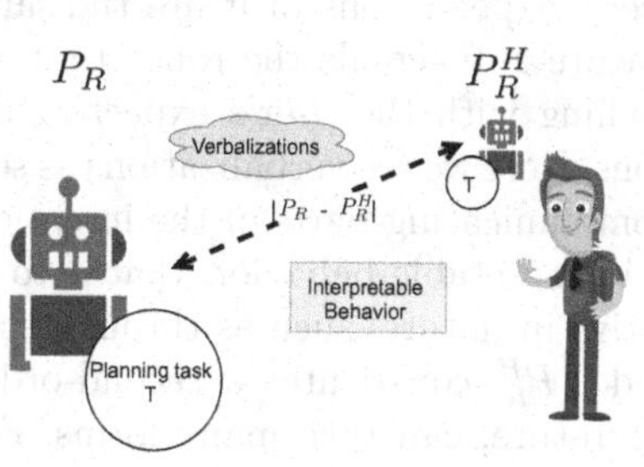

Fig. 1. P_R: model of the robot working on task T. P_R^H: second-order theory of mind of the robot. The goal of interpretable behavior and verbalizations is to reduce the distance $|P_R - P_R^H|$. Here we consider the minimum amount of actions, and their order, that the robot should communicate such that $|P_R - P_R^H| < \theta$.

Informativeness in explanations is still sparsely considered inside the literature, and previous work on explanations focuses more on the consistency of explanations from the agent's perspective, rather than generating explanations that are informative to the user [4,12]. With the goal of addressing this gap, in this paper we propose an algorithm to communicate a robot's plan using a criteria based on the informativeness of communications. We achieve this by firstly grounding the understanding that the user has about the agent as a measure of difference between agent model and user expectation model. Later, we select which actions of the plan to communicate, and their order, based on how their communication affect this distance measure. In addition, by the same concepts we define what is informative in the case of explanations of robot plans.

The rest of the paper is structured as follows. In Sect. 2 we provide brief, relevant background in theory of mind for robotics and verbalizations of robot plans. In Sect. 3 we present our method for informative communication of the robot plan. Section 5 describes experiments and measures performed on different tests. Finally, Sect. 7 and Sect. 8 contains discussion on the results and conclusions.

2 Background

Previous research in understandable robots [6] propose to consider the concept of *understanding* as a distance measure between a robot's intentional model P_R

and the user's model of P_R, P_R^H. The more similar these models are, the higher is the degree of understanding between user and robot. The limit case where the distance is 0 signals the robot that it is being fully understood in the sense that the user's expectations of it are the same as its actual intentional model, while a measure > 0 signals the robot that some parts of its intentional model are mismatching with the user's expectation, and therefore require additional verbalizations. Here we see verbalizations as sequences of communicative actions[1] aimed at communicating parts of the intentional model. While having the same function of interpretable behavior, that is to reduce $|P_R - P_R^H|$, they are purely communicative in nature, such as through speech, text, images, etc.

The model P_R^H constitutes a second-order theory of mind [6], and shown in recent literature, can take many forms. For example, in [18] and in [5] it is a context-dependent label describing whether the user understands the robot. After a training phase through human annotations, predicting the label's value allows to augment the cost function of the planning procedure with explainability awareness. Alternatively, more structured forms are for example presented in [3], where the theory of mind is a complete planning instance.

The work on understandable robots has connections also to research in interpretability and explainability. Given that a model of the user's expectations P_R^H is provided to the robot (Fig. 1), interpretable behaviors keep the distance measure $|P_R - P_R^H|$ low by modifying its behavior, while explanations through sequences of communicative actions (that we refer to as verbalizations) [7,16].

In this paper we focus on explanations, and in particular on the verbalizations of the robot's task experience, such as its recent course of action, its goal, or plan. For this type of question, the strategies to verbalize explanations that are proposed in the literature are often incremental i.e. orderly from the first to the last actions. For example, [11,15] propose strategies to verbalize robot plans. In addition, the authors keep into consideration possible categories of users by predefining, for a given plan, multiple types of explanations, one for every type of user. The resulting explanations span over standardized dimensions of verbalization such as abstraction, locality, and specificity. However, while these strategies can consider different types of users and what can be informative to them, they don't consider the information that users (in any given category) possess prior to the explanations, and therefore verbalizations can only be incremental, or with hand-coded strategies. [19] addresses this problem by a manual approach: we can ask the users which elements of the plan are of interest before its verbalization, in this way, the successive incremental verbalization can be filtered to contain only elements that are relevant to the specific user.

As we show in this paper the order by which actions are verbalized can be controlled to maximize the amount of information that verbalizations produce inside the second-order theory of mind. A similar idea is explored in [17], where the authors propose how the explanation process can be re-ordered by keeping into consideration the cognitive load of the user. While we also confront the

[1] A communicative action is an action, either verbal or physical, intended to decrease the models distance $|P_R - P_R^H|$ [6].

question of ordering verbalizations, in this paper we are interested in making the user understand the robot's internal state with a minimum amount of utterances.

3 Method

We consider the case in which the robot's model P_R and user's estimated model of the robot model, P_R^H, are probabilistic Belief-Desire-Intention (BDI) models, described by two Equivalent Bayesian Networks and forming a second-order theory of mind setting (Fig. 2). The networks use the same random variables, however, these variables can be differently distributed in P_R and P_R^H, thus possibly reflecting a mismatch between the user's beliefs over the robot model and the true robot model. We refer to this setting as the *Mirror Agent Model* because defining the second-order theory of mind of the agent as a "mirror" of the agent's true model. This model is easy to deploy and can be obtained *as a service* [1] on a variety of agents, which is an important property for its usability.

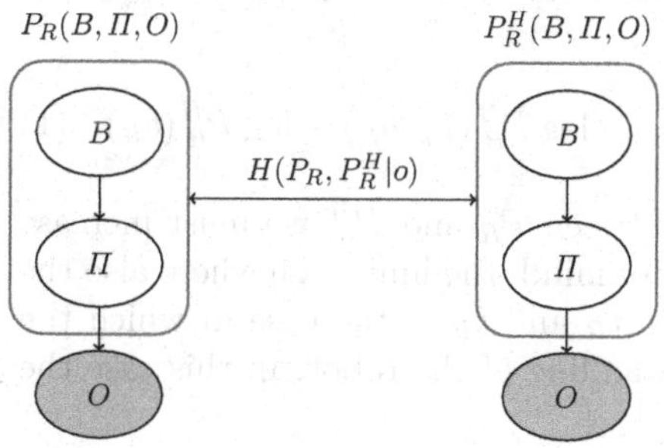

Fig. 2. Robot model (P_R) and second-order theory of mind of the user (P_R^H) as equivalent Bayesian Networks. The cross-entropy H measures the difference between robot's and user's estimated state of mind a posteriori of a verbalization o.

A setting which mirrors P_R and P_R^H has clear advantages when the robot decides what to communicate in order to increase the models similarity: if we are able to directly compare the robot and its theory of mind, we could immediately know what part of the model is being understood, and which part instead requires a verbalizations. However, the assumption this setting makes is that the user has internalized a robot model of the same form of the original. For this paper we take this assumption to hold, and model the user as knowing the exact robot model[2]. The robot's probabilistic BDI model is defined $P_R(O, \Pi, B) = P_R(O|\Pi)P_R(\Pi|B)P_R(B)$ where every $b \in B$ include both belief and goal of the robot, $\pi \in \Pi$ a possible intention (we consider intentions as plans) and $o \in O$ the observations that plans yield to the user. Since we here consider the case where the robot verbalizes its plans, observations are verbalizations of actions, that in our case have the form of textual descriptions of sequences of actions. The only observable random variable is O, while B and Π are variables internal to the robot's

[2] This assumption doesn't make the proposed method to lose generality, because from two different P_R and P_R^H we can always create a super-agent which comprehend both models, and that is used in the mirror model. Then, we would set inside P_R and P_R^H the corresponding probabilities to 0.

state of mind [6], and can be interacted with only through observations. P_R^H is similarly defined.

As a simplified case, we don't consider how the robot forms and updates its beliefs through its sensors, and we assume a fixed probabilistic belief $P_R(B)$. The robot can form plans using the planning model $P_R(\Pi|B)$, where the probability of a plan $P_R(\pi|b)$ is > 0 only if the plan is consistent with both belief and goal condition of b. While computing plans we model the robot to be a rational agent i.e. associating higher probabilities to cheap plans, and accordingly set $P_R(\pi|b) \propto R(\pi, b)$ where $R(.)$ is a function measuring the rationality of π when executed in b [14]. The model $P_R(O|\Pi)$ instead describes how executing plans create observations. $P_R(o|\pi) > 0$ means that o verbalizes a set of actions $o = \{a_1, ..., a_n\}$ that are a subset of the plan π, with $P_R(o|\pi) = \prod_i P_R(a_i|\pi), P_R(a_i|\pi) > 0$ **iff** $a_i \in \pi$. The model P_R^H is similarly defined. The cross-entropy measure $H(P_R, P_R^H)$ determines the similarity between P_R's and P_R^H's states of mind (i.e. their corresponding intentions and beliefs). For simplicity, we consider the case of a deterministic P_R, with $P_R(B = b_R) = 1$ and $P_R(\Pi = \pi_R) = 1$, and probabilistic P_R^H. In this setting, the cross-entropy between P_R and P_R^H is:

$$H(P_R, P_R^H) = \sum P_R(\pi, b) \log P_R^H(\pi, b) = -\log P_R^H(\pi_R|b_R) - \log P_R^H(b_R) \quad (1)$$

Therefore, to increase the similarity between P_R and P_R^H we must increase the probability of π_R and b_R in the theory of mind; the limit case where also the theory of mind deterministically produces π_R and b_R is the case in which the user is estimated to have an exact understanding of the robot. In this case the cross-entropy is 0.

3.1 Informative Communication

As described previously, the main objective of a verbalization $o \in O$ is to make P_R^H as similar as possible to P_R. This is achieved by decreasing the cross-entropy measure between the models. The associated Information Gain (IG) of the verbalization is $IG(P_R, P_R^H, o) = H(P_R, P_R^H) - H(P_R, P_R^H|o)$. Using the information gain, the most informative verbalization can be selected as the one with maximal information gain:

$$\begin{aligned} \hat{o} &= \arg\max_{o \in O} H(P_R, P_R^H) - H(P_R, P_R^H|o) \\ &= \arg\max_{o \in O} \log P_R^H(\pi_R, b_R|o) \\ &= \arg\max_{o \in O} \log P_R^H(o|\pi_R) - \log \mathbb{E}[P_R^H(o|\pi)] \end{aligned} \quad (2)$$

Two important properties of informative communication emerge from Eq. 2. The first is that only verbalizations that correctly reflect the model of the robot are informative. Communicating an action not belonging to the robot's plan, with $P_R^H(a_i|\pi_R) = 0$, induce an informativeness of $-\infty$ of the full verbalization.

The second is that actions that are informative to communicate are those that tend to appear exclusively in π_R.

A simple way to find which is the best verbalization of N actions to communicate is to enumerate all the possible combinations of actions belonging to π_R, to then select the combination with highest IG. Algorithm 1 implements this procedure. The output of the algorithm is the sequence of the N most informative actions ordered in plan order.

Algorithm 1. Find the most informative communication of size N, by enumerating and sorting the combinations of actions of size N

---

procedure VERBALIZE-PLAN(P_R, P_R^H, N)
  $\pi_R \leftarrow$ PLAN(P_R)
  $o \leftarrow$ FIND-MOST-INFORMATIVE(π_R, P_R^H, N)
  $o_{sorted} \leftarrow$ PLAN-SORT(o)
  VERBALIZE(o_{sorted})
end procedure
procedure FIND-MOST-INFORMATIVE(π_R, P_R^H, N)
  $C \leftarrow$ COMBINATIONS(π_R, N) ▷ $|C| = \binom{|\pi_R|}{N}$
  $Q \leftarrow \emptyset$
  for $c \in C$ **do**
    $h_c =$ INFORMATION-GAIN($P_R^H | o = c$) ▷ Eq. 2
    APPEND($Q, \langle h_c, c \rangle$)
  end for
  $Q \leftarrow$ SORT(Q)
  $h_{best}, c_{best} \leftarrow$ POP(Q)
  yield c_{best}
end procedure

---

4 Implementation in PDDL

We implemented the probabilistic BDI models $P_R(O, \Pi, B)$ and $P_R^H(O, \Pi, B)$ by specifying planning instances using the Planning Domain Description Language (PDDL). PDDL [10] is a standard language to specify planning domains for what is usually referred to as classical planning. A planning instance for the robot is obtained by specifying the tuple $\langle \mathcal{P}_R, \mathcal{A}_R, I_R, \mathcal{G}_R, \mathcal{O}_R \rangle$. Where I_R and $\mathcal{G}_R$ are set of ground predicates and correspond to the initial and goal state respectively, $\mathcal{O}_R$ is the set of objects available to ground the predicates $\mathcal{P}_R$, while $\mathcal{A}_R$ is the set of available actions to transition between states. Similarly, the second order theory of mind model has components $\langle \mathcal{P}_R^H, \mathcal{A}_R^H, I_R^H, \mathcal{G}_R^H, \mathcal{O}_R^H \rangle$.

We set the descriptive components of the planning instances of robot and theory of mind to be equivalent. i.e. $\mathcal{P}_R = \mathcal{P}_R^H, \mathcal{A}_R = \mathcal{A}_R^H$ and $\mathcal{O}_R = \mathcal{O}_R^H$, with the only probabilistic parts being I_R, $\mathcal{G}_R$, I_R^H and $\mathcal{G}_R^H$. In this setting, the corresponding probability distribution over the possible PDDL instances describing the robot state is obtained by a combination of Bernoulli distribution for the beliefs I_R, and a categorical distribution for the possible goals $\mathcal{G}_R$ (the same for I_R^H and $\mathcal{G}_R^H$ respectively).

$$\begin{array}{ll} P_R(B) = P_R(I)P_R(G) & P_R(G;\theta_R) = P(G|\{g_0, ..., g_m\}) \\ P_R(I;\theta_R) = \Pi_i P(p_i \in I_R; \theta_{p_i}) & P_R(G = \langle \mathcal{G}_j \rangle | \{g_0, ..., g_m\}) = \theta_j \\ P(p_i \in I_R) = \theta_i & \sum_j \theta_j = 1 \end{array}$$

where θ are the distribution parameters. Sampling a belief from $P_R(B)$ yields a initial state and a goal state for the PDDL planner. The planning model $P_R(\Pi|B)$ is instead implemented by a planner of choice compatible with the underlying PDDL requirements. The probability of a plan $P_R(\Pi = \pi|B = b)$ is defined as a function of rationality [14]. Sampling from the planning model can for example be done through Diverse Planning techniques [8]. $P_R^H(B)$ and $P_R^H(\Pi|B)$ are similarly defined.

5 Experiments

We test our algorithm for informative communication over two sets of tests. First, we run a set of automated benchmarks on the PUCRS dataset, which is a curated dataset of planning domains [13], discussing then some generally valid metrics and results. After that we show the results of a user study simulating the case where an operator meets a robot working in a warehouse, and not knowing what it is doing, asks for its plan.

5.1 Tests on the PUCRS Dataset

We benchmarked Algorithm 1 on the PUCRS dataset [13], that is a dataset of PDDL planning domains and problems, with the goal to search for properties of informative communication that generalizes across domains. We selected 6 standard PDDL domain: *logistics, intrusion-detection, rovers, satellite, blocks-world, satellite.* Table 1 shows relevant average measures of the domains, such as number of predicates and operators, size of the initial state, number of tested goals and length of optimal plans.

For every domain we perform the tests on 10 planning instances, averaging the results. In each test P_R is initialized by randomly selecting a goal from the pool of available goals and using the original instance's initial state. P_R^H is initialized by randomly selecting 3 goals from the goal pool plus the goal of P_R, for a total of 4 possible goals. These goals are used with equal probabilities in $P_R^H(G)$. In addition, 4 random predicates belonging to the robot plan's preconditions are made as probabilistic i.e. $P_R^H(I) = \prod_{i \in 1..4} P(p_i)$, with $P(p_i = 1) = 0.5$.

Two baseline communication strategies are tested alongside informative communication: increasing order, which communicates actions in plan order, and decreasing order, which communicates the actions in reversed plan order. Figure 3 shows the average measures of the benchmark for the tested strategies. On the first row is shown the gain on entropy obtained by using the informative communication strategy rather than the others, measured as $G_{\text{inf}} = H(P_R, P_H^R) - H_{\text{inf}}(P_R, P_H^R)$. The second row instead shows the distance measure $D_G(a_i)$ between the predicates affected by a communicated action a_i and the goal predicates of the instances. $D_G(a_i) = \frac{k}{|\pi_R|}$ means that, along the plan and starting counting from a_i, the first action directly affecting the predicates of the instance's goal is the k-th, e.g. $D_G(a_i) = 0$ if a_i has in its effects a predicate contained in the instance's goal.

Table 1. Average instance measures over the tested planning domains. The columns, from left to right are: number of operators, number of predicates, size of the initial state, number of tested goals, length of optimal plans.

Domain	$\|\mathcal{P}\|$	$\|\mathcal{A}\|$	$\|I\|$	$\|G\|$	$\|\pi\|$
miconic	8	4	517	6	35.57
logistics	3	6	22.16	10.39	24.41
intrusion	11	9	1	16.67	13.07
blocks-world	5	4	14.58	20.28	14.50
rovers	32	9	172.71	6	24.93
satellite	12	5	58	6.43	16.89

The plots highlight an additional relevant property of the informative strategy, that is a consistent low distance-to-goal measure for the actions communicated earliest. This means that the informative strategy tends to communicate earlier the actions that directly affect the predicates of the goal. If we think about it, these actions are clearly informative, because communicating the goal predicates (namely, communicating the goal) of the plan clearly mostly disambiguates the goal from the others. This order of communication is similar to the decreasing strategy in its early actions, and as an average, after communicating the first 10% of actions (that roughly correspond to one or two depending on the domain) the informative and the decreasing strategies are equally informative ($G_{\text{inf}} = 0$). Notice also that because of this reason the decreasing strategy is consistently more informative than the increasing strategy.

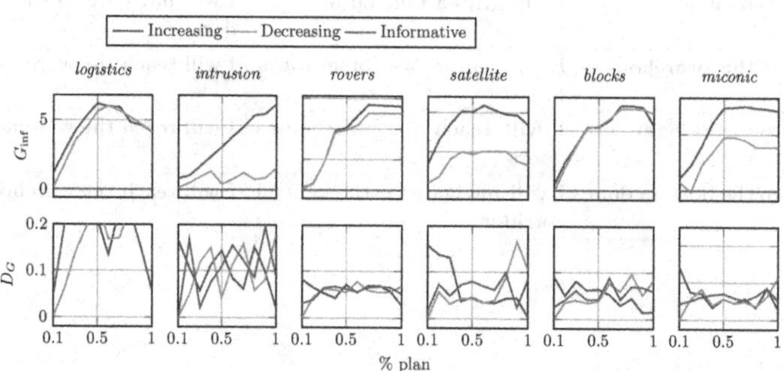

Fig. 3. Entropy gains and distance-to-goal measures for the automated benchmarks.

6 User Study

To further test our method, we performed a user study that simulates the case in which an operator encounters a robot in a corridor of a warehouse, and not knowing what it's doing asks it to verbalize its plan. The study's participants were given 12 scenarios of this type, illustrated on a Graphical User Interface (Fig. 3). In each of the scenarios there are two rooms connected by a corridor and containing 1 to 3 random objects of the same color. Objects can be circles, squares or triangles, and can be either red or blue. There are 3 possible exit doors at the corners. A recharge station is in the central corridor. The robot has 3 possible actions: moving from corridors and rooms, grabbing objects and recharging at the recharge station. In every scenario the robot had the goal of grabbing two random objects from those available, and exit the floor from a random door. It was also set to need to recharge at the recharge station in half of the scenarios. Both participants and robot had full observability on the initial state of the scenario, with robot position and available objects. However, the participants weren't informed on the belief of the robot, its goal or its plan.

Table 2. Verbalizations of a plan from the user study, sorted by the increasing, decreasing and informative strategies.

Increasing order	Decreasing order	Informative order
I will navigate to the central corridor	I will exit from the bottom door	I will grab a red circle
I will reach the warehouses doors	I will navigate to the right corridor	I will grab a blue cube
I will enter the blue warehouse	I will reach the warehouses doors	I will exit from the bottom door
I will grab a blue cube	I will grab a red circle	I will enter the blue warehouse
I will reach the warehouses doors	I will enter the red warehouse	I will enter the red warehouse
I will enter the red warehouse	I will reach the warehouses doors	I will navigate to the central corridor
I will grab a red circle	I will grab a blue cube	I will navigate to the right corridor
I will reach the warehouses doors	I will enter the blue warehouse	I will reach the warehouses doors
I will navigate to the right corridor	I will reach the warehouses doors	I will reach the warehouses doors
I will exit from the bottom door	I will navigate to the central corridor	I will reach the warehouses doors

Table 3. Graphical user interface utilized during the user study. The interface shows the positions of robot, objects and doors (left). For every step of a scenario the participants could select a prediction about the robot's goal (right) from a verbalization as a written sequence of actions (bottom).

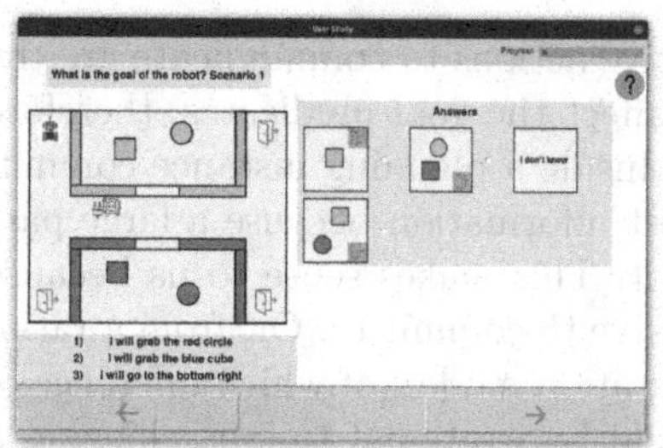

Table 4. Hit ratio of the participants as a function of percentage of communicated actions.

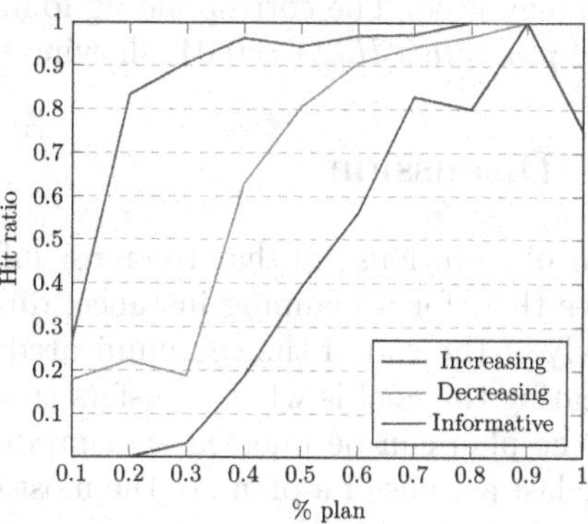

At every step of a scenario participants were given a picture of the scenario and a verbalization of the robot's plan, in the form of its plan in textual form (see Table 2). The verbalization was of increasing size at each of the scenario's steps (at the first step of size 1, second step of size 2, etc.), but, randomly for every scenarios, the verbalization could be given in one of the strategies *informative, increasing* and *decreasing*. Using picture and verbalization at every step the participant were asked to predict the robot's goal among a set of 3 possible goals, or to state they didn't know. Participants utilized the GUI to see the current scenario and verbalization, and to provide their prediction—for example, Fig. 3 shows the participants view of a scenario after the third verbalization of the robot.

We conducted the experiments with 10 participants. The participants were given a thorough introduction to the domain and the task they were asked to perform. At any time they could ask any additional clarification. In the attempt of better simulating an online interaction, the participants were told that the experiment was going to be evaluated also in term of the time required to answer the questions, and that they should have been both accurate and fast. Figure 4 shows the average hit ratio of the participants as a function of the percentage of communicated plan. The hit ratio was measured as the number of times the correct goal was predicted divided by the number of predictions, averaged among all the participants. The average length of plans was 9.14 actions.

The results highlight the effectiveness of the informative communication strategy among the participants. After communicating 20% of the plan, corresponding to 2 actions as an average, the hit ratio for the informative strategy was already measured as 0.85. In comparison, the decreasing strategy takes half of the plan to be as effective, while the increasing strategy almost all of the plan. The statistical significance of the informative strategy is tested against the null hypotheses H_{inc}: no difference with the increasing strategy ($\mu_{\text{inf}} = \mu_{\text{inc}}$), and H_{dec}: no difference with the decreasing strategy ($\mu_{\text{inf}} = \mu_{\text{dec}}$). μ is the average earliest step at which the participants answered correctly, depending on the strategy used. The corresponding found p-values are: $p(n \leq \mu_{\text{inf}}|H_{\text{inc}}) = 0.0014$ and $p(n \leq \mu_{\text{inf}}|H_{\text{dec}}) = 0.04$, showing statistical significance of the results.

7 Discussion

Our observations are that the most informative actions to communicate are the ones that, for a planning instance, directly affect the goal predicates, therefore likely at the end of the communicated plan. Inside a planning instance communicating the goal is what transfers the highest information because a large part of the plan can be inferred as a product of it. This makes sense to us because the last actions of a plan are the most expensive to commit to. Or, from a rationality perspective inside the observer's expectation model (of which inference of plans inside the models is based on), it would be irrational to see achieving a goal and then commit to another, excluding the case where the first goal is a sub-goal of the second. After the actions affecting the goal predicates have been communicated, the actions that mostly discriminate the beliefs become the most informative. This is reflected also in tests of the user study, where the informative strategy systematically selected as first actions to communicate the robot's exit point and the gathered objects.

Overall, the proposed informative communication works by communicating what most discriminates the robot's true state of mind among the set of other candidates, inside the estimated user's second-order theory of mind. The user study demonstrated that this strategy is effectively informative also for human participants. The proposed order of communicating plans based on informativeness, and formalized by the delivered algorithm, is mostly different from the seemingly natural way of communicating incrementally, that is also what is commonly used in the literature. Surprisingly, from our tests it results that the incremental strategy is the most inefficient among those being tested. To deepen the investigation, future work could probe whether human-human communication in task-driven scenarios follows more an informative rather than incremental strategy.

8 Conclusion

In this paper we proposed a strategy for the communication of robot plans that is based on the informativeness of verbalizations when contextualized inside a theory of mind. We compared the informative communication strategy with two baselines that followed increasing and decreasing plan order, finding that the informative strategy was effectively better at making users understand the robot's state using the least amount of verbalizations.

Our results further indicated that the communication strategy most commonly proposed in the literature, namely incremental in plan order, was the most inefficient at transferring information compared to the others. This is because the informative strategy (and partly the decreasing strategy) leverage the fact that the plan is grounded in a planning instance, and communicating as earliest key parts of it such as its goal allows the explainee to infer most of the remaining parts. This was also confirmed by a user study showing an effective correlation between informativeness and the capacity of participants to predict the robot's state.

There are several interesting directions for future work based on informative communication. A first direction is about a deepened investigation on how informative communication relates to human communication in task-driven scenarios. e.g. is it more natural to use an incremental or an informative strategy? Additionally, tests in a real human-robot interaction setting could be performed. And finally, additional tests using the proposed theory of mind model on more complex scenarios could also be performed.

References

1. Cashmore, M., Collins, A., Krarup, B., Krivic, S., Magazzeni, D., Smith, D.: Towards explainable AI planning as a service. arXiv preprint arXiv:1908.05059 (2019)
2. Chakraborti, T., Kulkarni, A., Sreedharan, S., Smith, D.E., Kambhampati, S.: Explicability? legibility? predictability? transparency? privacy? security? the emerging landscape of interpretable agent behavior. In: Proceedings of the International Conference on Automated Planning and Scheduling, vol. 29, pp. 86–96 (2019)
3. Chakraborti, T., Sreedharan, S., Zhang, Y., Kambhampati, S.: Plan explanations as model reconciliation: moving beyond explanation as soliloquy. arXiv preprint arXiv:1701.08317 (2017)
4. Gavriilidis, K., Carreno, Y., Munafo, A., Pang, W., Petrick, R.P., Hastie, H.: Plan verbalisation for robots acting in dynamic environments (2021)
5. Gong, Z., Zhang, Y.: Robot signaling its intentions in human-robot teaming. In: HRI Workshop on Explainable Robotic Systems (2018)
6. Hellström, T., Bensch, S.: Understandable robots-what, why, and how. Paladyn J. Behav. Robot. **9**(1), 110–123 (2018)
7. Kambhampati, S.: Synthesizing explainable behavior for human-AI collaboration. In: Proceedings of the 18th International Conference on Autonomous Agents and MultiAgent Systems, pp. 1–2 (2019)
8. Katz, M., Sohrabi, S.: Reshaping diverse planning. In: AAAI, pp. 9892–9899 (2020)
9. Lawless, W.F., Mittu, R., Sofge, D., Hiatt, L.: Artificial intelligence, autonomy, and human-machine teams-interdependence, context, and explainable AI. AI Mag. **40**(3), 5–13 (2019)
10. McDermott, D.: PDDL-the planning domain definition language (1998)
11. Meza, I., Flores, J.G., Gangemi, A., Pineda, L.A.: Towards narrative generation of spatial experiences in service robots. In: IJCAI 2016 Workshop on Autonomous Mobile Service Robots (2016)
12. Moon, J., et al.: Towards explanations of plan execution for human-robot teaming. In: CEUR Workshop Proceedings (2019)

13. Pereira, R., Oren, N., Meneguzzi, F.: Landmark-based heuristics for goal recognition. In: Proceedings of the AAAI Conference on Artificial Intelligence, vol. 31 (2017)
14. Persiani, M., Hellström, T.: Inference of the intentions of unknown agents in a theory of mind setting. In: Dignum, F., Corchado, J.M., De La Prieta, F. (eds.) PAAMS 2021. LNCS (LNAI), vol. 12946, pp. 188–200. Springer, Cham (2021). https://doi.org/10.1007/978-3-030-85739-4_16
15. Rosenthal, S., Selvaraj, S.P., Veloso, M.M.: Verbalization: narration of autonomous robot experience. In: IJCAI, vol. 16, pp. 862–868 (2016)
16. Sreedharan, S., Kambhampati, S., et al.: Balancing explicability and explanation in human-aware planning. In: 2017 AAAI Fall Symposium Series (2017)
17. Zakershahrak, M., Marpally, S.R., Sharma, A., Gong, Z., Zhang, Y.: Order matters: Generating progressive explanations for planning tasks in human-robot teaming. arXiv preprint arXiv:2004.07822 (2020)
18. Zhang, Y., Sreedharan, S., Kulkarni, A., Chakraborti, T., Zhuo, H.H., Kambhampati, S.: Plan explicability and predictability for robot task planning. In: 2017 IEEE International Conference on Robotics and Automation (ICRA), pp. 1313–1320. IEEE (2017)
19. Zhu, Q., Perera, V., Wächter, M., Asfour, T., Veloso, M.: Autonomous narration of humanoid robot kitchen task experience. In: 2017 IEEE-RAS 17th International Conference on Humanoid Robotics (Humanoids), pp. 390–397. IEEE (2017)

Improving the Connectivity of Multi-hop Communication Networks Through Auction-Based Multi-robot Task Allocation

Félix Quinton(✉), Christophe Grand, and Charles Lesire

ONERA/DTIS, University of Toulouse, Toulouse, France
{felix.quinton,christophe.grand,charles.lesire}@onera.fr

Abstract. A key step in the execution of any multi-robot mission is solving the multi-robot task allocation problem. It consists in assigning the tasks of the mission to the robots and might be described by an integer programming problem. To solve multi-robot task allocation, researchers have proposed many approaches. Among these, auction-based approaches received a lot of attention from researchers, as they are able to quickly reallocate tasks when needed. In this paper, we introduce a new term in the evaluation of bids for an auction-based task allocation protocol. This new term enables us to account for the connectivity of the communication network, which represents the communication links between the robots. The connectivity of the communication network is key to the efficiency of auction-based methods, as they need to share data as broadly as possible to produce efficient allocations. We evaluated our method in a surveillance scenario. We derived theoretical bounds of the time complexity of the evaluation of the bids and of the size of the data shared during the mission. We demonstrated through simulation experiments that our approach improves the robustness of the multi-robot system to dynamic events.

Keywords: Multi-robot systems · Task allocation · Market-based approach

1 Introduction

The applications of Multi-Robot Systems (MRSs) to surveillance missions have interested researchers for a long time [11]. As MRSs consist in several robotic agents working towards a common goal, a reliable coordination strategy is needed to ensure they operate safely and efficiently. An important part of MRSs coordination is the Multi-Robot Task Allocation (MRTA) problem, which consists in assigning the tasks of the mission to the MRS agents [6]. As MRTA is NP-hard, most of the research interested in solving it in real-time scenarios focus on approximate methods.

© The Author(s), under exclusive license to Springer Nature Switzerland AG 2022
F. Dignum et al. (Eds.): PAAMS 2022, LNAI 13616, pp. 345–357, 2022.
https://doi.org/10.1007/978-3-031-18192-4_28

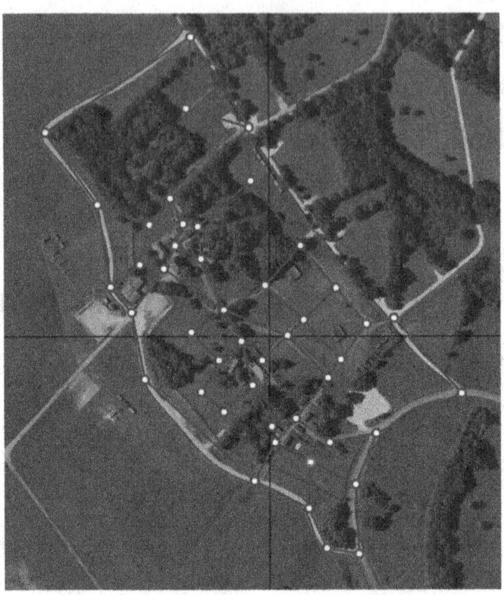

Fig. 1. Real-world surveillance scenario. The graph's nodes must be visited by the robots, but require specific sensors. Buildings and vegetation block communications.

Among the many approaches proposed throughout the years to solve MRTA, the Market-Based Approaches (MBAs) stand out, as they received a lot of interest from the researchers. In MBAs, the robotic agents composing the MRS compete to execute the mission's tasks through a market scheme that emulates real-world economic transactions. In particular, a sub-category of MBAs that received much attention are the Auction-Based Approaches (ABAs): the tasks are sold through an auction scheme in which the bidders are the robots [14]. ABAs excel at efficiently and robustly allocating single tasks [1]. However, ABAs require a reliable Communication Network (CN) for the market scheme to operate properly. For instance, if a robot is disconnected from its teammates, it might be unable to communicate its bids, causing the ABA to allocate no task to this robot. Hence, a poorly connected CN leads to a surge in inefficiencies. Moreover, the CN typically evolves dynamically, as robots move farther apart. Yet, few works are dedicated to the improvement of the CN's connectivity when solving MRTA through an ABA.

In this paper, we will study a surveillance scenario taking place in the environment displayed in Fig. 1. In this environment, physical obstacles such as buildings and vegetation can block teammates from communicating, even if they are very close. To address this issue in the context of ABAs, we introduce a pricing method that aims at preserving a well-connected CN by considering the CN's topology. Our method consists in penalizing allocations that may partition the CN into smaller components connecting disjoint robotic sub-teams (i.e. sub-CNs), while rewarding allocations that merge CN components into larger components connecting robots through multi-hop communications. We apply this pricing method to a dynamic surveillance mission performed by a team of heterogeneous robots with different sensing capabilities. During the mission, the requirements for surveying some positions evolve dynamically.

After a review of the relevant literature, we will present the mission that we study and describe the ABA scheme that we use. We detail the auction-related processes we used in our study, including the evaluation of our connectivity-preserving term, and evaluate their complexity. Next, we detail our experiments and discuss our experimental results. We conclude our paper by summarizing our main results and proposing directions for future research.

2 Related Work

MBAs have been used to solve MRTA since many years [1], and many improvements to ABAs were introduced to adapt them to the specific requirements of multi-robot surveillance missions. For instance, managing robots joining or leaving the team [12], or re-auctioning tasks to robots with lengthy patrol paths [4]. However, the quality of the allocations obtained through ABAs depends on the reliability of the communications between the agents of the MRS. In general, the performances achieved by ABAs decrease as the CN becomes less reliable [5]. Otte et al. [10] compared many ABAs, in scenarios with poor communications characterized by the probability of a message to be lost before its reception. The authors showed that all ABAs perform worst as the message loss probability increased. Their numerical experiments produced mixed results, as no ABA variant was better than the others across the whole spectrum of message loss probabilities. However, they showed that unreliable communications are very detrimental to the quality of the MRTA solutions produced by ABAs. This motivates us to develop and assess strategies accounting for the reliability of communications when solving MRTA. To address the issue on unreliable communications, many authors have focused the improvement of the communication protocols. Researchers proposed to limit the number of robots receiving announcement messages, based either on their closeness to the auctioneer [2], or on an estimation of the bids they might emit [9]. Other studies proposed to filter bids before relaying them to the auctioneer [8].

An alternative to ensure a reliable CN would be to design a bid valuation formula that accounts for the network's connectivity, and encourages robots to favor allocations that would maintain a well connected CN. To the extend of our knowledge, the only study proposing such a communication-related bid formula was published by Sheng et al. [13]. In their study, the authors defined the nearness measure, whose purpose is to evaluate the proximity of a robot to its neighbors. More precisely, robots receive rewards that increase when the distances between them and their teammates decrease. This measure is used in the bid formula and aims to maintain a connected CN during the task allocation process. Simulation experiments showed that it improved the quality of the MRTA solutions [13]. However, this method takes the distance between robots as the sole metric for the CN quality. This is a strong assumption that does not hold if one accounts for obstacles blocking communications, as discussed in our introduction.

In this paper, we propose to integrate in the bid formula a new communication preserving term based on the connectivity of the CN, and in particular on the number of robots in the connected components of the CN, rather than on the distance between robots. We evaluate and discuss the interest of this new term in both real-world and randomly generated scenarios. We account for obstacles blocking communications, which prevents neighboring robots from communicating, even if they are very close.

3 Problem Formulation

Multi-robot Surveillance Scenario: In this paper, we consider an area surveillance mission performed by a team $\mathcal{R}$ of heterogeneous robots. Robots are able to communicate via a multi-hop CN. We also assume that robots are able to determine precisely their position. The mission takes place in a known area represented by a graph $\mathcal{G} = \{\mathcal{W}, \mathcal{E}\}$. Robots must survey the waypoints $\mathcal{W}$ as often as possible and are only allowed to move through the edges $\mathcal{E}$ of the graph. Waypoints model areas of interest, e.g. road crossings or building surroundings.

To evaluate the quality of an MRTA solution, we consider the instantaneous idleness of the waypoints, defined by Eq. (1).

$$\mathrm{I}_w(t) = t - t_{last}^w \tag{1}$$

where $t \in \mathbb{R}_+$ is the current time, and $t_{last}^w \leq t$ is the last visit date of waypoint w. We denote by $\mathbf{t}_{last}$ the vector of last visit times $t_{last}^w, w \in \mathcal{W}$. The mission's objective is to minimize the maximum idleness among all waypoints during the whole mission, as described by Eq. (2). Many authors used a similar modeling for multi-robot surveillance missions [7,16].

$$\mathrm{I}^{\max}(t) = \min \max_{w \in \mathcal{W}} \mathrm{I}_w(t), \quad \forall t \in [0, t_e] \tag{2}$$

With t_e the ending date of the mission. Note that any allocation leaving any waypoint without surveillance results in the worst maximum idleness during the whole mission, that is, $\mathrm{I}^{\max}(t) = t$, $\forall t \in [0, t_e]$. Each robot $r \in \mathcal{R}$ is described by its type $T \in \mathcal{T}$. Robots of the same type share the same moving speed v_T and communication range c_T. They are also equipped with the same set of sensors $\mathcal{S}_T$. Also, each waypoint $w \in \mathcal{W}$ requires a specific set of sensors to be surveyed, that we denote $S_w \subset \mathcal{S}$. Given a waypoint $w \in \mathcal{W}$ and a robot $r \in \mathcal{R}$ of type $T \in \mathcal{T}$, r is able to survey w if and only if it is equipped with a least one relevant sensor, i.e. if $\mathcal{S}_T \cap \mathcal{S}_w \neq \emptyset$. However, robots have no global knowledge of the sensors able to survey each waypoint, i.e. the sets $S_w, w \in \mathcal{W}$. In consequence, they carry local knowledge of these sets, that we denote S_w^r.

Dynamic Events: In real-world environments, robots encounter unexpected events while executing their tasks. Such events are unpredictable and cannot be accounted for when solving the MRTA problem. In this study, we focused on dynamic events representing real-world situations that modify the S_w sets. For instance, a change in lighting conditions may prevent standard visual cameras to survey a waypoint, while night vision cameras will still be able to do so. Also, if smoke appears during the mission on a given waypoint, a specific sensor, such as a thermal camera, is needed to survey it.

A dynamic event is then characterized by the triplet $(w \in \mathcal{W},\ t > 0,\ \mathbf{s}^- \in \mathcal{S}_w)$. The location of the event is given by w, and its date by t, while $\mathbf{s}^-$ represents a set of sensors unable to survey w. In other words, this means that at time t, the list of sensors able to survey w will be updated such that $\mathcal{S}_w \leftarrow \mathcal{S}_w \setminus \mathbf{s}^-$. We consider that the robots are only able to detect these events when trying to survey the concerned waypoint.

4 Auction Protocol

To solve the problem described in Sect. 3, we use a Sequential Single-Item Auction (SSIA) scheme [15]. SSIAs are a simple scheme to consider task synergies in an ABA. In SSIA, robots auction tasks one after the other, in subsequent auction rounds. In each auction round, a new task is, and the robots consider their current plan to value the auctioned task. The auctioneer closes a round after waiting for bids for a fixed amount of time. In the following, we denote by A_r the list of items robot r must auction, and by $exec_r$ the list of tasks it must execute. When a robot r reaches a waypoint $w \in exec_r$, it evaluates the sensors needed to survey it. If r founds that $\mathcal{S}_T \cap \mathcal{S}_w \neq \emptyset$, it surveys w, setting its idleness to 0. Then, r removes w from $exec_r$ and adds it to A_r so that it is auctioned. Re-auctioning waypoints after they are surveyed allows for reallocations whenever they improve the robot's utility. Auction round may be initiated by any robot r with $A_r \neq \emptyset$. In this case, r becomes the auctioneer for the duration of the auction round. The auctioneer r starts an auction round by emitting an announcement message containing the waypoint's details and removing it from A_r. Then, it waits a given time for the bids on its teammates. At the end of the auction round's duration, it determines the bidder that emitted the highest bid, and awards it the waypoint. If no robot was able the survey the auctioned waypoint, then the auctioneer does not received any bid. In this case, it puts the waypoint back into A_r so that it is auctioned again later.

Proposition 1. *Given t_e the end date of the mission, and $\bar{t}$ the duration of an auction round. The SSIA scheme emits at most $\frac{t_e}{\bar{t}}|\mathcal{R}|\,(|\mathcal{R}|+1)$ messages.*

Proof. In the worst case, there are $\frac{t_e}{\bar{t}}$ auction rounds. Each round includes 1 announcement message, 1 award message, and at most $|\mathcal{R}| - 1$ bid messages, if all robots except the auctioneer emit a bid. That results in at most $1 + |\mathcal{R}|$ messages per round. In addition, robots may relay their teammates' messages. If the CN is connected, each message is relayed at most $|\mathcal{R}| - 1$ times: once per robot, except by its initial emitter. Hence, each message is emitted at most $|\mathcal{R}|$ times. We obtain the maximum number of messages by multiplying these results.

The bid valuation is a key element in determining the quality of the MRTA solution, because it determines the winner of each auction round. In the following, we present the bid valuation terms we studied, including our novel term that evaluates the CN quality based on its connected components.

Expected Idleness: First, we present the expected idleness term that we adapted from Yan et Zhang [16]. The expected idleness term computed by a robot $r \in \mathcal{R}$ of type $T \in \mathcal{T}$ for given waypoint $w \in \mathcal{W}$ is given by $I_r(t,w)$ as described in Eq. (3). It is the ratio between w's instantaneous idleness and r's travel time to w.

$$I_r(t,w) = \frac{J_r(t,w)}{1 + J_r(t,w)} \quad ; \quad J_r(t,w) = 1 + \frac{t - \mathbf{t}^r_{last}(w)}{d(r,w)/v_T} \tag{3}$$

With $\mathbf{t}^r_{last}(w) \leq t$ the last visit date of w according to r's local knowledge, and $d(r,w) \in \mathbb{R}_+$ the length of the shortest path from r's last target to w. As $J_r(t,w)$ takes values much greater than the other terms that we use in our bidding process, that we will detail below, it makes them negligible. To address this issue, we normalize J_r so that it takes values in $[0,1]$. The normalized version ofJ_r is denoted I_r.

Proposition 2. *The time complexity of computing I_r is: $\mathcal{O}(|\mathcal{E}| + |\mathcal{W}| \cdot log|\mathcal{W}|)$*

Proof. All the terms involved in I_r's computation can be accessed in $\mathcal{O}(1)$, except for $d(r,w)$, which requires to perform a shortest path search. To do so, we use the Dijkstra algorithm, whose complexity is $\mathcal{O}(|\mathcal{E}| + |\mathcal{W}| \cdot log|\mathcal{W}|)$ [3].

Nearness Measure [13]**:** The nearness measure presented by Sheng et al. [13] aims at evaluating the effect that task allocations have on the CN. To do so, it accounts for the distances between robots at the future date at which the bidder will survey the auctioned waypoint, as described in Eq. (4).

$$S_r(t,w,\mathbf{d}) = e^{-\frac{d_1}{c_T}} + \lambda e^{-\frac{d_2}{c_T}} + ... + \lambda^{n_k-2} e^{-\frac{d_{n_k}}{c_T}} \tag{4}$$

With $\mathbf{d} = \{d_1, ..., d_{n_k}\}$ the pairwise distances between robot r and its neighbors, sorted in increasing order. $\lambda \leq 1$ is a scalar that allows that subsequent $\mathbf{d}$ contributes exponentially less than its predecessor to the measure's value [13].

Proposition 3. *The time complexity of computing S_r is:*

$$\mathcal{O}(|\mathcal{E}| + (|\mathcal{W}| + |\mathcal{R}|) \cdot log|\mathcal{W}| + |\mathcal{R}| \cdot log|\mathcal{R}|)$$

Proof. To compute S_r, three algorithms are executed sequentially. A Dijkstra shortest path search is necessary to determine the date $t^\star$ at which the bidder will reach the auctioned waypoint. This has time complexity $\mathcal{O}(|\mathcal{E}| + |\mathcal{W}| \cdot \log|\mathcal{W}|)$ [3]. The bidder must also determine the positions of its neighbors given their plan. There are at most $|\mathcal{R}| - 1$ neighbors, and their plans contain at most $|\mathcal{W}|$ waypoints. Estimating the neighbor's position requires finding the latest waypoint in its plan reached before $t^\star$, which can be done in $\mathcal{O}(log|\mathcal{W}|)$ as the plans are sorted in arrival dates. Hence, this step has time complexity $\mathcal{O}(|\mathcal{R}| \cdot log|\mathcal{W}|)$. Finally, we need to sort the list of pairwise distances, which has time complexity $\mathcal{O}(|R| \cdot log|R|)$. Adding these three results gives the total time complexity of S_r's computation.

Rewarding Robots for Staying in Touch: To preserve the CN's connectivity during the whole mission, we introduce the term $K_r(t, w)$, de tailed in Eq. (5).

$$K_r(t, w) = \frac{\left|C_{\mathcal{N}\left(t+\frac{d(r,w)}{v_T}\right)}(r)\right|}{\left|C_{\mathcal{N}(t)}(r)\right|} - 1 \tag{5}$$

With = $(\mathcal{R}, \mathcal{F})$ the CN at time t, and $C_\Gamma(r)$ the connected component of graph Γ containing r. Note that the evaluation of $\mathcal{N}(t)$ by robot r is based on the limited, local knowledge its neighbors' behavior. The denominator of K_r is the number of robots in the same sub-CN as r at the beginning of the auction. This corresponds to the number of nodes in the connected component of the RC containing r. The numerator of K_r is an estimate of the number of robots in the same sub-CN as r at the future date $t + \frac{d(r,w)}{v_r}$ when r will attain w. To compute it, r needs to predict its neighbors' positions, which requires to know their plan. We subtract 1 to this ratio to ensure that $K_r(t, w) \leq 0$ if assigning w to r decreases the number of robots in its sub-CN.

Proposition 4. *The time complexity of computing* K_r *is:*

$$\mathcal{O}(|\mathcal{E}| + (|\mathcal{W}| + |\mathcal{R}|) \cdot log|\mathcal{W}| + |\mathcal{R}|^2)$$

Proof. To compute, three algorithms are executed sequentially. The two first algorithms are a Dijkstra shortest path search and the prediction of neighbor's future positions. As discussed in the previous proof, these have time complexity $\mathcal{O}(|\mathcal{E}| + |\mathcal{W}| \cdot \log |\mathcal{W}|)$ and $\mathcal{O}(|\mathcal{R}| \cdot log|\mathcal{W}|)$, respectively. Lastly, we compute the number of nodes in the CN's connected component that contains the bidder robot. To do so, we must perform a depth first search on the CN. In the worst case, the CN is a complete graph with $|\mathcal{R}|$ nodes. In this case, the time complexity on the depth first search is $\Theta\left(|\mathcal{R}| + \frac{|\mathcal{R}|(|\mathcal{R}|-1)}{2}\right)$. Summing the time complexities of these three algorithms, we get the result.

Combining Terms into a Bid Valuation: In the following simulation experiments, we combine I_r, which allows is to account for waypoints' idleness with either S_r et K_r, which are designed to account for the CN's connectivity. In particular, we want to assess the performances yielded by the SSIA scheme when evaluating bids with a combination of I_r and K_r as expressed in Eq. (6a). To do so, we compared our approach with a bid valuation that does not account for the CN's quality, that uses only I_r, and with a bid valuation combining I_r and S_r as described in Eq. (6b).

$$B_r(t, w) = I_r(t, w) + K_r(t, w) \tag{6a}$$

$$B_r(t, w, \mathbf{d}) = I_r(t, w) + S_r(t, w, \mathbf{d}) \tag{6b}$$

Shared Data: In order to compute their bids, the robots need to share data about the current state of the mission. Robots share their local knowledge to the best of their abilities through multi-hop communications, i.e., to all teammates in the same sub-CN. First, to evaluate the idleness cost I_r described in Eq. 3, robots have to share their knowledge of the last visit dates for each waypoint w in order to assess the idleness of the waypoints. To do so, each robot $r \in \mathcal{R}$ maintains a local version of $\mathbf{t}_{last}$, denoted $\mathbf{t}^r_{last}$, that is updated when receiving this value from another robot. Robots send an updated version of $\mathbf{t}^r_{last}$ to their teammates after surveying a waypoint. Upon reception of such message, robots update their list of last visit dates by keeping the element-wise minimum of the received list and their local list.

Proposition 5. *Let d^{min} be the length of $\mathcal{G}$'s shortest edge and v^{max} the moving speed of the fastest robot. The total size of last visit messages sent during the whole mission does not exceed:*

$$\frac{t_e}{d^{min} \cdot v^{max}} \cdot |\mathcal{R}|^2 \cdot |\mathcal{W}|$$

Proof. Last visit messages are emitted after a robot surveyed a waypoint. The frequency of such event is bounded by $d^{min} \cdot v^{max}$. Hence, the number of waypoints surveyed by a given robot throughout the mission is less than $\frac{t_e}{d^{min} \cdot v^{max}}$. In the worst case, all robots move at speed v^{max} and all edges are of length d^{min}. In this case, the MRS surveys $|\mathcal{R}| \cdot \frac{t_e}{d^{min} \cdot v^{max}}$ waypoint during the mission. Last visit messages are of size $|\mathcal{W}|$, as they carry the last visit date of each waypoint. Also, each message is relayed at most $|\mathcal{R}| - 1$ times, if the CN is connected. The result is obtained by multiplying the maximum number of messages by their size, and by the number of times they are emitted.

In addition to the last visits dates, robots also need to know the plans, i.e. expected paths, of their teammates, as they are needed to predict the robots' future positions to compute K_r and S_r. The plan of a robot is modified only when it receives an award after winning an auction. In consequence, sharing it does not add much to the communication load, as only one message per auction round is necessary to maintain an up-to-date version of the plans among all robots. Note that the maximum size of these messages is attained when a single robot is awarded all the waypoints, and is therefore $|\mathcal{W}|$.

Proposition 6. *Let $\bar{t}$ be the duration of an auction round. The total size of plan messages sent during the whole mission does not exceed:*

$$\frac{t_e}{\bar{t}} \cdot |\mathcal{R}| \cdot |\mathcal{W}| \tag{7}$$

Proof. As stated above, we need only one message per auction round, and its size is at most $|\mathcal{W}|$. Also, as discussed in the previous proof the message is relayed at most $|\mathcal{R}| - 1$ times. Finally, remark that if auction rounds start one after the other without interruption, there are $t_e/\bar{t}$ auction rounds during the whole mission. The result is obtained by multiplying the maximum number of messages by their maximum size, and by the number of times they are emitted.

5 Simulation Experiments

Simulation Set Up: To evaluate the effect of including K_r into the bid valuation formula as described by Eq. (6a), we compared it to using only the idleness term I_r and with the bid formula described in Eq. (6b) that includes the nearness measure S_r. To that end, we simulated multi-robot surveillance missions in the real-world scenario (RWS) described in Fig. 1, which has 46 waypoints, and in randomly generated scenarios with two topologies for $\mathcal{G}$: 7×7 grids scenarios (GSs) and stars scenarios (SSs) with 10 branches of depth 5. In order for the generated scenarios to be comparable to the RWS, we used the same team of 10 robots equipped with regular cameras. Additionally, 4 robots were equipped with night vision cameras and 2 others with thermal cameras.

We also parameterized the random generation of GSs and SSs so that they reproduce two key characteristics of the RWS. First, the densities of waypoints must be equal in all types of scenarios. This ensures that scenarios are equivalent in terms of travel time from a waypoint to another. Second, the ratio between the area covered by the robots' communication ranges and the mission's area must also be equal. This ensures that scenarios have the same likelihood of communication links appearing randomly. For GSs, this yielded an edge length of 67 and $c_T^{\text{RWS}} \approx c_T^{\text{GS}}$. For SSs, this yielded an edge length of 37 and $c_T^{\text{RWS}} \approx 1.04 c_T^{\text{GS}}$. In addition, we set up dynamic events to ensure that the scenarios are dynamic, as described in Sect. 3. Events are randomly generated such that in average, half the waypoints will require a night vision camera, and a fourth will require a thermal camera. These events have an occurrence date distributed from $t = 1200$ s to $t = 1500$ s, and each run lasts 3600. This allows the MRS to settle on a first allocation before encountering the events, and to settle again after the events. Finally, we explored values for the communication ranges from $c_T^{\text{RWS}} \in \{60, 75, 100, 200\}$.

Results: As can be seen in Fig. 2, in the RWS, the allocations produced using our bid valuation formula described in Eq. (6a) and represented by the blue lines, yielded lower values for $\text{I}^{\max}$ when compared with the alternatives, except when $c_T = 200$. To study this results in details, we must break down the mission into four phases. In the first phase, from $t = 0$ to $t \approx 500$, robots are not yet distributed on the area, so $\text{I}^{\max}$ increases linearly with t. This phase lasted longer when using $B_r = I_r + S_r$, except when $c_T = 200$, in which case it lasted longer when using our bid formula. In the second phase, which lasts until $t = 1200$, the MRS has settled into a quite stable MRTA, so $\text{I}^{\max}$ is mostly flat. In this phase, the baseline $B_r = I_r$ represented by the green lines is very efficient, as there is no need to optimize anything else than the idleness. Our bid valuation represented by the blue lines is equally efficient when $c_T \in \{60, 75, 100\}$, but not when

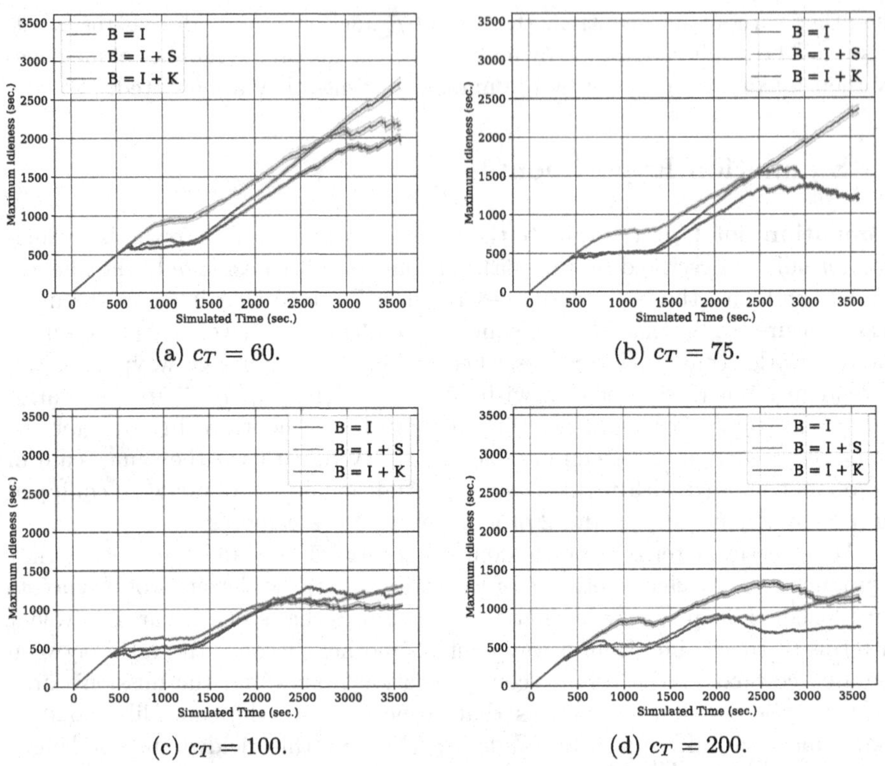

(a) $c_T = 60$.

(b) $c_T = 75$.

(c) $c_T = 100$.

(d) $c_T = 200$.

Fig. 2. Maximum idleness in the real-world scenarios. 50 runs were averaged to obtain each curve. The band around each curve represents the 99% confidence interval of the corresponding mean.

$c_T = 200$. The bid valuation using S_r performs poorly when $c_T \in \{60, 75, 100\}$, but is as efficient as the baseline when $c_T = 200$. In the third phase, starting at $t = 1200$, dynamic events are introduced and disturb the MRTA. This leads to an increase in $\mathrm{I}^{\max}$, as some waypoints are not surveyed. This increase is most dramatic in the baseline's results, which is not surprising as it does not attempt to reconnect with neighboring robots to reallocate the waypoints. However this is not true when $c_T = 200$, because the communication range is so large that robots do not need to intentionally try to reconnect. Finally in the fourth phase, the MRS has settled into a new stable MRTA, and $\mathrm{I}^{\max}$ is quite flat again. This phase starts at different times depending on the value of c_T. In this phase, our bid valuation allows for faster convergence into MRTAs yielding lower $\mathrm{I}^{\max}$, except when $c_T = 200$.

For conciseness purposes, we displayed the results of the generated scenarios in Table 1. We explored three performance metrics. $\overline{\mathrm{I}^{\max}}$ is the average maximum idleness along the mission's duration. $\mathrm{I}^{\max}(t_e)$ is the maximum idleness at the end of the mission. $\overline{\#CC}$ is the averaged number of connected components of the

Table 1. Results of the simulation experiments. 50 runs were averaged to obtain data for each combination of scenario type, communication range (denoted c_T), and bid valuation formula (denoted B).

B	Real-world scenarios				Generated grid scenarios				Generated star scenarios			
	c_T	$\overline{I^{max}}$	$I^{max}(t_e)$	$\overline{\#CC}$	c_T	$\overline{I^{max}}$	$I^{max}(t_e)$	$\overline{\#CC}$	c_T	$\overline{I^{max}}$	$I^{max}(t_e)$	$\overline{\#CC}$
$I+K$	$c_T=60$	**1071**	**1956**	4.99	$c_T=60$	**1462**	**3052**	**6.38**	$c_T=62$	**1100**	**2166**	**4.86**
$I+S$		1301	2167	5.70		1713	3414	7.24		1674	3272	5.77
I		1247	2715	**4.98**		1631	3332	8.81		1633	3302	5.10
$I+K$	$c_T=75$	**842**	**1189**	**4.26**	$c_T=75$	**1302**	**2737**	5.79	$c_T=78$	**1318**	**2601**	4.81
$I+S$		1012	1247	4.58		1633	3074	**5.60**		1563	2914	**4.51**
I		1090	2355	5.81		1411	2991	6.34		1571	3145	5.22
$I+K$	$c_T=100$	**754**	**1043**	**2.68**	$c_T=100$	**1106**	**1624**	4.37	$c_T=104$	**1151**	**1588**	3.30
$I+S$		842	1301	3.24		1342	2863	**4.27**		1330	1776	**3.16**
I		790	1217	4.25		1229	2463	4.92		1347	2270	4.23
$I+K$	$c_T=200$	919	1098	**1.07**	$c_T=200$	1236	2030	**1.17**	$c_T=208$	1129	1533	**1.06**
$I+S$		725	1230	1.09		1032	1378	1.29		1196	1410	1.14
I		**601**	**739**	1.22		**775**	**1138**	1.52		**1002**	**1319**	1.16

CN, i.e. the number of sub-CNs it is divided in. As expected, Table 1 shows that in the RWS, our approach outperformed the alternatives when $c_T \in \{60, 75, 100\}$, but performed poorly when $c_T = 200$. It produced the best $\overline{\#CC}$, except when $c_T = 60$ as the baseline outperformed it by a very slim margin. These results are confirmed by the results derived from GSs and SSs, as our approach produced the best results in terms of $\overline{I^{max}}$ and $I^{max}(t_e)$ when $c_T \in \{60, 75, 100\}$ but not when $c_T = 200$. While our approach produces consistently better results in terms of the idleness metrics, this is not always correlated with a more connected network. This means that we are not properly measuring the effect of our approach on the easiness for robots to reallocate waypoints that sustained an event.

6 Conclusion

In this paper, we studied a dynamic surveillance MRS mission accounting for physical obstacles blocking communications. State of the art methods to solve MRTA for such MRS missions include ABAs, that need a highly connected CN to perform reliably. However, there is no contribution that aims at improving the connectivity of the CN in the existing literature.

To address the issue of keeping the CN connected throughout the mission, we proposed the network connectivity term. We considered three types of scenarios: real-world inspired scenarios, and randomly generated grids and stars topologies. In all scenarios types, a number of dynamic events were randomly generated, causing most of the waypoints to require a specific sensor to be surveyed. To handle these events, robots had to re-allocate their tasks through an SSIA scheme. However, their communication capabilities were limited by their communication range, and by physical obstacles blocking messages. We produced simulation experiments to compare SSIA schemes using our network connectivity term with alternatives that either do not consider communication at all, or try to improve communication using the nearness measure, that relies on the pairwise distance between robots [13].

The results obtained from these experiments show that monitoring the connectivity of the CN using our network connectivity term yields better MRTA solutions. However, our term should not be used when the robots' communication ranges are so large that the connectivity of the CN is almost guaranteed. When connectivity is not guaranteed, our approach allows for an efficient handling of dynamic events and yields lower overall idleness.

In future work, we must design metrics to accurately evaluate the easiness of reallocating waypoints. It would also be useful to define new metrics, in addition to the maximum idleness, that account for the robustness of the approach. Finally, it would be interesting to compare the performances of auction-based approaches with some decentralized optimization-based approaches.

References

1. Dias, M.B., Zlot, R., Kalra, N., Stentz, A.: Market-based multirobot coordination: a survey and analysis. Proc. IEEE **94**(7), 1257–1270 (2006)
2. Ferri, G., Munafo, A., Tesei, A., LePage, K.: A market-based task allocation framework for autonomous underwater surveillance networks. In: OCEANS (2017)
3. Fredman, M.L., Tarjan, R.E.: Fibonacci heaps and their uses in improved network optimization algorithms. J. ACM (JACM) **34**(3), 596–615 (1987)
4. Hwang, K.S., Lin, J.L., Huang, H.L.: Cooperative patrol planning of multi-robot systems by a competitive auction system. In: ICCAS-SICE International Joint Conference (2009)
5. Kalra, N., Martinoli, A.: Comparative study of market-based and threshold-based task allocation. In: International Symposium on Distributed Autonomous Robotic Systems (DARS), Minneapolis/St. Paul, Minnesota, USA (2006)
6. Khamis, A., Hussein, A., Elmogy, A.: Multi-robot task allocation: a review of the state-of-the-art. Coop. Robots Sens. Netw. (2015). https://doi.org/10.1007/978-3-319-18299-5_2
7. Machado, A., Ramalho, G., Zucker, J.-D., Drogoul, A.: Multi-agent patrolling: an empirical analysis of alternative architectures. In: Simão Sichman, J., Bousquet, F., Davidsson, P. (eds.) MABS 2002. LNCS (LNAI), vol. 2581, pp. 155–170. Springer, Heidelberg (2003). https://doi.org/10.1007/3-540-36483-8_11
8. Madhyastha, M., Reddy, S.C., Rao, S.: Online scheduling of a fleet of autonomous vehicles using agent-based procurement auctions. In: International Conference on Service Operations and Logistics, and Informatics (SOLI) (2017)
9. Mezei, I., Malbasa, V., Stojmenovic, I.: Auction aggregation protocols for wireless robot-robot coordination. In: International Conference on Ad-Hoc Networks and Wireless (2009)
10. Otte, M., Kuhlman, M.J., Sofge, D.: Auctions for multi-robot task allocation in communication limited environments. Auton. Robots **44**, 547–584 (2019). https://doi.org/10.1007/s10514-019-09828-5
11. Parker, L.E.: Adaptive heterogeneous multi-robot teams. Neurocomputing **28**(1–3), 75–92 (1999)

12. Poulet, C., Corruble, V., El Fallah Seghrouchni, A.: Auction-based strategies for the open-system patrolling task. In: International Conference on Principles and Practice of Multi-Agent Systems (PRIMA) (2012)
13. Sheng, W., Yang, Q., Tan, J., Xi, N.: Distributed multi-robot coordination in area exploration. Robot. Auton. Syst. **54**(12), 945–955 (2006)
14. Smith, R.G.: The contract net protocol: High-level communication and control in a distributed problem solver. IEEE Trans. Comput. **C-29**(12), 1104–1113 (1980)
15. Sujit, P.B., Beard, R.: Distributed sequential auctions for multiple UAV task allocation. In: American Control Conference (ACC) (2007)
16. Yan, C., Zhang, T.: Multi-robot patrol: a distributed algorithm based on expected idleness. Int. J. Adv. Robot. Syst. **3**(6), 1729881416663666 (2016)

Optimal Inspection Trajectories for 3D Printed Objects

Bruna Ramos[1,2(✉)], Diana Pinho[1,3], and A. Ismael F. Vaz[1]

[1] ALGORITMI Research Center, University of Minho, Campus of Gualtar, 4710-057 Braga, Portugal
{bruna.ramos,diana,aivaz}@dps.uminho.pt

[2] COMEGI, Centro de Investigação em Organizações Mercados e Gestão Industrial, Universidade Lusíada-Norte, 4760-108 Vila Nova de Famalicão, Portugal

[3] Research Centre in Digitalization and Intelligent Robotics (CeDRI), Instituto Politécnico de Bragança, Campus de Santa Apolónia, 5300-253 Bragança, Portugal
diana@ipb.pt

Abstract. The 3D printing technology is innovative, allowing the creation of customized objects. Due to the possible reduction of manufacturing costs, 3D objects printing becomes increasingly attractive to several industrial areas. High levels of customization are achieved at low cost on a wide variety of materials. Despite of high levels of reliability and performance of this technology, it is still necessary to ensure that printed objects meet industrial standard quality requirements. Non–destructive tests are a class of possible tests that may be performed to verify if the industrial standard quality requirements are met. Some non–destructive tests require sampling the object at predefined positions. This paper aims to present an automatic procedure to perform non–destructive sampling of the object, by computing the optimal trajectory planning of the sampling equipment. The procedure is suitable to any inspection machine with three standard XYZ axes and two additional axes allowing the adjustment of the inspection head (e.g. a thermographic camera) to better inspect the object. Inspection trajectories to be computed are to be optimal w.r.t. the total time of inspection, while avoiding collisions between the object and the inspection head/camera. While any (3D printed or not) object can be considered, we take advantage of the 3D object representation (in the STL format used for printing) to determine the optimal inspection trajectories. Strong and weak points of the proposed methods are analyzed through a case study.

Keywords: 3D printing · Inspection trajectory · Optimization · Complex objects · Heuristic and exact approaches

1 Introduction

Additive manufacturing (a.k.a. 3D printing) is an innovative technology that allows the creation of custom objects. This technology allows to build complex structures and designs, with applications in several industrial areas such as

© The Author(s), under exclusive license to Springer Nature Switzerland AG 2022
F. Dignum et al. (Eds.): PAAMS 2022, LNAI 13616, pp. 358–370, 2022.
https://doi.org/10.1007/978-3-031-18192-4_29

automotive, aerospace, medicine, among others. Despite the high level of fidelity and performance of 3D printers, it is still necessary to ensure that manufactured objects meet quality requirements, especially when used in areas requiring high standards of safety and reliability. Non-destructive tests (e.g. thermographic camera) may be used in industrial inspection machines to determine if the object was built according to industrial requirements. Camera movement trajectories is not trivial and standard tools do not provide a single and efficient method for this purpose, especially in objects with complex structures. Techniques to compute adequate object inspection trajectories is, therefore, of most importance.

This work aims to propose a technique to compute inspection trajectories for complex objects created on a 3D printer when using non-destructive tests. The proposed technique can be used in any inspection machine that is able to perform the standard XYZ movements and two degrees of freedom in the inspection head/camera. By selecting a proper inspection head (and a proper non-destructive inspection test), the proposed technique is valid for any type of materials used for printing. The two additional degrees of freedom for the inspection head are only requested if the positioning of the inspection head/camera is to be perpendicularly to the object facet to be inspected. Given a set of inspection parameters (e.g. sampling distance to the object and number of samples) the main goal is to compute the inspection trajectory that minimizes the total inspection time, while avoiding collisions between the inspection head and the object under analysis. An optimization heuristic and an exact approach are proposed to determine the optimal inspection trajectory. The strengths and weaknesses of the approaches are analyzed through a relevant case study.

The remaining of the paper is organized as follow: in Sect. 2 a literature review concerning the three-dimensional inspection problem is performed; in Sect. 3 we describe our settings and the used approach to generate the inspection trajectories; Sect. 4 presents two algorithms to generate valid inspection trajectories; in Sect. 5 a discussion about the developed algorithms performance is made through a case study; finally, in Sect. 6 the main conclusions are drawn and lines for future work are defined.

2 Related Work

The combined use of modern Computer-Aided Design (CAD) and Computer-Aided Manufacturing (CAM) allows large items to be produced [8,11]. Components with complex geometries are becoming very common in several industries, like aerospace, where wide complex shaped parts are very frequently used. This new demand of complex curved surfaces provides significant motivation and challenges to develop new strategies for object quality inspection [11]. Li and Gu [10] provided a review of existing methodologies, techniques, and processes for inspection of parts with free-form surfaces, using specific types of measurement data acquiring methods. Scott *et al.* [13] perform the inspection of the surface of physical objects using laser scanning range sensors for high-precision and high-density. For products with regular features the inspection techniques and equipment are mature in industrial applications, but new algorithms are expected to be developed for more robust and efficient processing of various types of measurement data [10].

Improvements of efficient and effective inspections may be obtained by optimizing the path inspection on a 3D object, taking into account the camera distances range from the object and the view surface angle. Larsson and Kjellander [9] developed a method for automatic path planning using a laser scanning with an industrial robot, capable of planning paths along 3D curves with continuously changing viewing direction, i.e. the method automatically adapts to the shape of the object and scans the object with a proper orientation of the scanner. This gives the most accurate result, while occlusions are avoided. Weyrich *et al.* [18,19] proposed an industrial methodology that employs a camera and a robotic system in order to identify a defective surface and its corresponding location. The strength of this methodology is the combination of vision-based defect detection and automated path planning that makes it flexible to objects with variant geometries without the expense of operation time [18].

More recently, Mineo *et al.* [11], proposed a robotic path planning for non-destructive testing (NDT) of complex shaped surfaces. The proposed NDT approach provides significant motivation for the use of 6 axes robots. This system has the novelty of a flexible robotic trajectory planning, which was coordinated with the NDT data acquisition. Ding *et al.* [5] prove the feasibility of a CAD-based path planning for 3D laser scanning of complex surfaces. The proposed method is able to generate and optimize the scanning path of complex surfaces. However, when subsurface defects are to be detected, thermography strategies are one of the most commonly used tools for the NDT [4]. Dizeu *et al.* [6] use infrared thermography for the quantitative non-destructive evaluation of a long cylindrical object. In the work of Akhloufi *et al.* [1], the captured 3D images and their thermal infrared counterparts are aligned and fused using automatically detected features, allowing 3D visualization of subsurface defects on a 3D model. Ciampa *et al.* [4] provide an exhaustive review of the most recent active thermographic methods for aerospace applications.

3 Inspection Settings

The proposed approach is developed taking into account that it can be used under any conceptual machine settings. Therefore, we consider an inspection machine with five degrees of freedom: three degrees of freedom corresponding to the traditional movement along the XYZ axes and two additional degrees of freedom placed at the inspection head, allowing a correct positioning of the inspection equipment w.r.t. the object to be inspected/sampled.

We consider the object to be provided as a STL format file, which is used as input for the slicer software (e.g. Slic3r [16]) that provides the necessary (G) code to print the object, layer by layer.

To produce the (G) code for inspection one requests a number of parameters to be provided. These parameters are related with the type of inspection to be carried on. The object is sliced along the z-axis (or slicing direction), which corresponds to the intersection of the object facets with a plane perpendicular to the z-axis (or to the slicing direction). These intersections originate a set of (closed) polygons for each layer, being the distance between layers a requested parameter. For the inspection process we only consider the polygons that define the object exterior, i.e., polygons defining inner holes are discard. The inspection distance to the object and the sampling distance are two parameters to be considered when generating the inspection points. The set of points followed by the inspection head defines the inspection path, which defines the path along the current layer with movements along the z-axis (or along the slicing direction). Circular movements are not allowed in our settings, since we assume the printer head to be connected to the structure by a set of cables. The inspection distance, also known as lift-off, represents the distance to which the inspection head must be placed in order to avoid collisions with the object. Another parameter is the sampling distance, defining the distance between samples in the same layer. The lift-off, sampling, and slicing distances define the area to be captured by the inspection head. The computational complexity of the optimization algorithms used for computing the inspection path is high dependable on these parameters, since they define the (possible huge) set of inspection points. The inspection path complexity can also increase for high complex objects such as the ones composed by more than one inspection polygon per layer.

When computing the inspection points, corresponding to projected points of the polygon, one is able to provide the facet normal, which is used as the inspection machine head direction, if an object perpendicular position is to be obtained. The complete inspection path is formed by inspection paths for each layer obtained from slicing the object.

A simple object is an object that is composed by a unique (convex) polygon per layer. Whereas we consider an object to be complex if any layer obtained from slicing has more than one polygon or if a single (nonconvex) polygon shape includes a point where sampling leads to a collision with the inspection machine head. The polygon is obtained by the intersection of a plane with the object facets, resulting in a set of line segments. These line segments can be used to form a segmented parametric function, i.e. a linear spline. One of the vertex is taken as the initial and end point of the spline, since we have a closed polygon. Determining the points to be inspected for simple objects is done by computing a projection of the polygon vertices along the facets normal directions (ignoring the z-axis), considering the lift-off distance. Inspection points are points in the new projected polygon at sampling distances in original polygon, which may be obtained by sampling the polygon linear spline at equidistant parametric values. Figure 1a illustrates this approach, where I is the polygon initial point (selected among the polygon vertices), S is the sampling distance, and a and b are inspection points obtained from the projection along the facet normal direction (dashed line), where sampling is to take place, and L is the lift-off distance.

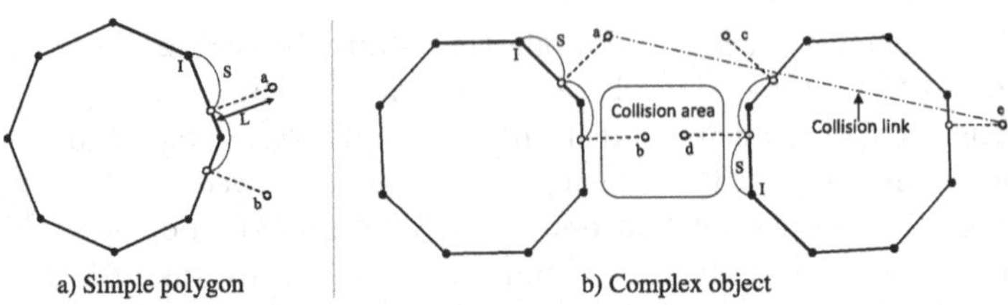

Fig. 1. Inspection points projection

Figure 1b presents the case of two polygons where the inspection points b and d will lead to a collision with the inspection head (assuming an inspection head size bigger enough than the space between polygons). Inspection points a and c are still available for sampling.

Still, considering only valid points may lead to an inspection path where a collision takes place. Figure 1b also illustrates the case where a link, i.e. a linear movement of the inspection head, may lead to a collision if one decides to take sample point a and e to be consecutive inspection points. A valid link is obtained when a linear movement is possible between two inspection points (e.g. a–c is a valid link, while a–e and c–e are not).

4 Inspection Path Computation

An inspection path corresponds to a solution of the traveling salesman problem, considering a graph whose nodes are valid inspection points and arcs are valid links between nodes. We aim to visit only once all the inspection points following valid links. Graphs are computed for each layer of the object, obtained from the slicing procedure. The initial node for the first graph/layer to be considered is also to be computed, i.e. the start city of the traveling salesman problem is not fixed, and returning to the start city is not mandatory, since we aim to proceed to the next layer/graph without visiting the starting valid inspection point. Path must take into account the inspection machine characteristics in order to minimize the total inspection time. We assume arc costs to be proportional to the total travel time, i.e. we use the Euclidean distance between points that form the arc to represent the arc cost. We further assume that movements along the z-axis are to be avoided, since these movements usually imply more stress and energy consumption to the machine (since a high load must be moved).

To compute a graph for a given layer, in a first step, all valid inspection points are computed. For each putative inspection point a collision between the inspection head and the object is checked, where the inspection head is oriented towards the normal direction of the facet that originated the corresponding line polygon line segment. If a possible collision is detected then the point is not considered for inspection and is discarded. The second step considers all the valid points as nodes in the graph and computes all the arcs formed by valid links between all valid points. A link is considered between each two possible valid inspection points and is tested for collisions against any existent object polygon and inspection head. One may consider the full object to check for collisions when following the link. If a possible collision occurs the link is not added to the graph. After executing all described steps it is obtained two lists, $\mathcal{N} = \{i \in \mathcal{S} : \mathcal{S} \in \mathcal{L}_{sub}\}$, $\mathcal{G}$, where $\mathcal{N}$ is a list of valid inspection points, $\mathcal{L}_{sub}$ the list of valid sub-paths, and $\mathcal{G}$ is a list of links.

Collision functions are implemented using a method developed by Möller [12] to compute if two triangles intersect. One considers a possible collision between the printer head and the object at the inspection points, whereas the other checks for a collision while transversing from an inspection point to another.

An example of a graph for the first object layer is illustrated in Fig. 2.

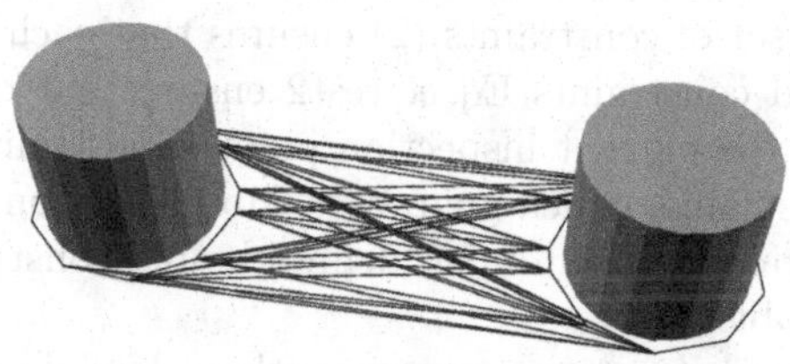

Fig. 2. Inspection graph for the first inspection layer of a complex object

Dropping not valid inspection points and links still leads to a NP-hard problem to be solved for the (optimal) inspection path. In this section we explore a mathematical model and a heuristic to obtain (optimal or near optimal) solutions. Since we assume movements along the z-axis to be prohibitive (high cost machine movement) the proposed strategies compute layer by layer inspection path together with the determination of the initial inspection point for the first inspection layer, while the starting inspection point for the remaining layers is the closest (Euclidian distance) point to the previous layer end point.

4.1 Mathematical Integer Programming Approach

In this section we describe a Mathematical Integer Programming (MIP) model to obtain an optimal inspection path. As already stated, compute an optimal inspection path is equivalent to solve a classic traveling salesman problem, since the main goal is to visit all inspection points minimizing the total travel time. Let, $\mathcal{N} = \{ip_1, \ldots, ip_n, d\}$ be the set of valid inspection points and T_{ij}, $(i, j) \in \mathcal{G}$, a symmetric cost matrix. The inspection point d is a dummy inspection point that is linked with a zero cost to all other inspection points.

The mathematical model presented in (1)–(6) is based on the Miller-Tucker-Zemlin [3,17] formulation, where x_{ij}, $(i, j) \in \mathcal{G}$ are binary variables and u_i, $i \in \mathcal{N}$ are support integer variables, which allows the elimination of sub-tours.

$$\min_{x,u} \sum_{(i,j)\in\mathcal{G}} T_{ij}x_{ij} \tag{1}$$

$$s.t. \sum_{\{j:(i,j)\in\mathcal{G}\}} x_{ij} = 1, \quad \forall i \in \mathcal{N}, \tag{2}$$

$$\sum_{\{i:(i,j)\in\mathcal{G}\}} x_{ij} = 1, \quad \forall j \in \mathcal{N}, \tag{3}$$

$$u_i - u_j + nx_{ij} \leq n - 1, \quad \forall i \in \mathcal{N}, (i,j) \in \mathcal{G} \text{ and } i,j \neq \{ip_1\}, \tag{4}$$

$$u_i \leq n - 1, \quad i \in \mathcal{N}, \quad \text{non-negative integer} \tag{5}$$

$$x_{ij}, \quad (i,j) \in \mathcal{G}, \quad \text{binary} \tag{6}$$

The objective function represents the total time of the inspection path given in equation (1). The set of constraints (2) ensures that each inspection point is visited only once and constraints Eq. eq:rest2 ensure that only one inspection point is visited from the current inspection point. Constraints (4) are the sub-tour elimination constrains, which guarantee sub-inspection paths infeasibility. The last set of constraints ((5) and (6)) defines bound constraints on u and our type of problem variables.

The mathematical formulation assumes, without loss of generality, ip_1 as the start inspection point and obtains a closed path, i.e., a path ending at ip_1. For the first layer and from the optimal solution of the MIP, using an arbitrary starting inspection point as ip_1, one is able to obtain the optimal inspection path by removing the links associated to the d inspection point from the MIP optimal solution [2]. Recall that our inspection path does not need to return to the initial inspection point, since it has already been visited, and the path proceeds to the next layer.

4.2 Heuristic Approach with Spline Orientation

Inspection points are computed from the parametric spline that represents each polygon, obtained from the slicing procedure (see [7]). Each spline is therefore a parametric function that starts at $t = 0$ and ends at t_{end}, where t_{end} corresponds to the perimeter of the polygon. A natural order for the inspection path is to follow the order which occurs in the inspection points computation

Clearly, for the simple object presented in Fig. 1a, we obtain an optimal inspection path since consecutive inspection points are visited by taking a linear movement following the spline orientation. For more complex objects (Fig. 1b) this simple strategy is unlikely to produce a solution. The herein approach considers the spline orientation in order to establish consecutive points inside a sub-path, i.e. it uses the spline orientation to divide the set of inspection points into sets of points forming sub-paths. When removing collisions inspection points we create a sub-path (Fig. 3), but this approach is not enough to provide a set of useful sub-paths to construct an (optimal) inspection path.

When invalid inspection points are not present and we have more than one polygon in the layer, following the spline orientation may not present a solution for the inspection path. A possible strategy is to consider a predefined number

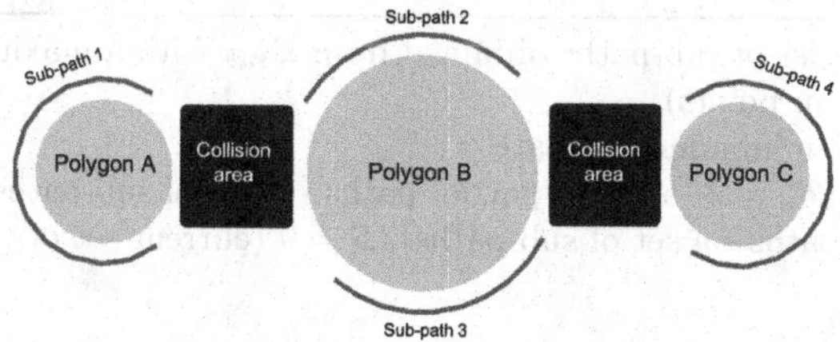

Fig. 3. Example of sub-paths generated due to collision constraints

(α) of valid inspection points to define a sub-path. Taking into consideration the spline orientation one build a set of sub-paths with a maximum of α valid inspection points. Indeed, if a previous generated sub-path with length of n points, with $n > \alpha$, then it is divided into $\lceil n/alpha \rceil$ sub-paths. A sub-path may have less than α valid inspection points due to the existence of invalid inspection points, e.g. sub-paths in Fig. 3 could be further subdivided into other sub-paths with less inspection points.

The k Nearest Neighbor Sub-path Heuristic (k-NNSH) approach consists in building the inspection path by considering the possible combinations of sub-paths. When $k = 1$, the algorithm takes a local view of the problem and attempts to complete the inspection path by looking for the nearest sub-path of a polygon that has not yet been visited, as long as it does not represent a possible collision. For $k > 1$ this approach has a more global view of the problem, not only concerned with the closest path in each step, but also with the k possible paths that has not been visited in each decision. The k-NNSH is presented in Algorithm 1 and the inspection points are replaced with sub-paths. The algorithm is divided in two steps and considers the sub-paths obtained from the $\mathcal{L}_{sub}$ sub-paths further divided into sub-paths with a maximum of α inspection points.

The `kSortS`(i, k, L_{sub}) is a function that computes the k shortest sub-paths not yet taken that is connected to the sub-path i. The function `lastSubPath`(p) returns the last sub-path considered in p. Function `completePathS`(p) is used to check if a path p includes all sub-paths (and therefore forms a complete inspection path). Finally, function `bestPath`$(\mathcal{F}_p)$ returns the best inspection path.

5 Results and Discussion

The proposed approaches, to compute optimal inspection trajectories, only consider valid inspection points and links, i.e. inspection trajectory passing points and links that do not lead to a collision. These approaches are able to determine an inspection path for an object given a set of user defined inspection parameters (e.g. sampling distance S). The proposed algorithms parametrization must be done according to the characteristics of the object and inspection machine. All proposed algorithms are implemented in the FIBR3DApp software, which can be obtained from the last author or visiting the GitHub FIBR3DApp project.

```
Input: L_sub (a list of sub-paths obtained from ℒ_sub with a maximum of α
       inspection points)
Output: p (the minimum cost path)
Initialization: 𝒫_p = ∅ (a list of partial paths - a set of sub-paths), ℱ_p = ∅ (a
list of possible paths - a set of sub-paths), 𝒮 = ∅ (current set of valid sorted
sub-paths).

for i ∈ L_sub do
    𝒮 = kSortS(i, k, L_sub)
    for s ∈ 𝒮 do
        p = {i ∪ s}
        𝒫_p = {p} ∪ 𝒫_p
    end
end
while 𝒫_p ≠ ∅ do
    for p ∈ 𝒫_p do
        i = lastSubPath(p)
        𝒮 = kSortS(i, k, L_sub)
        for s ∈ 𝒮 do
            p' = p ∪ {s}
            if completePathS(p') then
                ℱ_p = ℱ_p ∪ {p'}
            else
                𝒫_p = {p'} ∪ 𝒫_p
            end
        end
    end
    𝒫_p = 𝒫_p \ {p}
end
return bestPath(ℱ_p)
```

Algorithm 1: Nearest Neighbor Sub-path Heuristic (*k-NNSH*)

Since the complexity of the optimal inspection path computation depends on the number of layers and inspection points, the computational results' table reports the number of layers (column l) and the total number of valid points (column N) to be inspected. Column *#T* reports the number of valid links between valid inspection points available in the inspection path graph. The column *#SP* shows the number of sub-paths created in each layer. Please note that *#T* is only used in the *MIP*, while *#SP* is only used in the *1-NNSH* approach. The objective function value for each layer is presented in column f_l. The travel distance between layers is reported in column f_u, while column f_{eval} reports the total inspection distance for the complete object. The computational time used by the approach to find the optimal inspection path is reported in column t, in milliseconds. These results were obtained in an Intel Core i7-3615QM with 2.3 GHz and 16 GB of RAM computer. All algorithms were coded in the *C++* programming language and the objects presented in the case studies were created in OpenSCAD [15] and exported to STL format. The LPSolve [14] solver was used to solve the MIP model.

The case selected study considers a table with four legs depicted in Fig. 4. This case provides different polygons between layers leading to a different number of inspection polygons per layer. The first layer provides an inspection path for the table top while the remaining layers provide an inspection path for the table legs. To determine the inspection trajectory of this case study, a lift-off of 100 mm and a sampling distance of 45 mm were used, whereas the slicing was performed every 40 mm, leading to a total of 5 layers.

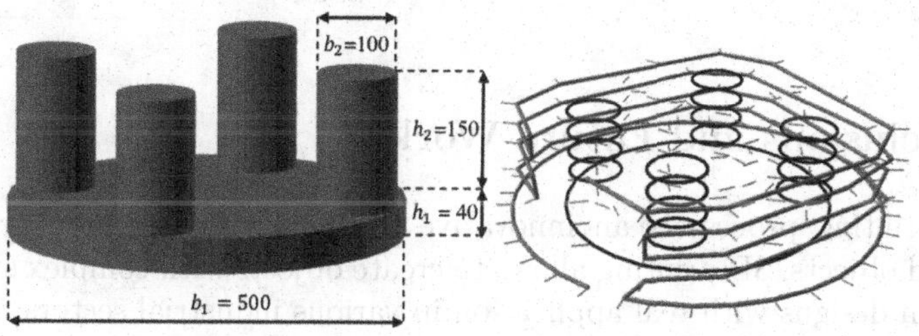

Fig. 4. Best path for the selected case study

As shown in Table 1, not all methods converged to the same solution. The heuristic approach *1-NNSH* with $\alpha = 3$ obtained the best inspection path with a total 9235.16 mm distance. Despite of achieving a slightly longer distance for the first layer, the *1-NNSH* with $\alpha = 3$ approach clearly improves the total distance since the distance taken to change between layers is smaller. Having selected a better quality starting point, which is not necessarily reflected in the best layer inspection path, the approach is able to find a more promising path.

The complexity of the inspection path computation is related with the number of valid inspection points and links. The number of valid inspection points and links are related with the object size and inspection parameters. For moderate number of inspection points and links, efficient solutions can be obtained through the *MIP* approach. For a high number of inspection points and links, then the most appropriate approach is the *k-NNSH* with $1 \leq k < n$ and $\alpha \geq \lceil 0.1n \rceil$.

Table 1. Computational results for the Case Study

Approach	l	N	$\#T$	$\#SP$	f_l	f_u	f_{eval}	t
MIP	1	35	35	-	2123.27	60.17	9341.07	47
	2	10	26	-	1783.48	40.00		
	3	9	24	-	1720.63	71.41		
	4	10	26	-	1780.80	40.00		
	5	10	32	-	1721.30	-		
1-NNSH ($\alpha = 3$)	1	35	-	12	2123.39	53.94	9235.16	31
	2	10	-	4	1706.19	40.62		
	3	9	-	4	1695.48	40.00		
	4	10	-	4	1696.58	40.00		
	5	10	-	4	1838.95	-		

6 Conclusions and Future Work

The 3D printing process is an innovative technology that allows printing of customized objects. 3D printing allows to create objects with complex structures and custom designs with real application in various industrial sectors. However, industries operating in sensitive and high precision areas, like e.g. aeronautics, have to achieve high quality standards in objects.

Although 3D printers may create reliable objects, it is necessary to ensure that they reach desired levels of quality. Non-destructive tests can be performed (e.g. thermographic chambers). The 3D inspection process is a relatively common task, however trajectories for the camera movement are not trivial. Standard tools do not provide an efficient and uniform method to inspect objects with complex structures.

This work provides different techniques to compute optimal inspection paths for complex 3D objects using non-destructive tests. Taking into consideration user defined parameters, two approaches have been proposed to generate valid optimal inspection trajectories. The main objective is to compute the inspection trajectory that minimizes the total inspection time (proportional to the distance used to visit all valid inspection points), while avoiding collisions between the inspection head and the object being analyzed. The quality of the obtained solution is dependent on the type of object and inspection parameters.

As future work, one could consider the global optimization of the inspection path, i.e. optimizing the full inspection path taking into consideration all the layers to be inspected. Please note that this strategy would lead to a higher number of valid inspection points and link, with possible prohibitive computational costs for complex objects.

Acknowledgements. This work has been supported by FCT - Fundação para a Ciência e Tecnologia within the R&D Units Project Scope: UIDB/00319/2020 (ALGORITMI).

References

1. Akhloufi, M.A., Guyon, Y., Castanedo, C.I., Bendada, A.: Three-dimensional thermography for non-destructive testing and evaluation. Quant. InfraRed Thermogr. J. **14**(1), 79–106 (2017). https://doi.org/10.1080/17686733.2016.1229245
2. Applegate, D.L., Bixby, R.E., Chvatál, V., Cook, W.J.: The Traveling Salesman Problem: A Computational Study. Princeton University Press, Princeton (2006). http://www.jstor.org/stable/j.ctt7s8xg
3. Bektaş, T., Gouveia, L.: Requiem for the Miller-Tucker-Zemlin subtour elimination constraints? Eur. J. Oper. Res. **236**(3), 820–832 (2014). https://doi.org/10.1016/j.ejor.2013.07.038
4. Ciampa, F., Mahmoodi, P., Pinto, F., Meo, M.: Recent advances in active infrared thermography for non-destructive testing of aerospace components. Sensors **18**(2), 609 (2018). https://doi.org/10.3390/s18020609
5. Ding, L.J., Dai, S.G., Mu, P.A.: CAD-based path planning for 3D laser scanning of complex surface. Procedia Comput. Sci. **92**, 526–535 (2016). https://doi.org/10.1016/j.procs.2016.07.378
6. Dizeu, F.D., Hesabi, S., Laurendeau, D., Bendada, A.: Three-dimensional nondestructive evaluation of cylindrical objects (pipe) using an infrared camera coupled to a 3D scanner. In: NDT in Canada 2016 & 6th International CANDU In-Service Inspection Workshop (2016). http://www.ndt.net/?id=20408
7. Duarte, J., Santo, I.E., Monteiro, T., Vaz, A.I.F.: Curved layer path planning on a 5-axis 3D printer. Rapid Prototyp. J. (2021)
8. Gibson, I., Rosen, D.W., Stucker, B.: Additive Manufacturing Technologies. Springer, Boston, MA (2010). https://doi.org/10.1007/978-1-4419-1120-9
9. Larsson, S., Kjellander, J.: Path planning for laser scanning with an industrial robot. Robot. Auton. Syst. **56**(7), 615–624 (2008). https://doi.org/10.1016/j.robot.2007.10.006
10. Li, Y., Gu, P.: Free-form surface inspection techniques state of the art review. Comput.-Aided Des. **36**(13), 1395–1417 (2004). https://doi.org/10.1016/j.cad.2004.02.009
11. Mineo, C., Pierce, S.G., Wright, B., Nicholson, P.I., Cooper, I.: Robotic path planning for non-destructive testing of complex shaped surfaces. In: AIP Conference Proceedings, vol. 1650, pp. 1977–1987 (2015). https://doi.org/10.1063/1.4914825
12. Möller, T.: A fast triangle-triangle intersection test. J. Graph. Tools **2**(2), 25–30 (1997). https://doi.org/10.1080/10867651.1997.10487472
13. Scott, W.R., Roth, G., Rivest, J.F.: View planning for automated three-dimensional object reconstruction and inspection. ACM Comput. Surv. **35**(1), 64–96 (2003). https://doi.org/10.1145/641865.641868
14. The LPSolve project: Lpsolve - Mixed Integer Linear Programming (MILP) solver (2003). http://lpsolve.sourceforge.net/5.5/
15. The OpenSCAD project: Openscad - the programmers solid 3D cad modeller (2010). http://www.openscad.org
16. The Slic3r project: Slic3r - Open source 3D printing toolbox (2011). http://slic3r.org

17. Velednitsky, M.: Short combinatorial proof that the DFJ polytope is contained in the MTZ polytope for the asymmetric traveling salesman problem. Oper. Res. Lett. **45**(4), 323–324 (2017). https://doi.org/10.1016/j.orl.2017.04.010
18. Weyrich, M., Wang, Y., Winkel, J., Laurowski, M.: High speed vision based automatic inspection and path planning for processing conveyed objects. Procedia CIRP **3**, 442–447 (2012). https://doi.org/10.1016/j.procir.2012.07.076
19. Weyrich, M., Laurowski, M., Klein, P., Wang, Y.: A real-time and vision-based methodology for processing 3D objects on a conveyor belt. Int. J. Syst. Appl. Eng. Dev. **5**(4), 561–569 (2011). http://www.naun.org/main/UPress/saed/20-686.pdf

Retrograde Behavior Mitigation in Planner-Guided Robot Swarms

Michael Schader(✉) and Sean Luke

George Mason University, Fairfax, VA 22030, USA
{mschader,sean}@gmu.edu

Abstract. Using an automated planner to guide the behavior of a robot swarm is an effective way to control a decentralized multi-robotic system so that it can accomplish complex tasks. Although classical planning assumes that the actors are unitary agents performing atomic actions, the virtual agents in a planner-guided swarm are groups of individuals. When those individuals have differing beliefs about what step of the plan they are on, so-called *retrograde behavior* can occur, slowing or stopping progress and potentially causing catastrophic failure. We formally define this issue, explain several approaches to mitigate it, and report the results of experiments in simulation across three different swarm robotics scenarios. We determine that this problem can be solved by combining a plan analyzer with either offline programming changes or some form of additional online coordination, and present a decision tree for choosing the best mitigation method.

Keywords: Agent-based simulation and prediction · Agent cooperation and negotiation · Multi-robot systems and real world robotics

1 Introduction

Robotic swarms provide several advantages over other multi-robotic systems, including scalability, robustness, and decentralization [1]. The long-standing challenge, however, is the difficulty of getting the agents in a swarm to coordinate effectively so the group can accomplish complex tasks [8]. In earlier work, we introduced the idea of *planner-guided robot swarms*, applying classical planning to the challenge of robotic swarm coordination and control [20,21]. This concept combines the power and flexibility of a centrally-directed multiagent system with the scalability and robustness of a decentralized swarm architecture. We later showed the effectiveness of such a swarm in the face of unreliable or unavailable communications, using observational capabilities as needed to support situation awareness when interagent information sharing is impossible [22].

In this paper we examine an underlying question about the planner-guided swarm approach: what happens when individual agents get out of sync with each other and execute actions from the wrong plan step, and how can any unwanted effects be mitigated? We first review the relevant work done by others on multi-agent planning and on swarm control and coordination with complicated objectives. Next we describe the unsynchronized actions problem, formally define its

© The Author(s), under exclusive license to Springer Nature Switzerland AG 2022
F. Dignum et al. (Eds.): PAAMS 2022, LNAI 13616, pp. 371–384, 2022.
https://doi.org/10.1007/978-3-031-18192-4_30

circumstances, and explain several potential methods to mitigate it. We report the results of experiments performed in simulation on various robot swarm scenarios: constructing a barrier out of scavenged bricks, pressurizing a moonbase that has multiple airlocks, and farming crops on a set of fields. Finally, we propose a decision tree for mitigation methods based on the experimental evidence.

2 Previous Work

This paper sits at the intersection of research into the distinct areas of multiagent planning and swarm robot coordination, and the published literature generally originates from one of these two disciplines. Within the first area there is a spectrum of inherent difficulty, ranging from work about managing fully-cooperative agents with common objectives, to efforts to control true multiagent systems in which agents can have differing (possibly contradictory) goals and private information that they cannot or will not share.

Some researchers limit aspects of the general problem in order to produce plans more simply and quickly. Boutilier [4] worked on "collective single-agent planning" in which fully-cooperative agents that share a joint utility function were managed using game theory and Markov decision processes. Brafman et al. [5] quantified the degree of coupling among agents so as to bound the difficulty of planning joint actions, then used that work to present a multiagent planning algorithm with manageable cost. Nissim et al. [16] developed a fully-decentralized multiagent planner using distributed constraint satisfaction for interagent coordination and local planning to produce individualized plans, with prior knowledge about the planning problem structure speeding the solution.

Others keep the multi-agent planning challenge unconstrained. Borrajo [3] assigned agents a subset of the universal public goals, which they combined with their private goals to produce partial plans; the agents then exchanged and recombined these plan fragments along with obfuscated private information, ultimately converging on a set of plans that met all goals. Luis et al. [12] created algorithms to issue goals to individual agents, have them build plans for themselves, consolidate the plans centrally, and reconcile conflicts among them, finding a balance between centralized and decentralized activity. Muise et al. [15] presented a system that encoded individual agents' public and private information and synthesized the result into a classical planning domain and problem to be solved by a centralized planner without loss of privacy. Torreño et al. [25] built a system that used cooperative refinement to allow agents to develop plans with incomplete information and private knowledge, even in situations with a high degree of coupling among them.

Another concentration in this field is on the coordination aspect of multiagent planning. Chouhan et al. [6] investigated planning in cooperative situations with heterogeneous agent capabilities, developing an algorithm superior to existing methods that worked by converting multiagent planning problems into classical ones. Dimopoulos et al. [7] developed a planner that addressed multiagent coordination using a "planning as satisfiability" approach to manage positive and

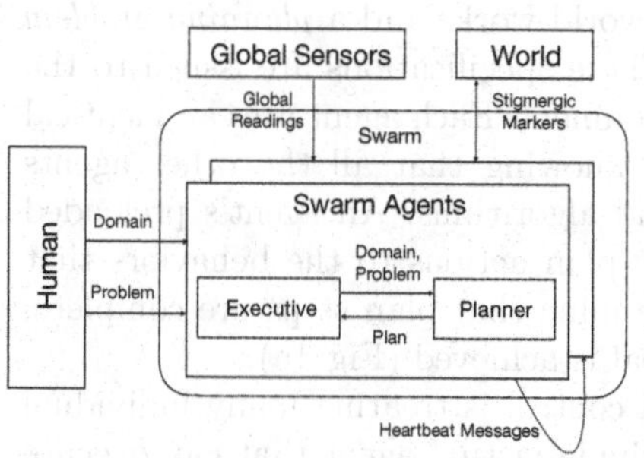

(a) Planner-guided swarm architecture.

Method	*Construction*	*Moonbase*	*Farming*
No Mitigations	100%	0%	0%
Behavior Adjustment	100%	N/A	100%
Heartbeat Shutdown	100%	61%	99%
Heartbeats and Checkpoints	100%	100%	96%

(b) Success rate by scenario and method.

Fig. 1. Architecture diagram and experimental success rate table.

negative interactions among agents pursuing the same goal, both with and without the need for true joint actions. Engesser et al. [9] used dynamic epistemic logic, a formal system that takes into account what agents know and when they know it, to build implicit coordination into decentralized planning.

Within the swarm robotics literature, much work focuses on synthesizing low-level agent behaviors, such as aggregating and navigating, into higher-level ones, like foraging and patrolling. Leng et al. [11] formally defined and then implemented a robot swarm with organizational layers for human-computer interaction, planning, and execution, along with a system to combine simple behaviors into more complex ones. Garattoni et al. [10] demonstrated a robot swarm that collectively learned the correct sequence for a collection of tasks, intriguingly combining reactive and deliberative behaviors. Sheth [23] closely examined multi-robot task allocation, finding that decentralization was necessary for effective scalability and parallelism. Tolmidis [24] used collaborative learning to optimize task allocation to robots as per multiple objectives. Petersen et al. [19] surveyed collective robotic construction techniques, finding examples of implemented systems that showed great promise for specific building environments, but only through tight vertical integration resulting in loss of generality.

Our work in this paper fits best into the collective single-agent planning area. However, we believe no one has explored the situation that we encounter in which certain members of a group of cooperative and homogeneous agents following the same classical and possibly parallel plan lose track of which step they should be executing, breaking traditional assumptions. As to swarm robotics research, there is no established general approach to accomplishing tasks more complex than foraging and the like; we seek an open-ended solution that can address a wide array of challenging swarm objectives.

3 Methods

In our approach, control over a planner-guided robot swarm is achieved by having a human use the Planning Domain Definition Language (PDDL) [14] to specify a *planning domain* that describes how the world works and a *planning problem* that states the goal to be accomplished. These specifications are issued to the agents when they are inserted into the environment. Each agent uses an identical planner to devise a plan for the mission, knowing that all the other agents are operating with the same knowledge and algorithms. An agent's preloaded programming includes a mapping from the plan actions to the behaviors that dictate how it is to act. As the agents determine that plan steps are complete, they advance through the plan until the goal is achieved (Fig. 1a).

A cornerstone of planner-guided swarm control is treating many individual real agents (members of the swarm) as a single virtual agent that can execute plan actions. This is a fiction, but a useful one: it lets us plan actions at a high level of abstraction and then wield the power of the many fungible individuals in the group to complete the prescribed steps. The mapping between macro-level actions and micro-level behaviors provides the bridge between the planning and execution layers of this scheme. Since we can allocate real agents to these groups however we wish, we are free to use a parallel planner to allow multiple groups to perform different actions simultaneously.

For an agent to coordinate properly with the other agents in the swarm, it must possess the same (ideally correct) understanding of the state of the world as they have. This implies the need for a communication mechanism to exchange precepts or an observational capacity to collect new information. When those two capabilities of an agent are interdicted, it can get stuck on a particular plan step while other agents move on to later steps. At minimum this causes a drop in performance since the affected agent is no longer contributing to the progress of the swarm.

More serious are cases in which an affected agent counteracts the actions of the group, to wit, *retrograde behavior*. Formally, this can occur when an action a_m in plan step m has an effect e, and a later action a_n in plan step n $(n > m)$ has an effect equivalent to $\neg e$. In this situation, any agents wrongly frozen on plan step m are undoing the work of those agents that are farther along on plan step n, causing a race condition in which success is dependent on whether the unaffected agents are able to work faster than the affected ones. In addition, it may be possible that performing a_m after a_n completely derails the mission with a catastrophic failure, for example by shorting an electrical circuit that has just been powered up.

To explore this problem, we built a custom Java implementation of the Graphplan algorithm [2] using the PDDL4J planner toolkit [18] for the front-end parser. We then added a plan analysis capability that identifies plan actions that may cause retrograde behavior issues. This analyzer detects exactly the situation described above: plan actions whose effects negate the effects of later plan actions. With that information in hand, we can attempt to reduce the potential damage. We examine three possible solutions: changing the particulars of how the agents perform an action, stopping the activity of out-of-touch agents, and coordinating to ensure that each agent group advances only when each of its individual agents are either ready or deactivated.

3.1 Behavior Adjustment Method

An offline approach that can mitigate or even eliminate retrograde behavior is to refine the low-level directives that the agents execute in order to carry out high-level actions specified in the plan. Although the plan itself is not changed, it is sometimes possible to introduce additional constraints on the agents' programming that prevents those that are incorrectly performing earlier plan actions from interfering with those engaged in later actions. For example, a plan might direct a group to search for test tubes in a chemical laboratory and clean them out, then fill them with a particular liquid. If some agents were performing the cleaning action while others were on the filling step, they could be wastefully working against each other. A suitable *behavior adjustment* might be to clarify the cleaning action as one that may only be performed on test tubes that do not already contain the liquid, thus obviating the conflict.

When it is available, this method can be ideal: a solution that always works and has no negative effect on performance. However, a behavior may or may not be modifiable in this fashion. The adjustment may require sensing beyond the capabilities of the agent, or it may limit the generality of the behavior and reduce its overall usefulness. It also must be done by the programmer ahead of time, which may be infeasible in some circumstances.

3.2 Heartbeat Shutdown Method

An online way to reduce the harm possible from retrograde behavior is to configure agents to shut themselves down if a specified amount of time has passed since the last receipt of a *heartbeat signal* from any other agent. The intent is for agents to self-identify as being disconnected from the rest of the swarm, and to stop all further activity on the grounds that it may be counterproductive. In practice, a robot in this situation might remain in place, revert to a harmless search mode, or return to its home base.

This solution limits the amount of time during which a retrograde agent can interfere with swarm progress, because the retrograde period ends once the agent determines that it is out of contact with the rest of the swarm. This mechanism takes advantage of the information exchanges that occur among agents when they are close enough to communicate with each other and requires no added sensing ability or offline programming. On the other hand, it is possible for a shutdown to occur when it should not, perhaps due to an agent being separated from its peers for too long, or to generalized communication failures inhibiting all interactions. This method also does not guarantee that no retrograde activity will take place, making it unsuitable for situations in which any out-of-sequence action can lead to disaster.

3.3 Checkpoints and Heartbeats Method

Another online approach to preventing retrograde behavior is to incorporate a *checkpoint* after each action identified by the plan analyzer as potentially problematic. This administrative action is injected into the plan itself and directs the

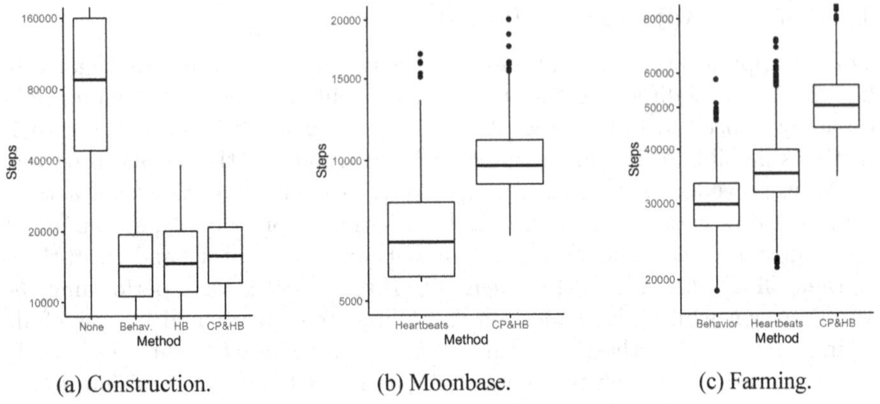

(a) Construction. (b) Moonbase. (c) Farming.

Fig. 2. Simulation steps to completion for each experimental scenario and method over 1000 successful runs.

agents not to advance to the next plan step until they have directly or indirectly learned that every agent in the swarm has reached the checkpoint step. Like a two-phase commit in a distributed database management system, the checkpoint ensures that the next action can only take place if every participant is poised to perform it.

While checkpointing alone eliminates retrograde behavior, it does so at the cost of stopping further progress if any agent fails to respond. To solve this problem, we combine checkpoints with heartbeats: agents on a checkpoint step wait to receive word that all functioning agents are on the same step, but they give up waiting for any that have not responded within a timeout period. Meanwhile, as in the Heartbeat Shutdown method, agents stop their own activity upon determining that they have been out of touch for too long.

This approach provides a guarantee against retrograde behavior, while preserving the ability of the swarm to continue executing the plan. Its main drawback is the added coordination time: each checkpoint slows down progress as each agent waits to learn the status of the others. Its main application is in situations where any unwanted action causes disaster, as in the electrical circuit example mentioned earlier.

4 Experiments

We conducted three experiments under different scenarios to examine retrograde behavior situations and evaluate various mitigation methods. First, we showed the core challenge using the simplest susceptible plan. Second, we raised the stakes by setting up a situation in which retrograde actions not only hurt performance, but could cause catastrophic failure. Third, we increased the sophistication of the domain, the problem, and the failure mechanism to see how our methods worked under more complex conditions. Each experiment exercised our retrograde-aware plan analyzer to detect potential issues.

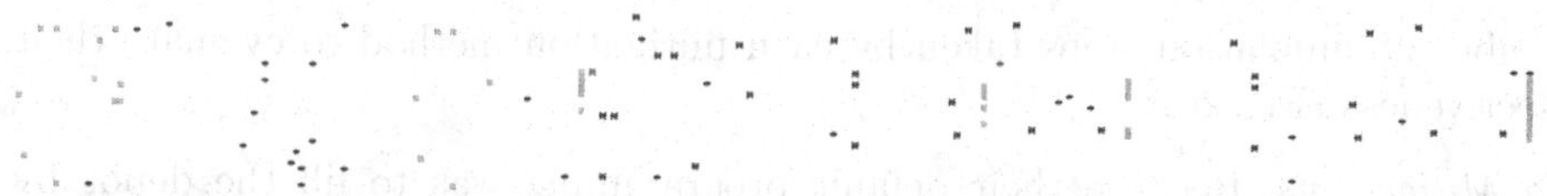

(a) Agents explore the field for bricks (grey).

(b) Some bricks have been brought to the depot in the center.

(c) Once the depot is filled, agents start moving bricks from it to the barrier to the right.

(d) Barrier complete.

Green dots are normally-functioning agents. Red crosses indicate retrograde agents.

Fig. 3. Stages of the construction scenario. (Color figure online)

All of our experiments were built using the MASON multiagent simulation toolkit [13] with discrete virtual environments and simulated non-point robots. The agents navigated using the common swarm mechanism of virtual pheromone trails [17]; that choice was incidental to the capabilities being explored and could have been replaced with robot localization, radio beacons, or some other wayfinding approach. Figure 1b summarizes the success rates for each scenario and mitigation method.

4.1 Construction: Reducing Slowdown Caused by Retrograde Behavior

The Construction scenario exemplifies the simplest possible retrograde behavior problem: a sequence of two actions in which all agents performing the first action should finish before any of them move onto the second action. The initial setup has bricks scattered in an open field. The agents need to move the bricks to a depot location where the bricks will be prepared for use. Once enough have been collected, the agents must use the bricks to build a barrier. They achieve success once the barrier is complete (Fig. 3).

The PDDL domain definition is 17 lines long with two predicates and two actions. The planner generates a short plan to accomplish the goal:

```
1  (fill-depot)
2  (build-barrier)
```

Our plan analyzer indicates that there is a potential retrograde behavior problem with step one: the (depot-full) effect of the (fill-depot) action negates the (not (depot-full)) effect of the later (build-barrier) action. Although the status of the depot is not specified in the goal, this negation means there is a possibility that agents performing those actions simultaneously would undo each others' work.

In our experiment, we had an outage strike ten of the fifteen agents soon after launching. Those agents lost the ability to communicate with any others, as well as the ability to observe the full or empty status of the depot. As a consequence, they were permanently stuck on plan step one. We measured the number of simulation steps taken by each mitigation method to evaluate their effectiveness (Fig. 2a).

No Mitigations. Because their default programming was to fill the depot by moving bricks to it from anywhere, the agents pulled bricks out of the barrier, undoing the progress being made by the other agents that had correctly moved onto plan step two. With no mitigations, the mission devolved into a race. Given enough time, random chance always eventually allowed the properly functioning agents to complete the barrier, but at a high cost in terms of extra work done: the average runtime was 125,150 simulation steps, over seven times longer than the other methods.

Behavior Adjustment. An offline approach to solving this issue was to recode the implementation of the micro-behavior mapped to the (fill-depot) action, adding a requirement for collected bricks to be found in the open field, not in any other location (such as the barrier-in-progress). This eliminated the conflict between the depot-filling and barrier-building activities. The average runtime was 15,462 simulation steps, the lowest that we observed.

Heartbeat Shutdown. Having each agent shut itself down upon detecting that 5000 time steps had elapsed since its last contact with another limited the harm caused by retrograde behavior. The average runtime was 15,968 steps, not significantly different from the Behavior Adjustment method, but clearly much faster than No Mitigations.

Checkpoints and Heartbeats. Based on the plan analyzer's output, under this method the planners added a (checkpoint) action between the two productive plan steps. The combination of checkpointing with a 5000-step heartbeat shutdown eliminated all backtracking caused by the retrograde agents, but at the cost of delaying the plan step transition. This led to an average runtime of 17,197 simulation steps, 11% higher than the Behavior Adjustment mitigation result.

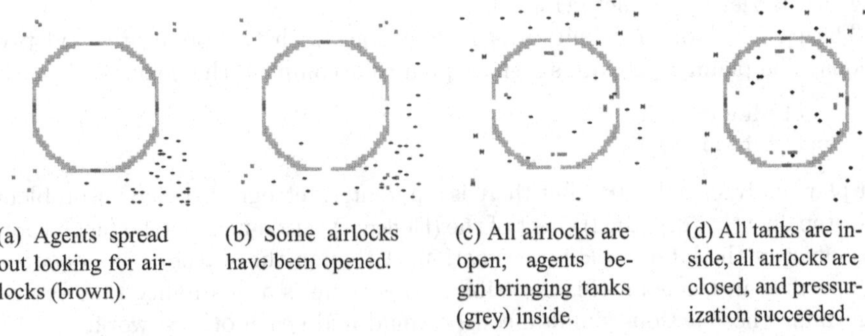

(a) Agents spread out looking for airlocks (brown).

(b) Some airlocks have been opened.

(c) All airlocks are open; agents begin bringing tanks (grey) inside.

(d) All tanks are inside, all airlocks are closed, and pressurization succeeded.

Agents turn black when plan execution is complete. Red crosses indicate retrograde agents.

Fig. 4. Stages of the moonbase scenario. (Color figure online)

We performed 1000 runs of each treatment with 100% completion. We tested the step counts for statistical significance using the two-tailed t-test at $p = 0.05$ with the Bonferroni correction, verifying that all were different from each other except for the Behavior Adjustment and Heartbeat Shutdown results, which were statistically indistinguishable.

4.2 Moonbase: Preventing Catastrophic Failure with Mitigations

The Moonbase scenario explores a situation in which retrograde behavior causes not mere delay, but instant disaster. The initial situation features a moonbase with closed airlocks and twelve full oxygen tanks scattered outside of it. The agents need to open the airlocks, bring the tanks inside, close the airlocks, and finally open the tanks to release the oxygen. It is critical that every airlock be closed when the tanks are opened, or else the oxygen will vent out of the building and be irreplaceably lost (Fig. 4).

The PDDL domain definition is 29 lines long with three predicates and four actions. The planner generates a four-step plan for a single virtual agent:

```
1 (open-airlocks)
2 (get-tanks)
3 (close-airlocks)
4 (open-tanks)
```

The plan analyzer identifies a possible retrograde behavior issue with step one: the (not (pressurized-dome)) effect of the (open-airlocks) action negates the (pressurized-dome) effect of the final (open-tanks) action. In this scenario, losing pressure after opening the oxygen tanks is a catastrophic event that immediately causes mission failure. If the fully-operational agents move onto the final step of opening the tanks while the retrograde agents are in the process of opening airlocks, disaster will ensue.

In this experiment, we injected a breakdown event similar to that used with the previous scenario: early in the run, ten of the 32 agents experienced an outage, preventing them from communicating or observing airlock and tank status. That caused them to remain on plan step one, the airlock-opening action, without regard to what any other agents were doing. We ran simulations to compare the performance of the two mitigation approaches that were ever able to succeed (Fig. 2b).

No Mitigations. With ten retrograde agents continually searching for airlocks to open, the properly-functioning agents had little opportunity to open the tanks while all the doors were closed. Although it was theoretically possible that random chance could have led to mission success with no mitigations, we never observed it happen, and so removed this method from the time step comparison.

Behavior Adjustment. Given the constraints of the scenario, there was no behavior change that would have eliminated the potential for depressurization disaster while still allowing the mission to succeed.

Heartbeat Shutdown. With a delay of 5000 time steps from last inter-agent contact to self-initiated shutdown, the swarm avoided catastrophic failure 61% of the time. The successful runs were completed in an average of 7,150 steps, the fastest of the methods we tested. However, the 39% disaster rate made this a poor option in terms of mission success.

Checkpoints and Heartbeats. The plan analyzer results prompted the addition of a (checkpoint) action after the initial (open-airlocks) step. Combining checkpointing with a 5000-step heartbeat timeout led to a 100% success rate with an average runtime of 10,149 simulation steps. Although this was 42% slower than the successful runs of the Heartbeat Shutdown method, the far better safety record made it the clear winner.

We performed 1000 runs of each treatment (omitting the Behavior Adjustment method due to having no usable adjustment to make) with 100% completion. We verified the step counts for statistical significance using the two-tailed t-test at $p = 0.05$ with the Bonferroni correction. We verified the success rates for statistical significance using the two-sided normal approximation to the binomial at $p = 0.05$.

4.3 Farming: Overcoming Probabilistic Failures in a Complex Multi-group Plan

The Farming scenario brings various complications into our exploration of retrograde behavior: there are three groups of agents working in parallel, the planning domain defines five different actions with dependencies among them, and individual agent failures can occur at any stage of the process. The scenario begins with three open fields ready to be farmed. The agents need to plow to churn up the soil, harrow the plowed fields into neat rows of dirt, seed the harrowed earth, fertilize the planted seeds, and finally weed the fertilized areas to remove any unwanted plants. The job is complete when all the operations have been performed in sequence on each section of each field. Any time an earlier step is performed on ground that has already been treated to a later step, that progress is lost and the later steps need to be repeated (Fig. 5).

The PDDL domain definition is 43 lines long with five predicates, five actions, and one variable. The planner generates a five-step plan for three virtual agents:

```
1 (plow field-a)      (plow field-b)      (plow field-c)
2 (harrow field-a)    (harrow field-b)    (harrow field-c)
3 (seed field-a)      (seed field-b)      (seed field-c)
4 (fertilize field-a) (fertilize field-b) (fertilize field-c)
5 (weed field-a)      (weed field-b)      (weed field-c)
```

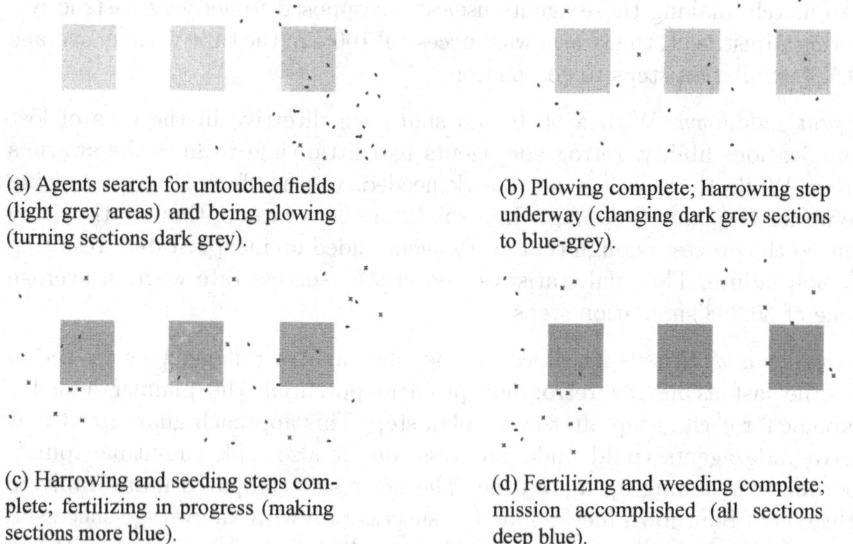

(a) Agents search for untouched fields (light grey areas) and being plowing (turning sections dark grey).

(b) Plowing complete; harrowing step underway (changing dark grey sections to blue-grey).

(c) Harrowing and seeding steps complete; fertilizing in progress (making sections more blue).

(d) Fertilizing and weeding complete; mission accomplished (all sections deep blue).

Green dots are normally-functioning agents. Red crosses indicate retrograde agents.

Fig. 5. Stages of the farming scenario. (Color figure online)

Every action in the first four plan steps is flagged by our plan analyzer as a potential retrograde behavior problem. The effects of each action, such as (not (harrowed field-a)) due to (plow field-a), can negate the effects of later actions, as with (harrowed field-a) resulting from (harrow field-a). The harm done is not catastrophic, since any retrograde action, e.g. plowing an already-seeded patch, can be overcome by performing the succeeding actions on the same area, re-harrowing and re-seeding in this case. However, there is the potential for arbitrarily long delays due to necessary rework.

The breakdowns we induced in this experiment were neither simultaneous nor pre-scripted. Instead, at every scenario time step there was a chance that any of the 32 agents could lose communications and observation capabilities (these treatments used a probability of 0.002%). The longer the whole mission took, the more agents fell victim to the outage probability, sometimes leaving none operating correctly and causing the swarm to fail (Fig. 2c).

No Mitigations. Without mitigations, the swarm's progress was repeatedly rolled back by retrograde agents endlessly applying the wrong treatment to more advanced areas. Although success was theoretically possible due to random happenstance, we never observed it.

Behavior Adjustment. Adding strict conditions to the agents' low-level behavior yielded success. We required them to sense the state of the land around them, and to only perform their plow, harrow, etc. actions if the area was not already in a more advanced state. This limited the impact of being stuck on an earlier plan step to merely making those agents useless, as opposed to actively destructive. With this adjustment, the swarm was successful 100% of the time with an average of 30,524 simulation steps to completion.

Heartbeat Shutdown. With a 5000-step shutdown directive in the case of lost communications ability, retrograde agents had little time to hurt the swarm's progress. While there was some rework needed, the unaffected agents quickly made up for the limited damage. In a small number of cases, though, the delay prolonged the process enough that every agent ended up incapacitated, resulting in mission failure. The final statistics were a 99% success rate with an average runtime of 36,388 simulation steps.

Checkpoints and Heartbeats. Because the plan analyzer flagged every action before the last as having retrograde problem potential, the planner added a checkpoint for each group after every plan step. This approach guaranteed that no retrograde agents could undo progress, but it also added multiple rounds of coordination, taking up more time. The net result compared unfavorably to the Heartbeat Shutdown method: a 96% success rate with an average successful runtime of 51,602 simulation steps, resulting in 42% slower completion with 3% fewer successes.

We performed 1000 runs of each treatment with 100% completion. We verified the step counts for statistical significance using the two-tailed t-test at $p = 0.05$ with the Bonferroni correction. We verified the success rates for statistical significance using the two-sided normal approximation to the binomial at $p = 0.05$.

5 Conclusions and Future Work

Our efforts to define, quantify, and mitigate retrograde behavior were successful. Based on experiments in simulation with possible retrograde behavior scenarios, we showed that if a Behavior Adjustment solves the problem, it should be used; failing that, if catastrophic failure can occur due to out of order actions, then Checkpoints and Heartbeats is the correct solution; in all other situations, Heartbeat Shutdown is the best approach.

In future work, we will conduct a demonstration using real robots to verify that the planner-guided swarm approach is effective in the real world. This will show for the first time a widely-applicable method for building a robot swarm that can accomplish complex tasks.

References

1. Beni, G.: From swarm intelligence to swarm robotics. In: Şahin, E., Spears, W.M. (eds.) SR 2004. LNCS, vol. 3342, pp. 1–9. Springer, Heidelberg (2005). https://doi.org/10.1007/978-3-540-30552-1_1

2. Blum, A.L., Furst, M.L.: Fast planning through planning graph analysis. Artif. Intell. **90**(1–2), 281–300 (1997)
3. Borrajo, D.: Plan sharing for multi-agent planning. In: Proceedings of DMAP Workshop of ICAPS 2013, pp. 57–65 (2013)
4. Boutilier, C.: Planning, learning and coordination in multiagent decision processes. In: TARK, vol. 96, pp. 195–210. Citeseer (1996)
5. Brafman, R.I., Domshlak, C.: From one to many: planning for loosely coupled multi-agent systems. In: ICAPS, vol. 8, pp. 28–35 (2008)
6. Chouhan, S.S., Niyogi, R.: MAPJA: multi-agent planning with joint actions. Appl. Intell. **47**(4), 1044–1058 (2017)
7. Dimopoulos, Y., Hashmi, M.A., Moraitis, P.: μ-satplan: multi-agent planning as satisfiability. Knowl.-Based Syst. **29**, 54–62 (2012)
8. Dorigo, M., Theraulaz, G., Trianni, V.: Reflections on the future of swarm robotics. Sci. Robot. **5**(49), eabe4385 (2020)
9. Engesser, T., Bolander, T., Mattmüller, R., Nebel, B.: Cooperative epistemic multi-agent planning for implicit coordination. In: ICAPS Proceedings of the 3rd Workshop on Distributed and Multi-Agent Planning (DMAP-2015), pp. 68–78 (2015)
10. Garattoni, L., Birattari, M.: Autonomous task sequencing in a robot swarm. Sci. Robot. **3**(20), eaat0430 (2018)
11. Leng, Y., Yu, C., Zhang, W., Zhang, Y., He, X., Zhou, W.: Task-oriented hierarchical control architecture for swarm robotic system. Nat. Comput. **16**(4), 579–596 (2016). https://doi.org/10.1007/s11047-016-9557-2
12. Luis, N., Fernández, S., Borrajo, D.: Plan merging by reuse for multi-agent planning. Appl. Intell. **50**(2), 365–396 (2019). https://doi.org/10.1007/s10489-019-01429-0
13. Luke, S., Cioffi-Revilla, C., Panait, L., Sullivan, K., Balan, G.: MASON: a multi-agent simulation environment. Simulation **81**(7), 517–527 (2005)
14. McDermott, D., et al.: PDDL: the planning domain definition language (1998)
15. Muise, C., Lipovetzky, N., Ramirez, M.: MAP-LAPKT: omnipotent multi-agent planning via compilation to classical planning. In: Competition of Distributed and Multi-Agent Planners (CoDMAP 2015), vol. 14 (2015)
16. Nissim, R., Brafman, R.I., Domshlak, C.: A general, fully distributed multi-agent planning algorithm. In: Proceedings of the 9th International Conference on Autonomous Agents and Multiagent Systems, vol. 1, pp. 1323–1330 (2010)
17. Panait, L., Luke, S.: A pheromone-based utility model for collaborative foraging. In: Proceedings of the Third International Joint Conference on Autonomous Agents and Multiagent Systems, pp. 36–43. IEEE (2004)
18. Pellier, D., Fiorino, H.: PDDL4J: a planning domain description library for Java. J. Exp. Theor. Artif. Intell. **30**(1), 143–176 (2018)
19. Petersen, K.H., Napp, N., Stuart-Smith, R., Rus, D., Kovac, M.: A review of collective robotic construction. Sci. Robot. **4**(28), eaau8479 (2019)
20. Schader, M., Luke, S.: Planner-guided robot swarms. In: Demazeau, Y., Holvoet, T., Corchado, J.M., Costantini, S. (eds.) PAAMS 2020. LNCS (LNAI), vol. 12092, pp. 224–237. Springer, Cham (2020). https://doi.org/10.1007/978-3-030-49778-1_18
21. Schader, M., Luke, S.: Fully decentralized planner-guided robot swarms. In: Dignum, F., Corchado, J.M., De La Prieta, F. (eds.) PAAMS 2021. LNCS (LNAI), vol. 12946, pp. 241–254. Springer, Cham (2021). https://doi.org/10.1007/978-3-030-85739-4_20

22. Schader, M., Luke, S.: Planner-guided swarm coordination with unreliable communications. In: AAAI Spring Symposium: Can We Talk? How to Design Multi-Agent Systems in the Absence of Reliable Communications, vol. 2 (2022)
23. Sheth, R.S.: A decentralized strategy for swarm robots to manage spatially distributed tasks. Ph.D. thesis, Worcester Polytechnic Institute (2017)
24. Tolmidis, A.: Multi mobile robot task allocation using multi-objective optimization techniques. Ph.D. thesis, School of Electrical and Computer Engineering, Aristotle University of Thessaloniki (2017)
25. Torreño, A., Onaindia, E., Sapena, O.: An approach to multi-agent planning with incomplete information. Front. Artif. Intell. Appl. **242** (2012)

A Declarative Modelling Language for the Design of Complex Structured Agent-Based Epidemiological Models

Vianney Sicard[1(✉)], Mathieu Andraud[2], and Sébastien Picault[1]

[1] INRAE, Oniris, BIOEPAR, 44300 Nantes, France
{vianney.sicard,sebastien.picault}@inrae.fr

[2] ANSES, Ploufragan-Plouzané-Niort Laboratory, Health and Welfare Research Unit, Ploufragan, France
mathieu.andraud@anses.fr

Abstract. To provide realistic accounts of disease spread in host populations, epidemiological modelling requires ever-finer details, including a complex spatio-temporal structuring. Multi-level agent based systems have proven effective in tackling such epidemiological dynamics, revealing nevertheless the need for coupling multi-level architectures and organizational features. The solution proposed here attempts to overcome this challenging task, through the development of a declarative domain-specific language to facilitate the separation of concerns and thus expert knowledge integration. We illustrate our approach with an application to the spread of the swine Influenza A between the batches and buildings of a pig farm, to demonstrate the impact of control measures based on modifications of the structural farm features.

Keywords: Epidemiological modelling · Multi-level agent-based simulation · Design patterns · Organizational system · Complex systems · Knowledge and software engineering

1 Introduction

Epidemiological modelling has been of growing interest for several years due to its relevance and support to decision-making. Applied to animal health, such models provide quantitative insights to evaluate and anticipate the implementation of control measures to curb the spread of pathogens, and represent decision-support tool for stakeholders. However, for these tools to be operational, they need to remain realistic in regard to field situation, accounting for the structure of contacts between animals, and the different levels of observation (farm, herd, individual, etc.). For this purpose, agent-based simulation (ABS) has proven its real value [12] to consider behaviours, interactions, and the monitoring of individuals. Furthermore, multi-level agent-based system (MLABS) provides solutions to deal with populations evolving at different scales and in different environments [9]. Especially, the introduction of MLABS-specific design patterns [7,8] allows for

© The Author(s), under exclusive license to Springer Nature Switzerland AG 2022
F. Dignum et al. (Eds.): PAAMS 2022, LNAI 13616, pp. 385–396, 2022.
https://doi.org/10.1007/978-3-031-18192-4_31

an explicit separation of concerns embedded in a generic approach. The EMULSION framework, developed for multi-level epidemiological modelling, is a proof of concept for this approach, offering a separation between a generic simulation engine implementing MLABS design patterns, and a declarative domain-specific language (DSL) [10].

However, to be as close as possible to the situation on the field, and thus implementing the most appropriate control measures, the modelling requires a very fine level of detail, the spatio-temporal structure and dynamics of the population being a key component for anticipating the spread of pathogens. For instance, in the case of pig farming systems, management with batch structuring, i.e. the evolution of groups of individuals according to their physiological statuses, was shown to be pivotal for several pathogens. However, such models present a very high programming complexity, implying difficulties to maintain, adapt or revise them. To tackle this issue, we identified the need to introduce organizational features in MLABS, discussed possible solutions and proposed an organizational multi-level agent-based pattern (OMLABS) [18].

In this paper, we focus on supporting this pattern through a DSL and demonstrate a concrete application to a complex epidemiological model. The paper is organized as follows: Sect. 2 introduces the proposed organizational design pattern with its specifications. Section 3 presents its implementation through a declarative DSL to extend EMULSION, which makes it possible for modellers to focus on the description of the spatio-temporal features of the model (Sect. 3). In Sect. 4, we demonstrate an application to the modelling of the spread of the swine Influenza A virus (SwIAV) within a pig farm.

2 An Organizational Design Pattern for Multi-Level Agent-Based Systems

To address the coupling between MLABS and organizational concepts, we proposed a solution based on a design pattern architecture [18]. Design patterns provide a generic, reusable and modular solutions to solve a specific problem [5]. Recent developments recommend design principles based on design patterns [7], as in other areas of agent-based simulation [6], to improve the genericity and reusability of conceptual solutions to recurring problems. The OMLABS pattern is based on previous MLABS patterns [7] coupled with organizational concepts [4], transcribed in the notion of organization-groups-atom, with an agentification by each of these levels of agents, which encapsulates an environment [18] (Fig. 1). The introduction of organizational concepts into MLABS allows organizations to have an explicit and flexible representation [18] and aims at addressing three issues: 1) to express and formalize the structural relationship between agents ; 2) to constrain the behaviours and interactions between agents ; 3) to be involved in controlling the environment, both structurally and functionally.

In addition to these general concepts, OMLABS implements specific features to handle multi-level environment dynamics and provide flexible modelling capabilities. The **recursivity**, a specific aspect of the pattern, allows for any sublevel

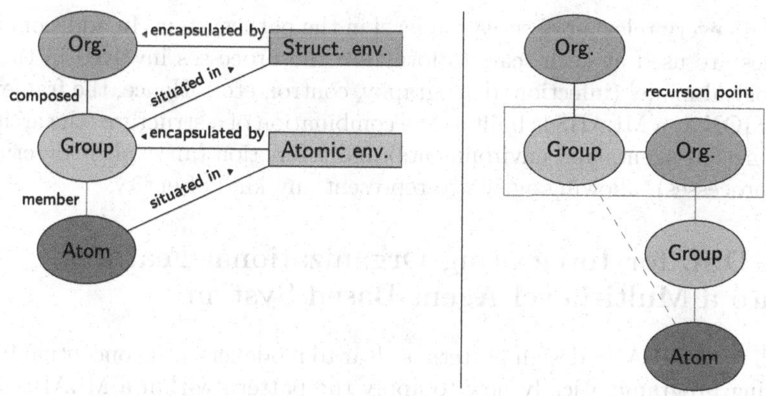

Fig. 1. Structure of the OMLABS pattern [18]. Agent *Organization* encapsulates a *structured environment* composed of *atomic environments*, themselves encapsulated by *Group* agents. Agents involved as *Atoms* belong to an organization by their location in an *atomic environment*, according to the constraints applied by the *Organization*. On the right, the recursive use of the pattern: for instance, a *Group* can itself be a new instance of the pattern. Spaces can be either spatial or social.

(group or atom) to play itself the role of an organization. The **consistent allocation** of atoms into an organization and its groups is managed by the *Organization agent*, according to explicit rules for acceptance, maintaining and location in spaces. **Information** can be stored by each environment and propagated to other environments. This information can be of two kinds: 1) *material*, i.e. with a transfer of information quantity during transmission, involving a loss of this quantity by the source (e.g. pheromone diffusion) ; 2) *informational*, i.e. with a conservation by the source of quantity of information during the transmission (e.g. message broadcast).

This OMLABS design pattern approach has been validated by a proof of concept [18] and proved efficient to interact with modellers. However, going from the conceptual model to its implementation presents real difficulties (allocation rules, recursivity, information propagation, etc.), and it is therefore necessary to provide modellers with an easier way to specify these features. From a model-driven engineering point of view, a convenient solution is to delegate the implementation part to a generic engine, in charge of instantiating several features of the pattern, which are themselves expressed through a convenient DSL, in a declarative way. To do so, we relied on the EMULSION framework, which is specifically built on this separation of concerns.

EMULSION is a generic framework for mechanistic epidemiological modelling, allowing modellers to focus on the modelling issues rather than on computer coding issues. It provides indeed an explicit description of the models through its own declarative DSL, allowing models to be flexible, revisable and modular [10]. The simulation engine of the framework relies on a MLABS architecture [11], based on environment and MLABS design patterns [7,8], which helps reify every relevant observation level in the pathosystem. In addition, state machines are used at each scale to formalize the processes involved in the epidemiological model (infection, demography, control, etc.). Hence, the framework EMULSION as a MLABS is built as the combination of a structure (the architecture of nested agents and environments) and a function (an explicit description of the processes), allowing agents to represent any kind of entity.

3 A DSL for Integrating Organizational Features into a Multi-Level Agent-Based System

Though the OMLABS design pattern is clear to modellers as a conceptual frame, specifying programmatically how to apply the pattern within a MLABS architecture for a given model is quite difficult, thus it requires a specific language to be independent of programming issues. Several agent-oriented programming languages are already used broadly [13,19,21], but require programming skills and thorough understanding of concepts specific to agent-based modelling, such as scheduling or behaviours. In contrast, modellers in epidemiology have no need to learn such general purpose languages if they are provided with a language dedicated to epidemiological modelling issues and focused on knowledge elicitation. Hence, we developed a declarative DSL, based on the YAML syntax and, as for EMULSION, built on main sections divided into indented blocks, representing OMLABS concepts and their features (e.g. the state machines, see Fig. 2).

This DSL for organizational features integrates with the existing EMULSION DSL [10], as the pattern architecture complements EMULSION metamodel. The coupling of the YAML syntax and the MLABS concepts simplifies the modification of the model structure by adding or removing blocks (e.g. adding states or transitions in a state machine).

```
health_state:
  desc: "The state machine which defines the evolution of health states"
  states:
      - S:
          name: 'Susceptible'
          desc: 'suceptible of becoming infected'
      - I:
          name: 'Infectious'
          desc: 'infected and able to transmit the disease'
          duration: 5
      - R:
          name: 'Resistant'
          desc: 'healthy again and resistant to infection'
    transitions:
      - {from: S, to: I, rate: force_of_infection}
      - {from: I, to: R, proba: 1}
      - {from: R, to: S, rate: immunity_loss}
```

Fig. 2. Example of the declaration of the state machine *health_state* with EMULSION DSL. The transition between each state depends on the values of the rates, or after five days for the transition between I to R.

3.1 Organization and Spaces

The core concepts of the OMLABS pattern, i.e. organization-group-atom with an agentification of environments, are transcribed with the notions of *spaces* corresponding to the *structured space* and *nodes* composed of *atomic spaces* where the atoms are located (Fig. 3).

```
farm:
  name: 'farm'
  description: 'organization level of the pattern'
  execute_process:
    - allocate
  spaces:
    name: 'buildings'
    description: 'the farm is composed of buildings'
    allocation:
      - if: 'is_S OR is_R'
        then: main_building
      - if: 'is_I'
        then: quarantine_building
    nodes:
      - main_building:
          informations:
            viral_load:
              value: 0
      - quarantine_building:
          informations:
            viral_load:
              value: 5
    graph:
      - 'main_building ->(viral_load: 0) quarantine_building'
      - 'quarantine_building ->(viral_load:0.6) main_building'
```

Fig. 3. Example of the declaration of an organization *farm*, which is composed of two buildings: *main_building* and *quarantine_building*. The environment can store an amount of viral load, initialized for each environment (0 and 5, resp.). The allocation rules depend on the health states of the individuals: infected ones are located in the *quarantine_building*, the others in the *main_building*. At the end, the graph section define the relation of propagation between each node.

In the main block of the organization statement, the section *execute_process* corresponds to the ordering of the organization processes, i.e. the dynamic of the environments (Fig. 3). Processes refer to predefined actions that need to be executed at the beginning of each simulation steps, e.g. *allocate*, *propagate*, *cleaning*, etc. The *spaces* block corresponds to the *group* level of the pattern, which is composed of nodes. The first subsection corresponds to the declaration of the allocation rules, and the second one to the description of the different nodes, i.e. the *atomic spaces*. Each of these spaces has information statements, with the specification of their initial values. The last block is the definition of the weighted graph handling information propagation between the *atomic spaces*. The distinction between material and informational propagation of information is defined by the two keywords *propagate_matter* and *propagate_information*.

3.2 Recursive Application of the Pattern

One of the specificities of the pattern is its ability to be used recursively: a group can itself be an organization composed of groups. Therefore, the node of the parent organization refers to a child organization (Fig. 1). Propagation between levels – the parent and the child organizations – is notified at the child level with two notions: *from_upper* and *to_upper*. It is thus possible to have a global coverage of the graph, and to know the value of an information at each level (Fig. 4).

```
farm:
  ...
    nodes:
      - main_building:
          reference: main_building

main_building:
  name: 'main_building'
  description: 'sub-organization'
  execute_process:
    - allocate
  spaces:
    name: 'room'
    description: 'buildings are composed of rooms'
    informations:
      viral_load:
        value: 0
        from_upper: 0.5
        to_upper: 0.4
    allocation:
      - 'alternate(spaces=ALL)'
    nodes:
    ...
```

Fig. 4. Example of recursive use. Parent organization *farm* is composed of buildings, and the *main_building* is itself an organization. The child organization *main_building* is composed of rooms. The statement of the child organization is the same as a "normal" organization. The allocation rule specifies that individuals are located in each room alternatively. The transmission between the rooms and the whole building is specified by *from_upper* and *to_upper*, so the graph covers all levels.

4 Application: Spread of Swine Influenza A Virus in a Farrow-to-Finish Pig Farm

To illustrate the complexity of structured systems in epidemiological modelling, more precisely the structuring of populations in space and time, the batch rearing management, commonly practised in pig production herds, is particularly suitable. Indeed, both physiological evolution and the groupings of individuals are closely linked to their location.

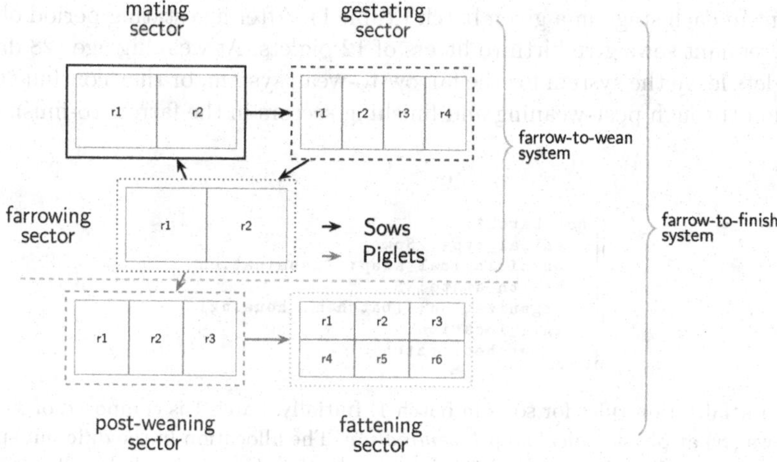

Fig. 5. Flow diagram of sows and piglets in the different sectors, each divided into several rooms.

4.1 Batch Rearing Management

Batch management is a specific feature of pig breeding, consisting in grouping sows that evolves at the same times. More precisely, a sow evolves through different physiological steps (insemination, gestation, farrowing). After farrowing, each sow returns to insemination while its offspring, i.e. the piglets constituting the litter, evolve separately (weaning, fattening). The grouping of litters and sows evolving at the same time constitutes a batch. Successive batches are separated by a constant delay. In our application case, we modelled a management in 7 batches with a between-batch interval of 21 days.

The farm is composed of sectors, and each sector is divided into rooms. Each sector corresponds to a physiological state for sows or piglets. Individuals are allocated in a room according to their batch, one batch per room at a time (Fig. 5). As batch management is known to impact the spread of pathogens, this complexity of setting up a highly structured population must be modelled explicitly.

4.2 Implementation in OMLABS

The model represents two kinds of pig farms: farrow-to-wean farms which sell weaned piglets, and farrow-to-finish farms which sell fattened piglets directly to slaughterhouses (Fig. 5). A parameter of the state machine *physiological_step* allows to easily switch between both systems. Both are driven according to a 7-batch rearing system, the allocation of sows to a batch is given in the initialization part (Fig. 6). Only piglets (new individuals) have to be allocated after farrowing, so the allocation rules obviously specify that piglets are put in the same batch as their mothers (Fig. 7). The time spent in each physiological step is constant in each stage in a given batch (Table 1). After a gestating period of 112 days, pregnant sows give birth to litters of 12 piglets. At weaning age (28 days), the piglets leave the system for the farrow-to-wean system, or they continue their evolution through post-weaning and finishing sectors in the farrow-to-finish context.

```
sow_batch1:
  animal_type: Sow
  physiological_step: Insemination
  health_state: S
  organization: [batches, housing]
  init_location:
    batches: batch1
```

Fig. 6. Initialization rules for sows in batch 1. Initially, batch 1 is composed of susceptible sows (S) at physiological step *Insemination.* The allocation in the different spaces of the sectors is directly managed by the organization *housing*, and the allocation in batches is explicitly defined in the *init_location.*

```
allocation:
  - if: 'is_Piglet'
    then: 'with_source()'
    else: 'alternate_by_group(group=batch, spaces=ALL)'
```

Fig. 7. New piglets are placed in the same room as their mother (*with_source*), and sows are alternately placed in rooms according to their batch, with one batch per room at a time.

Table 1. Duration for each physiological step [20].

Physiological step	Duration (days)
Insemination	35
Gestating	77
Suckling	28
Post-weaning	61 (for batches 1, 2, and 4) 54 (otherwise)
Fattening	121 (for batch 5) 114 (otherwise)

4.3 Epidemiological Model

The OMLABS pattern was used to model the spread of a Swine Influenza A virus (SwIAV) in a pig farm with batch rearing management. SwIAVs are widely spreading in pig production units, causing respiratory disorders and recognized as a main agent responsible for the Porcine respiratory disease complex (PRDC) [16]. It has been shown that SwIAV remains endemic in herds, inducing successive and regular infection waves in batches of growing pigs [3,14].

In what follows, we explain how we extended an existing model [20] by adding both a batch management and states to the epidemiological model to comply with a realistic French pig farm and investigate the impact of batch rearing. We developed the individual-based, discrete-time stochastic model through a MSEIR model with five health states: maternal immunity (M), susceptible (S), exposed (E), infectious (I), and recovered (R). Recovered/Immune sows deliver maternally derived antibodies (MDAs) to their piglets, conferring them a partial protection against infection [1,2,20].

Each scenario was run on two different farming systems: a farrow-to-wean system similar to the one described in White et al. [20] with a mating, gestating and suckling sector (piglets then leave the system after suckling), and a typical farrow-to-finish farm, including post-weaning and fattening sectors. Control strategies were based on increasing biosecurity levels, affecting the indirect transmission between rooms and sectors. For this purpose, three scenarios were developed [17]: 1) *Reference scenario* corresponds to the assumptions in [20], i.e. the same transmission level between rooms and between sectors ; 2) *Full isolation* assumes only direct transmission (i.e., no transmission between sectors nor between rooms) ; 3) *Partial isolation* represents a reduction of indirect transmission. Parameters values were modulated through a logarithmic scale from 10^0 to 10^{-5}.

The design of the different scenarios according to the two farming systems was facilitated by the DSL, allowing for the implementation of contrasted scenarios without programming code, and to switch from one scenario to another by modification of a single parameter.

4.4 Results

The simulations were run over 645 days with a burning period of two sow cycles (2×140 days), to reach a demographic equilibrium, after which the transmission process was initiated with the introduction of an infected sow in batch 1 at the very beginning of the third cycle (insemination stage), i.e., on day 280. Each scenario was repeated for 100 times.

The results show a first peak during the first 25 days after introduction of the virus and the persistence thereafter. The different waves correspond to the infection of successive batches, in line with field observations [15]. For the full isolation scenario, the infection was obviously contained into batch 1. For the farrow-to-wean system, the value of the decrease of the transmission parameter

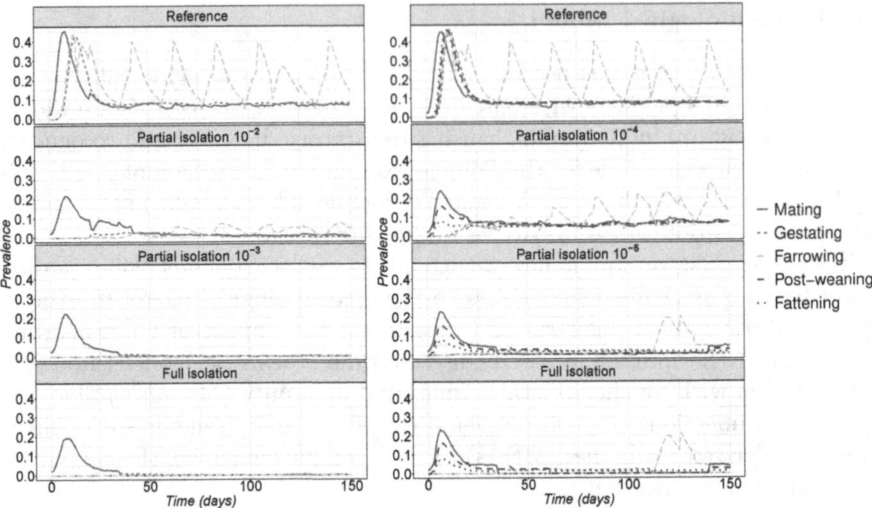

Fig. 8. Average prevalence per sector for the farrow-to-wean system (left), and for the farrow-to-finish (right). Each row represents a scenario.

was between 10^{-2} and 10^{-3}, and for the farrow-to-finish system between 10^{-4} and 10^{-5} (Fig. 8).

Not only did the results confirmed the major role of piglets and the airborne transmission on infection persistence – which are in line with White's model – but also that control measures based on the isolation of rooms and sectors should be really effective to prevent disease from spreading in the whole herd (Fig. 8).

5 Conclusion and Perspectives

We have presented an organizational multi-level agent-based pattern which, combined to the epidemiological framework EMULSION, makes it is possible to take into account the spatio-temporal structure of the population in mechanistic epidemiological modelling. By extending the DSL of this framework, our method gives the ability to model the complexity of highly structured population. The separation of concerns allows experts to easily express the knowledge integration with modularity, readability and revisability. It is thus possible to explicitly represent organizational aspects of the population (social and spatial), coupled with other processes, such as the spread of pathogens.

Models of SwIAV spread in pig farms had already been developed, but with a very high programming complexity, implying difficulties to maintain, adapt or revise [1,2,20]. In contrast, our modelling approach, with the ability to explicitly and easily represent a structured population, provides flexibility, revisability and reproducibility to the model. Assumptions can be explored using parameters (e.g. farming system, buildings division, contact structure, etc.) without compromising the system.

The application of the OMLABS pattern to the modelling of the swine Influenza A virus in batch rearing management highlighted specific behaviours of the pathosystem towards the application of various control measures. Indeed, the OMLABS pattern allowed to represent the dynamics of SwIAV in two different types of farms using a general modelling framework. Although the transmission dynamics were found similar in farrow-to-wean and farrow-to-finish pig farms, the inclusion of post-weaning and finishing sectors required much more biosecurity effort to mitigate the spread of the virus. This result, showing the impact of the structural configuration of the production site, evidences the benefit of the organizational pattern allowing for a direct comparison of selected scenarios through the modification of a single parameter in the DSL. This proof of concept will be applied to the modelling of several European pig farming systems, paving the way for the extension of use cases to broader eco-environmental issues.

Finally, the ability to handle complex systems with a solution coupling flexible MLABS patterns and DSL offers opportunities for the specification of complex multi-level agent-based simulations. This issue is all the more crucial as complex systems modelling often involve scientists from various fields, not necessarily skilled enough in computer science to dive into programming complex simulation architectures. A DSL approach appears then a relevant way to foster efficient interactions.

Acknowledgements. This work is supported by a grant from the Animal Health division of INRAE (French national research institute for agriculture, food, and environment) and the French region Pays de la Loire.

References

1. Allerson, M.W., Cardona, C.J., Torremorell, M.: Indirect transmission of Influenza A virus between pig populations under two different biosecurity settings. PLoS ONE **8**(6), e67293 (2013). https://doi.org/10.1371/journal.pone.0067293
2. Cador, C., et al.: Maternally-derived antibodies do not prevent transmission of swine influenza A virus between pigs. Vet. Res. **47**(1), 86 (2016). https://doi.org/10.1186/s13567-016-0365-6
3. Chastagner, A., et al.: Virus persistence in pig herds led to successive reassortment events between swine and human influenza A viruses, resulting in the emergence of a novel triple-reassortant swine influenza virus. Vet. Res. **50**(1), 77 (2019). https://doi.org/10.1186/s13567-019-0699-y
4. Ferber, J., Michel, F., Baez, J.: AGRE: integrating environments with organizations. In: Weyns, D., Van Dyke Parunak, H., Michel, F. (eds.) E4MAS 2004. LNCS (LNAI), vol. 3374, pp. 48–56. Springer, Heidelberg (2005). https://doi.org/10.1007/978-3-540-32259-7_2
5. Gamma, E., Helm, R., Johnson, R., Vlissides, J.: Design patterns: elements of reusable object-oriented software. Addison-Wesley (1994)
6. Juziuk, J., Weyns, D., Holvoet, T.: Design patterns for multi-agent systems: a systematic literature review. In: Shehory, O., Sturm, A. (eds.) Agent-Oriented Software Engineering, pp. 79–99. Springer, Heidelberg (2014). https://doi.org/10.1007/978-3-642-54432-3_5

7. Mathieu, P., Morvan, G., Picault, S.: Multi-level agent-based simulations: four design patterns. Simul. Model. Pract. Theory **83**, 51–64 (2018). https://doi.org/10.1016/j.simpat.2017.12.015
8. Mathieu, P., Picault, S., Secq, Y.: Design patterns for environments in multi-agent simulations. In: Chen, Q., Torroni, P., Villata, S., Hsu, J., Omicini, A. (eds.) PRIMA 2015. LNCS (LNAI), vol. 9387, pp. 678–686. Springer, Cham (2015). https://doi.org/10.1007/978-3-319-25524-8_51
9. Morvan, G.: Multi-level agent-based modeling - a literature survey. arXiv:1205.0561 (2012)
10. Picault, S., Huang, Y.L., Sicard, V., Arnoux, S., Beaunée, G., Ezanno, P.: EMULSION: transparent and flexible multiscale stochastic models in human, animal and plant epidemiology. PLOS Comput. Biol. **15**(9), e1007342 (2019). https://doi.org/10.1371/journal.pcbi.1007342
11. Picault, S., Huang, Y.L., Sicard, V., Ezanno, P.: Enhancing sustainability of complex epidemiological models through a generic multilevel agent-based approach. In: IJCAI 2017. AAAI (2017)
12. Roche, B., Guégan, J.F., Bousquet, F.: Multi-agent systems in epidemiology: a first step for computational biology in the study of vector-borne disease transmission. BMC Bioinform. (2008). https://doi.org/10.1186/1471-2105-9-435
13. Rodriguez, S., Gaud, N., Galland, S.: SARL: a general-purpose agent-oriented programming language. In: 2014 IEEE/WIC/ACM International Joint Conferences on Web Intelligence (WI) and Intelligent Agent Technologies (IAT) (2014). https://doi.org/10.1109/WI-IAT.2014.156
14. Rose, N.: Modélisation de la dynamique d'infection par le PCV2 en naissage-engraissement
15. Rose, N., et al.: Dynamics of influenza A virus infections in permanently infected pig farms: evidence of recurrent infections, circulation of several swine influenza viruses and reassortment events. Vet. Res. **44**, 72 (2013). https://doi.org/10.1186/1297-9716-44-72
16. Salvesen, H.A., Whitelaw, C.B.A.: Current and prospective control strategies of influenza A virus in swine. Porc. Health Manag. **7**, 23 (2021). https://doi.org/10.1186/s40813-021-00196-0
17. Sicard, V., Picault, S., Andraud, M.: Coupling spatial and temporal structure in batch rearing modelling for understanding the spread of the swine influenza A. In: Society for Veterinary Epidemiology and Preventive Medicine, p. 11. SVEPM (2022)
18. Sicard, V., Andraud, M., Picault, S.: Organization as a multi-level design pattern for agent-based simulation of complex systems. In: ICAAI, pp. 232–241. SCITEPRESS (2021). https://doi.org/10.5220/0010223202320241
19. Taillandier, P., et al.: Building, composing and experimenting complex spatial models with the GAMA platform. GeoInformatica **23**(2), 299–322 (2018). https://doi.org/10.1007/s10707-018-00339-6
20. White, L., Torremorell, M., Craft, M.: Influenza A virus in swine breeding herds: combination of vaccination and biosecurity practices can reduce likelihood of endemic piglet reservoir. Prev. Vet. Med. **138**, 55–69 (2017). https://doi.org/10.1016/j.prevetmed.2016.12.013
21. Wilensky, U., Rand, W.: An introduction to agent-based modeling: modeling natural, social, and engineered complex systems with NetLogo. The MIT Press (2015)

Multi-Agent Routing Optimization for Underwater Monitoring

Emiliano Traversi[1], Igor Zhilin[1], Alya Almarzooqi[1], Ahmed Alketbi[1], Abdulla Al Mansoori[1], and Giulia De Masi[1,2](✉)

[1] Technology Innovation Institute, Abu Dhabi, UAE
{Emiliano.Traversi,Igor.Zhilin,Alya.Almarzooqi,Ahmed.Alketbi, Abdulla.AlMansoori,giulia.demasi}@tii.ae

[2] College of Engineering, Khalifa University, Abu Dhabi, UAE

Abstract. The exploration of the underwater environment has always been a relevant field for science and technology, in order to enlarge our knowledge of this mainly unexplored environment.

Some of the main challenges in the underwater environment are the vehicles' limited battery life and the absence of infrastructures for communication or geo-positioning. Because of these reasons, large vehicles able to navigate collecting data for long distances underwater require performant and high-cost instruments.

In this paper, we propose a different approach applied to a fleet of small autonomous underwater vehicles (AUVs)*. We assume a coarse grained map is already available from satellite measurements and the set of robots is used to get detailed information on sea bottom features. A coverage path planning strategy is designed for the AUVs' fleet. This is based on an optimization problem belonging to the large class of vehicle routing problems. We provide an exact method for finding both the optimal routing for the fleet of drones and their starting position. This is a tool that can be applied on monitoring mission performed a fleet of AUVs. Specifically, a typical use case is the monitoring of health status and growth rate of corals on the coral reef near the coast.

Keywords: Underwater multi-robot system · Marine monitoring · Coverage path planning · Vehicle routing problem · Optimization

1 Introduction

Oceans cover around the 70% of the Earth's surface and they represent the largest basin of mineral and biological resources. For this reason, the exploration of the underwater environment has always been a relevant field for science and

Supported by Technology Innovation Institute, under the project "Heterogeneous Swarm of Underwater Autonomous Vehicles" developed with Khalifa University (contract no. TII/ARRC/2047/2020).

© The Author(s), under exclusive license to Springer Nature Switzerland AG 2022
F. Dignum et al. (Eds.): PAAMS 2022, LNAI 13616, pp. 397–409, 2022.
https://doi.org/10.1007/978-3-031-18192-4_32

technology. Moving from shallow to deep waters, specifically after the continental slope, the exploration and monitoring become always more challenging, being characterized by high hydrostatic pressure, turbidity, poor light, limited availability of communication technologies (the state of art technologies mainly rely on acoustic communications). Furthermore, the energy consumption and the limited battery life are crucial problems in any underwater mission, given the difficulty to have underwater recharging base stations. However, for the above-mentioned reasons, it is a priority to create new technologies for exploration of the oceans, particularly at deeper water depths.

Nowadays satellite images are increasingly available. They provide coarse-grained maps. To have higher resolutions images, we need to use underwater vehicles. In fact terrain based navigation is a common component in underwater exploration [6,14]. The monitoring of a wide area can be more efficient when performed with a fleet of underwater vehicles because it can cover larger distances than a single one and can achieve longer missions, being each robot equipped with its own batteries' system. More relevantly, at the perception level, the use of a fleet of robots is much more convenient than a single robot. In fact, in order to cover an area with an extension comparable with that of a fleet, the single robot should be equipped with much more advanced and costly sensors in order to perform long-range underwater navigation and exploration. For this reason an appropriate algorithm for marine coverage path planning is needed.

The goal of this paper is to determine the best path to be assigned to each robot of an underwater fleet in order to cover the most of the area and to enlarge the perception of specific features. We explore both cases where a single or many features are explored. When dealing with a group of robots the identification of the best path to be covered by each robot is in fact an optimization problem in the large class of Vehicle Routing Problems (VRPs), where the goal is to find the optimal routes for a number of vehicles visiting specific given locations.

The rest of the paper is organized as follows: In Sect. 2 we analyze the existing literature on similar problems, looking at applications both to the marine environment and different environments. In Sect. 3 the problem is clearly defined and outlined, while the mathematical formulation is given in Sect. 4. Finally, the data are presented in Sect. 5 and the experiment results are reported in Sect. 6. The Conclusions summarize the main results of our study.

2 Related Works

Coverage path planning is a well established task in Robotics where many approaches have been proposed [5]. Nevertheless, the extension to multi-robot system is a very active field of research with field applications [1,5,18].

In Marine Robotics, the topic of autonomous underwater robotic exploration and path planning attracted research attention, as summarized in a recent very comprehensive review [16]. A work quite similar to our approach, but applied to only one single AUV, is proposed by McMahon and Plaku [12,13]. They focus on trajectory planning for a vehicle that has to reach a few target regions within a specified time limit, with applications also to mine countermeasure missions.

They implement an algorithm based on the physical traveling salesman problem, including a complex bathimetry of the area and time-varying currents derived from the Operational Forecast System of Chesapeake Bay where they operate.

Nevertheless, the number of projects on underwater multi-vehicles systems or swarms [3] are increasing. In subCULTron project [20], an heterogenous swarm of AUVs is developed, including free to move a-fishes used for navigation and exploration, fixed a-mussels used for sensing and floating a-pads used to keep a connection with a base station. Within this project, they propose an algorithm of a decentralized exploration of interesting patches in an underwater environment with some randomly placed obstacles. This model is very interesting being decentralized and bio-inspired, but it is still quite simplistic. Another bioinspired monitoring system is proposed in [11], where a AUVs fleet is supported by a set of communication nodes connected to the sea surface. Based on the exploration of the AUVs, a kind of pheromone map is created and shared among the nodes, that is used by the AUVs to understand where the interesting targets are located. This approach is interesting from a theoretical point of view, but it cannot be adapted to different areas, relying on communication nodes that have to be deployed before the exploration starts. Li et al. [10] develop a strategy for AUVs' mission planning, generating sets of trajectories, including rendez-vous with energy-carrier agents and placements of recharging stations. Fu et al. [4] consider a mixed fleet of underwater and surface marine vehicles to perform data muling from measurements data obtained by underwater sensors. They applied Reinforcement Learning techniques to simultaneously maximize fairness in data transmissions and minimize the travel distance of the surface nodes.

In this paper, we suggest a methodology based on Vehicle Routing Problem (VRP). VRP is a well known combinatorial optimization problem that aims at finding the optimal set of routes for a fleet of vehicles [19]. The literature of exact [9] and heuristic [17] algorithms for the VRP and its variants is vast, both in terms of applications and methodologies. For more details we refer the reader to the following surveys: [7–9, 15, 19].

To the best of our knowledge, none of the mentioned works provide optimal exploration behaviour by a large number of robots. In this work, we present for the first time an exact method for finding simultaneously both the optimal routing for a fleet of drones and their starting point. Moreover, we apply this method to real case scenarios, for underwater exploration and monitoring, as explained in the Sect. 3.

3 Problem Formulation

In our real scenario, a first coarse resolution map is available to a centralized controller. The input data of our paper derive from satellite imagery, where bathymetry map with soil and vegetation description is provided by the Abu Dhabi Environmental Authority. The map distinguishes 3 features out of sand: grass, coral, rock. This first low resolution map allows the operator to identify the areas of interest.

In order to have higher resolution data, a fleet of robots has to be deployed. The exploring AUVs are "small" and equipped with simple sensors. Each one is able to get close to the sea bottom to get good resolution images but it can only cover a limited area. Therefore the single robot is unable to solve this task without cooperating with the other AUVs of the fleet. The full fleet, on the contrary, is able to guarantee the coverage of an extended area, collecting at the same time high resolution images and videos. For this reason, after an operator selects the area of interest, a centralized controller calculates the deployment point and the optimal path for each robot in order to maximize the coverage of one or more specific feature (rock, coral, sea-grass) to be monitored. The controller assigns to each robot the proper path and the low resolution map. An ultra-short baseline system (USBL) allows the localization of each AUV. The set of robots is subsequently deployed in the specific location from a service boat. The AUVs can move to explore the features taking pictures and videos, following the predetermined paths and eventually reaching back the deployment point within their individual battery life.

For example, a specific use case particularly relevant for environmental sustainability purposes is the monitoring of the health status of the coral reef and data collection (images and videos) of the 3D structure of this complex habitat, like in the sketch of Fig. 1 .

Fig. 1. Sketch of the underwater monitoring scenario, which is one of the main applications of the routing optimization here proposed. An USBL allows the localization of each AUV.

Paper Contributions. From a more technical perspective, this project aims at formulating a Team Orienteering Problem (TOP) [2] applied to an underwater multi-robot system, that would allow efficient underwater exploration. Many variants of the problem are present in the literature [15]. However, this is the first exact algorithm that includes the choice of the starting point as part of the decision process. The provided routes must satisfy a limit in terms of autonomy. Moreover, the speed of the vehicles is considered constant and equal for all the vehicles. Finally, being the focus on the exploration of the sea bottom, the space is considered 2-dimensional. In order to solve this problem, a new exact mathematical model has been developed, as described in the next section. To the best of our knowledge, this is the first exact algorithm that includes the choice of the starting point as part of the decision process.

4 Mathematical Model

Parameters and Variables. In Table 1 and Table 2 we present the decision variables and the parameters used in the models presented in this section. The space is divided in a grid of squares. Each square is represented by a node. A graph G is used to represent the seabed, where to each node i is associated a given quantity p_i^f of feature f, representing the abundance of the feature f on that node (i.e. square).

Table 1. Decision variables

Name	Definition	Range
$x^k_{i,j}$	1 if AUV k goes from i to j	$\{0;1\}$
w_i	1 if node i is used as a starting point	$\{0;1\}$
y_i	1 if node i is visited by at least one AUV	$\{0;1\}$
t^k_i	Arrival time at node i of AUV k	$\mathbf{R}_+$

In this section we present the mathematical models used to simultaneously compute the optimal starting point and routes for a fleet of underwater AUVs, according to different optimization criteria.

Parameters and Variables. In Table 1 and Table 2 we present the decision variables and the parameters used in the models presented in this section. The space is divided in a grid of squares. Each square is represented by a node. A graph G is used to represent the seabed, where to each node i is associated a given quantity p^f_i of feature f, representing the abundance of the feature f on that node (i.e. square).

Constraints. All the proposed mathematical models use the following sets of constraints:

$$y_i - \sum_{k=1}^{n_K} \sum_{j \in N^-(i)} x^k_{j,i} \leq 0 \qquad \forall i \in N \qquad (1)$$

$$\sum_{j \in N} w_i = 1 \qquad (2)$$

$$1 \geq \sum_{j \in N^-(i)} x^k_{j,i} \geq w_i \qquad \forall i \in N, k \in k \qquad (3)$$

$$1 \geq \sum_{j \in N^+(i)} x^k_{i,j} \geq w_i \qquad \forall i \in N, k \in k \qquad (4)$$

$$\sum_{j \in N^+(i)} x^k_{i,j} - \sum_{j \in N^-(i)} x^k_{j,i} = 0 \qquad \forall i \in N, k \in K \qquad (5)$$

$$\sum_{\{i,j\} \in A} d_{i,j} x^k_{i,j} \leq d^k_{max} \qquad \forall k \in K \qquad (6)$$

$$t^k_i + d_{i,j} - M(1 - x^k_{i,j} + w_j) \leq t^k_j \qquad \forall \{i,j\} \in A, k \in K \qquad (7)$$

$$t^k_i \leq M(1 - w_i) \qquad \forall i \in N, k \in K \qquad (8)$$

$$t^k_i \leq M \sum_{j \in N^-(i)} x^k_{j,i} \qquad \forall i \in N, k \in K \qquad (9)$$

Constraint (1) allows to count one node i as visited only if at least one of the arcs entering in i is equal to one. Constraint (2) imposes that one (and only one)

Table 2. Parameters

Name	Definition
$G = (N, A)$	Graph used for the routing of the AUVs
N	Set of nodes, $\|N\| = n_N$
A	Set of arcs, $\|A\| = n_A$
F	Set of features, $\|F\| = n_F$
K	Set of drones, $\|K\| = n_K$
$N^+(i)$	Set of nodes that are endpoints of outgoing arcs of node i
$N^-(i)$	Set of nodes that are endpoints of ingoing arcs of node i
p_i^f	Quantity of feature f associated to node $i \in N$
$d_{i,j}$	Length of arc $\{i,j\} \in A$
d_{max}^k	Maximum distance associated to AUV $k \in K$

node can be used as base station. Constraints (3) and (4) ensure that the route of each AUVs starts and end at the node selected as base station. Constraint (5) imposes that if a AUV visits node i it must also leave it. Constraint (6) imposes a limit on the maximum distance that each AUV can travel. Constraint (7) imposes the correct order of the nodes visited by vehicle k and avoids the generation of subtours. In our computation we used a value for the "big-M" constant equal to $M = d_{max} + \max_{(i,j)\in A} d_{i,j}$. Constraint (8) sets to zero the variable t associated to the base station. Constraint (9) sets to zero all the variables t associated to nodes that are not visited by any of the vehicles. In the Sect. 6 we show that the choice of the starting position is crucial for achieving good results in practice.
Single Feature Objective Function. In this work we have n_F features and to each feature f we associate a set of profits p_i^f, with $f = 1, \ldots, n_F$ and $i = 1, \ldots, n_N$. To obtain a model able to find the set of paths that allow to obtain the maximum collected quantity of a given feature f, we use the following objective function:

$$\max \sum_{i=1}^{n_N} p_i^f y_i \,. \tag{10}$$

The objective function (10) is used to sum up the profits of feature f associated to each node.
Multiple Feature Objective Function. On the other hand, we are also interested in finding solutions that allows to obtain a good mix of all the features considered. In this case it is not trivial to understand how to compare two solutions, because of the vectorial nature of the objective function. We therefore propose a *maxmin* approach, that maximizes the minimum amount of the gathered quantities of the n_F features. In this context, we add the following objective functions and

additional constraints:

$$\max \beta \tag{11}$$

$$\beta \leq \sum_{i=1}^{n_N} p_i^f y_i \qquad \forall f \in F\,. \tag{12}$$

Constraints (12) allows to the non-negative variable β to be equal to the minimum quantity gathered among all the considered features. To better investigate different solutions we also consider situation where we use the following generalization of constraints (12):

$$\beta \leq \sum_{i=1}^{n_N} \alpha^f p_i^f y_i \qquad \forall f \in F \tag{13}$$

where the coefficients αs are used to weight the contribution of each feature.
Model Improvements. To improve model (1)–(9) we add two set of inequalities. The first set of inequalities allows to have a tighter link between the y and the w variables. For each node $i \in N$, let $\mathcal{C}(i) \subseteq N$ be the set of nodes that are *reachable* from node i. A node i' is reachable from node i if there exists a path of length d_{max} that starts and ends in i that reaches node i'. With this definition, we define the following set of inequalities:

$$\sum_{j \in \mathcal{C}(i)} w_j \geq y_i \qquad \forall i \in N\,. \tag{14}$$

Inequalities (14) allows to have a variable y_i with a value of one only if at least one of the nodes that can be reached by i is selected as starting position.

5 Basic Data and Methodology

The experiments are based on a map provided by the Abu Dhabi Environment Agency based on satellite imagery (see Fig. 2). The habitat map reports 54 different features (*original features*) on both marine and terrestrial habitats.

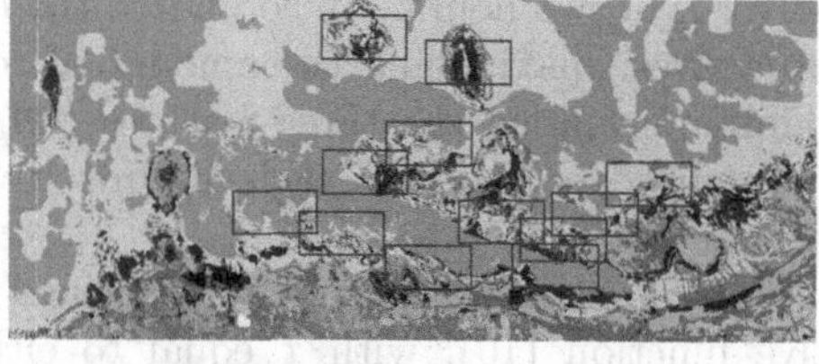

Fig. 2. Map showing the mainland and marine environment studied and the 12 different snapshots used in the experimental section.

The 54 starting features are grouped into three groups: relevant features (distinguished in *rock*, *coral* and *grass*), other *seabed* (not of interest) and *mainland*. We focus on 12 snapshots of size 16 km × 9 km providing an interesting combination of the three basic features considered.

We tested two options for the size of the square grids: *High granularity*, corresponding to squares of 200 × 200 and *Low granularity*, corresponding to squares of 1000 × 1000 m. In Figs. 3a, and 3b, we show an example of how a snapshot is preprocessed according to the chosen granularity. In both figures, each square is filled with four colors: light blue (seabed), dark green (sea grass), light green (rock), red (coral) and peach (mainland). The height of each color is proportional to the percentage of the abundance of the corresponding feature.

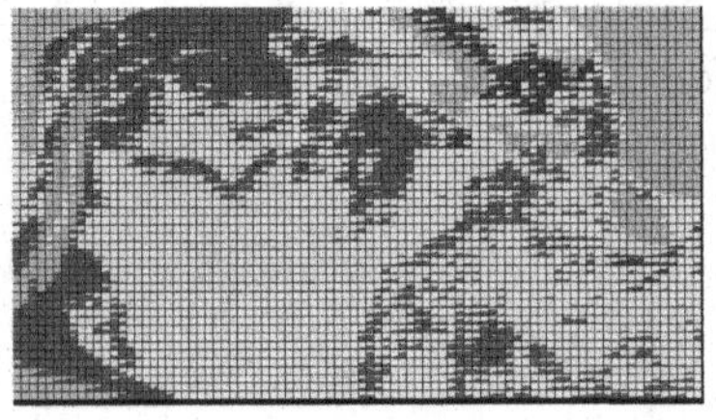

(a) High granularity: squares of 200 × 200 m

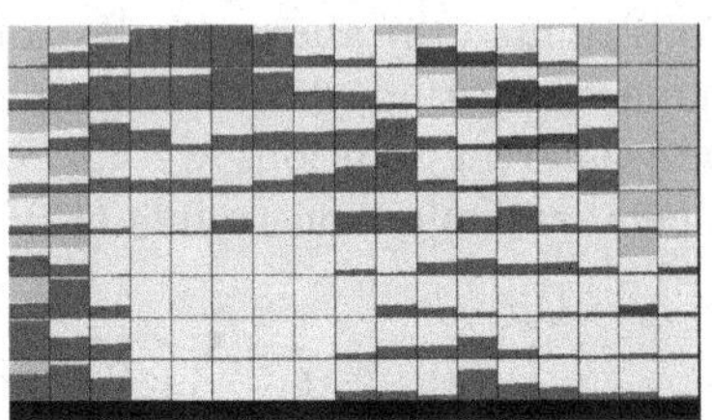

(b) Low granularity: squares of 1000 × 1000 m

Fig. 3. Low and high granularity (Color figure online)

6 Experimental Results

Impact of the Starting Point. As a first step in our analysis, we aim at assessing how the choice of the starting point can impact the overall quality of the obtained solution.

To assess the impact of the starting position it is not required to have an accurate description of the environment. For this reason, to perform this analysis we use the 12 snapshots presented in Sect. 5 with a low granularity and with a fleet of 3 AUVs and 4 km of autonomy each. The time limit imposed to the solver is of two hours. We computed the best solution according to the following objectives: maximizing the amount of rock (`R`), of coral (`C`), of grass (`G`), the minimum among the three features (`MM`), the minimum among the amount of normalized quantity of each feature, divided by the total availability of each feature (`MMN`).

The first three options are obtained by solving model (1)–(9) with objective function (10), with f equal to either *rocks, coral* or *grass*. The option `MM` is obtained by solving model (1)–(9) with objective function (11) and constraints (12). The option `MMN` is obtained by solving model (1)–(9) with objective function (11) and constraints (13) with $\alpha^f = \dfrac{1}{\sum_{i \in N} p_i^f}$. The goal of options `MM` and `MMN` is to search for a solution that balances the collected quantity of the three features. The option `MMN` is a normalized version of `MM`, where the contribution of each feature is divided by its total presence in the map, in order to better handle the situations where one feature is significantly more scarce than the others.

The results are presented in Table 3. Table 3a presents the amount of collected feature by each option. For example, if we consider the first row, associated with the option R, we have that the average quantity gathered of rocks is 7.11 and it is (as theoretically expected) the highest among the five options. However, a (relatively small) quantity of the other features is still gathered on average.

Table 3b shows the average distance (in Km) between the starting point selected by the solution of the given option and the starting point of the other options. In this table, we see for example that the distance between the optimal starting point that maximizes the rocks and the one that maximizes the corals is on average 7.04 Km. The results provided by Table 3b clearly show that a careful choice of the starting position has a strong impact on the overall performances. Preliminary studies also showed that for many instances it is sufficient to move 1 Km to have a drastic decrease/increase of the collected quantity of a given feature. *Coral* and *grass* are significantly scarcer in comparison to *rocks*. This implies that if we are not including the collection of them in the objective function, it is unlikely to collect a significant quantity of the feature. For example, the quantity of *coral* collected with the options R and G is 0.08 and 0.33; a similar behaviour happens for *grass*. For this reasons, it seems a good idea to consider also the more balanced solutions provided by MM and MMN.

Table 3. a) Amount of the collected features; b) Relative distance of the starting position and c) Amount of *rocks* gathered (km^2).

	Features		
Mode	rocks	coral	grass
R	7.11	0.08	0.26
C	3.18	2.87	0.50
G	2.37	0.33	4.17
MM	3.51	1.49	1.52
MMN	4.97	0.70	1.38

(a)

	Distance of init. position [Km]				
Mode	R	C	G	MM	MMN
R	0.00	7.04	6.82	6.01	4.78
C	7.04	0.00	5.88	2.72	5.70
G	6.82	5.88	0.00	4.93	5.88
MM	6.01	2.72	4.93	0.00	4.44
MMN	4.78	5.70	5.88	4.44	0.00

(b)

	autonomy [m]		
n_K	200	300	500
3	1.04	1.51	2.65
5	1.45	2.21	3.98
10	1.87	3.09	4.81

(c)

Impact of the Fleet Characteristics.

To assess the impact of the number of AUVs and their autonomy we need a more accurate description of the environment. For this reason, to perform this analysis we use snapshots with high granularity. To obtain more realistic information we run different combinations of number of AUVs $n_K \in \{3, 5, 10\}$ and autonomy $d^k_{max} = \{200\,m, 300\,m, 500\,m\}$. Such high granularity, combined with a significant number of AUVs leads to models that are really challenging to solve to optimality. To keep the computational effort under control, we focus only on 4 of the snapshots presented in Sect. 5 and we focus only on the solutions aiming at maximizing the quantity of collected *rocks*. In Table 3c we present the average collected quantity of rocks over the selected snapshots.

A possible issue of dealing with a variable fleet of AUVs is the risk that an increase of the size of the fleet does not produce the same increase of the observed feature, but a sublinear relationship is shown. The aim of Table 3c is to assess this sublinear behavior in our application. The table shows that the value of the gathered quantity scales well with the increase of the number of AUVs. Going from 3 to 10 AUVs allows to almost double the area covered. Therefore the use of a fleet of AUVs is highly recommended for large areas exploration. Moreover, Table 3c shows also that an increase of autonomy (represented in this paper by the maximum full path d_{max} covered by each AUV) is beneficial in terms of the gathered information. In fact the table shows that an increased autonomy is more effective than the fleet size.

Multi Objective Analysis - Pareto Frontier. To better understand the interaction between the three features we investigate in this section the Pareto frontier for pairs of features.

We focus on studying the Pareto frontier on instances with low granularity, with a fleet of 3 AUVs and 4 km of autonomy each. This allows us to work with a time limit of two hours. We consider the following combinations of α parameters: $(\alpha^{rocks}, \alpha^{coral}, \alpha^{grass}) \in \{$ (1, 5, 5), (5, 1, 5), (5, 5, 1), (1, 10, 10), (10, 1, 10), (10, 10, 1), (1, 5, 10), (1, 10, 5), (5, 1, 10), (10, 1, 5), (10, 5, 1), (5, 10, 1)$\}$. Figure 4 shows the three Pareto frontiers that we obtain when comparing pairs of features. We decided to show the Pareto frontier for only a single snapshot for conciseness reasons and because in general the plots do not change significantly from one snapshot to the other.

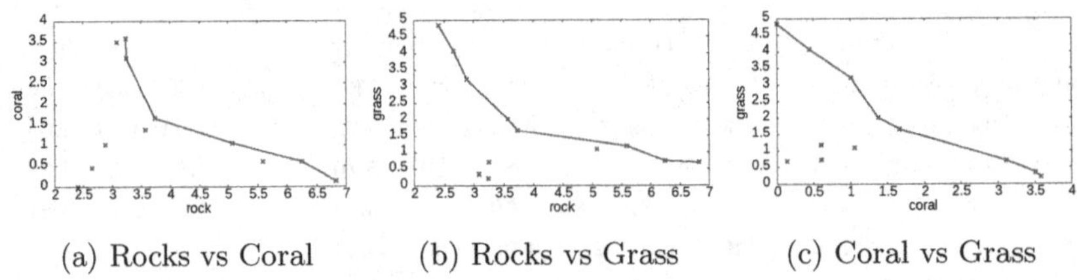

(a) Rocks vs Coral (b) Rocks vs Grass (c) Coral vs Grass

Fig. 4. Pareto Frontiers

Considering Fig. 4a, we notice that if we look for a solution with mixed quantities of rocks and coral it is likely to obtain solutions with significantly fewer quantities for both features. The same trend happens for Fig. 4b. Conversely, Fig. 4c shows that finding a mixed solution of coral and grass seems easier. This last behaviour is well explained by the nature of the two features: coral and grass are clearly more likely to be part of the same biome. The data seems to suggest that, when planning the exploration of an area, it is recommendable to plan a mixed exploration only if the two features involved are grass and coral. On the other hand, if we are interested in gathering information about rocks, it is more fruitful to plan a dedicated exploration.

7 Conclusions

In this paper, we propose the use of an underwater fleet for a cheaper and more reliable underwater area coverage. We provide a tool that can be used for real underwater monitoring, changing the input parameters based on the specific mission. Compared to the use of a single vehicle, a fleet is cheaper, more flexible, scalable and robust, and -most relevantly- has improved perception, because it can provide detailed information (images, videos) of large areas even in complex environment.

In our scenario, a detailed (high-resolution) exploration and mapping is performed by a fleet of AUVs. A centralized controller has a map with coarse resolution, as can be obtained from satellite's images. Based on this it runs an optimization algorithm able to identify the best paths each vehicle has to cover, in order to get the most possible information for a specific feature (coral, grass, rock) or a set of them, minimizing the energy consumption and guaranteeing all the robots complete their mission. Then, the controller transfers to each AUV its best path and the map. The fleet is deployed to get high resolution data.

The algorithm has been applied to real environmental data, specifically underwater maps based on satellite imagery and provided by the Abu Dhabi Environmental Authority. An example of a use case is the collection of detailed information on the health and conservation status of corals, or different species of seagrass, as it is needed by local Environmental Authorities. The optimization problem has been exactly solved. To the best of our knowledge, this is the first exact algorithm that includes the choice of the starting point in the decision process.

Our results show that the use of a fleet is beneficial, and this effect increases enlarging the size of the fleet. Larger fleets are able to collect more relevant information, as well as longer battery life increases the area covered by the fleet. We also observe that an increase of the fleet size is useful only if also the AUVs autonomy is increased. The Pareto frontiers have been analyzed, providing useful information for the mission decision plans: the monitoring missions of corals and seagrass can be performed together, while possible missions focused to investigate minerals and rocks need dedicated plans.

From a practitioner's point of view, we demonstrate that the proposed model is effective in representing the main salient aspects of submarine exploration. In case it is needed to solve scenarios with significantly larger dimensions than those considered in this paper, it will be more appropriate to use heuristic algorithms, which allow to obtain good solutions in a shorter time.

In the next future, we plan to improve our model introducing a more detailed environment (sea currents), by also considering communications, that guarantee the connection among the members of the fleet during the exploration.

References

1. Almadhoun, R., Taha, T., Seneviratne, L., Zweiri, Y.: A survey on multi-robot coverage path planning for model reconstruction and mapping. SN Appl. Sci. **1**(8), 1–24 (2019). https://doi.org/10.1007/s42452-019-0872-y
2. Chao, I.M., Golden, B.L., Wasil, E.A.: The team orienteering problem. Eur. J. Oper. Res. **88**(3), 464–474 (1996)
3. Connor, J., Champion, B., Joordens, M.A.: Current algorithms, communication methods and designs for underwater swarm robotics: a review. IEEE Sens. J. **21**(1), 153–169 (2020)
4. Fu, Q., Song, A., Zhang, F., Pan, M.: Reinforcement learning-based trajectory optimization for data muling with underwater mobile nodes. IEEE Access **10**, 38774–38784 (2022)
5. Galceran, E., Carreras, M.: A survey on coverage path planning for robotics. Robot. Auton. Syst. **61**(12), 1258–1276 (2013)
6. González-García, J., Gómez-Espinosa, A., Cuan-Urquizo, E., García-Valdovinos, L.G., Salgado-Jiménez, T., Cabello, J.A.E.: Autonomous underwater vehicles: localization, navigation, and communication for collaborative missions. Appl. Sci. **10**(4) (2020)
7. Khoufi, I., Laouiti, A., Adjih, C.: A survey of recent extended variants of the traveling salesman and vehicle routing problems for unmanned aerial vehicles. Drones **3**(3), 66 (2019)
8. Lahyani, R., Khemakhem, M., Semet, F.: Rich vehicle routing problems: From a taxonomy to a definition. Eur. J. Oper. Res. **241**(1), 1–14 (2015)
9. Laporte, G.: The vehicle routing problem: an overview of exact and approximate algorithms. Eur. J. Oper. Res. **59**(3), 345–358 (1992)
10. Li, B., Moridian, B., Mahmoudian, N.: Underwater multi-robot persistent area coverage mission planning. In: OCEANS 2016 MTS/IEEE Monterey, pp. 1–6. IEEE (2016)
11. Li, G., Chen, C., Geng, C., Li, M., Xu, H., Lin, Y.: A pheromone-inspired monitoring strategy using a swarm of underwater robots. Sensors **19**(19) (2019)
12. McMahon, J., Plaku, E.: Autonomous underwater vehicle mine countermeasures mission planning via the physical traveling salesman problem. In: OCEANS 2015-MTS/IEEE Washington, pp. 1–5. IEEE (2015)
13. McMahon, J., Plaku, E.: Autonomous data collection with limited time for underwater vehicles. IEEE Robot. Autom. Lett. **2**(1), 112–119 (2017)
14. Melo, J., Matos, A.: Survey on advances on terrain based navigation for autonomous underwater vehicles. Ocean Eng. **139**, 250–264 (2017)
15. Otto, A., Agatz, N., Campbell, J., Golden, B., Pesch, E.: Optimization approaches for civil applications of unmanned aerial vehicles (UAVs) or aerial drones: a survey. Networks **72**(4), 411–458 (2018)
16. Panda, M., Das, B., Subudhi, B., Pati, B.B.: A comprehensive review of path planning algorithms for autonomous underwater vehicles. Int. J. Autom. Comput. **17**(3), 321–352 (2020)
17. Pisinger, D., Ropke, S.: A general heuristic for vehicle routing problems. Comput. Oper. Res. **34**(8), 2403–2435 (2007)
18. Tan, C.S., Mohd-Mokhtar, R., Arshad, M.R.: A comprehensive review of coverage path planning in robotics using classical and heuristic algorithms. IEEE Access **9**, 119310–119342 (2021)

19. Toth, P., Vigo, D.: Vehicle routing: problems, methods, and applications. In: SIAM (2014)
20. Varughese, J.C., Thenius, R., Leitgeb, P., Wotawa, F., Schmickl, T.: A model for bio-inspired underwater swarm robotic exploration. IFAC-PapersOnLine **51**(2), 385–390 (2018)

An Agent-Based Model of Emotion Contagion and Group Identification: A Case Study in the Field of Football Supporters

Erik van Haeringen(✉), Gaia Liistro, and Charlotte Gerritsen

Vrije Universiteit Amsterdam, De Boelelaan 1111, 1081 HV Amsterdam, The Netherlands
e.s.van.haeringen@vu.nl

Abstract. When people who strongly identify with different competitive groups meet, this can result in negative affect and aggression. A significant body of work has applied agent-based modelling to study the spread of emotions in the crowds, called emotion contagion. Although some of these models consider the effect of pre-existing social relationships, this is mostly limited to dyadic relationships (e.g. friends) or clearly defined roles (e.g. police-civilian). In the present study we propose an extension of the agent-based model DECADE, that combines emotion contagion with continuous variation in how much an agent identifies with a group. We explore the spread of aggression among football supporters in the form of pitch invasions, in which spectators enter the playing field illegally. We test management strategies that alter the supporter composition on the stands with regards to placement (separating by teams and/or fanaticism) and composition (stadium bans, limiting the promotion of identification). The results show that measures that decrease the number of fanatics, or that promote a balanced mix regarding group identification, decrease collective aggression. Finally, the model is evaluated against recent footage and descriptions of a real pitch invasion. The simulations resembled the real incident in several behavioural patterns, but not all. We conclude that further research is required to determine which individual traits and processes are essential in simulating collective aggression among competitive groups, to come to a model that can be employed in society.

Keywords: Emotion contagion · Group identification · Crowd simulation · Supporter aggression · Agent-based model

1 Introduction

Group-based conflict and aggression are universal phenomena across societies and encompass many forms of groups [1]. Social identity theory offers an explanation for this behaviour by pointing to the nature of people to automatically identify with groups via self-categorisation, via which they develop a social identity that favours their own group in comparison to other groups [2]. By identifying with a group, the group becomes to an extent part of the psychological self, such that events that affect the group are also felt by the individual. People who identify stronger with a group are more susceptible

© The Author(s), under exclusive license to Springer Nature Switzerland AG 2022
F. Dignum et al. (Eds.): PAAMS 2022, LNAI 13616, pp. 410–422, 2022.
https://doi.org/10.1007/978-3-031-18192-4_33

for shared sentiment and empathy for group members compared to people outside the group [3, 4]. They are also more likely to interpret events that impact the group as if these were directed to themselves, feeling for example success and failure of the group as their own [3].

A familiar example of group identification is in supporting sports teams in competitive games as a viewer. Identifying with a team as a spectator is commonplace, and sports clubs aim to foster this process since it is an important driver for consumption [5]. However, when many people who identify strongly with opposing groups are part of the same crowd, friendly support and banter can quickly escalate into conflict [5]. Football matches are an example where the emotions of fans regularly run high and incidents of public disorder and aggression are frequent [6].

In this study we focus on a specific type of aggression by football supporters, called pitch invasions [6–8]. During pitch invasions, some spectators decide to leave their place and enter the playing field, even though this is explicitly forbidden. We chose this focus because supporter violence in pitch invasions is easier to observe relative to violence on the stands or around the stadium. Although a large share of the invasions occurs out of celebration, pitch invasions can also have severe consequences when negative sentiment is involved or develops. A particularly tragic example is a pitch invasion during 2012 in Egypt that resulted in at least 74 deaths and hundreds of wounded [9]. Large scale pitch invasions are particularly dangerous due to their sudden nature and because those that guard the crowd can be severely outnumbered by the spectators simultaneously participating in the invasion.

Agent-based modelling techniques may contribute to this challenge in the future by providing event organisers and security personnel tools to make (real-time) predictions, and practice without personal risk of injury or high costs. Among others, this requires the development of an accurate model of the relation between group identification and the spread of emotions in crowds, called emotion contagion. While significant work has been done on simulating emotion contagion in crowds, especially during evacuations, much less studies have considered the impact of social subgroups on this process [10]. Models of emotion contagion that consider social relationships often do so in a dyadic fashion, considering the impact of factors like intimacy and trust towards others [10]. Other studies have assigned binary roles to agents like leader-follower, parent-child and authority-civilian [10]. However, neither approach captures the variation in how strongly people identify with subgroups and how this affects patterns in collective emotion and behaviour.

The aim of this study is to use agent-based modeling to examine how individuals with varying levels of identification with rivaling group identities affect patterns in collective emotion and aggression during football matches. For this purpose, we extend an agent-based model of emotion contagion called DECADE [11]. Specifically, we add the desire of agents to belong to a social group as an agent parameter. The belongingness hypothesis states that people share an innate desire to belong to social groups, and can go to great lengths to obtain or keep these relationships, including violating their beliefs, norms and in extreme cases their well-being or that of others [12]. Furthermore, the desire to belong to a social group was found to be positively correlated with the degree to which people identify with a local team [5]. Building on this, in the proposed model the desire of an agent to belong determines the impact group identity has on emotion contagion and the appraisal of sport events, as well as the tendency of the agent to participate in collective aggression. To study the effect of several management strategies against supporter violence, we simulate scenarios with different supporter compositions and seating arrangements. Finally, the proposed model is evaluated against a real incident of supporter aggression that included pitch invasions, by using data collected from social and traditional media.

2 Methods

2.1 The DECADE Model

We build upon the DECADE (Dimensional Emotion Contagion via Agent-based Dyadic Exchanges) model [11], that is itself based on the ASCRIBE model [13]. DECADE was previously used to simulate the spread of emotions among supporters in a football stadium [11]. The agents in this model exchange emotion in the form of two continuous dimensions, valence and arousal (Fig. 1). These dimensions spread independently, yet together form the emotional state of the agent. How strongly valence and arousal can spread from one agent to the other is determined by the expressivity of the sender, the susceptibility of the receiver, the social and/or physical distance between the agents and the share of attention that the sender claims in competition with other stimuli.

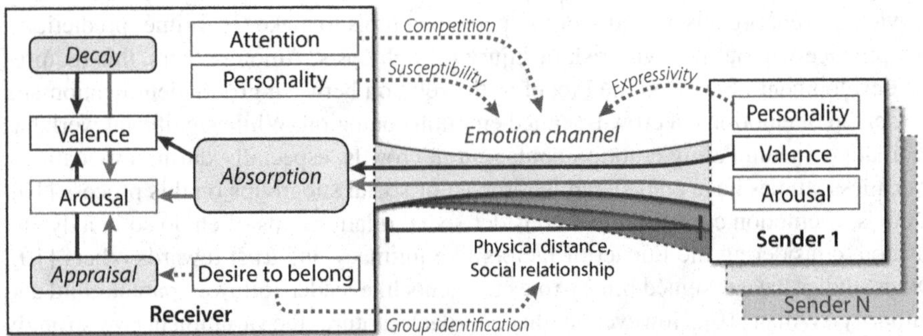

Fig. 1. Flow chart of the proposed emotion model. The 'desire to belong' and 'social relationship' factors are the additions to the DECADE model [11] proposed in the present study.

The effect of contagion on the valence and arousal of an agent is expressed as two components, 1) the total connection strength between a receiver and its neighbours and 2) the influence of the senders. Since the extensions introduced in this study only concern the connection component of DECADE, for brevity we will shortly explain this component below, while we refer to the previous study in its entirety for details about the influence of the senders [11].

$$\begin{aligned} \Delta E_{r valence} &= < connection > \cdot < influence_{valence} > \\ \Delta E_{r arousal} &= < connection > \cdot < influence_{arousal} > \end{aligned} \tag{1}$$

The total connection (Γ_r) of the receiver with its neighbours (N_r) is defined as the sum of each dyadic connection. The connection between each sender and the receiver (γ_{sr}) represents how well emotion can flow from the sender to the receiver. In the previous study [11], the strength of the connection was determined by the susceptibility of the receiver (δ_r), the physical distance between the agents (α_{sr}) and the weighted attention for the sender ($\theta_s{}^*$).

$$connection = \Gamma_r = \sum\nolimits_{s \in N_r} \gamma_{sr} \tag{2}$$

$$\gamma_{sr} = \delta_r \alpha_{sr} \theta_s{}^* \tag{3}$$

Susceptibility (δ_r) is a personality characteristic of the receiver. In the present study we set this parameter by drawing a random value from a normal distribution for each agent ($\mu = 0.5, \sigma = 0.2$), limited between 0 and 1. The physical distance (α_{sr}) is defined as the inverse of the Euclidean distance between the agents. The attention for a sender ($\theta_s{}^*$) is determined in competition with the other senders. A larger share of the receiver's attention is directed towards others with strong emotional expressions, yet all neighbours receive at least some amount of attention. Further in distributing its attention the receiver has a preference in the direction of valence and arousal, where $\mu_d < 0.5$ is a preference for negative valence or arousal, $\mu_d > 0.5$ for positive valence or arousal and $\mu_d = 0.5$ indicates no preference either way. In the present study we set no preference for valence and a positive preference for arousal ($\mu_{val} = 0.5$, $\mu_{aro} = 0.7$). This setting is motivated by a study that found that participants looked longer at stimuli higher in arousal, but attention did not vary with the valence of the stimulus [14].

2.2 Social Relationship

When a person strongly identifies with a group, the emotional influence of in-group members was found to be stronger than that of people outside their group [3, 4]. Further, the tendency of a person to identify with a team was found to correlate with his/her desire to belong to a social group [5].

To reflect these findings in the model, we introduce the desire to belong as an agent parameter. The desire to belong affects emotion contagion via the connection strength between a receiver and a sender, depending on whether they share a group identity. In the present study, Eq. 4 of the DECADE model is extended with the social connection between the agents (σ_{sr}). When the sender belongs to the same group as the receiver, the social connection between the agents increases with the desire of the receiver to belong (d_r). In contrast, if the sender belongs to a different group, we assume the connection is weaker relative to the desire to belong of the receiver. When the receiver is not part of a group (neutral), its social relation with all agents is equal to a half.

$$\gamma_{sr} = \delta_r \alpha_{sr} \theta_s{}^* \sigma_{sr} \tag{4}$$

$$\sigma_{sr} = \begin{cases} g_r = g_s & 0.5(1 + d_r) \\ g_r \neq g_s & 0.5(1 - d_r) \\ g_r = \varnothing & 0.5 \end{cases} \tag{5}$$

2.3 Emotion Decay

Emotions decay over time due to self-regulation [15]. DECADE proposed a non-linear decay, where the emotion of the receiver decreases with decay rate λ_r for each dimension of emotion separately [11]. A higher λ_r results in a faster decay of emotion, while at a decay rate of zero there is no decay of emotions. The decay rate of the agents is set to 0.01 in the present study.

2.4 Perceived Threat

Feeling like your group has been targeted or done injustice can pose a threat when the degree of group identification is high and may result in aggressive behaviour [5, 16, 17], for example due to police actions, ridicule or shame. How much an individual feels his identity is threatened, was found to be positively correlated to the desire to belong of that person [5]. Further, it stands to reason that the display of aggression by others can also present a threat, especially if this is displayed nearby. Perceiving a threat in turn positively affects arousal [18]. We hypothesise that this may be the case whether aggression comes from group members or not; when the aggressor does not belong to someone's group, this poses a direct threat to the individual's safety, while aggression by a group member signals that one's group is threatened [4]. For simplicity, we did not consider the effect of perceiving anxiety on identifying threats.

To reflect this description, we define the perceived threat (χ_r) as the inverse of the distance to the nearest aggressive neighbour, combined a logistic function of the impact of external events on the group identity (Ext_{group}) modified by the agent's desire to belong (d_r). Due to the logistic function, negative group events are perceived as a threat by an agent that identifies strongly with this group, while positive and neutral events for the group result in a threat perception close to zero.

$$X_r = \frac{1}{\min\limits_{s \in N_{agr}} D_s} + \frac{e}{1 + e^{-2(-d_r Ext_{group} e - e)}} \tag{6}$$

Finally, to model the emotional effect of the external event on the agent, perceiving a threat increases the arousal of the agent proportional to the size of the threat. Additionally, the appraisal of the external event affects the agent's valence depending on its desire to belong (e.g., a red card for their team decreases valence, while their team winning the game increases valence).

$$\begin{aligned} \Delta E_{aro} &= 0.1\chi_r \\ \Delta E_{val} &= 0.1 d_r e_{group} \end{aligned} \tag{7}$$

2.5 Decision Model

To model supporter aggression, a simple decision tree is implemented that is chance-based. To travel through the tree, a random number is drawn (P) that is compared to a threshold determined by parameters of the agents, where P_1 and P_3 are drawn from a uniform distribution and P_2 from an exponential distribution ($\mu = 0.25$). First, the perceived threat and the arousal of the agent determine whether the agent remains seated calmly or reacts. When the agent decides to react, it decides whether it responds with aggression or fear, depending on its desire to belong. When the agent reacts with aggression, the tendency to invade the field comes from perceiving aggression nearby and a strong group identity. Otherwise, the agent will display aggression on the stands and move to the border between the stands and the field without passing it. When the agent reacts anxiously, the chance it moves toward the exit increases with negative valence and nearby aggression. Otherwise, the agent remains seated anxiously.

$$act = \begin{cases} P_1 < E_{aro}\chi_r & \begin{cases} P_2 > 1 - d_r & \begin{cases} P_3 < d_r \frac{1}{\min_{s \in N_{agr}} D_s} & \textit{Invade field} \\ else & \textit{Aggression on stand} \end{cases} \\ else & \begin{cases} P_2 < \frac{1+E_{val}}{2} \frac{1}{\min_{s \in N_{agr}} D_s} & \textit{Leave stadium} \\ else & \textit{Static anxiety} \end{cases} \end{cases} \\ else & \textit{Static calm} \end{cases} \tag{8}$$

2.6 Analysis

The proposed model was implemented in the agent-based simulation environment Netlogo [19]. We made a stadium setup with 3000 agents located in a rectangle around the pitch. Each agent supports either the home team, the away team or no team (neutral). A supporter is either fanatic or a regular supporter. Based on these characteristics its desire to belong is drawn from a normal distribution, where neutral spectators draw from a distribution with a low mean, regular supporters from a distribution with an intermediary mean and fanatic supporters from a distribution with a high mean. To represent variation in personality types, the susceptibility and expressivity of all agents are drawn from the same normal distribution at the start. The valence and arousal of the agents start at zero. We chose a general setting for the simulations and studied the effect of varying the proportion of fanatic supporters (default is 0.2 and 0.4 for the home and away team respectively) and the seating arrangement (default is a loose separation of fanatic and away supporters) over 500 time-steps. To setup the model for the validation, we used the same general setting as for the other results, but with a larger crowd (n = 6000) and a seating arrangement that only separates the away supporters. Then we manually tuned the model to the observations via the parameter that represents the impact of events on the identity of the home team. The complete settings are available in Appendix 1. To account for the variation due to stochastic factors in the model, each condition was repeated 16 times. The figures are produced in RStudio using the Ggplot2 package. The model, scripts and data are included in the supplementary material.

2.7 Validation

While negative feelings may be shared broadly in a stadium, only a (small) share of the spectators is actively involved in incidents of supporter aggression, while others remain calm or distance themselves from the aggression. Our validation of the model focusses on the behaviour of the crowd as opposed to its emotion, as to our knowledge no datasets are available of the emotional development of spectators during pitch invasions. For this purpose, we examine two cases of pitch invasions with the use of descriptions, videos and photos from both traditional and social media. We compare several qualitative patterns from our observations of the real incident to the simulation output from the proposed model. Additionally, we measure the percentage of spectators on the field at the height of pitch invasion. For this, we counted the spectators on half of the field and divided this by the estimated total number of spectators to get the percentage of spectators that entered the field. See Appendix 2 for more details about the validation.

3 Results

3.1 Spectator Composition

To study the impact of stadium bans and limits on the promotion of team identification, the effect of the percentage of fanatics is considered on the percentage of spectators that invades the pitch for both a positive and negative event for the home team ($Ext_{home} = 0.4$ and -0.4, $Ext_{away} = -0.4$ and 0.4 respectively). All measures are with the away fans and home fanatics being loosely separated in the stadium (see next subsection). For the away team we assumed the percentage of fanatic supporters is double that of the home team. This assumption is inspired by literature suggesting that people who identify less with a team are more likely to favour practicality in their decision to attend a game [3], while away games generally require higher costs and effort.

A higher proportion of fanatic supporters increases the number of agents that invade the pitch and that leave the stadium, especially in the case of a home loss (Fig. 2). Most of the supporters that invaded the pitch are fanatic supporters. Further, the model predicts that pitch invasions following a home loss almost exclusively involve fanatic supporters of the home team, while those following a loss by the away team more often involve supporters from both teams. These findings suggest that measures to limit the total number of fanatics in the stadium, particularly those of the home team, are effective in lowering the scale of the pitch invasions as well as the threat to other supporters, as illustrated by the proportion of agents that left the stadium.

3.2 Seating Arrangement

It is common practice in European football stadiums to keep the home and away team fans separated to avoid conflict, among others by assigning a section of the stadium specifically to the fans of the away team. Moreover, fanatic fans of the home team usually also sit together in a section of stadium. In many cases these sections are not adjacent. However, while this arrangement is generally followed by the spectators, it is usually not strictly enforced. Supporters on the main stand can be fanatic too or can (openly) support the away team.

To study the impact of management strategies based on the seating arrangements, the location of the spectators is varied by type, while the total number per type and the

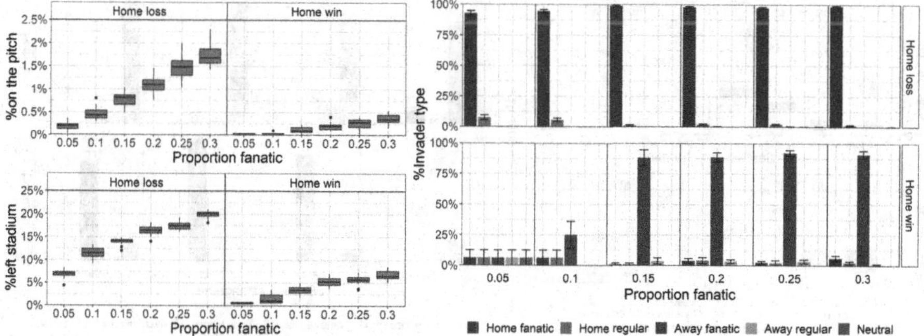

Fig. 2. Effect of the proportion fanatic home supporters (double for the away supporters) on the percentage of spectators that invades the pitch, leaves the stadium, and the supporter type of the agents that invade the pitch (±SE). Note that invader type does not add up to 100% for all conditions due to runs without pitch invaders.

density are kept equal. We tested four types of seating arrangements. In the 'random' condition, spectators are mixed throughout the stadium. In the 'away only' condition, the neutral spectators and home supporters are mixed, but the away supporters have their own section. In the 'strict' condition the fanatic home supporters also have their own section in the stadium on the opposite side of the section for the away supporters. In the 'loose' condition we assume that not all spectators will conform to the previous arrangement. In this arrangement the fanatic section is occupied by 50% of the fanatic home supporters, 20% of the regular home supporter and 5% of the neutral spectators, while the away section is occupied by 95% of the fanatic away supporters, 80% of the regular away supporters and 5% of the neutral spectators.

Contrary to common practice, our findings indicate that the tendency to separate fanatic fans might promote the severity of pitch invasions (Fig. 3). The loose and strict arrangements resulted in a higher percentage of pitch invaders and spectators that left the stadium than when all spectator types are mixed or when only the away supporters were seated separately. The fanatic supporters seem to amplify each other when placed together, while a more diverse mix downregulates the negative sentiment. The flipside is that in the 'random' condition pitch invasions are more likely to consist of rivalling supporters, increasing the opportunity for violence.

3.3 Case Study: Nigeria – Ghana

On March 29th 2022, Nigeria and Ghana played a game to determine which of their national teams would go to the world cup next summer, with a general expectation that this would be Nigeria. A strong rivalry exists between the countries with a long history, that has led to pitch invasions before and is not limited to sports [20, 21]. It was therefore not a complete surprise that when the most recent match in Nigeria ended in a draw, meaning that Ghana would go to the world cup, Nigerian supporters stormed the pitch upset. The stadium was vandalised and the police clashed with the invading supporters, using force and teargas [22].

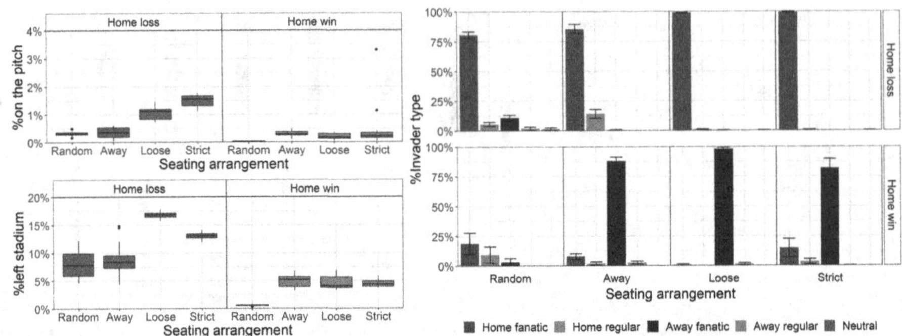

Fig. 3. Effect of seating arrangement on the percentage of spectators that invades the pitch, leaves the stadium, and the supporter type of the agents that invade the pitch (±SE).

From footage uploaded to social media, we observed several patterns in collective behaviour, the details and sources of which can be found in Appendix 2. First, before people entered the field, aggression was already displayed on the stands, where Nigerian supporters threw objects towards players and supporters of Ghana. Second, while a large number of people entered the pitch, many more presumably left the stadium as the majority of the seats are empty (Fig. 4). Many of the people that remained in the stadium are concentrated on and around the stairs toward the exits and appear relatively calm. Finally, we did not observe any Ghanaian supporters visibly participating in the pitch invasion, although a group was escorted over the pitch towards an exit by the police at some point. Based on a count of half the field and an estimated attendance of 60000 in the stadium, we conclude that around 1.5% of the spectators invaded the pitch.

Fig. 4. Photo taken shortly before the police intervened [23]. The pink dots are the counted spectators, the blue dots are stadium staff.

The patterns of collective behaviour in our simulations resemble several of the observed patterns. The average percentage of individuals that entered the pitch matches closely to our count of the real incident with 1.66% (SE 0.06). On average 87.7% (SE

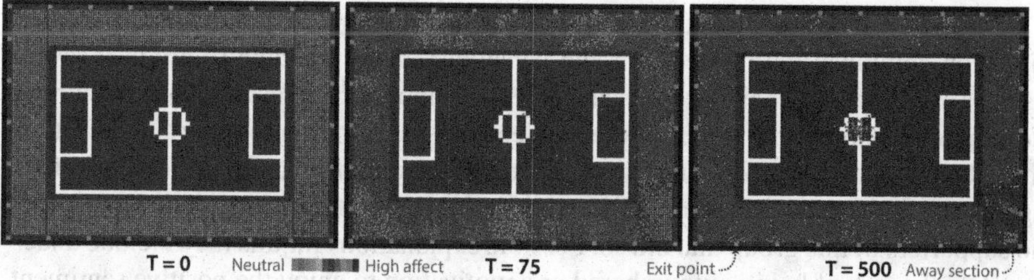

Fig. 5. Simulation output of the Nigeria – Ghana pitch invasion, for three time-steps showing the start, main onrush and end of the simulation. One agent represents 10 real supporters in scale. The colours of the agents indicate the strength of their emotions as the distance in valence-arousal space to the neutral state. A video of this simulation is included in the supplementary materials.

0.40) left the stadium in the simulations. We could not make an exact estimate of the people on the stands in the real incident via counts from the available material, but based on the area of visible seats in Fig. 4 at least the majority of people seem to have left their seat. Moreover, the simulation matches the pattern that most of the people who don't leave, gather around the exits and are relatively calm compared to those on the pitch (Fig. 5). A point where the simulations significantly differ from the real incident is in the aggression by the away supporters. In our simulations on average 18.3% (SE 2.43) of the invaders belonged to the away team, while we did not observe pitch invasions by the real away supporters. Overall, we conclude that the combination of emotion contagion and group identity can produce some of the patterns observed in the real incident, but not all. We expect that this is partly due to several important factors that are missing in the decision-making process of the agents, like the ability to properly estimate risk.

4 Discussion

The proposed model in this study focusses on the exchange of affect and the impact of continuous variation in group identification with rival teams during events of supporter violence in stadiums. A wide variety of measures is employed by police, governments and sport clubs to combat violence in and around football matches [6]. We explored the effects of measures that alter the supporter composition on the stands with regards to placement (separating by teams and/or by fanaticism) and by composition (stadium bans, limiting the promotion of identification). The findings indicate that measures that lower the number of fanatic supporters (stadium bans, limits to promoting identification) decrease aggression, especially when the home team loses. Allowing, or even forcing, fanatic supporters of the home team to sit separately was found to increase the overall aggression due to amplification that occurred among these fanatic supporters. Mixing the fanatic supporters throughout the stadium resulted in less aggression, but when aggression occurred it was more likely to involve agents from both teams, which may increase the opportunities for violence. Based on these findings we hypothesise that also other measures aimed at separating fanatics from regular fans may work counterproductively, such as separate transport [6].

Moreover, the present study demonstrates that emotion contagion and group identification combined with a decision and behaviour model are able to produce several aspects of collective behaviour in a real incident of supporter aggression, based on written descriptions, photos and videos of the incident. Yet we also found important deviations in the behaviour of the away supporters. Agents in the minority group decided to join the aggression at the end of the simulation, while in footage of the real incident we observed no supporters of this group that did so. Possible explanations for this may include understanding the risk of being outnumbered or a motivation to enjoy the positive sentiment, neither of which are included in the model. With perhaps the exception of situations that are dominated by very strong emotions, cognitive processes and individual motivations, beliefs, knowledge and percept play important roles in human decision making. Due to the minimal representation of these factors in the proposed model, the results regarding the management strategies should not be interpreted as an evaluation of these strategies, but as suggestions for future study.

That being said, it is neither practical nor possible to capture the full complexity of crowds in a simulation. Ethics, privacy and the sheer amount of individual variation drive the development of models that can make reasonably accurate predictions based on limited input. This is an important challenge in the field of crowd simulation, and even more so for crowd models that include the spread of emotions. Emotions are highly challenging to detect accurately in a crowd and are seen as private. This makes validation of models of emotion contagion at the individual level a steep challenge that has not been met for any current model yet as far as we are aware [10]. However, while this is important in order to develop an agent-based model of emotion contagion that is widely applicable, we argue that for the narrow use cases envisioned in this study, high accuracy at the emotion level may not be crucial. The model may overlook certain patterns of individual or collective emotion if these do not strongly contribute to the problematic collective behaviour. For example, a system indicating whether a match may escalate that is correct half of the time, or misses the emotional development of less relevant subgroups, might still be a useful tool for the police in planning if it outperforms currently available indicators. The same holds for a training simulator that shows the effects of a management strategy on the dominant behaviour of aggressive groups, even if not all groups will behave in this way.

To develop such tools, future study could look at which factors can significantly improve predictions over the current model driven by affect and group identification, without requiring the input of data of which the collection is prohibitive in the real world. Furthermore, future work can explore the role of the interaction between group identification and emotion contagion with the use of agent-based models for other crowd types where competitive subgroups play an important role, like in protests, riots and online crowds. Finally, this study focussed mainly on fight-flight behaviour following the spread of negative sentiment due to a threat to the group, while the positive fans remain calmly seated. However, fans are known for reacting passionately towards positive events as well. Combined with an inflated sense of superiority in the case of group identification, there are opportunities to further explore the dynamics of causing and perceiving threats between rival groups.

Acknowledgements. This work is part of the research programme Innovational Research Incentives Scheme Vidi SSH 2017 with project number 016.Vidi.185.178, which is financed by the Dutch Research Council (NWO).

Appendix

The supplementary materials can be found at: https://osf.io/4hvm5.

References

1. Al Ramiah, A., Hewstone, M., Schmid, K.: Social identity and intergroup conflict. Psychol. Stud. **56**, 1 56, 44–52 (2011)
2. Hogg, M.A.: Social identity theory. In: McKeown, S., Haji, R., Ferguson, N. (eds.) Understanding Peace and Conflict Through Social Identity Theory. PPBS, pp. 3–17. Springer, Cham (2016). https://doi.org/10.1007/978-3-319-29869-6_1
3. Clarke, E., Geurin, A.N., Burch, L.M.: Team identification, motives, and behaviour: a comparative analysis of fans of men's and women's sport. Manag. Sport Leisure 1–24 (2022)
4. van der Schalk, J., Fischer, A., Doosje, B., et al.: Convergent and divergent responses to emotional displays of ingroup and outgroup. Emotion **11**, 286–298 (2011)
5. Theodorakis, N.D., Wann, D.L., Nassis, P., et al.: The relationship between sport team identification and the need to belong. Int. J. Sport Manag. Mark. **12**, 25–38 (2012)
6. Schaap, D., Postma, M., Jansen, L., Tolsma, J.: Combating hooliganism in the netherlands: an evaluation of measures to combat hooliganism with longitudinal registration data. Eur. J. Crim. Policy Res. **21**(1), 83–97 (2014). https://doi.org/10.1007/s10610-014-9237-7
7. MacInnes, P.: The rise of disorder at football: why is it happening and what can be done?. In: The Guardian. https://www.theguardian.com. Accessed 20 Apr 2022
8. Ilett, R.: Football hooliganism, fan behaviour and crime. contemporary issues. British J. Criminol. **56**, 415–418 (2015)
9. Hussein, A.-R.: Egypt football match violence: dozens dead and hundreds injured. In: The Guardian. https://www.theguardian.com. Accessed 28 Apr 2022
10. van Haeringen, E.S., Gerritsen, C., Hindriks, K.V.: Emotion contagion in agent-based simulations of the crowd: a systematic review. Vrije Universiteit Amsterdam, Technical Report (2021)
11. van Haeringen, E., Gerritsen, C., Hindriks, K.: Integrating valence and arousal within an agent-based model of emotion contagion. In: Dignum, F., Corchado, J.M., De La Prieta, F. (eds.) PAAMS 2021. LNCS (LNAI), vol. 12946, pp. 303–315. Springer, Cham (2021). https://doi.org/10.1007/978-3-030-85739-4_25
12. Leary, M.R., Cox, C.B.: Belongingness motivation: a mainspring of social action (2008)
13. Bosse, T., Hoogendoorn, M., Klein, M.C.A.A., et al.: Modelling collective decision making in groups and crowds: integrating social contagion and interacting emotions, beliefs and intentions. Auton. Agent. Multi-Agent Syst. **27**, 52–84 (2013)
14. Vogt, J., De Houwer, J., Koster, E.H.W., et al.: Allocation of spatial attention to emotional stimuli depends upon arousal and not valence. Emotion (Washington, DC) **8**, 880–885 (2008)
15. Hatfield, E., Cacioppo, J.T., Rapson, R.L.: Emotional contagion. Editions de la Maison des Sciences de l'Homme (1994)
16. Pauwels, L.J.R., Heylen, B.: Perceived group threat, perceived injustice, and self-reported right-wing violence: an integrative approach to the explanation right-wing violence. J. Interpers. Violence **35**, 4276–4302 (2020)

17. Vasquez, E.A., Lickel, B., Hennigan, K.: Gangs, displaced, and group-based aggression. Aggress. Violent. Beh. **15**, 130–140 (2010)
18. Garrett, N., González-Garzón, A.M., Foulkes, L., et al.: Updating beliefs under perceived threat. J. Neurosc. Official J. Soc. Neurosci. **38**, 7901–7911 (2018)
19. Wilensky, U.: NetLogo. Center for Connected Learning and Computer-Based Modeling, Northwestern University (1999)
20. Wilson, J.: Nigeria out to scratch 15-year itch against Ghana in clash of great rivals. In: The Guardian. https://www.theguardian.com. Accessed 22 Apr 2022
21. BBC News: Letter from Africa: Behind Ghana and Nigeria's love-hate affair. In: BBC. https://www.bbc.com. Accessed 22 Apr 2022
22. Okeleji, O.: Nigerian fans riot after World Cup qualification defeat to Ghana. In: Al Jazeera. https://www.aljazeera.com. Accessed 22 Apr 2022
23. Anka, C.: Nigeria does sometimes come last – despite all the slogans, Ghana win World Cup place and local pride. In: The Athletic. https://www.theathletic.com. Accessed 21 Apr 2022

Smart Contracts for the CloudAnchor Platform

Eduardo Vasco[1], Bruno Veloso[2,3], and Benedita Malheiro[1,3(✉)]

[1] ISEP/IPP – School of Engineering, Polytechnic Institute of Porto, Porto, Portugal
{1141245,mbm}@isep.ipp.pt

[2] UPT – Universidade Portucalense, Porto, Portugal
brunov@upt.pt

[3] INESC TEC – Institute for Systems and Computer Engineering, Technology and Science, Porto, Portugal

Abstract. CloudAnchor is a multi-agent brokerage platform for the negotiation of Infrastructure as a Service cloud resources between Small and Medium Sized Enterprises, acting either as providers or consumers. This project entails the research, design, and implementation of a *smart contract* solution to permanently record and manage contractual and behavioural stakeholder data on a blockchain network. Smart contracts enable safe contract code execution, increasing trust between parties and ensuring the integrity and traceability of the chained contents. The defined smart contracts represent the inter-business trustworthiness and Service Level Agreements established within the platform. CloudAnchor interacts with the blockchain network through a dedicated Application Programming Interface, which coordinates and optimises the submission of transactions. The performed tests indicate the success of this integration: (*i*) the number and value of negotiated resources remain identical; and (*ii*) the run-time increases due to the inherent latency of the blockchain operation. Nonetheless, the introduced latency does not affect the brokerage performance, proving to be an appropriate solution for reliable partner selection and contractual enforcement between untrusted parties. This novel approach stores all brokerage strategic knowledge in a distributed, decentralised, and immutable database.

Keywords: Brokerage · IaaS · Multi-agent · Negotiation · Profiling · Smart contracts · Service level agreements · Trust & reputation

1 Introduction

Entities, who do not trust each other, typically rely on a Trusted Third Party (TTP) to transact with reduced risk. While such middle-man assistance services contribute to the success of transactions, they usually come with a price to the involved parties. The defining aspect of Blockchain Technology (BCT) is that it allows untrustworthy parties to interact and transact safely without the need of

© The Author(s), under exclusive license to Springer Nature Switzerland AG 2022
F. Dignum et al. (Eds.): PAAMS 2022, LNAI 13616, pp. 423–434, 2022.
https://doi.org/10.1007/978-3-031-18192-4_34

a central TTP as an authority. In this respect, Calvaresi *et al.* (2018) advocate the integration of Blockchain and Multi-Agent System (MAS) technologies to guarantee privacy, scalability, transparency, and efficiency [3].

Public blockchain networks are open and self-governed – anyone can read, write, and audit the ongoing activities. Private blockchains are restricted and have a single authority controlling the whole network. Private blockchain networks are thus for organisations oriented to data storage and concerned with protecting sensitive information, namely from cyberattacks. Moreover, they offer improved performance in terms of throughput, scalability, robustness, and efficiency compared with public networks.

This work reports the integration of CloudAnchor, a brokerage platform that allows businesses to lease Infrastructure as a Service (IaaS) resources, with a Smart Contract (SC) solution. Thus, the goal is to store the evolving trust-based business profiles and Service Level Agreements (SLA) celebrated within CloudAnchor as SC in a private blockchain network, providing trusted interactions among the agents and immutability to the celebrated contracts. This goal implies the selection and deployment of a SC solution as well as the design, development and assessment of a dedicated REST API to manage the requests delivery to the blockchain nodes, serving as a proxy. *This novel solution – the storage of behavioural and contractual data as SC – ensures the transparency, integrity, and legitimacy of all brokerage strategic knowledge.*

This paper is structured in five more sections Sect. 2 details the literature review; Sect. 3 describes the CloudAnchor platform; Sect. 4 presents the design and development of the proposed solution; Sect. 5 holds the experiments and results; and Sect. 6 draws the conclusion.

2 Background

This section reviews blockchain smart contract technology and related work on electronic marketplaces underpinned by multi-agent systems.

2.1 Smart Contracts

Smart contracts are computer programs running on blockchain nodes to facilitate, execute and enforce the terms agreed between untrusted parties without the involvement of any TTP [8]. According to Alharby (2017), there are deterministic and non-deterministic smart contracts. A deterministic smart contract executes without external inputs, whereas a non-deterministic smart contract needs information from external parties such as oracles or data feeds [1]. Since CloudAnchor smart contracts will be deployed on a private Fabric network and managed by the CloudAnchor platform, they fall into the private non-deterministic category.

Several blockchain platforms were evaluated to determine the most suited implementation to run a private network for the CloudAnchor smart contracts. Table 1 summarises the results of this analysis. The Fabric blockchain, together with its implementation client and library, have prevailed due to its Crash Fault

Tolerance (CFT) consensus mechanisms. Although Byzantine Fault Tolerance (BFT) mechanisms are excellent against malicious actors, CFT validates more transactions using fewer peers and recovers from system crashes as long as there are at least $2n + 1$ nodes available [5]. The Proof of Work (PoW), Proof of Authority (PoA), Proof of Stake (PoS) and Delegated Proof of Stake (DPoS) consensus mechanisms correspond to BFT instances, whereas Kafka and Raft to CFT. Besides, the performance of a Fabric network can be improved by optimising the number of transaction processing channels (application-specific) and adding endorsement peers [12]. The remaining aspects are largely equivalent.

Table 1. Platform comparison

	Ethereum[a]	Hyperledger[b]	Corda[c]	EOS[d]
Open source	Yes	Yes	Yes	Yes
Private network	Yes	Yes	Yes	Yes
Smart contracts	Yes	Yes	Yes	Yes
Consensus mechanisms	PoW, PoA BFT-Typed $(3n+1)$	Kafka, Raft CFT-Typed $(2n+1)$	PoW, PoS BFT-Typed $(3n+1)$	DPoS BFT-Typed $(3n+1)$
Clients	Geth, Besu	Fabric	CorDapps	Cleos, Eoslime
SDK	Web3j	Fabric SDK	N/A	N/A

[a] https://ethereum.org/
[b] https://www.hyperledger.org/
[c] https://www.corda.net/
[d] https://eos.io/

2.2 Related Work

Several agent-based platforms implement electronic marketplaces to automate business transactions, saving time and money. Below are a few application examples that resemble the CloudAnchor platform.

- Chichin et al. (2014) describe the Smart Cloud Marketplace (SCM), which is an agent-based cloud platform for trading cloud services [4]. Software agents represent cloud service consumers and providers in the marketplace and make intelligent judgements on their behalf. The platform allows the agents to use various trading policies to negotiate more efficiently in different situations.
- Cretan (2016) proposes an agent-based intelligent platform to model and support parallel and concurrent negotiations among organisations acting in the same industrial market [6]. The platform allows the negotiation of temporary coalitions to share skills and resources, allowing businesses to better respond to opportunities.
- Brousmiche et al. (2018) propose an agent-based simulation framework of blockchain-backed energy marketplaces. It combines MAS technology with

blockchain to offer a secure decentralised solution. Each agent, representing a household, models both its energy production and consumption profiles and offers to buy or sell energy in the platform market [2]. The platform defines two types of smart contracts: one for household account contracts and another for marketplace established contracts.
- Luo et al. (2019) advance a distributed electricity trading system to facilitate peer-to-peer electricity sharing among prosumers (entities acting both as producers and consumers). The two-layer system includes: (*i*) a MAS to model the prosumer network, support coalitions and the negotiation of electricity trading; and (*ii*) a blockchain-based transaction mechanism to enable the trusted and secure settlement of electricity trading transactions [10].
- Samuel et al. (2020) and a later update by Khalid et al. (2021) adopt a blockchain-based trust management system for a two-layered MAS. The lower layer enables agents to perform direct and indirect trust updates based on interactions and shares this interaction feedback with the blockchain. The upper layer implements a cooperation incentive mechanism and establishes the credibility of agents based on a weighted average of the chained agent trust. This credibility is then used to detect dishonest agents, securing the system against bad-mouthing and on-off attacks [9,11].
- Wang et al. (2021) suggest a blockchain trading framework for multi-agent cooperation and energy sharing. The market nodes are modelled in the physical layer through power system modelling and the transaction consensus strategy in the cyber layer. Moreover, the nodes are verified in a modified IEEE 13 distribution network testing feeder [16].

Table 2 summarises the characteristics of the surveyed platforms in terms of architecture, communication paradigm, smart contract support, SLA negotiation and negotiation strategy. All works adopt MAS technology and employ P2P communication, four use smart contracts (SC) and two rely on T&R profiling. Only CloudAnchor implements SC to represent and store inter-business trust profiles and SLA. The works by Luo et al. (2019) and Samuel et al. (2020) are similar to CloudAnchor. They adopt the same technologies as CloudAnchor, except for the SLA, and implement a double-layered design concerning SC and trust profiling of negotiating entities. In the case of these three platforms, entity agents rely on the chained trust-based profiles to negotiate. The main difference between the current proposal to the literature is that evolving inter-business SLA and trustworthiness are stored in a distributed, immutable and secure blockchain network, which is a distinct feature.

3 CloudAnchor

The CloudAnchor architecture, displayed in Fig. 1, comprises four layers – interface layer, contract layer, business layer, and market layer – and five agent types: (*i*) interface agents to interact with the actual consumer and provider businesses; (*ii*) contract agents to manage SLA instances; (*iii*) business agents to implement

Table 2. Platform comparison

Authors	MAS	P2P	SC	SLA	T&R
Chichin et al. (2014) [4]	Yes	Yes	No	No	No
Cretan (2016) [6]	Yes	Yes	No	No	No
Brousmichc et al. (2018) [2]	Yes	Yes	Yes	No	No
Luo et al. (2019) [10]	Yes	Yes	Yes	No	Yes
Samuel et al. (2020) [9,11]	Yes	Yes	Yes	No	Yes
Current Proposal	**Yes**	**Yes**	**Yes**	**Yes**	**Yes**

the business logic; (*iv*) market delegate agents to negotiate resources on behalf of their representatives; and (*v*) layer manager agents to manage the platform layers [15]. Each layer holds one layer manager agent.

Each registered SME business (consumer or provider) is represented in the platform by: (*i*) one interface agent located in interface layer; (*ii*) one agreement agent located in agreement layer; (*iii*) one business agent in the business layer; and (*iv*) an undetermined number of delegate agents involved in specific resource negotiations in the market layer [14]. This collection of agents works together on behalf of the SME to negotiate SLA regarding the provision of resources and build trust-based profiles of partners based on the outcomes of their interactions. For more details on the platform see [7,13–15]. The SLA terms are verified and guaranteed by the SLA layer manager agent, that controls the fulfilment of the terms and excludes and/or penalises defaulter provider and consumer businesses.

3.1 Service Level Agreements

To take advantage of CloudAnchor services, an SME needs to negotiate up to three types of SLA:

- brokerage SLA (bSLA) between business and platform to specify the fee for each successfully traded resource. These contracts are renegotiable.
- coalition SLA (cSLA) between one consumer and a collection of providers regarding large resource requests, which cannot be fulfilled by individual providers. These contracts detail the coalition and the resource supply terms.
- resource SLA (rSLA) between a consumer and a provider to specify the resource lease terms. These contracts are negotiated in the market layer between consumer and provider delegate agents.

The negotiation of an SLA starts by instantiating a template with the identification of the parties. If the negotiation succeeds, the contract is filled with the accorded terms; otherwise, the template is discarded.

Brokerage contracts (bSLA) are renegotiable. The renegotiation of the access terms to the platform can be triggered by default (contract termination deadline) or on-demand (consumer or provider request). If the negotiation fails, the business deregisters from the platform, and all representative agents are removed.

Coalition contracts (cSLA) establish virtual providers, which supply federated resources. Therefore, a virtual provider is a temporary coalition of providers established on the fly to provide federated resources, i.e., resources which cannot be offered by any single provider [14]. Nonetheless, once a virtual provider negotiates federated resources with a consumer, individual rSLA are celebrated between the actual provider and consumer.

3.2 Trust and Reputation Profiling

Trust and Reputation (T&R) modelling allows the platform to select the best partners for providing or consuming services. Trust is, by default, a subjective property of a direct one-to-one relationship attributed by a trustor to a trustee. Reputation is an indirect many-to-one relationship, which can be determined from the trust that many trustors have on the trustee. The trust a trustor has on a trustee is based on the outcomes of their past interactions and will be used to pre-assess any future interactions between them. Specifically, for each SLA established, there are two possible outcomes: success or failure. The platform maintains a registry of these outcomes between all parties (platform, consumers, providers, and virtual providers) to adjust the inter-business trust incrementally and derive reputation at anytime [7,14].

The platform maintains two behavioural models of each party – self-trust and inter-business trust. The self-trust, which corresponds to the global business reputation, is built from the outcomes of all past dealings with others. The inter-business trust represents how the business perceives a specific partner based on their past dealings. Note that inter-business trust is not commutative.

To minimise SLA failures, the platform rewards or penalises businesses based on these T&R profiles. This mechanism applies to all brokerage stages, namely bSLA renegotiation, partner lookup (invitation/acceptance) and resource negotiation. Businesses with higher T&R have more trading opportunities and better contract conditions, and those who violate contracts get fewer opportunities and higher fees. In the case of federated resources, the virtual provider propagates any incurred penalties to the members of the coalition. This way, the platform implements T&R-based brokerage to improve its overall performance. For more details, see [14].

4 Proposed Solution

CloudAnchor platform agents, specifically contract and business layer agents, must connect with a Fabric network to create, read and update the CloudAnchor smart contracts, representing inter-agent SLA and trust profiles. This way, CloudAnchor stores the strategic knowledge in a distributed ledger, protecting it against manipulation and, thus, ensuring its integrity. On the implementation side, rather than weaving a direct connection between CloudAnchor and the Fabric network, this solution implements a Fabric gateway through an external client, which exposes a dedicated API. This logic separation promotes interoperability and minimises the changes to CloudAnchor. Additionally, CloudAnchor and the API gateway can be hosted in separate machines, improving the hardware resource management efficiency and allowing the solution to be scaled horizontally. The API only accesses the Fabric network using generated identities to guarantee the security of the transactions. There are identities with different privileges, preventing malicious agents from taking control of the blockchain network.

4.1 Architecture

The system's architecture was designed with the goal of having the least amount of impact on the CloudAnchor platform's performance. The use of blockchain technology should be viewed as a third-party service that CloudAnchor utilises at its convenience. The agents behaviour should not be influenced by the blockchain integration. Figure 1 presents the proposed integration architecture between the CloudAnchor and Hyperledger Fabric. The gateway comprises the API module – with controller, service, modelling and repository layers – and relies on the fabric-gateway-java library to interact with the blockchain nodes.

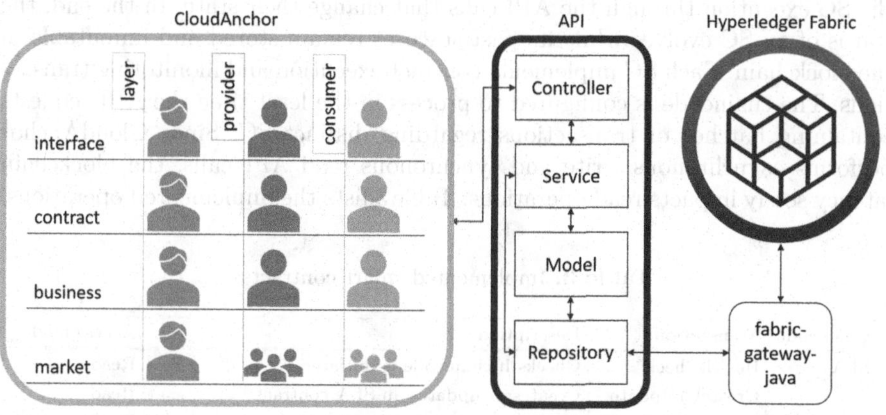

Fig. 1. Solution architecture

CloudAnchor – The platform agents create, read and update the smart contracts (bSLA, rSLA and trust) through the gateway API. The business agents update their smart contracts and, together with the layer managers, read business trust profiles from the blockchain when negotiating with others.

Gateway API – The API optimises transaction requests according to the Fabric network parameters. It queues the CloudAnchor requests to submit read and write requests separately, using optimised batch sizes to improve the overall system throughput.

Hyperledger Fabric – The Fabric network encompasses eight endorsement peers, three communication channels, one orderer node, five Certificate Authorities and four Membership Service Providers. To optimise the overall performance, the configuration of the blockchain network must consider the expected number of requests per time unit. Its goal is to be able to handle peaks of simultaneous requests, that are significantly greater than the average number of requests per second, without causing a bottleneck.

4.2 Smart Contracts

The negotiated contracts – bSLA and rSLA – and business behaviour – incremental self and inter-business trust – are stored in four types of SC:

BSlaTransfer manages bSLA instances (defined as BSlaContract data).
RSlaPairTransfer manages rSLA instances (defined as RSlaPair data).
OwnTrustTransfer manages self-trust instances (defined as OwnTrust data).
PairTrustTransfer manages inter-business trust instances (defined as PairTrust data).

The implemented SC are private and non-deterministic since they run on a private network and their execution is externally triggered. CloudAnchor commands the SC execution through the API calls that change their state. In the end, the status of an SC evolves while its past statuses remain stored and immutable in the blockchain. Each SC implements contract execution and monitoring transactions. The chaincode is configured to process in the least time the API requests containing batches of transactions regarding distinct SC. Since CloudAnchor performs asynchronous write and synchronous read API calls, the blockchain latency solely impacts read operations. Table 3 lists the implemented operations.

Table 3. Implemented smart contracts

Chaincode	Transaction	Description	Access mode
SLA	HealthCheck	Checks if chaincode is initiated	Read
	CreateOrUpdate	Creates or updates an SLA contract	Read
	ReadSLA	Returns an SLA contract by ID	Read
	GetAllSLA	Returns all SLA contracts	Read
	GetByEnterprise	Returns all SLA of an enterprise	Read
	UpdateStatus	Updates the status of an SLA	Write
	ValidateContracts	Synchronises the SLA state	Write
	CountContracts	Returns the number of SLA SC of the business	Read
Trust	HealthCheck	Checks if chaincode is initiated	Read
	Update	Updates a trust (own/pair)	Write
	ReadTrust	Returns a trust by ID	Read
	GetAllTrust	Returns all trust contracts	Read
	CountTrusts	Returns the number of trust SC of the business	Read

5 Experiments and Results

This experimental work aims to answer the following research questions regarding the impact on CloudAnchor of the SC integration:

(**Q1**) How does it affect brokerage (number and value of leased resources)?
(**Q2**) How does it affect run-time (blockchain latency)?

The experiments, which were repeated with and without the SC listed in Table 3, compare the overall performance considering brokerage and run-time metrics. The platform implements T&R-based brokerage, i.e., bSLA renegotiation, partner lookup (invitation/acceptance) and resource negotiation rely on the T&R profiles of the involved parties. To overcome the cold start, all metrics are collected after a five-month warm-up. The experiments are executed on a VM with a quad-core CPU, 2 threads per core, 20 GiB of RAM, and a 70 GiB of disk. They cover the four experimental scenarios summarised in Table 4.

Table 4. Experimental scenarios

Scenario	Businesses	Resource/Business	$\overline{T_E}$ (%)
1	30 consumers 30 providers	1000 × 1 Short term	10 × [60, 80, 100]
2	30 consumers 30 providers	1000 × 1 Long term	10 × [60, 80, 100]
3	30 consumers 30 providers	40 × 25 Short term	10 × [60, 80, 100]
4	30 consumers 30 providers	40 × 25 Long term	10 × [60, 80, 100]

There are thirty consumers and thirty providers. Consumers and providers are grouped into three sets of 10 businesses with 60%, 80%, and 100% of average SLA enforcement trustworthiness ($\overline{T_E}$). The simulation of these business profile data is stochastic. Each provider holds 1000 single resources, which, depending on the test, can be negotiated individually – one thousand single resources – or in groups of 25 resources – forty federated resources. The platform negotiates single and federated resources for both the short and long term. A one-month period corresponds to a short term lease and a five-month period to a long term lease. Short-term experiments last 10 months, while long-term experiments last 30 months, yielding 5 and 25 months of warm operation, respectively.

Finally, to decouple the effects of the processing overload generated by the execution on a single VM from that of the blockchain, the latency experiments consider two operation modes: (*i*) SC-Execution, which performs all SC transactions; and (*ii*) SC-Read-Delay, which introduces the delay of SC read transactions. Specifically, in SC-Read-Delay mode, the API maintains all SC data in memory and answers queries directly. Nonetheless, it forwards read queries to the blockchain and waits for the answer, which is ignored, to introduce the corresponding delay. SC-Execution tests were repeated five times and SC-Read-Delay three times per resource and lease period.

5.1 Brokerage

The main brokerage indicators are the value and quantity of resources leased. The collected metrics are average number bSLA, cSLA and rSLA established, fulfilled rSLA, corresponding to the supply and payment under the agreed terms of the leased resources, and the average transacted value ($\overline{TV}$) per resource. Table 5 displays the variation of these metrics in the SC-Execution mode, using as baseline the results without SC. As expected, the deviations are residual (<1%) and can be attributed to the stochastic simulation of the business profile data. The SC-Write-Delay mode does not affect these metrics.

Table 5. Brokerage Metrics Variation in SC-Execution Mode

Lease	Metric	Single resources Δ(%)	Federated resources Δ(%)
Short term	bSLA contracts	+0.0	+0.0
	bSLA (renegotiated)	−0.7	−0.9
	cSLA contracts		−0.5
	rSLA contracts	−0.9	−0.5
	Successful rSLA	−0.8	−0.8
	$\overline{TV}$ (€)	−0.3	+0.3
Long term	bSLA contracts	+0.0	+0.0
	bSLA (renegotiated)	−0.7	+0.4
	cSLA contracts		+0.1
	rSLA contracts	−0.6	+0.2
	Successful rSLA	−0.2	+0.2
	$\overline{TV}$ (€)	+0.0	+0.8

5.2 Latency

The integration of Cloudanchor with Hyperledger Fabric allows the adoption of SC at the cost of additional latency. Specifically, it affects all read API calls, which are synchronous. Table 6 compares the average latency per resource in SC-Execution mode and in SC-Write-Delay, using as baseline the results without SC.

In SC-Execution mode, the latency increases from 150% (short term and long term single resources) to 300% (long term federated resources). In SC-Write-Delay mode, latency ranges from a 20% increase (short term lease of single resources) to 23% growth (long term lease of federated resources).

Table 6. Average Latency Variation in SC-Execution and SC-Read-Delay Modes

Lease	Metric	Operation mode	Single resources Δ(%)	Federated resources Δ(%)
Short term	Latency	SC-Execution	+150.9	+148.6
		SC-Read-Delay	+20.1	+21.7
Long term	Latency	SC-Execution	+156.4	+293.0
		SC-Read-Delay	+20.9	+22.9

6 Conclusion

The representation and execution of inter-business behaviour and SLA changes as SC have several implications for the CloudAnchor platform. On the one hand, it enhances the security, integrity and traceability of the platform's strategic knowledge, i.e., SLA and business profiles. On the other hand, it introduces latency. While the blockchain integration does not affect the brokerage indicators, i.e., the number of resources leased an average transacted value per resource, run-time increases between 20% and 23%. Nonetheless, CloudAnchor remains largely unaffected by this higher latency since the established SLA, detailing the terms of business access to the platform and IaaS lease, and associated business profiles tend to last hours, days, months or even years.

When compared with related work, this integration makes CloudAnchor unique: it is the only MAS brokerage platform that adopts smart contracts to execute and store both behavioural and contractual strategic knowledge.

At the moment, CloudAnchor maintains a local copy of all SC. The plan is to use blockchain as the sole repository of CloudAnchor's strategic knowledge.

Acknowledgements. This work was partially supported by Portuguese National Funds through the FCT - Fundação para a Ciência e a Tecnologia (Portuguese Foundation for Science and Technology) as part of project UIDB/50014/2020.

References

1. Alharby, M., Aldweesh, A., van Moorsel, A.: Blockchain-based smart contracts: a systematic mapping study of academic research (2018). In: 2018 International Conference on Cloud Computing, Big Data and Blockchain (ICCBB), pp. 1–6 (2018). https://doi.org/10.1109/ICCBB.2018.8756390
2. Brousmichc, K.L., Anoaica, A., Dib, O., Abdellatif, T., Deleuze, G.: Blockchain energy market place evaluation: an agent-based approach. In: 2018 IEEE 9th Annual Information Technology, Electronics and Mobile Communication Conference (IEMCON), pp. 321–327. IEEE (2018). https://doi.org/10.1109/IEMCON.2018.8614924
3. Calvaresi, D., Dubovitskaya, A., Retaggi, D., Dragoni, A.F., Schumacher, M.: Trusted registration, negotiation, and service evaluation in multi-agent systems throughout the blockchain technology. In: 2018 IEEE/WIC/ACM International Conference on Web Intelligence (WI), pp. 56–63 (2018). https://doi.org/10.1109/WI.2018.0-107

4. Chichin, S., Chhetri, M.B., Vo, Q.B., Kowalczyk, R., Stepniak, M.: Smart cloud marketplace-agent-based platform for trading cloud services. In: 2014 IEEE/WIC/ACM International Joint Conferences on Web Intelligence (WI) and Intelligent Agent Technologies (IAT), vol. 3, pp. 388–395. IEEE (2014). https://doi.org/10.1109/WI-IAT.2014.193
5. Correia, M.: From Byzantine consensus to blockchain consensus, chap. 3. CRC Press, New York (2019). https://doi.org/10.1201/9780429674457-3
6. Cretan, A.G.: Intelligent multi-agent platform within collaborative networked environment. Challenges Knowl. Soc. 975–981 (2016)
7. Cunha, R., Veloso, B., Malheiro, B.: Renegotiation of electronic brokerage contracts. In: Rocha, Á., Correia, A.M., Adeli, H., Reis, L.P., Costanzo, S. (eds.) WorldCIST 2017. AISC, vol. 570, pp. 41–50. Springer, Cham (2017). https://doi.org/10.1007/978-3-319-56538-5_5
8. Hewa, T.M., Hu, Y., Liyanage, M., Kanhare, S.S., Ylianttila, M.: Survey on blockchain-based smart contracts: technical aspects and future research. IEEE Access **9**, 87643–87662 (2021). https://doi.org/10.1109/ACCESS.2021.3068178
9. Khalid, R., Samuel, O., Javaid, N., Aldegheishem, A., Shafiq, M., Alrajeh, N.: A secure trust method for multi-agent system in smart grids using blockchain. IEEE Access **9**, 59848–59859 (2021). https://doi.org/10.1109/ACCESS.2021.3071431
10. Luo, F., Dong, Z.Y., Liang, G., Murata, J., Xu, Z.: A distributed electricity trading system in active distribution networks based on multi-agent coalition and blockchain. IEEE Trans. Power Syst. **34**(5), 4097–4108 (2019). https://doi.org/10.1109/TPWRS.2018.2876612
11. Samuel, O., Javaid, N., Khalid, A., Imrarn, M., Nasser, N.: A trust management system for multi-agent system in smart grids using blockchain technology. In: 2020 IEEE Global Communications Conference, GLOBECOM 2020, pp. 1–6 (2020). https://doi.org/10.1109/GLOBECOM42002.2020.9348231
12. Thakkar, P., Nathan, S., Viswanathan, B.: Performance benchmarking and optimizing hyperledger fabric blockchain platform. In: 2018 IEEE 26th International Symposium on Modeling, Analysis, and Simulation of Computer and Telecommunication Systems (MASCOTS), pp. 264–276. IEEE (2018). https://doi.org/10.1109/MASCOTS.2018.00034
13. Veloso, B., Malheiro, B., Burguillo, J.C.: CloudAnchor: agent-based brokerage of federated cloud resources. In: Demazeau, Y., Ito, T., Bajo, J., Escalona, M.J. (eds.) PAAMS 2016. LNCS (LNAI), vol. 9662, pp. 207–218. Springer, Cham (2016). https://doi.org/10.1007/978-3-319-39324-7_18
14. Veloso, B., Malheiro, B., Burguillo, J.C., Gama, J.: Impact of trust and reputation based brokerage on the CloudAnchor platform. In: Demazeau, Y., Holvoet, T., Corchado, J.M., Costantini, S. (eds.) PAAMS 2020. LNCS (LNAI), vol. 12092, pp. 303–314. Springer, Cham (2020). https://doi.org/10.1007/978-3-030-49778-1_24
15. Veloso, B., Meireles, F., Malheiro, B., Burguillo, J.C.: Federated IaaS resource brokerage. In: Kecskemeti, G., Kertesz, A., Nemeth, Z. (eds.) Developing Interoperable and Federated Cloud Architecture, chap. 9, pp. 252–280. IGI Global, Hershey (2016). https://doi.org/10.4018/978-1-5225-0153-4.ch009
16. Wang, X., Liu, P., Ji, Z.: Trading platform for cooperation and sharing based on blockchain within multi-agent energy internet. Glob. Energy Interconnection **4**(4), 384–393 (2021). https://doi.org/10.1016/j.gloei.2021.09.009

Partial Swarm SLAM for Intelligent Navigation

Jawad N. Yasin[1,2(✉)], Huma Mahboob[1], Suvi Jokinen[1], Hashem Haghbayan[1], Muhammad Mehboob Yasin[3], and Juha Plosila[1]

[1] Autonomous Systems Laboratory, Department of Future Technologies, University of Turku, Vesilinnantie 5, 20500 Turku, Finland
{janaya,ssjoki,mohhag,juplos}@utu.fi
[2] ABB Oy, Helsinki, Finland
[3] Department of Computer Networks, College of Computer Sciences and Information Technology, King Faisal University, Hofuf, Saudi Arabia
mmyasin@kfu.edu.sa

Abstract. The focus of this work is to present a novel methodology utilizing the classical SLAM technique and integrating with the swarm agents for localizing, guiding, and retrieving the agents towards the optimal path while using only necessary tracker-based information between the agents. While navigating in an unknown environment with no-prior map information, upon encountering large obstacles (out of the field of view detection range of the onboard sensors, the swarm is divided into sub-swarms. This is done while dropping tracking points at every turn. Similarly, the time stamps for every turn taken and the gap width available between obstacles are recorded. Once an agent from any sub-swarm category reaches the destination, the agent broadcasts these tracker points to the rest of the swarm agents. Utilizing this broadcasted key information, the rest of the agents are able to navigate toward the destination without having to find the path. With the help of simulation examples, it is shown that the proposed technique is efficient over other similar randomized turn-based techniques.

Keywords: Swarm robotics · Distributed systems · Exploration schemes · SLAM

1 Introduction

Swarm robotics can be defined as the study of how a large group of agents or robots can be controlled in such a way to achieve an overall desired behavior or shape to perform a set of tasks. This overall emergence of the behavior is due to the interactions of the agents with other agents within the swarm as well as the objects in the environment [1]. A swarm of robots can be utilized for

This work has been supported by the Academy of Finland-funded research projects (AURORA: 330493, ADAFI: 335512).

© The Author(s), under exclusive license to Springer Nature Switzerland AG 2022
F. Dignum et al. (Eds.): PAAMS 2022, LNAI 13616, pp. 435–446, 2022.
https://doi.org/10.1007/978-3-031-18192-4_35

a wide range of tasks ranging from search and rescue to mapping to military purposes [2,3]. That is due to the ability of the agents within the swarm to self localize, self-organize, and communicate with other agents, as well as the flexibility and scalability of the overall swarm making the utilization of swarm of robots ideal for such unknown environments [4]. Similarly, for a swarm to navigate autonomously, in any environment introduces several research challenges, such as keeping or maintaining the formation, collision avoidance, localizing, inter-agent communication, path finding [5]. Among other approaches for localizing, the agents in the swarm can utilize simultaneous localization and mapping (SLAM) to autonomously self-localize and navigate in unknown environments with no prior map information [6]. SLAM is a known and fundamental technique in the navigation of autonomous robots. However, the focus of the studies and development in SLAM has been mostly from the perspective of individual robots and which leaves a gap for the development of SLAM with multiple robots or a swarm as a whole [7].

The existing multi-robot SLAM techniques focus on either collective production of maps or centralized map merging (due to limited onboard computational resources). Recently, an approach was introduced where the robots produce individual maps by utilizing different exploration methodologies and these maps were later integrated on a remote platform [8,9]. Moreover, SLAM, from computational perspective, is intensive and similarly for transferring the data between robots will also require a large amount of data to be transferred and processed [10]. However, none of the existing methodologies address the issue of utilizing the SLAM technique to facilitate the agents of the swarm to collaborate by exchanging minimum information required to direct the other agents towards a common goal. In order to develop an effective and efficient SLAM technique for a swarm, there are several questions that need to be addressed, ranging from the inter-agent communication of the swarm to the exploration of the environment to utilization of the acquired data and sharing of the necessary information between the agents.

In this article, we propose an algorithm in which only the necessary information is shared between the agents, i.e., reducing the overhead for communication, and subsequently is computationally light for the agents. Agents note the coordinates of the position where they disperse and the main swarm is divided into sub-swarms. This point of separation is noted by the respective agent as it navigates in a different direction. Upon approaching an available gap between the obstacles, the agent notes the coordinates of this point as well, the time it took to travel from the first point, the velocity with which the agent navigated, and the shape/width of the gap found between the obstacles. This process is continued until one of the agents of the sub-swarm finds a clear route to the destination. At this point, that agent broadcasts the recorded information to the rest of the sub-swarms for them to follow the tracker points and reach the destination.

The novelty of the proposed algorithm is as follows:

1. While navigating towards the destination, upon encountering obstacle(s) large enough to have their edges out of bounds from the sensor's range, the agents

are dispersed in different directions and individual agents keep a record of their movement
2. Only the necessary information is shared between the agents rather than sharing the whole acquired maps with other agents, i.e., reducing the overhead of the communication between the agents
3. When the agents disperse to find a route for reaching the destination, an agent upon finding an opening towards the destination only keeps a track of certain features and shares only that information with other agents for them to perform targeted pathfinding and navigate towards the destination in an efficient manner

The rest of the paper is organized as follows. Motivation is provided in Sect. 2. Section 3 describes the proposed approach. Simulation results are provided in Sect. 4. Finally, the concluding remarks, discussion, and some future work in given in Sect. 5.

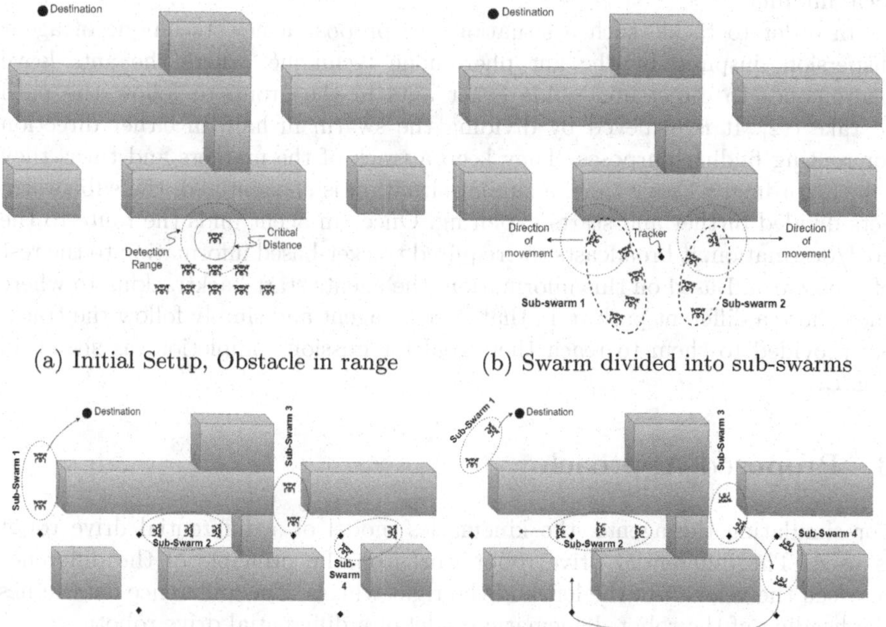

(a) Initial Setup, Obstacle in range

(b) Swarm divided into sub-swarms

(c) Swarm further divided into sub-swarms. Sub-swarm 1 finds path to destination

(d) All sub-swarms start tracking back utilizing the Tracker points

Fig. 1. Illustration of the Partial Swarm SLAM technique. (a) shows the swarm approaching a large obstacle with edges not visible in the ranging sensor's range. (b) Swarm gets divided into sub-swarms, and sub-swarm 1 and 2, start navigating in different directions to find the route. (c) All the sub-swarms have place pheromone trackers (coordinates) while navigating through the maze of unknown environment. (d) Sub-swarm 1, upon finding path to destination, broadcasts its placed pheromone trackers to the rest of the swarm agents

2 Motivation

While navigating in an unknown environment, with no prior map information, autonomous agents have to perform avoidance maneuvers by analyzing the information at hand, i.e., by utilizing the onboard sensors for observing the surroundings, evaluating the situation, and choosing the continuation trajectory as necessary [11]. However, in situations, where the encountered obstacle(s) are large and while utilizing the onboard ranging sensors, the agents cannot detect either edge of the obstacle, arguably the best course of action is to make a calculated guess (by keeping the direction of the destination under consideration) and turn or deviate accordingly [cite our paper]. In such a scenario, since the final destination is known, the agent draws a tangent from its own coordinates towards the destination and chooses the direction to turn accordingly. In such a manner, based on the information at hand, without any knowledge of the map, the agent takes the best/optimal decision. However, such an approach can also lead to a much larger deviation leading to longer mission time, battery drainage, or even local minima.

In order to tackle such a situation, we propose a new technique of agent dispersion, inspired by the ant pheromone technique, where the ants leave pheromones to direct and guide other ants in the group to follow the path to take [12]. It is achieved by dividing the swarm in half, in either direction for routing finding purposes. They keep a track of the markers and turns they take accordingly. Every time, a similar situation is encountered, the sub-swarm gets divided further and starts exploring. Once, an agent finds the route to the goal/destination, it broadcasts the required tracker-based information to the rest of the swarm. Based on this information, the agents start backtracking to where they chose a different path from that specific agent and simply follow the trackers provided to them to reach their goal for mission completion, as shown in Fig. 1.

3 Proposed Approach

For simulating the agents, the kinematics model of a differential drive robot is used. The differential drive robot works on the principle of the difference between the velocity of the left and the right wheels. This difference determines the heading of the robot. Kinematic model of a differential drive robot:

$$\begin{aligned} \dot{x} &= vcos\theta, \\ \dot{y} &= vsin\theta, \\ \dot{\theta} &= \frac{v_\Delta}{W} \end{aligned} \tag{1}$$

where $\dot{x}$ and $\dot{y}$ are the x and y positions of the robot, v is the velocity, $\dot{\theta}$ is the heading angle of the robot.

To calculate the turning curve of the robot, the following equation is used:

$$\Delta V = \frac{v_r - v_l}{W} \tag{2}$$

where ΔV is the difference between the left and the right wheel speed, v_r and v_l are the right and the left speeds respectively, and W is the width of the robot.

Algorithm 1. Global Routine

```
    procedure NAVIGATION & DETECTION
2:      B_Formation ← False;
        Destination ← False;
4:      if Self.ID == 1 then
            α ← Self;
6:          α_Alive ← False;
        else
8:          α ← Leader(Self);
            α_Alive ← True;
10:     end if
        while True do
12:         D = Scan();
            if D < ReactionRange then
14:             D_o, A_o ← Calculate obstacle distance and angles at which the edges lie;
                if D_o < γ && A_o < Γ then
16:                 Collision Avoidance(D_o, A_o);
                    if Destination == L.o.S. then
18:                     Self.Destination ← True
                        Broadcast Tracker points;
20:                 end if
                end if
22:             if B_Formation && Destination then
                    Traceback(PoB, t, G_w, T_D);
24:             else
                    Navigate();
26:             end if
            end if
28:     end while
    end procedure
```

The top-level pseudo code of the agents is given Algorithm algo1. In the initial setup, the agents are assigned their respective IDs. Every agent in the swarm executes this top-level algorithmic routine locally. In the beginning, the Boolean variables $B_{Formation}$ and *Destination* are initialized, whose roles are to notify the global routine if the swarm has been divided into sub-swarms and if the agent has reached the destination respectively (Lines 2-3). Then the algorithm checks if the global leader has been declared and if the leader-follower connection has been set up. If not, then the global leader is declared (α) and the followers are connected to their respective and immediate leaders accordingly. As the global leader does not have any leader, therefore, $\alpha Alive$ (My leader is Alive) is set to False. And for the followers, this flag is set to True (Lines 4-9). After this, the agents start scanning their surroundings while navigating toward the destination (lines 11-12). As soon as an object is detected, it is checked if the distance to the object (D) is less than the defined *ReactionRange* (line 13). If the detected obstacle lies within the *ReactionRange*, the distance (D_o) along with the angles at which edge(s) of the detected obstacle(s) lie are calculated (Line 14). If the calculated distance lies within the defined deviation range (γ) and the angles at which the edge(s) have been detected also lie within the defined ranges, indicating that continuing the current trajectory will lead to a potential collision, the control is transferred to Collision Avoidance algorithm (Lines 15-16). Every agent checks if the destination is in its line of sight ($L.o.S.$), if this is true, the agent then sets the destination flag to *True* for itself and broadcasts the tracker points to the rest of the agents (Lines 17-19). The algorithm then checks if the swarm was divided into sub-swarms ($B_{Formation}$ Flag indicates the break of formation) during any phase of the mission or while performing avoidance maneuvers and if the agent has reached the destination (implying that the route to the destination is now complete). In this case, the Traceback() function is called to provide the pheromone tracker points to other agents to allow them to simply follow and navigate towards the destination (Line 22-23). Otherwise, the agents continue the navigation process until the goal is achieved.

3.1 Collision Avoidance

Algorithm 2. Collision Avoidance

```
    procedure CollisionAvoidance(D_o, A_o)
2:      if A_o != NULL then                              ▷ Obstacle edge(s) detected
            β = detect_edges(D_o);
4:          if β > 2 then
                ζ ← calculated gap between obstacles;
6:              if ζ > R_c then
                    Align agent to pass through;
8:                  if B_Formation then
                        T_D[][] = Turn direction and number of turn;
10:                     G_w = Gap width;
                    end if
12:             else                                      ▷ out of bounds Obstacle
                    B_Formation = True;
14:                 Break Formation();
                end if
16:         end if
        else                                              ▷ No edges detected
18:         Break Formation();
            B_Formation = True;
20:     end if
    end procedure
```

In the collision avoidance phase in our proposed algorithm, it is first checked if there were any edges detected of the detected obstacle(s). If A_o (angles at which the edges have been detected) has real values, then it means that the edges have been detected and the obstacle is not large enough to be out of bounds from the ranging sensor's view (Line 2). Then the number of edges are detected (β) in order to check how many obstacles have been detected that can cause a potential collision if the current trajectory is continued (Line 3). If the detected edges are more than 2, it indicates multiple obstacles detected, and then the algorithm calculates the gap (ζ) that is available between detected obstacles (Lines 4-5). After calculating the available gap between the detected obstacles, it is checked if the gap is sufficient enough for the agents to pass through, i.e., the gap bigger than R_c. R_c is calculated based on the dimensions of the agent plus a defined safe distance that is to be allowed on either side of the agent, Eq. 1:

$$R_c = \delta + \tau \tag{3}$$

where $R_[c$ is the collision radius, and δ, and τ are the width and the minimum safe distance allowed from either side of the agent respectively.

Then agent(s) is aligned to pass through the available gap (Lines 6-7). Further, it is checked if the swarm has already broken down the initial formation to create sub-swarms for route finding, then the direction of the turn the agent is taking and the width of the gap which the agent is navigating through are noted as part of pheromone tracker pointers (Lines 8-10). These pheromone tracker pointers are later used to direct other agents to find the route. Whereas, if the available gaps are not wide enough for the agent to pass through or if there were no edges detected (Line 2), then in both cases, it is treated as a single obstacle out of bounds case, the $B_{Formation}$ flag is set to *True*, and the control is transferred to BreakFormation() algorithm (Lines 12-19).

3.2 Formation Breaking and Path Finding Mode

Algorithm 3. Break Formation

```
    procedure BreakFormation
2:      TangentLine = Calculate tangent to destination;
        PoB = current coordinates;
4:      t = time;
        T_D[][] = turn directions and number of turns;
6:      G_w = Gap width;
        G_1i, G_2j = Create sub-swarms();
8:      G_1i,G_2j ← Temporary sub-swarm leaders;
        Short term path planning(TangentLine);
10: end procedure
```

Algorithm algo3, Break Formation, starts by drawing a tangent line from the agents' coordinates to the destination for directional purposes (Line 2). Agents utilize onboard positioning systems (GPS) to determine the direction to the destination. Then the *PoB* (point of break) is noted, i.e., the current position (Line 3). The time stamps are noted starting from *PoB* onwards, a stamp for every turn taken (Line 4). This helps as a cross-check for tracing back the route for every agent, by allowing the agent to verify if at approximately the same amount of time it has arrived at the similar position. This is further cross-checked with the gap width (G_w) (Line 6), also noted in Algorithm algo2. The agent then notes the direction in which it is turning and further notes the number of the turns it has taken (Line 5). Then the swarm is divided into sub-swarms, by pooling the agents alternatingly into G_{1i} and G_{2j} (Line 7). The sub-swarms are assigned their respective temporary or sub-swarm leaders for continuing the mission and leading the rest of the follower agents (Line 8). After this, short term path planning is done by the sub-swarm leader by utilizing the calculated $TangentLine$ to resume navigating in the direction of the destination after bypassing the current obstacle (Line 9).

3.3 Trace Back Utilizing Tracker Points

Algorithm 4. Trace Back

```
   procedure TRACEBACK(PoB, t, G_w, T_D)
2:     if Self.Destination != True then
           Rcv(Tracker points(PoB));
4:         Set (speed);
           if Tracker[i] then
6:             cross-check t, G_w, T_D;
               Navigate;
8:         end if
```

Algorithm algo4 shows the pseudo-code for the *Traceback* function. the algorithm starts by checking if the agent performing the check has already reached the destination (Line 2). If the *Destination* flag is $False$, the agent receives the tracker points, and sets its speed accordingly by reading the speed of the broadcasting agent (Lines 3-4). Upon reaching a tracker point ($Traker[i]$), the agent cross-checks the provided data by checking the time it took for navigating between $Tracker[i]$ and $Tracker[i-1]$, the shape/width of the gap at the current position (G_w), and takes the respective turn to continue navigation towards the destination (Lines 5-7).

4 Simulation Results

The initial conditions defined for our work are as follows:

1. All agents obtain their position vectors utilizing their onboard localization techniques
2. The communication channel is lossless
3. The agents can communicate and broadcast their tracker-based information to other members of the swarm

For the simulation environment, we used python graphics. For the ranging sensor, we simulated the output of the LiDAR sensor in a 2-dimensional scale. The scaling of the environment closer to the real-world movement is performed by converting the distance traveled and the speed with which the agents are navigating from meters and meters per second to pixels and pixels per second.

Figure 2a shows the floor map of the environment used for testing the proposed methodology. The destination mark is shown by the hollow square in the right corner. Figure 2b the agent encountering the large obstacle and taking a priority-based left turn. The rest of the swarm follows in a similar manner. As shown in Fig. 2c, the swarm reaches a dead end. In this situation, the agents have to turn back and go to the point from where the swarm took the left turn. This not only drains more energy resources but is also time taking and results

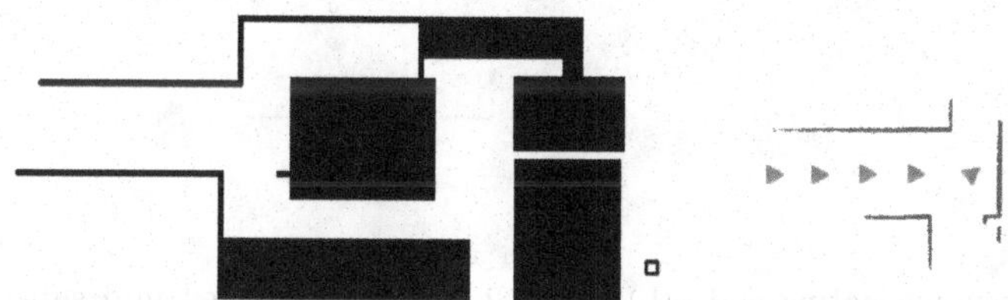

(a) The floor map of the environment used for verification

(b) Swarm comes across a large obstacle, i.e., out of bounds

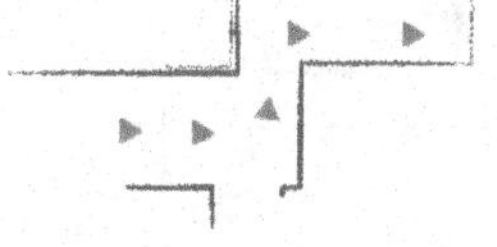

(c) With no-prior map information, the swarm utilizes the priority-based turning and turns left

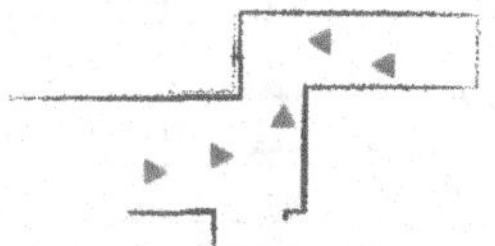

(d) Swarm is turning back after reaching a dead end, here the congestion is also faced

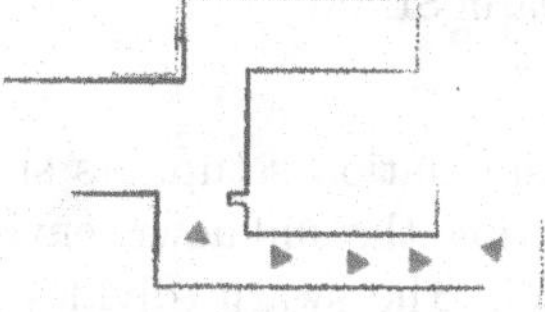

(e) Swarm keeps navigating in the other direction

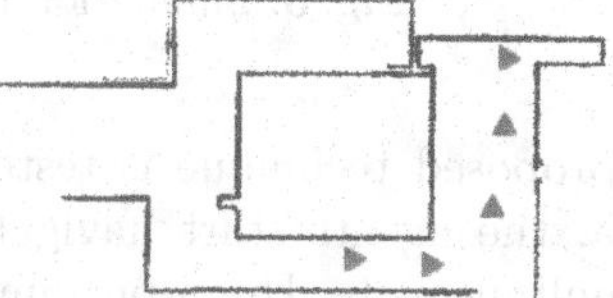

(f) Swarm once again faces the issue of reaching a dead end, rerouting the whole swarm, congestion and wastage of energy resources

Fig. 2. Simulation results: priority-based turn

in congestion (Fig. 2d). After the swarm reroutes back to the initial position, from where it turned left, the agents navigate in the other direction, where the swarm faces a similar situation again, Fig. 2e. Figure 2f shows the swarm facing another dead end. Upon tracking back, the swarm will finally find the path to the destination, in the considered simulation setup.

(a) Scene 1, swarm starts navigating and encounters a larger obstacle

(b) Scene 2, swarm is divided into sub-swarms and simultaneously navigating the environment to find the path

(c) Scene 3, one agent finds the destination, and other agents in the sub-swarms have started navigating towards that point

(d) Scene 4, all the agents of the sub-swarms have successfully reached the desired coordinates

Fig. 3. Simulation results: partial swarm SLAM

The proposed technique is tested in the same simulation setup. As shown in Fig. 3a, the agents start navigating while exploring the unknown environment simultaneously. Upon encountering an obstacle, the swarm divides into two sub-swarms and keeps on navigating in the pursuit of finding the path to the destination, as shown in Fig. 3b. Figure 3c, shows the swarm divided into further sub-swarms. Here, it can be seen that an agent of the sub-swarm found the unobstructed path to the destination. And the other agents in the sub-swarms have started navigating back by backtracking the tracker points. Figure 2d shows the final scene, where the agents (sub-swarms) have to regroup into the initial swarm setup and reached the destination.

As it is evident from the comparative simulation results, utilizing the proposed approach the time to mission completion can be significantly reduced in environments with no-prior map information available. In the considered setup, utilizing the priority-based turn technique, the longest distance any agent had to travel was approximately 1.5 times the longest distance any agent traveled utilizing the proposed Partial Swarm SLAM technique. The distances covered by individual agents are provided in Table 1. If only the traveled distance is considered, while employing the traditional method, the overall distance covered by the swarm was approx. 1.6 times more as compared to the distance covered by the swarm using the Partial Swarm SLAM method.

Table 1. Total distance (in meters) travelled by agents, comparison between Partial Swarm SLAM and traditional method

Agent No	PS-SLAM	Traditional
1	310 m	660 m
2	310 m	660 m
3	490 m	660 m
4	480 m	660 m
5	480 m	660 m

5 Conclusion

In this paper, we developed an algorithm for utilizing the SLAM technique partially in order to guide dispersed agents of the swarm towards the destination. The agents in the sub-swarms, keep a track of the vital information about their movements, such as tracker points (the coordinates) at which the swarm/sub-swarm gets divided into further sub-swarms, the timestamps between two adjacent tracker points, the velocity at which the agent traveled between the tracker points, the which direction the agent turned towards, the shape or the gap available between the obstacles/objects. This key information is then shared by the agent that finds a clear route to the destination. The agents in the rest of the swarm then utilized this information to quickly localize themselves while navigating and tracing back towards the tracker points left by the broadcasting agent. The simulation results provide sufficient proof that the proposed methodology works reliably in the simulated environments. The results evidently show that this technique helps navigate the swarm in an unknown environment with no-prior map information and without any communication with central servers for path-finding purposes. The chances for the swarm agents to reach a local minimum by utilizing this technique are minimized considerably in comparison to priority-based or randomized turning methods.

In the future, we plan to include detailed comparative and analytical results with other techniques, to show the efficiency of the proposed technique. Furthermore, the proposed approach will be further developed by injecting noise in the setup by including the IMU drift and limited range communication between the agents to analyze the efficiency of the proposed approach in-depth. The chain-linked limited range communication between the agents will restrict the extent to which the agents can disperse. It will also be interesting to analyze, which tracking back utilizing the broadcasted trackers, if an agent or a sub-swarm has to deviate, for instance, due to any newly added obstacle, and how computationally expensive the re-localization process will be.

References

1. Yasin, J.N., et al.: Energy-efficient formation morphing for collision avoidance in a swarm of drones. IEEE Access **8**, 170681–170695 (2020). https://doi.org/10.1109/ACCESS.2020.3024953
2. Shakhatreh, H., et al.: Unmanned aerial vehicles (UAVs): a survey on civil applications and key research challenges. IEEE Access **7**, 48572–48634 (2019). https://doi.org/10.1109/ACCESS.2019.2909530
3. Ladd, G., Bland, G.: Non-military applications for small uas platforms. https://doi.org/10.2514/6.2009-2046
4. Brambilla, M., Ferrante, E., Birattari, M., Dorigo, M.: Swarm robotics: a review from the swarm engineering perspective. Swarm Intell. **7**(1), 1–41 (2013)
5. Yasin, J.N., Haghbayan, M.H., Yasin, M.M., Plosila, J.: Swarm formation morphing for congestion-aware collision avoidance. Heliyon **7**(8), e07840 (2021)
6. Martínez, D., et al.: A mobile robot agent for gas leak source detection. In: Bajo Perez, J., et al. (eds.) Trends in Practical Applications of Heterogeneous Multi-Agent Systems. The PAAMS Collection. AISC, vol. 293, pp. 19–25. Springer, Cham (2014). https://doi.org/10.1007/978-3-319-07476-4_3
7. Kegeleirs, M., Grisetti, G., Birattari, M.: Swarm slam: challenges and perspectives. Front. Robot. AI **8**, 23 (2021). https://doi.org/10.3389/frobt.2021.618268
8. Park, S., Kim, H.: DAGmap: multi-drone slam via a DAG-based distributed ledger. Drones **6**(2), 34 (2022). https://doi.org/10.3390/drones6020034
9. Kegeleirs, M., Garzón Ramos, D., Birattari, M.: Random walk exploration for swarm mapping. In: Althoefer, K., Konstantinova, J., Zhang, K. (eds.) TAROS 2019. LNCS (LNAI), vol. 11650, pp. 211–222. Springer, Cham (2019). https://doi.org/10.1007/978-3-030-25332-5_19
10. Mattar, E.A.: Mobile robot feature-based slam behavior learning, and navigation in complex spaces. In: Hurtado, E.G. (ed.) Applications of Mobile Robots, IntechOpen, Rijeka (2018). https://doi.org/10.5772/intechopen.81195
11. Yasin, J.N., Mahboob, H., Haghbayan, M.H., Yasin, M.M., Plosila, J.: Energy-efficient navigation of an autonomous swarm with adaptive consciousness. Remote Sens. **13**(6), 1059 (2021). https://doi.org/10.3390/rs13061059
12. Sumpter, D.J., Beekman, M.: From nonlinearity to optimality: pheromone trail foraging by ants. Anim. Behav. **66**(2), 273–280 (2003)

Demonstrations

IRRMA: An Image Recommender Robot Meeting Assistant

Benoît Alcaraz[1(✉)], Nina Hosseini-Kivanani[1], and Amro Najjar[2]

[1] University of Luxembourg, 2 Av. de l'Université, 4365 Esch-sur-Alzette, Luxembourg
{benoit.alcaraz,nina.hosseinikivanani}@uni.lu

[2] Luxembourg Institute of Science and Technology (LIST), 2 Av. de l'Université, 4365 Esch-sur-Alzette, Luxembourg
amro.najjar@list.lu

Abstract. The number of people who attend virtual meetings has increased as a result of COVID-19. In this paper, we present a system that consists of an expressive humanoid social robot called QTRobot, and a recommender system that employs natural language processing techniques to recommend images related to the content of the presenter's speech to the audience in real time. This is achieved utilising the QTRobot's platform capabilities (microphone, computation power, and Wi-Fi).

Keywords: Robot assistant · Meeting assistant · Recommender system

1 Introduction

Presentations and meetings are recurrent tasks in today's workplace. Furthermore, the COVID-19 situation has shifted meetings modes and forced users to increase the number of meetings they attend [2]. As a result, technologies that improve the productivity of meetings are highly valuable. Some meeting assistant technologies have been developed in recent decades to help with this. Recommender systems (RSs) [1] are used to provide information for users and facilitate smooth decision-making when participants are overloaded with information. This issue has been addressed in the literature of smart assistants and intelligent personal assistants for decades. For instance, Augmented Multi-party Interaction (AMI) [3], a recommender system based on what the speaker says, provides participants with textual documents and resources from previous meetings in real time. However, we can identify two problems with this work.

First, the recommendations are often limited to those of previous meetings or what the speaker has provided. This makes the system unsuitable for meetings where the topic under consideration has not been previously discussed. It also requires additional work on the part of the speaker, who needs to provide

© The Author(s), under exclusive license to Springer Nature Switzerland AG 2022
F. Dignum et al. (Eds.): PAAMS 2022, LNAI 13616, pp. 449–453, 2022.
https://doi.org/10.1007/978-3-031-18192-4_36

resources to fill the database. Secondly, even though textual documents provide a lot of valuable information, they cannot be viewed during a presentation without the participants missing information from the speaker. Furthermore, reading documents is time-consuming. If the number of documents recommended during a meeting is too high, people may simply ignore them due to lack of time, and so the system is no longer valuable.

Addressing these issues requires expanding the recommendation database while also improving its fit for the meeting context. The database can be extended with data available on the Internet. It is possible to create a whitelist of documents from which appropriate recommendations can be taken. Websites like Wikipedia Commons[1], the Wikipedia image database, can be added to the whitelist. Furthermore, a recommendation fits a meeting context if it can be viewed without the audience being distracted from what the speaker is saying. Images fit such contexts perfectly as they can be viewed while listening to the speaker. A photo, a schema, or a statistical graph are all examples of recommended images.

This paper is a demonstration for PAAMS 2022 of our Image Recommender Robot Meeting Assistant (IRRMA). The information is displayed through the interface of an expressive humanoid social robot called QTRobot standing on the meeting table in front of the participants. Figure 1 shows IRRMA during a meeting. Figure 2 shows the architecture of our approach.

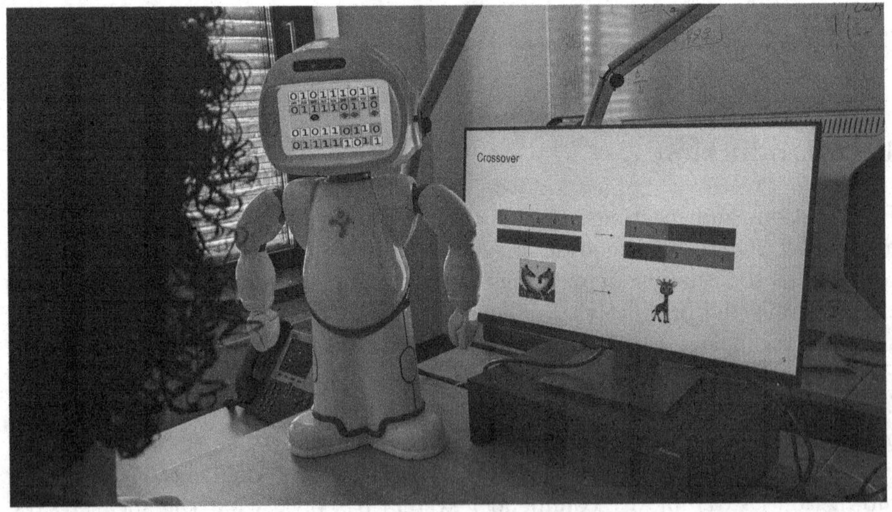

Fig. 1. QTRobot using IRRMA next to the main presentation monitor

In meeting situations, IRRMA can help users better retrieve information from the presenter, and it can fine-tune the assistance during usage. IRRMA

[1] https://commons.wikimedia.org.

will provide as information in an application domain (i.e. providing "live" recommendations during meeting sessions).

More specifically, the advantages of IRRMA are threefold: (i) it provides information that can be consulted during the meeting, (ii) it can catch the attention of the audience more effectively than a monitor showing recommendations, (iii) it can search for recommendations based on the contents of a large database without requiring too much preparation time from the speaker.

2 Main Purpose

IRRMA's aim is to suggest images that are related to what the speaker is saying. The goal is to add more information and references to a presentation in order to improve its quality. A statistical graph, for example, can be displayed to evaluate what the speaker is currently saying, or a photo can be used to illustrate the speech. A whitelist of websites can be used as a database to find images. This provides access to an enormous number of suitable images. Also, if the topic is known prior to the presentation, a whitelist can be created of websites strictly related to the topic. This would allow recommendations of a higher quality. We have chosen to use a QTRobot to represent IRRMA because it can grab the attention of participants when a recommendation is made. It also better fits the role of "assistant" in that way. We intend to design and develop an interactive user support system. Multiple challenges have been identified, including (i) speech processing and keyword extraction, (ii) developing the recommendation system, and (iii) how to share the recommendation with the audience. We propose an early stage demonstration of IRRMA in a meeting situation, with a focus on the recommendations and the way we present them.

3 Demonstration

Figure 2 depicts the architecture of our system. Our procedure can be broken down into several steps. To begin with, IRRMA has to extract the keywords of the speech. It uses the QTRobot microphone to listen to the speaker. It then uses speech-to-text technologies to convert the speech to text. It then extracts the keywords from the transcript using a custom-made algorithm. Next, it must choose a recommendation based on the keywords obtained. To do so, it uses the keywords to iterate and search through the images in its whitelist. If a suitable image is found, it is chosen as the recommendation.

Finally, the recommendation has to be presented to the audience. This step largely depends on the type of meeting (i.e. online, offline or hybrid). The QTRobot can be connected as a user of the remote meeting application, which then shares its screen with the online participants. It is placed on the table next to the presenter and faces the audience. The recommendation can then be displayed on the tablet held by the QTRobot. The QTRobot makes a movement with its arms when displaying the recommendation to attract the audience's attention. Although the speaker's monitor is present in our architecture, it is possible that the speaker has nothing to show.

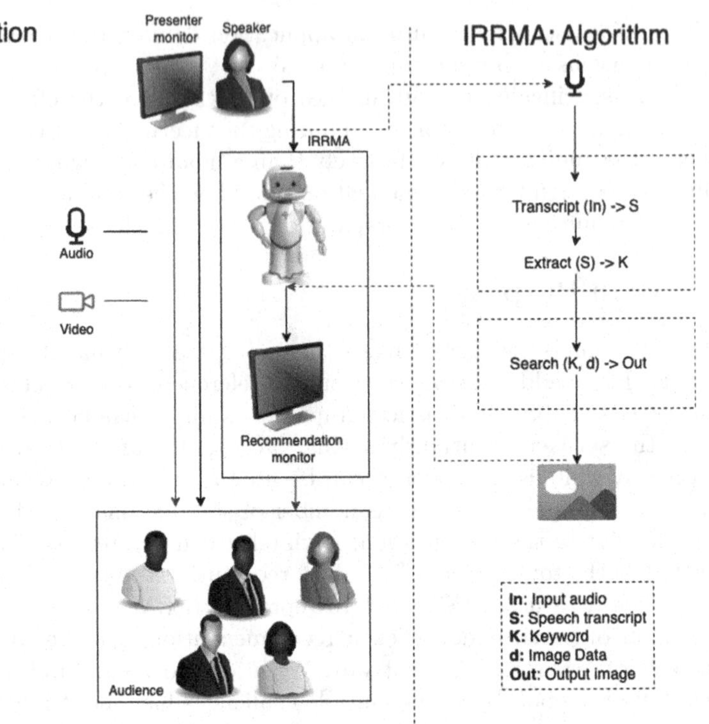

Fig. 2. Architecture of IRRMA in situ and its algorithm

4 Conclusion

Our system, an Image Recommendation Robot Meeting Assistant, aims to recommend relevant images in real time based on the contents of a presentation. Natural language processing technologies are used to accomplish this. We also use the possibilities that this embodiment provides to improve the trust among audience's into the system [4].

Our contribution is relevant for meetings where the speaker is giving a presentation, as well as for other situations where the speaker dose not necessarily have slides to show. We plan to improve the system in the future so that it can handle multimedia recommendations and follow a meeting with multiple speakers.

Acknowledgments. This work has been funded by the Luxembourg National Research Fund under Grant No. IS/14717072.

This work is partially supported by the Chist-Era grant CHIST-ERA19-XAI-005, and by *(i)* the Swiss National Science Foundation (G.A. 20CH21_195530), *(ii)* the Italian Ministry for Universities and Research, *(iii)* the Luxembourg National Research Fund (G.A. INTER/CHIST/19/14589586), *(iv)* the Scientific and Research Council of Turkey (TÜBİTAK, G.A. 120N680).

References

1. Bobadilla, J., Ortega, F., Hernando, A., Gutiérrez, A.: Recommender systems survey. Knowl.-Based Syst. **46**, 109–132 (2013)
2. DeFilippis, E., Impink, S.M., Singell, M., Polzer, J.T., Sadun, R.: Collaborating during coronavirus: the impact of Covid-19 on the nature of work. Technical report, National Bureau of Economic Research (2020)
3. Ehnes, J.: A tangible interface for the AMI content linking device-the automated meeting assistant. In: 2009 2nd Conference on Human System Interactions, pp. 306–313. IEEE (2009)
4. Stroessner, S.J., Benitez, J.: The social perception of humanoid and non-humanoid robots: effects of gendered and machinelike features. Int. J. Soc. Robot. **11**(2), 305–315 (2019)

Grouplanner: A Group Recommender System for Tourism with Multi-agent MicroServices

Patrícia Alves[1(✉)], Domingos Gomes[1], Catarina Rodrigues[1], João Carneiro[1], Paulo Novais[2], and Goreti Marreiros[1]

[1] GECAD – Institute of Engineering of Polytechnic of Porto, Porto, Portugal
{pat,1190534,cadra,jrc,mgt}@isep.ipp.pt

[2] ALGORITMI Centre – University of Minho, Guimarães, Portugal
pjon@di.uminho.pt

Abstract. To provide recommendations to groups of tourists is a very complex task, especially due to conflicting preferences and the group's heterogeneity. The introduction of Multi-Agent Systems (MAS) can be the leverage we are looking for. Their autonomy, isolated state, distribution, and loose coupling make them suitable for the development of distributed systems, being the concept similar to a Microservices architecture. This connection brought a new approach, the Multi-Agent Microservices (MAMS) architecture, which exposes agents as resources through REST endpoints, changing the way MAS are seen and implemented, facilitating the user ↔ agent interaction, with a more efficient interoperability, bringing faster and more intelligent systems. In this demonstration, we propose the use of a MAMS architecture to represent the tourists in a mobile Group Recommender System for Tourism prototype, Grouplanner, exposing their agents and knowledge as resources that can be consumed by HTTP clients by directly communicating with the tourists' agents using REST endpoints, in order to provide faster and better recommendations.

Keywords: Group recommender systems · Multi-agent microservices · Tourism

1 Introduction

Recommender Systems (RS) are an increasingly important tool to help users obtain personalized recommendations in a variety of domains. The travel and tourism domain are a good example, however, when groups of tourists are involved, conflicts related to the users' preferences and the group's heterogeneity arise. Several authors proposed the use of Multi-Agent Systems (MAS) to help with those limitations, and proactively make recommendations based on the tourists' profile and context, enriching the tourists' experience [1, 2].

It can be seen in literature that the use of MAS is becoming more frequent and applied to a variety of different domains [3–5]. One of the greatest advantages of using MAS is that their autonomy, isolated state, distribution, and loose coupling [6] allows the development of distributed systems [7], being the concept similar to MicroServices

© The Author(s), under exclusive license to Springer Nature Switzerland AG 2022
F. Dignum et al. (Eds.): PAAMS 2022, LNAI 13616, pp. 454–460, 2022.
https://doi.org/10.1007/978-3-031-18192-4_37

(MS), as argued by W. Collier, O'Neill, Lillis and O'Hare [6], who believe that "an agent can be viewed as a type of Microservice that can be deployed seamlessly within any Microservice ecosystem". According to the authors, there are many similarities between MAS and MS, such as the isolated state, distribution, elasticity, automated management, and loose coupling, as well as how easy it is for MS to meet the social ability, autonomy, and reactivity of agents, with the advantage that agents can be proactive. These similarities led to the Multi-Agent MicroServices (MAMS) architecture, that consists on Agent-Oriented MS exposed through REpresentational State Transfer (REST) endpoints [6], where requests can be responded asynchronously by the agents. This type of architecture can change the way MAS are seen and implemented, facilitating the implementation of agile development methods [6], and the way agents are accessed and used, bringing faster and more intelligent systems.

This paper presents an improvement and demonstration of part of our work, on modeling a mobile Group Recommender System (GRS) for tourism using the tourists' personality to predict their preference for tourist attractions [8] and intelligent agents with MicroServices [3, 9], where we propose the use of a MAMS architecture to expose the agents and their capabilities as resources, facilitating the user $\leftrightarrow$ agent interaction, the access to the agents' knowledge and capabilities, and a more efficient interoperability, to provide faster and more personalized recommendations.

2 Main Purpose

This demonstration intends to show how we managed to implement a MAS using MAMS in a mobile GRS for tourism prototype, Grouplanner, allowing direct communication with the tourists' agents using REST endpoints, and how the agents use their social abilities to interact with each other and provide individual and group recommendations.

Each tourist is represented by an agent in the MAMS (Tourist Agent), modelled with the tourist's profile (demographic data, personality, travel-related preferences and concerns, and motivations for traveling), which is accessible through a REST endpoint from the MAMS REST Application Programming Interface (API) (see Fig. 1). The objective is to expose Tourist Agents as resources through a REST API [6], so the information on the tourists can be shared easily and faster. The agents can share their knowledge and interaction data, either internally and externally, and collaborate to provide more accurate and satisfying recommendations to the tourists, reducing the group conflicts, without the need of a broker agent in the environment to communicate with the other agents.

.NET is one of the most used object-oriented programming frameworks for implementing web services and interoperable cross-platform applications, and it was therefore used to implement the Grouplanner prototype. As for the development of the MAMS, many multi-agent platforms can be found in literature [10]. We chose ActressMAS [11] for its simplicity and ease of use, and because it was one of the few agent frameworks that uses C# programming language, being more suitable for integrating with the.NET framework.

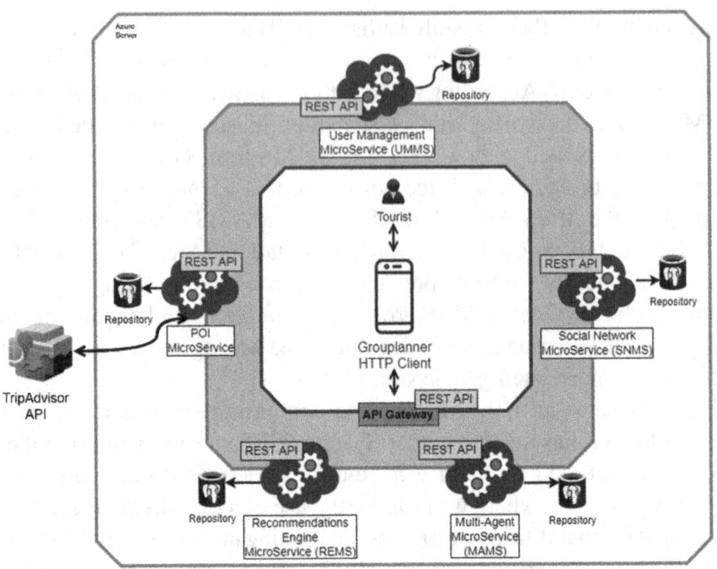

Fig. 1. Grouplanner MicroServices architecture.

3 Demonstration

When a tourist user registers in the Client App, he is first registered and authenticated/authorized in the system, using the ASP.NET Core Identity and JSON Web Tokens (JWT), through the API Gateway, which was developed using the ASP.NET Core framework, that acts as a single-entry point into the system, having all the HTTP Clients requests to pass through it.

After the registration, a JSON with the tourist's profile is built and sent at the same time to the User Management MS (UMMS) and the MAMS, via an HTTPS POST request. The MAMS parses the JSON file and brings life to a Tourist Agent (TourAg) in the environment, modelled with the tourist's profile, registering it in the environment's concurrent dictionary [11]. The UMMS stores the tourist's data in the corresponding repository, necessary for consults and updates in the app.

When a tourist requests individual recommendations of Points-Of-Interest (POI), a JSON message is sent, via HTTPS, directly to her TourAg in the MAMS, using the URL: "https://<domain>/mams/agents/tourists/<TourAg-name>/requestRecommendation". Having access to the tourist's knowledge base, the respective TourAg compiles the tourist's profile into a JSON and asks the Recommendations Engine MS (REMS) for the 10 best POI that match her personality[1], as predicted in the "Personality vs Tourist Attractions Preference" model proposed in our previous work [8], and according to a POI Ontology. The REMS responds to the TourAg with a JSON containing the suggested POI, after which the TourAg uses her social ability to ask the other

[1] To facilitate the demonstration, we are not considering the tourists' demographic data, motivations, nor travel-related preferences and concerns.

TourAg if there are better suggestions based on their current knowledge, updating them accordingly. The final recommendations are then sent to the requesting user.

When a tourist creates an excursion group (e.g.: "One Adventure"), becoming the group owner, a JSON containing the group's information is sent to the MAMS (URL: "https://<domain>/mams/groups/registerGroup"), which immediately creates a Travel Agent (TrvAg) with the group's data, responsible for that group (see next dialogue).

(12/05/2022 10:20:20) Travel Agent 1 has been added
(12/05/2022 10:20:20) [TrvAg-1]: Greetings, I am the Travel Agent for the "One Adventure" excursion group.

When the group owner requests recommendations for the group, an HTTPS request is sent to the group's TrvAg (URL: "https://<domain>/mams/agents/groups/OneAdventure/requestRecommendation"), which divides the group into subgroups with similar personalities, meaning a group can be divided into two or more subgroups, depending on the tourists' personality (if all the tourists have similar personalities the main group will not be divided). In the example (Fig. 2, left image), the group was divided into three subgroups, where one has more interest in Adrenaline activities, another in Gastronomy events, and the other in Museums, Boat trips & Viewpoints[2].

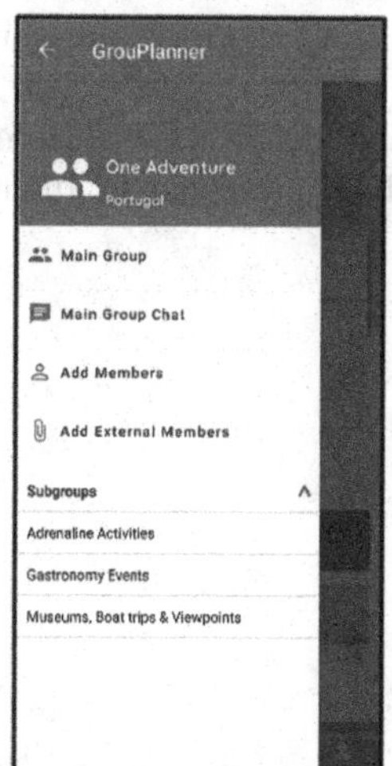

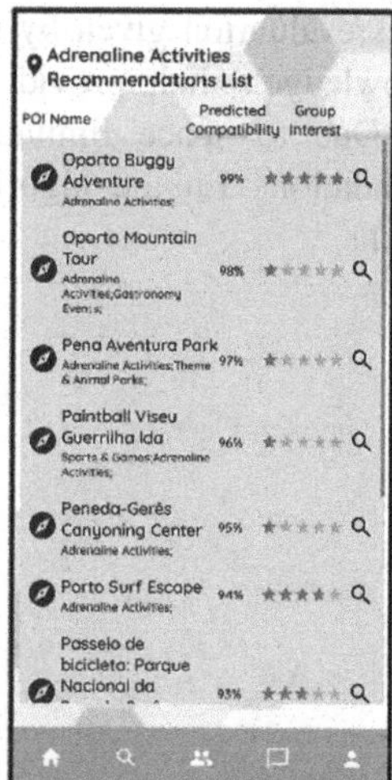

Fig. 2. Left: Grouplanner user interface showing the 3 subgroups formed; Center: Detail of the members in the "Adrenaline Activities" subgroup formed; Right: List of POI recommended to the "Adrenaline Activities" subgroup.

After creating the subgroups, they are sent via HTTPS in a JSON message to the REMS, which proceeds as in the individual recommendations previously mentioned.

[2] This division is also based on the "Personality vs Tourist Attractions Preference" model proposed in our previous work [8].

After assigning the 10 best POI to each subgroup, the service responds with a JSON message to the requesting TrvAg with the recommended POI list. The TrvAg then communicates with the Tourist Agents to learn what should, or should not, be recommended using the same strategy mentioned for the individual recommendations (as can be seen in the next dialogues).

The final POI list is then sent by the TrvAg to the Grouplanner HTTP Client, which creates the proposed subgroups and assigns their respective tourists, and at the same time to the group's Social Network MS (SNMS), responsible for persisting all the (sub)groups data, necessary for future consults within the app. Each subgroup can then consult its respective recommended POI list (see Fig. 2, right side image).

4 Conclusions

In this paper, we briefly demonstrated how we implemented a MAMS in a mobile GRS prototype using a MicroServices architecture, and how the agents were exposed as resources and exchanged information between them.

Just by using HTTP requests, the Tourist Agents knowledge and capabilities can be accessed by any HTTP client, meaning the proposed MAMS can be used by recommender systems exposing a REST API, to obtain knowledge on tourists' preferences according to their personality, demographic data, etc. The ability to make individual recommendations is a plus, as the respective Tourist Agent can learn with the feedback/evaluation given by the tourist to the suggested/visited POI, and therefore gain knowledge to help provide better group recommendations.

Due to space limitations, the remaining implementation details, the Recommendations Engine algorithms and the POI Ontology will be presented in future works.

(12/05/2022 10:20:30) [TrvAg-1]: margaridaXD, please tell me your score for each personality dimension.
(12/05/2022 10:20:30) [TrvAg-1]: user1, please tell me your score for each personality dimension.
…
(12/05/2022 10:20:31) [TourAg-margaridaXD]: Hi TrvAg-1, here are my personality scores: …
(12/05/2022 10:20:31) [TourAg-user1]: Hi TrvAg-1, here are my personality scores: ...
…
(12/05/2022 10:20:32) [TrvAg-1]: margaridaXD, you have a personality very similar to user1, joao_pedro12 and antonio, so I will put you together.
(12/05/2022 10:20:32) [TrvAg-1]: user1, you have a personality very similar to margaridaXD, joao_pedro12 and antonio, so I will put you together.
…
(12/05/2022 10:20:33) [TrvAg-1]: I finished analyzing the group members and decided to create 3 subgroups, one more motivated by "Adrenaline activities", other by "Gastronomy events", and another by "Museums", "Boat trips & Viewpoints".
(12/05/2022 10:20:33) [TrvAg-1]: margaridaXD, user1, joao_pedro12 and antonio, you were assigned to subgroup "Adrenaline activities".
… //After receiving the POI list for each subgroup from the REMS:
(12/05/2022 10:40:10) [TrvAg-1]: I have the following POI recommendation for these subgroups, does anyone has something against the recommendations?
(12/05/2022 10:40:12) [TourAg-margaridaXD]: I am afraid of water activities, can you please recommend other POI?
(12/05/2022 10:40:14) [TourAg- Joana]: I went to Nómadas Adventure Tours, but it's a 1 star to me.
…
(12/05/2022 10:40:24) [TrvAg-1]: According to the feedback received, I have changed the POI list recommendation and will send it to the group.
(12/05/2022 10:40:24) [TrvAg-1]: POI recommendations sent to "One Adventure" group.

References

1. Borràs, J., Moreno, A., Valls, A.: Intelligent tourism recommender systems: a survey. Expert Syst. Appl. **41**, 7370–7389 (2014)
2. Ravi, L., Devarajan, M., Sangaiah, A.K., Wang, L., Subramaniyaswamy, V.: An intelligent location recommender system utilising multi-agent induced cognitive behavioural model. Enterprise Inf. Syst. **15**, 1376–1394 (2021)
3. Carneiro, J., Andrade, R., Alves, P., Conceição, L., Novais, P., Marreiros, G.: A consensus-based group decision support system using a multi-agent MicroServices approach. In: Proceedings of the 19th International Conference on Autonomous Agents and MultiAgent Systems, pp. 2098–2100 (2020)
4. Zouad, S., Boufaida, M.: Using multi-agent microservices for a better dynamic composition of semantic web services. In: 2020 The 4th International Conference on Advances in Artificial Intelligence, pp. 47–52 (2020)
5. Neto, J., Morais, A.J., Gonçalves, R., Coelho, A.L.: Multi-agent-based recommender systems: a literature review. In: Yang, X.-S., Sherratt, S., Dey, N., Joshi, A. (eds.) Proceedings of Sixth International Congress on Information and Communication Technology. LNNS, vol. 235, pp. 543–555. Springer, Singapore (2022). https://doi.org/10.1007/978-981-16-2377-6_51

6. Collier, R.W., O'Neill, E., Lillis, D., O'Hare, G.: MAMS: Multi-Agent MicroServices. In: Companion Proceedings of the 2019 World Wide Web Conference, pp. 655–662 (2019)
7. Batet, M., Moreno, A., Sánchez, D., Isern, D., Valls, A.: Turist@: agent-based personalised recommendation of tourist activities. Expert Syst. Appl. **39**, 7319–7329 (2012)
8. Alves, P., et al.: Modeling tourists' personality in recommender systems: how does personality influence preferences for tourist attractions? In: Proceedings of the 28th ACM Conference on User Modeling, Adaptation and Personalization, pp. 4–13 (2020)
9. Alves, P., Carneiro, J., Marreiros, G., Novais, P.: Modeling a mobile group recommender system for tourism with intelligent agents and gamification. In: Pérez García, H., Sánchez González, L., Castejón Limas, M., Quintián Pardo, H., Corchado Rodríguez, E. (eds.) HAIS 2019. LNCS (LNAI), vol. 11734, pp. 577–588. Springer, Cham (2019). https://doi.org/10.1007/978-3-030-29859-3_49
10. Pal, C.-V., Leon, F., Paprzycki, M., Ganzha, M.: A review of platforms for the development of agent systems. arXiv preprint arXiv:2007.08961 (2020)
11. Leon, F.: ActressMAS, a. NET multi-agent framework inspired by the actor model. Mathematics **10**, 382 (2022)

Microblogging Environment Simulator: An Ethical Approach

Maria Araújo Barbosa(✉), Francisco S. Marcondes, Dalila Alves Durães, and Paulo Novais

ALGORITMI Centre, University of Minho, Braga, Portugal
pg42844@alunos.uminho.pt,
{francisco.marcondes,dalila.duraes}@algoritmi.uminho.pt,
pjon@di.uminho.pt

Abstract. Social media were originally created as a means of communication, but have eventually become an important way of producing and sharing information and news. Beyond that, the scientific community's interest in conducting studies in numerous fields using Twitter is growing daily. This paper presents a platform that simulates a microblogging, inspired by the Twitter layout, with the aim of creating an environment where social media-focused studies can be conducted without compromising ethical values. The end result is a in lab environment with the ability to present the content (in the format of post) to validate or investigate and record user interactions.

Keywords: Microblogging · Simulator · Prototyping · Research environment

1 Introduction

Currently, interest in microblogging platforms such as Twitter is high not only among users, but also among researchers who want to use this type of social media for their experiments or studies in different fields from fake-news detection [1,2] to hate speech classification [3]. However, conducting a study directly on social media can raise a complexity of ethical issues [4] related to **data**, **consent**, **traceability**, or even the **integrity of the human Person** [5].

With this project, the aim was that the dilemmas presented earlier would be resolved using a platform that simulates a social media interface. This way, in all interactions, participants know the context they are in and can be sure that no personal information is stored. The goal is to provide a platform that can present content (in the microblogging format of posts) to users and record all interactions. It also aims to ensure that the constructed experiment has been properly tested in a laboratory environment before being placed on the social network, so as not to jeopardise the success of the experiment by a bug that might be discovered in a lab environment.

© The Author(s), under exclusive license to Springer Nature Switzerland AG 2022
F. Dignum et al. (Eds.): PAAMS 2022, LNAI 13616, pp. 461–466, 2022.
https://doi.org/10.1007/978-3-031-18192-4_38

Since there are a variety of social networks with different functions, purposes, and audiences, this prototyping environment has modelled microblogging platforms and is inspired in *Twitter*. Examples of other social media that fall within this context are Weibo, GETTR or GAB.

2 System Architecture

This section describes the functionalities and requirements of the platform. Figure 1 shows the diagram of use cases and the three main blue scenarios with some sub-scenarios for each of them. The Researcher performs experiments and the *SuD* (System Under Development) has the task of creating the environment that allows the Subject to access and participate in the study. Thus, the Subject is a secondary actor who only provides a service to the SuD [6].

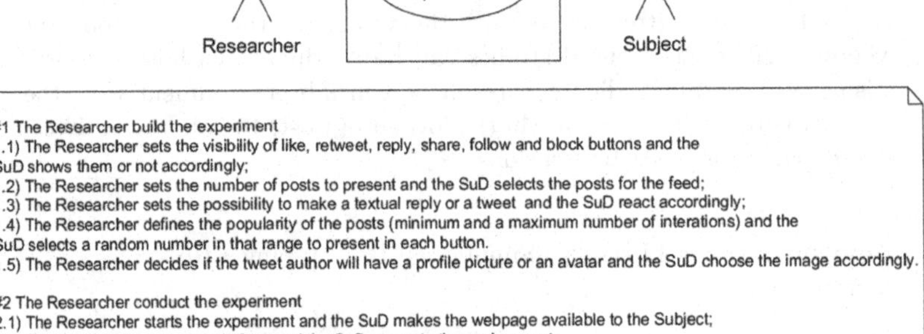

SuD
Conduct Experiments
Researcher
Subject
#1 The Researcher build the experiment
1.1) The Researcher sets the visibility of like, retweet, reply, share, follow and block buttons and the SuD shows them or not accordingly;
1.2) The Researcher sets the number of posts to present and the SuD selects the posts for the feed;
1.3) The Researcher sets the possibility to make a textual reply or a tweet and the SuD react accordingly;
1.4) The Researcher defines the popularity of the posts (minimum and a maximum number of interations) and the SuD selects a random number in that range to present in each button.
1.5) The Researcher decides if the tweet author will have a profile picture or an avatar and the SuD choose the image accordingly.
#2 The Researcher conduct the experiment
2.1) The Researcher starts the experiment and the SuD makes the webpage available to the Subject;
2.2) The Subject accesses the platform and the SuD generate the environment;
2.3) The Subject gives consent to participate and the SuD present them the page;
#3 The Researcher get data from the experiment
The Subject interact with the platform and the SuD record the data;

Fig. 1. System use case view

The object diagram in the Fig. 2 represents the second blue scenario and shows the Subject interaction with the experiment. When the SuD reacts to the instructions of the researcher (first blue scenario) creating the experiment and the Subject gives consent to participate, the environment is ready for the study. The application has a :Listener role that waits for interactions from the participant and send them to the :Database Handler, which is responsible for correctly record the data.

The class diagram in Fig. 3 shows the nature of the relationship between classes. The classes comprise of interaction, tweet, tweet frame, configuration, and feed. Interact with the platform can be done through one of the buttons whose visibility is set to True. But, different from the Twitter beyond liking, retweeting, and replying, the actions of blocking, following, and sharing are still

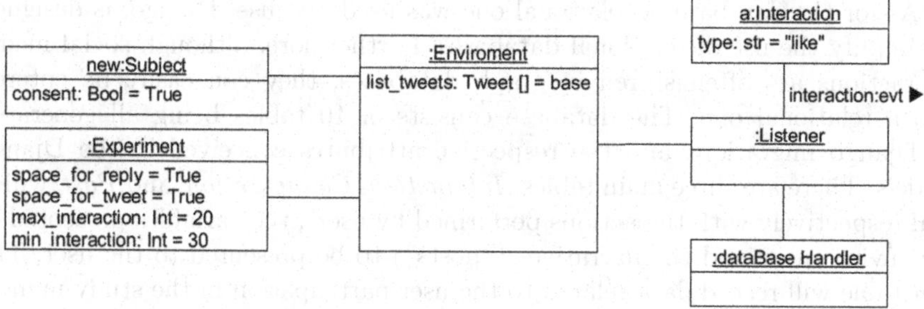

Fig. 2. Object diagram for the conduct the experiment scenario

considered interaction with a post. Moreover, these actions are incremental and are only used to measure engagement of the Subject participant with the post. A configuration is defined by the researcher and can be composted by the visibility of the interaction buttons, the engagement of each post, the length of the feed, and the characteristics of the post author.

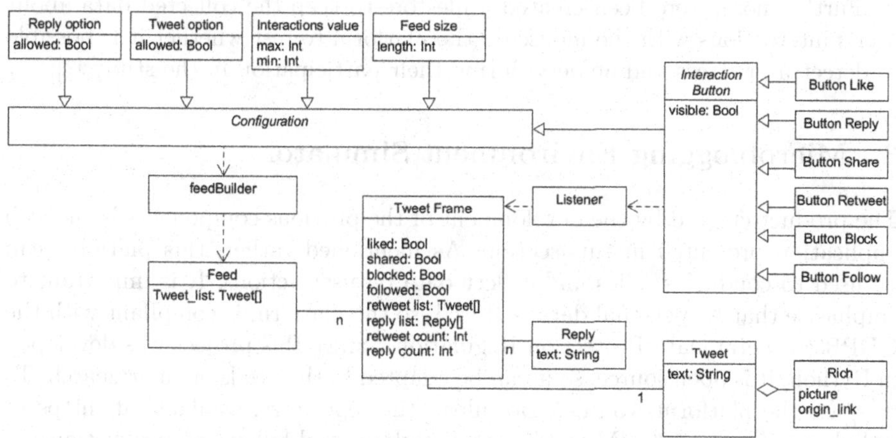

Fig. 3. Class diagram of the system

The platform has been developed using the framework Django. This choice is justified by the fact that it's inherent characteristics meet the previously defined requirements. It stands out for its high scalability, which allows adding more resources at any time, no matter at what stage of development. The frontend uses templates to provide a user interface that allows participation in this study. The backend is responsible for processing the requests sent by the frontend and providing a response.

As for the database, a relational one was used because, Django, is designed to simplify the use of relational databases. Furthermore, although social media interactions are often stored in graph databases, they can easily be entered into a relational one. The database consists of 10 tables being all generated by Django migrations and the respective attributes conceived in the Django models. There are three main tables, *Interaction*, *Configuration*, and *Post*, which deal respectively with the actions performed by users, the variables presented in the environment and the narratives ("posts") to be presented to the user. The user table will record data related to the user participation in the study namely time of participation and personality. This last field, it's kept with the intention to allow the research to look for patterns related to the user's personality and post content, this can be done, for example applying a personality test to the user. The *post_by_participant* table stores the content published by the user in the feed. Also, the *action_type* table stores the type of interaction performed by the user. A record is stored in the *action_reply* table if the *action_type.name* is a *reply* with the content written by the user. The *hashtag* and *image* tables, as the name suggests, contain the hashtags and images associated with a specific post. Figure 4 presents a better understanding of the data record by the system in a partial data model view.

Furthermore, were been created a filestore to keep the collected data about user's interactions with the mouse on the platform to test whether it is possible to detect user stress and anxiety during their participation in the study [7].

3 Microblogging Environment Simulator

The product created by the development of the previous components is the web application presented in this section. As mentioned earlier, this platform can be used to conduct studies and collect data on user actions. It is important to emphasise that no personal data is stored, so the platform is compliant with the GDPR (General Data Protection Regulation). Since this project was developed in Python, it is open source, so it can be adapted to the needs of any research. To test/use the platform, you can Download the repository, available at: https://github.com/maria85290/MicrobloggingSimulator and follow the instructions.

The participation page, in Fig. 5, presents a layout similar to Twitter, and show to the user a set of narratives in the form of posts with which it is possible to interact and allowing the researcher to validate the narratives that are being automatically created and record data.

It is important to note that although Twitter served as the inspiration for the developed interface, efforts were made so it would be similar but not exactly equal to Twitter. That ensures it is clear the post was not published on Twitter even if the posted content was widely distributed. In addition, some areas of microblogging platforms, such as the user profile or private message area, were not implemented, however, they are correctly labeled.

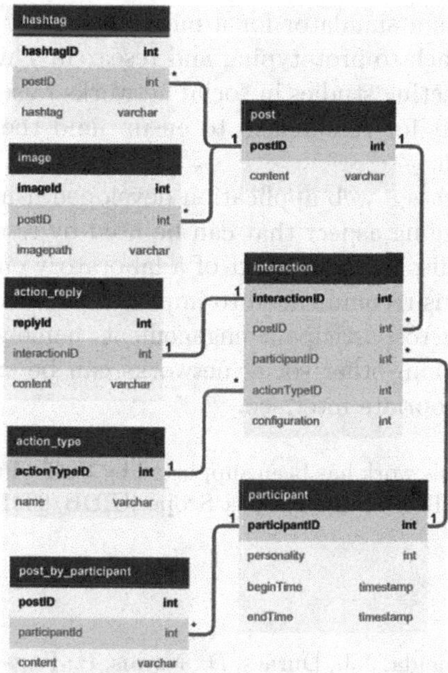

Fig. 4. Partial data model of the tables related to the prototype environment in First Normal Form

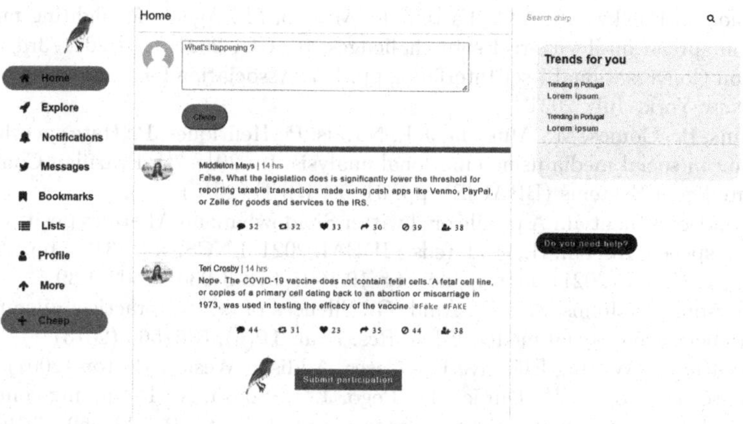

Fig. 5. Participation page

4 Conclusions and Future Work

Recently, the numerous studies that have been developed in social media, have given the perception of the ethical problems that can arise if the research doesn't have attention to that questions.

This paper presents a simulator for a microblogging environment that provides an ethical approach to prototyping and research. This tool arose from the recognition that conducting studies in social networks raises a number of ethical issues that are difficult for researchers to ensure and the goal is to overcome these issues in research.

The current version is a web application developed using the Django framework with a microblogging aspect that can be used by researchers interested in conducting online studies in the context of a laboratory environment.

For future work, it is recommended to implement some areas of the platform that could be relevant to participant engagement, namely the profile pages of post authors. In addition, other social networks can be explored and modeled by developing an appropriate interface.

Acknowledgment. This work has been supported by FCT - Fundação para a Ciência e Tecnologia within the R&D Units Project Scope: UIDB/00319/2020;

References

1. Marcondes, F.S., Almeida, J.J., Durães, D., Novais, P.: Fact-check spreading behavior in Twitter: a qualitative profile for false-claim news. In: Rocha, Á., Adeli, H., Reis, L.P., Costanzo, S., Orovic, I., Moreira, F. (eds.) WorldCIST 2020. AISC, vol. 1160, pp. 170–180. Springer, Cham (2020). https://doi.org/10.1007/978-3-030-45691-7_16
2. Piccolo, L., Blackwood, A.C., Farrell, T., Mensio, M.: Agents for fighting misinformation spread on Twitter: design challenges. In: CUI 2021: CUI 2021–3rd Conference on Conversational User Interfaces, pp. 1–7. Association for Computing Machinery, New York, July 2021
3. Martins, R., Gomes, M., Almeida, J.J., Novais, P., Henriques, P.: Hate speech classification in social media using emotional analysis. In: 2018 7th Brazilian Conference on Intelligent Systems (BRACIS), pp. 61–66. IEEE (2018)
4. Marcondes, F.S., et al.: A profile on Twitter Shadowban: an AI ethics position paper on free-speech. In: Yin, H., et al. (eds.) IDEAL 2021. LNCS, vol. 13113, pp. 397–405. Springer, Cham (2021). https://doi.org/10.1007/978-3-030-91608-4_39
5. Henderson, M., Johnson, N.F., Auld, G.: Silences of ethical practice: dilemmas for researchers using social media. Educ. Res. Eval. **19**(6), 546–560 (2013)
6. Cockburn, A.: Writing Effective Use Cases. Addison-Wesley, Boston (2001)
7. Carneiro, D., Novais, P., Durães, D., Pego, J.M., Sousa, N.: Predicting completion time in high-stakes exams. Future Gener. Comput. Syst. **92**, 549–559 (2019)

Toward an Agent-Based Model of Community of Practice: Demonstration

Amal Chaoui[1], Sébastien Delarre[2], Fabien Eloire[2], Maxime Morge[1(✉)], and Antoine Nongaillard[2]

[1] CNRS, Centrale Lille, UMR 9189 CRIStAL, University of Lille, 59000 Lille, France
amal.chaoui@centrale.centralelille.fr, maxime.morge@univ-lille.fr
[2] CNRS, UMR 8019 Clersé, University of Lille, 59000 Lille, France
{sebastien.delarre,fabien.eloire,antoine.nongaillard}@univ-lille.fr

Abstract. Communities of Practice services enable users that share same interests and exchange knowledge in an ongoing learning process. The Stack Overflow platform supports such communities where the majority of the content are produced by a small number of highly active users. We propose an agent-based model of a Community of Practice exhibiting a social dynamics which is compliant with this insight.

Keywords: Agent-based modeling · Social network analysis · Complex system

1 Introduction

A Community of Practice (CoP) is "a group of people who share a concern, set of problems, or passion for a given topic, and who deepen their knowledge and expertise in that area by interacting on an ongoing basis" [8]. The Internet has contributed to the creation of Distributed Community of Practice (DCoP) whose members are geographically distributed and use technological means to remotely interact with each other. For instance, Stack Overflow[1] is not only a simple Question and Answer (Q&A) website about programming, but also a collaborative work platform that structures DCoPs.

DCoPs are complex systems. The interleaving of microscopic elementary behaviors leads to complex mesoscopic dynamics (at the community level) and macroscopic ones (at the platform level). In particular, the identification of authorizative actors cannot be tackled by the classical algorithms `PageRank` and `HITS` for analyzing such networks whose topologies are heterogeneous and distinguish themselves from the web [2]. The individual-centered approach is more suitable since it allows to conceptualize and simulate such complex systems as self-organized systems of cooperative agents with limited perceptions and rationality, which are structured by the effect of interactions [4].

[1] https://stackoverflow.com.

© The Author(s), under exclusive license to Springer Nature Switzerland AG 2022
F. Dignum et al. (Eds.): PAAMS 2022, LNAI 13616, pp. 467–472, 2022.
https://doi.org/10.1007/978-3-031-18192-4_39

While multi-agents technologies supporting DCoPs are numerous and diverse [7], the agent-based models of a DCoP are much rarer. Zhang et al. adopt an individual-centered approach to generate the social network [12] and the `CommunityNetSimulator` [11] analyze it. Contrary to [1], links are not created solely on the basis of the preferential attachment principle whereby new nodes connect more easily to those having already a large number of connections, but the model considers links as the outcome of interactions (questions/answers) resulting from the individual behaviors, which are in turn guided by their expertise levels. However, the interaction model introduced by [12] does not reproduce a commonly observed insight: a small part of the members is responsible for a vast part of the community activity.

We propose here an agent-based model of a Community of Practice that exhibits a social dynamic where the activity is unfairly distributed among the members. The significance of our work consists in reproducing this phenomenon according to the principle of parsimony. By reducing the number of parameters and restricting the mechanisms to the simplest and most general ones, we propose an explainable model of this social phenomenon based on a clear understanding of the underlying local solidarity processes built upon a large real-world dataset. Our simulator `ABM4DCoP` (Agent-Based Modeling for Distributed Community of Practice) [6] is built upon NetLogo. Our experiments show that, our model, contrary to [11], reproduces the unfair distribution of posts observed on Stack Overflow.

2 Agent-Based Model

In order to simulate a DCoP, we model a constant population of N agents. Each simulation step t corresponds to a biweekly period. During such a period, each agent can publish a number of posts (questions or answers), bounded by a biweekly maximum number of questions (respectively answers), $maxQ$ (respectively $maxA$). The idiosyncrasy of an agent determines its actions. Concretely, the behavior of each agent a_i is specified by two individual parameters:

- $\overline{nQ(a_i)}$, i.e. the mean number of questions asked per period;
- $\overline{nA(a_i)}$, i.e. the mean number of answers replied per period.

The number of questions (respectively answers) posted at time t, denoted $nQ(a_i, t)$ (respectively $nA(a_i, t)$), is drawn from a normal distribution of mean $\overline{nQ(a_i)}$ (respectively $\overline{nA(a_i)}$).

In order to populate the simulation, we consider that the distribution of the biweekly number of posts of the agent is of power law type:

$$\overline{nA(a_i)} = maxA \times rank^{\overline{nA}}(a_i)^{k_A} \text{ with } k_A < 0 \tag{1}$$

where the degree of the law k_A is constant. As explained in [10], users motivated by gamification incentives mostly post answers. This is the reason why we generate $\overline{nQ(a_i)}$ as $\overline{nA(a_i)}$, and in such a way that the more answers an agent gives, the fewer questions it asks. The simulation of a period t is divided into two phases (cf. Figure 1). During the question phase, each agent a_i asks $nQ(a_i,t)$ questions. During the responding phase, each agent reacts to $nA(a_i,t)$ questions asked by the other agents[2].

Data: a_i, t: agent/timestep
H: history
Result: H': history
$nQ(a_i,t) = \mathcal{N}(\mu = \overline{nQ(a_i)}, \sigma^2 = 0.02)$;
if $randomU(0,1) \leq \{nQ(a_i,t)\}$ **then**
  $nQ(a_i,t) \mathrel{+}= 1$;
for $j \in [1; nQ(a_i,t)]$ **do**
  $H \cup= question(author = a_i)$;
return H

Data: a_i, t: agent/timestep
H: history
Result: H': History
$nA(a_i,t) = \mathcal{N}(\mu = \overline{nA(a_i)}, \sigma^2 = 0.02)$;
if $randomU(0,1) \leq \{nA(a_i,t)\}$ **then**
  $nA(a_i,t) \mathrel{+}= 1$;
$Q = \{question \in H \mid author(question) \neq a_i\}$
for $j \in [1; nA(a_i,t)]$ **do**
  $q = random(Q)$;
  $H \cup= answer(author = a_i, question = q)$;
return H

Fig. 1. Individual asker behavior (at left) and helper behavior (at right)

3 Simulator

Our `ABM4DCoP` simulator [6] is based on `NetLogo` [9] which is a multi-agents programming language and an integrated development environment for the design of agent-based simulations. Even if `Netlogo` is user-friendly, it allows the design of high-level models with complex behaviors.

As depicted in Fig. 2, the interface of our simulator consists of three types of components to:

- configure the simulation parameters;
- visualize agents, interactions and links;
- analyze the evolution of the metrics which are computed and displayed in real time during the simulation.

The agents are arranged in a circle in a clockwise direction in ascending order of $\overline{nA(a_i)}$. The graphical representation of the community in Fig. 3 allows us to observe the spatial distribution of the productivity of the agents (in purple) and of their links (in grey). An arc represents the help provided by the source

[2] The variances are small enough to maintain the shape of the power law type distribution for the mean number of posts published per period.

agent to the destination one. The outdegree of a node is the number of peers helped and the indegree is the number of advisors. During the simulation, the posts accumulate on the radial segment of its author: questions are in green and answers are in red.

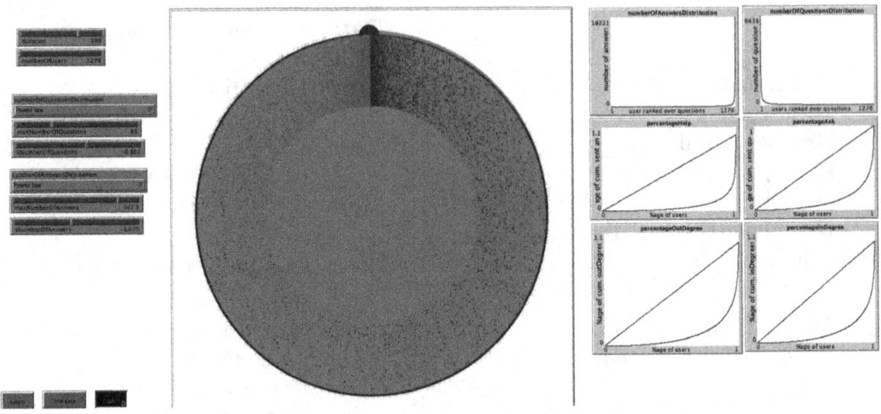

Fig. 2. Configuration (at left), visualization of agents arranged in a circle (at center) and reporting (at right) of the simulation (Color figure online)

4 Discussion

In order to explore our Stack Overflow study area, we have extracted, transformed and loaded the raw data produced from 2008 to 2021 (~50 GB) into a data warehouse [5]. Our multidimensional conceptual model allows the analysis of key performance indicators such as the number of posts, the debatability of questions or the response time. The multidimensional logic model is supplied by 6 face-to-face communities: `Hive/Pig`, `Hadoop/Spark` and `R/Pandas`. The latter two communities represent about 1,300,000 posts published by nearly 250,000 members. We have discarded 2,000 posts (0.15 %) involving 4,000 users who deleted their accounts and for whom we did not have attribute data.

Figure 4 represents the cumulative help of users from lowest to highest mean numbers of questions asked per period ($\overline{nA(a_i)}$). We have reimplemented `CommunityNetSimulator` [3] with `NetLogo`. According to this model, 20% of the most active members are responsible for up to 66% of the answers. However, we observe that 20% of the most active members of the `R` community are the authors of 94% of the answers on this topic. According to our model, the unfairness of the distribution is similar if the maximum biweekly number of answers is $maxA = 167.3$ (as in the `R` community) and $k_A = -1.2$. In online communities, very few users post the majority of content. This mesoscopic phenomenon is shared by all the DCoPs that we we have studied on Stack Overflow. The pseudo-random and sequential scheduler of our engine, which allows talkative

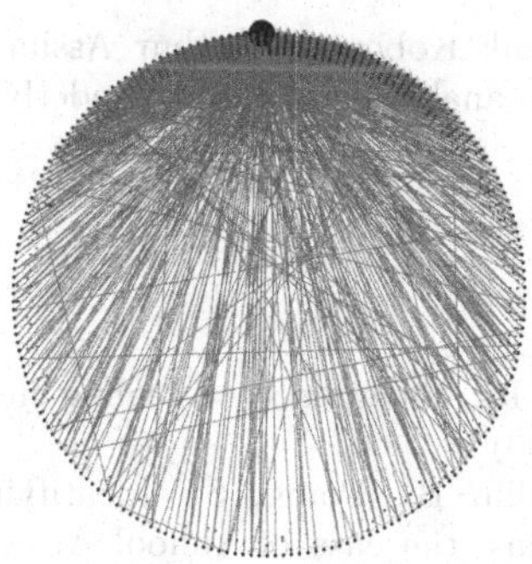

Fig. 3. Quasi-bipartite community network

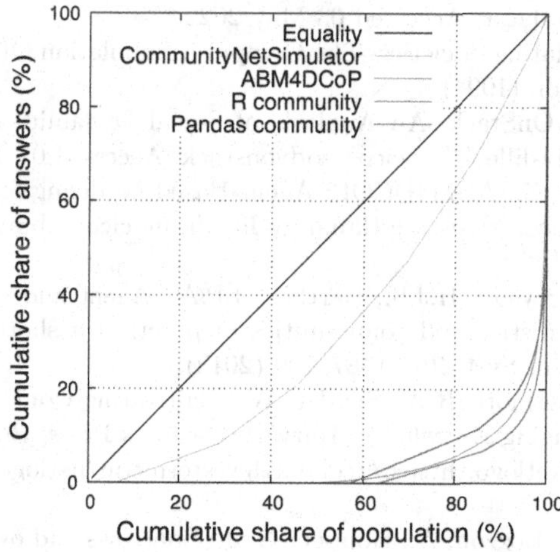

Fig. 4. Lorenz curves that show the number of answers observed (dotted line), simulated by CommunityNetSimulator (in red) and ABM4DCoP (in green) with the share of the population (Color figure online)

agents to speak more than once per period, purposely reproduces the inequality of the event-driven activity.

Our future work will focus on the statistical modeling of the distribution of idiosyncratic characteristics in order to calibrate the population of our simulations based on the large dataset we have collected. For now, the population of agents is homogeneous and their expertise is measured by their activities *ex post*. However, we wish to distinguish the most active individuals whose answers are not necessarily the most relevant ones (sparrows) from the domain experts who are not necessarily the most active (owls) [10]. In the longer term, we wish study and confront other mesoscopic phenomena such as: (a) the popularity - measured by the number of views of threads, (b) controversy - measured by the debatability of questions, and (c) the efficiency with the response time.

Acknowledgment. We thank Koboyoda Arthur Assima and Audrey Dewaele for their contribution on the data analysis and Jarod Vanderlynden for his work about the state-of-the-art.

References

1. Barabási, A.L., Albert, R.: Emergence of scaling in random networks. Science **286**(5439), 509–512 (1999)
2. Bouguessa, M., Dumoulin, B., Wang, S.: Identifying authoritative actors in question-answering forums: the case of Yahoo! Answers. In: Proceedings of the ACM Conference SIGKDD, pp. 866–874 (2008)
3. Chaoui, A., Vanderlynden, J., Morge, M.: CommunityNetSimulator: Agent-Based Model for Simulating a Community. https://gitlab.univ-lille.fr/mocicos/communitynetsimulator. Accessed 03 May 2022
4. Gilbert, N.: Simulating Societies: The Computer Simulation Of Social Phenomena. UCL Press, London (1994)
5. Morge, M.: SoDyOnStack: An Analysis of Social Dynamics on Stack Overflow. https://gitlab.univ-lille.fr/mocicos/sodyonstack. Accessed 01 June 2022
6. Morge, M., Amal, C.: ABM4DCOP: Agent-Based Modeling for Distributed Community Of Practice. https://gitlab.univ-lille.fr/mocicos/abm4dcop. Accessed 01 June 2022
7. Sato, G.Y., de Azevedo, H.J.S., Barthès, J.P.A.: Agent and multi-agent applications to support distributed communities of practice: a short review. Autonom. Agents Multi-Agent Syst. **25**(1), 87–129 (2012)
8. Wenger, E., McDermott, R.A., Snyder, W.: Cultivating Communities of Practice: A Guide to Managing Knowledge. Harvard Business Press, Boston (2002)
9. Wilensky, URI: Netlogo. https://ccl.northwestern.edu/netlogo. Accessed 01 June 2022
10. Yang, J., Tao, K., Bozzon, A., Houben, G.-J.: Sparrows and owls: characterisation of expert behaviour in stackoverflow. In: Dimitrova, V., Kuflik, T., Chin, D., Ricci, F., Dolog, P., Houben, G.-J. (eds.) UMAP 2014. LNCS, vol. 8538, pp. 266–277. Springer, Cham (2014). https://doi.org/10.1007/978-3-319-08786-3_23
11. Zhang, J., Ackerman, M.S., Adamic, L.: Community net simulator: using simulations to study online community networks. In: Steinfield, C., Pentland, B.T., Ackerman, M., Contractor, N. (eds) Communities and Technologies 2007, pp. 295–321. Springer, London (2007). https://doi.org/10.1007/978-1-84628-905-7_16
12. Zhang, J., Ackerman, M.S., Adamic, L.: Expertise networks in online communities: structure and algorithms. In: Proceedings of the International Conference on World Wide Web, pp. 221–230 (2007)

A Demonstration of BDI-Based Robotic Systems with ROS2

Devis Dal Moro(✉), Marco Robol, Marco Roveri, and Paolo Giorgini

University of Trento, Via Sommarive, 9, 38123 Povo, Italy
{devis.dalmoro,marco.robol,marco.roveri,paolo.giorgini}@unitn.it

Abstract. The paper demonstrates our BDI-based tool-kit built on top of ROS2. We present its main features by means of a realistic industrially-inspired scenario where a fleet of autonomous and heterogeneous robotic systems are asked to move and sort boxes to target destinations. The aim of the demo is to show the advantages of combining the expressiveness of the BDI architecture with an integrated planning system. We show how agents are able to find suitable solutions to achieve their goals in an evolving environment, and how agents communicate and cooperate to achieve common objectives.

Keywords: Real-time multi-agent systems · Planning & execution · ROS2

1 Introduction

Industry requires more and more robotics systems with higher degrees of autonomy and capabilities to cope with problems that cannot be exhaustively predicted at design time. This is particularly relevant for I4.0 where state-of-the-art robotic infrastructures, such as Robotic Operating System - ROS - [11], provide only means to reliably sense the environment and promptly react to stimuli without any possibility for robots to autonomously deliberate the best course of action [1–4,6,7,9]. Different development paradigms, such as the Belief-Desire-Intention architecture (BDI) [10], have been proposed in the literature to overcome the limitations of hard-coded algorithms with limited or no adaptive capabilities.

In our recent work [5], we proposed a first attempt to combine reasoning and planning capabilities with lower level reactive functionalities of a robotic system. The framework has been implemented on top of ROS2 exploiting the (temporal) planning capabilities of PlanSys2 [8]. In this paper, we demonstrate our work in a realistic industrially-inspired scenario. We show the potentialities offered by the tool-kit and its underlying architecture, its expressiveness and its adaptability to real-world problems. The demo focuses on capabilities related to planning, re-planning, and reactiveness, as well as interaction capabilities that allow robots to collaborate and reach common objectives.

© The Author(s), under exclusive license to Springer Nature Switzerland AG 2022
F. Dignum et al. (Eds.): PAAMS 2022, LNAI 13616, pp. 473–479, 2022.
https://doi.org/10.1007/978-3-031-18192-4_40

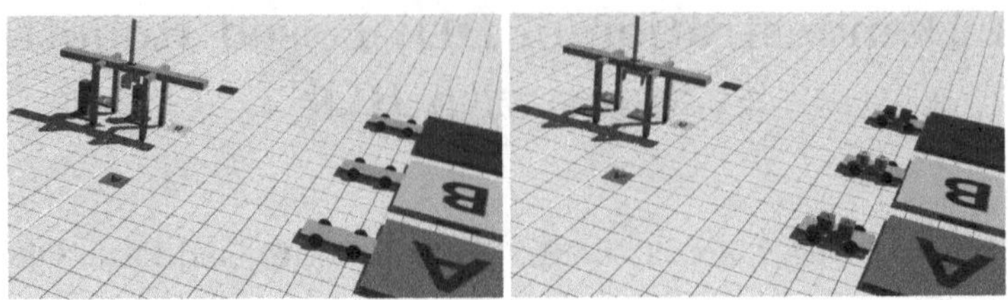

Fig. 1. The initial state with stacked boxes that need to be moved and sorted (left). The final state, where all boxes are delivered to the correct deposit (right)

The demonstration scenario is a logistic problem consisting in sorting and moving boxes to given destinations depending on the specific box type. Robotic agents with different capabilities and partial view of the environment are asked to collaborate one another to solve an overall warehouse problem. The underlying engine allows each agent to reason about the necessary steps for achieving its goals and finding new solutions in the case of a failure or unexpected events (e.g., a collaborator agent is not where it is supposed to be). Additionally, we show how agents can ask other agents to execute tasks (e.g., moving to a target location) for a distributed and adaptive collaboration, without any central control.

2 Main Purpose

In this paper, we demonstrate the BDI reasoning and planning system presented in [5]. The demonstration focuses on a very common industrial logistic problem with different collaborative robotic agents having the goal of moving goods. We leverage on a planning-based solution to improve the adaptability of agents so they can cope with unforeseen situations and contingencies. We will demonstrate our framework in two paradigmatic scenarios: the case where everything proceeds as expected, and the case with an unexpected event (anomaly) that forces agents to adapt their behaviour.

3 Demonstration

Figure 1 shows a typical logistic problem, where colored and labelled boxes are initially stacked on different piles. A robotic agent (hereafter `gripper`) can pick and put down boxes, holding a box at a time. It can move boxes between different stacks or load/unload them on "carriers" robots. Carriers can transport boxes back and forth between their assigned loading and deposit areas. Each box is labelled with the target destination: `A`, `B`, and `C`. The `gripper` asks carriers to move in the loading area when they are not there, and carriers when `fully_loaded` move to the deposit area. The final goal for all agents is to transport all boxes to the deposit accordingly to their labels.

Figures 2 and 3 show two timelines, each representing a different run. Each run is initiated by: i) specifying the static information regarding the environment,

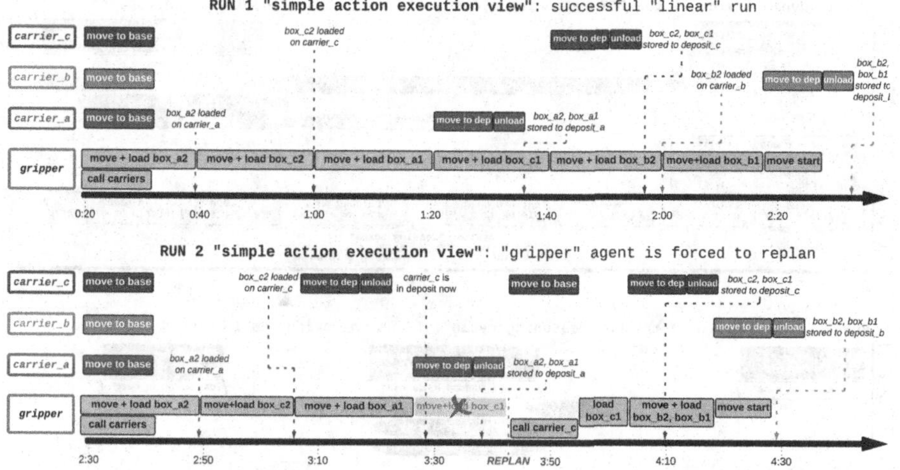

Fig. 2. Timeline of the two runs highlighting the key events and actions

and the initial configuration to then create the initial knowledge base; and, ii) assigning to the `gripper` agent the goal of loading boxes on "right" carriers. Figure 2 provides a schematic view of the sequence of actions performed over time by the different agents. Figure 3 details what happens in the different phases of the BDI reasoning framework within each agent. In Fig. 3, for the sake of readability, we've abbreviated the names of robotic agents, actions, artifacts and places as follows: `gripper` ↦ `grip`, `carrier_a` ↦ `c_a`, `deposit` ↦ `dep`, `base_a` ↦ `b_a`, `box_a1` ↦ `bx_a1`, and so on for the others.

In the first run (upper part of Fig. 2), starting from the configuration depicted in Fig. 1 (left), the `gripper` agent computes and executes a plan consisting in calling carriers to come to their respective base, picking up boxes and loading them on top of the "right" carrier. When a carrier is `fully_loaded`, it goes to unload boxes to the assigned deposit as depicted in Fig. 1 (right).

In the second run (lower part of Fig. 2), we show what happens in response to an unexpected event. Starting from the same initial state of the first run, the carrier of boxes `C` moves back to the destination area just after the first box has been loaded since it incorrectly believes being `fully_loaded` and that it can go. When the `gripper` attempts to load the second box, it detects that the `carrier` is not there anymore. The execution of its plan fails and the `gripper` has to re-plan from the current state. The new plan will initially require to call back the carrier `C` and then continue as before.

Figure 3 is a more fine grained version of Fig. 2 and it aims at providing a dynamic view of what happens in the different phases of the BDI reasoning framework. For instance, it complements the scheduled actions (filled rectangles) performed by each agent with the most relevant information of i) which belief and at what time instant it becomes true (filled ovals); ii) which desire and at what time instant it become active for the respective agent (parallelograms).

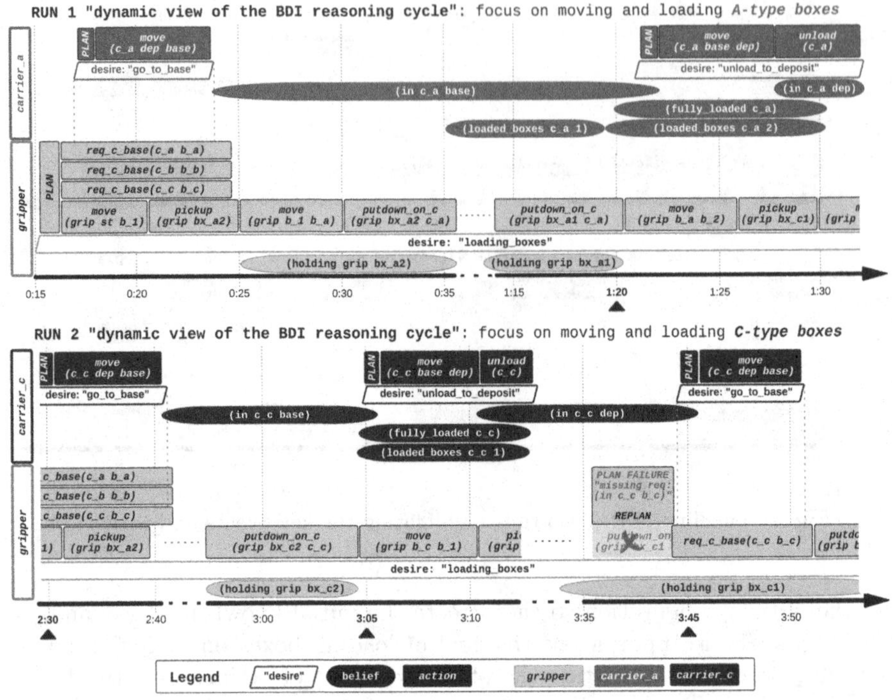

Fig. 3. Timeline of the two runs showing a dynamic view of what happens in the different phases of the BDI reasoning framework with focus on the boxes of type A (up), the re-planning triggered by the "misbehaviour" of the C-type carrier (down)

In autonomous multi-agent systems (MASs), agents act either autonomously or by cooperating/coordinating with other agents. Evidence of this is provided in Fig. 3. The phase around instant 2:30 describes a collaborative behaviour in which carrier_c and gripper communicate with one another. More in details, gripper makes a request to carrier_c, by posting him the goal go_to_base, and expecting him to act accordingly upon acceptance of the request. Then, carrier_c decides whether to accept or reject such request, based on static policies defined at agent's design time. In contrast to this, an autonomous behaviour occurs at instant 3:05, when carrier_c decides to leave the loading position, without coordinating with the gripper, who is still expecting to find carrier_c in that position. This behaviour of the carrier_c is incompatible with gripper current plan, whose action preconditions get invalidated when it is about to load the second type C box, therefore the plan execution is aborted. The gripper, still trying to achieve its goal, needs to adapt to this new scenario by re-planning and finding another suitable way to pursue it. Again, the newly recomputed plan assumes the collaboration of carrier_c, who is asked to move back to its loading base. The request consists in pushing the desire go_to_base (at instant 3:45).

The agents in our framework exhibit autonomous behaviours triggered by their reactive capabilities. This corresponds to equip the agents with "option generation" functions in compliance with statically-defined rules. For instance, when carriers are `fully_loaded` (e.g., see Fig. 3 `carrier_a` in `RUN 1` at about instant 1:20 and, `carrier_c` in `RUN 2` at instant 3:05), they activate the goal of unloading boxes and then compute and start to execute an adequate plan to fulfill it. Note how this happens also in the `RUN 2` where, in response to an incorrectly defined rule, `carrier_c` erroneously believes to be `fully_loaded` right after the first loaded box (see instant 3:45 in Fig. 3).

Figure 3 also provides a view of how the key[1] elements of the knowledge base evolve as result of executing actions, sensing the environment, do reasoning. The successful execution of an action updates the agent knowledge base according to the effect of the action itself. For instance, a successful `pickup` results in updating the knowledge base of the `gripper` agent in a way it knows it is holding the box; a successful `putdown` update the knowledge base to store that it is not holding the box anymore. This update builds on the PlanSys2 Executor [8]. The knowledge base is also updated at the beginning of each iteration of the BDI reasoning cycle by reading the sensors to associate a value to each symbol of the model used for reasoning (e.g., `(in c_c base)`, `(loaded_boxes c_c 1)`). Each sensor publishes its value into a ROS2 topic. The BDI reasoning cycle to acquire the sensor value, subscribes to the needed ROS2 topics, reads the values, processes them and uses them to update the knowledge base. The reading of all the sensors also triggers the "belief revision functions" (a set of static inference rules defined at design time to infer new knowledge). For instance, for the considered scenario a rule states that if carrier agent `c_a` is loaded with at least 2 boxes, it considers itself `fully_loaded`, i.e., the agent updates its knowledge base by adding the belief `fully_loaded` (e.g., if `(loaded_boxes c_a 2)` holds in the knowledge base, then add `(fully_loaded c_a)`).

The demo has been implemented using the Webots (https://cyberbotics.com) high-fidelity robotic simulation environment. We exploited its APIs and development toolkit for implementing the actions of the different robotic agents, and for retrieving relevant information at run time from the environment. Webots is one of the state-of-the-art 3D robot simulator to demonstrate the functionalities of a ROS2 application with a high level of fidelity, while providing an almost "out of the box" integration with the robotics middle-ware. Notice that all controls developed with Webots can be deployed with no changes directly to real robots, namely that all results of the simulations correspond to those we can obtain in real-world scenario.

All development and deployment details with instructions to reproduce the demo are available at https://github.com/devis12/ROS2-BDI, whereas its recording can be watched here https://youtu.be/zB2HvCR5H9E.

[1] For the scenario of this demonstration.

4 Conclusions

In this paper, we demonstrated the BDI reasoning and planning system presented in [5]. We focused on a very common industrial logistic problem with different collaborative robotic agents having the goal of moving goods. We showed the benefit of leveraging on a planning-based solution to improve the adaptability of agents to cope with unforeseen situations and contingencies. The demonstration considers two paradigmatic scenarios: the case where everything proceeds as expected, and the case with an unexpected event (anomaly) that force agents to adapt their behaviour. We also showed a deployment of the framework within the Webots high-fidelity robotic simulation environment. The framework allows for an off-the-shelf deploy of the same controls to real robots.

We envisage several possible directions for future work. Firstly, we will validate the framework in a real environment. Secondly, we will enhance the current BDI reasoning cycle to comply with scenarios where a greater degree of real-time compliance is required [12] or where optimizing a certain metric over time is taken into consideration, instead of blindly fulfill the next highest priority desire. Finally, we will enable a more tight integration between planning and execution, thus to avoid computing an entire plan and deciding only the next action.

References

1. Alzetta, F., Giorgini, P.: Towards a real-time BDI model for ROS 2. In: WOA. CEUR Workshop Proceedings, vol. 2404, pp. 1–7. CEUR-WS.org (2019)
2. van Breemen, A., Crucq, K., Krose, B., Nuttin, M., Porta, J., Demeester, E.: A user-interface robot for ambient intelligent environments. In: Proceedings of the 1st International Workshop on Advances in Service Robotics (ASER) (2003)
3. Bustos, P., Manso, L.J., Bandera, A., Rubio, J.P.B., García-Varea, I., Martínez-Gómez, J.: The CORTEX cognitive robotics architecture: use cases. Cogn. Syst. Res. **55**, 107–123 (2019)
4. CogniTAO-Team: CogniTAO (BDI). https://wiki.ros.org/decision_making/Tutorials/CogniTAO
5. Dal Moro, D.: A planning based multi-agent BDI architecture for ROS2. Master's thesis, DISI - University of Trento (2021). https://www.biblioteca.unitn.it/
6. Duffy, B.R., Collier, R., O'Hare, G.M., Rooney, C., O'Donoghue, R.: Social robotics: reality and virtuality in agent-based robotics. In: BISFAI-1999 (1999)
7. Gottifredi, S., Tucat, M., Corbata, D., García, A.J., Simari, G.R.: A BDI architecture for high level robot deliberation. Inteligencia Artif. **14**(46), 74–83 (2010)
8. Martín, F., Clavero, J.G., Matellán, V., Rodríguez, F.J.: PlanSys2: a planning system framework for ROS2. In: IROS, pp. 9742–9749. IEEE (2021)
9. Polydoros, A.S., Großmann, B., Rovida, F., Nalpantidis, L., Krüger, V.: Accurate and versatile automation of industrial kitting operations with SkiROS. In: Alboul, L., Damian, D., Aitken, J.M.M. (eds.) TAROS 2016. LNCS (LNAI), vol. 9716, pp. 255–268. Springer, Cham (2016). https://doi.org/10.1007/978-3-319-40379-3_26
10. Rao, A.S., Georgeff, M.P.: Modeling rational agents within a BDI-architecture. In: KR, pp. 473–484. Morgan Kaufmann (1991)

11. ROS2 - Robot Operating System version 2 (2022). https://docs.ros.org
12. Traldi, A., Bruschetti, F., Robol, M., Roveri, M., Giorgini, P.: Real-time BDI agents: a model and its implementation. In: Press, A. (ed.) IJCAI 2022 (2022, to appear)

Demonstrator of Decentralized Autonomous Organizations for Tax Credit's Tracking

Giovanni De Gasperis, Sante Dino Facchini(✉), and Alessio Susco

DISIM, Università degli Studi dell'Aquila, Via Vetoio, 67100 L'Aquila, Italy
giovanni.degasperis@univaq.it, santedino.facchini@graduate.univaq.it, alessio.susco@student.univaq.it

Abstract. Tax credit stimulus and fiscal bonuses had a very important impact on Italian economy in the last decade. Along with a huge expansion in constructions a relevant increase in scams and frauds has come too. The demonstrator implements a possible system to track and control the whole Superbonus 110 tax credit process from its generation to its redeem through a Decentralized Autonomous Organization architecture enriched with a Multi Agent Systems to implement controllers.

Keywords: Decentralized autonomous organizations · Multi agent systems · Tax credit tracking · Superbonus 110

1 Introduction: Tax Credit Stimulus in Italian Law

A Brief History. Italian energy policies and laws have a deep root into European Union guidelines, these mainly aim to improve the performance and to reduce the wastefulness of households energy production systems. During the last years the debate around energy efficiency rose in importance and is now central to determine the Next Generation EU funding policies, As a EU Member, Italy has taken steps to encourage energy efficiency increase of residential buildings. A program of tax deductions and fiscal bonuses, originally introduced in 1997 were relaunched since 2011 and renewed over the years till 2019. Finally during 2020 the actual system of 110% Superbonus tax credit has been introduced (Art. 119 DL Rilancio 34/2020)[1]. For the first time the lawmaker set up a system where energy efficiency and structural works are at no cost for residential properties.

The Actual Legislation. Superbonus 110, unlike other tax allowances for energy efficiency measures and reduction of seismic risks of buildings, provides for a higher-than-investment rate of deduction as well as a different way of allowances claim. In fact for each 100 euros spent on renovation works, the

[1] https://www.gazzettaufficiale.it/eli/id/2020/05/19/20G00052/sg.

© The Author(s), under exclusive license to Springer Nature Switzerland AG 2022
F. Dignum et al. (Eds.): PAAMS 2022, LNAI 13616, pp. 480–486, 2022.
https://doi.org/10.1007/978-3-031-18192-4_41

buyer will mature a 110 euros tax deduction to be used over the next 5 years and divided into 5 equal annual instalments. Since the annual deduction is discounted from the taxpayer's gross tax (IRPEF), it is therefore recoverable within the limit of such amount and cannot be carried forward or claimed back. Any deduction in excess of the gross tax would be lost. The legislator has thus provided two alternative solutions to the direct deduction: a discount on the invoice received for the works or assignment/selling of the matured credit to a third party. The option considered and modeled in this paper is the Invoice Discount as it is the most diffused solution and, differently from direct selling or direct deduction, requires credits to be tracked and managed as the benefits may be transferred through many subjects during the generation and redeem process. Another assumption we make in this paper is that the Costumers are using a General Contractor to manage the whole process of renovation on the construction yard and connected paperworks. This is both in order to simplify the level of the model (which in turn can be easily extended to a multi supplier situation) and to describe the most diffused scenario that is represented in Fig. 1.

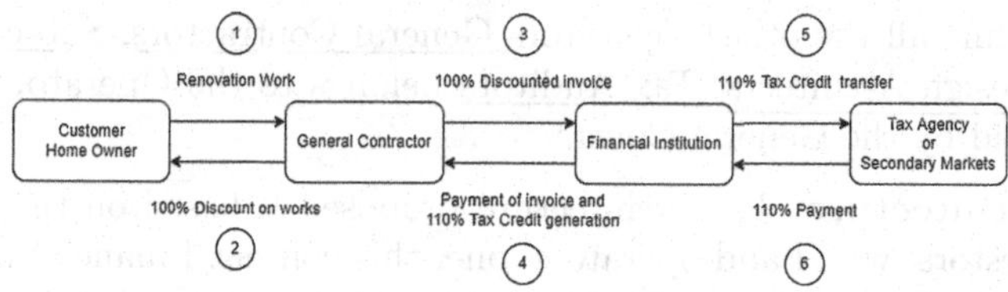

Fig. 1. Invoice Discount Tax Credit generation. The General Contractor will be the only subject dealing with the Costumer, coordinating and paying all the Subcontractors, Professionals and Suppliers involved in the works

Credit Tracking. In such an environment is of paramount importance being able to track the history of credits as well as the identity of all players involved in the process. Identity scams and credit assignment to fraudster recipients are in fact the main risks involved in Superbonus 110 process. Another risk, not connected necessary to willing to fraud, is represented by incorrect credit assignment where for example a client asks for a bigger amount than owed or more properties than allowed. In all of these situation back tracking of each euro of tax credit assigned is of key importance.

Distributed Autonomous Organizations. The idea of Distributed Autonomous Organizations (DAOs) has been outlined for the first time during the late 90s and was connected to the application of Multi-agent Systems to intelligent home sensors [1]. With the introduction of the Digital Autonomous Corporations concept (DACs) after 2008, a first transposition of a real company on the blockchain was defined; taking advantage from the introduction of Ethereum instruments like tokenization of shares, fully automated and incorruptible smart contracts along with transparent transactions register were finally applicable to the real governance process of a company [2]. The actual DAOs paradigm is an evolution of the DACs one, on the technical perspective it refers to a system able to model an organization through the deployment of a set of interacting smart contracts upon a blockchain network. It also inherit the properties of the underlying layers such as lack of centralized control, security through cryptographic keys and self-execution of smart contracts. All these properties make DAOs a reliable paradigm to operate a virtual organization modeling all functionalities and procedures of a real one.

2 Main Purpose: DAOs for Tax Credit's Tracking

Roles and Actors. The first step is to model the environment and the entities involved in the process, we identified to start two main areas: the Investors Group which includes all actors getting financial burdens and benefits in the process of Superbonus 110, and the operators group that in turns aggregate all actors with on-the-job interests in the Superbonus. Some actors may take both groups properties like Financial Institutions (Banks that buy/sell credits and lend money) or Costumers (House Owners that sell/transfer tax credits from works); Investors belongs to the Investors Group as invest money to buy credits and benefits from its selling, while all the others operators General Contractors, Sub-contractors, Suppliers, Design Architects, Tax Auditors belongs to the Operators Group as hired and paid by the General Contractor.

System Architecture. The architecture proposed is based on the separation between investors' world and operators' one, this consent Financial Institutions to raise fund from clients or investors and tokenize such assets. The process is designed assuming a simplified model where banks receive transfers of fiat on their accounts and mint the correspondent value of tokens on the Investors DAO. Another key feature is to guarantee that money anticipation performed by financial institutions and the correspondent underlying credit generation is backed by a fiat asset and is thus repayable when the credits' chain is closed. In brief this first DAO is meant to represent a simplified investing fund where participants get tokens proportionally to their investment, keep them blocked until the end of the fund duration and get a reward proportional to their initial quota at the end. Here we have Non Fungible Tokens (NFT) that are minted upon fiat deposit or credit selling by the Financial Institution and freezed or unfreezed when a guarantee from Operators DAO is requested or released (Fig. 2).

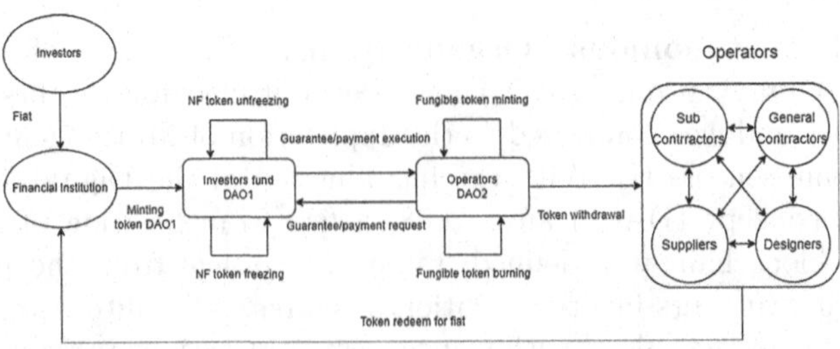

Fig. 2. DAOs interaction diagram. The architecture can be seen as a Distributed Trust and Reputation Management Systems (DTRMS) implemented through two DAOs

The second DAO is a marketplace for Financial Institution to distribute fungible tokens to General Contractors, these are minted and burned in order to satisfy credit request from Operators and spent for buying good and services. Each minting on Operators DAO correspond to a token freezing of the same amount on first DAO in order to guarantee the coverage. The tokens are redeemable by the Financial Institution that is also warrantor of the whole system. Once second DAO tokens are redeemed, first DAO NFTs are unfreezed. Each fungible token minted here is coupled via a unique code to the tax credit generated by that spending of money [5].

Aragon Platform. The framework chosen to develop our demonstrator is Aragon[2]. This is a second level platform based on the Ethereum network that is natively designed to model government systems of public and private entities, it is easy to use and allows to deploy test nets for application at very cheap costs using Ethereum's test nets such as Rinkeby[3]. Another feature of the Aragon framework is that completely manages the layers necessary for communication between the dApp and the Ethereum Virtual Machine (EVM); in this way it is possible to concentrate on the development of business logic and the interaction with external smart contracts via the Agent module of the framework.

Smart Contracts. The model described is implemented through several smart contracts written with Solidity[4] an object-oriented language specifically meant for contract contracts implementation. The choice of such stiff language is because we want the execution to be strictly what is supposed to be without possibility of modifications. A representation of Smart contract's states along with global and local constrain, data structures and actors involved is instead reported in Fig. 3

Integration of MAS. We have integrated a module composed of 4 Agents in order to control main aspects of the Investors an Operators DAOs and suggest the future behaviour of the Financial Institutes in terms of token needs of the system. Com-agents manage the data exchange with the DAOs, the Prediction-agent forecasts token needs on Operators DAO while Control-agent checks the correct behaviour of operators in claiming credits and points out potential fraud or incorrect schemes. We used the MESSAGE/UML paradigm to model the agent interaction and behaviour [3] in Fig. 4.

3 Demonstrator

The actual Superbonus 110 procedure has two weak point: the first is the difficulty to track the credits and the second is the disbursement of anticipated cash both from Financial Institutions and General Contractors. In this way we'll focus on two main features of the software in order to simulate the substitutions of

[2] https://aragon.org/.
[3] https://www.rinkeby.io/.
[4] https://soliditylang.org/.

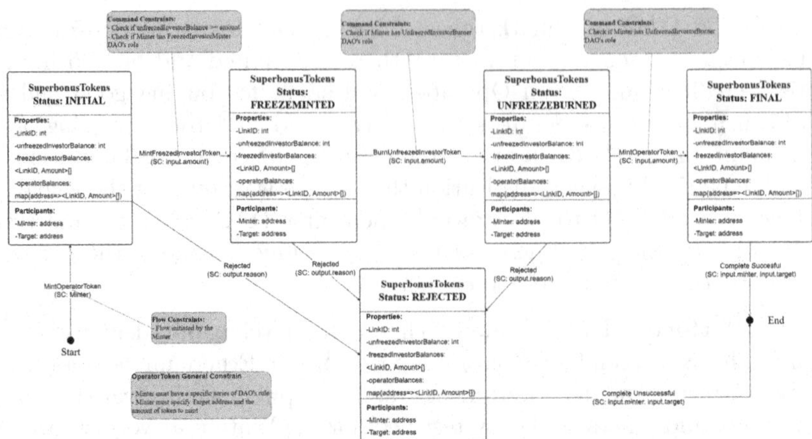

Fig. 3. Smart contract view

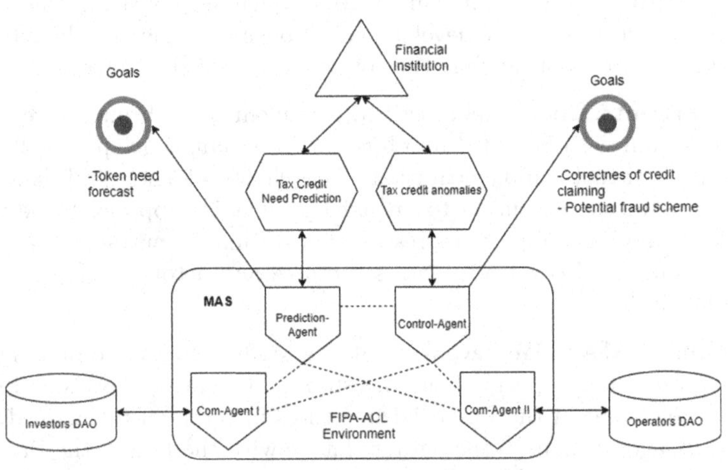

Fig. 4. Multi Agent System architecture. The demonstrator we have implemented is meant to illustrate the benefits of introducing the DAOs and MAS to Superbonus 110 environment

cash with Operators tokens and the tracking of the matured credits through a spreading tree. It will be possible to track the tokens coupled to tax credit and represent their path as a tree where the root is the first minting action. Furthermore the MAS modules will point out potential fraud situations and forecast the token request path in a certain time lapse. The user interface outline is represented in Fig. 5.

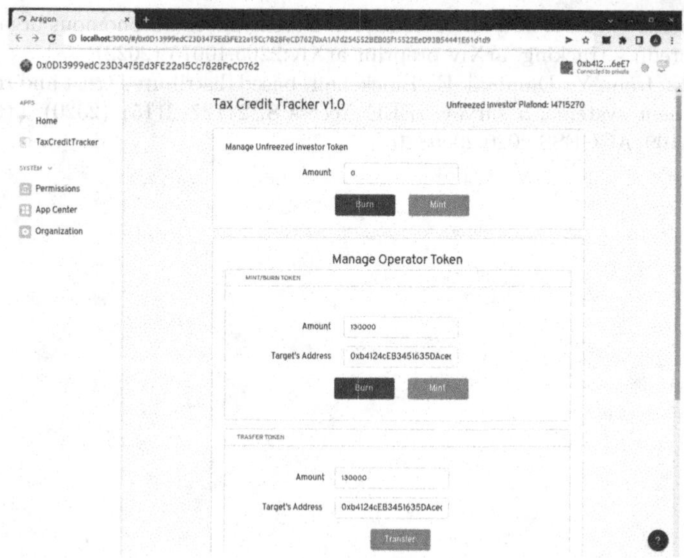

Fig. 5. Demonstrator user interface

4 Conclusions

The model used in our demonstrator could be easily exported to other areas both in the institutional and private sectors. In particular public administrations may benefit of a reliable governance and voting system to provide services that requires tracking of items and documents (e.g. Board resolutions, Certifications, etc.) [4]. More in general every process where a tracking of some asset or document is required could benefit from the architecture of Blockchain in the environment of Distributed Trust and Reputation Management Systems (DTRMS) [6]. Another possible future development may consider the integration of smart contracts and agents with IoT solutions such as sensors to monitor physical quantities.

References

1. Dilger, W.: Decentralized autonomous organization of the intelligent home according to the principle of the immune system. In: 1997 IEEE International Conference on Systems, Man, and Cybernetics. Computational Cybernetics and Simulation, pp. 351–356. IEEE (1997)
2. Buterin, V., et al.: A next-generation smart contract and decentralized application platform. White paper **3**(37), 2.1 (2014)
3. Ozkaya, M.: Analysing UML-based software modelling languages. J. Aeronaut. Space Technol. **11**(2), 119–134 (2018)
4. Chohan, U.W.: The decentralized autonomous organization and governance issues, 4 December 2017. Available at SSRN. https://ssrn.com/abstract=3082055. https://dx.doi.org/10.2139/ssrn.3082055

5. De Gasperis, G., Facchini, S.D., Susco, A.: Decentralized autonomous organizations for tax credit's tracking. arXiv preprint arXiv:2205.10075 (2022)
6. Bellini, E., Iraqi, Y., Damiani, E.: Blockchain-based distributed trust and reputation management systems: a survey. IEEE Access **8**, 21127–21151 (2020). https://doi.org/10.1109/ACCESS.2020.2969820

Agents Assembly: Domain Specific Language for Agent Simulations

Przemysław Hołda[1(✉)], Kajetan Rachwał[1], Jan Sawicki[1], Maria Ganzha[1], and Marcin Paprzycki[2]

[1] Faculty of Mathematics and Information Science, Warsaw University of Technology, Warsaw, Poland
{przemyslaw.holda.stud,kajetan.rachwal.stud}@pw.edu.pl
[2] Systems Research Institute Polish Academy of Sciences, Warsaw, Poland

Abstract. Researchers studying group behavior, social dynamics, or epidemiology lack an easy-to-use tool to run large-scale simulations. This contribution introduces a domain specific language (Agents Assembly; AASM) and a toolset for creating and running scalable simulations, using containerized environment. The proposed language supports describing abstract concepts, such as agent, message, and behavior. Its structure, resembling assembly mnemonics, is simple to understand. The language is supported by a code generation module with a graphical user interface, which allows defining simulations using instruction blocks. The AASM code is translated to Python and runs in a distributed containerized ecosystem, utilizing a slightly modified SPADE agent framework. The developed toolset includes also data storage and live visualization.

Keywords: Domain specific language · Multi-agent simulations · Scalable computing

1 Introduction

Multi-agent simulations have been used in multiple fields, ranging from supporting electoral campaigns [3] to analyzing the spread of viruses in a population [1]. However, creating such simulations requires both domain knowledge and programming skills (to code the simulation). It may hinder the potential use of simulations, as two different skills are required. Moreover, the development of large-scale agent-based simulations requires knowledge of the agent-based paradigm and tools, which are not common skills. For all practical purposes, only the Repast (for High Performance Computing[1]) is a mature tool capable of running large-scale agent simulations. However, earlier experiences with Repast [2] showed that its use is not simple. To address this problem, a domain specific language (DSL) called Agents Assembly (AASM) was developed. It allows users without advanced programming skills to define the structure and

[1] https://repast.github.io.

© The Author(s), under exclusive license to Springer Nature Switzerland AG 2022
F. Dignum et al. (Eds.): PAAMS 2022, LNAI 13616, pp. 487–492, 2022.
https://doi.org/10.1007/978-3-031-18192-4_42

behavior of a multi-agent system. The proposed language is complemented with a Runtime Environment, which facilitates running and analyzing simulations formulated using AASM. Moreover, since AAMS is executed on top of containerized instances of the Smart Python Agent Development Environment (SPADE)[2] agent platform, large-scale simulations can be realized.

2 Main Purpose

The starting point of this contribution was the authors' own experience in using a general-purpose programming language (Python) and an agent framework (SPADE) to create agent-based simulations. Upon reflection, it became apparent that the process may be difficult for researchers without an extensive computer science background. Hence, the idea of developing an environment that delivers "the same capabilities" as SPADE but without the need for in-depth knowledge of programming came to be. As a result, more researchers from all fields should be able to use multi-agent-based simulations. In this context, the following objectives were identified by analyzing the process of developing large-scale agent-based simulations.

1. To allow users to define simulations using simple logic, arithmetic, and concepts of the simulation domain (e.g., agent, behavior).
2. To create a user-friendly environment in which a simulation may be prepared, run, and analyzed.
3. To ensure that large-scale simulations (consisting of thousands of agents) can be executed in an architecture that is simple to set up.

To satisfy these objectives, the proposed ecosystem consists of: (1) domain specific language (AASM), (2) runtime that translates it to Python and runs on a (slightly modified) SPADE platform, (3) possibility to run multiple SPADE instances, in separate dockerized containers, on networked computers, (4) user-friendly front-end, (5) data storage (for result persistence and further analysis), and (6) live visualization.

3 Demonstration

The authors will now describe the Agents Assembly DSL and its ecosystem. The main features of the proposed approach will be presented using two simulations during the live demonstration.

3.1 Agents Assembly – Key Concepts

Agents Assembly has been developed based on analysis of literature and own experiences gathered when developing agent-based simulations. The language

[2] https://github.com/javipalanca/spade.

structure is divided into agents, messages, and a network, which creates a skeleton, upon which a multi-agent simulation will be realized.

The **agent** instruction defines agents. The AASM allows declaring the structure and the initial state of agents using a carefully selected set of parameters. Parameters may be numbers, enums, lists of connections, numbers, or messages. Enums and numbers may be initialized using set values or random values drawn from the specified distribution. Inside the agent scope behaviors are defined with the **behav** keyword. An agent's behavior is a sequence of actions performed by the agent when certain conditions are met. The language supports running behaviors during agent setup, after a specified delay, periodically, and upon receiving a message from another agent.

The definition of an action starts with the **action** keyword. Two types of actions are supported: modifying the internal state and sending messages to other agents. The body of an action includes a list of instructions to be executed. AASM includes more than thirty instructions, such as mathematical operations, control statements, and array procedures. Their style was heavily inspired by the design of the assembly mnemonics.

Listing 1.1. Autonomous car AASM listing

```
agent autonomous_car
  prm current_speed , float , dist , uniform , 0, 120
  behav speed_communication , cyclic , 15
    action inform_cars , send_msg , speed_alert , inform
      set send.speed , current_speed
      send connections
    eaction
  ebehav
eagent
```

The code in Listing 1.1 defines the blueprint for the agent `autonomous_car`, which has one parameter and one behavior. Parameter `current_speed` is a floating-point number, initially drawn from the uniform distribution. The agent's behavior (`speed_communication`) runs cyclically. Inside it, there is an action `inform_cars`, used to send messages of a specific type (`speed_alert inform` defined in Listing 1.2). The first instruction sets the message parameter `speed` with the value of `current_speed`. Finally, the message is sent to the list `connections` that represent the recipient agents. The initial content of the list `connections` depends on the agent network definition (see Listing 1.3).

AASM supports defining messages, using the **message** instruction. They are identified by their name and an ACL performative (as specified in the FIPA00037J Standard)[3]. Messages contain numerical parameters.

[3] http://www.fipa.org/specs/fipa00037/SC00037J.html.

Listing 1.2. Speed alert

```
message speed_alert , inform
    prm speed , float
emessage
```

Code snippet in Listing 1.2 declares a message `speed_alert` with the performative `inform` and a parameter `speed`.

The **graph** keyword is used to describe the graph structure of the agent network. In its scope, the connections of each agent are defined.

Listing 1.3. Agent network

```
graph statistical
    defg autonomous_car , 300, dist_exp , 0.1
egraph
```

The code in Listing 1.3 defines a network of type `statistical`. This name refers to the fact that the size of each agent's initial connection list is drawn from a statistical distribution while the connections are assigned randomly. Here, for agents of type `autonomous_car`, the numbers are drawn from the exponential distribution, with $\lambda = 0.1$. The network's size totals 300, and `autonomous_car` instances constitute the complete simulation environment.

To facilitate the use of the AASM, a translator capable of validating an AASM program, and generating a run-time code, was developed. Specifically, a target-agnostic intermediate representation is created first. Next, it is translated to Python code, for the SPADE agent framework. Interestingly, the Python code generated from the snippets above is approximately six times longer than the AASM code. Note that the translation, using the intermediate representation, delivering code for other agent platform(s) can be instantiated.

The language structure is, by design, simple and block-like. It allows for easy generation of code with graphical user interface (GUI) modules. A custom AASM code generator can be seen in Fig. 1.

New parameter

Name

Alignment

Draw from distribution

Normal

miu

50

sigma

10

ADD PARAMETER

Fig. 1. GUI code generator

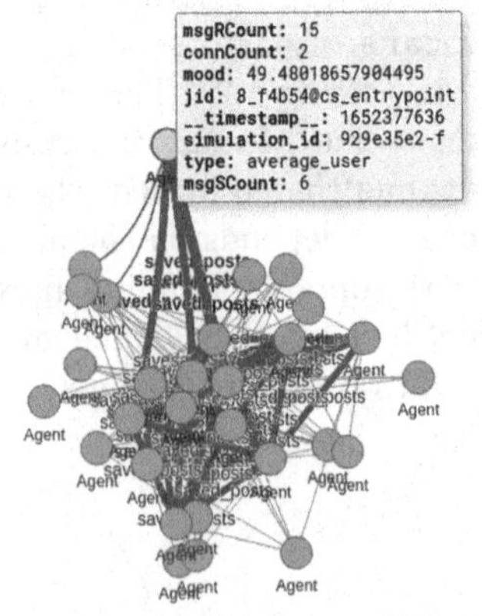

Fig. 2. Simulation visualization

3.2 Implementing AASM Ecosystem

The AASM ecosystem consists of three main components: the Interface, the Simulation Run Environment (SRE), and the Communication Server. Each component corresponds to a Docker[4] Swarm stack, running multiple microservices. Through the Interface, a user may define a simulation using the GUI code generator, run it and analyze it using management and visualization modules. The Interface interacts with SRE mainly through HTTP requests (although Bolt Protocol[5] connection with the database is possible). When a user creates an AASM simulation, SRE translates it, generates the network structure, and distributes agents between Agent Containers. Agent Containers are dockerized microservice processes that run the translated code using the SPADE agent platform. Each container holds the number of simulation agents assigned by the Simulation Load Balancer (one of the microservices in the SRE stack). Agents send their states to the database through Kafka[6], which ensures that the database does not get overloaded by write requests. Agents send messages through the Communication Server, an instance (or a cluster, as they may be freely scaled) of Tigase XMPP Servers[7]. The containerized approach allows an easy increase in the computational resources used by the simulation.

During the experiments, the system was deployed on a cluster of 15 physical computers, running 120 Agent Containers. It was also deployed on 5 virtual machines, running 5 Agent Containers each. A single agent container is capable of running multiple agents. Experimental results indicated a limit of around 1000 agents per container and a good (stable) performance at 100 agents (tested on Intel Core i7-6700HQ @ 2.6 GHz and 24 GB DDR4 RAM). The exact number of agents depends on agents' complexity (number of operations per minute) and the hardware.

In the system, the Interface may be accessed from any node in the dockerized network. Its connection to a graph database (neo4j[8]) grants live access to the simulation data (values and aggregates of agent and message parameters). The agents' state is visualized directly through a dedicated module that presents an interactive graph of data available in the database (depicted in Fig. 2). The visualization module also supports live plotting of data streams during the simulation. Data can be requested directly through Cypher (neo4j's query language) queries or via GUI query creator providing a user-friendly alternative.

3.3 Demonstrations

During the demonstration, the attendees will be able to see running simulations prepared in AASM. They will also have the possibility to modify the details of the simulations through the code generating GUI, observing its simplicity.

[4] https://docker.com.
[5] https://boltprotocol.org.
[6] https://kafka.apache.org.
[7] https://tigase.net.
[8] https://neo4j.com.

The presentation will be performed on 2 computers, starting with 2 agent containers and scaling to 8. The simulations will be verified in terms of the validity of the results and the system's stability.

4 Concluding Remarks

The purpose of the work was to ease the development of agent-based simulations. In this context, a domain specific language, Agents Assembly, was proposed. The design of Agents Assembly was based on the evaluation of actual user needs. Thanks to translation to an intermediate code, it is possible to develop support for other agent platforms and frameworks.

The system is being tried by a group of students at the Warsaw University of Technology to develop a complex traffic simulation. Their initial feedback has been positive. However, it was suggested that the number of available mathematical functions should be increased, which resulted in adding built-in **sin**, **cos**, **log**, and **pow** instructions. Their experiences, collected at the end of the semester, will be used to further improve the AASM ecosystem.

Separately, during experiments, it has been noticed that the system's stability can be affected in the case of vast numbers of connections. Specifically, during a simulation (running on 15 networked workstations) with an agent network with more than 399 million connections (large, dense, all-to-all graph), congestion in the system has been identified. However, it should be stressed that even when the communication bottleneck has been detected, the system did not crash. Nevertheless, this problem requires addressing in future development.

The current version of the Agents Assembly ecosystem can be found at https://agents-assembly.com. The web page gives access to an online version of the translator, links all pertinent repositories, and the language documentation. Contributions to its further development are welcome and requested.

References

1. Castro, B.M., de Abreu de Melo, Y., Fernanda dos Santos, N., Luiz da Costa Barcellos, A., Choren, R., Salles, R.M.: Multi-agent simulation model for the evaluation of COVID-19 transmission. Comput. Biol. Med. **136**, 104645 (2021)
2. I Ciecierski, J., Mai, V.B., Słupczyński, M., Zyskowski, W.: Multi-agent simulation of the world found in the G. R. R. Martin's novel "Sandkings". In: Ganzha, M., Maciaszek, L., Paprzycki, M. (eds.) Position Papers of the 2015 Federated Conference on Computer Science and Information Systems. Annals of Computer Science and Information Systems, vol. 6, pp. 249–256. PTI (2015). https://doi.org/10.15439/2015F417
3. de Sola Pool, I., Abelson, R., Popkin, S.: Candidates, Issues and Strategies: A Computer Simulation of the 1960 and 1964 Presidential Elections. M.I.T. Paperback Series. Massachusetts Institute of Technology Press (1965)

Digital Twin Assisted Decision Making

Vinay Kulkarni, Souvik Barat(✉), Abhishek Yadav, Dushyanthi Mulpuru, and Anwesha Basu

Tata Consultancy Service Research, Pune 411013, India
{vinay.vkulkarni,souvik.barat,y.abhishek1,dushyanthi.mulpuru, anwesha.basu1}@tcs.com

Abstract. You have heard extensively about digital twins and how they can be applied in a range of domains and for a range of different purposes. A particularly pressing problem that you are wrestling with is understanding how digital twin technology can be applied to aid in your decision-making requirements in the face of uncertainty. Do you need help in understanding how digital twins can be used? This demonstration provides you with a detailed understanding of how digital twins can serve as an important technology that subject matter experts can use to arrive at quantitative justification-backed decisions with reasonable confidence about their effectiveness when implemented in real-world context. The demonstration presents a human-in-loop automation aid and how it has been used to effectively address complex decision-making problems in socio-techno-economic space.

Keywords: Digital twin · Decision-making · Simulation

1 Motivation

We live in a hyperconnected world experiencing unprecedented changes along multiple dimensions that open up new opportunities or pose threats. Ability to arrive at the right decisions and their effective implementation has emerged as a key need. The ever-shortening window of opportunity provides little room for later course correction. Determining the right response often requires a deep understanding of aspects such as structural decomposition into subsystems, relationships between these subsystems, and emergent behaviour. The scale, socio-technical characteristics, and fast dynamics make this a challenging endeavor.

For decision-making, the system can be viewed as a transfer function from input value space to output value space as shown in Fig. 1. System exists to meet the stated goals while operating in an environment which may constrain inputs and/or system behaviour. System goals are an objective function over output value space and may have temporal characteristics. Moreover, the goals can have a complex decomposition structure with inter-dependent and cross-cutting goals as shown in Fig. 1. Designing a suitable transfer function is in itself a challenging task. The transfer function needs to be continually modified in response to changes in the environment and/or goals – the decision-making

© The Author(s), under exclusive license to Springer Nature Switzerland AG 2022
F. Dignum et al. (Eds.): PAAMS 2022, LNAI 13616, pp. 493–499, 2022.
https://doi.org/10.1007/978-3-031-18192-4_43

problem. This problem is further exacerbated when the available information is incomplete, and the environment is uncertain. Traditionally, decision-making is formulated as a multi-variate optimization problem when the system behaviour is known and amenable to purely analytical specification. However, socio-techno-economic systems are characterized by emergent behaviour that's not amenable to rigorous mathematical specification. Other prominent approach is to use past data. The idea is to (machine) learn a model from the past data and use it for predictive analysis. This approach works well if the past data captures all possible behaviours of the system which is difficult to ascertain. Therefore, the machine learnt model is likely to be a subset of real model thus leading to sub-optimal analysis at best and incorrect results at worst. As a result, current practice relies extensively on subject matter experts for decision-making. Typically, the decision maker operates with a fixed set of interventions to nudge the system toward the desired state. This is an iterative process based largely on expertise and experience. Given the large size, complex goal decomposition, interfering goals, and incomplete knowledge, the decision-making endeavor is typically an art. However, subject matter experts have no way to foretell system wide ramifications of a specific intervention being introduced locally.

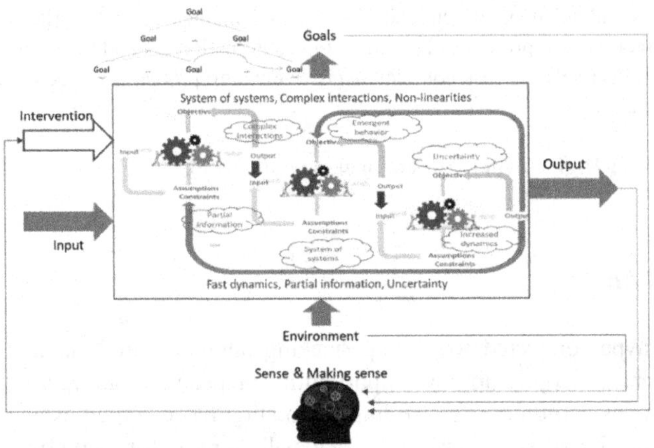

Fig. 1. Decision-making in complex systems

2 Our Solution

We envisage a line of attack that borrows proven ideas from modeling & simulation, control theory and artificial intelligence, and builds upon further to be able to use them in an integrated manner. At the heart of this line of attack is the concept of Enterprise Digital Twin [1] – a virtual hi-fidelity machine processable representation of enterprise. It is amenable to solution space exploration through what-if/if-what analysis. Thus, it can be used as "in silico" experimentation aid where experts subject the digital twin to a variety of perturbations. As the digital twin is a hi-fidelity representation of the system, its response to a perturbation is in the ballpark of actual system response. Experts can interpret this response in the light of their knowledge and experience to arrive at a candidate set of suitable interventions. The set can be validated for correctness and efficacy using the digital twin itself by running appropriate simulations thus leading to identification of the most suitable intervention. Thus, digital twin considerably reduces the need for real life experimentation with the system and leads to significant savings in time, cost and effort. In essence, digital twin supports a knowledge-guided tool-assisted approach to decision-making for complex systems whose key tenets are:

Analysis: Data-backed explanation of why things are the way they are
Design: Exploring the solution space in evidence-backed manner
Adaptation: Bring the system back to the desired state in response to changes in the environment or goal or input
Transformation: A sequence of interventions to nudge the system from as-is state to the desired to-be state in a data-driven justification-backed manner

Moreover, these capabilities are supported "in silico" thus resulting in significant savings on real life experimentation. We use Reinforcement Learning (RL) techniques to train a controller through interactions with the digital twin that acts as an "experience generator". The controller may nudge the system directly (self-adaptation) or through human agent. We propose use of suitable learning techniques to derive knowledge from historical data collected from system operations as well as digital twin simulations. Going forward, this knowledge can be used to improve subsequent usage of digital twin. Also, the system can be made resilient to "known unknowns", and to some extent even to "unknown unknowns" by imagining the future.

We have developed a Java based actor-based language called ESL[1] [2] to specify and simulate digital twin of a complex system. It helps model the system as a set of autonomous actors where an actor tries to achieve its stated goal by responding suitably to the events of interest and by exchanging messages with other actors. We address uncertainty through stochastic behaviour of actor i.e. there could be a probability distribution of actions associated with an event. We provide two ways of validating the digital twin: (i) Certification of correctness by experts, and (ii) Through simulation wherein the models (suitably initialized) are subjected to known past events leading to a simulation trace which is then examined to ascertain the resultant behaviours are identical to the ones from the past. Our simulation engine generates rich execution traces containing detailed information necessary for analysis. We have developed a pattern language to specify the desired behaviour and a pattern matching engine to look for the specified patterns in the simulation trace.

We have validated the approach and supporting technology on several real-world use cases from telecom [3], retail [4], and societal [5] domains. Next section describes the use cases from societal domain in detail.

[1] http://www.esl-lang.org.

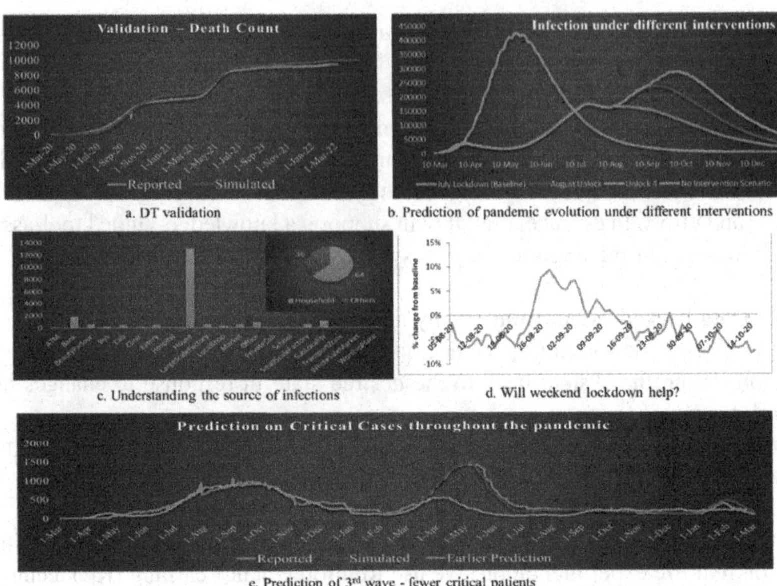

a. DT validation

b. Prediction of pandemic evolution under different interventions

c. Understanding the source of infections

d. Will weekend lockdown help?

e. Prediction of 3rd wave - fewer critical patients

Fig. 2. Prediction and control of Covid19 pandemic in a city

3 Demonstration

3.1 Prediction and Control of Covid19 Pandemic in a City

During Covid19 pandemic, one of the key priorities of the public health administration is to understand the dynamics of the transmission of the pathogen and use that knowledge to design effective control measures to keep its impact on public health within manageable and tolerable limits. Spread of Covid19 is related to people's movement, the nature of the area where people congregate, and number and frequency of proximal contacts. The demographic factors and comorbidity also play a role in the spread of infection as well as its lethality.

While statistical and mathematical models [6] are useful in predicting evolution of pandemic at a macro level, they are found wanting in identifying appropriate interventions for pandemic control. This is principally because their underlying model is not fine grained enough to capture the heterogeneity as regards people, places, movements, routine set of activities etc. We developed a purposive fine-grained agent-based model of a city – City Digital Twin – that captures heterogeneity in terms of people, places, transport infrastructure, health care infrastructure, etc. The digital twin is amenable to what-if and if-what scenario playing. We populated the city digital twin with data made available by city administration. The fine-grained nature of digital twin enabled us to address the critical concerns such as the rate and the extent of the spread of the epidemic, load on the healthcare infrastructure in terms of specific needs such as number of admissions requiring critical care (supplementary oxygen, ventilator support, intensive care, etc.), load on institutional quarantine centers, and so on. We set up appropriate what-if scenarios to identify the most effective NPIs from the candidate set to control epidemic as well as bring back normalcy [5].

Figure 2 depicts sample simulation results obtained using the city digital twin. We validated correctness of city digital twin using number of reported Covid deaths as the primary criterion (Fig. 2a). One of the first requests from city administration was about the need to enforce a lockdown. Our simulation supported the need for enforcing a strict lockdown highlighting the load on health infrastructure otherwise (Fig. 2b). Relaxation of lockdown – which places to open when and to what extent – remained an important question throughout the pandemic. Ability to pinpoint the source of infection (Fig. 2c) helped us provide precise answers. It was important to strike the right balance between infection control and revival of economy. Keeping shops closed over the weekend was an alternative being mulled. Simulating the city digital twin for this situation rendered this alternative quite ineffective (Fig. 2d). Omicron variant induced 3rd wave caught everybody unaware. When will it peak and to what extent were the principal concerns expressed by city authority. We were able to address these concerns through simulation-based prediction (Fig. 2e). Thus, overall, the city digital twin came out as a useful aid for city authority to come up with locality-specific pandemic control measures in a justification-backed manner.

3.2 Helping Organizations Transition from Work-From-Home to Work-From-Office Mode

Organizations are struggling to ensure business continuity without compromising on delivery excellence in the face of Covid19 pandemic related uncertainties. The uncertainty exists along multiple dimensions such as virus mutations, infectivity and severity of new mutants, efficacy of vaccines against new mutants, waning of vaccine induced immunity over time, and lockdown/opening-up policies effected by city authorities. Moreover, this uncertainty plays out in a non-uniform manner across nations, states, cities, and even within the cities thus leading to highly heterogeneous evolution of pandemic. While Work-From-Home (WFH) strategy has served well to meet ever-increasing business demands without compromising on individual health safety, there has been an undeniable reduction in social capital. With Covid19 pandemic showing definite waning trends and employees beginning to miss the office environment, several organizations are considering the possibility of safe transition from WFH to Work-From-Office (WFO) or a hybrid mode of operation. An effective strategy needs to score equally well on possibly interfering dimensions such as risk of infection, project delivery, and employee (& their dependents) wellness. As large organizations will typically have a large number of offices spread across a geography, the problem of arriving at office-specific strategies be-comes non-trivial. Moreover, the strategies need to adapt over time to changes that cannot be deduced upfront. This calls for an approach that's amenable to quick and easy adaptation.

We developed a Digital Twin centric approach that: (i) Leverages pure data-centric statistical model, coarse-grained system dynamic model, and fine-grained agent-based model, (ii) Helps human experts arrive at pragmatic strategies to effect WFH to WFO transition keeping the key stakeholders satisfied, and (iii) Easily adapt the strategies over time. We have validated the approach with a large organization and the results are encouraging.

Figure 3 depicts results of sample simulations carried out while arriving at city plus office specific strategies for effecting WFH to WFO transition that ensures timely delivery to customers without compromising health of employees and their dependents. Figure 3a depicts daily office-induced infections whereas Fig. 3b depicts cumulative infections. While there is a possibility of significant rise in office-induced infections with 50% occupancy, this sudden rise is rather miniscule in absolute numbers.

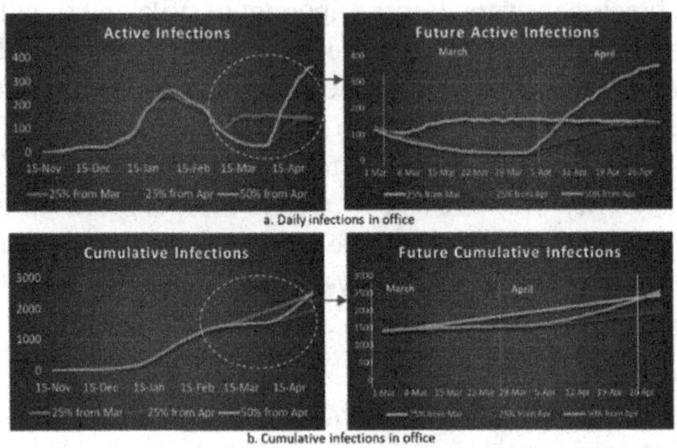

Fig. 3. WFH to WFO transition

4 Conclusions

We motivated the importance of data-driven justification-backed decision-making. We argued the need for a new approach as the current state of practice is found wanting. We presented a digital twin centric simulation-based approach to overcome the limitations of current practice. We briefly illustrated the efficacy of the proposed approach and supporting technology on two business-critical use cases from socio-techno-economic space.

References

1. Grieves, M., Vickers, J.: Digital twin: mitigating unpredictable, undesirable emergent behavior in complex systems. In: Kahlen, J., Flumerfelt, S., Alves, A. (eds.) Transdisciplinary Perspectives on Complex Systems. Springer, Cham (2017). https://doi.org/10.1007/978-3-319-38756-7_4
2. Clark, T., Kulkarni, V., Barat, S., Barn, B.: ESL: an actor-based platform for developing emergent behaviour organisation simulations. In: Demazeau, Y., Davidsson, P., Bajo, J., Vale, Z. (eds.) PAAMS 2017. LNCS (LNAI), vol. 10349, pp. 311–315. Springer, Cham (2017). https://doi.org/10.1007/978-3-319-59930-4_27

3. Souvik, B., et al.: Towards effective design and adaptation of CSP using modelling and simulation based digital twin approach. In: Proceedings of the 2020 Summer Simulation Conference (2020)
4. Souvik, B., et al.: Actor based simulation for closed loop control of supply chain using reinforcement learning. In: Proceedings of the 18th International Conference on Autonomous Agents and Multiagent Systems (2019)
5. Souvik, B., et al.: An agent-based digital twin for exploring localized non-pharmaceutical interventions to control COVID-19 pandemic. Trans. Indian Natl. Acad. Eng. **6.2**, 323–353 (2021)
6. He, S., Peng, Y., Sun, K.: SEIR modeling of the COVID-19 and its dynamics. Nonlinear Dyn. **101**(3), 1667–1680 (2020). https://doi.org/10.1007/s11071-020-05743-y

Intelligent Artificial Agent for Information Retrieval

Michael Pulis[1(✉)], Joel Azzopardi[1], and Jeffrey J. Micallef[2]

[1] University of Malta, Msida, Malta
{michael.pulis.18,joel.azzopardi}@um.edu.mt
[2] RS2 p.l.c, Mosta, Malta
jeffrey.micallef@rs2.com
http://www.rs2.com

Abstract. Throughout the day of the average employee at RS2, there will often be a need to search one of the company's information repositories. Finding the information will often force employees to perform a context switch and search within the appropriate repository. We propose a system that will facilitate this process by creating a ChatBot that can perform the search within the company's chat client by making use of the latest machine learning techniques, alongside several NLP techniques and established industry standard information retrieval technologies to allow for a single consolidated, optimised searching system. Results on benchmark datasets show that our system was able to achieve the best results when making use of a combination of traditional and modern techniques.

Keywords: Deep learning · Information retrieval · S-Bert · Document embeddings

1 Introduction

Employees at RS2[1] often run different types of processes that will sometimes fail due to errors or issues in the process. To identify the issue with their process, or to obtain helpful information about the task they are trying to carry out, the employees will look up similar issues that others encountered in the past manually, from a system called JIRA[2]. It contains issues that were raised, as well as the possible solution found by previous employees within the comments for the issue. The issue could also be resolved by looking up the issue in the documentation repository (Confluence[3]).

Performing this search manually is time consuming and inefficient, and often leads to the proposed solution or the ideal document being overlooked. In order to

[1] https://www.rs2.com/, May 2022.
[2] https://www.atlassian.com/software/jira, May 2022.
[3] https://www.atlassian.com/software/confluence, May 2022.

© The Author(s), under exclusive license to Springer Nature Switzerland AG 2022
F. Dignum et al. (Eds.): PAAMS 2022, LNAI 13616, pp. 500–506, 2022.
https://doi.org/10.1007/978-3-031-18192-4_44

identify the correct document, users must first search within the correct information repository, after which they must also use the correct query language since the different repositories sometimes utilise different keywords to achieve the same functionality. Thus, we propose a centralised system that can perform an optimised search for a given user query within the company's information repositories at once. This proposed solution would allow the user to carry out the query and obtain the relevant documents from within the company chat client itself, thus simplifying the process of obtaining the required information. We also propose the usage of both traditional and modern AI based IR techniques to enhance the quality of the results when compared to the searching algorithms employed by the current services used by the company.

2 Background Research and Literature Review

2.1 Document Search

Term Frequency - Inverse Document Frequency (TF-IDF) is a method used to identify which documents within a corpus are most relevant to a query word. The score given to a document in relation to a word is based on how much the word appears within the particular document more than it appears in other documents. By using cosine similarity on the extracted TF-IDF vectors of the query and the documents, the relevance of each document can be found. Okapi Best Matching 25 (BM-25) is another method that aims to find the most relevant documents for a particular query. It also contains considerations for how common the word is, and how long the document itself is [10].

Whilst TF-IDF is one of the most popular algorithms used for information retrieval, powering roughly 83% of online text-based recommendation systems within digital libraries [1], BM-25 is considered to be an improvement upon it. This is shown in literature as BM-25 often outperforms TF-IDF at information retrieval related tasks [5,7].

2.2 Document Embeddings

Recent advances in IR utilise document embedding systems to obtain better results than traditional IR methods, whereby a model is trained to output a vector representation of a particular section of text that aims to encapsulate the general meaning and sentiment of the text. The Bi-directional Encoder Representations from Transformers (BERT) model developed by Google is a deeply bidirectional model [3]. Traditional NLP models are structured unidirectionally, meaning that to represent the context of the current word, only the previous words are considered. However in BERT, a deep representation of both the preceding and the following contexts are used to understand the meaning of the current word. The BERT model itself has previously been used in document retrieval [13].

Further work was carried out on the BERT model to improve its computational cost when extracting embeddings, whilst also obtaining the semantic meaning from sentences, which was called Sentence-BERT (S-BERT) [9]. In this work, the authors made use of a Siamese Neural Network structure to input sentence pairs containing either similar, or dissimilar sentence pairs to train a pair of BERT models to identify thematically similar or dissimilar sentences. The authors use this architecture to obtain embeddings from BERT that are more suited for semantic similarity calculations. The results show that the S-BERT model produces embeddings that perform better in IR tasks [2,4]. This is also corroborated by experiments carried out in real world industrial scenarios[4], where both inference speed and result quality were found to be better when using S-BERT.

2.3 Incorporating Artificial Agents in IR

One of the most noteworthy contributions in the field was the Ask Alice system [12]. In this work, the authors developed an agent capable of identifying the state and intentions from the query, which was then used to enhance the IR aspect of the project, highlighting the importance of understanding the query for IR. Further work into the implementation of artificial agents being used for IR was carried out in [8]. In this work, the authors made use of the Google DialogFlow system, which can carry out complex NLP and ML tasks. By utilising DialogFlow, the authors were able to create an intelligent artificial agent that could process user queries and match them with an adequate internship role.

3 Methodology

3.1 Datasets

To create the dataset that was used for searching on, the company's information repositories *(Jira and Confluence)* were scraped. This was carried out using their respective APIs, after which the BeautifulSoup library[5] was used to strip the HTML markup and obtain the raw text. The obtained data consists of the Project title, issue title, issue body, and the comments. However, this dataset does not contain ground truth values that can be used to fine-tune the algorithms. Thus, evaluation was carried out on two standard IR datasets that are commonly used in literature, namely the CACM and CISI datasets [6,11]. Both of these contain a set of documents, a set of queries, and a ground truth set that pairs queries with relevant documents in no particular order.

3.2 Document Search

For this project, Apache Solr was chosen as the basis for our system, since it is slightly more suited to static text data searches than ElasticSearch[6]. Searching within Solr is typically performed using the **lucene**, **dismax** or **e-dismax**

[4] https://github.com/nadjet/sentence_similarity, May 2022.
[5] https://pypi.org/project/beautifulsoup4/, May 2022.
[6] https://logz.io/blog/solr-vs-elasticsearch/, May 2022.

query systems. The **dismax** search scheme was used since it perform searches in a similar fashion to traditional search engines, where the entire query string is compared against all the text present within each document in the collection. To integrate vector embeddings within Solr, the Solr-Vector-Scoring plugin[7] was integrated. Thus, each document within Solr will also contain a vector representation of itself.

This allowed searches to be performed based on the extracted document embedding. By using the **boost-query** functionality within Solr, it was also possible to incorporate both BM-25 and Document embeddings into a single search, whereby the results obtained from the traditional technique are boosted by the vector embedding system. The embeddings used were derived using S-Bert, as they were found to perform better than embeddings extracted from BERT [9]. Query expansion was achieved within Solr by including modules that pre-process the query with **stop word removal** and **stemming**. Another step that was developed was to make use of DialogFlow's ML toolkit to automatically extract sections of the query such as the Project and the Issue itself. These are fed into Solr's **boost query** to boost when certain strings appear in certain fields. This is useful as identifying the project name allows the search to boost the project name if it is found in the query's project field.

3.3 Chat Component

To comply with the standards set by the company, the entire system was integrated within Google Chat. The challenge with implementing the system within Google Chat is that any company APIs that are required must be made public to the internet to parse queries sent from Google Chat directly. To avoid making sensitive information available through a public endpoint, Google Pub/Sub was used. This allowed data to be relayed to private networks (Fig. 1).

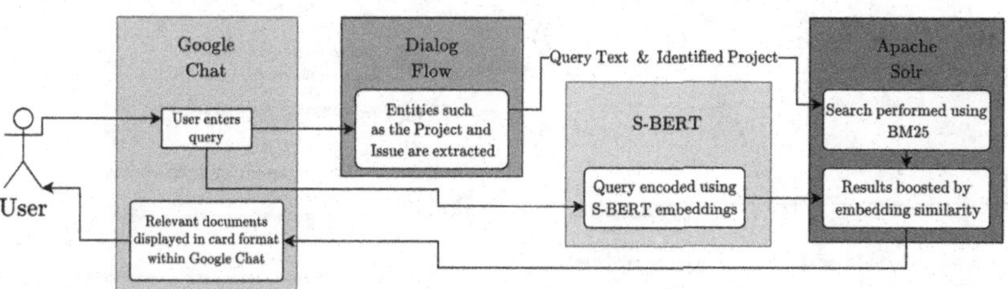

Fig. 1. System overview

[7] https://github.com/saaay71/solr-vector-scoring, May 2022.

4 Results and Evaluation

Since the CACM and CISI datasets do not have explicit Projects, the DialogFlow implementation was not integrated in these results, however it is included in the real world scenario.

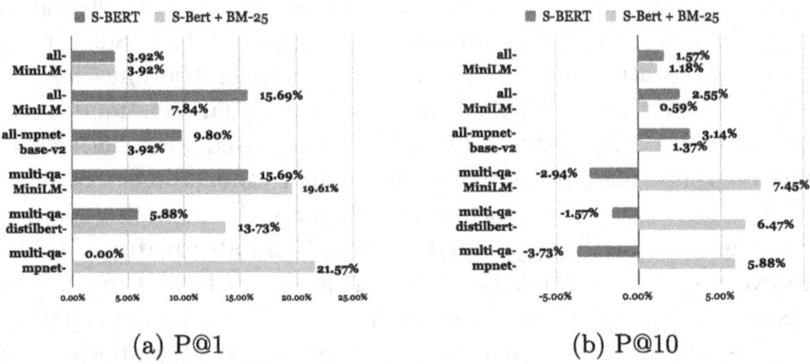

Fig. 2. Increase in percentage points over baseline BM-25 (CACM)

The data in Fig. 2 shows the percentage point increase in P@K over the baseline BM-25 system against the P@K obtained from the S-BERT embeddings alone, as well as the S-BERT + BM-25 system. The results show that the S-BERT model consistently outperformed the baseline implementation, however the best results are achieved when utilising the boost-query functionality to enhance the results of the BM-25 system with the results from the S-BERT vector similarity. To obtain further context, the precision-recall curve was drawn for the models, which can be seen in Fig. 3.

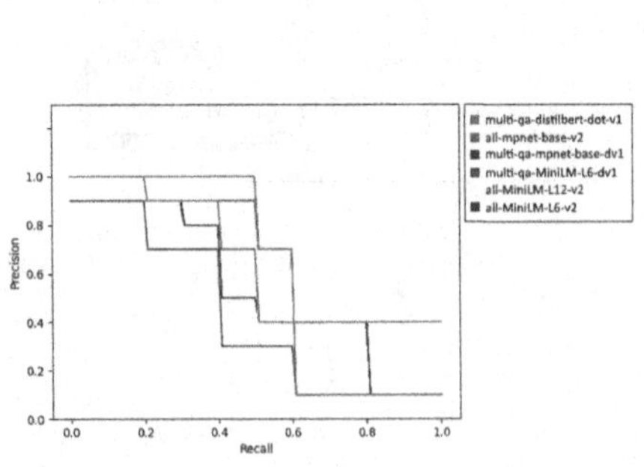

Fig. 3. PR curve for various S-BERT+BM25 models

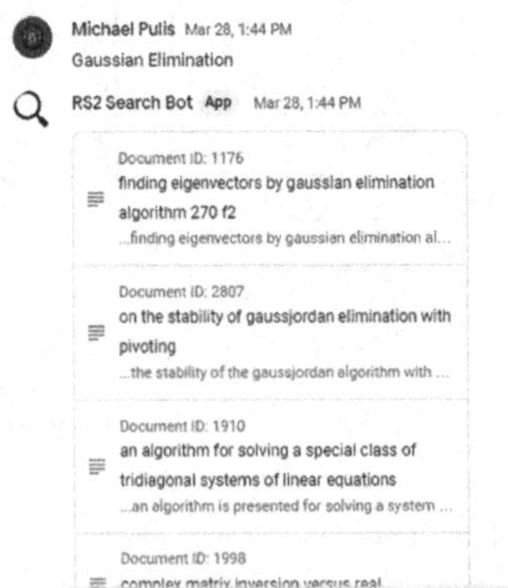

Fig. 4. Sample system output

The graph shows that several models perform well at lower levels of recall, however there is a tendency for rapid decay after a certain threshold is reached. When considering the results presented, the **multi-qa-distilbert-dot-v1** model appears to be the best candidate since the top results are usually more important to the user. However the model for use will be confirmed through empirical tests carried out on internal company data. A demonstration of the system can be seen in Fig. 4, where a user makes a query and after obtaining the relevant documents, a card containing the results is returned.

5 Conclusion and Future Work

Throughout this document, the issue of having information stored within different repositories has been identified. A solution has also been proposed and implemented that will allow employees to perform a comprehensive search directly within the communication application used by the company thus addressing the issue. To attempt to improve the system's performance, future work could be carried out to attempt different models for encoding the documents, as well as to experiment with more query expansion techniques. Future work could also include relevance feedback, allowing the system to improve performance over time.

References

1. Beel, J., Gipp, B., Langer, S., Breitinger, C.: Research-paper recommender systems: a literature survey. Int. J. Digit. Libr. **17**(4), 305–338 (2015). https://doi.org/10.1007/s00799-015-0156-0
2. Deshmukh, A.A., Sethi, U.: IR-BERT: leveraging BERT for semantic search in background linking for news articles. arXiv preprint arXiv:2007.12603 (2020)
3. Devlin, J., Chang, M.W., Lee, K., Toutanova, K.: BERT: pre-training of deep bidirectional transformers for language understanding. arXiv preprint arXiv:1810.04805 (2018)
4. Esteva, A., et al.: Co-search: COVID-19 information retrieval with semantic search, question answering, and abstractive summarization. arXiv preprint arXiv:2006.09595 (2020)
5. Kadhim, A.I.: Term weighting for feature extraction on Twitter: a comparison between BM25 and TF-IDF. In: 2019 International Conference on Advanced Science and Engineering (ICOASE), pp. 124–128. IEEE (2019)
6. Lee, D.L., Chuang, H., Seamons, K.: Document ranking and the vector-space model. IEEE Softw. **14**(2), 67–75 (1997)
7. Marwah, D., Beel, J.: Term-recency for TF-IDF, BM25 and USE term weighting. In: WOSP (2020)
8. Ranavare, S., Kamath, R.: Artificial intelligence based chatbot for placement activity at college using dialogflow, December 2020
9. Reimers, N., Gurevych, I.: Sentence-BERT: sentence embeddings using siamese BERT-networks, pp. 3973–3983 (2019). https://doi.org/10.18653/v1/D19-1410
10. Robertson, S.E., Walker, S., Jones, S., Hancock-Beaulieu, M., Gatford, M.: Okapi at TREC-3. In: TREC (1994)

11. Sharma, D.K., Pamula, R., Chauhan, D.S.: A hybrid evolutionary algorithm based automatic query expansion for enhancing document retrieval system. J. Ambient Intell. Human. Comput. **4**, 1–20 (2019). https://doi.org/10.1007/s12652-019-01247-9
12. Valstar, M., et al.: Ask Alice: an artificial retrieval of information agent. In: Proceedings of the 18th ACM-ICMI, pp. 419–420 (2016)
13. Yilmaz, Z.A., Wang, S., Yang, W., Zhang, H., Lin, J.: Applying BERT to document retrieval with birch. In: Proceedings of the 2019 Conference on EMNLP and IJCNLP: System Demonstrations, pp. 19–24 (2019)

From Research to Crisis Management: Multiagent Simulation for Local Governments

Alexander Schewerda(✉), Veronika Kurchyna, Jan Ole Berndt, and Ingo J. Timm

German Research Center for Artificial Intelligence (DFKI), Cognitive Social Simulation, Universitätsring 15, 54296 Trier, Germany
{alexander.schewerda,veronika.kurchyna}@dfki.de

Abstract. During the COVID-19 pandemic, a rise of (agent-based) simulation models for predicting future developments and assessing intervention scenarios has been observed. At the same time, dashboarding has become a popular way to aggregate and visualise large quantities of data. The *AScore Pandemic Management Cockpit* brings together multiagent-based simulation (MABS) and analysis functionalities for crisis managers. It combines the presentation of data and forecasting on the effects of containment measures in a modular, reusable architecture that streamlines the process of use for these non-researcher users. In this paper, the most successful features and concepts for the simplification of simulation usage are presented: definition of scenarios, limitation of parameters, and integrated result visualisation, all bundled in a web-based service to offer a low-barrier entry to the usage of MABS in decision-making processes.

Keywords: Multiagent-based simulation · COVID-19 pandemic · Crisis management · Decision-making cockpit

1 Introduction

With the beginning of the COVID-19 pandemic, the need for easily available information for the population and governments increased. Thus, a large number of pandemic dashboards was proposed by companies and research groups across the globe. Infection numbers, hospital capacities, vaccination rates and other statistics were displayed in graphs and coloured maps. However, the scope of data processing was usually limited to simple visual presentation and basic aggregation without interpretation, requiring additional expert knowledge to assess the presented results accurately [1].

Furthermore, forecasts on the course of the pandemic were required in addition to the current data and facts presented in those dashboards, especially for making political decisions. Different simulation models were presented, including a number of agent-based models (ABMs) [2]. ABMs compete against established equation-based models. As a result, the usage of mutliagent-based simulation (MABS) for policy decisions was not particularly widespread [3]. Easy access

© The Author(s), under exclusive license to Springer Nature Switzerland AG 2022
F. Dignum et al. (Eds.): PAAMS 2022, LNAI 13616, pp. 507–513, 2022.
https://doi.org/10.1007/978-3-031-18192-4_45

to information and its interpretation, as well as forecasts, are the three main features needed by governments to manage the pandemic. This work presents the simulation-based cockpit *AScore*, which combines these spheres of dashboarding and multiagent-based simulation to support policy-makers in local government with the assessment of the pandemic situation in their region and possible outcomes of different intervention decisions. Section 2 outlines the main purpose and goals of AScore, Sect. 3 demonstrates its application and in Sect. 4 we conclude on the lessons learned from bringing agent-based simulation into practice.

2 Purpose of the AScore Pandemic Management Cockpit

The simulation-based cockpit AScore was developed in cooperation with crisis managers in Germany during the COVID-19 pandemic. Its main purpose is to help local governments manage the pandemic with a holistic approach [4]. This includes the presentation of up-to-date data and information that is aggregated and evaluated to allow for assessing the overall situation in a chosen region. However, AScore aims not only at providing an overview of the current situation, but also at the possibility to evaluate future developments using an agent-based simulation approach. For that, an ABM based on population data is used to produce understandable and explainable results in real-world scale of a German city – such that each inhabitant is represented by an agent in the simulation. Accessibility of the underlying simulation used for predictions when examining possible impacts of policy decisions is a major factor in determining whether people are willing to take advantage of MABS or not [5,6]. By streamlining the process of running meaningful simulations and viewing their results, users experience reduced entry barriers to the use of AScore in their workflows.

AScore supports these objectives with modular architecture that can be used for different models, even outside of the pandemic context. Such a modular architecture includes visualisation of results which addresses an issue often encountered by developers of ABMs: easily understandable visualisation and presentation of simulation results is often time consuming [7]. As such, this kind of architecture, which emphasises reusability and interchangeability of components, is an important approach to addressing the high cost and effort associated with the presentation of different simulations to stakeholders.

3 From Research to Practice: Demonstration of AScore

In this section, we present the architecture of the simulation-based cockpit and how its design contributed towards the overall quality and usefulness of the system in its practical application during crisis management counselling.

3.1 AScore Architecture

Figure 1 displays the general architecture of the AScore dashboard. The ecosystem consists of four major components: the actual management cockpit, which

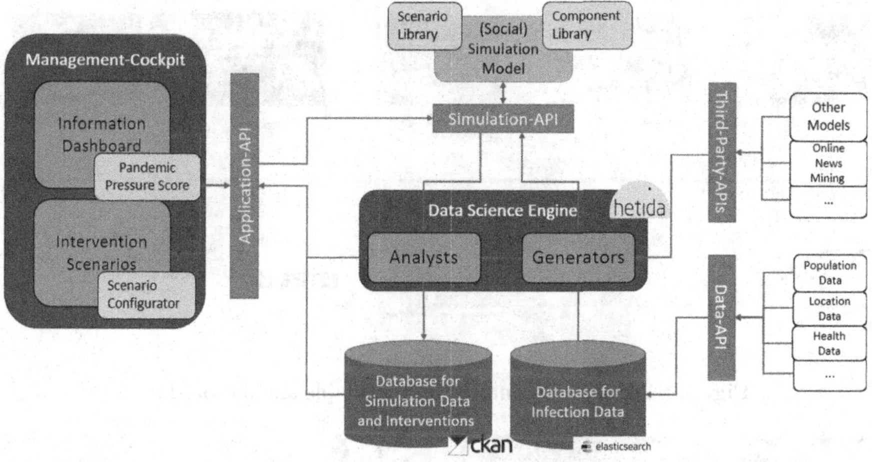

Fig. 1. AScore architecture diagram

is the frontend presented to users, and the three underlying backend components. There is the agent-based simulation, along with metadata on its scenarios and components, which is connected to the system by an API. This means the simulation is a modular component which can be switched with another model, increasing the reusability of this architecture. A CKAN [8] database and an Elasticsearch [9] instance are used for the management of unstructured, file-based data, both for the dashboard visualisations and for simulation inputs, as well as the results of a simulation which can be viewed in the dashboard. To process this needed input and also the output data, a data science engine, such as the open source framework *hetida designer* [10] serves as a connecting component. Different APIs serve as connectors between the four components, ensuring modularity.

3.2 Agent-Based Simulation Scenarios

Based on active use for decision making, simulations are usually conducted with respect to specific issues. Typically, these are if-then questions that examine the impact of specific decisions such as the mandated home office. To facilitate such targeted simulations, scenarios of particular interest were identified in collaboration with members of rapid response groups, local governments, and other potential users. The following were deemed of particular importance: *Impact of home office*, *Impact of alternate instruction and different testing strategies at schools*, and *Impact of lockdown.* Figure 2 shows the overview of the different scenarios under which users can find previous simulation results that, when requested for analysis, are loaded from the CKAN database. In addition, it is also possible for users to freely design own scenarios using more than twenty parameters. However, to lower the complexity of the model there are also fixed

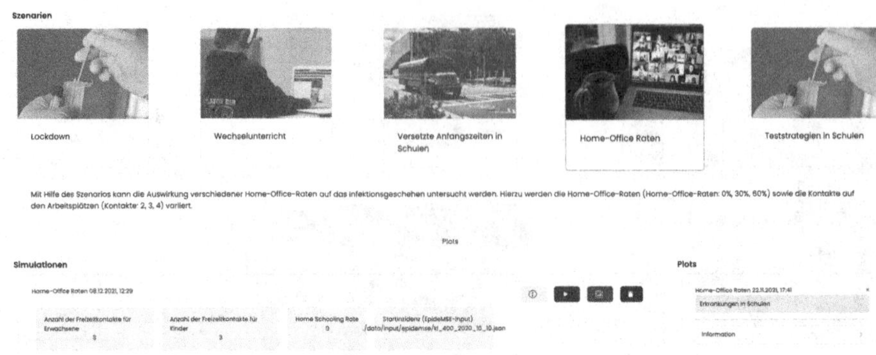

Fig. 2. Selection of scenarios and available simulation data

Fig. 3. Configuration interface of the *home office*-scenario

parameters, which are usually verified by experts, scientific data, data drawn from other sources (i.e. population data) or parameters not needed for the specific scenario studied. Figure 3 shows the interface for the configuration of the home office scenario in this case – while users may want to adjust the contact behaviour of the population, constants are not displayed at all, reducing the complexity of the configuration process.

3.3 Simulation Result Visualisation

Once a simulation has is done, the output data is processed and visualised using custom workflows in hetida, allowing for the selection of relevant data to be displayed. Figure 4 shows a selection of plots that compare the infection dynamics for three different home office rates and different contact behaviours among adults. The graphs display both case numbers in the general population and in schools, allowing the examination of different population groups or metrics besides simple case numbers. Apart from infection dynamics, there are a number of other output data that can be used to create charts such as hospitalisation, mortality and more. In addition, users can view the results of the scenarios with their respective progress in the simulation player in Fig. 5. This player visualises

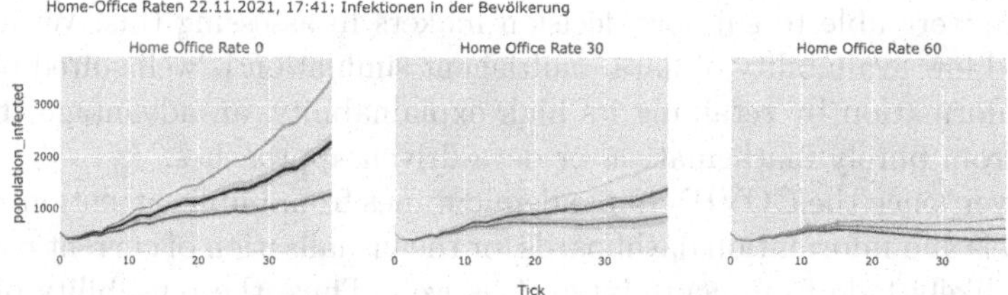

Fig. 4. Visualisation of results for the *home office*-scenario

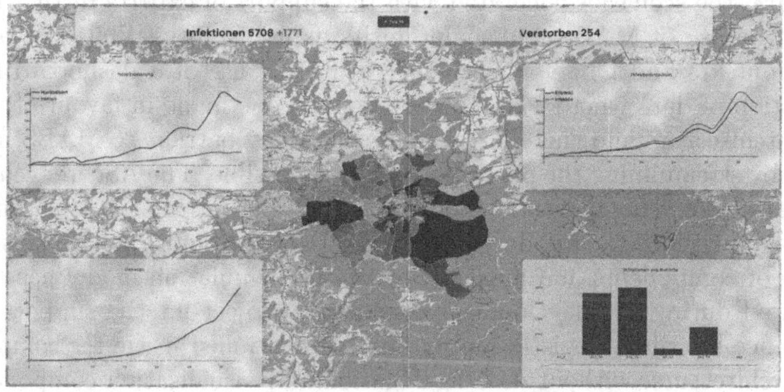

Fig. 5. Simulation player for the visualisation of individual experiment setups

the results of a parameter combination (averaged across different random seeds) step by step, increasing the transparency of the simulation results and making it more accessible and explainable to users. This model, based on the city of Kaiserslautern in Germany, maps locations and their 100'000 inhabitants to the statistical districts of the city as provided in the population data. This allows the model to map the case numbers to their specific districts and cohorts allowing an identification of possible hot-spots. This gives the user insights that cannot be obtained from a static set of plots.

4 Lessons Learned

Due to the unique combination of data presentation, evaluation of results and simulation-based forecasting, the AScore Cockpit contributed to pandemic management. Over the course of the pandemic, the authors actively participated in municipal crisis management and gave counsel on different topics, such as schooling strategies, opening of public swimming pools or extended holidays at the start of the new year. An important aspect of this success is the flexibility of such a system, allowing quick adaptation to unexpected events, such as new variants [11], recent policy changes and interventions. Especially with the emergence of the Omicron variant, the demand for forecasts was high. The forecasts by AScore were able to support decision makers in assessing this. With uncertainty and low availability of data, multiagent simulation is well suited to adapt to new information by retaining its high explainability, an advantage that sets it apart from purely mathematical or data-driven approaches.

However, once the COVID-19 pandemic wanes from public attention, simulation models and information dashboards for the visualisation of current pandemic data will likely fade from acute interest as well. Thus, the reusability of different technologies is an important topic not just for disease scenarios, but other, especially regarding civil security contexts. Like the visualisation and analysis of the data, the scenarios generated with the support of experts further help to simplify the use of MABS and maintain its explainability. While not all simulation contexts and models may benefit from the use of a dashboard for the visualisation of data, there is still an argument to be made in favour of using a generic architecture and therefore decrease the entry barriers to MABS in practical use by streamlining the process as much as possible. The AScore technology stack is also promising due to its modular nature, permitting the replacement of components without forcing developers to start over from scratch. The successful reuse of components and inclusion of another simulation model has already been tested during the development of another project for the support of crisis resilience in critical logistic supply lines. A continued usage for components of this architecture, without data aggregation and visualisation components, is planned in the context of future projects involving MABS.

Acknowledgements:. The AScore project was funded by the German Federal Ministry of Education and Research (BMBF) under grant number 13N15663.

References

1. Peeples, L.: Lessons from the COVID data wizards. Nature **603**, 564–567 (2022)
2. Lorig, F., et al.: Agent-based social simulation of the COVID-19 pandemic: a systematic review. JASSS **24**(3), 5 (2021)
3. Alsharhan, A.: Survey of agent-based simulations for modelling COVID-19 pandemic. Adv. Sci. Technol. Eng. Syst. J. **6**(2), 439–447 (2021)
4. Memmel, M., Berndt, J.O., Timm, I.J.: AScore - developing a cockpit for regional pandemic management in Germany with agent-based social simulation. In: REAL CORP 2021, pp. 65–75 (2021)
5. Liu, C.-H., Huang, Y.-M.: An empirical investigation of computer simulation technology acceptance to explore the factors that affect user intention. Univ. Access Inf. Soc. **14**(3), 449–457 (2015). https://doi.org/10.1007/s10209-015-0402-7
6. Meechang, K., et al.: The acceptance of using information technology for disaster risk management: a systematic review. Eng. J. **24**(4), 111–132 (2020)
7. An, L., Grimm, V., Turner, I.I., Billie, L.: Editorial: meeting grand challenges in agent-based models. JASSS **23**(1), 13 (2020)
8. CKAN - The Open Source Data Management System. https://ckan.org/
9. Elasticsearch: the official engine for distributed search and analytics. www.elastic.co/de/elasticsearch/
10. hetida-designer. https://github.com/hetida/hetida-designer

11. Tapp, L., Kurchyna, V., Berndt, J.O., Timm, I.J.: School's out? Simulating schooling strategies during COVID-19. In: MABS@AAMAS 2022 (2022)

Author Index

Printed in the United States
by Baker & Taylor Publisher Services

Printed in the United States
by Baker & Taylor Publisher Services